Authority and Political Culture in Shi'ism

SUNY Series in Near Eastern Studies
Said Amir Arjomand, Editor

Authority and Political Culture in Shi'ism

Edited By
Said Amir Arjomand

State University of New York Press

Published by
State University of New York Press, Albany

Printed in the United States of America

For information, address State University of New York Press, State University Plaza, Albany, N.Y., 12246

Library of Congress Cataloging-in-Publication Data

Authority and political culture in Shi'ism.

(SUNY series in Near Eastern studies)
Includes index.
1. Shīʻah—Government. 2. Shīʻah—Doctrines.
3. Islam and state. 4. Islam and state—Iran.
5. Iran—Politics and government. I. Arjomand, Said Amir. II. Series.
BP194.9.G68A94 1988 297'.1977 87-10064
ISBN 0-88706-638-0
ISBN 0-88706-639-9 (pbk.)

10 9 8 7 6 5 4 3 2 1

Contents

Part II: Selected Sources

Preface

The conspicuous entry of Shi'ism onto the contemporary political scene has underlined the need for the historical treatment of Shi'ite political ideas and institutions. The essays in the volume address this need. Furthermore, this is a topic for which the primary sources are inaccessible to all but a small number of specialists. I have therefore supplemented the historical essays with a selection of primary sources in English translation.

I am most grateful to Mr. Albert Hourani for his kind organizational advice at an earlier stage of the project as well as his comments on the essays, to Professor Wilferd Madelung for his corrections and valuable comments on my own contribution, and to Professor Sayyed Hossein Modarresi Tabataba'i for his helpful advice and comments on the sources.

I also wish to express my gratitude to the editors of *Studia Islamica* for their kind permission to incorporate some of the material previously published in that journal into Chapter IV, and to Mrs. Veronica Abjornson for her patience and care in the typing of successive drafts of most chapters. Special thanks are due to Ms Liora Gvion for her work on the Index.

The terms Shi'ism, Shi'ite and Shī'a in this book always refer to Imāmī or Twelver Shi'ism. Zaydī and Ismā'īlī Shi'ism are not covered. For consistency, Persian words have been transliterated in conformity with the Arabic, except in that 'v' is used for the *waw* in preference to 'w'. Usually, both the Islamic and the common era dates are given together in the text. Whenever only one date is given, it refers to the common era. Finally, I have added a few comments and notes to the chapters by other contributors. These have been marked off by (Ed.).

S.A.A.

Contributors

Abbas Amanat is Assistant Professor of History at Yale University and the author of *Resurrection and the Renewal of the Age. The Emergence of the Bābī Movement in Qājār Iran* (Cornell University Press, 1988.) He is a Consulting Editor of *Encyclopaedia Iranica* and a member of the Council of the Society for Iranian Studies.

Kathryn Arjomand is a doctoral student in the Department of English at the State University of New York at Stony Brook.

Said Amir Arjomand is Professor of Sociology at the State University of New York at Stony Brook, and the author of *The Shadow of God and the Hidden Imam* (University of Chicago Press, 1984) and *The Turban for the Crown. The Islamic Revolution in Iran* (Oxford University Press, 1988.)

William C. Chittick was assistant editor of the *Encyclopaedia Iranica* and teaches at the State University of New York at Stony Brook. He is the author of *A Shi'ite Anthology, Fakhruddin 'Iraqi: Divine Flashes*, and *The Sufi Path of Love: The Spiritual Teachings of Rumi.* His translation of the fourth Shi'ite Imam's prayer book, *al-Sahifat al-sajjadiyya*, is forthcoming.

John Cooper studied Islamic philosophy and law for four years at Qumm in Iran. He recently completed the first part of an abridged translation of Ṭabari's Commentary on the Qur'ān, and is at present working on a doctoral thesis on theories of language in Shi'ite philosophy of law at the University of Oxford.

Hamid Dabashi is Lecturer in Sociology at the University of Pennsylvania. His publications include "Symbiosis of Religious and Political Authorities in Islam," in Thomas Robbins and Roland Robertson (eds.) *Church-State Relations: Tensions and Transitions*, and "The Poetics of Politics: Commitment in Modern Persian Literature," *Iranian Studies*, Spring-Autumn 1985.

Mohammad-Taqi Danishpazhouh, Professor Emeritus at the University of Tehran, is the *doyen* of Iranian librarians famed for his photographic memory. He is the author of numerous bibliographies, historical and philosophical essays and the editor of various Persian and Arabic texts.

Etan Kohlberg is Chairman of the Institute of Asian and African Studies and Professor of Arabic Language and Literature at the Hebrew University in Jerusalem. He is the author of numerous articles on Shiʿite doctrine and history, and has edited a number of early Sufi texts.

Abdol Karim Lahidji obtained his doctorate from the University of Tehran and taught Private Law between 1970 and 1980. A practicing lawyer, he is the Founder and Secretary of the Society of Iranian Lawyers (founded in 1978), Founder and Vice-President of the Iranian Human Rights Society (founded in 1978) and President of the Iranian Society for Human Rights (in Exile-Paris) which he founded in 1983.

Mohammad-Djaʿfar Mahdjoub was Professor of Persian Literature at the University of Tehran, and has also taught at the University of Strasbourg. He is the author of various articles in scholarly journals and editor of several historical, literary and Sufi texts.

Andrew Newman received his Ph.D. in Islamic Studies from the University of California, Los Angeles. He is the author of a recent article on the seventeenth-century Imāmī cleric Shaykh Bahāʾī in *Studia Iranica*, and is completing a book on Imāmī law and theology in the ninth and tenth centuries.

John R. Perry is Associate Professor of Persian Language and Civilization at the University of Chicago. He is the author of *Karim Khan Zand: A History of Iran, 1747-1779* (Chicago, 1979), and a number of articles on Iranian history and Persian linguistics.

Yann Richard, permanent researcher at the Centre National de la Recherche Scientifique (Paris), spent many years in Iran at the Institut Francais d'Iranologie which he left after the Islamic Revolution. He has published mainly on the ideological conflicts between secularism and traditional Islam in twentieth century Iran.

CHAPTER 1

Introduction: Shi'ism, Authority, and Political Culture

SAID AMIR ARJOMAND

If we take the right or legitimate claim to obedience as the essential component of the notion of authority,[1] the search for its roots in Islam takes us to Verse 4:59 of the Qur'ān: "O believers, obey God, and obey the Messenger and those in authority among you. . . ." The phrase translated as "those in authority" is *ulu'l-amr"*. It means those entitled to command (*amr*). The referent of the term is nowhere defined in the Qur'ān itself. Sunni Islam considered the Caliphs (*khalīfa*, deputy or successor) the heirs to the Prophet and Imams (*imām*, leader), making them, together with their appointees, beneficiaries of this Verse and thus entitled to obedience.

One can argue that even in the Qur'ān, the implicit notion of authority had two basic points of reference—that its matrix already pointed to *dīn* (religion) on the one hand, and to *mulk* (temporal rule) on the other. It is true that Verse 4:59 mentions "those in authority" after God and the Prophet, but it is also true that temporal domination provides the model for divine power. The very vocabulary used to describe and conceptualize the majesty of God in the Qur'ān is borrowed from the tradition of sacral kingship which it sought to destroy: God is "the true King" (20:114 and 23:116); "to God belongs the kingdom (*mulk*) of the heavens and the earth";[2] and "His is the kingdom (*mulk*)" (6:73 and 64:1). The invidious contrast between divine and human kingship in the Qur'ān could only delegitimize the latter. The term *mulk* was thus tainted and another Qur'ānic term, *sulṭān*, was employed to denote legitimate political authority.[3] The term appears in the seventh/first century Egyptian papyri for governor,[4] and was used by the Umayyad Caliphs. In the eighth/second century, the 'Abbasid Caliph al-Manṣūr, following this usage, declared himself "the authority of God on His Earth" (*sulṭān Allāh fī arḍihi*).[5] Furthermore, the idea of kingship was not destroyed and reemerged in the eighth/second century as a result of Iranian influences. It soon reconstituted itself in Islamic form as *dawla*(*t*)—God-ordained "turn" in power,[6] usually linked with the Qur'ānic Verse 3:26: "Say, oh God, possessor of kingship (*mulk*), you give kingship to whomever you choose and take it from whomever you choose."[7] The interdependence of religion and kingship became a major theme in the Islamic theories of government. Thus, *dīn* (religion) and *dawla*(*t*) (temporal rule) became the two distinct sources of legitimate authority in medieval Islamic culture.

During the first centuries of Islam, religious authority became differentiated from political authority as a result of the recording and study of the Traditions (*ḥadīth*) of the Prophet and the rise of the schools of law. The *'ulamā'* (literally, the learned, from *'ilm* [science/knowledge]), too, because of their legal learning and their knowledge of the Qur'ān and the Traditions of the Prophet, were His heirs and therefore their legal injunctions were to be obeyed. They possessed authority as the interpreters of the *sharī'a* (Sacred Law). Thus had emerged in Sunni Islam the notion of authority in religion (*dīn*) as distinct from that of temporal authority, authority in *mulk* or in *dawla*(*t*). However, unlike political authority which was exercised by the persons of the Caliph and the Sultan, the authority of the *'ulamā'* was both impersonal and collective. Furthermore, it was institutionally amorphous. In law, it was sanctioned as the principle of *ijmā'* (consensus). But *ijmā'* as a source of legitimate authority never found any conciliar or other concrete institutional embodiment.

With the bifurcation of supreme political leadership that resulted from the Buyid conquest of Baghdad in the mid-tenth/fourth century,[8] and with the subsequent rise of Sultanate, the Caliph remained the heir to the Prophet while the actual power of command passed to the *amīr al-umarā'* (commander of the commanders). The retention of the mantle of the Prophet endowed the office of Caliphate with the authority to legitimize the actual holder of power, the *amīr al-umarā'* who subsequently assumed the title of *sulṭān*. *Sulṭān* came to mean 'ruler,' and Sultanate came to mean kingship and became nearly synonymous with *dawla*(*t*). Justice (*'adl*) and the observance of the *sharī'a* were made the condition of legitimacy of temporal rule by the *sulṭān*.[9]

It can no longer be doubted that Sunni and Shi'ite Muslims shared the idea of the legitimate Caliph as the "Imam of guidance" [to salvation] in the first two centuries.[10] Nevertheless, the Shi'ite conceptions of authority developed along a radically divergent path. The Shī'a vehemently rejected the legitimacy of the established Caliphate and considered 'Alī and his descendants the rightful successors of the Prophet—and as such, entitled to *khilāfa*(*t*)—and the divinely inspired and infallible (*ma'ṣūm*) Imams (leaders) of the community of believers. Divine appointment (*naṣb*) and divinely sanctioned designation (*naṣṣ*) by the Prophet or the preceding Imam became the distinctive mark of the Shi'ite theory of Imamate. Consequently, "those in authority" in Verse 4:59 could be no other than the Imams.[11] Furthermore, as Kohlberg shows in Chapter 2, from the eighth century onward, the charismatic authority of the Imams as the supreme political leaders and teachers of religion became intimately linked to their *'ilm* (science/knowledge). This partial derivation of the authority of the Imams from *'ilm* had no counterpart in the Sunni theory of Caliphate and constituted another distinctive feature of the Shi'ite theory of authority. This distinctive feature becomes all the more important for later developments in the period of Occultation (*Ghayba*), as the portion of the authority of the Imam that was most easily transferrable to the Shi'ite *'ulamā'* in his absence was precisely that derived from *'ilm.* In the process of transfer, the notion of *'ilm* became detached from that of the infallibility of the Imam and equated with the knowledge of the *'ulamā'.* Thus, the two most important distinctive features of the Shi'ite notion of authority, which formed the basis of the later theories of the juristic authority of the *'ulamā',* were (1) its derivation from Imamate as the immediate extension of Prophecy and (2) its partial derivation from *'ilm.*

Much confusion in the scholarly literature[12] could have been avoided by the recognition of a crucial fact. The distinctive Shi'ite theory of authority, according to which the authority of the Prophet passed on to the Imams and devolved upon the *'ulamā'* after the Occultation of the Twelfth Imam, could easily be reconciled with the theories of Sultanate so long as the ruler did not claim to be the heir to the Prophet. It was irreconcilable with Caliphate precisely because the Caliph *did* claim to be the heir to the Prophet and thus usurped the legitimate authority of the holy Imams. This claim was retained while the Caliphs were forced to give up their political authority after the bifurcation of Caliphate and Sultanate in the tenth century. The eleventh-century jurists such as al-Māwardī and al-Ghazālī emphasized the Imamate of the powerless Caliph as the heir to the Prophet all the more as temporal power was held not by them but by the *sulṭān.* The distinction is as important in fact as it is neglected in current scholarship. The Shi'ite jurists could never accept the authority of the Caliph as the heir to the Prophet, but as early as the eleventh century they had no compunction in granting legitimacy to the authority of the just ruler (*al-sulṭān al-'ādil*).[13] The first three Caliphs, the Umayyads and the 'Abbāsids, were thus illegitimate (*jā'ir*) because they falsely claimed the position of the Imams. This is the logic of the *fatwa* (ruling) by the eminent Shi'ite theologian and jurist Ibn Ṭāwūs that the Mongol conqueror, Hülegü, an infidel but a just ruler, was better than the 'Abbāsid Caliph, who claimed to be the successor of the Prophet and thereby usurped the right of the Imams.[14] After the overthrow of the 'Abbāsids in 1258, no ruler in Iran claimed Caliphate and the Shi'ite theory of authority coexisted with the theories of *salṭanat* and kingship as temporal rule.

The first component of our title, *Authority and Political Culture in Shi'ism*, is free from ambiguity. Ever since *'ilm* was closely linked to the principle of leadership of the community of believers under the Imams, there has been a distinctly Shi'ite theory of authority. Authority in Shi'ism has in principle been conferred upon the possessors of *'ilm*, the *'ulamā'*, though its nature and area of jurisdiction and the qualifications for its possession have varied from period to period. The major theme of this book is precisely the treatment of authority in Shi'ism, with special emphasis on its institutionalization in different historical periods. In Chapter 2, Kohlberg examines the crucial relationship between Imamate and the notions of *'ilm* and *'ulamā'* under the Imams which is fundamental for the understanding of all subsequent developments in the Shi'ite theory of authority. Although the politically powerless Imams never gave up their claim to political rule as the designated descendants of the Prophet, in practice, religious guidance and the teaching of the *sharī'a*—activities covered by the notion of *'ilm*—became their predominant function and the chief expression of their authority.

Given the Shi'ite belief that the Imam was the *ḥujja* (proof) of God among mankind, we can imagine how serious the crisis caused by the disappearance of the Twelfth Imam in 874/260 must have been for the Shi'ite community.[15] The community, however, survived this crisis, and the idea of Occultation eventually became an established doctrine in which the Imam was not really absent from the earth but was alive and merely hidden from the eyes of mankind. This last tenet completed the Twelver doctrine of Imamate which was reset in the framework of rational theology adopted from the Mu'tazila in the eleventh/fifth century. In Chapter 10, we have an authoritative statement of this doctrine by the 'Allāma al-Ḥillī (d. 1325/726) which concisely sets forth the Shi'ite principle of the divinely inspired authority of the infallible

Imams, the last of whom is in Occultation until the end of time.

In the sphere of religion it was natural for much of the authority of the Imams to devolve on the *'ulamā'* during the Occultation. This they justified by a decree purportedly issued by the Twelfth Imam from concealment.

> Concerning the new cases that occur, refer to the transmitters of our Traditions, for they are my *ḥujja* (proof) unto you and I am God's proof unto them.[16]

However, at the theoretical and doctrinal level, the definition and legitimation of the authority of the *'ulamā'* required a radical reorientation of Shi'ite thought. The authority of the Sunni *'ulamā'* derived from their qualifaction as jurists, from their knowledge of the *sharī'a*. Under the Imams as the infallible interpreters of the *sharī'a*, the Shi'a had totally rejected the Sunni legal methodology, the nascent science of jurisprudence (*uṣūl al-fiqh*). After the Occultation of the Twelfth Imam, the task of interpreting the *sharī'a* devolved upon the fallible jurists who needed the rules and methods of the *uṣūl al-fiqh* for deriving valid legal norms. The great *'ulamā'* of the eleventh century, Shaykh al-Mufīd, Sharīf al-Murtaḍā, and Shaykh al-Ṭūsī, adopted the science of jurisprudence for Shi'ism. Yet they upheld the principle that all valid legal norms could be known with certitude. As stated concisely by Madelung:

> They indeed maintained that the law was complete and comprehensive as it had been laid down by the Imams. The task of the *'ulamā'* could merely be to find it, not to derive any new norms. *Ijtihād* was not needed but was expressly rejected, just as it had been in the time of the presence of the Imams.
>
> This attempt to maintain the principle of certitude in the law during the absence of the infallible Imam could not permanently be sustained. In the 6th/13th century, the Muḥaqqiq al-Ḥillī (d. 1277/676) admitted that the Imāmī scholars, though rejecting legal analogy, were practicing *ijtihād* in deriving legal norms since these were "most often based on theoretical considerations not deduced from the literal meaning of the texts." His pupil, the 'Allāma al-Ḥillī (d. 1325/726), elaborated the methods of Imāmī *ijtihād*.[17]

With the 'Allāma al-Ḥillī's acceptance of *ijtihād*, the principle of certitude was formally given up. His definition of *ijtihād* is often cited in later Shi'ite works on the science of jurisprudence as their starting point, and centers on the capacity of the jurist for the acquisition of probable opinion (*ẓann*).[18] The text of this earliest explicit acceptance and discussion of *ijtihād* in translation is presented in Chapter 10. The Shi'ite jurists could henceforth legitimately derive new legal norms on the basis of preponderant probability. Al-Ḥillī's acceptance of *ijtihād* thus constituted a crucial step in the enhancement of the juristic authority of the Shi'ite *'ulamā'*. By the time the Safavids had created the first Shi'ite empire in Iran, the Shi'ite jurists "had become *mujtahids* in name as well as in fact."[19] The principle of *ijtihād*, vigorously condemned in early Shi'ism, became the vital and distinctive feature of its legal system. Furthermore, by becoming firmly coupled with *taqlīd* (following/imitation), it constituted the foundation of clerical authority in Shi'ite Iran. Chapter 12 reproduces one of the earliest discussions of *taqlīd* as the correlative of *ijtihād* by Mullā Aḥmad Ardabīlī, the Muqaddas (d. 1585/993). The passage shows how clerical authority came to mean the authority of the jurist over the layman who was now under moral/legal obligation to follow the former's legal opinion.[20]

The Safavid rulers (1501-1722) who made Shi'ism the state religion of Iran did not claim to be heirs to the Prophet but only to rule on behalf of the Hidden Imam. With the establishment of the Safavid *dawlat* in Iran, the Shī'a ceased to be a sectarian minority and came to possess their own state. The problem they now faced was the institutional translation of the Shi'ite theory of authority, which in turn raised the issue of articulation of authority in religion with political authority. The foremost representative of Shi'ism in the early decades of Safavid rule was Shaykh 'Alī al-Karakī (d. 1534) from the Jabal 'Āmil. The Arab *mujtahid* was warmly received by the Safavid rulers; and in 1533, the young and pious monarch Ṭahmāsp issued several *farmāns* (decrees) granting al-Karakī extensive powers as the "Seal of the *mujtahidīn*" and the "Deputy of the Imam" (*nā'ib al-imām*). However, the accommodation of the foremost *mujtahid* as the representative of the Imam in the new Shi'ite polity met with strong resistance on the part of the holders of the office of the *ṣadr*, the highest office of the state in charge of religious administration, an office inherited by the Safavids from the previous Sunni rulers of Iran.[21]

Shāh Ṭahmāsp's *farmān* concerning the Shaykh al-Karakī, often referred to by the Shi'ite *'ulamā'* subsequently, is translated in Chapter 11, Section 1, while the issue of the institutional articulation of religious and political authority is addressed in Chapter 4. The issue is approached from the viewpoint of political developments, especially at the end of the Safavid era and the beginning of the Qājār period (1785-1925), a period of critical transition in the history of Shi'ism in Iran. I have characterized this transition as one from the Safavid "caesaropapism" to the Qājār dualism—dualism in the structure of authority being the result of the consolidation of an independent Shi'ite "hierocracy."[22] Here, as well as elsewhere, the employment of the terms "caesaropapism" and "hierocracy" is not a gratuitous act of introducing a category from the increasingly fashionable Weberian sociology to the discussion of authority in Shi'ism. The subject of the chapter is organization or institutionalization of authority in the first important Shi'ite state. Generally speaking, some developments can be explained in terms of evolution of ideas, others in terms of material interests of their bearers. There is yet another type of development which can be best explained in terms of a transition from one form of organization to another. This last type of explanation can subsume the earlier ones, but it would have to go beyond them. Hence the intrusion of such unwonted terms as "caesaropapism" and "hierocracy" to explain, first, the transition from the honorific position of "the *Mujtahid* of the Age" to the office of *Mullā-bāshī*, and then the eclipse and eventual disappearance of the latter, which was in turn a prerequisite for the unchallenged growth of power of the *mujtahidīn* and the enhancement of their authority in nineteenth-century Iran.

One interesting fact presented in Chapter 4 is the initial attempt by the Qājārs to claim Safavid descent, implausible as that must have seemed. The attempt demonstrates the astounding persistence of Safavid legitimacy through more than six decades of anarchy and internecine war. On the basis of the evidence on this point, it can be argued that it was the failure of this attempt as much as the piety and rational calculations of Fatḥ 'Alī Shāh (1797-1834) that sealed the fate of caesaropapism and made the ruler willingly and fully acknowledge the autonomous hierocratic authority of the *mujtahidīn*, who in turn legitimized the rule of the new dynasty. Be that as it may, the reign of Fatḥ 'Alī Shāh witnessed the consolidation of a dual structure of authority in Shi'ite Iran, whose normative foundations I have examined elsewhere.[23]

Before turning to the nineteenth century, it is interesting to note that the memory of Safavid caesaropapist legitimacy indeed died hard under the dualistic authority structure of the Qājār period. In the 1840s, we hear of agitation instigated by Safavid descendants with clerical support.[24] As late as 1907, the *mujtahid* of Tehran, Sayyid 'Abdallāh Bihbahānī, then at the height of his popularity for championing the cause of the Majlis, would not cease to dream of reviving the absolute religiopolitical dominion of the Safavid rulers and *sayyids* on behalf of the Hidden Imam. The following passage records his ambition during the summer of 1907:

> Sayyid 'Abdallāh is beating the drum of 'I and none else.' His court in Dizāshūb [a suburb north of Tehran] is more colorful than that of the government. He is the pillar of the Majlis and the lord of a cause (*ṣāḥib-i dā'īya*). He had once asked Ṣāḥib Ikhtiyār to which side of the turban the Safavids would affix the regal jewel (*jiqqa*).[25]

But die it did, as we shall see, under the impact first of Constitutionalism and then of *étatisme*.

Unlike the periods covered by the first four chapters, much has been written on the Shi'ite *'ulamā'* in the nineteenth century.[26] In Chapter 5, Amanat offers new insights into the problem of clerical leadership in nineteenth-century Shi'ism. He challenges the view that sees the emergence of the institution of *marja'-i taqlīd* (source of imitation/emulation) as the establishment, de facto, of a hierarchy among the *mujtahidīn* under one supreme authority.[27] As the issue of the leadership of the Shi'ite community could not be resolved on the basis of legal criteria established in the *madrasa*, Amanat argues, it continued to depend on popular acclamation, and hence on the respective influence of the *mujtahidīn* in the marketplace.

The key legal concepts elaborated by the Shi'ite *'ulamā'* of the nineteenth century in their effort to centralize clerical authority are already familiar to us from Kohlberg's account of pristine Shi'ism and from al-Ḥillī's tract. The notion of *a'lamiyyat* (superiority in learning), used for establishing a ranking order among the *mujtahidīn*, derives from *'ilm*, the foundation of the distinctive Shi'ite theory of authority since the time of the Imams. However, as Amanat demonstrates, the notion of *a'lamiyyat* was too weak in its practical legal implications to achieve the aim of centralization of clerical authority. In practice, it was not the *marja'iyyat-i taqlīd* on the basis of *a'lamiyyat*, but *riyāsat* (leadership), acknowledged by popular acclamation and payment of religious taxes, that made for a measure of centralization of clerical authority in nineteenth-century Shi'ism. The concept of *riyāsat* can also be traced back to Imamate. Kohlberg mentions that before the Occultation, the Imam was the only legitimate leader (*ra'īs*) of the Shi'ite community.[28] As can be seen in Chapter 10, the 'Allāma al-Ḥillī uses the term leadership (*riyāsa*) in his definition of Imamate. The attempts to centralize clerical authority during the Safavid period bypassed the notion of the leadership of the community of believers.[29] Nevertheless, the notion remained in use. Shaykh Bahā' al-Dīn 'Āmilī (d. 1621/1030), for instance, is referred to as the leader (*ra'īs*) of the Imāmiyya.[30] With the autonomy of religious authority from the state in the nineteenth century, the notion of the leadership of the community—now on behalf of the Imam—once more came to the fore. However, as Amanat points out, throughout the nineteenth century the notion of *riyāsat* remained linked to distinct ethnic communities and was frequently used to denote the leadership of the 'Arab, the Turkish-speaking, and the 'Ajam communities.[31]

Chapters 4 and 5, on the institutionalization of religious authority of the *mujtahidīn* in Shi'ite Iran, do not cover an important trend which disputed the very foundation of their juristic authority, namely, the Akhbārī movement. The transfer of the authority of the Twelfth Imam to the *'ulamā'* had not been unproblematic from the very beginning. For decades after his disappearance, the prevailing attitude was one of staunch traditionalism; only the explicit statements (*akhbār*) of the Imams had legal validity and no legal norms could in principle be derived by any jurist who could only arrange the *akhbār* according to topics. Despite the progressive development of *uṣūl al-fiqh* in the subsequent two centuries and the eventual acceptance of *ijtihād* by the fourteenth century, the traditionalist orientation did not disappear in the Shi'ite scholarly community and was vigorously reasserted in seventeenth-century Iran. Akhbārism became a major force in the second half of the seventeenth century, completely dominated Shi'ism from the collapse of the Safavid empire in 1722 well into the second half of the eighteenth century, and survived well into the nineteenth century. The Akhbārīs revived the principle of certitude in law and rejected the validity of probable opinion and, therefore, the practice of *ijtihād.* The rise of the movement clearly occurred in the context of the continuation of the struggle between the *ṣadr* and the *mujtahid* covered in Chapter 4. The *ṣadr* of the first half of the seventeenth century who gleefully remarked that no Shi'ite *mujtahid* remained in Iran or the Arab world in his time[32] would not have failed to support Akhbārī traditionalism against the *mujtahidīn.* Elsewhere, [33] I have put forward a hypothesis on the socio-political determinants of the rise of Akhbārī traditionalism which awaits scholarly reaction. Here it suffices to say that in addition to the political and organizational difficulties discussed in Chapter 4, important doctrinal and theoretical obstacles also had to be surmounted before the unchallenged prevalence of the juristic authority of the *mujtahidīn* in the nineteenth century.

This brings us to the chapters covered by the second component of our title. The phrase "political culture in Shi'ism" is inevitably ambiguous and especially problematic in a historical collection that covers the period from the Middle Ages to the present century. Why then adopt it? Because the historical reality it bears on is equally ambiguous and open to interpretation. There are two basic reasons for this ambiguity. The first is that what is political in the Shi'ite culture in one period may not be so in another. The theme of the martyrdom of Imam Ḥusayn and the extolling of the virtues of the Imam had clear political implications during the seventh and eight centuries but had become the largely apolitical ritual of *manāqib-khwānī* later in the Middle Ages—the period covered by Mahdjoub in Chapter 3. Given the minority status of the Shi'a in medieval Iran, these recitations of the eulogies of the Imams had a political aspect as the chief instrument of intersectarian rivalry and often led to clashes between the Shi'a and the followers of the Sunni *madhhabs* (Schools of Law). Incidentally, in the long run, popular eulogies of the Imams had a considerable impact on the popular culture of Sunni Iran as documented by Mahdjoub. They created groups of "Twelver Sunnis," and facilitated the eventual conversion of Iran to Twelver Shi'ism by the Safavids. Once the Shi'a had become dominant in Iran under the Safavids, these popular recitations, now transformed to *rawḍa-khwānī*, became largely apolitical, and the theme of the martyrdom of Imam Ḥusayn underwent a soteriological transposition.[34] Yet the same theme was intermittently politicized, and has become a major element in the contemporary political culture of Shi'ism with the onset of the Islamic revolutionary movement in Iran.

The second reason for the inevitable ambiguity of the title stems from the difference between the phrases "the political culture *of the Shī'a*" and "political culture in Shi'ism." The two expressions are not strictly the same, and the latter is often used when the former is intended. The latter expression is the more convenient, but it also has a built-in danger of reifying Shi'ism, and of attributing to Shi'ism as a religion aspects of the life and culture of the Shī'a which have nothing directly to do with it. The danger is only too real, as every student of Islam and of Shi'ism should know.

In the medieval period, the Shī'a were a minority in the Islamic empires but shared much of the political culture of the mainstream; above all, they shared the notions of government and statecraft whose origins were, in any event, independent of Islam. From the sixteenth century onwards, these notions of government and statecraft constituted the core components of the political culture of the Shī'a in Iran. Chapter 9, by Danishpazhouh, is a bibliographical guide to the extensive literature on statecraft. I hope it acts as an antidote to the widespread tendency to discard elements of culture and social life which do not derive directly from Islam in general or Shi'ism in particular. Among these elements are the principles of government and statecraft. Their neglect in the scholarly literature, by omission, conveys the impression of monolithic comprehensiveness that Shi'ism or Islam do not possess as a matter of historical reality. The literature surveyed in Chapter 9 merits the attention of the reader lest he or she be misled into thinking that the Shi'ite theory of authority was tantamount to the political culture of the Shī'a. There were notions of political authority, justice, and tyranny current among the Shi'ite and Sunni Muslims alike which were accepted as such without being considered part of the religious doctrine.[35]

As Danishpazhouh points out in Chapter 9, the Sasanian and Indian ideas on statecraft entered the political culture of medieval Islam through such works as the ninth/third century *Kitāb al-Tāj* (Book of the Crown). These ideas made their impact on the Shi'ite literature, and many of them were given religious sanction in the tenth/fourth century by being attributed to the first Imam, 'Alī, in the form of a letter of instruction to the man he appointed governor of Egypt.[36] This important document was included in the collection of 'Alī's sayings, *Nahj al-Balāgha* (completed in 1009/400) and became known as 'Alī's political testament (*'ahd*). It was translated into Persian by the Safavid *'ulamā'* several times.[37] A similar letter contains the instructions of the sixth Imam, Ja'far al-Ṣādiq to the Shi'ite governor of Ahvāz.[38] Such documents assured the incorporation of the patrimonial theory of just rule into the Shi'ite literature. The theory included notions pertaining to the fair treatment of the subjects, to political economy of patrimonial government, and to the stratification of society into classes. It should be emphasized, however, that the incorporation of the pre-Islamic patrimonial ideas of just government into the Shi'ite culture entailed some change in their original meaning. Perhaps the most significant and broadest change shown in 'Alī's political testament was the devaluation of earthly authority when juxtaposed to the divine.[39]

Chapters 11 and 13 cover the political culture of Iran during the two centuries after the establishment of Shi'ism. Practical rules for government and statecraft are given in the ordinance issued by Shāh Ṭahmāsp in the sixteenth century (Chapter 11, Section 2). These reflected the customary practice and were, at best, only tangentially related to the Shi'ite Sacred Law.[40] The two seventeenth-century tracts presented in Chapter 13, by contrast, focus on the general principles of kingship and seek to interpret them on the basis of the sources of the Shi'ite religion and Sacred Law. The tract by Mullā Muḥsin Fayḍ, is the more philosophical and consists of a statement on the significance of kingship at the highest level of generality. It is especially noteworthy for placing earthly authority and political rule in the total context of life—i.e., in relation to the spiritual and the mundane, to this-worldly and other-worldly action. The devaluation of earthly power through its juxtaposition to divine authority, found in 'Alī's political testament, is thus given elaborate philosophical form. Although the tract begins with the conventional praise for the Safavid King and the typical prayer that God join his rule to that of the Hidden Imam, kingship is placed quite low in the cosmic order. Political sovereignty is put at the level of common law, whose goal is the maintenance of order, and below the Sacred Law. Acts of the rulers are oriented to this world and need to be complemented by the Sacred Law, not vice versa. Sovereignty to the Sacred Law is therefore the body to the spirit, the slave to the master. Only if the ruler obeys the Sacred Law is the harmony of the universe imitated and Dominion realized.[41] Incidentally, Mullā Maḥsin Fayḍ is the only representative in this collection of Akhbārī Shi'ism and of gnostic philosophy (*'irfān*) that tended to be associated with it. As an Akhbārī, Fayḍ rejects *ijtihād*, considering it the mixing of imperfect intellect and the Sacred Law, and hence a confusion of "Commanders."[42] Elsewhere, Fayḍ restricts the function of the General Deputy (*al-nā'ib al-'āmm*) during the Occultation of the Imam to reference to the reliable and recorded Traditions.[43] As a gnostic philosopher, Fayḍ puts the Intellect above the Sacred Law, if perfected. He adds, however, that Perfect Intellect as the revealed law within is identical with the *sharī'a*, and pertains exclusively to the Prophet and the saints (*awliyā'*).[44]

With the second tract in Chapter 13 by Mullā Muḥammad Bāqir Majlisī, we move from philosophy of sovereignty to political ethics. In this tract, the rights and duties of kings and subjects are discussed according to the teachings of the Imams as recorded in their Traditions. It has become fashionable for the modernists in the present century to denounce the writings of the Safavid *'ulamā'* as politically motivated fabrications.[45] As Chittick points out, however, Majlisī's documentation cannot be faulted, and his *isnād* goes back to the canonical works of the tenth/third century. The first section presents the Traditions on the duties of those in authority. It stresses the necessity of avoidance of tyranny and injustice, and the accountability of the holders of authority—both religious (*fuqahā'*) and temporal (*umarā', salāṭīn*)—in the hereafter. The rights of the subjects to justice, fair treatment, and access to the ruler are discussed in the next section. Majlisī then turns to the rights of the kings. Most notable among these is the right to unconditional obedience, except in violation of the *sharī'a*. It is also interesting to note that Traditions numbered 41 and 42 state that obedience to the rulers is incumbent as self-protection because God forbids self-affliction. These latter Traditions pave the way for the transition from the abstract moralism of the earlier sections to the stark pragmatism of what follows on the "corruption caused by proximity to kings"—this being "loss in this world and the next." The focus of the discussion is on the evils of tyranny and injustice by the holders of power and those who associate with them. Nevertheless, Majlisī does bring in the theme of acceptance of authority from a tyrannical ruler (*jā'ir*),[46] and maintains that association with the rulers becomes obligatory for self-protection, or for furthering the cause of the believers, or for the guidance of kings.

Between them, Chapters 11 and 13 depict most aspects of the political culture of Shi'ite Iran in the Safavid era. Perhaps one important aspect should be added: the reaffirmation of the conventional theme of the interdependence of religion and government in medieval theories of kingship.[47] Here is a passage on this theme of the interdependence of religious and temporal authority from yet another seventeenth-century treatise on ethics:

> If the *'ulamā'* are the builders of religion after the Prophets, the Kings are the protectors of that building. The construction of religion is done by the lords of knowledge (*'ilm*) but its protection by the lords of command as in: "The kings are the protectors of religion"[48] .... Justice is the pillar of the arcade of sovereignty and equity the guarantor of the order of the kingdom. The army is the stronghold of the kingdom and the nation, and the protector of the property, honor and life of the subjects.[49]

An important genre of ethico-political writing not included in our selection consists of mirrors for princes. One such mirror, *Qavā'id al-Salāṭīn*, written by an *'ālim* who was a descendant of Shaykh 'Alī al-Karakī in 1670/1081, mentions twelve principles of rulership, illustrating each with edifying stories of the exemplary behavior of past kings and occasionally with Traditions of the Imams. First and foremost among these principles is justice (*'adālat*). The author defines justice as the treatment of each class according to its station and deserts and as prevention of the domination of any class by any other.[50] He then proceeds to identify the classes of the body politic in a manner which throws considerable light on the position of the Shi'ite *'ulamā'* in Safavid society and brings out the concrete implications of the interdependence of temporal and religious authority.

Society is divided into five classes. The first four are compared to the four elements and are said to constitute the *body* politic: men of the sword—the military, men of the pen—scribes and bureaucrats, men of affairs—merchants and craftsmen, and the cultivators of land.[51] To these four components of the traditional conception of society, already to be found in the Testament of 'Alī,[52] the author adds a fifth reflecting the growth of the clerical class and its aspirations in the late Safavid period. The *'ulamā'* constitute the fifth class. It is the *soul* (*rūḥ*) of the body politic consisting of the other classes.[53] It follows from this conception of society that

> the kings, who are the shadow of God, should improve the position of the *'ulamā'* so as to strengthen the perspicuous religion and the order of the nation of the Lord of Messengers. They should also treat the other classes, which are like the four elements, with justice and equity so as to strengthen the order of the kingdom and [thus have] all [their subjects] engaged in praying for the person and benefactions (*barakāt*) of the royal majesty.[54]

The author praises the Safavid kings for following this principle of rulership by their constant and unfailing support for the Shi'ite *'ulamā'* since the foundation of their empire.[55] This is followed by a blatant request for personal favor and augmentation of the author's stipend addressed to the young Shāh Suleymān (1666-1694).[56]

Gratitude for benefaction (*shukr-i ni'mat*), an important element in the ethos of Islamic patrimonialism,[57] is duly praised and ingratitude (*kufrān-i ni'mat*) and disloyalty to the benefactor decried at some length.[58] Other important principles of rulership are forbearance (*ḥilm*) and removal of tyranny (*zulm*). The wrongdoers (*zalama*) and their helpers are denounced and threatened with the fire of hell, without, however, being identified with the rulers or their functionaries as a class.[59]

The traditional theories of kingship were restated in the Qājār period (1786-1925) and remained an important component of the political culture of Shi'ite Iran in the nineteenth century. However, given the dualism of the Qājār structure of authority and the tremendous enhancement of clerical power in the early nineteenth century, the culture of the *'ulamā'* itself acquired political significance. Henceforth, depending on the circumstances, one or another of its elements bore political consequences by virtue of the fact that the *'ulamā'*, with their considerably enhanced religious authority, were inevitably drawn into politics in an era characterized by the weakness of central government. This is the main reason for including the candid and engaging account of the lives of the prominent *'ulamā'* of the first half of the nineteenth century in Chapter 14. These biographies from the *Qiṣaṣ al-'Ulamā'* also illustrate the nature of clerical authority in that period, and they are replete with instances of competition among clerical authorities and of confrontation between religious and political authority. Furthermore, Section 5 consists of the biography of a Mullā who played an important role in the development of *ta'ziya:* the popular religious ceremonies that centered on the commemoration of the martyrdom of Imam Ḥusayn, and represent the latest transformation of the popular eulogies of the Imams.

Chapter 15 consists of an exchange of letters from the latter part of the nineteenth century. It offers a rare glimpse of the routine operation of the notions of religious and political authority in the dualistic Qājār polity, and it completes our picture of the political culture of Qājār Iran by throwing considerable light on the articulation of religious and political authority in practice.

If the theories of statecraft and government surveyed in Chapter 9 formed the politicocultural context of the Shi'ite theory of juristic authority until the end of the nineteenth century, Constitutionalism (of the first decade of the present century), *étatisme* (of the Pahlavi era), and the Marxist ideology of the Tudeh Party constituted the political culture to which Shi'ite clerical authorites had to adapt themselves in the twentieth century. The last three chapters deal with developments in the twentieth century when Shi'ism was exposed to strong international currents—political and cultural currents that posed a serious threat to the authority of the Shi'ite *'ulamā'*. Chapter 6 deals with the exposure of Shi'ism to Constitutionalism and the compromise between the principles of parliamentary law-making and the juristic authority of the interpreters of the Sacred Law during the Constitutional Revolution of 1906-11.

The Constitutional Revolution marks the advent of modern politics and thus constitutes a watershed separating old and new Iran. The prominence of the *'ulamā'* in that revolution seemed striking from the very beginning. A participant in the revolutionary events observed the following:

> One remarkable feature of this revolution here . . . is that the priesthood have found themselves on the side of progress and freedom. This, I should think, is almost unexampled in the world's history.[60]

In his major history of the Constitutional Revolution, Kasravi[61] considered the alliance of the two *mujtahids* of Tehran, Ṭabāṭabā'ī and Bihbahānī, against the state the starting point of the revolution without, however, considering the *'ulamā'* as champions of progress and freedom. To explain the paradoxical appearance of the Shi'ite *'ulamā'* on the side of a revolution against the traditional order, a number of Western scholars sought a partial explanation in the Shi'ite theory of authority.[62] The tendency to see the Shi'ite *'ulamā'* as the opponents of the state on doctrinal grounds, which exaggerated the extent and constancy of clerical support for Constitutionalism, remained unchallenged for some time. However, serious doubts regarding its validity have been raised more recently.[63] In Chapter 6, Lahidji follows the recent line of reassessment of the role of the *'ulamā'* in the Constitutional Revolution. He argues that the *'ulamā'* did not initiate the Constitutionalist movement, nor did they determine its goals. Furthermore, their participation in the movement did not entail their acceptance of the principle of national sovereignty. Once the movement had gathered momentum, the *'ulamā'* became divided in their attitudes towards Constitutional government. One group, typified by Muḥammad Ḥusayn Nā'īnī, legitimized constitutional government n Shi'ite terms—i.e., by reconciling it with the Shi'ite theory of the authority of the Hidden Imam. The second group, typified by Shaykh Faḍlallāh Nūrī, developed embryonic notions for an Islamic government in contradistinction to constitutional government and parliamentary democracy whose secularizing implications had by now become abundantly clear. The opposite views of these two groups are represented by two tracts in Chapter 16, one for and one against constitutional government.

In Chapter 6, Lahidji also examines a neglected feature of the period, namely, the acceptance of the Shi'ite juristic theory of authority by the Constitutionalists and its accommodation, both in the Constitution (the Fundamental Law and especially its Supplement) and in the early legislations regarding the judiciary system. Thus, it is argued that the *'ulamā'* did *not* initiate the Constitutionalist movement, as is still commonly believed, and that they *did* exact a price for joining it once it was underway, which is not generally recognized. The price was the recognition of the principles of clerical authority and some of the prerogatives of the *'ulamā'* which necessitated considerable modification of the principles of parliamentary democracy. If some of the *'ulamā'* legitimized the authority of constitutional government in accordance with Shi'ite principles, the legislation of the First and the Second Majlis legitimized clerical authority in accordance with the principles of Constitutionalism, and gave it considerable scope.

Of all the chapters in this book, Chapter 7 is probably the one that deals with political issues least directly. Yet, it does represent an important mode of adaptation of Shi'ism to the modernizing *étatisme* of Riḍā Shāh, and, more generally to the European culture which began to penetrate Iran more deeply. Richard describes the belated intellectual impact of the Enlightenment and of Victorian rationalism in the person of Sharī'at Sangalajī, one of the *'ulamā'* who advocated reform of Shi'ism. Furthermore, Sharī'at's project for the reform of Shi'ism included the discarding of *taqlīd*, the correlate of *ijtihād* and the true foundation of clerical authority in Iran. His message constituted a serious challenge to clerical authority and thus made a deep and disturbing impression on the custodians of Shi'ism, many of whom excommunicated him.

Finally, in Chapter 8, I analyze the eventual response of the militant *'ulamā'* who followed Āyatallāh Khumeinī to the cumulative effect of the wide spread of modern political ideas and the creation of a secularizing modern bureaucratic state. The vigor of this response made up for some six decades of relative passivity with a vengeance. The serious erosion of juristic authority of the Shi'ite *'ulamā'* that had resulted from the growth of a variety of competing secular political theories was countered not only with the reassertion of the traditional Shi'ite theory of juristic authority (*ijtihād*) but also with its categorical extension to government and the political sphere in the theory of *vilāyat-i faqīh* (mandate of the jurist).[64] The Shi'ite *'ulamā'*, it is now claimed, are "those in authority" referred to by the Verse 4:59 of the Qur'ān. Furthermore, an Islamic response to the whole gamut of issues raised by modern political ideas and ideologies has been put forward in the form an increasingly coherent ideology. The result, not surprisingly, has been no less than an ideological revolution in Shi'ism.

From the perspective of the evolution of the Shi'ite theory of authority, the Islamic Revolution of 1979 in Iran completes the medieval revolution in Shi'ite thought which consisted in the adoption of the principle of *ijtihād*. From the perspective of institutionalization of clerical authority in Shi'ite Iran, it completes the amazing trajectory "from the state's theologians to the theologians' state."[65] It can thus be viewed as the culmination of the intermittent growth of Shi'ite clerical authority which, having survived the onslaught first of Akhbārī traditionalism and then of modern political ideas and ideologies, has transformed Iran into the first Shi'ite theocracy in history. The Articles relating to clerical authority in the Constitution of this theocracy are presented in the final chapter of the book.

The purpose of the preceding pages has been to describe the general theme of this book and to show how and where the individual contributions fit into its overall framework. The essays offered in Part I either cover new topics or present a new interpretation of significant issues that are at the center of current scholarly debate. They share the common theme of authority and political culture in Shi'ism but differ in their scholarly style and analytical approach. No attempt has been made to summarize their rich content. Nor is the amount of attention paid in passing to different contributions in any way related to their respective significance. Part II, on the other hand, consists of important documents and primary sources I have selected to represent the major trends in the history of Shi'ism. With one exception, these sources have not been available in English translation, or for that matter, easily accessible in the original Arabic or Persian. They are assembled here and offered to the scholarly community in the hope of stimulating further research and enquiry in this important field.

Notes

1. The notion of authority—or more precisely *auctoritas* and its complement *potestas*—comes from Roman law and has no equivalent in Arabic or Persian. Its meaning is approximated by the terms discussed in this chapter, as it is by some other terms such as *ḥukm* (command, verdict) and *siyāda* (authority, originally of the tribal chief).

2. 2:107, etc. The phrase is exactly repeated twelve times, and with slight modification in several other instances. See H. E. Kassis, *A Concordance of the Qur'ān* (Berkeley and Los Angeles: The University of California Press, 1983), pp. 766-767.

3. Kassis, op. cit, pp. 1081-1082. It is interesting to note that of all the terms discussed, *sulṭān* is the one which corresponds most closely to the abstract form 'authority.'

4. T. W. Arnold, *The Caliphate*, New York: Barnes & Noble, 1966 [1924], pp. 202-203.

5. Cited in P. Crone and M. Hinds, *God's Caliph. Religious authority in the first centuries of Islam*, Cambridge: Cambridge University Press, 1986, p. 85.

6. B. Lewis, "Hukûmet and Devlet, "*Belleten*, C.XLVI (1982), pp. 418-21.

7. R. P. Mottahedeh, *Loyalty and Leadership in an Early Islamic Society*, Princeton: Princeton University Press, 1980, pp. 185-86.

8. The Buyids, incidentally, came from Daylam, the stronghold of Zaydī Shi'ism in Iran. After conquering Baghdad in 945/334, the Buyids did not abolish the 'Abbāsid Caliphate and retained the Caliph as a figurehead representing Islam with supreme authority over the application of the *sharī'a*.

9. A. K. S. Lambton, *State and Government in Medieval Islam*, Oxford: Oxford University Press, 1981: Chapter VII.

10. Crone and Hinds, op. cit., esp. pp. 34, 80-82.

11. See below, pp. 192-93.

12. See S. A. Arjomand, *The Shadow of God and the Hidden Imam* (Chicago: The University of Chicago Press, 1984), pp. 21-23, 279-280.

13. Ibid., pp. 63-64 for citations and sources.

14. W. Madelung, "Authority in Twelver Shi'ism in the Absence of the Imam," in G. Makdisi et al., eds., *La notion d'autorité au Moyen Age Islam,*

Byzance, Occident (Paris: Presses Universitaires de France, 1982), p. 172, n. 9. See also Arjomand, op. cit., pp. 62-64.

15. E. Kohlberg, "From Imāmiyya to Ithnā 'Ashariyya," *Bulletin of the School of Oriental and African Studies*, XXXIX (1976).

16. Reported by Ibn Bābūya (d. 991/381) in *Ikmāl al-Dīn wa Itmām al-Ni'ma*, Najaf, 1389/1970, p. 451.

17. Madelung, loc. cit., p. 168.

18. Chapter 10, below, p. 243.

19. Madelung, loc. cit., p. 169.

20. See Chapter 12 below.

21. Arjomand, op. cit., pp. 132-135.

22. Ibid., pp. 12-15.

23. Ibid., Chapter 10.

24. Ibid., pp. 250-251.

25. Mahdī-qulī Hidāyat, *Khāṭirāt va Khaṭarāt* (Tehran: Zavvar, 1344/1965), p. 155.

26. Notably, A. K. S. Lambton, "*Quis Custodiet Custodes:* Some Reflections on the Persian Theory of Government," *Studia Islamica*, V-VI (1956); *ead.*, "The Persian *'ulamā'* and Constitutional Reform," in *Le Shi'isme imamite* (Colloque de Strasbourg) (Paris: Presses Universitaires de France, 1970); N. R. Keddie, "Religion and Irreligion in Early Iranian Nationalism," *Comparative Studies in Society and History*, IV (1962); *ead.*, "Roots of the "Ulama's Power in Modern Iran," in *Scholars, Sufis and Saints. Muslim Institutions since 1500* (Berkeley: University of California Press, 1972); H. Algar, *Religion and the State in Iran 1785-1906* (Berkeley: University of California Press, 1969); J. R. Cole, "Imāmī Jurisprudence and the Role of the *'Ulamā'.* Murtaḍā Anṣārī on emulating the Supreme Exemplar," in N. R. Keddie, ed., *Religion and Politics in Iran. Shi'ism from Quietism to Revolution* (Yale University Press, 1983).

27. To strengthen Amanat's argument, it can be said that, down to the present time, it is accepted Shi'ite doctrine that every jurist must personally investigate the legal source before ruling on any issue. Furthermore, "imitation of the opinion of a *mujtahid*, however great he is, by another *mujtahid* in legal matters is unlawful." See H. Modarressi, "Rational and Traditional in Shī'ī jurisprudence: a preliminary survey," *Studia Islamica*, LIX (1984), p. 143.

28. See below, p. 36.

29. See Chapter IV. It is interesting to note that Muḥammad Bāqir Khātūnābādī, the *Mujtahid* of the Age and the *Mullā-bāshī*, is said to be "The leader

(*ra'īs*) of all the *'ulamā'* rather than the leader of the Shi'ite community. See below, p. 87.

30. Sayyid 'Abd al-Ḥusayn Khātūn-ābādī, *Vaqāyi' al-Sanīn va'l-A'vām* (Tehran: Islamiyya 1352/1973-4), p. 482.

31. See below, p. 113.

32. Cited in Modarressi, loc. cit., p. 155.

33. Arjomand, op. cit., Chapter 5.

34. Ibid., p. 165.

35. It is interesting to note that Āyatallāh Khumeinī proved his familiarity with this literature by "citing an old Persian belief that the rulers should be close to their people [when he] had his home telephone numbers in the holy city of Qum published in this afternoon's newspapers." *The New York Times*, March 19, 1979. See Lambton, 1981, p. 123 on the accessibility of the ruler.

36. See below, pp. 215-16. See also W. al-Qadi, "An Early Fatimid Political Document," *Studia Islamica*, XLVIII (1978), pp. 71-108.

37. For instance, see below, p. 224, #27.

38. See below, p. 216, #5.

39. See W. C. Chittick's translation in his *Shi'ite Anthology* (Albany: SUNY Press, 1981), p. 69.

40. See below, p. 252.

41. See below, pp. 274-75.

42. See below, p. 280.

43. Mullā Muḥsin Fayḍ, *Kalamāt Maknūna* (Tehran, 1316/1898-9), p. 195.

44. See below, p. 279.

45. These accusations are as old as the century. Nūrī refuted them in 1909 along the same line as Chittick (see below, p. 364). Nevertheless, they have persisted and were voiced with particular vehemence by the late 'Alī Sharī'atī (d. 1977).

46. For the earliest systematic treatment of the topic, see W. Madelung, "A treatise of Sharīf al-Murtaḍā on the legality of working for the government (*Mas'ala fi'l-'amal ma'a'l-sulṭān*), *Bulletin of the School of Oriental and African Studies*, XLIII (1980).

47. Arjomand, op. cit., Chapter 3.

48. Tradition of the first Imam, 'Alī. (*Ghurar al-Ḥikam*)

49. Muḥammad Sāliḥ b. Muḥammad Bāqir Qazvīnī, *Ḥikmat-i Islām*,

J. Muḥaddith Urmavī, ed. (Tehran: Bungāh-i Tarjuma va Nashr-i Kitāb, 1354/1975), p. 38.

50. Muḥammad b. Aḥmad al-'Āmilī al-'Alavī, *Qavā'id al-Salāṭīn*, Library of the Majlis, Tehran, manuscript # 516, f.12.

51. Ibid., ff. 12-13.

52. Chittick, op. cit., pp. 71-72. In the Testament of 'Alī, the class comprising the cultivators is identified as the taxpayers. It is interesting to note that the fifth class in the Testament consists of the poor and the needy. In *Qavā'id al-Salāṭīn*, this class is replaced by the *'ulamā'* who are now differentiated from the men of the pen and elevated above the other classes of society as the soul to bodily organs.

53. Ibid., f. 14. By the twentieth century, *rūḥāniyyūn* had become the common term for Shi'ite clerics. See Ch. 8, p. 184 below.

54. Ibid., ff. 14-15.

55. Ibid., ff. 156-165.

56. Ibid., ff. 165-168.

57. Mottahedeh, op. cit., Ch. 2.

58. *Qavā'id al-Salāṭīn*, ff. 86 ff.

59. Ibid., ff. 109-112.

60. E. G. Browne, *The Persian Revolution. 1905-1909* (London, 1910), p. 123.

61. A. Kasravī, *Tārīkh-i Mashrūṭa-yi Īrān* (Tehran, 1320/1941).

62. See the works of Lambton, Keddie, and Algar cited in n. 20 above.

63. F. Ādamiyyat, *Ideology-yi Nahḍat-i Mushrūṭiyyat dar Īrān* (Tehran: Payām, 1976); and, implicitly, Hairi, who documented the increasing clerical opposition to Constitutionalism. (A.-H. Hairi, *Shi'ism and Constitutionalism in Iran* [Leiden: Brill, 1977]). The editor, too, has offered an alternative interpretation of the role of the *'ulamā'* that underscores their progressive opposition to the legislative power of the Majlis (Iranian Parliament). S. A. Arjomand, "The *'Ulamā*'s Traditionalist Opposition to Parliamentarianism, 1907-1909," *Middle Eastern Studies*, XVII (1981), pp. 174-190.

64. The terms *vilāya*(*t*) and *vālī* (from the same root) were used in the medieval period for provincial governorships and governors, respectively. Khumeinī's followers constantly link *vilāyat-i faqīh* with *vilāyat-i amr* and *ulu'l-amr* (those in authority) of Verse 4:59. The suggested etymological derivation of *valī* from the Qur'ānic phrase is in fact incorrect, but the terms are becoming wedded in the minds of the contemporary Shī'a.

65. This suggestive phrase is borrowed from the title of B. Fragner, "Von

den Staatstheologen zum Theologenstaat: religiöse Führung und historischer Wandel in schi'itischen Persien," *Wiener Zeitschrift für die Kunde des Morgenlandes*, 75 (1983), pp. 73-96.

PART I

Essays

CHAPTER 2

Imam and Community in the Pre-Ghayba Period

ETAN KOHLBERG

The period preceding the disappearance (in 260/874) of the Twelfth Imam affords an interesting glimpse into the interrelationship between a superhuman but politically impotent spiritual leader and members of his community. Ideally, such an interrelationship ought to be investigated with both the doctrinal and historical aspects in mind. It is, however, in the nature of the Imāmī sources that the former is given virtual exclusivity, while whatever item is presented as a historical fact is often colored by doctrinal considerations and must accordingly be treated with caution. Despite these limitations, there is much that can be learned about the self-image of the Imāmī community from the manner in which its role vis-à-vis the Imam is portrayed.

I

The unique position of the Imam is based essentially on two factors: first, he is viewed as a divinely appointed successor to the Prophet; second, he alone is seen as invested with personal qualities which make him the undisputed leader of all believers. For our purposes, one quality in particular should be emphasized: his possession of knowledge (*'ilm*). The great importance attached to this is reflected in the fact that the Imam is often described as the *'ālim* (learned) par excellence, and that the words *imām* and *'ālim* appear on occasion to be interchangeable. In one account, for example, a question is raised as to the position of the *'ulamā';*[1] a second version of this account is identical, except that for *'ulamā'* there appears the word *a'imma.*[2] The term *al-'ālim* is often used when, for reasons of *taqiyya* (self-protection through dissimulation), it is deemed best to conceal the Imam's name.[3] It is also employed as an honorary appellation of both the sixth and seventh Imams, Ja'far al-Ṣādiq and Mūsā al-Kāẓim.[4] The Imams, we are told, do not belong within the ranks of the prophets, yet they are *'ulamā'.*[5] Similarly, the celebrated tradition that "the *'ulamā'* are the successors of the prophets" is interpreted as referring to the Imams.[6]

Two main issues are discussed in Imāmī texts with a view to establishing the unrivalled position of the Imams as possessors of *'ilm:* the sources of the Imam's knowledge, and the nature and scope of this knowledge. The sources are essentially four, all of a kind denied to ordinary mortals: transmission from the previous Imam, knowledge acquired in hereditary fashion, knowledge acquired from books whose contents are known only to the Imams, and knowledge acquired through direct contact with an angel. This last manner of transmission is often referred to as 'inspiration' (*ilhām*), and its recipient is described as a *mufahham* or *muḥaddath* (one addressed by a divine messenger). Unlike a prophet, the Imam does not see the messenger, but only hears his voice in a dream. The precise nature of the divine messenger whose voice is thus heard is a moot point. In some traditions, he is described as the spirit of holiness (*rūḥ al-qudus*), which is one of five spirits possessed by the Imam; unlike the other four, the *rūḥ al-qudus* "neither sleeps nor is negligent or distracted,"[7] and is always available to inform the Imam on any issue.[8] Elsewhere, it is identified with the Qur'ānic *rūḥ* (e.g., 42:52, 97:4). This *rūḥ* is "a creature (*khalq*) of God larger than Gabriel or Michael; it was present with the Messenger of God, informing and guiding him, and is now with the Imams."[9] In some variants, this *khalq* is described as actually inhering in the Imam's body (*wa innahu la-fīnā*).[10] Against those who insist that the *rūḥ* is not an angel ("Gabriel is an angel, while the *rūḥ* is a creature larger than the angels"),[11] others maintain that it clearly is.[12]

Views concerning the nature and scope of the Imam's knowledge range from the minimalist position, according to which the Imam's *'ilm* is largely confined to a superior knowledge of the law (*al-ḥalāl wa'l-ḥarām*),[13] to the popular conception of the Imam as partaking of many of the divine mysteries (*ghayb*), such as knowledge of all languages (including those of animals and plants), future events, and the innermost thoughts of other persons. This latter position is adopted by Muḥammad b. 'Alī Ibn Bābawayhi (d. 381/991), who emphasizes that the Imam's superior knowledge has been conferred on him by the

Prophet.[14] Ibn Bābawayhi's renowned pupil al-Shaykh al-Mufīd (d. 413/1022) opts for a more moderate position and maintains that the Imams do not always know the future or people's hidden thoughts, but that God on occasion provides them with such knowledge as a divine favor.[15] Al-Sharīf al-Murtaḍā (d. 436/1044) and his pupil Abū Ja'far al-Ṭūsī (d. 460/1067) appear to restrict even further the extent of the Imam's knowledge. They argue, first, that before assuming office (i.e., when he is still a "silent" [*ṣāmit*] Imam) he does not necessarily know all the legal precepts.[16] Secondly, even after becoming a "speaking Imam" (*imām nāṭiq*) he is not omniscient, and is at liberty to consult experts on non-*shar'ī* matters such as commercial transactions or the value of certain items.[17] Both al-Mufīd and al-Ṭūsī apply the notion of the Imam's limited knowledge of the *ghayb* in addressing a central issue faced by the community following the disappearance of the Twelfth Imam: If, as was claimed, the Imam had to go into hiding for fear of his enemies, why could he not stay in touch with his devoted followers? The answer, according to the two scholars, is that the Imam cannot know his followers' thoughts or predict their actions, and so cannot tell which of them might reveal his whereabouts, through inadvertence or for some other reason.[18]

A central question in this connection is whether al-Ḥusayn, when setting out for Kūfa, knew what fate would await him and his entourage at Karbalā'. Al-Mufīd, in keeping with his system, implies that al-Ḥusayn had no advance knowledge of what would happen there;[19] others, however, insist that he was fully aware of the impending tragedy.[20] In fact, the most common view among Imāmī scholars appears to be that all the Imams predicted the place and manner of their own deaths. Often the Imams are credited more generally with knowledge of the place and manner of death of various persons, particularly from among their supporters (*'ilm al-balāyā wa'l-manāyā*).[21]

The majority view among the Imāmiyya is that the Imams are more excellent than any of the prophets except Muḥammad.[22] Since excellence is defined largely in terms of the possession of knowledge, the Imams are thus taken to be more knowledgeable than the prophets (Muḥammad excepted). At the same time, the belief that Muḥammad and the Imams possess equal authority rests on the assumption that they also possess equal knowledge. A related notion is that there was an increase in the amount of knowledge possessed by successive prophets. Various traditions support this notion: Solomon knew more than David;[23] Moses knew only some of the contents of the Tablets (though he thought he knew them all), while Muḥammad and the Imams possess knowledge of every aspect of the Qur'ān (and so also of the Tablets);[24] the *ulū'l-'azm* (prophets of resolution) knew only about past events, while the Imams (following Muḥammad) also know what will happen in the future. When an (unidentified) listener dared to ask the fifth Imam, Muḥammad al-Bāqir, whether 'Alī was more knowledgeable than one of the prophets, the Imam answered sharply: "Listen to what he says! God chooses whose ears to open. I have told him that God gathered for Muḥammad the knowledge of all the prophets and that Muḥammad placed all this with the Commander of the Faithful (i.e., 'Alī), yet he asks me whether 'Alī is more knowledgeable or one of the prophets!"[25]

In contrast to the situation obtaining in the prophetic era, the majority view among the Imāmiyya is that no difference exists in the amount of knowledge possessed by each Imam. The reason for upholding this view is obvious enough; if knowledge during the era of the Imams is cumulative (as it was in the prophetic era), then later Imams are inevitably more knowledgeable than their predecessors, whether prophets or Imams, and this is a conclusion clearly to be avoided. Now the assumption underlying the majority view would at first appear to be that the body of knowledge available to the Imams after Muḥammad's death became immutable. Such an assumption would, however, entail an awkward problem: If the Imam is granted precisely the same knowledge as his predecessors, then he cannot possibly be the recipient of new information. The concept of *muḥaddath*, so central to Imāmī doctrine, would thereby be rendered meaningless. Imāmī scholars were acutely aware of this problem, and the solution which they devised for it will be mentioned presently; but it should first be noted that in the view of these scholars, the Imams' knowledge does increase. "Had we not continually been granted an increase of knowledge, then all our previously gained knowledge would have dissipated," the Imam Ja'far al-Ṣādiq declared.[26] Every week, the Imam is reportedly lifted to heaven, where he is supplied with knowledge in addition to that already in his possession.[27] According to some traditions, each Imam knows five things (*ashyā'/ajzā'*) in addition to those known to his predecessor.[28] Ja'far al-Ṣādiq said: "'Alī was a man of knowledge (*'ālim*), and knowledge is transmitted in hereditary fashion; whenever an *'ālim* dies there remains behind someone (i.e., an Imam) who possesses the same knowledge as he, or whatever God wishes."[29] The final *aw mā shā'a llāh* ("or whatever God wishes") points to the possibility of the knowledge possessed by one Imam not being identical to that possessed by another.

A particularly propitious time for the revelation of knowledge to the Imams is considered to be the *laylat al-qadr* (Night of Determination), the holiest night of Ramaḍān. According to Ja'far al-Ṣādiq, various matters known to the Imam in general terms only (*jumalan*) are given their *tafsīr* on that night.[30] The precise meaning of the term *tafsīr* here is not clear. It might mean "detailed information." Support for this interpretation may be found in a declaration of al-Ṣādiq to the effect that on each *laylat al-qadr* the *tafsīr* regarding all events of the coming year is revealed to the Imams (as it was to Muḥammad before them).[31] The implication, then, is that *tafsīr* involves knowledge not previously possessed by the Imam. Such a conclusion seems borne out by other traditions stating clearly that on the *laylat al-qadr* the Imam receives new information.[32] Yet when pressed by a disciple, al-Ṣādiq categorically denies that *tafsīr* constitutes new knowledge. He argues that both *jumal* and *tafsīr* are known to the Imam beforehand; all that happens on the *laylat al-qadr* is that God orders the Imam to act on a specific issue already known to him, and provides an explanation (*tafsīr*) as to how this action is to be carried out.[33] In other words, *tafsīr* belongs to the existing arsenal of the Imam's knowledge. The disciple, however, persists and wants to know whether there are any new items of knowledge (not covered by the term *tafsīr*?) which the Imam acquires that night. Here al-Ṣādiq draws the line and refuses to answer: "This is a matter which the Imams have been ordered to conceal"; and again: "You may not ask this question."[34]

There is clearly a problem here. For, on the one hand, the Imam denies receiving new information; on the other, there is a definite sense of something extraordinary taking place on the *laylat al-qadr*, perhaps transcending what the Imam is ready to reveal. An interesting attempt to resolve the question is made by Muḥammad Bāqir al-Majlisī (d. 1111/1699-1700) in his analysis of this tradition. Al-Majlisī relates the tradition to the tenet that God may postpone the revelation of certain information; this tenet constitutes one formulation of the doctrine of *badā'*.[35] Since *badā'* is a complicated issue tending to cause confusion among the uninitiated, the Imam chose not to mention it. Al-Majlisī's reading of the tradition is that before the *laylat al-qadr* the Imam knows what God intends to do in a particular year, but he is not certain whether God will actually carry out His intention. At this point, in other words, the Imam is unable to distinguish God's irreversible decisions (*maḥtūm*) from those subject to change; this is the meaning of *jumal*. On the *laylat al-qadr* the Imam is told which of the divine decisions relating to the coming year are final and irreversible, and will therefore come to pass; this is the *tafsīr*.[36] If this is a sound interpretation, then the Imam, in denying receipt of new information, was correct in a narrow sense only, since on a deeper level, the ability to distinguish between reversible and irreversible divine decisions implies the acquisition of additional knowledge.

Let us now turn to the device employed to show that traditions referring to an increase in knowledge do not run counter to the doctrine of the Imams' equal knowledge. This device is based on the notion that no new item of knowledge is divulged to the Imam unless it is first presented (*'urida*) and made known to his predecessors.[37] The divine messenger carrying it is described as an angel (*malak*) or, more mysteriously, "a rider"[38] or "a rider on his beast."[39] This messenger informs Muḥammad and orders him to pass the information on to 'Alī. 'Alī in turn passes it on to al-Ḥasan, and so on down to the incumbent Imam.[40]

In order for this to make sense, two Imāmī doctrines must be borne in mind. The first maintains that the physical demise of Muḥammad and the Imams does not spell the end of their activities: After their death they are transported body and soul to Paradise, where they enjoy heavenly bliss while staying in continuous contact with their followers on earth;[41] every day (or every Thursday), the actions of all human beings are presented to them for judgment.[42] The acquisition of additional knowledge thus fits in with their other activities.[43] The second doctrine is the previously mentioned *badā';* the assumption is that all knowledge posthumously imparted to the Imams forms part of God's *ghayb* which He had initially decided to withhold from them, but which later He chose to divulge to them: "When God changes His mind concerning some matter of the *ghayb* we are informed of this" (*fa idhā badā lillāh fī shay' minhu u'limnā dhālika*).[44]

While most Imāmī scholars subscribed to this view of the Imams' knowledge, others appear to have diverged from it. In their opinion, all Imams possess equal knowledge of the Qur'ān and the *sharī'a;* beyond that, some Imams might acquire knowledge denied to others (*al-a'imma ba'ḍuhum a'lamu min ba'ḍ*).[45] The logic behind this position seems to be that the authority of the Imams rests on their mastery of the legal and religious sciences; individual variations in their knowledge of other matters do not affect their authority and are therefore possible. A similar train of thought may lie behind early traditions which emphasize that all Imams are equal in their knowledge but that Muḥammad and 'Alī occupy a position of particular excellence (*faḍl*).[46] The tenet that some Imams are superior to others is still found in a creed of al-Mufīd's pupil Abū'l-Fatḥ Muḥammad b. 'Alī b. 'Uthmān al-Karājakī (d. 449/1057), which he included in his *Kanz al-fawā'id.* In al-Karājakī's system, 'Alī is the most excellent Imam, followed by al-Ḥasan, al-Ḥusayn, the Mahdī, and finally the rest of the Imams.[47] Such views appear, however, to have been largely discarded in favor of the doctrine stipulating complete equality of the Imams in all fields.

II

The unique position of the Imam poses an intricate problem regarding the status of his community: On the one hand, the unbridgeable gap between the infallible leader and his flock has to be maintained; on the other, there are obvious reasons for wishing to glorify the Shīʿī community as a whole by elevating it to a lofty plane approximating that of the Imams. The tension between these two perceptions comes to the fore in traditions which deal with the creation of the Imams and their followers (*shīʿa*). According to some texts, the bodies of the Imams and the spirits of their *shīʿa* were created of the heavenly substance *ʿilliyyūn* (or, more precisely, of a heavenly substance taken from *ʿilliyyūn*); yet while the spirits of the Imams were created of a substance superior to *ʿilliyyūn*, the bodies of their *shīʿa* were created of a substance inferior to it.[48] In other traditions the spirits of the Imams are described as having been created from the light of God's greatness; their bodies were then created from a special clay (*ṭīna*) concealed under the Throne, into which God infused His light. The spirits of the *shīʿa* were created from the *ṭīna* of the Imams (and are thus suffused with light), while their bodies were created from a *ṭīna* inferior to that of the Imams; all the prophets (except Muḥammad) were created in like manner.[49] Here, then, Shīʿa and prophets (except Muḥammad) are placed on the same level, while the Imams (and Muḥammad) are on a higher plane. In somewhat different descriptions, the two constituent elements are body and heart (*qalb*): In the case of the Imams, both are made of the highest (*aʿlā*) and most excellent part of *ʿilliyyūn*, while in the case of the Shīʿa only the heart is thus constituted, while the body is made of a substance inferior to it.[50] Some of these traditions, then, emphasize that the spirits (or hearts) of Imams and followers are made of the same substance; others deny such identity. All traditions in question agree that the Imams' bodies were created of a substance superior to that of their *shīʿa*. In this way, both the affinity of the Shīʿa with their Imams and the gulf separating them are highlighted. A similar effect is achieved through traditions maintaining that Muḥammad and ʿAlī were created of the same piece of clay (*ṭīna*); the Shīʿa were then created from the remnants (*faḍla*) of this clay.[51] A variant of this theme has it that the clay of which the Imams were made had first been saturated for seven days with sweet water; after the water had dried up, the Shīʿīs were created from the lowest part (*asfal*) (or the dregs, *thufl*) of this clay. "Had God left your clay in the same state as ours, we and you would have been one and the same," al-Bāqir told his disciple Abū Isḥāq Ibrāhīm al-Laythī.[52]

The two facets of the Imam-Shīʿa relationship are evident in various traditions dealing with their respective positions in this world. Both Imams and Shīʿīs are described as possessing *firāsa*, the ability to tell a man's character from his outward appearance. In order to emphasize that there is nevertheless a difference between the two, the point is sometimes made that the degree of *firāsa* is determined by the individual's faith and knowledge, and that the Imams possess the combined *firāsa* found in all believers.[53] Various Qur'ānic expressions are interpreted as referring to both Imams and Shīʿīs, as for instance the *muttaqīn* (the pious) of 43:67[54] or the *ʿibād* (servants) of 15:42, 17:65.[55] In other passages, a distinction is drawn between the two: Thus *al-ṣiddīqīn wa'l-shuhadā'* in 4:69 are the Imams, while *al-ṣāliḥīn* are the Shīʿa.[56] Similarly, *alladhīna yaʿlamūna* in 39:9 are the Imams, and *ulū'l-albāb* are their followers.[57] A favorite image used to describe the relationship between Imams and Shīʿīs is a tree whose branches are the Imams and whose leaves are the Shīʿa.[58]

While the vastly different levels of knowledge of Imam and followers are emphasized, both are sharply distinguished from the outside world: "We are the possessors of knowledge (*ʿulamā'*), our Shīʿa are those who acquire it (*mutaʿallimūn*), the rest of humanity are scum (*ghuthā'*)."[59] When it comes to comparing the Shīʿa with all others, the differences between Imam and Shīʿa tend to be played down, so as to bring out more strongly the elements common to both. Muḥammad al-Bāqir declares in a typical statement: "We and our Shīʿa were created from clay from *ʿilliyyūn*, while our enemies were created from the stinking mud of Hell."[60]

The traditions emphasizing the common origins of Imams and followers imply that the Shīʿīs also resemble their Imams in their moral fiber. Indeed, the Shīʿīs are described as God-fearing ascetics (*ahl al-zuhd wa'l-ʿibāda*) who perform fifty-one *rakʿas* (sections of the prayer) a day, fast, give alms, go on the pilgrimages to Mecca, and refrain from forbidden acts.[61] Their asceticism is underscored in a large number of traditions in which they are portrayed as pale-faced from nights of wakefulness, thin-bellied from fasting, their lips parched from supplication.[62]

Such a uniform and idealized picture of the community could not, however, be sustained for long, particularly once it became evident that not all Shīʿīs lived up to these lofty standards. One method of overcoming this discrepancy between theory and reality was to draw a distinction between true Shīʿīs and other loyal followers of the Imams, termed *mutashayyiʿūn*,[63] *muḥibbūn* or *muwālūn* (sympathizers). The essential difference between the two groups is that the Shīʿīs, in addition to being loyal, also follow their Imams in deed and action by refraining from the commission of sins. Such true Shīʿīs are few and far between. Muḥammad, Fāṭima, and all the Imams are quoted as condemning the practice of persons who in too facile a manner call themselves Shīʿīs, when in fact they are mere *muḥibbūn.* Unlike the Shīʿīs (who automatically go to Heaven), *muḥibbūn* who have sinned are punished by a temporary stay in the uppermost (and so least painful) level of Hell.[64] The trouble with this solution is that it reduces the number of true Shīʿīs to an unacceptable level. A different approach overcomes this difficulty by admitting that not all Shīʿīs are spiritually and morally impeccable, and that some may have been tainted by the evil characteristics of their adversaries.[65] Alternatively, it is argued that the term *shīʿa* may be broadened to include those who are in fact sympathizers.[66] In a radical departure from the notion of the Shīʿa as a group of which membership is predetermined and hereditary, it is acknowledged that Shīʿīs and Nāṣibīs (anti-ʿAlid Sunnīs) may be found in the same family. Thus the ninth Imam is said to have advised one of his supporters not to reveal his Shīʿī allegiance to his Nāṣibī father (*wa'l-mudārāt khayr laka min al-mukāshafa:* concealment is preferable to disclosure). As a result of the Imam's prayers, the father subsequently softened his anti-Shīʿī attitude.[67] According to Imāmī law, the only case where a Nāṣibī may perform the *ḥajj* on behalf of an Imāmī obtains when the Nāṣibī is the Imāmī's father.[68]

Differences between Shīʿīs, once admitted, were not restricted to the moral sphere, but extended also to their knowledge and understanding of the traditions of the Imams: "You can recognize the ranks (*manāzil*) of our Shīʿa on the basis of their transmission from us," Jaʿfar al-Ṣādiq is quoted as declaring.[69] In this evolving hierarchy, pride of place was reserved for those most closely associated with the Imam of the day. In Shīʿī biographical works, various utterances of the Imams are recorded in which one or more members of the community are singled out for special praise. "But for Zurāra, all my father's traditions would have disappeared," Jaʿfar al-Ṣādiq declared,[70] referring to his disciple Zurāra b. Aʿyan (d. 150/767). Although such disciples are mere *mutaʿallimūn* (students) when compared to the Imams, they may quite properly be regarded as *ʿulamā'* when contrasted with those (both inside and outside the Imāmī community) who do not possess their knowledge. The question must now be raised as to the kind of authority enjoyed by these disciples. Was their task limited to the preservation and propagation of the Imam's sayings, or did they also serve as authorities in their own right?

No single answer was given to this question during the pre-*Ghayba* period; instead, Imāmī thinking on the subject underwent significant modifications. The initial phase coincides with the crystallization of the Imāmī doctrine of the Imamate in the mid-second/eighth century. The position at this stage was straightforward: As long as the Imam lives among his followers and is available to them, he is the ultimate authority who lays down the law and acts as sole arbiter in any dispute or problem. He is also the ultimate source of all Imāmī texts: The four hundred *uṣūl* (collections of traditions), regarded as the basis of subsequent Imāmī *ḥadīth*, consist of utterances of the Imams; the various disciples who gave their names to the titles of individual *uṣūl* are viewed as mere compilers.[71] The same holds true for other forms of literary expression. A relatively late example is provided by al-Faḍl b. Shādhān (d. 260/873), who is credited with a treatise detailing the reasons (*'ilal*) for the performance of various religious duties.[72] The complete treatise appears to be preserved in two of Ibn Bābawayhi's works.[73] When al-Faḍl was asked whether he had arrived at these *'ilal* through a process of logical reasoning, he replied that he had repeatedly heard them from the Imam al-Riḍā and had decided to collect them (*fa jama'tuhā*).[74] In other words, al-Faḍl, too, was keeping to the role of transmitter and compiler.

The ideal disciple, then, was the *musallim*, who unquestioningly received, transmitted, and abided by the Imam's rulings.[75] Thus al-Bāqir is said to have been particularly complimentary regarding one of his followers whose habit of exclaiming *"sallimū!"* whenever he heard a *ḥadīth* earned him the nickname "Sallim."[76] Under such a system, any manifestation of independent reasoning was condemned as leading to chaos and anarchy; numerous traditions decry the use of *qiyās* (regarded as a favorite tool of Iblīs), *ra'y*, and *ijtihād* (the latter two often being regarded as synonymous).[77] It is in keeping with this position that the repeated pleas of the disciple Muḥammad b. al-Ḥakīm for permission to use reasoning were turned down by the Imam Mūsā al-Kāẓim.[78] Another disciple, Muḥammad b. al-Ṭayyār, was rebuked by al-Bāqir for using his own arguments while debating with his opponents, instead of relying on what the Imam had said.[79] Since the Imam served as the ultimate legal authority, there was no room for judges. When Shurayḥ became a *qāḍī* (judge), 'Alī upbraided him[80] and ordered him not to execute any legal decision without first referring it to the Imam (in this case, 'Alī).[81]

Two qualifications must, however, be borne in mind. The first concerns some of the earliest adherents to Islam, who in the Imāmī view attained a special position. Fāṭima, for example, was a member of the *ahl al-bayt* and possessed the same divine knowledge as her husband 'Alī; she is therefore regarded as an authority in her own right (though it appears that only women came to her for advice on legal matters).[82] Other examples are provided by some of 'Alī's closest followers: Salmān al-Fārisī, who enjoys a special status among Shī'īs, is considered as possessing a great amount of knowledge (esoteric and other), and so is often regarded as an authority.[83] Another disciple, Rushayd al-Hajarī, also had some knowledge of the *ghayb*, which enabled him to tell people when and how they would die. As noted before, this *'ilm al-balāyā wa'l-manāyā* is normally restricted to the Imams; Rushayd's knowledge was transmitted to him directly from 'Alī, who referred to him as Rushayd al-balāyā.[84]

The second qualification is that even after the doctrine of the Imamate took shape, it was not immediately accepted by all adherents of the *ahl al-bayt*. Some acknowledged the special position of the Imam, but regarded him as *primus inter pares* rather than yielding all authority to him. This was particularly true of those who had only recently joined the ranks of the believers and who had brought with them clearly formed views on specific legal or theological issues.[85] When such persons were in addition independent-minded and strong-willed, they were not as a rule likely to abandon their views without an argument. There is also a psychological factor to be considered: It is not a simple matter for persons who regard themselves, and are regarded by others, as experts in their field, willingly to forego any role of leadership and submit to a higher authority. The level of independence shown by disciples of the Imams is expressed in hyperbolical fashion by al-Bāqir, who is said to have lamented that if everyone belonged to the Shī'a, then judging by the quality of his present supporters, three-quarters would entertain doubts about the Imams and the rest would be fools.[86]

While this complaint need not be taken at face value, it is true that some of the best-known figures of early Shī'ism either did not accept the Imam's superiority in all fields, or else did not automatically conform to the official line. Hishām b. al-Ḥakam, a major figure of early Imāmī *kalām* (theology), refused to take for granted al-Ṣādiq's mastery of *kalām*, and subjected him to a series of questions on the subject.[87] The previously mentioned Zurāra b. A'yan held independent views on several theological questions: He argued in favor of the position (subsequently adopted by various Mu'tazilīs) that the ability to act existed independently of the actual performance of the act. His views on this matter were set out in the lost *Kitāb al-istiṭā'a*.[88] While these views gained a measure of support among the later Imāmiyya, they were frowned upon by Ja'far al-Ṣādiq as a harmful innovation (*bid'a*).[89] Zurāra also argued (against the Imam al-Bāqir) that there was no intermediate position between believer and unbeliever.[90] It is of interest to note that Zurāra's grandfather was a Byzantine monk; it appears that Zurāra's father adopted Islam, but it is not clear whether the father or only the son embraced Shī'ism.[91] The question whether Zurāra's Christian origins in any way affected his theological views may be worth pursuing.

Zurāra's views on *istiṭā'a* were shared by two of his associates, Muḥammad b. Muslim and Burayd b. Mu'āwiya al-'Ijlī, and both were severely criticized as a result.[92] Muḥammad b. Muslim is further blamed for holding that God does not know things before they come into being—a position also held by Hishām b. al-Ḥakam.[93] Muḥammad, Burayd, and Zurāra, together with Ismā'īl b. Jābir al-Ju'fī and a fifth, unnamed person, are described as *al-mutara''isūn* (or *al-mutarayyisūn*) *fī adyānihim*—those who set themselves up as leaders in matters of their religion.[94] The pejorative sense in which *'mutara''isūn'* is used here is established when Ja'far al-Ṣādiq wishes perdition on them all.[95] The choice of this term is significant in that it reveals the basic reason for the condemnation of this group: The only legitimate *ra'īs* is the Imam; those who voice independent views or give their own doctrinal interpretation (*ta'wīl*) are thereby guilty of challenging the Imam's authority, as well as of a lack of humility. This latter point is made abundantly clear when al-Bāqir quotes for Muḥammad b. Muslim the verse, "Give good tidings to the humble" (Qur'ān 22:34), and follows it by telling him, "Be humble (*tawāḍa'*)!"[96] The same verse is quoted by al-Ṣādiq when he mentions other *mutara''isūn*.[97]

There is, however, another side of this coin, for most of these *mutara''isūn* were loyal supporters of the Imāmī cause and mainstays of Imāmī *fiqh*. The selfsame Ja'far al-Ṣādiq praises not only Zurāra (as already noted), but also Muḥammad b. Muslim, Burayd b. Mu'āwiya, and Abū Baṣīr Layth b. al-Bakhtarī for preserving and propagating the Imāmī *madhhab*.[98] Many of these early disciples engaged their non-Shī'ī opponents in theological debates, with the blessing and approval of the Imam. The assumption, however, was that the official Imāmī doctrine would be defended in these debates. Likewise, the Imams on occasion encouraged some of their supporters to display their knowledge of Imāmī law. Al-Bāqir, for instance, told Abān b. Taghlib (d. 141/758-59): "Sit in the Prophet's mosque in Medina and provide answers to legal questions (*wa afti 'l-nās*); for I would like it to be known that people like yourself belong to my *shī'a*".[99] What the Imam could not condone was any deviation from approved theological or legal positions. There were practical considerations, however, which militated against too harsh a condemnation of maverick supporters of the Imams. The attitude toward Mu'min al-Ṭāq is a case in point. When al-Ṣādiq was told that this famous disciple of his was expressing independent views while engaged in theological disputations, he declared, "If I were to approve of and express satisfaction with the theological views which you (i.e., Mu'min al-Ṭāq and his followers) express, I should be guilty of error (*ḍalāl*). On the other hand, it would be hard for me to dissociate from these views. After all, we are few and our enemies legion."[100] Dissociation (*barā'a*), then, is a luxury which the Imams can ill afford, even if Mu'min al-Ṭāq, Zurāra, and their ilk deserve it in principle.

Later generations of Imāmī scholars were loath to admit that such strictures were addressed by the Imams to leading lights of the early Imāmiyya; hence the attempts to explain them away as manifestations of *taqiyya*. In this vein, al-Ṣādiq is said to have told Zurāra: "I criticize you because I wish to protect you (*anā a'ībuka difā'an minnī 'anka*)."[101] In other words, too close an association with the Imam might alert the authorities to Zurāra's importance in the Imāmī community, and might lead to his arrest or worse; by publicly rebuking Zurāra, al-Ṣādiq was therefore acting to ensure his safety.

By the beginning of the third/ninth century, the number of adherents who dared challenge the Imam on any given issue appears to have declined sharply. The reason may well be that his position had become invulnerable with the firm establishment of the Imāmī doctrine. Later Imams thus had their authority more completely and unquestioningly accepted than earlier Imams such as Ja'far al-Ṣādiq. The irony is that al-Ṣādiq enjoyed greater latitude than any of his successors. Yet by the time these successors had assumed the Imamate, they were no longer in a position to exercise their leadership in an effective manner because of the severe restrictions placed on their movements by the 'Abbāsids; they were often incarcerated or placed under house arrest, and so had little direct contact with their followers. It is no coincidence that the later Imams had a significantly smaller number of disciples than their predecessors, and that much of what we have from them is in the form of written *responsa* sent (or smuggled) out of their place of confinement.

The diminishing physical contact between Imam and followers coincided with the numerical growth and the geographical expansion of Imāmī Shī'ism. No longer was it a case of only two centers, as Medina and Kūfa had been in the days of al-Bāqir and al-Ṣādiq; by the third/ninth century new communities had risen to prominence, such as Qumm and Baghdad.[102] This fact, coupled with the increasing difficulty of communication with the Imam, led naturally to the growth of a local leadership. The Imams themselves encouraged this process: When the Shī'ī scholar Zakariyyā b. Ādam told al-Riḍā of his desire to leave his native Qumm which had, he argued, become a hotbed of insolent fools (*sufahā'*), the Imam dissuaded him by saying that his role as defender of the Shī'īs of Qumm equalled that of Mūsā al-Kāẓim as defender of the Baghdādī Shī'a.[103] And when al-Riḍā's disciple 'Alī b. al-Musayyab told the Imam that he could not always make the long journey (apparently from his native Hamadhān to Medina) to see the Imam, al-Riḍā told him that he could consult Zakariyyā b. Ādam on all points.[104] In Zakariyyā's case, at least, al-Riḍā was acting in accordance with his own maxim: "We provide you with the general principles of religion, and it is for you to elaborate the detailed points of law" (*'alaynā ilqā' al-uṣūl wa-'alaykum al-tafrī'*).[105] The permissibility of the use of analytical reasoning by competent scholars is hereby sanctioned—a significant shift from the earlier position. The same maxim, in a slightly different formulation, is ascribed to Ja'far al-Ṣādiq.[106] It is doubtful, however, whether he actually uttered it, given the rigid attitudes to questions of authority prevailing at his time. The attitude to the appointment of Imāmī judges also changed: The believers were urged to avoid, whenever possible, bringing legal disputes before a Sunnī judge. Instead they should look for a member of the community who was conversant with Imāmī law and tradition, and appoint him as judge (*qāḍī*) or arbiter (*ḥakam*); this appointment would automatically be sanctioned by the Imam.[107] Al-Majlisī maintains that the Imams themselves appointed judges to act on their behalf in the various provinces;[108] the extent of this practice remains, however, to be investigated.

The basic assumption, shared by all later Imāmī scholars, is clear; all actions undertaken by the disciples of the Imams in the pre-*Ghayba* period carried the Imam's stamp of approval. In this vein, al-Sharīf al-Murtaḍā argues that the Imams were at liberty to appoint one or more lieutenants (*khalīfa*) who would serve as military leaders (*umarā'*), judges, or arbiters. Each would be responsible for the implementation of a particular segment of the holy law; all would be answerable to the Imam, who would intervene and set things right whenever an error was committed by one of them.[109]

Yet, what should the believer do when faced with an urgent legal problem, with neither the Imam nor a competent Imāmī scholar being within reach? The answer, as given by al-Riḍā to his disciple 'Alī b. Asbāṭ, is that he should solicit the legal opinion of the local (Sunnī) *faqīh* and should then do the opposite, since Sunnī *fiqh* is based on falsehood.[110] The claim that Sunnī legal traditions are automatically to be discarded, though current in Imāmī literature, has obvious polemical overtones; in reality, of course, Sunnīs and Imāmīs agree on many points of law.

The practice of delegating authority to trusted disciples was maintained by al-Riḍā's successors. In a typical conversation, Aḥmad b. Isḥāq b. Sa'd al-Ash'arī al-Qummī is reported to have asked the tenth Imam, 'Alī al-Naqī (d. 254/868): "I constantly come and go; even when I am present (presumably in Sāmarrā) I do not always get a chance to see you. Whose words should we accept (when you are unreachable) and whose orders should we obey?" In reply, the Imam referred Aḥmad to Abū 'Amr 'Uthmān b. Sa'īd al-'Amrī (the future first *safīr* [representative]), saying: "Whatever he tells you is on my authority, and whatever he transmits to you comes from me." These words were reiterated by al-Naqī's son Ḥasan al-'Askarī (d. 260/873).[111]

The independence of local scholars appears at times to have gone beyond the Imam's wishes. It is significant that with the growing importance of Qumm it was precisely Qummī scholars who tended to play down the extent of the Imam's knowledge and to argue that he often had to fall back on his personal judgment. This attitude was condemned by others as *taqṣīr* (falling short).[112] Perhaps the most dramatic evidence for the change which began in al-Riḍā's time concerns Aḥmad b. Muḥammad b. 'Īsā al-Ash'arī, a disciple of the eighth, ninth, and tenth Imams.[113] He was not only a highly respected scholar with various works to his credit, but also served as leader of the Imāmī community in Qumm in the mid-third/ninth century, and in this capacity used to welcome government representatives on their visits to the city.[114] Yet al-Ash'arī also took upon himself the task of deciding on the orthodoxy of particular individuals. The need for decisions of this kind became pressing in view of the constant danger to mainstream (i.e., Imāmī) Shī'ism from dissident Shī'ī groups, such as the *wāqifīs* and various extremists (*ghulāt*). A common mechanism for dealing with such dissidents was dissociation, by which they were effectively removed from the community. This was a natural prerogative of the Imam; yet al-Ash'arī appears to have had no hesitation in assuming it himself. In at least two cases he ordered the expulsion from the city of persons known for their extremist Shī'ī views, apparently without first consulting the Imam. The first was Abū Sumayna Muḥammad b. 'Alī b. Ibrāhīm al-Ṣayrafī,[115] and the second, Sahl b. Ziyād al-Ādamī, a disciple of the ninth, tenth, and eleventh Imams. In Sahl's case, al-Ash'arī also forbade anyone to hear or transmit traditions from him.[116] He further expelled from the city Aḥmad b. Muḥammad b. Khālid al-Barqī (d. 274/887 or 280/893) for transmitting traditions by "weak" authorities; later, however, he allowed this renowned scholar to return, apologized to him, and even walked barefoot at his funeral as a mark of repentance.[117]

Al-Ash'arī was not the only one to make use of *barā'a:* during the imamate of the eleventh Imam Ḥasan al-'Askarī, certain unnamed leaders of the Imāmī community declared their dissociation from the extremist Shī'ī Abū Muḥammad al-Sharī'ī (or Shuray'ī), who claimed that he was the Imam's representative (*wakīl*). Their action was subsequently endorsed in a document (*tawqī'*) composed by the Imam.[118]

A tentative conclusion to be drawn from these admittedly sparse data is that the position of the religious leaders in the latter part of the pre-*Ghayba* period was not very different from their position in the century immediately following the Occultation. The fact that the later Imams were unable fully to exercise their authority largely contributed to this state of affairs and, paradoxically enough, proved beneficial to the community in the long run: By the time the Occultation took place, a tradition of administrative and scholarly independence from the Imam had established itself, thus making for a smoother and less painful transition to the era of the *Ghayba.*[119]

An important element which contributed to this process was the doctrine of the two *Ghaybas*, according to which the "greater" Occultation would be preceded by a shorter, "lesser" one. The realization of this doctrine occurred between the years 260/874-329/941, which are known as the period of the Lesser Occultation. At that time, the community was led by a series of four representatives of the Imam (*safīrs*). According to al-Shaykh al-Mufīd, these *safīrs* were appointed by Ḥasan al-'Askarī shortly before his death as intermediaries (*wasā'iṭ*) between the community and the Twelfth Imam. In this capacity, they transmitted answers which the Hidden Imam had provided to questions addressed to him by members of the community. They were aided in this by other close associates of Ḥasan al-'Askarī, who hailed from a variety of Shī'ī communities: al-Ahwāz, Kūfa, Baghdad, Qazwīn, Qumm, and the Jibāl. The mandate of these persons was not limited to the scholarly field, but included also the collection of dues paid to the Imam by the believers. This must have required at least some financial and administrative expertise, since considerable sums were involved. Such expertise had long been available to the community, for the position of *wakīl* (financial agent of the Imam) is attested at least since the days of Ja'far al-Ṣādiq. The extrascholarly aspect of this activity is underlined by al-Mufīd when he refers to its practitioners as *umarā'* (commanders) and *wulāt* (governors).[120]

The twin functions of administrator and scholar were united in the person of the *safīr*, who was superior in rank to other leading personalities not only by dint of his appointment by the Imam but also because he was believed to be in direct touch with the Hidden Imam. The first and second *safīrs*, 'Uthmān b. Sa'īd al-'Amrī and his son Abū Ja'far Muḥammad b. 'Uthmān (d. 304/916 or 305/917), had been financial agents for the tenth and eleventh Imams, and retained this position after their elevation to the office of *safīr*. At the same time, they did not neglect their scholarly duties: The second *safīr* is credited with works on *fiqh* which he transmitted from the tenth, eleventh, and twelfth Imams, directly or via his father.[121] The *safīrs* thus proved to be pivotal figures in paving the way for the period of the Greater Occultation.

III

The increasing significance of the *'ulamā'* is reflected in an important text, the *Tafsīr* ascribed to Ḥasan al-'Askarī. If this work really was composed by the eleventh Imam, it would constitute one of a small number of texts predating the Lesser Occultation. Its authenticity remains, however, to be investigated; for now all that can be said with certainty is that it was compiled no later than the mid-fourth/tenth century, since it was transmitted by Ibn Bābawayhi, who also cites it in various works.[122] In this *Tafsīr*, two distinct groups within the Imāmiyya are identified: *'ulamā* and *ḍu'afā'*. The *ḍu'afā'* are those whose knowledge of the doctrine is weak and who are therefore in danger of falling under the spell of Sunnism.[123] The term is also used in this sense by al-Khazzāz al-Rāzī al-Qummī (d. 381/991), one of Ibn Bābawayhi's pupils. In his case, the alien doctrine against which Shī'īs whose religious knowledge is weak or only moderate (*qawm min ḍu'afā' al-shī'a wa mutawassiṭīhim fī'l-'ilm*) ought to be protected is that of the Mu'tazila, who deny the line of twelve Imams.[124] Other terms for "weak" members are *mustaḍ'afūn, 'awāmm, aytām*, and *masākīn*. All are used in Imāmī texts in more than one sense. *Mustaḍ'afūn*, for example, often refers to the Imams (and occasionally to the entire Shī'ī community), whose weakness renders them unable to resist and defeat evil and oppression. Thus the Quranic *mustaḍ'afūn* (e.g., 4:75) is interpreted as referring to the Imams as a whole, or specifically to 'Alī, al-Ḥasan, and al-Ḥusayn.[125] In the second place, this term refers to those who are unsure of the identity of the Imam, and who are thus in an intermediate position between belief and unbelief.[126] The term *mustaḍ'afūn* as employed in the *Tafsīr al-'Askarī* may be said to constitute a third category. It has parallels elsewhere: Al-Karājakī, for one, mentions the *mustaḍ'afū'l-shī'a* who lend a ready ear to Sunnī claims that 'Alī had been an unbeliever before adopting Islam.[127] *'Awāmm* (or, more commonly, the singular form *'āmma*) is often used in Shī'ī texts to describe non-Shī'īs, but it can also on occasion be found in the sense employed here. The meaning given in the *Tafsīr* to *yatīm* and *miskīn* (both of which are Qu'rānic) appears to be idiosyncratic. The term *yatīm* is used in this work to denote a believer whose spiritual father (the Imam) has been imprisoned or is in hiding. Such a believer does not know how to conduct himself, and is thus in a worse plight than the orphan who has lost his parents.[128] Similarly, the *miskīn* is too weak (*sakanat jawāriḥuhu*) to be able to respond to arguments put forward by Sunnī opponents, and is thus worse off than the destitute.[129] It is the duty of the *'ulamā'* (or *fuqahā'*) to guard over these *aytām* and *masākīn*, to protect them from the darkness of ignorance, and to save them from falling into the Satanic net of the enemies of Shī'ism. The *'ulamā'* are described as warriors (*murābiṭūn*) who guard the frontiers against Iblīs and his devils. In so doing, they safeguard the Shī'ī religion; their actions are therefore more commendable than those of regular *mujāhidūn*, whose role is limited to defending the physical existence of the believers by fighting the infidels.[130] The *'ulamā'* are also placed above pious men; unlike the latter, they are not merely concerned with the performance of good deeds which would lead to their own salvation, but are engaged in saving others as well.[131] Those *'ulamā'* who have faithfully executed their duty have thereby saved Shī'ism from wholesale apostasy, and will be amply rewarded in the world to come; luminous crowns will be placed on their heads, and they will join the Imams in the highest parts of Paradise.[132]

Not all *'ulamā'*, however, belong to this category; there are also evil scholars (*'ulamā' al-saw'*) who have reneged on their duty, and who instill doubts and misgivings in the *ḍu'afā'*. Here, an interesting parallel is drawn with the situation of the Jewish community in Arabia at the advent of Islam. According to the Imam Ja'far al-Ṣādiq, the Jews were also divided into *'ulamā'* and *ḍu'afā'* (or *mustaḍ'afūn*). The latter are identified with the *ummiyyūn* of Qur'ān 2:78, who cannot read and write and are therefore dependent on others for information about the contents of books and documents. When Muḥammad began to spread his message, the Jewish *'ulamā'* became worried that the *ḍu'afā'* might follow him and deprive them of their position of leadership. In order to forestall this eventuality, they circulated among the *ḍu'afā'* false descriptions of what the true Prophet would be like: In contrast to Muḥammad, he would be tall, full-bodied and reddish-haired, and would only be sent at the end of time—namely five hundred years hence.[133]

A listener asked the Imam: If the Jewish *ḍu'afā'* received all their information from their *'ulamā'* and had no access to any other source of knowledge, surely they cannot be blamed for following their teachings (*taqlīd*)! If Jewish *'awāmm* may not follow their *'ulamā'*, why should ours be allowd to practice *taqlīd*? In his reply, the Imam draws a distinction between the two cases: The Jewish *'awāmm* had been aware all along that their leaders were a sinful, deceitful lot; the *'awāmm* knew therefore that they were not to follow them, but instead use their own judgment. Had they done so, they would surely have joined the Prophet, since the proofs (*dalā'il*) confirming his prophecy were there for all to see. The Shī'ī *'awāmm*, on the other hand, might be confronted by either pious or evil *'ulamā'*, and it was their duty to distinguish between the two. The implication, then, is that even the *'awāmm* are expected to use reasoning.[134] Shī'īs following evil scholars are no better than their Jewish counterparts; but *taqlīd* is permissible when it has been established that the *'ālim* in question is a just, God-fearing person.

The Imam distinguishes three kinds of evil scholars operating in the community: First, there are those engaged in the pursuit of worldly pleasures and the persecution of all who might stand in their way; their evil nature is often coupled with ignorance of Shī'ī tradition, and so they misconstrue the words of the Imams. Worse still are those *'ulamā'* who know the truth but deliberately spread falsehoods about the Imams in order to curry favor with the rulers. Finally, there are anti-'Alid (*nuṣṣāb*) scholars with some knowledge of the Shī'ī heritage. They pose as loyal Shī'īs, and, having insinuated themselves into the confidence of the uneducated masses (here referred to as *al-mustaslimūn min shī'atinā*—those of our Shī'a who uncritically accept whatever they are told), they then proceed to mislead them by attributing countless lies to the Imams. The harm which scholars of this group inflict on the Shī'ī *ḍu'afā'* is seen as worse than the misfortune visited by Yazīd on al-Ḥusayn and his entourage: After all, those killed or imprisoned at Karbalā' were all loyal Shī'īs who will be compensated for their sufferings in the world to come; but those *ḍu'afā'* who are led astray in this world will as a result be punished in the next.[135]

It is difficult to assess the historical significance of these passages from the *Tafsīr*, owing to the uncertainty regarding its precise date of composition. Several points are, however, worth mentioning. The reference to an apparently large body of *ḍu'afā'* would appear to agree with the actual state of the Imāmī community both before and immediately after the Occultation. As mentioned above, the believers were beset, in the pre-*Ghayba* period, by two major problems: persecution from without and doubts and splits from within. With the onset of the *Ghayba*, a major crisis was added; the sudden loss of the supreme spiritual leader must have caused profound disquiet and raised some agonizing questions among ordinary Imāmīs. The early Firaq literature attests to the extent of division which this event caused, and much effort was expended by the best-known Imāmī scholars of the fourth/tenth century to explain and justify the Imam's disappearance. The pressures upon the community were not confined to the *ḍu'afā'*. Learned Shī'īs were subject to similar doubts, as attested by the numerous defections to the *wāqifī* and *ghālī* camps. There was, in addition, the ever-present temptation to go over to the Sunnī side, or at least to work for the government for mere personal gain. The blanket term *'ulamā' al-saw'* would thus seem to cover all of these cases. It was essential for the official leadership to distance itself from these scholars and to establish its own credentials as the sole guardian of true faith.[136]

Abbreviations

'A = *Tafsīr al-'Askarī*, Tabriz, 1314-15/1896-98.
B = al-Majlisī, *Biḥār al-anwār*, [Iran], 1305-15.
Ḥ = Aḥmad al-Ṭabarsī, *al-Iḥtijāj*, [Iran], 1268.
K = al-Kulīnī, *al-Kāfī*, ed. 'Alī Akbar al-Ghaffārī, Tehran, 1377-81.
L = Abū 'Amr al-Kishshī, *Rijāl*, Najaf, n. d.
M = al-Mufīd, *al-Ikhtiṣāṣ*, Najaf, 1390/1971.
Q = al-Barqī, *al-Maḥāsin*, ed. Jalāl al-Dīn al-Ḥusaynī al-Muḥaddith, Tehran, 1370/1950-51.
R = Ibn Bābawayhi, *Ma'ānī l-akhbār*, Najaf, 1391/1971.
Ṣ = al-Ṣaffār al-Qummī, *Baṣā'ir al-darajāt*, Tehran, 1285.
U = Hāshim al-Baḥrānī, *Kitāb al-burhān fī tafsīr al-qur'ān*, Tehran, 1375.
Y = al-'Ayyāshī, *Tafsīr*, ed. Hāshim al-Rasūlī al-Maḥallātī, Qumm, 1380-81.
Z = al-Karājakī, *Kanz al-fawā'id*, Mashhad, 1322.

Notes

*This paper was written while I was a Fellow of the Institute for Advanced Studies at the Hebrew University of Jerusalem in 1984-85. I should like to express my gratitude to the Institute staff for their unfailing help and generosity.

1. Ṣ, p. 106; K, I, p. 268.

2. K, I, p. 398; see also Ṣ, p. 2.

3. See Muḥsin al-Fayḍ's comment in the introduction to his *Wāfī*, Tehran, 1375/1955-56, I, part 1, p. 12. A case in point may be the traditions which al-Kulīnī, in his introduction to the *Kāfī*, cites on the authority of *al-'ālim*, without identifying him further (K, I, pp. 7-9, cited in Yūsuf al-Baḥrānī, *al-Ḥadā'iq al-nāḍira*, I, Najaf, 1376/1957, p. 107).

4. *Al-'ālim* does not appear in the usual lists of honorific appellations of these two Imams (see B, XI, pp. 107f, 233, and the sources cited there). It is attested, however, in various texts (though it is not always clear which of the two is meant). See R, pp. 241f; 'A, pp. 46, 47; M, p. 137; and especially al-Mas'ūdī, *Ithbāt al-waṣiyya*, Najaf, 1374/1955, pp. 9 (where the *'ālim ahl al-bayt* is Ja'far al-Ṣādiq, as can be seen from a parallel tradition in K, I, p. 21), 13, 14, 59, 76, 160, 164f, 172, 178, 248. For *al-'ālim* as an appellation of the tenth Imam, 'Alī al-Naqī, see al-Faḍl b. al-Ḥasan al-Ṭabarsī, *I'lām al-warā*, Najaf, 1390/1970, p. 355.

5. Ṣ, p. 106.

6. K, I, p. 32.

7. Ṣ, p. 133, cited in B, VII, p. 194; K, I, p. 272; Ḥasan b. Sulaymān al-Ḥillī, *Mukhtaṣar baṣā'ir al-darajāt*, Najaf, 1370/1950, p. 2; U, I, pp. 238f. The other four spirits are the *rūḥ al-īmān, rūḥ al-quwwa, rūḥ al-shahwa* and *rūḥ al-ḥayāt* (or *al-badan*).

8. The question whether prophets preceding Muḥammad also possessed the *rūḥ al-qudus* is discussed by al-Majlisī in B, VII, p. 197, and in *Mir'āt al-'uqūl*, III, Tehran, 1404/1984, pp. 172f. The evidence of the texts is contradictory. According to some traditions, the spirit of holiness accompanied all prophets; according to others, only Muḥammad and the Imams possessed it. See, e.g., K, II, p. 282; Ibn Bābawayhi, *'Uyūn akhbār al-Riḍā*, Najaf, 1390/1970, II, p. 200, cited in B, VII, p. 214.

9. Ṣ, p. 134, cited in B, VII, p. 197; K, I, p. 273; al-Ḥillī, *Mukhtaṣar*, pp. 2, 3; U, IV, pp. 132f; B, VII, pp. 193f. See also al-Qummī, *Tafsīr*, Najaf, 1386-87, cited in B, VII, p. 192; al-Mas'ūdī, *Ithbāt*, p. 186. For an eighteenth-century Sunnī attack on this view, see Shah 'Abd al-'Azīz al-Dihlawī, *Al-tuḥfa'l-ithnā 'ashariyya*, pp. 104f in the Istanbul 1401/1981 edition of the Arabic *Mukhtaṣar* of Maḥmūd Shukrī l-Alūsī; see also A. A. Rizvi, *Shah 'Abd al-'Azīz: Puritanism, Sectarian Polemics and Jihād*, Canberra, 1982, pp. 291f, 393f.

10. Ṣ, p. 134, cited in B, VII p. 195; K, I, p. 273; al-Ṭabarsī, *Majma' al-bayān*, Beirut, 1374-77, XXV, p. 66; al-Ḥillī, *Mukhtaṣar*, p. 3; U, IV, p. 133.

11. Ṣ, p. 136, cited in B, VII, p. 196; al-Ḥillī, *Mukhtaṣar*, p. 4; U, IV, p. 481. See also al-Riḍā's statement: "God has supported us with a pure and holy spirit which is not an angel" (Ibn Bābawayhi, *'Uyūn akhbār al-Riḍā*, II, p. 200, cited in B, VII, p. 214).

12. For example, S, p. 134: *malak, mundhu unzila dhālika'l-malak lam yaṣ'ad ilā'l-samā';* al-Ṭabarsī, loc. cit. For attempts at harmonization, see B, VII, pp. 193f; Abū l-Ḥasan al-'Āmilī al-Iṣfahānī, *Tafsīr mir'āt al-anwār*, Tehran, 1374, pp. 156f.

13. For details see H. Modarressi Ṭabāṭabā'ī, *An Introduction to Shī'ī Law*, London, 1984, pp. 27-29.

14. Ibn Bābawayhi, *Khiṣāl*, Najaf, 1391/1971, p. 398, R, p. 101, both cited in B, VII, p. 216. See also 'Alī b. Ṭāwūs, *Kashf al-maḥajja*, Najaf, 1370/1950, pp. 41f; Rajab al-Bursī, *Mashāriq anwār al-yaqīn fī asrār amīr al-mu'minīn*, Beirut, n. d., pp. 70ff, 135ff.

15. Al-Mufīd, *Awā'il al-maqālāt*, Tabriz, 1371, pp. 36-38; M. J. McDermott, *The Theology of al-Shaykh al-Mufīd*, Beirut, 1978, p. 108.

16. Al-Murtaḍā, *al-Shāfī fī'l-imāma*, Tehran, 1301/1884, pp. 76, 78; al-Ṭūsī, *Talkhīṣ al-shāfī*, Najaf, 1383/1963, I, p. 263.

17. Al-Murtaḍā, *Shāfī*, pp. 188-89; al-Ṭūsī, *Talkhīṣ al-shāfī*, I, p. 252.

18. Al-Murtaḍā, *al-Fuṣūl al-mukhtāra*, n. pl., n. d., I, pp. 80f; al-Ṭūsī, *Talkhīṣ al-shāfī*, I, p. 94; id., *Kitāb al-ghayba*, Najaf, 1385/1965, pp. 66f; McDermott, *Theology*, pp. 125-27.

19. Al-Mufīd, *al-Masā'il al-'ukbariyya*, cited in McDermott, *Theology*, p. 109.

20. See, e.g., al-Bursī, *Mashāriq*, p. 88, and in general my article "Some Imāmī Shī'ī Interpretations of Umayyad History," *Studies on the First Century of Islamic Society*, ed. G. H. A. Juynboll, Carbondale and Edwardsville, 1982, pp. 145-59, 249-54, at pp. 149f.

21. Ṣ, pp. 32, 53f, 74; K, I, p. 223; Ibn Bābawayhi, *'Uyūn*, II, p. 207.

22. Al-Mufīd, *Awā'il al-maqālāt*, pp. 42f; McDermott, *Theology*, p. 106. See also al-Ḥillī, *Mukhtaṣar*, p. 108; B, I, p. 125 (citing al-Rāwandī, *al-Kharā'ij wa'l-jarā'iḥ*). Cf. al-Karājakī, *Kitāb al-tafḍīl*, Tehran, 1370, pp. 31-33.

23. *K. Ja'far b. Muḥammad b. Shurayḥ*, MS Tehran University no. 962, fol. 44b; al-Ḥillī, *Mukhtaṣar*, p. 61.

24. Ṣ, p. 61; Y, II, pp. 28, 266; M, p. 252, cited in B, I, p. 125; al-Ḥillī, *Mukhtaṣar*, p. 109.

25. Ṣ, pp. 31f; K, I, pp. 222f; al-Ḥillī, *Mukhtaṣar*, p. 108; shorter version: Ṣ, p. 61.

26. *K. Ja'far b. Muḥammad b. Shurayḥ*, fol. 44b; Ṣ, pp. 35, 115f; K, I, p. 254; al-Ṭūsī, *Amālī*, Najaf, 1384/1964, II, p. 23; Āghā Najafī, *Ḥaqā'iq al-asrār*, Tehran, 1296/1879, p. 4.

27. K, I, p. 254, no. 2.

28. Ṣ, p. 124.

29. Ṣ, p. 31; K, I, pp. 221f, 379. Similar versions: Q, p. 235; Ṣ, pp. 31f; K, I, pp. 222f; Ibn Bābawayhi, *'Ilal al-sharā'i'*, Najaf, 1385/1966, p. 591.

30. K, I, p. 251, cited in B, VII, p. 201.

31. K, I, p. 250, cited in U, IV, p. 484. Cf. Murtaḍā al-Zabīdī, *Tāj al-'arūs*,

s.v. *fsr: wa qīl: al-tafsīr sharḥ mā jā'a mujmalan min al-qaṣaṣ fi'l-kitāb al-karīm*, etc.

32. Ṣ, pp. 59f.

33. K, I, pp. 251f, cited in B, VII, p. 201, and U, IV, pp. 248f. See also K, I, p. 248, cited in U, IV, p. 483.

34. K, I, pp. 251f, cited in B, VII, p. 201, and U, IV, pp. 484f.

35. *EI*, new edition, art. "Badā'" (I. Goldziher-A. S. Tritton); McDermott, *Theology*, pp. 329-39.

36. B, VII, p. 205; id., *Mir'āt al-'uqūl*, III, p. 97. See also Ibn Bābawayhi, *'Uyūn akhbār al-Riḍā*, I, pp. 145f; Muḥammad Ṣāliḥ al-Māzandarānī's *Sharḥ* on al-Kulīnī's *Uṣūl al-kāfī*, VI, Tehran, 1385, pp. 16-19. Cf. al-Bursī, *Mashāriq*, p. 137; Madelung, "The Shiite and Kharijite Contribution to Pre-Ash'arite *kalām*," *Islamic Philosophical Theology*, ed. P. Morewedge, Albany, 1979, pp. 120-39, at p. 131, n. 25.

37. K, I, p. 255; Ṣ, p. 115; M, pp. 261f, 306, 307.

38. Ṣ, p. 116.

39. M, p. 308.

40. Ṣ, p. 115; M, p. 307; al-Ṭūsī, *Amālī*, II, p. 23. See also al-Bursī, *Mashāriq*, p. 138; al-Majlisī, *Mir'āt al-'uqūl*, III, p. 99; Muḥammad b. Muḥammad Karīm Khān, *al-Kitāb al-mubīn*, Tabriz, 1324/1906, I, p. 281.

41. Al-Mufīd, *Awā'il*, p. 45; id., *al-Masā'il al-'Ukbariyya*, as quoted in *Awā'il*, p. 45, n. 1.

42. *K. Ja'far b. Muḥammad b. Shurayḥ*, fol. 44b; Ṣ, pp. 124-26; K, I, pp. 219f; cf. al-Mufīd, *Amālī*, Najaf, 1367, p. 115; 'Alī al-Ṭabarsī, *Mishkāt al-anwār fī ghurar al-akhbār*, Najaf, 1385/1965, p. 72. For a Sunnī view, cf. Muḥammad Rashīd Riḍā, *Fatāwā*, ed. Ṣalāḥ al-Dīn al-Munajjid, I, Beirut, 1390/1970, pp. 262-64.

43. For a somewhat different description, see Ṣ, p. 35; K, I, p. 254.

44. K, I, p. 255; Ṣ, p. 115; M, p. 308. See also Āghā Najafī, *Ḥaqā'iq al-asrār*, pp. 25-40.

45. Ṣ, p. 140; M, pp. 261f (*al-a'imma yatafāḍalūn*), 306f; al-Ḥillī, *Mukhtaṣar*, p. 6.

46. *K. Ja'far b. Muḥammad b. Shurayḥ*, fol. 43b; Ṣ, p. 140; K, I, p. 275. See also al-Ḥillī, *Mukhtaṣar*, p. 109, where al-Bāqir declares: "'Alī is the first among us, the most excellent and most knowledgeable (*akhbarunā*) after the messenger of God."

47. Z, pp. 112f. As al-Majlisī points out, al-Karājakī's position is based on a number of Īmāmī traditions (*Mir'āt al-'uqul*, III, p. 178). Al-Majlisī thus

appears to acknowledge the validity of this position, even though he himself does not explicitly adopt it.

48. Ṣ, p. 6; K, I, p. 389, no. 1; ʻAlī al-Ṭabarsī, *Mishkāt al-anwār*, pp. 95f; Muḥsin al-Fayḍ *Wāfī*, I, part 2, pp. 155f, I, part 3, p. 6; id., *Uṣūl al-maʻārif*, ed. Jalāl al-Dīn Āshtiyānī, Mashhad, 1354 Sh/1975, p. 188. In these traditions, *ʻilliyyūn* is used not merely to refer to a place in Paradise but also to the substance found in it. For the various interpretations of ʻIlliyyūn, see B, III, p. 65; *EI*, new edition, s.v. (R. Paret). Cf. in general U. Rubin, "Pre-existence and Light," *IOS*, 5 (1975), pp. 62-119.

49. Ṣ, p. 6; K, I p. 389, no. 2. In some traditions, prophets and Shīʻīs are said to have been created of the same *ṭīna* (Q, I, p. 133; K, II, p. 3, cited in B, XV/i, p. 26; cf. Warrām b. Abī Firās, *Tanbīh al-khawāṭir*, Najaf, 1384/1964, p. 317); but elsewhere it is emphasized that the prophets were created of the purest element (*ṣafwa*) of this *ṭīna* (K, II, p. 3, cited in B, XV/i, p. 23).

50. Q, I, pp. 132f, and al-Qummī, *Tafsīr*, II, p. 411, both cited in B, III, p. 65; Ṣ, p. 4, cited in B, III, p. 63; K, II, p. 4. Cf. M, p. 186.

51. Al-Mufīd, *Amālī*, p. 183; al-Ṭūsī, *Amālī*, I, p. 77; ʻAlī al-Ṭabarsī, *Mishkāt al-anwār*, p. 80; see also al-Ṭurayḥī, *Muntakhab*, Beirut, n. d., p. 268; al-Bursī, *Mashāriq*, p. 199; Āghā Najafī, *Ḥaqāʼiq al-asrār*, p. 6; al-Nūrī al-Ṭabarsī, *Nafas al-Raḥmān*, Tehran, 1285, p. 34. Cf. al-Ṭūsī, *Amālī*, I, p. 305: *shīʻatunā juzʼ minnā khuliqū min faḍl ṭīnatinā;* II, p. 188.

52. Ibn Bābawayhi, *ʻIlal al-sharāʼiʻ*, pp. 607f, cited in B, III, pp. 63f. See also Q, I, p. 282, cited in B, III, p. 70; al-Bursī, *Mashāriq*, p. 152; Muḥsin al-Fayḍ, *Wāfī*, I, part 3, pp. 12f (with a *bāṭin* interpretation); B, XV/i, pp. 28f.

53. Ṣ, p. 22; Ibn Bābawayhi, *ʻUyūn akhbār al-Riḍā*, II, p. 200.

54. M, p. 102.

55. Ibn Bābawayhi, *Faḍāʼil al-shīʻa* (with a Persian translation by Ḥusayn Fashāhī), Tehran, 1342 Sh, p. 23; M, p. 103. Cf. Q, I, p. 171.

56. Y, I, p. 256, cited in B, XV/i, p. 110; Ibn Bābawayhi, *Faḍāʼil al-shīʻa*, pp. 23f; M, p. 102. Contrast Q, I, pp. 163f, where *al-ṣiddīqūn waʼl-shuhadāʼ* of Qurʼān 57:19 are the Shīʻīs. See the discussion in B, XV/i, p. 103.

57. Q, I, p. 169, cited in B, XV/i, p. 110; Ṣ, p. 16; K, I, p. 212; ʻAlī al-Ṭabarsī, *Mishkāt al-anwār*, p. 95.

58. Ṣ, p. 17; R, pp. 92, 380, cited in B, XV/i, p. 109; al-Ṭūsī, *Amālī*, II, p. 223.

59. Ṣ, pp. 2f (different versions). Cf. Q, I, p. 227; Ṣ, p. 6; K, I, p. 389, no. 2; al-Ṭūsī, *Amālī*, I, p. 19; Muḥammad Amīn al-Astarābādī, *al-Fawāʼid al-madaniyya*, Tehran, 1321/1904, p. 120; Muḥsin al-Fayḍ, *al-Maḥajjaʼl-bayḍāʼ fī tahdhīb al-iḥyāʼ*, ed. ʻAlī Akbar al-Ghaffārī, Tehran, 1339-42 Sh, IV, p. 373; id., *Kitāb al-uṣūl al-aṣīla*, ed. Jalāl al-Dīn al-Ḥusaynī al-Urmawī al-Muḥaddith, Tehran, 1390, pp. 132, 170.

60. Al-Ṭūsī, *Amālī*, I, p. 148.

61. Ibn Bābawayhi, *Ṣifāt al-shī'a* (in the same volume with the *Faḍā'il al-shī'a*, continuous pagination), p. 52.

62. Ibn Bābawayhi, *Ṣifāt al-shī'a*, p. 53; al-Ṭūsī, *Amālī*, II, pp. 188f; Warrām b. Abī Firās, *Tanbīh al-khawāṭir*, p. 317; 'Alī al-Ṭabarsī, *Mishkāt al-anwār*, pp. 58, 62f, 79, 89. See in general K, II, pp. 226-42; Z, pp. 29-34; Muḥsin al-Fayḍ, *Maḥajja*, I, p. 74, IV, pp. 352-70; B, XV/i, pp. 69-103, and the sources cited there.

63. Ibn Bābawayhi, *Ṣifāt al-shī'a*, p. 53.

64. 'A, pp. 124-31. For a threefold division of *muḥibbūn*, see al-Ḥasan b. 'Alī Ibn Shu'ba, *Tuḥaf al-'uqūl*, Beirut, 1394/1974, p. 240. Cf. Warrām b. Abī Firās, *Tanbīh al-khawāṭir*, pp. 347f.

65. Q, I, pp. 136-38 (*bāb ikhtilāṭ al-ṭīnatayn*); Ibn Bābawayhi, *'Ilal al-sharā'i'*, pp. 82-84, 116f, 607-9; al-Ḥillī, *Mukhtaṣar*, pp. 150f, 157f.

66. Muḥsin al-Fayḍ, *Maḥajja*, IV, p. 372.

67. Al-Mufīd, *Amālī*, p. 113.

68. K, IV, p. 309; al-Ṭūsī, *Tahdhīb al-aḥkām*, Najaf, 1377/1957ff, V, p. 414; my "Non-Imāmī Muslims in Imāmī *fiqh*," *Jerusalem Studies in Arabic and Islam*, 6 (1985), pp. 99-105, at p. 101.

69. L, pp. 9, 10; Muḥsin al-Fayḍ, *Uṣūl*, p. 56.

70. L, pp. 122, 124; Muḥsin al-Fayḍ, *Uṣūl*, p. 55.

71. See my *al-Uṣūl al-arba'umi'a, Jerusalem Studies in Arabic and Islam*, 10 (1988).

72. Early sources listing the *Kitāb al-'ilal* among al-Faḍl's writings include al-Najāshī, *Rijāl*, Bombay, 1317, p. 217, and al-Ṭūsī, *Fihrist*, Najaf, 1380/1961, p. 150.

73. *'Ilal al-sharā'i'*, pp. 251-75, *'Uyūn akhbār al-Riḍā*, II, pp. 97-119, both cited in B, III, pp. 108-15. See also Jalāl al-Dīn al-Ḥusaynī al-Urmawī's introduction to his edition of al-Faḍl b. Shādhān's *Īḍāḥ*, Tehran, 1392/1972, pp. 30-32. A passage from the *'Ilal* is quoted (via Ibn Bābawayhi) by al-Khumaynī, *al-Ḥukūma l-islāmiyya*, Najaf, 1389, pp. 37f.

74. Ibn Bābawayhi, *'Ilal al-sharā'i'*, pp. 274f; id., *'Uyūn akhbār al-Riḍā*, II, p. 119; B, III, p. 115.

75. Ṣ, p. 151, referring to Qur'ān 4:65 (*wa yusallimū taslīman*), cited in B, I, pp. 112, 123f, al-Nūrī al-Ṭabarsī, *Mustadrak al-wasā'il*, II, Tehran, 1383, p. 373; al-Ḥillī, *Mukhtaṣar*, pp. 71-77; U, I, pp. 389-91, IV, p. 72. Cf. Q, I, pp. 270-72; Muḥsin al-Fayḍ, *Maḥajja*, I, p. 260; id., *Uṣūl*, p. 175.

76. Ṣ, p. 152, cited in B, I, p. 123; al-Ḥillī, *Mukhtaṣar*, pp. 73f.

77. T. Nagel, *Staat und Glaubensgemeinschaft im Islam*, Zürich and München, 1981, I, pp. 185-92; Modarressi, *Introduction*, pp. 29-31, and the sources cited there.

78. Q, I, p. 212, cited in B, I, pp. 154f.

79. Q, I, p. 213, cited in B, I, p. 155.

80. K, VII, p. 406, cited in Muḥsin al-Fayḍ, *Maḥajja*, VI, p. 194.

81. K, VII, p. 407, cited in B, IX, pp. 495f.

82. ʻA, pp. 136, 138f.

83. M, pp. 216f; al-Nūrī al-Ṭabarsī, *Nafas al-raḥmān*, pp. 31, 59. See also al-Ḥillī, *Mukhtaṣar*, p. 125; "Salmān belongs to the *ʻulamā'* because he is one of us, the *ahl al-bayt*."

84. M, pp. 72f; al-Ṭūsī, *Amālī*, I, p. 167. See also al-Masʻūdī, *Ithbāt*, p. 191.

85. The reasons for conversion to Imāmī Shīʻism in the early period and the social background of the converts are issues still to be investigated. It appears that the Imams encouraged Shīʻī missionary activities, provided these were restricted to areas of unbelief. See L, p. 292; al-Ṭūsī, *Amālī*, I, pp. 44f.

86. L, p. 179. The following four paragraphs are largely extracted from my "*Barā'a* in Shīʻī doctrine," *Jerusalem Studies in Arabic and Islam*, 7 (1986), pp. 139-75, at pp. 158-61.

87. L, p. 233; al-Ṭūsī, *Amālī*, I, p. 45.

88. Al-Ṭūsī, *Fihrist*, p. 100.

89. L, pp. 134, 208. See also Ibn Bābawayhi, *Tawḥīd*, n. pl., 1321, pp. 354f.

90. K, II, pp. 402f; L, pp. 128f.

91. Al-Ṭūsī, *Fihrist*, p. 100.

92. L, pp. 151, 208.

93. *EI*, new ed., art. "Hishām b. al-Ḥakam" (W. Madelung); W. Madelung, "Contribution," pp. 12f.

94. L, pp. 151, 174, 208.

95. Ibid. Cf. K, II, pp. 297-99. Al-Bāqir is said to have admonished his disciple Abū Nuʻmān al-ʻIjlī: "Do not set yourself up as a head lest you become a tail (*lā tar'as fa takūna dhanaban*) (al-Mufīd, *Amālī*, p. 108). For an analysis of the various types of *ri'āsa*, consult B, XV/iii, pp. 102-4.

96. L, pp. 148, 152, 207.

97. L, p. 152. On the merits of *tawāḍuʻ* see K, II, pp. 121-24; Muḥsin

al-Fayḍ, *Maḥajja*, VI, pp. 222-26.

98. M, p. 61; L, pp. 124, 152; Muḥsin al-Fayḍ, *Uṣūl*, pp. 55-57.

99. Al-Ṭūsī, *Fihrist*, p. 41; al-Najāshī, *Rijāl*, p. 7; al-Astarābādī, *Fawā'id*, p. 152; Muḥsin al-Fayḍ, *Uṣūl*, pp. 54f, 154; al-Tustarī, *Qāmūs al-rijāl*, I, Tehran, 1379, pp. 73f.

100. L, p. 168.

101. L, p. 126.

102. Shī'īs are known to have resided in Qumm as early as the mid-second/eighth century. 'Īsā b. 'Abd Allāh al-Qummī, for instance, was regarded by Ja'far al-Ṣādiq as an honorary member of the *ahl al-bayt*. See al-Mufīd, *Amālī*, p. 83; M, p. 63; L, pp. 281f (where 'Īsā describes himself as a *rajul min ahl Qumm*), cited in al-Quhpā'ī, *Majma' al-rijāl*, Iṣfahān, 1384-87, IV, p. 303, al-Māmaqānī, *Tanqīḥ al-maqāl*, Najaf, 1349-53, biography no. 9316. Mālik's pupil Abū Muḥammad 'Abd Allāh b. Abī Ḥassān al-Yaḥṣubī refers to the Shī'ī religion as *dīn ahl Qumm*. See Abū Bakr 'Abd Allāh al-Mālikī, *Riyāḍ al-nufūs fī ṭabaqāt 'ulamā' al-Qayrawān wa Ifrīqiya*, ed. Ḥusayn Mu'nis, I, Cairo, 1951, p. 202. I owe this reference to Mr. Yehoshua Frenkel.

103. M, p. 83; L, p. 496. For Imāmī definitions of a *safīh*, see K, II, pp. 322f.

104. M, pp. 83f; L, p. 496.

105. Aḥmad B. Muḥammad b. Abī Naṣr al-Bizanṭī (fl. early third/ninth century; cf. al-Māmaqānī, *Tanqīḥ al-maqāl*, biography no. 452), *Jāmi'*, cited in Ibn Idrīs, *Sarā'ir*, Qumm, 1390, p. 477, al-Astarābādī, *Fawā'id*, p. 154, Muḥsin al-Fayḍ, *Uṣūl*, p. 66, B, I, 136; Modarressi, *Introduction*, p. 24.

106. Ibid. See the discussion in Muḥsin al-Fayḍ, *al-Ḥaqq al-mubīn fī taḥqīq kayfiyyat al-tafaqquh fī'l-dīn*, ed. Jalāl al-Dīn al-Ḥusaynī al-Urmawī al-Muḥaddith, Tehran, 1390, pp. 7f.

107. K, I, p. 67, VII, pp. 411f; al-Astarābādī, *Fawā'id*, p. 151; Muḥsin al-Fayḍ, *Uṣūl*, pp. 52f, 91, 150. See in general N. Calder, "Judicial Authority in Imāmī Shī'ī Jurisprudence," *BRISMES Bulletin*, 6 (1979), no. 2, pp. 104-8, at p. 104; A. K. S. Lambton, *State and Government in Medieval Islam*, O. U. P., 1981, p. 252.

108. Al-Majlisī, *Mir'āt al-'uqūl*, cited in K, VII, p. 406, n. 1.

109. Al-Murtaḍā, *Shāfī*, pp. 42, 67, 76, 78.

110. Ibn Bābawayhi, *'Uyūn akhbār al-Riḍā*, I, p. 214; id., *'Ilal al-sharā'i'*, p. 531, cited in al-Astarābādī, *Fawā'id*, p. 190, Muḥsin al-Fayḍ, *Uṣūl*, p. 97, B, I, p. 133. This principle is attributed already to al-Bāqir, al-Ṣādiq, and al-Kāẓim. See Muḥsin al-Fayḍ, *Uṣūl*, pp. 87, 95f.

111. K, I, p. 330; al-Ṭūsī, *Kitāb al-ghayba*, pp. 146f, 215, 218f; al-Astarābādī,

Fawā'id, p. 48; Muḥsin al-Fayḍ, *Uṣūl*, p. 51; al-Māmaqānī, *Tanqīḥ al-maqāl*, biography no. 7783; Javad Ali, "Die beiden ersten Safīre des Zwölften Imāms," *Der Islam*, 25 (1939), pp. 197-227, at p. 199. Since this tradition legitimizes the first *safīr*, the possibilities of retrojection cannot be ruled out. No date is given in the sources for 'Uthmān b. Sa'īd's death. Jassim M. Hussain (*The Occultation of the Twelfth Imam*, London, 1982, p. 97) is probably correct in arguing that he died before 267/880 and not in 280/893, as maintained by Javad Ali (op. cit., p. 205).

112. Al-Mufīd, *Taṣḥīḥ al-i'tiqād*, Tabriz, 1371, pp. 65f; al-Nūrī al-Ṭabarsī, *Nafas al-Raḥmān*, p. 29.

113. Al-Ṭūsī, *Fihrist*, pp. 48f; al-Najāshī, *Rijāl*, pp. 59f; al-Quhpā'ī, *Majma' al-rijāl*, I, pp. 161-65.

114. Al-Najāshī, *Rijāl*, p. 60.

115. H. Halm, "Das 'Buch der Schatten,'" *Der Islam*, 55 (1978), pp. 241f.

116. Al-Najāshī, *Rijāl*, p. 234, al-Ghaḍā'irī, *Ḍu'afā'*, cited in al-Quhpā'ī, *Majma' al-rijāl*, III, p. 179, V, pp. 264f.

117. Al-Tustarī, *Qāmūs al-rijāl*, I, pp. 189, 390, 420; al-Māmaqānī, *Tanqīḥ al-maqāl*, biography no. 508.

118. Al-Ṭūsī, *Kitāb al-ghayba*, p. 244.

119. Whatever practical authority the scholars wielded in the period under discussion, they neither claimed nor sought to justify clerical rule. The notion of *wilāyat al-faqīh* was still a very long way off.

120. Al-Mufīd, *al-Fuṣūl al-'ashara fī l-ghayba*, Najaf, 1370/1951, pp. 17f, 28; al-Ṭūsī, *Kitāb al-ghayba*, pp. 209-43; Muḥsin al-Fayḍ, *al-Nawādir fī jam' al-aḥādīth*, Tehran, 1339 Sh/1960, pp. 157f; in general, B, XIII, pp. 93-100; Javad Ali, "Die beiden ersten Safīre"; Nagel, *Staat und Glaubensgemeinschaft im Islam*, I, pp. 207f; Hussain, *Occultation*, pp. 79ff. The wealth amassed by the Imams through the network of revenue collectors laid them open to attacks by opponents. See, for instance, the charges levelled by the Zaydī Imam al-Qāsim b. Ibrāhīm (d. 246/860) in his *Kitāb al-radd 'alā l-rawāfiḍ* against his contemporary, the tenth Imam, 'Alī al-Naqī (quoted by Madelung, *Der Imam al-Qāsim ibn Ibrāhīm und die Glaubenslehre der Zaiditen*, Berlin, 1965, p. 147).

121. Al-Ṭūsī, *Kitāb al-ghayba*, p. 221. Al-Ṭūsī relies for this information on Ibn Nūḥ, i.e., the Baṣran scholar Aḥmad b. 'Alī b. al-'Abbās b. Nūḥ al-Sīrāfī (fl. beginning of fifth/eleventh century), who is credited with a work on the *safīrs* entitled *Akhbār al-wukalā' al-arba'a* (al-Najāshī, *Rijāl*, p. 63) or *Kitāb akhbār al-abwāb* (al-Ṭūsī, *Fihrist*, p. 62).

122. The renowned Imāmī author Muḥsin al-Fayḍ al-Kāshānī (d. 1091/1680) refers to this work as *al-Tafsīr al-mansūb ilā'l-imām Abī Muḥammad al-'Askarī*. See his works *al-Nawādir fī jam' al-aḥādīth*, p. 3, *Tafsīr al-ṣāfī*, [Iran],

1266, p. 19, and *Wāfī*, II, part 9, p. 137. For a contemporary Shī'ī view of *Tafsīr al-'Askarī*, see al-Ṭihrānī, *al-Dharī'a ilā taṣānīf al-shī'a*, Najaf and Tehran, 1355/1936-1398/1978, IV, pp. 285-93, no. 1295.

123. 'A, p. 137; Ḥ, p. 5; B, I, p. 70.

124. Al-Khazzāz al-Rāzī, *Kifāyat al-athar*, [Persia], 1305, p. 289. See also my "From Imāmiyya to Ithnā 'ashariyya," *BSOAS*, 39 (1976), pp. 521-34, at p. 522.

125. Y, I, p. 257; al-'Āmilī al-Iṣfahānī, *Tafsīr*, p. 219.

126. Y, I, p. 257; K, II, pp. 404-6; B, XV/iii, pp. 19-22; al-'Āmilī al-Iṣfahānī, *Tafsīr*, p. 219.

127. Z, p. 118.

128. 'A, p. 136; Ḥ, p. 217; Muḥsin al-Fayḍ, *Maḥajja*, I, pp. 29-32; id., *Uṣūl*, pp. 51f; B, I, pp. 70, 71. See also al-'Āmilī al-Iṣfahānī, *Tafsīr*, p. 345, where additional usages of *yatīm* are mentioned.

129. 'A, p. 138; Ḥ, p. 5.

130. 'A, p. 137; Ḥ, p. 211.

131. 'A, p. 137.

132. 'A, pp. 136, 138; Ḥ, pp. 3f, 211; al-Astarābādī, *Fawā'id*, p. 151; Muḥsin al-Fayḍ, *Maḥajja*, I, pp. 29-33; B, I, p. 71; Hāshim al-Baḥrānī, *Ḥilyat al-abrār*, Qumm, 1397, II, pp. 455; U, IV, p. 306.

133. For variants of this tradition, see, e.g., al-Ṭabarsī, *Majma' al-bayān*, I, pp. 327f, whence Muḥammad Ḥusayn al-Ṭabāṭabā'ī, *Kitāb al-mīzān fī tafsīr al-qur'ān*, Tehran, 1375-76, I, p. 219.

134. Contrast al-Mufīd's view according to which this requirement should be limited to those Shī'īs who have the capacity to use *naẓar*. Al-Murtaḍā, *al-Fuṣūl al-mukhtāra*, I, pp. 78f; 'Alī b. Yūnus al-Bayāḍī, *al-Ṣirāṭ al-mustaqīm*, ed. Muḥammad Bāqir al-Bihbūdī, I, Qumm, 1384, p. 12. Cf. al-Mufīd, *Taṣḥīḥ al-i'tiqād*, pp. 27f; Z, pp. 98f.

135. 'A, pp. 120-22; Ḥ, pp. 256-58; Muḥsin al-Fayḍ, *al-Nawādir fī jam' al-aḥādīth*, pp. 16-18; id., *al-Ḥaqā'iq fī maḥāsin al-akhlāq*, ed. Ibrāhīm al-Miyānjī, Tehran, 1378/1959, pp. 43f; B, I, p. 93; Yūsuf al-Baḥrānī, *Kashkūl*, Bombay, 1292, I, pp. 61f; Murtaḍā al-Anṣārī, *Farā'id al-uṣūl*, Qumm, 1374, p. 86.

136. I should like to thank Professors Michael A. Cook and Frank H. Stewart for their useful comments.

CHAPTER 3

The Evolution of Popular Eulogy of the Imams Among the Shi'a

MOHAMMAD-DJA'FAR MAHDJOUB
Translated and adapted by John R. Perry

From the earliest days of the Shi'i-Sunni split—starting with the death of the Prophet—each of the two factions apparently set out to prove the justice of its cause by propagating its tenets and publishing documentary evidence. At a meeting convened before the Prophet's burial in order to choose a successor, a faction that had been known as the *shī'a* "party" (sc. of 'Alī) even during the Prophet's lifetime opposed the election of Abū Bakr and championed 'Alī, the cousin, son-in-law, and legal heir of Muḥammad, as the automatic choice.[1] On the day that Abū Bakr formally entered the mosque as Caliph of Islam, these men rose one after the other, detailing 'Alī's merits and proclaiming him to be the rightful ruler. The author of the *Kitāb al-Naqḍ*, 'Abd al-Jalīl Rāzī, ennumerates twelve of them.[2]

The dispute over succession continued and became more serious as time went on. Even before the massacre of Ḥusayn at Karbalā' and the establishment of Umayyad rule, 'Alī b. Abī Ṭālib was being publicly cursed by order of Mu'āwiya, which unedifying practice was kept up throughout the Umayyad period, except for the brief reign of 'Umar b. 'Abd al-'Azīz (A.H. 99-101/717-20 C.E.)

At present, we have no information on the nature of the propaganda employed by the Shi'a and other partisans of 'Alī against the Umayyads. We know that after the martyrdom of 'Alī's son Ḥusayn there arose a band of men sworn to avenge him, under the leadership of Mukhtār b. Abī 'Ubayda al-Thaqafī b. al-Jarrāḥ,[3] who indeed exacted a grim vengeance from Ḥusayn's killers; he assassinated 'Ubaydullāh b. Ziyād, who had been governor of Kufa at the time of the massacre of Karbalā', and was himself killed soon after (d. 67/687) by Muṣ'ab b. Zubayr.[4] There followed numerous revolts against the Umayyad Caliphs, who were considered by most Muslims to be usurpers and debauchees who openly flouted the religious law and had exceeded all bounds in their oppressive misrule. The Umayyads were finally defeated and their dominion swept away by Abū Muslim of Khurasan. Since the revolt of Abū Muslim and its antecedents constitute an important area of this discussion, we will return to them in greater detail below.

The first and oldest extant documentation of *manāqib-khwānī* and *faḍā'il-khwānī* (lit., recitation of merits/virtues, sc. of 'Alī or his kin) comes likewise from 'Abd al-Jalīl Rāzī, writing in the middle of the sixth century A.H./twelfth century C.E. The motivation for his *Kitāb al-Naqḍ* was as follows. A zealous Sunni and anti-Shi'ite (such as the Shi'ites disparagingly dubbed *nāṣibī* or malefactor) wrote a book in refutation of the Shi'a under the title *Ba'ḍu faḍā'iḥi'l-Rawāfiḍ* (Vices of the Recusants, i.e., the Shi'a, who were called *rāfiḍī* [pl. *rawāfiḍ*], rejector, dissenter, recusant, by their detractors). 'Abd al-Jalīl nowhere names the author of this tract, perhaps to protect him from assassination at the hands of some Shi'ite fanatic and to save the Shi'a—at that time in the minority—from the resulting outrage; but according to evidence adduced by the editor of the *Naqḍ*, this writer was one Shihāb al-Dīn al-Tawārīkhī al-Shāfi'ī. The original manuscript happened to come into the possession of Imām Shihāb al-Dīn Muḥammad b. Tāj al-Dīn, a leading Shi'ite of Rayy, who sent it to 'Abd al-Jalīl Rāzī. In his own book, the latter first sets out the premises of the hostile tract and then answers each attack, calling the whole *Ba'ḍu mathālibi l-Nawāṣib fī naqḍi faḍā'iḥi'l-Rawāfiḍ* (Defects of the Malefactors [Sunnites], in Refutation of the "Vices of the Recusants"). This unwieldy title was abbreviated in common usage to *Kitāb al-Naqḍ*.

One of the many virtues of this unique book is the description it provides, after the *Faḍā'iḥ al-Rawāfiḍ*, of the popular eulogists of the time.

> In the market places they [sc. the Shi'a] send round foulmouthed *manāqib-khwānān* who claim to be lauding the merit [*manqabat*] of the Commander of the Faithful ['Alī], and who recite Shi'ite odes [*qaṣīdahā*] and the like, while a crowd of Shi'ites gathers. Their subject matter is nothing less than the deeds of the pure Companions and the caliphs of Islam and the fighters for the Faith [*ghāzīān*]; they talk of

> the attributes of transcendence—which belong to God—and of infallibility—which belongs to the apostles of God—and recount tales of miracles—which are proper only to the prophets—attributing all these to 'Alī b. Abī Ṭālib![5]

'Abd al-Jalīl answers "Mr Malefactor" (*Khwāja Nāṣibī*) as follows:

> How odd that the Khwāja should see eulogists in the bazaars reciting *manāqib!* Have you not also seen *faḍā'il-khwānān* who are far from idle and silent? Or some good-for-nothing drunkard and gambler without a penny to his name, and who in fact has no idea of the virtues of Abū Bakr or the merits of 'Alī, who in order to earn a living and a reputation has committed to memory a few verses in vituperation of the Shi'ites, reviles [true] Muslims and takes what he earns to dens of vice to spend it on revelry and fornication, and laughs in the faces of Determinists and Predestinarians?[6] This is no new practice, for *manāqib-khwānān* and *faḍā'il-khwānān* to recite the merits and virtues [of the heroes of Islam] in the market places; the former, however, speak only of justice, divine unity, prophethood, and innocence, while the latter are full of predestination, anthropomorphism, and anathemas....[7]

Elsewhere, during a disquisition on the status of Murtaḍā Sharaf al-Dīn Muḥammad b. 'Alī, the author writes, "Qavāmī Rāzī dedicated an ode on divine unity and *manāqib* to him, and complimented him thus: 'Until [the coming of] the Expected One [*ṣāḥib al-zamān*]/The greatest champion of the Faith is Sharaf al-Dīn Murtaḍā.'"[8] Again, 'Abd al-Jalīl mentions a number of Shi'ite poets.

> Firdawsī and Fakhr-i Jājarmī were Shi'ites, and there is no doubt that Kisā'ī's works are full of praise of the merits [*manāqib*] of the Prophet and his family, and 'Abd al-Malik Bayān... and Kāfī Ẓafar-i Hamadānī, though he was a Sunnī, wrote many eulogies [*manāqib*] of 'Alī and 'Alī's kin... there is even a disclaimer in his divan, that he should not be suspected of being a Shi'ite; and As'adī of Qumm and... Amīr Qavāmī and others... all of whom wrote countless verses in praise of the One God, and asceticism, and moral homily, and *manqabat.* To list all the Shi'ite poets would be impossible.... The incomparable poet and prose writer Khwāja Sanā'ī of Ghazna, hailed as the Seal of the Poets, wrote many eulogies [*manqabat*], of which the following is but one verse: "Whoever is hostile to 'Alī,/Whoever he be, I am no friend of his."[9]

The author of the *Naqḍ* elsewhere replies sarcastically to the charge that Shi'ism has recourse for its support to certain dubious bits of doggerel about the early conquests.

> No wonder that when he hears in the bazaar such brilliant verses as this: "Thank God we are Muslims born/Not from Qumm nor from Kāshān!"—it puts him [sc. "Khwāja Nāṣibī"] in mind of the great poems and verses of such as Kisā'ī or As'adī or 'Abd al-Malik Banān Mu'taqid and Khwāja 'Alī Mutakallim and . . . Amīr Qavāmī and Qā'imī, whose every verse is worth a whole world; no-one can object to any of their praise of God and asceticism and *manāqib* except an agnostic, a libertine, or a Kharijite![10]

This is all that the *Kitāb al-Naqḍ* has to offer concerning *manāqib*- and *faḍā'il-khwānān* (also called *manāqibīān* and *faḍā'ilīān*), and by way of definition or exemplification of this genre of verse. From it we may deduce the following:

1. Popular eulogists of the early heroes of Islam called *manāqibīan* and *faḍā'ilīān* used to tour the bazaars; adherents respectively of the Shi'ite and the Sunni sects would gather round them and pay for their performances, and the performers were able to acquire a certain reputation.

2. This was already a standard and long-established practice when 'Abd al-Jalīl was writing, in the middle of the sixth century A.H. (late twelfth century C.E.)

3. The verses he attributes to the *manāqibīān* are all in Persian of the highest literary standard, as witness his quotations from Sanā'ī and Qavāmī Rāzī; although the latter is not a poet of the first rank, his verse can by no means be described as doggerel. Whereas the verse he cites as that of the *faḍā'ilīān* and ironically describes as "brilliant" (*gharrā*) is indeed doggerel and characteristic of vernacular versification.

4. Concerning Kisā'ī, 'Abd al-Jalīl claims: "Everyone agrees that his divan is full of praises and eulogies of Muḥammad and his family." Kisā'ī is a Persian writer of the first magnitude; no less a poet than Nāṣir Khusraw compares his own verse with that of Kisā'ī. Unfortunately his divan has been lost, and of all his eulogies only these four lines are extant:

> Praise and laud one whom the Prophet praised and to whom he gave all responsibility.
> Who is this so characterized, who was he, who might he be? None other than the Lion of the Lord of the world, the aggressive Ḥaydar [Alī].
> Look on this Religion of revelation as a circle: our Prophet is the center, and 'Alī is the circumference.
> The Prophet gave to 'Alī the knowledge of every sage, as the spring cloud waters the meadow.[11]

One or two odes in this vein can also be found in the divan of Qavāmī Rāzī. Sanā'ī, too, in his *Ḥadiqat al-Ḥaqiqa*, has many verses in praise of the Prophet and his family, 'Alī, and Imams Ḥasan and Ḥusayn, and devotes a section to an account of the massacre of Karbalā', vituperation of Yazīd and his army, and a description of the misfortunes suffered by the Prophet's kin, which is probably the earliest treatment of the Karbalā' episode in Persian poetry.

Two further inferences concerning the recital of *manāqib* and *faḍā'il* may be deduced from 'Abd al-Jalīl's work—one about the subject matter of the eulogies, and the other about the obstacles encountered by the reciters and the reprisals taken against them.

Regarding the topics that comprise *manāqib* poetry, 'Abd al-Jalīl's opponent claims that the *manāqib-khwānān* attribute prophetic miracles to 'Alī. 'Abd al-Jalīl responds:

> From this statement one would gather that the writer is a recent convert to Sunnism and does not properly understand the tenets of the sect, since he says somewhere that Shaykh Junayd went in a single day from Baghdad to Damascus, and that Shaykh Shiblī journeyed in one hour from Kufah to Mecca, and that Ma'rūf-i Karkhī was fed from a stone, and that Abu'l-Ḥasan [sic; sc. Abu'l-Ḥusayn] Nūrī was saluted by a tree. These Sufi masters never made any such claims or encouraged the circulation of such superstitious gibberish; it is the Khwāja, in his zeal for his new religion, who has attributed these miracles to them—which are more far-fetched than those of the prophets! Even Moses, prophet though he was, took a week to travel from Egypt to the land of Midian, and the Prophet Muḥammad himself took several days to get from Mecca to Medina! Thus if the Imāmī Shi'a occasionally impute prophetic miracles to an Imam to prove a point, this can hardly be considered novel. Either one must eschew this device altogether, or if one admits it on behalf of one side, one must accept it also for the other.[12]

Evidently this sort of miracle-mongering found its way into the recitals of the (Sunni) *faḍā'il-khwānān*. 'Abd al-Jalīl's opponent continues his diatribe on Shi'ite *manāqib:*

> They recount fictional adventures such as that at God's command 'Alī was shot from a catapult into the fortress of Dhāt al-Salāsil and single-handedly captured the fortress with its garrison of five thousand armed men, and that 'Alī tore open with one hand the city gates of Khaybar, which a hundred men had not been able to budge, and held it so that the Prophet's army could walk over it into the city—and that Abū Bakr, 'Umar, 'Uthmān and the other Companions walked to and fro on the

> end of the gate as 'Alī held it, in order to tire him and force him to show weakness.[13]

Again, "the Rāfiḍīs say that as [the Imam] 'Alī b. Mūsā al-Riḍā was being brought before the Caliph al-Ma'mūn, the picture of a lion that was embroidered on a cushion suddenly came to life and sprang at Ma'mūn—which is utter nonsense!"[14] And, again "another of the fantastic stories circulated by the Rāfiḍīs is that 'Alī went down a well and fought with jinn, felled many of them with his sword and returned with the blade bloody, announcing that he had slain so many jinn and devils. This is the sort of superstitious nonsense they attach to 'Alī; their chapbooks [*daftar*] are chock-a-block full of this balderdash."[15]

'Abd al-Jalīl's response to this attack adds nothing to our knowledge of *faḍā'il-* and *manāqib-khwānī.* In answer to the first charge, he claims that Umayyad fanatics and Marwānids, jealous of 'Alī's popularity, had gathered a body of Khārijites and pagans and made up fake stories about Rustam, Suhrāb, Isfandyār, Kai Kā'ūs, and Zāl to tell in the bazaars.[16] As regards the tale of 'Alī's ballistic entry into Dhāt al-Salāsil, he says that this is not recorded in reliable books by respectable Shi'ite writers, though he admits that the legend of the embroidered lion is found in Shi'ite literature as well as in oral tradition. As is evident, he is on the defensive against these charges, and as a result does not reproduce anything of his own from the popular eulogists' material.

Incidental reference is also made to the reprisals suffered by *manāqib-* and *faḍā'il-khwānān.* 'Abd al-Jalīl's antagonist here reports that

> when the *manāqib-khwānān* ply their trade in the bazaar, the Turks [i.e., the Seljuk rulers] listen to them without knowing what they are about; but those who have learned to distinguish Shi'ites by their symbolism and allusions have cut out the tongues of some of these Shi'ite eulogists. In Sārī, Malikshāh's daughter Khātūn Sa'īd Salqam, the wife of Isfahbud 'Alī, ordered a *manāqibī* called Abū Ṭālib to have his tongue cut out, alleging that he had fled there in order to satirize the Companions and criticize the wives of the Prophet.[17]

Elsewhere he mentions another *manāqib-khwān* by name.

> There was another scoundrel, one Bu'l-'Amīd the *manāqibī,* who also recited parables. Under suspicion of atheism [i.e., Isma'ilism] he fled from Rayy to Sārī and went to ground there; he recited scurrilous tales about the Companions and was held in high esteem by the atheists of Sārī and Iran. Finally toward the end of his life he became paralyzed and deformed, so that his face resembled that of a pig, and he died.[18]

'Abd al-Jalīl comments on the punishment of the *manāqibī* Abū

Ṭālib: "Khwāja Abū Bakr Khusrawābādī the Sunnī, who was governor of Qazvin, was told that one Ṣiddīq-i Faḍā'ilī, who was hostile to 'Alī and his kin, was calling down curses on him (the governor); he ordered the Sunnī *faḍā'ilī* to be torn limb from limb in the *Dār al-Sunna*, Qazvin." He concludes that "rulers everywhere often did such things, and still do, regardless of religious or sectarian concerns."[19]

Apparently the Shi'a believed that a miracle intervened in the case of Abū Ṭālib, the *manāqibī* whose tongue was cut out, since 'Abd al-Jalīl says of him that "'Khwāja Sunnī' should not forget that on that same night he [Abū Ṭalib] had a dream in which 'Alī put his tongue in his mouth and by God's will his tongue at once became whole again, and for forty years more he contined in asceticism and poverty to recite *faḍā'il* and *manāqib* in Rayy, Qumm, Kāshān, Ābeh, Nīshāpūr, Sabzavār, Jurjān, and the towns of Māzandarān."[20]

By contrast, 'Abd al-Jalīl also mentions one "Pangānak-i Nāṣibī the *faḍā'il-khwān*" who "did not die until stricken with ten dreadful diseases, all of which the people of Rayy witnessed, and one of which was this same paralysis. He indeed loved Abū Bakr and 'Umar, and should surely not have been afflicted with paralysis and fetid breath and leprosy . . . !"[21]

Evidently the *faḍā'il-* and *manāqib-khwānā*, instead of wandering around the bazaar, sometimes plied their trade at a fixed spot. Qavāmī of Rayy, a Shi'ite poet of the sixth/twelfth century mentioned above, although dignified by the author of the *Naqḍ* as "Amīr" Qavāmī—implying by this title that he held a government post—was actually a baker. This trade had a considerable influence on his verse; many of his tropes involve flour, dough, ovens, granaries, and bakeries.[22] He would recite his eulogies in a regular spot, and in one of his occasional verses he threatens to satirize someone if he does not pay him or tries to oust him from his pitch.[23]

In the Bibliothèque Nationale at Paris are preserved three Persian manuscripts of the popular epic (*dāstān*) known as the *Abū Muslim Nāma*, each of which shows special peculiarities. One of them (*Supplément persan* 843) is a defective MS written in India. Though the basic structure of the tale is identical in all three, they differ in narrative detail, length, and style. This most interesting Indian MS includes a few odes in *manqabat-khwānī* style, amid the various exploits of Abū Muslim and friends. The basic plot of the *Abū Muslim Nāma* is as follows. After the martyrdom of the Imām Ḥusayn and the consolidation of the oppressive Umayyad rule, revolts by groups vowing vengeance for Ḥusayn erupted throughout the Umayyad period. Even before these revolts, individuals from the Prophet's family had prophesied that the Umayyads would reign for less than a thousand months (950 months to be precise; or "one thousand months less fifty," in the words of the *dāstān*); during this period seventy-two persons would rise in revolt to avenge Ḥusayn b. 'Alī, but all would be defeated except the seventy-second. The leader of this revolt would overthrow the Umayyads and avenge Ḥusayn.[24]

Accordingly, at the beginning of the tale, Abū Muslim vows repeatedly that if he is victorious in a forthcoming contest (e.g., his fight to the death with the "forest lion of Kushmīhan") he will be the leader of the seventy-second revolt. Needless to say, he is victorious in every case. Abū Muslim's principal objective and the constant tenor of his rallying-cry are thus to overthrow the oppressive Umayyad usurpers, put an end to the public cursing of the Prophet's kin, and avenge the martyrs of Karbalā'. Both in their deliberations and preparations for the uprising and in the battlefield, Abū Muslim and his comrades encourage each other by recounting the injustices suffered by the family of the Prophet, especially Ḥusayn, by conjuring up the plain of Karbalā' and by praising the Prophet's descendants, particularly the Commander of the Faithful 'Alī and his son Ḥusayn. And although the author of this particular manuscript is a Sunnī Muslim, this does not prevent his incorporating eulogies of the Imāms in his book.

There are three *manqabat*-odes in the MS, one in praise of Sayyid Qaḥtaba (one of Abū Muslim's warriors).[25] In the course of the ode, Abū Bakr, 'Umar, Uthmān, and 'Alī are praised, and then the writer adds: "When he had ended his recital he uttered a shout, and said, 'O wretched Khārijites, alas that you call such a being ['Alī] unworthy, by reason of sensuality and ambition! Come on, and behold [the wages of] your own unworthiness!' "[26]

Another supporter of Abū Muslim was Muḥammad Ismā'īl "Sarbarahna" (the Bareheaded, of Khwārazm. The epic tells how he dreamed that the Commander of the Faithful 'Alī made him his favorite and told him that henceforth no weapon would ever harm his head, and that any steel that touched his head would be shattered. From that day forth, Muḥammad Ismā'īl would go into battle bareheaded and would fight on foot, felling his foes with a blow of his head. This Muḥammad Ismā'īl was a berserker, and generally fought in a state of ecstatic frenzy. It is he who recites the second *manqabat*-ode on the battlefield.

> On that day the emir Abū Muslim was dressed all in black. He carried the banner of the Family of the Prophet above his head, and wore the Prophet's turban round his own black headcloth and the robe of the Imām Muḥammad al-Bāqir over his own clothes; the sword of the Imām Ḥusayn girded his waist, about his neck hung the Koran of the Amīr

> ['Alī] and over his shoulder was the blue-steel ax of his relative [Ḥusayn];[27] to right and left of him men who had memorized the Koran recited the words of (God) the Omniscient King, muezzins intoned prayers, and 120 pairs of kettledrums and sidedrums were beaten. Suddenly, Muḥammad Ismā'īl Sarbarahna sprang out in front of the ranks of footsoldiers,[28] bowed to the emir Abū Muslim, and turned to face the enemy. The emir asked why it was he went to battle bareheaded, and was told the story. Muḥammad Ismā'īl began reciting verse eulogies [*manāqib*] in battle, face to face with the Khārijites, with a fine voice and beautiful diction, as follows: "O my heart, after praising God and the grace of the Prophet/Sing to the Faithful of the virtues [*manāqib*] of the Companions."

The poem continues for twenty-three lines, after which the writer concludes:

> Upon concluding this *manqabat*, he began to recite invective against the Marwānids. Muḥtāj, one of the Khārijite leaders, said "I have never heard Abū Turāb ['Alī] praised so effectively! Whoever brings me his head shall have anything he desires." Faḍl b. Rabī' Baghdādī stepped forth [to challenge Muḥammad Ismā'īl], saying, "O madman, why did you not bring a pinch of wild rue to burn on a potsherd before fighting warriors?" Muḥammad Ismā'īl replied, "That rue is your heart and liver, which I shall burn today!"[29]

But the longest *manāqib*-ode, of which this *qaṣīda* of Muḥammad Ismā'īl Khwārazmī forms a part, is recited at a feast and council-of-war of the rebels by Abū Muslim himself. The rubric of one of the tales in the *Abū Muslim Nāma* reads thus: "Account of Khwāja Sulaymān's entertainment of all the Believers and of the arrival of Sahlān-i Ardabīlī, and the emir Abū Muslim's donning the ceremonial robe given to him by the Imām Ibrāhīm, and his mounting the rostrum and addressing his comrades and administering the oath of fealty." We then have the eulogy of the Lord of Created Beings:

Appreciation of the Universal intellect stems from the perfection of Muḥammad; the magnification of the Faith is from the dignity and glory of Muḥammad.
The moon is a ray from the flame of the Pure One [sc. Muḥammad]; the sun is an atom of the beauty of Muḥammad.
The *Ṭūbā* tree [in Paradise] is a sprig from the tree of the Seal of the Prophets; [The paradisiacal stream] Kauthar takes its source from the limpid stream of Muḥammad.
Fortunate is he who follows the principles of the sacred law; happy is

he who seeks after the (blessed) state of Muḥammad.
The carpet [of Earth] is laid in place by virtue of the dust of his street;
the heavenly throne is ennobled by virtue of the dust of his shoes.
The divine court, which is the goal of ascension to the Glorious One, is
exclusively and indubitably the place and abode of Muḥammad.

After this encomium, he recited a eulogy (*manqabat*) of the Companions, as was appropriate,[30] and despite the contempt of the Khārijites for the King of Men ['Alī] he eulogized the Commander of the Faithful 'Alī (God ennoble his visage) all the more energetically, to encourage the partisans to greater efforts, as follows:

O heart, after praising God and eulogizing Muḥammad, recite to the
believers the praises (*manāqib*) of the Companions.
The first Companion is Abū Bakr, who is noble enough to place his
foot on the crown of the dwellers in the firmament;
The head of the circle of chivalry and fount of generosity, leader of the
roster of knightliness and chief of the company of saints.
Next is 'Umar, from whom issues a sea of awesome steadfastness; from
him the law of the Prophet gained lustre and brilliance.
Bastion against paganism, when the battle waxed, preventer of immorality, staunch defender of the law and bulwark of the battle-ranks.
'Uthmān, the collator of the canonical Koran, was destined to be twice
the father-in-law of Muḥammad;
Sea of generosity, mine of magnanimity, abode of serenity, ocean of
existence, quarry of nobility, and fount of life.
Next, in spite of the Khārijites, as is only proper, open your mouth in
eulogy (*manqabat*) of the King of Saints ['Alī]:
That rising star of beneficence, that depository of nobility, that miracle-
worker, that guardian of friendship,
That royal falcon of the tower of the sacred law, so noble that his throne
extends from *hal 'atā*, his crown from *'innamā*.[31]
That mine of justice so mighty and superior that the pillars of the Faith
take their splendor and effulgence from him.
The law (*qānūn*) of God, a gesture (*ishārat*) from him frees a hundred
captives and heals (*shifā*) two hundred wounded.[32]
His light is derived[33] from the light of the chosen Aḥmad [Muḥammad];
from that candle the sacred law takes its effulgence through his light.
In the middle of the sacred precinct [of Mecca] and the Ka'ba he came
into existence,[34] and by his light the face of the Ka'ba was purified.
Bare-handed in the cradle wth his mighty arms he tore apart the dragon's
jaws.[35]

On campaign, he heard with the ear of truth a call from Muḥammad's mouth at a distance of forty days' march.
Nimbly he sprang on foot across a seventy-yard moat, tore open the gate of Khaybar, and tossed it aside.
He risked sitting in the sling of a ballista, and landed from mid-air in the fortress of [Dhāt al-] Salāsil.
To bring down an idol from the roof of the Ka'ba, by God's command he placed his foot on Muḥammad's shoulder.
He bought camels from Malik and sold them to Malik in order to entertain the chief and lord of prophets.
So that he might repay his debt to a merchant, out of his kindness, camel-trains came from the hill of Ḥaṣā.
He solved the world's problems such that a four-month-old child bore witness to his edicts.
In a year of famine he fed the army of the Faith; on a hot day in Mecca he kept his fast.
At the well of Jābir the head of a decapitated ox said to him, "You have spoken truly, O Imam, and are far from [the risk of] calumny!"
Of his generosity he gave a suppliant four hundred camels, two-humped, fleet-footed, black-eyed, and fully loaded.
Recite the stories of the skull of Ibn Kirkira, what happened on the plain of Arzhan, and of Salmān-i Pārs.
For all his great strength, up to the age of sixty-three he ate no more than seventeen *raṭl* of barley flour in all.[36]
His is this bliss, his this honor, without favor or hypocrisy, by virtue of his kindness and nobility.[37]

This eulogy has a total of forty-nine lines. The first section, in praise of God, and the third section, the *manqabat* proper, have the same monorhyme and meter,[38] while the *ghazal* in between, in praise of the Prophet, has the same meter but a different rhyme. Following the close of this eulogy, the story continues.

> After this, he commenced a eulogy of the two Princes of Both Creations and darlings of the Prophet of Men and Jinn, the Princes of the Faithful Ḥasan and Ḥusayn (God be pleased with them), and described the injustices of Yazīd and the cruelties inflicted by the Marwānids upon those princes and their companions, so affectingly that a wailing arose from that throng. He told of the seventy persons, men and women, who faced the final onslaught, and eulogized the souls of those believers who had not attained the goal thus pursued for love of those dear ones and whose heads were veiled by the dust, and asked God's mercy upon them, saying, "May they remain with You for as long as the dust lies

> over them . . . ." Then in moving and ringing tones he declared, "We can no longer tolerate insults to the Prophet's family. It is now one thousand less fifty months since these insults have been continuing, and we must end them!" Then a roar arose from the believers and many of them rent their clothes, and Khwāja Sulaymān wept bitterly, and all declared their unanimous support and renewed their oaths of loyalty.[39]

Though the narrator puts these sentiments into the mouths of Abū Muslim and his comrades, it is obvious that they are fundamentally his own convictions. The beliefs of Abū Muslim, who lived at the beginning of Islam's second century, remain vague for us; all we know is that he tried to unite all the factions opposed to the Umayyads about his person under the slogan *al-riḍā min āl Muḥammad* (that scion of Muḥammad's family acceptable [to all]). This is not the place to discuss the problem further; the fact remains, however, that the ambiguity of Abū Muslim's slogans, and the confusion, vacillation, and changes in what he professed are reflected even in the text of a popular epic composed centuries after his death.

In every copy of the various manuscripts of the *Abū Muslim Nāma* (of which this writer knows twenty-two, and has seen many of them) there is direct evidence for this claim. In every instance where the narrator—more precisely, the oral reciter of the tale who later began to write it down—was a Shi'ite, Abū Muslim also espouses Shi'ite sentiments. Conversely, where the narrator was a Sunni, there is no trace of Shi'ite beliefs in the text; all four of the Prophet's chief Companions, the later Orthodox Caliphs, are celebrated equally. Even the degree to which the narrator is a hardened or fanatical partisan is revealed in the various scenes of the story.[40]

The manuscript of the *Abū Muslim Nāma* in the Bibliothèque Nationale (Suppt. pers. 843), as used here, was written in India between A.H. 1145 and 1146/1732-34 C.E., and demonstrates that, even if the custom of *manqabat-khwānī* in religious assemblies had by then been discontinued, at least traces of it remained in the literature. As has been noted above, *manqabat-khwānī* took the form mainly of verse, and the few extant samples are of the genres *qaṣīda, ghazal,* and *qiṭ'a.*[41] Despite 'Abd al-Jalīl Rāzī's contention that masters of the art such as Kisā'ī of Marv and Sanā'ī produced *manāqib* poetry, the examples that have come down to us are technically poor, stylistically simple, and comprehensible to the masses.

It is important to note that composers and reciters of *manāqib* verse need not be formal adherents of the Shi'ite sect. The eulogies contained in the *Abū Muslim Nāma* are the work of a Sunni poet.

During the eighth to tenth centuries there were Sunni factions known as the *Sunnī-yi tafḍīlī* (Preferentialist Sunnites) and *Sunnī-yi davāzdah imāmī* (Twelver Sunnites). The "Preferentialists" accepted the legitimacy of the three Caliphs before 'Alī, but reckoned him superior to them; the "Twelvers" accepted 'Alī's twelve descendents as successors to the Caliphate after him and considered the Umayyads and 'Abbāsids both as usurpers. The narrator of the *Abū Muslim Nāma* used here tells us about his own beliefs.

> The way of truth is that after the Prophet, his caliph, deputy and successor is by right Abū Bakr al-Ṣiddīq . . . and next the Commander of the Faithful 'Umar . . . and next the Commander of the Faithful 'Uthmān . . . and next the Commander of the Faithful 'Alī (God ennoble his visage), and next the Commander of the Faithful the Imām Ḥasan (God be pleased with him), and next the Commander of the Faithful Ḥusayn (God be pleased with him), from whom Yazīd wrested the caliphate by force and killed that Prince of Both Worlds so basely and perfunctorily at wretched Karbalā'; whereupon *the caliphate was terminated in the line of the Prophet*, and foul Yazīd through that wicked action never enjoyed the fruits of rulership and empire . . . .[42]

Notable by its absence here is any mention of Mu'āwiya. Although he was the first to take up arms against 'Alī, obtained the Caliphate by trickery from Ḥasan, made it hereditary in his family, and devoted all his efforts to securing the succession for his son Yazīd, nevertheless he was the brother of Umm Ḥabiba, daughter of Abū Sufyān and wife of the Prophet; as the Prophet's brother-in-law or "Uncle of the Faithful" (*khāl al-mu'minīn*, an epithet evidently devised for Mu'āwiya to demonstrate his affinity with the Prophet), he was for most Sunni Muslims immune from opprobrium.

It would not be amiss to give some account of the practices associated with the mourning of the martyrs of Karbalā' and the commemoration of their courage, self-sacrifice, and sufferings at the hands of Yazīd as these are observed among Sunni Muslims. The *Abū Muslim Nāma*, for all its legendary character, is in this respect a reliable and accurate document. The Sunni author repeatedly describes how Abū Muslim and his men attracted people who were disgusted with the injustice and impiety of the Umayyads by reminding them vividly of the carnage of Karbalā', aroused their religious fervor, and persuaded them to join battle against the Umayyad Caliphs; a scene of this type has been described above. Ample evidence of this can also be gleaned from works of history, belles-lettres and religion, and indeed it appears that from the very first days after Karbalā' the horror and tragedy of the event were widely felt. The author of the *Tajārib al-Salaf* (A.H. 723/1323 C.E.), under the heading "The Martyrdom of Imam Ḥusayn," begins his account as follows:

> It is impossible to exaggerate in telling this tale, for *never has a more disastrous event befallen Islam.* The murders of 'Umar and 'Uthmān, hard as they were on Muslims, pale beside the horrors of Ḥusayn's tragedy. Before his head was taken to Damascus, his infant child at his side was shot through with arrows, his nephews and cousins were slain before his eyes, his womenfolk and children were led as captives into the towns as slaves are led from Africa or India. In short, *when Yazīd besmirched the throne*, he devoted all his energies to depriving Ḥusayn, and the three others whom Mu'āwiya had named as successors, of their right to rule.[43]

The author next relates how the Kufans wrote to Imam Ḥusayn inviting him to govern them, and how they subsequently deserted him.

> 'Umar b. Sa'd b. Abī Waqqāṣ advanced [against Ḥusayn] with a huge army, consisting mostly of Kufans, who had written the letter of invitation to Ḥusayn. Ḥusayn asked, "Was it not you who wrote inviting me to come?" They replied, "We do not know what you are talking about," and ignored him, and opened hostilities. Ḥusayn, together with his cousin and brothers and companions, fought desperately, but all were killed (God be pleased with them). Ḥusayn was killed last of all; they tossed his precious person onto the ground and drove so many horses over his body that it disappeared from sight.[44]

The following describes the reaction of the people of Damascus, all of whom had been supporters of [Yazīd's father] Mu'āwiya, to this massacre.

> They say that when Ḥusayn's precious head was brought into Damascus, and his son Zayn al-'Ābidīn 'Alī . . . was among the captives . . . together with the womenfolk of the Prophet's family, all seated on camels . . . and all were paraded through Damascus, . . . an old Syrian came up and stood in front of Zayn al-'Ābidīn, reviling him and ridiculing his plight. Zayn al-'Ābidīn said, "Shaykh, do you read the Koran?" He replied, "Yes." Zayn al-'Ābidīn asked, "Have you read this verse: 'Say, I ask of you no fee therefor, save loving kindness among kinsfolk'?"[45] "Yes," he replied. Zayn al-'Ābidīn asked, "Do you recognize me?" He answered, "No." Zayn al-'Ābidīn said, "I am a kinsman," and told him his lineage. The old man made him swear that he was indeed Zayn al-'Ābidīn, and when he did, the old man said, "By God, I never knew that Muḥammad had any relatives [living] other than Yazīd and his kin!" Then he burst into

> tears and begged forgiveness of Zayn al-ʿĀbidīn. It is said that seventy shaykhs of Damascus swore solemn oaths that they had not known the Prophet had any living relatives other than Yazīd; that they all wept and begged Zayn al-ʿĀbidīn's pardon, and he forgave them all.

At the end of this story, the author of the *Tajārib al-Salaf* depicts even the Byzantine envoy as protesting to Yazīd.

> The Greek said, "Glory be to almighty God! When this is how you treat the grandchild of your own prophet, what will you do to others? Christians revere the ground on which Jesus' donkey walked; you claim to be Muslims, yet visit such injustices upon the grandson of your prophet!" And he rose and angrily walked out.[46]

This is but one example of Sunni writers' judgments of this event and public reaction to it. The author of the *Naqḍ*, moreover, states plainly that Sunni Muslims commemorated Karbalā' with weeping, wailing, and rioting. He first reproduces his Sunni opponent's criticisms of Shiʿite attitudes in these terms:

> On the day of ʿĀshūrā [the tenth of Muḥarram] this sect raises a great hullabaloo and goes into mourning (*taʿziyat*), reliving the misfortunes of the martyrs of Karbalā; they recount the story from the *minbar*, the *ʿulamā'* bare their heads, the common people rend their clothing, the women lacerate their faces and lament.

In reply to this brief and jaundiced view of Shiʿite practices during Muḥarram in the sixth century A.H./twelfth century C.E., ʿAbd al-Jalīl states:

> First, all the world knows that the great and respected scholars of both sects, followers of Abū Ḥanīfa and al-Shāfiʿī as well as scholars and legists of various communities, have observed this practice and maintained this custom. In the first place, al-Shāfiʿī himself, the founder of the rite which is named for him, as well as writing eulogies . . . wrote many elegies of Ḥusayn and the martyrs of Karbalā.

The author then cites the opening verses of two odes by al-Shāfiʿī, which he describes as "elegies of a poetic order no other could match," and further claims:

> There are innumerable elegies on the martyrs of Karbalā composed by Abū Ḥanīfa and al-Shāfiʿī. So if this is wrong, the fault is first theirs, then ours. On a lower plane, it is common knowledge that Khwāja

> Bū Manṣūr Māshāda in Isfahan—an impeccable Sunni, a model for his contemporaries—went into mourning every year on this day with much weeping and wailing and breast-beating, and would praise 'Alī, Ḥasan and Ḥusayn (God be pleased with them), and publicly curse Yazīd and [his henchman] 'Ubaydullāh in Isfahan. Likewise Sharaf al-Islām Ṣadr al-Khujandī and his brother Jamāl al-Dīn kept this anniversary with noisy public lamentations, which every visitor witnessed and nobody has ever denied.[47]
>
> Then again, in Baghdad, the capital of Islam and seat of the Caliphate, Khwāja 'Alī Ghaznavī, the Hanafite [preacher], is known to have taken this mourning so far as to curse the Sufyānids vehemently. Someone stood up and asked him, "What do you think of Mu'āwiya?" He answered in a loud voice, "O Muslims! He asks 'Alī what he thinks of Mu'āwiya! You know very well what 'Alī thinks of Mu'āwiya!"
>
> Amir 'Iyādī, the greatest scholar of his age, master of meaning and monarch of eloquence, was asked in the presence of [the 'Abbāsid Caliph] al-Muqtafī li-Amrillāh [sixth century A.H./twelfth century C.E.] —on the eve of the 'Āshūrā—what he thought of Mu'āwiya. He made no reply until his interlocutor had asked him three times, then answered: "Sir, your question is equivocal; I do not know which Mu'āwiya you mean. Is it the Mu'āwiya whose father broke Muḥammad's teeth and whose mother chewed on Ḥamza's liver? Who himself drew sword a score of times against 'Alī, and whose son cut off the head of 'Alī's son Ḥusayn? Muslims, what do *you* think of this Mu'āwiya?" All those in the caliphal audience—Sunni, Ḥanafī and Shāfi'ī alike—broke into curses and contumely [against Mu'āwiya]. There are many such examples, and on every 'Āshūrā at Baghdad Ḥusayn is mourned with renewed weeping and lamentation.
>
> Even in Hamadan, though it is populated mostly with anthropomorphists . . . Majd al-Dīn Mudhakkir Hamadānī commemorates the 'Āshūrā in a way that would surprise [even] the people of Qumm.[48] And Khwāja Imām Najm . . . Nīshāpūrī, though he was a Ḥanafī, used to celebrate the Muḥarram mourning to the utmost, . . . taking his turban off, keening, strewing dust over his head, and lamenting wildly.

'Abd al-Jalīl, the author of the *Naqḍ*, originating from Rayy, gives a more detailed description of the way 'Āshūrā was commemorated by the Sunnis of Rayy, who constituted half the populace and were partly of the Shāfi'ī and partly of the Ḥanafī rite. He mentions by name the Sunni *'ulamā'* and the places where they would lead their assemblies in mourning.[49]

'Abd al-Jalīl Rāzī's valuable accounts of the Sunni mourning rites during 'Āshūrā reliably document many of the details of these practices as they were during the sixth/twelfth century, including particular case histories with names and affiliations of the promoters of these rites, the cities and quarters where they were held, and the names of Sunnī notables (not excluding the Caliph al-Muqtafī) who were involved in such gatherings.

A study of this unique document suggests the following conclusions:

1. In his otherwise detailed account, and frequent allusion to Shāfi'ites and Ḥanafites, 'Abd al-Jalīl makes no mention of Ḥanbalites or Mālikites. Evidently, the adherents of these two schools disapproved of the Muḥarram mourning rites.

2. The military and civilian elite of the cities and their wives, all the way up to the Caliphate, and likewise the leading *'ulamā'* and *qāḍīs*, were present at these gatherings of mourners; the author claims that sometimes the number of participants at these [Sunni] assemblies exceeded twenty thousand.

3. Mu'āwiya, by virtue of his having written down divine revelation and being called "the Uncle of the Faithful", was generally exempt from criticism and curses, which the orators were content to direct at Yazīd. Occasionally, however, someone in the congregation would try to trap a preacher by asking him his opinion of Mu'āwiya; whereupon the preacher, if he were endowed with sufficient wit and boldness, without giving vent to open vituperation, would answer in such a way as to elicit his hearers' opprobrium against Mu'āwiya.

4. At the gatherings organized by Sunni Muslims to mourn the martyrs of Karbalā', the murder (or martyrdom) of 'Uthmān was generally commemorated also (as the Shi'ite 'Abd al-Jalīl does in his book, pp. 388-92).

Characteristic of this kind of gathering were extremes of weeping, keening, clamoring, rioting, laceration of the face and tearing of hair and garments (by the lay populace), baring the head (an extreme action in the case of the turbaned *'ulamā'*), and scattering dust over the head, much as the author of *Faḍā'iḥ al-Rawāfiḍ* attributed to the Shi'a.

6. In almost all of the towns and regions populated by Ḥanafites or Shāfi'ites—even in "fanatical" Hamadan, which according to the *Naqḍ* was a hotbed of "Anthropomorphists," that is, probably Sunni Muslims other than Ḥanafite or Shāfi'ite—similar mourning rites were performed, in some cases more extreme than those of Shi'ite populations.

7. The author of the *Naqḍ* implies that in Khuzistan and Kurdistan these rites were disapproved, when he advises the writer of the "Vices of the Recusants"—whom he regards as hostile to the Prophet and 'Alī and their progeny—to go there if he wishes to avoid hearing or seeing any Muḥarram mourning rites. 'Abd al-Jalīl incidentally characterizes the inhabitants of these two provinces as "Kharijites," but this probably represents polemical propaganda rather than historical reality.

Other interesting aspects of *manāqib-khwānī* are the conventional etiquette of its performance and the costume and accoutrements of the performer. In two out of three scenes of *manāqib-khwānī* in the extant texts of the *Abū Muslim Nāma*, the narrator carefully describes the reciter's donning of special clothes and martial panoply ("Sa'īd b. Qaḥtaba . . . mounted on a noble steed . . . wielding a forty-*man* mace, wearing a scholar's turban wound with a fine linen cloth woven with gold thread . . ."). In another scene, that of Abū Muslim's eulogy, the performer puts on black clothing and a black *durrā'a* (headcloth), a robe of honor that he had received when imprisoned by his enemies from the hands of the Imām Ibrāhīm, and mounts a throne or rostrum (*kursī*) to deliver his eulogy. In a third scene, the eulogy of Muḥammad Ismā'īl Sarbarahna of Khwārazm, instead of describing Muḥammad Ismā'īl, who has no special costume, the narrator turns to Abū Muslim's accoutrements: "He carried the banner of the family of the Prophet above his head. . . and the blue-steel ax of [Ḥusayn]."

The descriptions are no coincidence; the reciters evidently intended to impress their audience at first sight. At the turn of the tenth century A.H./sixteenth century C.E., Mawlānā Ḥusayn Vā'iẓ-i Kāshifī included in his *Futuvvat-nāma-yi Sulṭānī* a chapter on "Biographies of popular entertainers. . . and the etiquette of public speakers," in which he described the various types of public entertainment (*ma'raka*). He devotes the second subsection of this chapter to the subcategory of storytellers, reciters, and so forth (*ahl-i sukhan*), and divides them into three categories:

1. *Maddāḥ* (verse eulogist), *gharrā-khwān* (prose eulogist), and *saqqā* ("water-carrier").
2. *Khavāṣṣ-gū* ("encomiast") and *bisāṭ-andāz* ("entertainer").
3. *Qiṣṣa-khwān* and *afsāna-gū* (reciters of "secular" folktales and legends).[50]

The first three (category 1) were the remnants of the *manāqib-khwānān*, forming an intermediate class between the latter and the *rawḍa-khwānān*. The different appellations here correspond to peculiarities of insignia and accessories.

> If you ask what are the special characteristics of the *maddāḥ*, they are these: the *maddāḥ* is not distinguished by his robe or other clothing. They are permited to wear any kind of apparel. They are distinguished instead by carrying a lance, a *tūq*, a *shadda*, a napkin, a lamp, and a battle-ax.

The writer goes on to describe each of these insignia and explain when and how, in his view, they came to be associated with the *maddāḥ*. In the case of the lance, for instance, he states that the Negus of Abyssinia sent 'Alī "an exceedingly massive lance" which 'Alī sometimes wielded in battle.

> One day Ḥassān b. Thābit told the Amir ['Alī] that the Hypocrites of Medina were plotting with the Jews to kill him [Ḥassān] because he was always singing the Prophet's praises, and that he was afraid of them; the Amīr gave Ḥassān that lance and said, "Keep it always with you so that they will fear you too." Ḥassān accepted the lance, which thus became the insignia of the *maddāḥ*.[51]

He relates a similar legend about the *tūq*, namely, that this is none other than the lance with a pennon tied to it,[52] "because Ḥassān one day had attached a few long, narrow felt strips (*alif-i namad*) to the lance; the Amīr came up and asked Ḥassān what this meant, and Ḥassān replied, 'I have made this lance into a banner (*'alam*) to signify that we have become a byword (*'alam*) throughout the world (*'ālam*) for love and devotion to you.'"[53]

The *tūq* is explained by Kāshifī as a part of the apparatus and ornaments of the bands of male mourners (*sīna-zan*) in the Muḥarram processions. It is a pole about twelve feet high topped by a wooden hoop about three feet across, from which hangs a multicolored silk streamer or pennon almost to the foot of the pole, so that from a distance the whole stands out like a brightly colored column. It is carried before the procession of mourners like a banner, and the bearer is called the *'alāmat-kash* or *tūq-kash.* This is still the practice in present-day Iran. Evidently, the *tūq* used to be carried to a given locality as a rallying point, from where the crowd thus assembled would march in procession, the banner held aloft to attract more marchers along the way. The word *pātūq* (meeting-place, [leisure-time] hangout), used nowadays in reference to a café, club, restaurant or the like, is derived from the same *tūq* (*pā*—"foot of," "at").

The *Futuvvat-nāma-yi Sulṭānī* provides similar explanations for *sufra* (napkin), *chirāgh* (lamp), and *shadda* (tie), most of which may be dispensed with here.[54] Concerning *chirāgh*, there is one point worth noting: When entertainers solicit a sum of money from some of the onlookers at the outset of their pitch (an activity called *ṭalab kardan*), they call this initial sum *chirāgh*, "the lamp," and enumerate additions to it accordingly (*chirāgh-i avval*, "lamp no. 1," etc.); this payment of earnest-money they call "lighting the lamp." The adoption of the lamp as a badge of office by the *maddāḥān* is not explained, nor is the reason for the application of the word to their earnest-money. The author observes only that during the ritual of "lighting the lamp" the storyteller urges the audience to call out *"Allāhu akbar!"*

The battle-ax, however, has its own special legend.

> One day Ṣafiyya Khātūn [one of the Prophet's wives] had been brought some presents from her kinsfolk. Among these was an exceedingly massive battle-ax, and Prince Muḥammad ibn al-Ḥanafiya used to wield it. One day he saw Ḥassān b. Thābit reciting the praises of the Prophet and his legatee ['Alī]. This pleased the prince, and he gave the battle-ax to Ḥassān, saying, "Take it, and if anyone hinders you from praising ['Alī], take issue with him with this!" Thus the *maddāḥān* have their battle-ax from Muḥammad ibn al-Ḥanafiya.[55]

Such legends were, of course, made up centuries later. The earliest reference to the battle-ax (*tabarzīn*), and to its peculiar fishtale form, occurs in the epic of Abū Muslim. Here the ax is Abū Muslim's weapon par excellence, though we have no way of knowing whether the historical Abū Muslim used one or not. We do know that during the Umayyad period, the Mawālī, or non-Arab Muslim converts, were prohibited from bearing weapons of war such as the sword, lance, and bow; therefore, when they rebelled, they of necessity had recourse to implements such as knives, slings, and axes, which—while not technically weapons—could serve as such. Another of Abū Muslim's weapons is the knife, and one of the chapters of the epic concerns Abū Muslim's acquisition of a coveted miraculous knife, the "knife of Khwāja Muḥammad Māhān Mushtarī-zar."[56]

In later times, *maddāḥān* did not carry the *tabarzīn;* though up until living memory the public eulogists known as *sukhanvar*, who worked in pairs and may be classed together with storytellers in mixed prose and verse (*murraṣṣa'-khwān*),[57] used to carry a *tabarzīn* on their shoulder while declaiming, and, when it was their partner's turn, would hand the ax to him. As we saw in the scene of Abū Muslims's *manqabat-khwānī*, he too carried his battle-ax over his shoulder.

Kamāl al-Dīn Ḥusayn Sabzavārī, with the pen name of Kāshifī, better known as Ḥusayn-i Vā'iẓ (d. 910/1504), is a well-known literary figure of the fifteenth century, and indeed of Persian literary history as a whole. He was an athlete, a local hero (*javānmard*), a preacher, a scriptural commentator, a government official, and at the same time a prolific author. In the introduction to his famous book the *Rawḍat al-shuhadā'* ("Garden of the Martyrs") he is credited with thirty-three works,[58] to which may be added numerous others such as the *Futuvvat-nāma-yi Sulṭānī.* Not only was he versed in all the sciences of his time, including sorcery and alchemy, but his writings on them have come down to us. Moreover, we are fortunate that succeeding generations have appreciated him even more than is justified by his works. His *Makhzan al-Inshā'* ("Thesaurus of Composition") was for many years the sole *vade mecum* of secretaries and scribes, and his *Anvār-i Suhaylī* ("The Lights of Canopus") is a reworking of *Kalīla and Dimna.*[59] His brief commentary on the Qur'ān, the *Mavāhib-i 'Aliyya*, has been published and reprinted repeatedly in Iran and India. Perhaps more celebrated than any of these works is his *Rawḍat al-Shuhadā'*, dealing with the sufferings of the prophets and of the family of the Prophet of Islam, especially the martyrs of Karbalā'. This genre of books, concerning the martyrdom of saints and rebellions by champions of religious beliefs unacceptable to the authorities, is called *maqtal* or *maqtal-nāma* (massacre-literature). Initially, such episodes were recorded like other events under the rubric of history, but since the recording and recitation of them came to have special political or sectarian significance for certain factions, an independent genre of *maqtal* (pl. *maqātil*) books evolved. Like other compilers, Ḥusayn-i Vā'iẓ undoubtedly relied on various sources for this work, and he names many of them in the body of his text; they may be gleaned from the index of literature in the printed editions of the *Rawḍat al-Shuhadā'*.

It is certain, however, that up until the *Rawḍat al-Shuhadā'* no book had appeared that purported to treat all the martyrdoms and misfortunes of all the prophets and all of Muḥammad's descendents. Ḥusayn-i Vā'iẓ makes this clear in his introduction: "Every book written on the topic, however adorned with tales of martyrs, in respect of a total accounting of the virtues of Ḥasan and Ḥusayn and of what befell them, is empty."[60] He goes on to say that he undertook to compile the book on the instance of a certain prince "Sayyid Mīrzā," who was both of royal descent and of the Prophet's house.[61]

Kāshifī lived to a respectable age, perhaps over eighty, and is said to have written this book in 908/1502, only two years before his death (he refers in the preface to his advanced age).[62] The book was thus composed barely a year after the Safavids came to power with the accession of Shāh Ismā'īl, and proclaimed Twelver Shi'ism as the official state religion of Iran. This event was to contribute greatly to the unparalleled success of the *Rawḍat al-Shuhadā'*.

Soon after its appearance, the *Rawḍat al-Shuhadā'* was presented to Shi'ites and other Iranians who had recently converted to Shi'ism as the only comprehensive martyrology. Shi'ites would assemble on holidays and Fridays, and a *muraṣṣa'-khwān* or someone with a good voice would take up a copy of the *Rawḍat al-Shuhadā'* and read, while the assembly wept. Such meetings came to be called *Rawḍa-khwānī*, that is, occasions for reading the *Rawḍat* [*al-Shuhadā*'].[63] The convention of reading from the text of the *Rawḍat al-Shuhadā'* was adhered to for some time, just as in the nineteenth century actors in the *ta'ziya* passion plays that were performed during Muḥarram were to read aloud from a hand-held libretto. After the *Rawḍat al-Shuhadā'*, other works of *maqātil* appeared, the most notable being the *Ṭūfān al-Bukā'* (Tempest of Tears) of Muḥammad Ibrāhīm Jawharī, and the *Asrār al-Shahāda* ("Mysteries of Martyrdom") of 'Alī Aṣghar Ṭabāṭabā'ī. Reciters varied the source of their *rawḍa* and turned to the newer books, and also changed their technique, memorizing their material and emulating the acknowledged experts in order to perfect their delivery. But the name of this institution remained *rawḍa-khwānī*, after the first Persian compendium of martyrology.

Notes

1. See Sayyid Muḥammad Ḥusayn Ṭabāṭabā'ī, *Shi'ite Islam*, tr. & ed. Seyyed Hossein Nasr (Albany: SUNY Press, 1975), 40-44. The meeting took place at the *saqīfat Banī Sā'ida* (the covered porch of the Banū Sā'ida), a place near Medina; 'Alī b. Abī Ṭālib and several other members of the Prophet's family were not present.

2. 'Abd al-Jalīl Rāzī, *al-Naqḍ*, ed. S. Jalāl al-Dīn Muḥaddith (Tehran, 1331/1952), 656-64. The editor pursues this point further in his notes, citing Shaykh Ṭabarsī (Aḥmad b. 'Alī b. Abī Ṭālib, *Kitāb al-Iḥtijāj*) to the effect that twelve of the Emigrants (*muhājirūn*) spoke out against the election of Abū Bakr; see also pp. 28, 307, 315, 551, 652.

3. The author of the Naqḍ states that Abū 'Ubayda "three days later [i.e., after the election of Abū Bakr] approached 'Alī and said, 'O 'Alī, you are more worthy of this position by virtue of your merit and achievements and kinship, but I abide by what the Muslims have decided.'"

4. Muṣ'ab b. al-Zubayr: son of Zubayr, one of the Prophet's Companions and relatives, and brother of 'Abdullāh b. al-Zubayr, who during the reign of Yazīd b. Mu'āwiya laid claim to the caliphate and was killed at Mecca.

5. *Al-Naqḍ*, p. 33.

6. The *mujabbirūn* (Determinists) and *muqaddirūn* (Predestinarians) were both followers of the puritan Ash'arite school; their opponents were the liberal Mu'tazilites, who emphasized the attributes of divine justice and human free will.

7. *Al-Naqḍ*, p. 33; emphasis supplied.

8. Ibid., p. 230; see Qavāmī Rāzī, *Dīvān*, Ed. S. Jalāl al-Dīn Muḥaddith (?Tehran, 1334/1955), pp. 73-77.

9. *Al-Naqḍ*, p. 252.

10. Ibid., p. 628.

11. Dihkhudā, *Lughatnāma*, s.v. *Kisā'ī*, citing the *Ganj-i Bāz-yāfta* of Muḥammad Dabīr-Siyāqī. Further on Kisā'ī and his verse, see Badī' al-Zamān Furūzānfarr, *Farhang-i Sukhanvarān*, p. 22; *Majma' al-Fuṣahā*, pp. 482ff; the notes to the *Chahār Maqāla* by the late Muḥammad Mu'īn, pp. 89ff; Dhabīḥullāh Ṣafā, *Tārīkh-i Adabiyāt dar Īrān* I, pp. 444ff; Sa'īd Nafīsī, *Aḥvāl va Ash'ār-i Rūdakī*, p. 1197.

12. *Al-Naqḍ*, p. 34. This legend is also mentioned in the *Futuvvat-nāma-yi Sulṭānī.*

13. Ibid.

14. Ibid., p. 38.

15. Ibid., p. 39.

16. This reference to tales of the legendary heroes of Iran shows the public recitation of stories from the national epic in the bazaars was already well established; however 'Abd al-Jalīl's explanation of their motivation is not to be taken seriously.

17. *Al-Naqḍ*, p. 77.

18. Ibid., p. 78.

19. Ibid.

20. Ibid.

21. Ibid., p. 81. Pangānak: *pangān* is the older, Persian form of the word now current under the Arabicized form *finjān*, used here as a name, and with the suffix *-ak*, probably as a diminutive used pejoratively.

22. Qavāmī Rāzī, *Dīvān*, pp. 3, 6, 12, 44, 76, 81.

23. Ibid., p. 24: "Do me one of two favors, my fine fellow,/Or you'll make me bare my privates [i.e., force me publicly to humiliate you]:/Either give me a little something/Or else clear off my pitch!"

24. The Shi'a regard Mukhtār as the avenger of the martyrs of Karbalā'. Among Sunni Muslims, however, and especially the Ottoman Turks, if an avenger is himself killed, his vengeance is nullified; thus they consider Abū Muslim, the author of the ultimate downfall of the Umayyads, to be the avenger of Karbalā'.

25. *Abū Muslim Nāma*, Bibliothèque Nationale MS, Supplément persan

843, fol. 303ab.

26. Ibid.

27. The sectarian champions of Iranian popular epics, such as Ḥamza or 'Alī, traditionally possess weapons and accessories, or a steed, inherited from prophets or heroes of the past. Thus Ḥamza's horse came to him from the prophet Isḥāq (Isaac, the father of Jacob), his helmet (*khūd*) from the (Qur'ānic) prophet Hūd, and his boots from the (Qur'ānic) prophet Ṣāliḥ. Part of the narrative tells how the hero acquired these accoutrements. Abū Muslim's characteristic weapon is a miraculous battle-ax; the story of how he acquired it is told in a separate chapter of Abū Muslim's adventures.

28. Original: *bijastand*, sc., *bijast*.

29. *Abū Muslim Nāma*, fol. 278b-279a. Wild rue (*isfand*): the insult is an allusion to the practice of beggars in calling attention to themselves by sprinkling a few seeds of the aromatic wild rue onto coals which they held in a potsherd.

30. Viz., the first three Caliphs, Abū Bakr, 'Umar, and 'Uthmān.

31. *Hal 'atā:* Qur'ān 76/1, "Hath there come upon man (ever) any period of time in which he was a thing unremembered?" *'Innamā:* Qur'ān 5/55, "Your friend can be only Allah; and His messenger and those who believe, who establish worship and pay the poor due, and bow down (in prayer)." (Pickthall's translation.)

32. The allusion is to three of the works of Ibn Sīnā (Avicenna), the *Ishārāt*, the *Qānūn*, and the *Shifā'*.

33. Original: *mushfaq*, sc., *mushtaqq*.

34. 'Alī is traditionally supposed to have been born inside the Ka'ba.

35. A reference to another legend, in which 'Alī as an infant in his crib tore a huge serpent in two. The three following verses likewise refer to legends of this type; the fourth verse alone makes reference to a historical event, and the rest of the poem consists of allusions to tales of the miraculous and supernatural, some of which are recorded in respectable works (e.g., the tale of Salmān, and the conversation with the skull) while others are not found in such sources.

36. Tradition has it that 'Alī never ate more than 17 *raṭl* (17 × 6 lb/2.65 kg = 102 lb/45 kg) of barley flour in his whole life. For someone who reached the age of sixty-three, this would have required a daily intake of less than 2 gm, which is highly unlikely.

37. *Abū Muslim Nāma*, fol. 150b-153a.

38. I.e., *muḍāri' muthamman akhrab maqṣūr/maḥdhūf*.

39. *Abū Muslim Nāma*, fol. 150b-153a.

40. By way of example, we may compare the present MS of the *Abū Muslim Nāma* and that in *Āstān-i Quds* library at Mashhad. The peculiarities of the Paris MS will be further noted below. The writer of this was a "Preferentialist" Sunni (see below) who revered the Orthodox Caliphs and the twelve Imāms, whereas the Mashhad MS was written in Turkistan in a fanatically Sunni milieu and shows no trace of Shi'ite proclivities.

41. This MS furnishes another short eulogistic *qiṭ'a* beginning: "Dear one, speak of your friendship for [A]bū Turāb ('Alī); rebuild the Ka'ba, and demolish Khaybar" (fol. 394a).

42. *Abū Muslim Nāma*, fol. 173b-174a. For another instance of the "Twelver Sunnis," see M. Dj. Mahdjoub, *"Bustān-i Khayāl," Īrān Nāmeh* Vol. II, No. 1 (1362/1983), pp. 43-93. The author of this romance, Muḥammad Taqī Ja'farī Ḥusaynī, with the pen-name "Khayāl," was a Twelver Sunnī.

43. *Tajārib al-Salaf*, ed. 'Abbās Iqbāl Āshtiyānī (Tehran, 1313/1934), p. 67.

44. Ibid., p. 68.

45. Qur'ān 42/23 (Pickthall's translation).

46. *Tajārib al-Salaf*, p. 69.

47. *Al-Naqḍ*, pp. 402-3. Khwāja Bū Manṣūr Māshāda was the leading Shāfi'ite in Isfahan of his time, as Sharaf al-Islām Ṣadr al-Khujandī and his brother Jamāl al-Dīn were the leading Ḥanafites; and a keen rivalry and open hostility subsisted between the two factions. Ṣadr al-Khujandī was the head of the well-known Khujandī family of Isfahan, and is referred to by name in Sa'dī's *Būstān:*

> He took out a thorn from the orphan's foot, and saw in a dream Ṣadr-i Khujand[ī];
> He was wont to say, as he strolled through the gardens, "What roses bloomed for me from that thorn!" (*Būstān*, ed. Yūsufī, Tehran, 1359/1980, Chapter 2 (*Iḥsān*), verses 1153-54).

48. *Al-Naqḍ*, pp. 403-4. The Hamadānīs were known as zealous Sunnis, as Qumm was from the earliest Islamic period a Shi'ite center. The "Anthropomorphists" (*mutashabbiha*, also *ahl-i tashbīh*) were a hardline Sunni sect who insisted on a literal exoteric interpretation of Koran and Ḥadīth, and attributed to God human hands, eyes, ears, etc.

49. *Al-Naqḍ*, p. 406.

50. See my article in *Sukhan*, vol. 20, pp. 583ff.

51. *Sukhan*, vol. 20, p. 589.

52. The word *parcham*, here translated "pennon," originally refers to a bushy black yak's tail, which was tied to the neck of a lance as a good-luck charm.

The tassels in use today, which are what is meant by *parcham* in this text, are the residue of the yak's tail.

53. *Sukhan*, loc. cit. Ḥassān's reply involves a play on the original meaning of *'alam* (symbol, token), hence (in Arabic) "proper noun, name, byword." To become an *'alam* (*'alam shudan*) thus means to become characterized by, famous for, something.

54. According to the *Futuvvat-nāma-yi Sulṭānī*, the *shadda* is "a good-luck favor (*tabarruk*) tied to a *tūq* at the shrine of one of the Imams or, better, placed separately from the *tūq*, for two reasons: first, because of the veneration accorded the *shadda*, it should not be attached to anything else; and second, because these two symbols were originally set up separately. The *shadda* appears to have been a belt or a cloth sash that was tied to the top of a pole.

55. *Sukhan*, vol. 20, p. 591.

56. Khwāja Muḥammad Māhān "Mushtarī-zar," i.e., "the buyer of gold," a character in the *Abū Muslim Nāma*, was a wealthy merchant. In some MSS it is stated that this knife originally belonged to Siyāvush, the son of Kay Kāvūs, the famous legendary king of Iran; he is also referred to as "Siyāvush Valī," i.e., ranked as a Muslim saint.

57. For *sukhanvarī*, see *Sukhan*, vol. 9, nos. 7-9; for the entertainers known as *maddāḥ, gharrā-khwān, muraṣṣa'-khwān*, see *Sukhan*, vol. 20, p. 588.

58. *Rawḍat al-Shuhadā'* (Tehran: Khāvar, 1341/1962), pp. 7-8.

59. M. J. Maḥjūb, *Dar bābat-i Kalīleh va Dimna* (Tehran: Khwārazmī, 1349/1970), pp. 196-200.

60. *Rawḍat al-Shuhadā'*, p. 13.

61. Ibid., p. 14.

62. Ibid., *Muqaddima*, pp. 4, 8.

63. *Rawḍat/rawḍa:* the form *Rawḍat al-Shuhadā'*, with *t*, reproduces the Arabic contextual form of the phrase in Persian as a citation form or *Fremdwort*, ending in the Arabic dotted *h* known as the *tā' marbūṭa* and pronounced as *t;* the form *rawḍa* represents the lexically assimilated loan-word in Persian, written with undotted *h*, and used in isolation or in Persian compounds to mean "a session/selection of readings from the *Rawḍat al-Shuhadā'*."

CHAPTER 4

The Mujtahid of the Age and the Mullā-bāshī: An Intermediate Stage in the Institutionalization of Religious Authority in Shi'ite Iran

SAID AMIR ARJOMAND

I

The Safavids (1501-1722) inherited and preserved many of the religious institutions of Sunni Iran; more precisely, of the Timurid and the Āqqūyūnlū period. Consequently, in the sixteenth and the most part of the seventeenth centuries, the structural relationship between the religious and the political institutions in Shi'ite Iran did not differ appreciably from the "caesaropapist" pattern to be found in the Sunni world. The mosques and the educational system under clerical control were integrated into the caesaropapist state through the centralized administration of the religious endowments (*awqāf*) by the highest clerical functionary of the state, the *ṣadr*, on behalf of the king. Furthermore, the *qāḍīs*, appointed by the ruler, manned the judiciary branch of the Safavid state. Caesaropapism in Safavid Iran had two sources: the legitimacy of *dawlat* as God-ordained turn in power in common with Sunni Islam, and the charisma of Safavid lineage as the putative descendants of the Imam and the Vicegerents (*nuvvāb*) of the Hidden Imam. This second source was specific to Shi'ite Iran, and outlived the Safavid *dawlat* in the form of the charisma of Safavid descendants as *nuvvāb* (corrupt singular form, *navvāb*).

Close scrutiny of Safavid sources reveals that until the last decades of the seventeenth century, the religious and judiciary institutions remained under the firm control of a distinct status group whom we may refer to as the "clerical estate." This group consisted of a landed nobility with strong local roots who were incorporated into Safavid political organization as an estate of clerical administrators, engaged in judiciary and quasi-administrative quasi-religious functions.[1]

However, the introduction of Shi'ism as the established religion was not without serious institutional consequences. The foremost representative of Shi'ism in the early decades of Safavid rule was the theologian and jurist Shaykh 'Alī al-Karakī (d. 1534) who entered the service of the rising Shi'ite state under its founder, Isma'il I (1501-1524). Karakī gained unrivalled eminence under Ṭahmāsp (1524-1576), who succeeded to the throne at the age of ten. Ṭahmāsp bestowed a variety of honorific titles upon Karakī—most notably "the *Mujtahid* of the Age" (*mujtahid al-zamān*) and "Seal of the *Mujtahidīn*"—and in the early 1530's (between A.H. 936 and A.H. 940), sought to establish him as the supreme religious authority in the Shi'ite state. Ṭahmāsp's attempts to institutionalize the authority of the *Mujtahid* of the Age over the religious establishments controlled by the *ṣadr* is reflected in a prolix edict (*farmān*) issued in July 1533, in which the young Ṭahmasp granted Karakī extensive power over the *ṣadrs*, and indeed over all state functionaries, alongside *suyūrghāl* (land grant) and tax immunities.[2] This edict was issued shortly after the banishment of Karakī's opponent, the *ṣadr* Mīr Ni'matallāh Ḥillī.[3] The banishment order is instructive in the section where Ṭahmāsp commands the dissident Shi'ite *mujtahid*, Shaykh Ibrāhīm al-Qaṭīfī, to obey Karakī.

> Shaykh Ibrāhīm is hereby ordered to desist from opposing the world-incumbent command. If the contrary should occur, let the deputies (*vukalā'*) of the Seal of the *Mujtahidīn* and the Heir to the sciences of the Lord of the Prophets, the Exemplar of the people of Islam, the Deputy/Vicegerent of the Imam (*nā'ib al-imām*), the Ornament for beneficence, 'Alī 'Abd al-'Ālī [al-Karakī] prevent and punish him in the clearest way so as to set a lesson for others.[4]

It would appear from this order, that Karakī had representatives responsible to him independently of the *ṣadrs* and their subordinate officials.

Ṭahmāsp's attempt to subordinate all religious functionaries to Karakī's authority generated intense opposition among the Persian clerical estate, and it ultimately failed.[5] There is even a hint that Karakī's death might have resulted from the hostility of the *ṣadr* faction.[6] In any event, the office of the *ṣadr* escaped subjugation to the authority of the *Mujtahid* of the Age, and henceforth continued to be subordinate only to the king. Nevertheless, with the support of the Safavid kings, a Shi'ite hierocracy of incoming doctors and their native trainees was accommodated into the Safavid polity in the sixteenth and early seventeenth century to the sufferrance of the clerical estate. The offices of the *qāḍī*, and the prerogative of the clerical estate, declined sharply, while the immigrating Shi'ite doctors were accommodated, usually as *shaykh al-Islāms* of the important cities.[7]

As *shaykh al-Islāms* of the major cities and as professors at the *madrasas*, the incoming Arab Shi'ite *'ulamā'* and their Persian students were administratively and financially dependent on the *ṣadr* and his subordinates or deputies (singular, *nā'ib al-ṣidāra*). However, given the Shi'ite theory of clerical authority—that is, the doctrine of *ijtihād* as developed by the 'Allāma al-Ḥillī and the First Martyr in the fourteenth century, and by Karakī, the Second Martyr and Bahā, al-Dīn 'Āmilī in the sixteenth and early seventeenth centuries[8]—the *ṣadr* and his deputies did not have any *religious* (as distinct from administrative) authority over the Shi'ite *'ulamā'*. Consequently, even though the notion and title of the *Mujtahid* of the Age was retained, Ṭahmāsp failed to institute it as an office of the state. The concept denoted supreme religious authority and implied a structure of hierocratic authority in the community of Shi'ite scholars distinct from the underlying structure of the administration of religious organizations under *ṣidārat*.

The term "Deputy of the Imam" did not gain currency in the Safavid era but the designation *Mujtahid* of the Age was used to confer supreme religious authority. It was bestowed upon Karakī's son, Shaykh 'Abd al-'Ālī (d.1585/992). Even Ismā'īl II (1576-77), who reverted to Sunnism, acknowledged the supreme religious authority of Shaykh 'Abd al-'Ālī, albeit with pointed sarcasm. Upon ascending the throne, Ismā'īl II

> summoned his Excellency Shaykh 'Abd-al-'Ālī, the *Mujtahid* of the Age, with the most important of the men of learning and said: "In reality sovereignty belongs to the Lord of Time, the [Hidden] Imam, peace be upon Him. As you are His deputy and are authorized by Him to spread the commandments of Islam and the Sacred Law, spread my rug and seat me upon it so that I be established upon the throne of sovereignty and government by your will and your judgment.

While bending down to perform the humiliating task of spreading the rug, the Shaykh murmured, "My father was not anybody's carpet-layer (*farrāsh*)," an utterance which, incidentally, the king did not forgive or forget.[9] After 'Abd al-'Ālī, the title of *Mujtahid* of the Age was conferred upon Karakī's grandson through a daughter, Mīr Sayyid Ḥusayn (d. 1592/1001) who also assumed one of Karakī's more sonorous titles, the Seal of the *Mujtahidīn*. However, neither 'Abd al-'Ālī nor Mīr Ḥusayn had any deputies operating independently of the *ṣidārat*. Although the bestowal of this title signified the recognition by the state of one of Karakī's descendants as the foremost among the Shi'ite dignitaries, it did not amount to a formal appointment. Nor was this recognition binding on other *mujtahidīn* according to the doctrine of *ijtihād*.[10] Indeed, we are told the *'ulamā'* demurred in acknowledging Mīr Sayyid Ḥusayn's state-endorsed supremacy, even though none apparently dared challenge it publicly.[11]

Thus, throughout the sixteenth century the Karakī family retained the title of the *Mujtahid* of the Age and the official state endorsement it implied. But this designation entailed neither a systematic doctrinal justification of centralized supreme religious authority nor any formal organization of such authority over the administration of religious establishments which remained under the undisputed control of the *ṣadrs*. It represented a compromise between the Shi'ite juristic theory of authority, as reflected in the designation *mujtahid*, and the Persian patrimonial theory of authority, reflected in the elevation of the jurist to primacy—"of the Age"—by the king. This solution to the problem of supreme religious authority in a Shi'ite state, representing a compromise between the juristic and the patrimonial principles, can be considered a failure in that it did not succeed in institutionalizing supreme religious authority. Nor did the seventeenth century witness a satisfactory solution to this problem. The eighteenth century, by contrast, offered two opposite solutions: a patrimonial solution at the beginning of the century and a juristic solution at the end of the century. Both these solutions succeeded in institutionalizing Shi'ite religious authority in a more satisfactory way than was possible for Ṭahmāsp and his successors in the sixteenth century. Needless to say, these solutions institutionalized religious authority along different—in fact opposite—lines.

II

Although, in the person of Mīr Dāmād (d. 1631), the Karakī family remained prominent among the Shi'ite *'ulamā'*, the seventeenth century is characterized by a different development in the institutionalization of religious authority. Several *mujtahidīn* are simultaneously recognized without any being designated the *Mujtahid* of the Age. At the same time, the importance of the family of the Master Propagator (*mawlā muravvij*)[12] of Shi'ism as its official representatives declined; religious authority became more dispersed and tended to be invested in the office of the *shaykh al-Islām*. As was pointed out, from the latter half of the sixteenth century onward, incoming Shi'ite theologians were appointed *shaykh al-Islāms* of the important cities in Iran. More than any other office, that of *shaykh al-Islām*, foremost among the religious offices with ceremonial and judiciary functions, came to represent Shi'ism officially. Shaykh al-Islamates thus constituted the most important institutional basis of the emergent Shi'ite hierocracy in Iran. With development of Isfahan as the permanent capital of the Safavid empire under 'Abbās the Great (1587-1629), the *shaykh al-Islām* of Isfahan emerged as the *primus inter pares* of the Shi'ite dignitaries and thus tended to be regarded as the foremost religious authority of the realm. The importance of the Shaykh al-Islamate of Isfahan as the highest office is clear in Chardin's account for the 1660s.[13] This development culminated in the appointment of Muḥammad Bāqir Majlisī (d. 1699) as the *shaykh al-Islām* of Isfahan in 1687/1098, a post he held for the next twelve years, util the last year of the seventeenth century.

Majlisī's achievement consisted in the consolidation of a Shi'ite hierocracy of religious professionals in the last decades of the seventeenth century which continued, after his death, through the first two decades of the eighteenth century. Through the state, he set out to suppress Sufism and Sunnism, while personally devoting himself to the propagation of the Shi'ite doctrine and the elaboration of directives for a wide variety of rituals as the basis for the creation of a specialized hierocracy of religious professionals. He did so by replacing the Sufi Shaykhs and by establishing exclusive control over the religious lives of the masses without the intermediary of the state which had hitherto sustained the clerical notables as its religio-administrative functionaries. With his efforts at the final phase of a prolonged struggle between two distinct groups with competing pretentions to religious authority—i.e., the Shi'ite *'ulamā'* and the clerical notables—a Shi'ite hierocracy relatively independent of the caesaropapist state, though still in uneasy coexistence with the countervailing power of the clerical notables, finally consolidated itself. In short, Majlisī paved the way for the creation, in the early eighteenth century, of the office of *Mullā-bāshī*, an office that embodied the patrimonial solution to the problem of institutionalization of supreme religious authority in the Shi'ite state.

III

According to Minorsky, the title of *Mullā-bāshī*

> was first officially conferred on Muḥammad Bāqir Majlisī by Sulṭān-Ḥusayn, who ascended the throne in 1105/1694. . . . The office of *Mullā-bāshī* survived down to Nādir Shāh's [1736-1748] time. . . . In later times the title seems to have been applied chiefly to the teachers of the Princes.[14]

Minorsky goes on to express his surprise at "the strange dislike of the author [of the *Tadhkira*] for. . . Majlisī, the all-powerful restorer of the Shī'a orthodoxy," and identifies the last incumbent at the office as Mīr Muḥammad Ḥusayn ibn Mīr Muḥamad Ṣāliḥ Khatūnābādī (d. 1739/1151).[15] Here is the text of the *Tadhkirat al-Mulūk* on which Minorsky's comments are based:

> During the reigns of the previous Safavid rulers, the Office of *Mullā-bāshī* was not a specific office, rather the most excellent of the scholars of each age was *in effect* the *Mullā-bāshī*. . . . *Towards the end* of the reign of Shāh Sulṭān-Ḥusayn, a scholar named Mīr Muḥammad Bāqir, even though he was inferior to Āqā Jamāl in learning, was appointed to the office of *Mullā-bāshī*, . . . and founded the *madrasa* of Chahār-Bāgh and himself became its rector. After his death a certain Mullā Muḥammad Ḥusayn became *Mullā-bāshī*.[16]

The statement that Mīr Muḥammad Bāqir was appointed *towards the end* of Shāh Sulṭān-Ḥusayn's reign (1694-1722) predisposes us to question Minorsky's identification of Mullā Muḥammad Bāqir Majlisī, who died in 1699/1111. Furthermore, as Danishpazhouh has pointed out, Majlisī was neither a Mīr nor a Sayyid.[17] In fact, the identification of Majlisī as the first *Mullā-bāshī* is incorrect. The new *madrasa* in Chahār-Bāgh was inaugurated in 1710/1122, some eleven years after Majlisī's death, and its rector for life whom the passage in the *Tadhkirat al-Mulūk* refers to is not Muḥammad Bāqir Majlisī but Mīr Muḥammad Bāqir Khātūn-ābādī (d. 1715/1127).[18] After his death,[19] Mullā Muḥammad Ḥusayn, son of Mullā Shāh-Muḥammad Tabrīzī, who had been appointed the *shaykh al-Islām* of Isfahan in 1715/1126, was promoted to the rank of *Mullā-bāshī*.[20]

We may remark in passing that Āqā Jamāl Khwānsārī (d. 1710/1122) was among the last representative of the philosophically oriented School of Isfahan, whose influence was on the wane, while Mīr Muḥammad Bāqir Khātūn-ābādī had succeeded Majlisī as the head of the emergent hierocracy of the religious professionals after an interval of some thirteen years. The rivalry between Mīr Muḥammad Bāqir and Āqā Jamāl as the leading personalities of the contending camps is evident from a contemporary account of the inauguration of the royal *madrasa* in Chahār-Bāgh.[21] His dislike for Mīr Muḥammad Bāqir indicates that the author of the *Tadhkirat al-Mulūk* must have sided with the clerical estate and with Āqā Jamāl Khwānsārī as its intellectual representatives.

More light is thrown on the coining and significance of the title of *Mullā-bāshī* by the passage describing the office in the *Dastūr al-Mulūk*.

> [The *Mullā-bāshī*] was the head and the president and the most excellent and the most learned of the *'ulamā'* and of the entire learned community of the age. As the king enquired about religious problems and scientific subtleties through him, and he would be addressed by the title of *Mullā-bāshī;* and in assemblies and gatherings, he would sit above the *'ulamā'* and close to the seat of the king. He was required to be in attendance in the company of the victory-favored (king) in all journeys.[22]

Having thus clarified the proximity to the king as the essential feature of the office, and the mode of royal address as the origin of the title, *Dastūr al-Mulūk* gives us important additional information about the salary of the two *Mullā-bāshīs* during the last decade of Safavid rule. The *Mullā-bāshī* was in charge of distributing some charitable funds, and his office carried the annual salary of two hundred *tūmāns.* It is worth noting that this figure is equal to the salary of the *shaykh al-Islām* of Isfahan, and to that of the *qāḍī* of the capital. It is much lower than the "supplementary" salary of 1,360 *tūmāns* received by the *ṣadr-i khāṣṣa* who must be assumed to have had an even larger basic revenue from his commissions on the *suyūrghāls* and the *awqāf.*[23] It is safe to conclude from these figures, and from other indications, that despite this eventual institutionalization of supreme religious authority in the office of *Mullā-bāshī* along the lines suggested by the patrimonial principles of kingship, *ṣidārat* retained its importance to the last day of the Safavid regime, and that the two *ṣadrs*, of the *Khāṣṣa* and of the *Mamālik*, remained the most powerful officials of the Safavid state after the Grand Vazir.

A passage in the *Vaqāyi'* establishes 1712/1124 as the year of the creation of an office for the leader (*ra'īs*) of the Shi'ite hierocracy who became designated as the *Mullā-bāshī* soon thereafter.

> On the last Sunday of the month of Rabī' al-Thānī of the year 1124 (June 15, 1712), the Noblest Vicegerency (*nuvvāb-i ashraf*) [of the Hidden Imam] and Exalted Majesty ordered that His Excellency the *Mujtahid* of the Age, Amīr Muḥammad Bāqir, may God protect him

> from harm, be the leader (*ra'īs*) of all the *'ulamā'* and the religious notables, and the dignitaries and that in the assembly of His Majesty no one have priority over the *Mujtahid* of the Age in seating or standing. That he deliver the reports, and that everyone give precedence and priority to that most learned of the *'ulamā'*. In short, that none of the *ṣadrs* and the *'ulamā'* and the *sayyids* have precedence over him in any matter.[24]

Note the persistence of the title "the *Mujtahid* of the Age." By contrast, the title of *Mullā-bāshī* is not yet mentioned. On his tombstone, however, Mīr Muḥammad Bāqir Khātūn-ābādī is identified as the first rector of the *madrasa* in Chahār-Bāgh, the tutor of Shāh Sulṭān-Ḥusayn and the *Mullā-bāshī*.[25] Therefore, the office formally instituted for him in 1712 is no other than the one to be described in the *Tadhkirat al-Mulūk* as that of "the leader (*sar-karda*) of all *mullās*. . . [who] had a special place near the throne, and none of the learned or the *sayyids* would sit closer than him to the kings."[26]

Throughout the *Vaqāyi' al-Sanīn*, Mīr Muḥammad Bāqir Khātūn-ābādī is still referred to as the *Mujtahid* of the Age. A distinct office is created, but without the proper designation. The title of *Mullā-bāshī* does not make its appearance until after the death of Mīr Muḥammad Bāqir in 1715/1127, when we are informed that "the learned Mullā Muḥammad Ḥusayn, son of Mullā Shāh-Muḥammad of Tabriz, was appointed *Mullā-bāshī*."[27]

It is important to note that Mīr Muḥammad Bāqir had been the king's tutor. According to our source, the king consulted him regularly "and the manner of the Noblest Vicegerency (*nuvvāb-i ashraf*) with the most learned of the *'ulamā'* and the manner of our mentor with the Noblest Vicegerency was the manner of the pupil with the mentor, and of the mentor with the pupil, may God continue his sovereignty (*dawlat*) until the rising of the Redresser (*al-Qā'im*—i.e., the Hidden Imam), may peace be upon Him."[28]

The *Mullā-bāshī* is mentioned in connection with the intrigues during the seige of Isfahan by the Afghans in 1722 by a later source. He reportedly accompanied men in the sorties and raised objections to their touching the heads of decapitated Afghans which he considered polluting (*najis*). The prince in charge of the troops ordered the *Mullā-bāshī* not to accompany them.[29]

Thus, Minorsky's incorrect attribution of the title to Majlisī is an instructive mistake: it can justifiably be said that Muḥammad Bāqir Mājlisī was *in effect* the first Safavid *Mullā-bāshī*, as the position he had carved for himself as the head of a Shī'ite hierocracy of religious professionals was that to be made into a formal office some eleven years after his death—that is, in 1712/1124—for the benefit of the homonymous Muḥammad Bāqir Khātūn-ābādī, and for Mullā Muḥammad Ḥusayn after him. Once formally instituted, the monarch's teacher would be the most likely occupant for the office. Furthermore, owing to the patrimonial organization of Safavid government and the caesaropapist character of the ruler's authority, the office of the *Mullā-bāshī* as the head of an institutionally differentiated but hetercephalous hierocracy would naturally tend to assume the character of the mentorship of the king and the chaplaincy of the royal household.

IV

Minorsky's assertion that the office survived only down to the reign of Nādir Shāh should also be corrected. Though Karīm Khān Zand (1747-1779), owing to his indifference to religious matters, did not appoint a *Mullā-bāshī*,[30] the office survived into the Qājār era. It is true that *Mullā-bāshī* did become a title for the teachers of the Princes towards the mid-nineteenth century, and depreciated even further, being applied to a provincial governor's buffoon by the beginning of the twentieth.[31] Nevertheless, in the last decade of the eighteenth and the beginning of the nineteenth century, we do encounter the *Mullā-bāshī* among the officials of the Qājār patrimonial state.

The office of *Mullā-bāshī* was retained after the Afghan invasion. The Afghan rulers appointed a certain Mullā Za'farān who acted as an intermediary between Ashraf and Ṭahmāsp II during the final hours before the collapse of Afghan rule in Isfahan in 1729.[32] Ṭahmāsp II (1729-1732) had his own *Mullā-bāshī*, Mīrzā 'Abd al-Ḥasan. Mīrzā 'Abd al-Ḥasan was strangled with a bow-string because of his Safavid loyalty on the eve of Nādir's "election" as king in March 1736.[33] Mullā 'Alī Akbar was thereupon appointed *Mullā-bāshī* and held the office until Nādir's assassination in 1748/1160, when he too was killed along with Nādir's other close associates.[34] Nādir's "pan-Islamic" religious policy and the demotion of Twelver Shi'ism from the religion of the state to the fifth School of Law (*madhhab*) cannot be dealt with here.[35] What is important for us to note is the crucial role of the *Mullā-bāshī*, 'Alī Akbar, in Nādir's religious policy and its consequences. Mullā 'Alī Akbar was closely involved in Nādir's negotiations with the Ottomans even before his appointment as *Mullā-bāshī*.[36] According to the official historian of Nādir Shāh, in 1741/1155, "the *Mujtahid* of the Age, Mullā 'Alī Akbar, the *Mullā-bāshī*," helped clear all doubt in the king's mind—

i.e., assented to the latter's view—that Ismā'īl the Safavid's denigration of the Rightly-guided Caliphs was the source of all subsequent troubles. The *nā'ib al-ṣidāra* of the realm, Mīrzā Muḥammad 'Alī, was sent to all quarters of the country to propagate Nādir's opinion.[37] Two years later (1743/1156), the *Mullā-bāshī* played a crucial role in the conference with the Sunni *'ulamā'* in which the first document of "Islamic unity" was signed and sealed. As a part of the arrangement to secure the recognition of Shi'ism by the Sunnis, on the twenty-sixth of Shawwāl 1156/thirteenth of December 1743, Mullā 'Alī Akbar mounted the pulpit of the grand mosque of Kūfa to pronounce, for the first time in Shi'ite history, the legitimacy of the first three Rightly-guided Caliphs.[38]

Curiously, it was under Nādir that the office of the *Mullā-bāshī* reached its apogee. The office of the *ṣadr* had been abolished, and the *nā'ib al-ṣidāra* was clearly a lesser official than the *Mullā-bāshī.* It is also worth noting that the *Mullā-bāshī* was still designated the *Mujtahid* of the Age.[39] On the other hand, Nādir's anti-Shi'ite religious policy irreparably alienated the Shi'ite hierocracy from the Afshār state, and from its chief religious official, the *Mullā-bāshī.*

As has already been pointed out, Karīm Khān Zand made no effort to reincorporate the Shi'ite hierocracy into the state. The latter subsisted on its own resources in the Arab Iraq, and showed signs of inner vigor and revival during the anarchic 1770s and 1780s. This revival took the form of the Uṣūlī movement under the leadership of Āqā Muḥammad Bāqir Bihbahānī (1705-1790), a descendant of Majlisī through his daughter.[40] After more than six decades of intervening anarchy, on the basis of the goundwork laid by his illustrious predecessor, Bihbahānī's leadership assured the reemergence and consolidation of hierocratic power independently of the state.

Āqā Muḥammad Khān, the founder of the Qājār Dynasty who ruled most of Iran from 1785 to 1796, affirmed the continued adherence of his state to Twelver Shi'ism established in Iran by the Safavids. As a new dynasty, the need to legitimate their rule was felt acutely by the first Qājār monarchs. As the Qājārs lacked the Safavids' charisma of holy lineage as the putative descendants of the Imams, it was all the more imperative for Āqā Muḥammad to establish the legitimacy of his rule and that of his Dynasty. Āqā Muḥammad Khān did not live long enough after his coronation to deal with this problem, but his successor, Fatḥ 'Alī Shāh (1796-1834), did. As Weber remarks, "if the legitimacy of the ruler is not clearly identifiable through hereditary charisma, another charismatic power is needed; normally this can only be hierocracy."[41] At first, the Qājārs made a serious, if desperate, effort to claim Safavid descent. Their ancestry was traced to Shāh Sulṭān-

Ḥusayn through Muḥammad Ḥasan Khān and his mother Khayr al-Nisā' Khānum, who had allegedly been given to the chief of the Qājār tribe Fatḥ 'Alī Khān by the Safavid Shah when pregnant with Muḥammad Ḥasan by him! On the basis of the fantastic and unflattering story, Āqā Muḥammad Khān would call the *sayyids* "brethren," and the contemporary historian Rustam al-Ḥukamā' refers to him as Sulṭān Muḥammad Shāh al-Mūsavī al-Ṣafavī, and to his father as Muḥammad Ḥasan Khān Ṣafavī Qājār. Even Fatḥ 'Alī Shāh is referred to as al-Mūsavī al-Ṣafavī.[42] It is said that the latter intended to wear the Safavid turban several times but was opposed by the Qājār emirs.[43] Be that as it may, Fatḥ 'Alī Shāh gave up the attempt to claim Safavid descent and turned to the alternative of obtaining legitimacy from the Shi'ite hierocracy. Many of the prominent *'ulamā'* responded favorably to the initiative taken by the first Qājār rulers, but they firmly insisted on the differentiations of religious from the political authority, and hence on the autonomy and autocephaly of the hierocracy. They legitimized kingship, but legitimized it as authority pertaining to the temporal sphere. The religious sphere was left to the exclusive hierocratic authority of the *mujtahidīn*, and Safavid caesaropapism was definitively discarded in principle.[44]

The rejection of the Safavid caesaropapist rule on behalf of the Hidden Imam, as well as the *de jure* and *de facto* autonomy and autocephaly of the Shi'ite hierocracy, spelled the demise of the highest religious office of their state, that of the *Mullā-bāshī.*

In 1791/1205, Āqā Muḥammad Khān Qājār sent his *Mullā-bāshī*, Mullā Muḥammad Ḥusayn Māzandarānī, to Kirmānshāh to invite Āqā Muḥammad 'Alī *Mujtahid*, the son of Āqā Muḥammad Bāqir Bihbahānī, to the capital.[45] This mission marked the beginning of the rapprochement between the Qājār state and the Shi'ite hierocracy, and decisively sealed the fate of the office of the *Mullā-bāshī.* The *Mullā-bāshī* still remained the chaplain of the royal household, but, given the autocephaly of the Shi'ite hierocracy and its independence from the patrimonial government, his jurisdiction no longer extended beyond the Qājār household. The office was noted by a European traveller in the early nineteenth century.[46] Mullā Muḥammad Ḥusayn's son, Mullā 'Alī Asghar, in due course succeeded him as the *Mullā-bāshī.*[47]

Mullā 'Alī Asghar appears as a miserable figure in the royal household. His duties seem to have been so restricted as to have given him ample opportunity for dissolute drunkenness. *Mullā-bāshī* 'Alī Asghar was often reprimanded for his bibulousness, and was even bastinadoed for this propensity by the order of Fatḥ 'Alī Shāh.[48] The office of the *Mullā-bāshī*, however, was not abolished. We know that a certain

Ḥājjī Mullā Muḥammad Amīn (d. between 1826 and 1828/1241 and 1243) held the title.[49] A certain Mullā Karīm ibn Muḥammad Ṣāliḥ Sarābī Tabrīzī served as the *Mullā-bāshī* of the Sufi and anticlerical Muḥammad Shāh (1834-1848).[50] In this period, the title was also used by the tutor of the Crown Prince, Nāṣir al-Dīn, who resided in Tabriz. Even so, this tutor, Ḥājjī Mullā Maḥmūd Tabrīzī (d. 1855/1272)—who subsequently moved to Tehran with the new monarch, Nāṣir al-Dīn Shāh (1848-1896), and retained his privileged position—was much more commonly addressed by the title of Niẓām al-'Ulamā'. Furthermore, it was this latter title of Niẓām al-'Ulamā' which came to be officially used, in preference to *Mullā-bāshī*, to designate Mullā Maḥmūd's successors to the privilege of being "the first among the *'ulamā'* in royal audiences."[51]

Already during the Afshar period, some Princes appear to have appointed their own *Mullā-bāshī* in the provinces they ruled.[52] During the early decades of the nineteenth century, replicas of the office of *Mullā-bāshī* were set up in some of the provincial capitals as tutors and chaplains of the princes acting as their governors. In Shiraz, for instance, Mīrzā Muḥammad Bāqir Mūsavī Shīrāzī (d. 1824-5/1240), a student of Bihbahānī returning from his studies in the holy cities of Iraq, was appointed *Mullā-bāshī* of Fatḥ 'Alī Shāh's son, Prince Farmānfarmā, who was the governor of Fars. The office, or more probably the title as a sinecure, was passed on to his son, and then to his grandson who died in 1902/1320.[53] In Tabriz, Ḥājj Mīrzā 'Abd al-Karīm and Mullā 'Abd al-Laṭīf Ṭasūjī were appointed *Mullā-bāshīs* and tutors to the sons of the Crown Prince and Regent, 'Abbās Mīrzā.[54] In the second half of the nineteenth century, the title of *Mullā-bāshī* continued to be held by the tutors of the Crown Prince in Tabriz, Mīrzā Maḥmūd Ṭasūjī (d. 1878/1295) and his brother Mīrzā Muḥammad who succeeded him.[55]

In the middle of the nineteenth century, the office of *Mullā-bāshī* was still a respectable sinecure. Mullā Muḥammad Malik al-Kuttāb, the *Mullā-bāshī*, was appointed to the Consultative Chamber (*Maṣlahat-Khāna*) set up by Nāṣir al-Dīn Shāh in 1858.[56] By the latter part of the century, however, the title had so depreciated as to be bestowed on certain clerics and men of learning by common acclamation.[57] By the beginning of the twentieth century, we have the provincial governor's buffoon mentioned by Minorsky. But the fact that the *Mullā-bāshī*, like other courtly functions, could degenerate into buffoonery does not justify our ending with an entirely pejorative note. Let us rather end our history of the office with one last dignified appearance of a *Mullā-bāshī* in the twentieth century.

During the Constitutional Revolution, the first popular provincial assembly (*anjuman*) was opened in Isfahan on December 22, 1906. It was dominated by the influence of the powerful *mujtahid*, Āqā Najafī, and presided over by his brother, Ḥājj Shaykh Nūrallāh. Prince Ẓill al-Sulṭān, the governor of the province, authorized the *Mullā-bāshī* to represent him at its meetings.[58]

V

The office of the *Mullā-bāshī* was not the only casualty of the demise of the Safavid caesaropapism. The office of the *ṣadr* collapsed after Nādir Shāh. The *qāḍīs*, who were appointed by the Safavid ruler, also disappeared fairly fast, and very few of them are mentioned in the local histories of the early nineteenth century. In fact, in so far as the sources on the early nineteenth century mention the office of judgeship at all, this office tends to be attached to that either of the *shaykh al-Islām* or of the *imām jum'a* (congregational prayer leader).[59]

This brings us to the one caesaropapist institution of Shi'ite Iran which did not decline to any comparable extent. The state-appointed *shaykh al-Islāms* of the major cities continued their prominence among the local notables. In the fall of 1790/1205, for instance, the inhabitants of the city of Kirman sent the *shaykh al-Islām*, accompanied by the *qāḍī*, to the camp of Lutf 'Alī Khān, the last Zand ruler, to intercede for them.[60] The Qājārs either confirmed the *shaykh al-Islāms* or appointed new ones, as in the city of Kashan.[61] The ruler thus continued to appoint—or, given the strong hereditary tendency to the appropriation of the office by the same family, to confirm—the *shaykh al-Islāms*, who played an important role in the dualistic Qājār polity as intermediaries between the state and the independent hierocracy of *mujtahidīn*. Thus, in the early decades of the nineteenth century, the office of the *shaykh al-Islām* was the connecting link between the temporal and the religious structures of authority. As the intermediary officials between the state and the independent hierocracy, the *shaykh al-Islāms* played an important role in the politics of the first half of the nineteenth century, a role that deserves further study. Even more deserving of a systematic study is the gradual rise of the office of *imām jum'a* and the progressive transfer of the functions of the *shaykh al-Islām* to it in the course of the nineteenth century. As a consequence of this unexplored process, it was the office of the *imām jum'as*, appointed by the ruler in the cities, that had become the intermediary institution between the state and the hierocracy in the latter part of the nineteenth century.[62] Like the offices of the *Mullā-bāshī*, the *ṣadr*,[63] and the *qāḍī* before it, Shaykh al-Islamate had by then become a sinecure and a title, preserved as a source of honor and pride by the families who were its presumptive inheritors. By 1914, even family pride and honor seemed barely sufficient for extending the tenuous life of the functionless office. Sardār Muḥyī, the peculous governor of Kurdistan demanded the earlier price of 7,000 *tūmāns* from a certain Mullā 'Abd al-Fattāḥ who expected to inherit the office of the *shaykh al-Islām* of Kurdistan. The latter only offered 300 *tūmāns* and raised it to 1,500 for a package deal which also included two lesser titles for his relatives. Still, the deal was clenched and Mullā 'Abd al-Fattāḥ was appointed *shaykh al-Islām* on June 11, 1914/Rajab 17, 1332.[64]

VI

With a handful of eminent *mujtahidīn* acquiring enormous power and prestige as the leaders of an autonomous Shi'ite hierocracy during the reign of Fatḥ 'Alī Shāh, the office of the royal chaplain, the *Mullā-bāshī*, thus withered away. In the institutionalization of religious authority, the juristic principle had triumphed over the patrimonial. The societal structure of authority in Shi'ite Iran had become distinctly dualistic. The religious authority of the *mujtahidīn* was fully institutionalized in the form of an autonomous hierocracy. However, as a consequence of this mode of institutionalization, the centralization of supreme religious authority disappeared. The institutionalization of a centralized supreme authority in terms of the juristic principle was not to occur until after the Islamic revolution of 1979.[65]

Notes

1. S. A. Arjomand, "The Clerical Estate and the Emergence of a Shi'ite Hierocracy in Safavid Iran. A Study in Historical Sociology," *Journal of the Economic and Social History of the Orient*, XXVIII (1985): 169-219.

2. See Chapter 12 below.

3. In Muḥammad Taqī Dānishpazhouh, "Yak parda az zindigānī-yi Shāh Ṭahmāsp-i Ṣafavī" [A Scene from the Life of Shah Tahmasp the Safavid], *Majallah-yi Dānishkada-yi Adabiyyāt va 'Ulūm-i Insānī-yi Mashhad*, VII.4 (1972/1350), p. 972.

4. Ibid., p. 973, from al-Karakī's obituary in *Khulāḍat al-Tavārīkh* under the year 940. Also see below, Chapter 9, p. 224.

5. S. A. Arjomand, *The Shadow of God and the Hidden Imam. Religion,*

Political Order and Societal Change in Shi'ite Iran from the Beginning to 1890 (Chicago: University of Chicago Press, 1984), pp. 133-37. For a more detailed account, see C. J. Beeson, "Origins of Conflict in the Ṣafavī Religious Institution," unpublished Princeton University Ph.D. Dissertation, 1982.

6. Dānishpazhouh, op. cit., p. 975.

7. Arjomand, *The Shadow of God*, p. 302, n.30.

8. Ibid., pp. 140-41.

9. Maḥmūd Afūshta-yi Naṭanzī, *Nuqāwat al-Āthār fī Dhikr al-Akhyār*, Iḥsān Ishrāqī, ed., Tehran, 1971/1350, p. 41. This conversation is not reported in any other source. According to Qāḍī Aḥmad Qummī, the royal rug was spread two *'ulamā'*, Mīr Sayyid 'Alī 'Arab Jabal-'Āmilī and Mīr Raḥmat-Allāh Fattāl Najafī, the prayer leader. (*Khulāṣat al-Tavārīkh*, Deutsche Staatbibliothek, Berlin, MS Orient, fol. 2202, f.255a.)

10. Karakī's primacy as the spokesman for Shi'ism was vigorously disputed by the rival *mujtahid*, Ibrāhīm al-Qaṭīfī. See W. Madelung, "Shi'ite Discussions on the Legality of *Kharāj*," in R. Peters, ed., *Proceedings of the Ninth Congress of the Union Européenne des Arabisants et Islamisants* (Leiden: E. J. Brill, 1981), pp. 193-202; Arjomand, *The Shadow of God*, pp. 135-36.

11. Iskandar Beg Turkamān, Munshī, *Tārīkh-i 'Ālam-ārā-yi 'Abbāsī*, I. Afshār, ed., Tehran, 1971/1350, vol. 1, pp. 145, 458.

12. Dānishpazhouh, op. cit., p. 974.

13. J. Chardin, *Les Voyages du Chevalier Jean Chardin en Perse*, L. Langlès, ed. (Paris, 1811), vol. 9, p. 515.

14. V. Minorsky, ed., *Tadhkirat al-Mulūk* (London: E. J. W. Gibb, Memorial Series, N.S., XVI, 1943), Commentary, p. 110.

15. Ibid., pp. 110-11.

16. Cf. ibid., p. 41. This and the subsequent passage from the *Tadhkirat al-Mulūk* have been translated from the original because of minor inaccuracies in Minorsky's translation. Emphasis added.

17. M. T. Dānishpazhouh, "*Dastūr al-Mulūk-i* Mīrzā Rafī'ā va *Tadhkirat al-Mulūk-i* Mīrzā Samī'ā, I," *Majalla-yi Dānishkada-yi Adabiyyāt va 'Ulūm-i Insānī*, XV 5-6 (1968/1347), pp. 487, 497, 500.

18. Sayyid 'Abd al-Ḥusayn Khātūn-ābādī, *Vaqāyi' al-Sanīn va'l-A'vām*, M. B. Bihbūdī, ed. (Tehran: Islāmiyya, 1973/1352), pp. 559-61.

19. Cf. H. Muddarisī Ṭabaṭabā'ī, *Mithālha-yi Ṣudūr-i Ṣafavī* (Qumm: Ḥikmat, 1974/1353), p. 21.

20. Khātūn-ābādī, pp. 567-69.

21. Ibid., pp. 559-62.

22. Dānishpazhouh, *"Dastūr al-Mulūk," Majalla-yi Dānishkada-yi Adabiyyāt va 'Ulūm-i Insānī*, XVI (1 & 2), p. 64.

23. Ibid., pp. 64-69.

24. Khātūn-ābādī, p. 566.

25. Sayyid Muṣḥiḥ al-Dīn Mahdavī, *Tadhkirat al-Qubūr yā Dānishmandān va Buzurgān-i Iṣfāhān* (Isfahan: Thaqafī, 1969-70/1348), p. 158.

26. Cf. Minorsky, p. 41.

27. Khātūn-ābādī, p. 569.

28. Ibid., p. 557.

29. Muḥammad Hāshim Āṣif, Rustam al-Ḥukamā', *Rustam al-Tavārīkh*, M. Mushīrī, ed. (Tehran, 1969/1348), pp. 144-67.

30. J. R. Perry, *Karīm Khān Zand. A History of Iran*, 1747-1779 (Chicago: University of Chicago Press, 1979), pp. 220-22.

31. Minorsky, Commentary, p. 111, n. 2.

32. Riḍā-Qulī Khān Hidāyat, *Rawḍat al-Ṣafā-yi Nāṣirī* (Tehran: Khayyām, 1960-61/1339), vol. 8, pp. 525-26.

33. J. Hanway, *An Historical Account of the British Trade Over the Caspian Sea* (London, 1753), p. 127.

34. M. Bāmdād, *Tārīkh-i Rijāl-i Īrān* (Tehran: Zavvār, 1968/1347), vol. 2: p. 435.

35. See R. Sha'bānī, "Siyāsat-i Madhhabī-yi Nādir," *Vaḥīd* 7, no. 9 (1970/1348).

36. Abu'l-Ḥasan ibn Muḥammad Amīn Ghulistāna, *Mujmal al-Tavārīkh*, Mudarris Raḍavī, ed. (Tehran: Intishārāt-i Dānishgāh-i Tihrān, 1977/1356), Commentary, p. 373.

37. Muḥammad Mahdī Astarābādī, *Jahānqushā-yi Nādirī*, 'A. Anvār, ed. (Tehran: Anjuman-i Āthār-i Mellī, 1962/1341), p. 375.

38. 'Abdallāh ibn al-Ḥusayn al-Suwaydī, *Mu'tamir al-Najaf* (Cairo, 1973/1393), pp. 50-53.

39. Fatḥ 'Alī Shāh, by contrast, would use the designation not for his *Mullā-bāshī* but for the eminent *mujtahid* of Qumm, Mīrzā Abu'l-Qāsim. See Chapter 5, p. 105 below.

40. J. R. I. Cole, "Shi'i Clerics in Iraq and Iran, 1722-1780: The Akhbārī-Uṣūlī Conflict Reconsidered," *Iranian Studies XVIII* (1985): pp. 3-34.

41. M. Weber, *Economy and Society*, G. Roth and C. Wittich, eds. (Berkeley: University of California Press, 1978), vol. 2, pp. 1147.

42. Rustam al-Ḥukamā', pp. 51-60, 174, 237-240.

43. Ibid., pp. 51-52, n. 1.

44. Arjomand, *The Shadow of God*, Chapter 10.

45. Mīrzā Muḥammad Taqī Siphir, *Nāsikh al-Tavārīkh*, M. B. Bihbūdī, ed. (Tehran: Islāmiyya, 1965/6/1344), vol. 1, p. 60; Hidāyat, vol. 9, p. 241.

46. Tancoigne, *A Narrative of a Journey into Persia* (London, 1820), p. 191.

47. Aḥmad Mīrzā 'Azud al-Dawla, *Tārīkh-i 'Azudī*, K. Kūhī Kirmānī, ed. (Tehran, 1949/1328), p. 37.

48. Ibid. We hear of Mullā 'Alī Asghar's son in 1833/1247, but as an administrator of the province of Kirman and no longer as the *Mullā-bāshī*. (Sipihr, 2:111; Hidāyat, 10:44).

49. Professor Hossein Modarresi Tabataba'i has kindly informed me that he has seen a manuscript of *Zahr al-Rabī'* written for Muḥammad Amīn the *Mullā-bāshī*. Interestingly—as if to acknowledge the transfer of religious authority discussed in this paper—the *Mullā-bāshī* donated the book to the *'ulamā' imāmīyya* after his death ca. 1828 (Library of Masjid-i A'ẓam, Qumm, MS No. 190).

50. Mīrzā Riḍā-qulī ibn Mahdī-qulī Sarābī Tabrīzī, *Lajjat al-Ilam fī Ḥujjat al-Umam*, n.d., p. 6. I am grateful to Dr. Kamran Amir Arjomand, the Librarian at the Shi'ite Library of Cologne University, for supplying me photocopies of the relevant pages of this work and of the preface to the work cited in note 53 below.

51. Mīrzā Ḥasan I'timād al-Salṭana, *al-Ma'āthir va'l-Āthār* (Tehran, 1888), p. 24; Hidāyat, vol. 10, p. 603. Mullā Maḥmūd was the chief questioner at the examination of the Bāb in the presence of the Crown Prince in Tabriz in 1847/1263.

52. Bāmdād, vol. 6 (1972/1351), p. 248, n. 5.

53. M. A. Mudarris, *Rayḥānat al-Adab*, Tabriz: Shafaq, n.d., vol. 1, p. 303; Mīrzā Muḥammad Bāqir al-Mūsavī al-Shīrāzī, *Lawāmi' al-Anwār al-'Arshīyya*, copied by Sayyid Muḥammad Bāqir Mūsavī Āyatallāhī in 1974/1394, the editor's preface.

54. Bāmdād, vol. 2, pp. 275-76; vol. 6, p. 143.

55. Bāmdād, vol. 4, p. 50; vol. 6, p. 186.

56. K. Iṣfahāniān, ed., *Majmū'a-yi Asnād va Madārik-i Farrukh Khān Amīn al-Dawla* (Tehran: Tehran University Press, 1970/1350), vol. 3, pp. 331-47.

57. I'timād al-Salṭana, p. 211.

58. A. K. S. Lambton, "Persian Political Societies, 1906-11," *St. Antony's Papers, 16, Middle Eastern Affairs*, 3 (1963), p. 48.

59. See, for instance, Nādir Mīrzā, *Tārīkh va Jughrāfiyā-yi Dār al-Salṭana-yi Tabrīz* M. Mushīrī, ed. (Tehran, 1972/1351), p. 222-27; 'Abd al-Raḥīm Kalāntar-i Ḍarrābī, *Tārīkh-i Kāshān*, I. Afshār, ed. (Tehran, 1963/1341), pp. 296-300.

60. Ḥasan Fasā'ī, *History of Persia Under Qajar Rule*, H. Busse, tr. and ed. (New York: Columbia University Press, 1972), p. 37.

61. Kalāntar-i Ḍarrābī, pp. 305-6.

62. See further Amanat's remarks in Chapter 5, especially pp. 107-108, on the rivalry between the *imām jum'a* and the *mujtahidīn* resident in Iranian cities.

63. For *ṣadr* as sinecure and title, see, for instance, Nādir Mīrā, p. 116-225; for *nā'ib al-ṣidāra*, see, for instance, Kalāntar-i Ḍarrābī, pp. 303-4.

64. Bāmdād, vol. 6, pp. 133-34.

65. See Chapter 8 below.

CHAPTER 5

In Between the Madrasa and the Marketplace: The Designation of Clerical Leadership in Modern Shi'ism

ABBAS AMANAT

I

"The order of the clerical community (*rūḥanīyat*) is in its disorder." Whether genuine or apocryphal, this dictum—popular in clerical circles—expresses cynicism of those who saw the lack of a well-defined Shi'ite hierarchy an inherent blessing.[1] This anarchic discipline—if such contradiction in terms can be employed—is an important clue for the study of clerical leadership over the past two centuries.

The theory of *ijtihād* as first introduced to Shi'ism in pre-modern times, and elaborated in Safavid and post-Safavid eras, established a functional relationship between the *mujtahid* (one who applies limited deductive methods to arrive at reasonably practical legal norms) and the *muqallid* (one who emulates the *mujtahid* in his legal rulings).[2] By late eighteenth century, *mujtahids* were distinguished as a religious elite, and qualifications for acquiring the status of *ijtihād* were formulated in some detail. Most notable among these were three qualities: *'ilm* (knowledge of law; more specifically *uṣūl* [jurisprudence] and *furū'* [branches or the actual body of law]), *'adl* (justice in the practice of law), and *vara'* (piety) or *taqvā* (godliness).[3] Such formulation was sufficient to designate a body of *mujtahids* with substantial juristic authority, but it was barely adequate to create an ecclesiastical hierarchy.

To compensate for this structural handicap, first the concept of *marja'-i taqlīd* (the source of emulation, the authority to which one turns, or appeals, for legal guidance) and then the notion of *marja'īyat-i taqlīd-i tāmm* (complete authority [of one *mujtahid*] over the community, the supreme exemplar) were proposed in the latter part of the nineteenth century. In turn, the respective nuances of the three moral qualities mentioned above—knowledge, justice, and piety—were highlighted to demonstrate not only the relativity of *ijtihād* but the superiority of one *mujtahid* over the others. Thus *a'lamīyat* (superiority in learning) was held by most later jurists as the key prerequisite for *marja'īyat-i tāmm*, though no practical set of criteria was ever established for determining its definition.[4]

Indeed, the theoretical obstacles inherent in Imami Shi'ism posed a serious obstacle to any clear definition of superiority in learning and, in effect, to the fuller institutionalization of the religious authority. The inescapable presence of the Hidden Imam made any attempt towards theoretical elaboration of a supreme authority a matter of controversy and conflict. The theological grounds for the designation of leadership, therefore, remained inherently limited. The fact that the degree of such legal knowledge could not be determined by any empirical means may not have facilitated the emulator's difficult task of choosing a *marja'*, but it clearly established one point: There was no theoretical justification —even in the jurisprudence (*fiqh*) of the dominant Uṣūlī school—for absolute legal authority. Even the greatest of the nineteenth-century legal scholars, Shaykh Murtaḍā Anṣārī (d. 1864), who is often regarded by posterity as the first *marja'-i taqlīd-i tāmm*, is careful to interpret *a'lamīyat*, without ever clearly defining its boundaries, as a comparative quality. Several commentators of Anṣārī also agree with him on this issue. Anṣārī delineates this point in his *Ṣirāṭ al-Najāt*.[5]

> What is intended by [the term] *a'lam* (superiority in learning), is the one who is more skillful (*ustādtar*) in deducing God's law (*ḥukm*) and comprehending it from the lawful evidence (*adalla-yi shar'īya*). For recognition of the *a'lam* and obligation of referring to him, testimony of a single just man (*'adl-i vāḥid*) who is one of the people of insight is sufficient to provide reasonable presumption (*ẓann*).

In their commentaries on Ansārī's tract, none of the seven juristic authorities of later generation challenge the main premises of the above statement. The first of these commentators, Mīrzā Ḥasan Shīrāzī (d. 1896), remarks that, in the absence of positive knowledge (*'ilm*), any degree of presumption (*ẓann*) would suffice. Even if there is a slight probalility (*iḥtimāl*) that one *mujtahid* is superior to another, it is not unreasonable to honor that probalility.[6] Ismā'īl Ṣadr Iṣfahānī, on the other hand, maintains that "the sufficiency of a single just man is open to doubt," presumably implying that two just men (*'adlayn*) are needed.[7] Mullā Muḥammad Kāẓim Khurāsānī sustains the same position: presumption (*ẓann*) is acceptable "where positive knowledge and proof (*bayyina*) is absent."[8] In contrast, Muḥammad Taqī Shīrāzī maintains that in this juncture, *ẓann* has absolutely no validity.

What is at issue is the relative rather than absolute superiority of the jurist. Even though some disagreement does exist on the validity of presumption (*ẓann*), there is no dispute on the literal meaning of *a'lam* as more learned (*ustādtar* rather than *ustādtarīn*, the most learned). Nor is there any major difference regarding the method of observing priorities in choosing a *marja'*. Except for Muḥammad Taqī Shīrāzī, who denies the validity of *ẓann* (an un-Uṣūlī position), all three major figures—Anṣārī, Shīrāzī, and Khurāsānī—admit that presumption (*ẓann*), and even probability (*iḥtimāl*), which is based on the testimony of one just man would be adequate to establish the *a'lamīyat* of a *mujtahid.*

The rudiments for designation of the *a'lam* is thus laid on such shaky grounds that even most scrupulous followers can make a choice of *marja'* by merely relying on the testimony of one or two just men. It is difficult to exaggerate the vulnerability of such formulation. The main guideline for the lay emulator is to follow the rule of priority as Anṣārī states and others agree (with minor variations in Muḥammad Taqī Shīrāzī). The follower is left at the discretion of just men who may recommend diverse choices of *marāji'*. Beyond this, there is little to guide the laity in its choice, nor is there a precise definition of "the people of the insight" beyond its conventional meaning. In effect, the process of observing the priorities and thus choosing one *a'lam* is entirely delegated to the individual emulator (*muqallid*). Even other conditions of *marja'īyat*, namely, justice (*'adl*) and godliness (*taqvā*), are subordinated to prime quality of knowledge. Echoing Uṣūlī jurists before him, Anṣārī maintains "a more learned [but less] just [*mujtahid*] is preferable to a more just [but less] learned [*mujtahid*]."[10] The same rule applies to the quality of godliness.[11]

Though in theory the order of priorities are knowledge, justice, and piety, in practice the determination of these priorities is made by the emulator and his "just consultants." Besides the above conditions, no other prerequisites for becoming an eligible *marja'* have been set except that of being a fully recognized *mujtahid* (*musallam al-ijtihād*) or fully qualified *mujtahid* (*jami' al-sharāyiṭ*)—a quality which is implicit in the notion of *a'lamīyat*. There is no institutional scheme, as for instance in the Catholic church, to govern the choice of the supreme clerical authority.

Two conclusions may be drawn. First, based on the evidence in the work of Anṣārī and later experts, there is no logical ground for constituting a systematic line of juristic authority. The three theoretical prerequisites are subjective ideals which are open to arbitrary interpretations. There are no institutional authorities, such as the church or the state, to verify these prerequisites or to designate their possessors. The ultimate arbiter, therefore, is the follower (*muqallid*) who would decide upon, and thus present his loyalty to, the *mujtahid* of his choice. This would allow the follower considerable room to maneuver; to shift from one *marja'* to another as he pleases (e.g., upon the necessity of obtaining favorable opinions) and to direct religious dues and other funds to the appropriate recipient. The *marja'* is in effect the willing dependent of the *muqallid*.[12]

Second, the evidence presented in Anṣārī and others in fact tends to remove the justification for emergence of a supreme *marja'* on doctrinal grounds. This has more to do with the limitations of the Shi'ite hierarchical theory—Uṣūlī or otherwise—rather than failure of prominent experts. Uṣūlism no doubt encouraged rationalization through deductive premises of conventional logic and thus legitimized clerical elitism by distinguishing a body of *mujtahids* for their expert knowledge. However, it never developed an institutionalized process for creating a complete pyramid. The emergence of supreme authority, which seems the logical culmination of any hierarchy in pre-modern times, was thus held back, at least in theory, by the presence (more accurately, the material absence) of the Imam. It can be asserted that in no time during the history of post-formative orthodox Shi'ism, prior to Khumeinī's doctrine of the Guardianship of the Jurist (*Vilāyat-i Faqīh*), the doctrinal barriers were crossed to create a centralized leadership in the same way that *ijtihād* was institutionalized a century before the death of Anṣārī. The rudimentary regulations for *taqlīd* (as they appeared in treatises for public consumption) never indicated—let alone assumed—that "the order of priority" (*al-a'lamu fī al-a'lam*) should be taken to its logical conclusion. What emerged in the second half of the nineteenth century and later came to be known as *marja'-i taqlīd* was therefore an informal status based on practicalities of leadership rather than on doctrinal grounds. Interestingly enough, the most renowned holders of this office, Shaykh Murtaḍā Anṣārī and Mīrzā Ḥasan Shīrāzī, were cautious not to attach a doctrinal justification to their own seniority.

Shaykh Murtaḍā Anṣārī has often been considered the first recognized *marja'-i taqlīd kull* (supreme source of emulation). But a closer examination of the available historical evidence would pose a question as to the very existence of such a notion at the time of Anṣārī. The author of *Rawḍāt al-Jannāt*, one of the more reliable biographical dictionaries, who was a contemporary of Anṣārī, gave a typical description of the celebrated scholar when he distinguished him as the one "to whom at this time came the leadership (*riyāsat*) of the Imamīyya";[13] a title by which the author refers to at least three other immediate predecessors of Anṣārī.[14] The first explicit reference to Anṣārī's supreme authority, however, appears much later in the sources of the twentieth century, where, somewhat retrospectively, his leadership (*riyāsat*) was taken synonymously with the later-coined *marja'īyat-i taqlīd tāmm.*[15]

The absence of the *marja'īyat*, therefore, stands against the later assumptions that from the time of Anṣārī onwards, there existed a unified leadership with unchallenged jurisdiction over the whole community, both *mujtahid* and lay. But if *a'lamīyat* in its theoretical context is not a decisive criteria, what else has determined the course of evolution of clerical authority over the past century? In other words, what factors have influenced the designation of certain leaders and allowed them to maintain some prominence over the rest of the *mujtahids*? We have already mentioned the mandate of the laity as a major factor. Such a mandate could hardly materialize in isolation from a social context. Rather, it was the outcome of a process in which a set of social, economic, and political factors permitted a prominent figure to stand above the others.

Though much has been said in the writings of the jurists on the qualifications and functions of the *mujtahids*, almost nothing has been mentioned about the status of *riyāsat;* a fact which strongly confirms the practical nature of this status.[16] Indeed the evolution of *riyāsat* before Anṣārī was due to several important elements of the prevailing historical climate. Perhaps one of the most evident features of *riyāsat* was the transformation of *mujtahids'* function from mere teachers of the *madrasa* to powerful figures in the life of urban centers. Consequently, the actual situation which emerged in this period was considerably distant from the scholastic seniority of the Uṣūlī elite of the 'Atabāt in the closing decades of the eighteenth century.

II

The Uṣūlī school, even from the early days of its formation in the last decades of the eighteenth century, had nurtured the seed of a more organized clerical body; but even after the eclipse of the rival Akhbārī school, it could hardly overcome the traditional Shi'ite resistance to institutionalization. Teachers such as Āqā Muḥammad Bāqir Bihbahānī and his early colleagues rose to prominence primarily because of their effective control over the teaching circles of Najaf, and later, Karbalā' and Kāẓimayn.[17] Bihbahānī (d. 1205/1790-91) was posthumously singled out by the *'ulamā'* of later generations as the renovator (*mujaddid*), the unique (*vaḥīd*), the master of all (*ustād-i kull*), and he was addressed as the *āqā* (sometimes *āghā*) not only to reflect reverence and gratitude towards the founder (*mu'assis*) of neo-Uṣūlism but more significantly in order to create a patron saint for the emerging clerical "corporation."[18] The professional designation was complemented by some degree of support from Shi'ite merchants of Baghdad who presumably found the Persian Uṣūlīs more cooperative and useful for their business than the Akhbārīs. The pro-Shi'ite Mamluks of Iraq, sometimes in rivalry with the Zand rulers of Iran, were also willing to extend their patronage to Uṣūlī *'ulamā'*.

Prior to the turn of the nineteenth century, therefore, the Uṣūlī group in Iraq was content with no more than academic independence. Ambitions of senior *mujtahids* hardly ever exceeded their scholastic means. After the establishment of the Qājārs, and especially after the accession of Fatḥ 'Alī Shāh (1797-1834), the royal patronage became more frequent, and the attention of Uṣūlī *'ulamā'* further tilted towards Iran. The Wahhābī sack of Karbalā' (1802) and the Ottomans' brief restoration of direct rule in Iraq (1810), and the ensuing decades of power struggle, tribal conflict, and insecurity (up to 1843), changed the political climate. Moreover, the diversion of Persian supply routes from Basra-Baghdad-Kirmanshah to Persian Gulf ports of Bushihr and Muḥammarah dried up local commercial resources, thus affecting the self-sufficiency of the 'Atabāt community.[19]

The flow of funds from Iran, India, and elsewhere required a more robust and determined *mujtahid* with a stamina for dealing with the laity (*'avāmm*) and the despotic monarch (*sulṭān-i jā'ir*). A prototype for such jurists was Shaykh Ja'far Najafī (d. 1228/1813), a disciple of Bihbahānī and the famous author of *Kashf al-Ghiṭā'*; the first comprehensive Uṣūlī work of *fiqh* in modern times.[20] Tours for collection of pious alms through Iran, the warm reception and generous gifts by the monarch, Fatḥ 'Alī Shāh, and by prince governors and notables, gave a special veneer to the image of this flamboyant Arab *mujtahid*.[21] Najafī is often considered as the first to contemplate the *niyābat 'āmm* (general deputiship) of the Imam mostly as the collective function of the *'ulamā'* body. The reemergence of the old Shi'ite notion of "deputiship" in a new context, and at times even with the undertone of specific deputiship (*niyābat-i khāṣṣ*), consolidated *mujtahids'* status and helped to legitimize the regular reception of religious dues. The revival of the *sahm-i Imām* as a regular pension assigned to the *'ulamā'* became a necessary component of deputiship.[22]

Thus, the diffuse leadership was shared among a number of Bihbahānī's students. Sayyid Muḥammad Mahdī-Baḥr al-'Ulūm (Ṭabāṭabā'ī) was renowned for his comprehensive learning (*jāmi'īyat*); while a son-in-law of Bihbahānī, Sayyid 'Alī Ṭabāṭabā'ī, and Mīrzā-yi Qummī specialized in the methodology of jurisprudence (*uṣūl al-fiqh*). Others such as Najafī and Muḥammad Ṭabāṭabā'ī (son of Sayyid 'Alī) became prominent owing to their control of teaching circles and reception of funds. For more than half a century, close family ties, often with remote but vital genealogical links to the Majlisīs of Isfahan, guaranteed the domination of three families—Bihbahānīs, Ṭabāṭabā'īs, and Najafīs—over the clerical establishment. At least up to the third decade of the nineteenth century, this collective leadership maintained its scholastic facade predominantly as a body of learned men engaged in jurisprudential studies. Founding of new endowments, especially in Najaf, and increasing pilgrimage enhanced the 'Atabāt as academic center of Shi'ism, with a large turnover of works on Uṣūlī themes and a larger body of *mujtahids* authorized by scions of the 'Atabāt.

With all the reverence these teachers enjoyed, from the early decades of the nineteenth century onwards, they were overshadowed, at least in some respects, by their own students who returned to Iran after the completion of their studies. A reverse process to that of the eighteenth century brought many *mujtahids* back home where relative security and recovering economy provided attractive alternatives to the overcrowded circles of the 'Atabāt. Benefitting from patronage of central government and local powers, *mujtahids* like Mīrzā-yi Qummī in Qumm, and Mullā Mahdī Narāqī in Kashan were among the first to achieve national prominence. In contrast to the 'Atabāt clerical elite, these were representatives of a new generation of *'ulamā'*, often with humble peasant background, who had risen in rank chiefly as a consequence of their cooperation with the government and of their mediatory functions at a time when Qajars were still consolidating their urban base.

Treatment of Mīrzā Abu'l-Qāsim Qummī (d. 1231/1815-16) by Fatḥ 'Alī Shāh demonstrates the latter's efforts to maintain amicable relations with celebrated *'ulamā'*. Qummī, an expert in *uṣūl al-fiqh*, was chiefly responsible for revitalization of teaching circles in the old pilgrimage town of Qumm.[23] The Shah's support was extended to him mostly by means of cash consignments delivered as religious dues. In one instance, a royal decree specifies payment as "lawful portion of the gift (*pīsh-kish*) received from the rulers of Farang and agent of frontier provinces of Rum (i.e., Ottoman Empire)."[24] Other forms of patronage included construction and agricultural projects to revive Qumm and its environs. Precious gifts to the shrine of Fāṭima and frequent visits enhanced Shah's image as a protector of Islam and supporter of its venerable representatives. Mīrzā-yī Qummī was addressed by the monarch as "the refuge (*marja'*) of the East and the West," "the *mujtahid* of the age," "the most learned (*'allāma*) of the time," "the source of emulation to the people (*muqtadī al-anām*)," and "the refuge of Islam."[25]

The respectful tone by which the Shi'ite *mujtahid* was addressed demonstrates the Shah's intention to foster a cooperative religious leadership in Qumm. The use of the titles *marja'* and *muqtadī al-anām* by the monarch seems to have been calculated for the promotion of Qummī and the deliberate undermining of the authorities of the 'Atabāt at a time when many prominent *mujtahids*, including some of the latter's teachers, were still active. This is also apparent in the royal contributions Qummī was assigned to distribute among the distressed, the needy, and the *sayyids* of Qumm, for which receipts were to be produced. Part of the contributions, however, was allotted to Qummī's own personal use. Implicit in his responsibilities was his mediatory role between the state and its domestic adversaries, sometimes to prevent political crises (as in the case of Ḥusayn Qulī Mīrzā's revolt against his brother Fatḥ 'Alī Shāh) and endemic urban riots.[26]

Cooperation over a broad range of juristic and political issues guaranteed mutual legitimacy for the Shah and the *mujtahids*, and it is largely in this context that their veneration by the state can be fully understood. Designation of prominent *mujtahids* by the early Qajar state proved to be a successful adoption of late Safavid policy. With slight variations, the *'ulamā'* of the early Qajar period upheld positions and discharged duties not wholly unsimilar to their late seventeenth-century predecessors. One major difference, however, became more apparent during the reigns of Fatḥ 'Alī Shāh and his successor, Muḥammad Shāh (1834-48). The gradual consolidation of the Persian *mujtahids'* socioeconomic base in effect made them less dependent on the state patronage and more assertive in the pursuit of their own vested interests. This is not unrelated to the apparent decline in the authority of the central government during the second quarter of the century. The growing sphere of the *mujtahids'* power is particularly visible in the latter years of Fatḥ 'Alī Shāh and throughout the years of Muḥammad Shāh. Symbolically, this falls in between the second round of Russo-Persian wars (1826-1828), when high ranking *mujtahids* for the first time made their collective presence felt in the political arena, and the accession of Nāṣir al-Dīn Shāh, when the dual effect of the state's centralization policies and the rise of the anti-clerical Bābī movement engendered some noticeable setbacks for clerical power.

By the second decade of the century, the emergence of a new generation of *mujtahids* made some kind of collective leadership desirable. The *mujtahids* such as Sayyid Muḥammad Bāqir Shaftī and Ḥājjī Ibrāhīm Karbāsī in Isfahan, Mullā Aḥmad Narāqī in Kashan, the Baraqānī brothers in Qazvīn, and others in Tabriz, Tehran, Yazd, and Shiraz created a vast network of jurists who boasted their years of study under Najafi teachers and held a sense of "old boy" solidarity. What allowed them to hold sway over major urban centers of Iran, however, was not merely their academic credentials or their pragmatic application of Uṣūlī jurisprudence to the needs of their constituencies. The key to their success perhaps was the timely exploitation of the growing political vacuum in the provinces. Even more significant was their direct participation in the economic market. The not long before peasant boys of remote villages of Gīlān, and later the impoverished *ṭullāb* of the seminaries of Najaf and Karbalā', turned into major investors, landowning magnates, and money lenders. The flow of pious bequests, alms, and the newly revived *sahm-i Imām* (the portion of the income received by prominent *'ulamā'* as lawful *de facto* deputies of the Imam), resumption of the trusteeship of endowments, and even direct participation in the economic market turned a few of Anṣārī's predecessors from humble teachers of the *madrasas* into sizable financiers and investors.[27]

Benefitting from the *mujtahids'* financial support, numerous seminarians (*ṭullāb*) crowded their teaching circles. A large body of the religious students was considered an indispensable asset, since their diffusion after the completion of their studies broadened the *mujtahids'* network of patronage and influence, and boosted the *mujtahids'* public image. Equally essential was the ability to maintain amicable relations with the government while at the same time putting on public display a combination of austerity and independence in legal judgment. In this respect, the support of some urban groups, among them the merchants, was vital and in some instances decisive in *'ulamā'*'s political behavior vis-à-vis the state. Furthermore, the ability of some of the *mujtahids* to patronize and protect the *sayyids* and the *lūtīs* (the urban brigands) put at their disposal an effective force. With such support, control over the pulpits of the mosques was secured and old accounts with the government, notables, and other *mujtahids* were settled; heretics were punished, mobs incited, and city quarters divided.

The most notorious example of the rapid social mobility of the new generation of *mujtahids* was Muḥammad Bāqir Shaftī (d. 1260/1844), who owed his fortune and position in Isfahan in the 1820s and 1830s to his skillful blend of juristic acrobatics and economic speculations. The widening gap between the Isfahan government and the central authorities, and the efforts of a semiautonomous class of bureaucrats, merchants, tribal chiefs, and notables to seek clerical support, provided golden opportunities for Shaftī to exploit the delicate balance of power in the city and to forge ephemeral alliances with ultimate advantage to himself.[28]

Indeed Shaftī was not alone amongst *mujtahids* of his time in benefitting from the generous interpretation of jurists' functions. The restoration of Safavid *waqfs* under Fatḥ 'Alī—the reverse of Nādir's policy—brought a large portion of *ruqabāt-i Nādirī* under clerical control. Skillful justification for repossession of unclaimed property (*ghaṣb-i bila-ṣāḥib*), as well as actual participation in trade and agriculture, gave them a substantial economic base.

These successes enhanced the authority of the *mujtahids* resident in Iran. Though the teachers of the 'Atabāt were still regarded as their nominal superiors, the real power rested with the former. In addition to their reliable economic resources, the advantage of the Iranian *'ulamā'* over their 'Atabāt counterparts was their control of the judiciary—especially under Fatḥ 'Alī when they were given almost a free rein. Moreover, there was the proximity to large constituencies, direct supervision of endowment, and ample supply of local students. Close contact with the government and its provincial agents, however, was a mixed blessing. On the one hand, it furnished the *'ulamā'* with funds, titles, and functions; and on the other, it obliged them to comply with the government's wishes, either by persuasion, by coercion, or by fostering rivalries.

A reflection of the growing importance of the *'ulamā'* of Iran can be seen in the adoption of more grandiose titles. Shaftī, who probably was the most significant among them, was addressed as *Ḥujjat al-Islām* (the Proof of Islam), an epithet apparently with no precedent in the history of Shi'ism.[29] Use of this title suggests a degree of reverence reserved for a *de facto* head. He created an appealing image of a leader who combined material wealth and power with utterances of devotion and independence. Yet his authority did not remain unchallenged even in his home base, Isfahan. Sayyid Muḥammad Khātūn-ābādī, the *imām jum'a* of the city, who carried an equally pompous title of Sulṭān al-'Ulamā', was a sufficient match to Shaftī's power.[30] The government's desire to counterbalance the influence of major *mujtahids* often meant the appointing or reinstating of rival jurists to the semiofficial office of *imām jum'a* in the hope of preventing full autonomy from state control.

Diverse as they were, all the above elements—a growing body of high ranking *mujtahids*, accumulation of wealth, and inherent competition between *'ulamā'*—were instrumental in the division of labor and the emergence of a collective leadership. While the high ranking *'ulamā'* of Iran primarily enjoyed wealth and sociopolitical influence, the teachers of the 'Atabāt were reputed for their scholarship and teaching qualities, even after the eclipse of the "aristocratic" clerical families in the middle of the century. This naturally encouraged competition for public following and government attention. The Qājār rulers on their own part fostered such diversity with some success, hence avoiding the rise of a major clerical figure outside their reaches. For them, the hazards of the *'ulamā'*s minor insubordinations at home were still surmountable. Occasional conflict of interest could result in spasmodic turmoils (as in the case of the Shaftī and Isfahan riots of the 1830s and 1840s), but most of the time the bulk of the *'ulamā'* remained loyal to, albeit not uncritical of, the Qājārs.

Most *mujtahids*, whether in Iran or the 'Atabāt, were aware of their limitations and thus willing to comply with a diffused leadership, however loose and implicit that leadership might have been. The *esprit de corps* was particularly strong whenever the clerical community was threatened and its legitimacy challenged. Responding to the claims for spiritual guidance of Ni'matullāhī leaders—who even during their gradual decline in the 1830s still posed a threat to the *'ulamā'*—Shaftī held the "concillium of the *'ulamā'* of the time (*qāṭiba-yi 'ulamā-yi zamān*)" solely responsible for "delving into the roots (*uṣūl*) and the branches (*furū'*) (i.e., jurisprudence and applied law) until the day of Resurrection." He made it incumbent upon believers to refer all matters of religion to "the righteous *'ulamā'* (*'ulamā-yi abrār*)" and denounced other claims of religious guidance as "abrogated, void, corrupt, and futile." He further asserted that "the rightly guided *'ulamā'* are the trustees of the illustrious creed and vicars (*khulafā'*) of the virtuous Imams.[31]

The sense of monopoly and exclusive clerical rights apparent in Shaftī's statement was basically the reassertion of the doctrine of *taqlīd* and the duty of the followers to comply with the *mujtahid* in order to avoid the danger of schism. This standpoint was defended with greater clarity and vehemence during the Bābī resurgence of the 1840s and 1850s, when the *'ulamā'* faced serious defection within their own ranks. Curiously, with all its vigorous denunciations of the Bābīs in this period, which would logically have implied unification of leadership, the clerical establishment barely departed from its pattern of diffuse leadership. Instead, the "synodic" consensus achieved among the leading *mujtahids* resulted in further stratification of the religious body along socioeconomic lines. Such division, however, was not devoid of a strong ideological content. The lower and middle ranks already exposed to Shaykhi revisionism became increasingly critical of the privileged Uṣūlī *mujtahids.* Their grievances eventually erupted in radical tendencies which denied the very basis of the *mujtahids'* legitimacy and in effect weakened the solidarity of the clerical class.[32]

The reign of Muḥammad Shāh was particularly critical in the polarization of the clerical community. Under Ḥājjī Mīrzā Āqāsī, a self-styled Sufi adept with profound influence over the Shah, the Qājār government reduced its support for the mainstream Uṣūlī school and even sought to curb its influence. This in turn facilitated, somewhat unintentionally, the growth of anticlerical tendencies at a time when the unusually rapid loss of the high-ranking leaders made the collective leadership more vulnerable.

During the 1840s—in less than a decade—the death of a number of eminent jurists created a vacuum not immediately filled by a younger generation. In Isfahan, the alliance of prominent jurists, already weakened during the governorship of Manūchihr Khān Mu'tamid al-Dawla, came to an end with the death of Shaftī in 1844 and that of his ally, Ḥājjī Muḥammad Ibrāhīm Karbāsī, in 1845. Another prominent *mujtahid,* Sayyid Ṣadr al-Dīn 'Āmilī, died in 1846, giving Mīr Sayyid Muḥammad Imām Jum'a (d. 1874-75) an obvious advantage over Asadullāh Shaftī (d. 1873), son of Muḥammad Bāqir, and other heirs to clerical positions. In the 'Atabāt, the leader of the Shaykhī school, Sayyid Kāẓim Rashtī, died at the end of 1843; his notorious opponent Sayyid Muḥammad Mahdī, the last of the influential Ṭabāṭabā'īs, died in 1844. Shortly thereafter, Sayyid Ibrāhīm Qazvīnī, one of the leading authorities in Karbalā' and another opponent of the Shaykhīs, died in 1846.[33] His counterpart, Shaykh Ḥasan Āl-i Kāshif al-Ghiṭā', the leader of the Arab Shī'a of Iraq, died in the same year. The leadership (*riyāsat*) of the two latter figures had been acknowledged particularly by the Ottoman pashaliq, who held them responsible for the religious affairs of the Shi'a in Iraq. After them, the only significant survivor of the older group, Shaykh Muḥammad Ḥasan Najafī Iṣfahānī (the author of *Jawāhir al-Kalām,* d. 1850) rose to *riyāsat* in the late 1840s.[34] In other centers, Shaykh 'Abd al-Vahhāb Qazvīnī, a respected leader with Shaykhī leaning, died in 1847; his rival Mullā Muḥammad Taqī Baraqānī, an archenemy of the Shaykhīs, was assassinated in the same year by Shaykhī-Bābī elements. In the same year, Mullā Muḥammad Ja'far Astarābādī, another troublesome opponent of Shaykhīs, died in Tehran.

The death of a considerable number of leading jurists, partly because of the plague of 1845-1847 in Iran and Iraq, had serious repercussions. Their successors—inheritors of their fathers' wealth, pulpits, and religious courts—could not rapidly master the political arena, as had their predecessors. Not infrequently, they were uncannily victims of local intrigues and targets of sharp criticisms. The absence of prominent figures in the Uṣūlī camp gave new dimensions to the deep rooted Shaykhī-*faqīh* schism which since the 1820s had polarized the religious community. After the death of Sayyid Kāẓim Rashtī, the younger and more radical students of the Shaykhī school were reorganized under the banners of the Bābī movement and began an all-embracing campaign against the very foundation of orthodox Shi'ism.

The Bābī movement advocated a messianic revelation—the externalization of Shaykh Aḥmad Aḥsā'ī's theory of *Shī'a Kāmil*—in the person of the Bāb Sayyid 'Alī Muḥammad Shīrāzī as the only legitimate source of spiritual guidance. The Bābīs criticized the *mujtahids* for their moral conduct, their usurpation of Imam's authority, and their worldly attachment. Recruiting from Shaykhī ranks most of its ardent supporters, the movement's rapid growth was accelerated by defections from clerical ranks and the conversion of middle rank merchants, guilds, and peasantry. Though the ratio of the active Bābīs to the entire population of the country was relatively small, the potentials for the Bābī breakthrough alarmed the *'ulamā'*. This jeopardized, at least temporarily, the position of the juristic elite. The supply of the newly authorized *mujtahids*—products of Shaykhī teaching circles—could hardly be absorbed in the clerical establishment so long as inherited positions and privileges were closely guarded by the established *mujtahids* and their heirs.

Faced with the prospects of an internal revolt, the jurists and their allies had little choice but to turn to a government which was essentially unsympathetic to their plight, and yet was equally apprehensive of the Bābīs' popularity. The outcome of this realignment with the state was as fateful to the Bābīs as it was disheartening to the *'ulamā'*. The Bābī experience proved to the jurists their precarious dependence on the state and made the government more conscious of its vital role. The decades following the final episode of the Bābī movement (1848-52) thus witnessed the gradual diminution of clerical prestige in Iran and the reversal of the earlier autonomous trend. Though the *mujtahids* still exercised considerable influence (e.g., the Najafī family in Isfahan, Shaykh al-Islāms in Tabriz, and Raḍavīs in Mashhad), the clerical elite throughout Nāṣir al-Dīn's reign was evidently more prone to Qajar pressure. Not until the time of Mīrzā Muḥammad Ḥasan Shīrāzī and the Tobacco protest (1891-92) did the *mujtahids* of Iran stage a united stand against the state. Nor did they venture a major confrontation with the government on policy measures and their implementations.

Thus, the evolution of clerical leadership from the late eighteenth century to the middle of the nineteenth century could be best summed up as a vigorous move from the *madrasa* to the marketplace. In this process, academic seniority was transformed into a collective leadership, with no ultimate place reserved for a supreme authority. The *'ulamā'* grew more autonomous, but serious perils from within compelled them to remain loyal to the state.

III

The new climate in state-*'ulamā'* relations and the conciliatory mood that resulted from the defeat of the Bābīs and the fall of Mīrzā Taqī Khān Amīr Niẓām (posthumously known as Amīr Kabīr, d. 1851) was bound to find reflection in the conduct of the later jurists. The earlier generations of the *mujtahids* of Iran could not always convince the public of their overall moral immaculacy, judicial imparitiality, and material detachment. Hence the aspirations for a morally reformed leadership, both among the *'ulamā'* and the public at large, found expression in the idealized image of a religious figure distant from familiar market environment. Recognition of the religious headship (*riyāsat shar'īya*) for Shaykh Murtaḍā Anṣārī in the late 1850s was not a mere coincidence. Earlier in the century, public desire for nonclerical saintly figures had already given rise to a wide range of charismatic personages. The Ni'matullāhī Sufi Nūr 'Alī Shāh, theosophist Shaykh Aḥmad Aḥsā'ī, the ascetic-scholar Sayyid Mahdī Baḥr al-'Ulūm, and above all the prophet-mystic Sayyid 'Alī Muḥammad the Bāb, are only a few examples. Such aspirations, as well as denunciation of unacceptable practices among the *'ulamā'*, gave an exceptional veneration to Anṣārī's public image at a time when all alternative heterodoxies were effectively suppressed.

The circumstances that led to Anṣārī's ascendency pose two interrelated problems. First, what elements in Anṣārī's background and personality qualified him for this exceptional reverence? Secondly, to what extent did he symbolize a shift from collective consensus of earlier times to the leadership of a single individual with which he was associated? The answer to the first question perhaps is best summed up by his contemporaries who repeatedly praised him for two distinct qualities: piety (*wara'*) and scholarship (*'ilm*).[35] Reassertion of traditional values—already defined in the Uṣūlī literature of earlier decades—had a peculiar resonance in the religious milieu of the time and was symptomatic of a moral crisis within the Shi'ite establishment. There seems to be a direct relation between emphasis on Anṣārī's piety and his growing popularity. The image of a serious scholar with the austerity of an ascetic and the sagacity of a statesman needed a certain dissociation, though not total isolation, from worldly affairs. He was particularly admired for avoiding accumulation of personal wealth.[36] His reluctance to issue controversial legal opinions[37] and his effort toward depoliticizing the clerical community[38] make him an advocate of political acquiescence and nonintervention, often in sharp contrast to the entrepreneurial image of some earlier *mujtahids.* Impartiality and fairness, underscored by frequent references to his justice (*'adl*), permitted him to enjoy the support of influential groups—the merchants, landowners, and other contributors to religious funds—who preferred to see more judicial cooperation and less hinderance and competition. Reverence demonstrated toward Anṣārī in Najaf thus may be seen as a sign of discontent with the *mujtahids'* economic ventures and the extravagance of their lifestyle at home.

Equally crucial was the support of the Qajar government. The growing independence of Nasir al-Din Shah after the fall of his prime minister, Mīrzā Āqā Khān Nūrī, in 1858 required greater cooperation and coexistence between the state and the *'ulamā'.* Interdependency made the latter more accomodating, and Anṣārī's political quietism was a timely reflection of such a mood. This policy did not remain unrewarded as the flow of funds—alms, *sahm-i Imām*, and bequests from private and government sources—flooded Najaf. At one stage in the late 1850s, the figure of two hundred thousand *tūmāns* has been given for the lawful funds (*vujūhāt-i shar'īya*) annually received by Anṣārī;[39] a substantial figure, taking into account government's total revenue of about three million *tūmāns* for the same period. And this, in spite of Anṣārī's reported disapproval of the concentration of funds in Najaf.

Administration of the incoming funds and methods of disbursement proved to be formidable, as Anṣārī strongly detested the private use or the investment of such funds. The alternative was the immediate distribution among the growing crowd of deserving recipients clustered in Najaf. Barring relatives and proxies from misappropriation was not an easy task, especially as bureaucratic procedures were kept to a bare minimum. Haphazard and irregular as it was, the payment of pensions and alms created a large following for Anṣārī in Najaf and beyond. The large number of students attending his classes were the prime beneficiaries. According to one witness, at one time as many as five hundred attended his lectures,[40] though the number of students who systematically studied under him over a period of two decades may have been in excess of one thousand.[41]

The reputation of Shaykh Murtaḍā as a serious teacher and his academic prominence made every student in Najaf impatient with the prospects of obtaining his authorization (*ijāza*). Popularity and large attendance in turn gave wider circulation to his works.[42] His collection of treatises and his work on laws of commerce became text books in the Najaf curriculum. His systematic discourses of *uṣūl al-fiqh* in *Farā'id al-Uṣūl*, a complex subject which for long baffled students of the *madrasas*, was a noticeable improvement compared to the works of Bihbahānī and Mīrzā-yi Qumī.[43] His *Makāsib* was equally attractive for the *ṭullāb*, who considered its study a useful exercise for their future career.[44] Though the theoretical speculations of these works were not easily applicable to the rapidly changing economic market, they nevertheless witnessed the author's awareness of the role of the jurists vis-à-vis their mercantile clients.

Reassertion of all three qualities—piety, justice, and knowledge—contributed, each in its own way, to the designation of Anṣārī into the broadly acknowledged status of leadership (*riyāsat*). The root of his success lay in his ability to attract funds and divert them for the upkeep of his educational and social network—almost the functions of a rudimentary welfare system—both to the satisfaction of the contributors and the recipients. This *riyāsat* was a modest step beyond the collective leadership of "the concilium of the *'ulamā'* of the time" which nonetheless did not undermine the inherent diversity of the institution of *ijtihād*. It remained an informal status reserved for one or several prominent *mujtahids* whose social conduct, popularity, and assured moral qualities granted them supervision of practical affairs of the clerical community.

In this respect, Anṣārī followed what had already been laid down by his immediate predecessors. Both his teachers, Shaykh Muḥammad Ḥasan Najafī and Shaykh 'Alī Najafī (Āl-i Kāshif al-Ghiṭā', d. 1838), exercized *riyāsat* of the same nature over Persian and Arab Shi'ite communities of Iraq, respectively.[45] The ethnic division—at times, rivalry—among the *ṭullāb* as well as among merchants, the notables, and nomads often determined loyalties. The Ottoman *millat* system, for all practical purposes, honored such diversity and recognized Shi'ite leaders of Arab and Persian origins as the head (*ra'īs*) responsible for their constituencies. Anṣārī, being originally from Dizfūl, a region with a mixed Perso-Arabic environment, enjoyed an advantage over his predecessors. Teaching in both vernaculars, his appeal lay partly in his ability to bridge over the ethnic division and emerge, as Muḥammad Ḥasan Najafī put it, "the point of union between two rivers and the choice of two factions" (*majma' al-baḥrayn wa pasandīda-yi farīqayn*).[46]

Initial hesitation on the part of Anṣārī to assume the *riyāsat* and become the recipient of funds in Najaf does not seem to have stemmed purely out of his prudence (*iḥtiyāt*) or modesty, but also from the fear of an internal revolt in the high ranks. Perhaps it is not a coincidence that he first invited the chief *mujtahid* of Mazandaran and an old school mate, Mullā Sa'īd Bārfurūshī (Sa'īd al-'Ulamā', d. ca. 1270/1854-55), to assume *riyāsat* of the 'Atabāt.[47] The latter made a career for himself out of vigorous persecution of the Bābīs during the uprising of Ṭabarsī (1848-49). He was a remarkable example of the *mujtahids* whose active clamp down on the heretics secured them both prominence among *'ulamā'* and amicable relations with Nāṣir al-Dīn Shāh.[48] By securing Bārfurūshī's approval, Anṣārī defused a potential source of opposition. Yet he remained aware of the limitations of his status. Once questioned as to the lawfulness of the Friday congregational prayer—an issue heatedly debated among jurists—he reinstated the non-Uṣūlī disapproval but went as far as to state that he can only perform Friday prayers with the authorities of the ruler (*sulṭān*, presumably the Ottoman Sultan) and possessors of authority (*ulu'l-amr*).[49]

In his overcautious judicial conduct Anṣārī seems also to have deliberately swum against the mainstream of Uṣūlī practice by showing reluctance—almost to the point of refusal—to issue a legal opinion (*fatvā*) even on matters of such seemingly obvious consensus as refutation of the Bābīs.[50] Refraining from issuance of *fatvā*, Anṣārī followed his predecessor, Shaykh 'Alī Kāshif al-Ghiṭā', in distinguishing between the scholarly elaboration of law and the actual passing of legal judgments. Highlighting the former as the essential undertaking of his career, he seems to have recommended a return to the scholarly pursuits within the walls of the *madrasa*. It is in this context that his discourse on *a'lamīyat* could be better understood. These exegetical and deductive skills were confined to the *madrasa* and did not account for the universality of *marja'iyat*. He was highly praised as the "Seal of the *mujtahids*" (*khātam al-mujtahidīn*) and "the Chief of the Party [of the Shi'a]" (*shaykh al-ṭā'ifa*) but even his keenest eulogists did not include *marja'īyat* —whether relative or absolute—in their long list of honorifics.[51]

IV

By the time Anṣārī died in 1864, the Shi'ite *riyāsat* had acquired a more scholarly form. The collective leadership was transformed into a single headship with far greater acceptance among Arabs and Persians and with financial backing chiefly diverted towards the 'Atabāt. The supremacy of Najaf over other centers was firmly established, and amicable relations with the state was achieved. Yet Anṣārī's success was in many ways ephemeral. The struggle which started in the wake of his death and continued for almost a decade (1864-74) demonstrated the precarious nature of *riyāsat*. The struggle meant a return to traditional plurality. This in due course challenged the hard earned superiority of Najaf. The ethnic divisions—this time, more significantly between the *ṭullāb* of Azarbaijan (and Caucasus) and the Persian-speaking students —polarized the 'Atabāt and led to the emergence of an independent *riyāsat* for Turkish-speaking followers in the person of Ḥajjī Sayyid Ḥusayn Kūh-Kamara'ī (d. 1299/1881-82), who, reputed for his systematic teaching of *Uṣūl*, increased his attendance to more than six hundred.[52]

Such popularity understandably reduced the *riyāsat* of his chief contestant, Mīrzā Ḥasan Shīrāzī, and restricted the latter's sphere of influence to predominantly Persian-speaking students and followers.[53] Shīrāzī's credentials as a teaching assistant and aid to Anṣārī was impeccable. Reportedly, he was praised by the late teacher, together with Mīrzā Ḥabīballāh Rashtī, as the most promising of his students.[54] He was also admired by his biographers, particularly for his endeavors towards facilitating the livelihood of the *ṭullāb*, the needy, and the distressed. Manifestation of such public concern during the famine of 1871, and the setting up of an emergency relief center, boosted his reputation.[55]

Competition in Najaf, nevertheless, proved to be too intense. Though Shīrāzī had already secured the blessing of many ex-classmates, he evidently lacked total support and saw little chance of wider recognition.[56] In 1874, when he "emigrated" from Najaf to the nearby Sunni-dominated Samarra, he reportedly intended "to resign his *riyāsat* and relieve himself from its restraints" in order to pursue the life of an ascetic.[57] Whether he was testing the loyalty of the student body or genuinely frustrated with being one of many in Najaf is difficult to know. What is certain, however, is the effectiveness of this move. A faction of Persian-speaking students who followed him to Samarra later became the most prominent *'ulamā'* of the next generation. Among them were Mīrzā Ḥusayn Nūrī, the author of *Mustadrak*, and his son-in-law Shaykh Faḍlullāh Nūrī; Muḥammad Kāẓim Khurāsānī; Muḥammad Ṭabāṭabā'ī; and Sayyid Ḥusayn Ṣadr.[58]

The growing popularity of the new center overshadowed Najaf, particularly after the death of Kūh-Kamara'ī in 1881-82. Yet Najaf survived as a center of learning and even thrived through the last quarter of the century. The Azarbaijanis found a new *marja'*: Shaykh Muḥammad Ḥasan Māmaqānī (d. 1905-6), a student of Kūh-Kamara'ī.[59] Meanwhile, Mīrzā Ḥabibullāh Rashtī emerged as the most scholarly-minded teacher of the 'Atabāt.[60] Though neither of the two matched Shīrāzī, the diversity in leadership continued to contrast the unanimity of Anṣārī's time. Mīrzā Ḥabībullāh Rashtī is quoted as having said that of Anṣārī's three distinguished qualities, the learnedness (*a'lamīyat*) was inherited by himself (i.e., Rashtī) and the leadership (*riyāsat*) by Shīrāzī; but the piety, Ḥabībullāh believed, Anṣārī took with him to the grave.[61] Such a remark is particularly revealing, as it reflects a division of labor which had emerged as a result of clerical competition. Rashtī denies exemplary piety to himself and Shīrāzī, perhaps to contrast the idealized immaculateness of Anṣārī's time with the shady realities of his own. At the same time, he draws a distinction between leadership and scholarship. Indeed, if the volume of written works could be a standard for *a'lamīyat*, Shīrāzī's meager record as a writer could have hardly qualified him as the *a'lam*.[62] He was nevertheless successful in drawing the support of a large portion of contributors—primarily merchant-landowners of Fars, his home province—who sought in his *riyāsat* a reassertion of the traditional bonds between *'ulamā'* and the merchants.

Throughout the 1880s, the fame of Shīrāzī surpassed any other *mujtahid*, chiefly because of his more systematic endeavors to achieve two objectives: first, to attract merchant support and funds, and second, to expand his own network of students. Most effective in his first task was Shīrāzī's own mercantile background. He was coming from a Shīrāzī family of petty clerics with long-established links with the closely woven network of merchants of southern Iran. From the same family came the *imām jum'a* of Kirman, Sayyid Javād Shīrāzī (d. ca. 1264/1848), and more significantly, Sayyid 'Alī Muḥammad the Bāb, a paternal second cousin of Shīrāzī.[64] The merchant connection almost automatically put Shīrāzī in an advantageous position, making him an ideal candidate of Persian *tujjār* and their counterparts in India and elsewhere, as the recipient of large sums. The flow of religious dues and bequests, which probably included the Oudh bequest administered by the British Consul-General in Baghdad, symbolically materialized in various building projects under his auspices in Samarra. A bridge over Tigris at the cost of ten thousand Turkish golden lira, two *madrasas* in Sāmarra, and a new market (*sūq*) financed by some Indian bequests testify to Shīrāzī's success in generating funds for the improvement of his educational center.[65]

The fruits of thirty years of teaching generations of students and often funding their long years of study, on the other hand, finally ripened by the late 1880s, when these students occupied high places throughout Iran, Iraq, India, and the Caucasus. Such a network of *mujtahids* with prime allegiance to Shīrāzī secured him a more comprehensive and powerful *riyāsat*. Both of these factors were contributory to what his student Sayyid Ḥasan Ṣadr calls "the monopolization of the *riyāsat* of the Ja'farī denomination throughout the world." In the latter part of his life, Ṣadr asserts, "the death of the [previous] heads and sources of public emulation all over the [Shi'ite] lands left amongst that denomination no head (*ra'īs*) except him."[66]

If the above factors paved the way for the wider recognition of *riyāsat*, the participation in the tobacco protest of 1891-92 sealed its unanimous acceptance. More crucially, it also furnished the *riyāsat* with a political dimension without precedent since the *jihād* proclamation of 1825-26. The shift in the policy of noninterference did not come without a great deal of hesitation. Any political commitment would have meant the abandonment of the neutrality of *riyāsat* and a disturbance of the equilibrium achieved under Anṣārī. But if the pressure exerted upon Shīrāzī by the prominent *mujtahids* of the major cities during the Regie episode was resistible, he could not afford to ignore the unmistakable signals coming from his financial backers—the merchants and landowners of Fars, Isfahan, Tabriz, and elsewhere. The implementation of the Regie Concession was a direct threat to the prosperity and financial viability of this class. The gloomy prospects of the Regie intrusion, reflected in the merchants' petitions and repeated inquiries, compelled Shīrāzī to cast off his customary prudence and to side with his constituency against the Qājār's sale of the concession.[67]

This decision was only a prelude to what became a familiar characteristic of *riyāsat* in the following decades. The reciprocal interdependency demonstrated in the tobacco protest had far-reaching consequences for both parties. It became increasingly in the merchants' interest to support a united *riyāsat* rather than merely to back local *mujtahids* in their hometowns. Greater centralization of the government brought further pressure upon the mercantile community through the sale of concessions, taxation, and customs, and intervention in the market. On the other hand, the growing volume of foreign trade in the latter part of the century made long-distance merchants more dependent on the export of cash crops (more precisely, cotton, opium, and tobacco), and, in turn, on heavy investment in the production of these commodities. Organization of the production and exports brought handsome profits to some, but it also increased their exposure and vulnerability to the government's arbitrary measures. The merchants' allies and beneficiaries, the local *mujtahids*, were effective so far as government intervention was within the recognized boundaries of coercion and compromise. The odds against the merchants increased gradually as the state resorted to the sale of concessions on a national scale. In response, investors in land and trade sought a more potent agent of influence and protection; a source of authority more immune from the state which could, if need be, reflect their grievances and speak out on their behalf.

This gradual shift to the universal *riyāsat* was further facilitated by the need for arbitration by a superior authority in cases of disputes between the *mujtahids* and their chief clients, the merchants. In the absence of an overall state judiciary, the *mujtahids* of cities had at their disposal the only available judicial machinery and the registry of contracts and deeds, without which the merchants could hardly operate. A constant change in the otherwise amicable relations between the two groups was the merchants' complaints of the *mujtahids'* lack of impartiality in judicial proceedings, and of their contradictory rulings. These charges were not helped by the notoriety some *'ulamā'* acquired for receiving double bribes in litigations to rule in favor of one party and then to overrule their own verdict in favor of the other. These and other irregularities, particularly in the guardianship of minors, orphans, and imbeciles, and the supervision of their assets, harmed the already tarnished image of religious courts. The privileged groups were critical of local *mujtahids* for the increasing price of their favor and influence, which, in any case, could not be secured for long if a higher bidder emerged. The gradual shift to a superior arbiter in the 'Atabat may be explained in terms of this crisis of confidence as reflected in the shift of religious funds to Samarra. The *mujtahids* in urban centers were thus overshadowed in significance by the grand *mujtahids* of Iraq. By the end of the century, many of them performed the role of agents for the 'Atabāt leadership.

Other external elements also facilitated the prominence of the 'Atabāt. The expansion of the trade network and better means of communication (including the expansion of the telegraph system) ensured regular receipt of funds as well as regular contact with the followers. More convenient means of transport brought pilgrims to the holy cities who otherwise visited local shrines. The memories of the 'Atabāt pilgrimage, which often included visits to the prominent divines, helped to spread their fame to remote places. Even prior to Regie, the government preferred to see a moderate and uncontroversial head in the 'Atabāt in order to ensure subordination of the other *mujtahids* at home.

This more direct relation between the public and the *ra'īs*, with other *'ulamā'* serving as agents, created a new setup in which the aspirations of the contributors were reflected more clearly than ever before in their choice of the head. The conspicuous presence of a patron-client relationship is unmistakable, but what makes such a relationship specifically important is the way it acquired a pronounced expression in the concept of universal juristic authority (*marja'īyat-i tāmm*). Even prior to the Regie episode, the official Qājār almanac, *al-Ma'āthir v'al-Āthār*, in 1888 defines Shīrāzī not only as "the proof of Islam" (*ḥujjat al-Islām*), "the Deputy of the Imam" (*nā'ib al-Imām*) and "the renovator of [Islamic] ordinance (*mujadid-i aḥkām*) whose prior status is recognized by other *mujtahids*," but as "the most learned of *mujtahids* whose opinions (*fatāvī*) are the standard of sound practice by Shi'ite emulators."[68] One can hear an echo of public reverence augmented by the government's desire to create a shadow authority superior to any *mujtahid* at home—a necessary step to bring the prominent jurists into rank.

The aspirations of the followers are more clearly evident in the way the alleged declaration by Shīrāzī concerning the prohibition of the use of tobacco during Regie ws interpreted as a "ruling" (*ḥukm*) binding on all Shi'a rather than a legal opinion (*fatvā*) binding only on the *mujtahid*'s emulators.[69] Throughout the Regie episode—from first petitions by merchants and dealers of tobacco, agitations in Shiraz, Isfahan, and Tabriz, and correspondence between the *'ulamā'*, to rumors concerning Shīrāzī's issuance of the prohibition and finally his confirmation of the ban on the use of tobacco—it is possible to detect a clear attempt by the merchants, the *'ulamā'*, and the radical laity, all for their own varying reasons, to increase Shīrāzī's involvement. Either by persuasion, by pressure, or by unsolicited delegation on his behalf, the latter was obliged to throw his support behind the movement of protest against the concession.

The network of merchants throughout Iran and Iraq—among them, tobacco producers from Lar as well as merchants and dealers of Shiraz—was the first to urge clerical involvement by inducing popular preachers like Sayyid 'Alī Akbar Falāsīrī, a son-in-law of Shīrāzī, to appeal to public sentiment.[70] Later on, after his exile to Iraq, Falāsīrī was instrumental in providing the link between his father-in-law and the other opponent of Regie, Sayyid Jamāl al-Dīn Asadābādī (al-Afghānī). In Iran, the clerical-merchant family network was hard at work to promote Shīrāzī and to magnify the significance of his objection to Regie. Shīrāzī's letters to Nāṣir al-Dīn Shāh bears clear reflection of his prime concern with the fate of the merchants and their trade.

> In spite of the fact that for centuries the guardians of religion, the kings of the Muslims—pray to God for their endeavors—sacrificed souls and

> spent fortunes towards promotion of the cause of Islam, why is it that today, for the sake of trifling profits and regardless of its corrupt consequences, they allow the infidels to dominate the livelihood and commerce (*ma'ayish va tijārat*) of the Muslims? It was uncharacteristic of your royal prudence to permit your subjects, who indeed are abundant treasures of the state, to be deprived of controlling their own trade and business, and instead to bow to the subjugation of the infidels.[71]

Shīrāzī's letters reflected the merchants' concern but also the exhortations of the religious activist, Sayyid Jamāl al-Dīn Asadābādī. After his disgraceful expulsion from Iran, Jamāl al-Dīn, who was enraged with fresh wounds of humiliation, found in Shīrāzī a tactical ally and an effective platform against Nāṣir al-Dīn and his policies. The implicit elevation of Shīrāzī by the merchants soon found explicit acknowledgment in Jamāl al-Dīn's famous letter to the grand *mujtahid.* The impact of this letter upon Shīrāzī's action should not be exaggerated; yet the endorsement of Shīrāzī and the magnification of his position must have given the *mujtahid* some reassurance. Moreover, the wide circulation of its Persian translation must have exulted Shīrāzī's position in the eye of the Iranian population. The modernist Afghānī seems to have had no hesitation in conferring upon the traditional *mujtahid* the ultimate religious authority and in showering him with honorifics.[72] Addressing him as "the pontiff of the people, the ray of Imams' light, the pillar of the edifice of religion [and] the tongue attuned to the exposition of the prespicuous law,"[73] Afghānī, with a flattery close to adulation, attributes to Shīrāzī "the vicegerency of the Most Great Proof" (*niyābat al-'uẓma 'an al-ḥujjat al-kubrā*), "the throne of general leadership" (*arīkat al-riyāsat al-'āmm*), and "supremacy over people" (*siyādat 'ala khalqih*).[74] He goes further to say what amounts to recognition of Shīrāzī's universal authority.

> Thine is the word which will unite them [i.e., people of Iran] and thine the proof which shall decide, that thy command is effective, and that none will contest thy wits by a word on thy part.[75]

Afghānī therefore should be credited for being the first to realize the potentials of Shi'ite *riyāsat*. He reminded the *'ulamā'* of the possibility of utilizing such leadership, not for limited and often personalized gains but for explicit political ends.

The chief *mujtahids* of Iran—among them Mīrzā Ḥasan Āshtīyānī (d. 1319/1901-2) in Tehran, Muḥammad Taqī Najafī (Āqā Najafī) in Isfahan, and Mīrzā Javād Mujtahid in Tabriz—viewed Shīrāzī's direct involvement as a mixed blessing. It has been said that Āshtīyānī himself composed the text of the famous declaration prohibiting the use of tobacco in the name of Shīrāzī, thus obliging the latter to confirm what amounted to be a *fait accompli.*[76] Whatever the circumstance, Shīrāzī's involvement greatly improved the *mujtahids'* overall stance vis-à-vis the government, and for a while returned unity to their ranks. Yet, as far as the long-term interests of these *mujtahids* were concerned, such involvement had the potentials of undermining their position not only as champions of antigovernment action but as the only religious authorities present in their constituencies. Āshtīyānī, an old classmate of Shīrāzī and a prominent commentator of Anṣārī's discourses in *Uṣūl al-fiqh*, was well aware of this threat. He was canny enough to use the occasion to attract Shīrāzī's confidence and at the same time to dictate his own objectives through that channel. This collaboration worked throughout the Regie period, but it soon collapsed after the cancellation of the concession, when the government gained enough confidence to buy back the loyalty of Āshtīyānī and others. Once the major crisis was over, disagreement over the future course of action between Shīrāzī and Āshtīyānī, and between the latter and more junior figures, may be taken as symptoms of fragmentation.[77]

In the years following the death of Shīrāzī in 1312/1895, the problem of *riyāsat* remained unresolved. The sole *riyāsat* of the Régie episode was once again changed to plurality in leadership. The absence of an influential head brought a number of leading *mujtahids* into the limelight. While Mīrzā Ḥasan Āshtīyānī relied on his connections with the court and the notables in the capital, Shaykh Muḥammad Sharābīyānī (d. 1904-5) in the 'Atabāt attained considerable authority chiefly for being an effective mediator between the Turkish-speaking populace and governments in Iran and the Ottoman empire.[78] Mīrzā Ḥusayn Tihrānī (ibn Mīrzā Khalīl) was largely emulated by the Persian-speaking population. Shaykh Ḥasan Māmaqānī (d. 1905) and Shaykh Muḥammad Kāẓim Khurāsānī (d. 1911) both relied on their *ṭullāb* support, the latter being the mentor of Persian-speaking students and for a while the recipient of the Oudh bequest. As the constitutional revolution brought Khurāsānī in the forefront of pro-Constitutional forces, there emerged Sayyid Kāẓim Yazdī (d. 1918-19) as the representative of the anti-Constitutional tendency.[79] As a whole, they represented a broad spectrum of religious leaders with limited jurisdiction.

What survived from Shīrāzī's time, however, was the legacy of political *riyāsat* which became more explicit under his successors. In the wake of the Constitutional Revolution, the *marāji'-i 'uzam* (grand authorities) is the most common reference to these high-ranking *mujtahids*, often with extended legal authority in the political sphere. The collective action of the senior *'ulamā'* and joint issuance of *fatwās* on matters of national significance would confirm the tendency to maintain a facade of unity.[80] For a brief period, a pronounced political dimension became the determined factor in the process of designation. But during the Constitutional period, unlike Shīrāzī's time, no unanimously accepted leadership emerged. What was apparent, however, was that political participation rather than customary practice became the norm in the way funds were located and students were attracted.

During the Constitutional period, the widening rift within the ranks of religious leaders can best be explained in terms of their willingness to represent conflicting interests and divergences in their followers' political views and actions. Though ideological division on the nature of the Constitution can not be overlooked, for the most part it was the contest for popularity and support of the laity that determined the political orientation of the *'ulamā'*. Faced with challenges of secular Constitutionalists and popular preachers of lower ranks, the *marāji'* were hardly able to maintain their unanimity. Unlike the Bābī episode, where the *'ulamā'* preserved their unity and survived the revolt of the lower ranks, the Constitutional Revolution had a far larger mass appeal and could not be safely ignored or rejected. Even after the split in the *'ulamā'*'s ranks became apparent in 1907, the Constitutionalists continued to receive not only the backing of the lesser mullas but that of a few celebrated jurists such as Khurāsānī and Ṭabāṭabā'ī.

Yet, political disagreements and defections weakened the hard-earned unity of Shīrāzī's time. The bulk of the *'ulamā'* either withdrew their earlier support for the constitution and abstained from politics, or else actively backed the absolutist monarchy. The best example of the polarization of the *'ulamā'* in this period is the secret war waged between Khurāsānī and Yazdī during 1909-11.[81] Ironically, the shift from nonintervention to activism not only resulted in internal division but also in a long-term social decline and loss of popular support. Unable to keep pace with the accelerating secularization of the Iranian polity, the prominent *mujtahids* after the Constitutional period quietly returned to their scholastic retreat.[82] Save for sporadic attempts, the majority of the surviving *marāji'*, bitter with the memories of the Constitutional experience and cautious not to endanger their dwindling financial and public backing, chose to maintain a low profile and to watch jealously from the safety of their *madrasa* the rising tides of anticlerical modernity and the gradual loss of their monopolies and privileges.

V

The interaction between the Shi'ite scholarly milieu, on the one hand, and the economic, social, and political forces which shaped the Shi'ite society of the nineteenth century, on the other hand, was subject to a complex set of factors. First, whenever the adverse forces of political anarchy (as in the first and the second interregnum in the eighteenth century), state opposition (as under Ḥājjī Mīrzā Āqāsī's regime), or anticlerical revolt (as in the Bābī movement) posed a threat to the religious leadership, it tended to retreat to the *madrasa* and undertake the safe practices of teaching and scholarship. Greater involvement in the affairs of the marketplace, however, came whenever there was a relative degree of social and economic stability, state cooperation, and royal patronage (as in Fatḥ 'Alī Shāh's reign), or when there was a willingness on the side of the interest groups, most notably the merchants, to render to the *mujtahids* nonacademic functions, whether judicial, financial, or political. The alternating shifts of leadership between the 'Atabāt and the religious centers of Iran may also, to some extent, be explained in terms of this changing climate. The 'Atabāt leadership, with its emphasis on legal scholarship, gained ground at times when direct involvement in the worldly affairs was not desirable. On the other hand, the *mujtahids* resident in Iran, as the actual representatives of the religious law, enhanced their position at times when the overall conditions for this worldly involvement were suitable.

Second, the informal hierarchy that evolved within the *'ulamā'* establishment recognized an equally informal status of *riyāsat* with almost caretaker responsibilities towards the clerics and the laity. In the second half of the century, this status gained prominence under the *mujtahids*, who were able to combine successfully the support of the community with the backing of the state, to enhance their popular image as the models of piety and knowledge, and to strengthen their control over the teaching circles. Contrary to conventional interpretations, the transition from plural to singular leadership during Anṣārī and Shīrāzī was not so much owing to the recognition by the community of the most learned (*a'lam*), which, at any rate, was institutionally inconceivable. Nor was it at the outset owing to the *mujtahids'* greater involvement in political affairs. Rather, it was the mechanics of the *madrasa*-bazaar interaction which allowed the designation of a senior *mujtahid* as the sole head; one who could best monopolize the academic and nonacademic spheres by having the largest constituency of emulators and agents. Such a supreme authority thus enjoyed the greatest access to financial resources and the endorsement of the state, and of the other *mujtahids*.

Third, the notion of the *riyāsat* gained further substance only when the changing political situation in the last decade of the century obliged the religious leaders to take a markedly antigovernmental position in the interest of their lay clients. In the period between the Regie protest and the end of the Constitutional period, the position of *marja'īyat-i taqlīd* came to represent not only the traditional *riyāsat* but also a supreme religious authority with marked political concerns on behalf of the entire community. Though the sole *marja'īyat* received almost universal recognition during the Regie episode, this development proved to be ephemeral. The institutional provisions in the doctrine of *taqlīd* made it practically impossible for any future clerical figure (except perhaps Āyatallāh Burūjirdī in the 1950s) to claim undisputed authority. During the Constitutional period, the diverse choices of the emulators remained the determining factor in the rise of the competing exemplars (*marāji'*); a fact which contributed to the exhaustion of clerical power and the hasty return of the *marāji'* to the previous nonpolitical position in the aftermath of that revolution.

Therefore, it is not unrealistic to suggest that in no time before the establishment of the Islamic Republic of Iran and the institutionalization of the Guardianship of the Jurist, the designation of the religious leadership, be it *riyāsat* or *marja'īyat*, was done by the *mujtahids* themselves. Rather, it remained at the discretion of the emulators—more the laity than the lower-rank clerics—to employ the loosely defined provisions for *taqlīd* and to bring the *marja'* in line with their own diverse wishes. From this historical perspective, Āyattallāh Khumeinī's thesis of the Guardianship of the Jurist is an innovation as much in revolt against the authority of a secular ruler as it is against the hegemony of the emulator.

Notes

1. Cited in N. Amīr Ṣādiqī Tihrānī, *Rūḥānīyat dar Shī'a* (Tehran (?), 1349/1970), 91. The author, a critic of clerical establishment, attributes this saying to "one of the Shi'ite scholars of the past."

2. On the evolution of the doctrine of *ijtihād* in pre-eighteenth-century Shi'ism, see N. Calder, "The Structure of Authority in Imami Shī'ī Jurisprudence," Ph.D. thesis, School of Oriental and African Studies, University of London, 1980; S. A. Arjomand, *The Shadow of God and the Hidden Imam* (Chicago, 1984), pp. 51-56, 137-44; J. Eliash, "The Ithna 'Asharī-Shī'ī Juristic Theory of Political and Legal Authority," *Studia Islamica* 29 (1969): 17-30; E. Kohlberg, "From Imamiyya to Ithna-'Ashariyya," *Bulletin of SOAS* 39 (1976): 521-34.

For the survey of the Shi'ite literature on *ijtihād*, see H. Modarressi Tabataba'i, *An Introduction to Shī'ī Law; a Bibliographical Study* (London, 1984), pp. 1-11, 39-50.

3. More recent Shi'ite works of *uṣūl al-fiqh* under the heading of *ijtihād* specify certain conditions for the jurist to be eligible as "absolute" (*muṭlaq*) or "fully qualified" (*jāmi' al-sharāyiṭ*) *mujtahid.* To be able to possess the "power" (*quwwa*) of *ijtihād*, the jurist must have command of Arabic grammar and syntax, the jurisprudence (*fiqh*), and the precedence for opinions (*fatāwī*) and consensus (*ijmā'*) on legal and doctrinal issues, as well as a fair knowledge of Qur'ānic exegesis, *ḥadīth* and its narrators (*rijāl*), logic, and theology (*kalām*). The "partial" (*mutajazzī*) *mujtahid* would only be qualified to express authoritative opinions on the specific areas of his expertise. For a summary of the conditions of *ijtihād*, see Ghulām-Riḍā 'Irfānīyān, *al-Ra'y al-Sadīd fī al-Ijtihād wa al-Taqlīd* (based on lectures by Sayyid Abu'l-Qāsim Khū'ī) (Najaf, 1386/1967), pp. 9-22; M. Rashād, *Uṣūl al-Fiqh* (Tehran, 1355/1976), pp. 585-89.

4. The final recognition of superiority in learnedness (*a'lamīyat*) as chief requisite for *sole marja'īyat* may have emerged as late as the time of Āqā Ḥusayn Burūjirdī in the late 1950s. An example of retrospective classification of the past Shi'ite scholars as *marāji'* (plural of *marja'*) may be found in 'Alī Davānī *Zindigānī-yi Za'īm-i Buzurg . . . Āyatallāh Burūjirdī* (Qumm, 1340/1961, pp. 18-35) which takes the chain of *marāji'* as far back as the time of Muḥammad Kulaynī (d. 940). However, as Āqā Buzurg Tihrānī takes care to point out, unified authority emerged under Burūjirdī when the "majority of people" turned towards him "until he came to be recognized as the source of the emulation for all" (*Ṭabaqāt A'lām al-Shī'a, I: Nuqabā' al-Bashar fī Qarn al-Rābi' 'Ashar* [Najaf, 1373/1954], pp. 606-7). After Burūjirdī (d. 1960), the doctrine of the sole *marja'* was questioned by a number of *'ulamā'* and the laity, including contributors to *Marja'īyat va Rūḥānīyat* (Tehran (?), 1341/1962). For a critical study of this work, see A. K. S. Lambton, "A Reconsideration of the Position of the *Marja' al-Taqlīd* and the Religious Institution," *Studia Islamica* 20 (1964): 116-35.

5. First published in 1291/1874-75 in Tehran, this Persian catechism on *taqlīd* and other related issues was compiled by Ḥajjī Mullā Muḥammad 'Alī Yazdī on the basis of his teacher's legal rulings. It is annotated and endorsed by Mīrzā Ḥasan Shīrāzī and carries the subtitle *Risālat al-Tāj al-Ḥujjaj*. (The above-mentioned statement appears on page 2.) The significance of this *risāla* may be gauged by its wide circulation. Between the date of the first publication and 1327/1909-10, at least ten editions of this work were produced (see K. Mushār, *Fihrist-i Kitābhā-yi Chāppī-yi Fārsī* [Tehran, 1352/1973], II, pp. 2219-21). The 1323/1906 edition entitled *Majma' al-Rasā'il* contains additional annotations in the margin by six leading *mujtahids* of the Constitutional period (see below). The section dealing with *taqlīd* (but not the marginal commentaries) has been studied by J. R. Cole in his "Imami Jurisprudence and the Role of the 'Ulama: Murtaza Ansari on Emulating the Supreme Exemplar," in *Religion and Politics in Iran; Shi'ism from Quietism to Revolution*, N. R. Keddie, ed. (New Haven

and London, 1983), pp. 33-46. Cole comes close to suggesting that indeed the learnedness was the determining factor in the emergence of the sole *marja'īyat*. I am thankful to J. Cole and to S. Arjomand for providing me with two different editions of this *risāla*.

6. *Majma' al-Rasā'il*, 9.

7. Ibid.

8. Ibid.

9. Ibid.

10. *Sirat*, 2; *Majma'*, 10.

11. Ibid.

12. A number of contributors to *Marja'īyat va Rūhānīyat*—particularly, the editor (introduction pp. jim-dal), M. Muṭahharī (pp. 105-30), and M. Jazāyirī (pp. 136-47)—have pointed out the relativity of *a'lamīyat* and have implicitly acknowledged the inadequacy of such criteria in determining the *marja'*.

13. Muḥammad Bāqir Khawānsārī, 2d ed. (Tehran, 1367/1947), p. 28 (under the biography of Mullā Aḥmad Narāqī). It is interesting to note that the author did not allocate an independent entry for Anṣārī. See also pp. 132 and 637. [It is worth noting that the entry on Anṣārī in *Qiṣas al-'Ulamā'* is very brief, but refers to him as *a'lam* to all the *'ulamā'* and describes his position as *riyāsat*. See below, p. 324. (Ed.)]

14. These are Shaykh Muḥammad Ḥasan Najafī Iṣfahānī the author of *Jawāhir al-Kalām* (*ibid.*, 182), Shaykh Ḥasan Najafī son of Shaykh Ja'far Kāshif al-Ghiṭā' (*ibid.*, 182) and Sayyid Ibrāhīm Qazvīnī (*ibid.*, 12).
[For the biography of Sayyid Ibrāhīm and anecdotes on his rivalry with Shaykh Muḥammad Ḥasan Najafī, see Chapter XIV, Section 3 below. (Ed.)]

15. See, for instance, Muḥammad 'Alī Mudarris Khayābānī, *Rayḥānat al-Adab*, 3 vols (Tehran, 1324/1945), p. 116, who identifies the "absolute scholarly leadership" (*riyāst-i muṭlaqa-yi 'ilmīya*) with the position of "*marja'-i taqlīd* of all the Shi'a."

16. The term *ḥubb-i riyāsat* (drive for leadership) is often applied pejoratively by the critics—mostly the lay writers, mystics, and nonconformists—to denote the exceedingly worldly ambitions entertained by some religious leaders.

17. On the Uṣūlīs' gradual rise to prominence under Bihbahānī and his disciples, see 'Alī Davānī *Vaḥīd-i Bihbahānī*, 2d ed. (Tehran, 1362/1983), particularly pp. 122-28 and 169-252; H. Algar, *Religion and State in Iran, 1785-1906* (Berkeley and Los Angeles, 1969), pp. 32-36.

18. For these and other titles, see Davānī, *Vaḥīd*, pp. 109-10, 131-36; Muḥammad 'Alī Mu'allim Ḥabībābādī, *Makārim al-Āthār* (Isfahan, 1337/1958), I, 222.

19. See 'A. al-'Azzawī, *Tārīkh al-'Irāq Bayn Ihtilālayn*, 8 vols. (Baghdad, VII [1375/1955]), pp. 10-60; 'A. Wardī, *Lamahat Ijtimā'iyya min Tārīkh al-'Irāq al-Ḥadīth*, 3 vols. (Baghdad, II [1971]), pp. 15-111; S. T. Longrigg, *Four Centuries of Modern Iraq* (Oxford, 1925), pp. 216-49. For economic condition in the first half of the nineteenth century, see J. G. Lorimer, *Gazetteer of the Perian Gulf, Omamn and Central Arabia*, 2 vols. (Calcutta, 1915), I, parts I and II; C. Issawi, *The Economic History of the Middle East, 1800-1814* (Chicago, 1966), pp. 131-36.

20. Āqā Buzurg Tihrānī, *al-Dharī'a ilā Taṣānīf al-Shī'a*, 25 vols. (Najaf and Tehran, 1387-1898/1968-1978), XVIII, p. 45; cf. Modarressi, *Shi'i Law*; p. 91.

21. See Muḥammad Tunikābunī, *Qiṣaṣ al-'Ulamā'* (Tehran, 1378/1967), pp. 183-98, for an interesting account of Najafī's life and personality. See also Tihrānī, *Ṭabaqāt*, II: *al-Karam al-Barrāra* (Najaf, 1374/1954), pp. 248-52; Khawānsārī, *Rawḍāt*, pp. 154-56.

22. Arjomand, *The Shadow of God*, pp. 224-45 and 230-32, and cited sources.

23. For his biography, see *Ṭabaqāt*, II, pp. 52-54, and cited sources. Passing through Qumm in 1812, Mīrzā Ṣāliḥ Shīrāzī notes the dilapidated state of *madrasas* in the town, but also new religious buildings under construction with Fatḥ 'Alī Shāh's patronage. He also notes that the students in the *madrasas* of Qumm, are solely engaged in the study of *fiqh* and *uṣūl*, since Mīrzā Abu'l-Qāsim Qumī does not permit the teaching or the study of any other subject (*Rūznāma-yi Mīrzā Ṣāliḥ Shīrāzī*, MS. Ouseley Collection, no. 159, Bodleian Library, Oxford, fol. 25b).

24. Fatḥ 'Alī Shāh to Mīrzā Abu'l-Qāsim Qummī, "Panj Nama az Fatḥ 'Alī Shāh bi Mīrzā-yī Qummī," letter no. 5, H. Modarressi Tabataba'i, ed., supplement to *Barrasīha-yi Tārīkhī* X, 4, p. 274.

25. Ibid., p. 270 (letter no. 3).

26. Ibid., pp. 1-18.

27. Beside Muḥammad Bāqir Shaftī who has often been singled out as the most prosperous *mujtahid* of the nineteenth century (see Chapter XV, Section 2 below), other Uṣūlī mujtahids also amassed large fortunes. Among the better known, though by no means the only examples, are: in Isfahan, Mīr Muḥammad Ḥusayn *imām jum'a* and his family, and later the Najafī family (Shaykh Muḥammad Bāqir and Shaykh Muḥammad Taqī, known as Āqā Najafī); in Tabriz, Mullā Murtaḍā 'Alam al-Hudā, Shaykh 'Alī-Asghar, Shaykh al-Islām and his family, and the *imām jum'a* Mullā Aḥmad and his family; in Qazvin, Mullā Muḥammad Taqī Baraqānī and his brothers; in Mashhad, the *imām jum'a* Mīrzā-yī 'Askarī; in Shiraz, Ḥajjī Muḥammad Ḥasan Mujtahid; in Kashan, Mullā Mahdī Narāqī and his family; and in Tehran, Mullā 'Alī Kanī. Because of the government backing, some holders of official and semi-official positions such as *imām jum'as*, and *shaykh al-Islāms* were the benefi-

ciaries of this favorable economic climate; however, the independent mujtahids were no less eager to have a share of the material wealth. [For an example of money lending by Shaftī, see below, p. 312. (Ed.)]

28. On Shafti and his economic ventures in Isfahan, see *Qiṣaṣ al-'Ulamā'*, pp. 135-67 (translated in Chapter XIV, Section 2 below). Together with *Rawḍāt* (pp. 125-26), they are the chief sources for later accounts. See also 'A. Jazzī, *Rijāl-i Iṣfahān ya Tadhkirat al-Qubūr* 2d ed., M. Mahdavi, ed. (Isfahan, 1328/1949), pp. 146-53; Ḥabībābādī, *Makārim*, III, 1614-20; Tihrānī, *Ṭabaqāt*, II, pp. 192-96. For a summary, see Algar, *Religion and State*, pp. 59-63; 'A. Iqbal, "Ḥujjat al-Islām. . . Shaftī," *Yadgar* V, 10, pp. 28-43.

29. Ḥabībābādī, *Makārim*, V 1614. It is not clear whether this title was adopted by Shaftī or had been conferred upon him.

30. On Sayyid Muḥammad and the Khatūnābādīs, see Ḥabībābādī, *Makārim*, II, pp. 314-20; Asadallāh Fāḍil Māzandarānī, *Zuhūr al-Ḥaqq* (Tehran, n.d.), III, pp. 94-96.

31. Sayyid Muḥammad Bāqir Shaftī, *Kitāb-i Su'āl va Javāb*, 2 vols., rev. ed. (Tabriz, 1247/1832), I, 6.

32. On the sociopolitical aspects of the Bābī movement see A. Amanat, *Resurrection and the Renewal of the Age; the Emergence of the Babi Movement in Qajar Iran, 1844-1850* (forthcoming); M. Momen, "The Social Basis of the Babi Upheavals in Iran (1848-53)," *IJMES* (1983): 157-83; D. M. MacEion, "From Shaykhism to Babism: A study in Charismatic Renewal in Shi'i Islam," Ph.D. thesis, Cambridge University, 1979; M. S. Ivanov, *The Babi Uprising in Iran (1848-1852)* (Moscow, 1939 [in Russian]).

33. [For the biography of Sayyid Ibrāhīm Qazvīnī, see Chapter XIV, Section 3 below. (Ed.)]

34. His leadership is attested by most contemporary sources. See Khawānsārī, *Rawḍāt*, pp. 181-82; Muḥammad Ḥasan Khān I'timād al-Salṭana, *al-Ma'āthir wa al-Āthār* (Tehran, 1306/1888-89), pp. 135-36.

35. A collection of anecdotes and praiseful statements about Anṣārī's scholarship and moral accomplishments appears in Murtaḍā al-Anṣārī, *Zindagānī va Shakhṣīyat-i Shaykh-i Anṣārī* (Tehran (?), 1339/1960), pp. 75-105.

36. Anṣārī, *Zindigānī*, pp. 85-86.

37. In this respect he was reportedly following his teacher Shaykh Ḥasan Āl-i Kāshif al-Ghiṭā'. See Ibid., pp. 89-90, citing N. Turāb Dizfūlī, a confidant of Shaykh Murtaḍā.

38. Ibid., pp. 79-80.

39. I'timād al-Salṭana, *Ma'āthir*, 137; cf. Anṣārī, *Zindagānī* which gives the figure of one hundred thousand *tūmāns*.

40. Anṣārī, *Zindagānī*, 169. This source gives the short biography of 277 of his students (pp. 168-322).

41. Ibid., p. 169; cf. *Ma'āthir*, p. 137.

42. Anṣārī, *Zindagānī* (pp. 354-87) lists 144 scholars who wrote commentaries on Anṣārī's works.

43. Tihrānī, *al-Dharī'a*, XVI, p. 132.

44. Ibid., XXII, p. 151.

45. Anṣārī briefly visited Shaykh Asadallāh Burūjirdī, a scholar with esoteric inclinations (possibly a student of Shaykh Ja'far Kashfī, a renowned scholar-mystic with Akhbārī tendencies) who had claims to be the *a'lam* and a "gate of knowledge" (*bāb-i 'ilm*) to the Imam. This encounter may not have been without influence in Shaykh Murtaḍā's pietistic tendencies (see *Ma'āthir*, p. 140; *Zindagānī*, pp. 66-67).

46. Anṣārī, *Zindagānī*, pp. 77; cf. 110-11 (citing *Luma'at* of Dizfūlī). This report asserts that Anṣārī was endorsed by his teacher Muḥammad Ḥasan Najafī, when, in his death bed, the latter addressed a gathering of the learneds, saying, "This is your *marja'* after me" (*Ibid.*, p. 73).

47. Anṣārī, *Zindagānī*, p. 74.

48. For his biography, see *Rayḥānat al-Adab*, I, pp. 201-2; Tihrānī, *Ṭabaqāt*, II, p. 599. For his anti-Bābī campaign, see Muḥammad Nabīl Zarandī, *The Dawn Breakers*, S. Effendi, trans. (Wilmette, 1932), pp. 430-33; Māzandarānī, *Zuhūr al-Ḥaqq*, III, pp. 430-33; Muḥammad Ṭaqi Sipihr, Lisān al-Mulk, *Nāsīkh al-Tawārīkh (Qājārīya)* (Tehran, 1385/1965), III, pp. 240ff.

49. Anṣārī, *Zindagānī*, p. 84.

50. E. G. Browne, ed., *A Traveller's Narrative* (Cambridge, 1891), p. 86; cf. Mīrzā Ḥusayn 'Alī Bahā'ullāh, *Lawḥ-i Sulṭān-i Īrān* (Tehran, 1976); E. G. Browne, ed., *The New History* (Cambridge, 1893), pp. 187-88.

51. Anṣārī, *Zindagānī*, p. 120.

52. 'Ali Vā'iẓ Khayābānī Tabrīzī, *Kitāb-i al-'Ulamā' al-Mu'aṣirīn* (Tabriz, 1366/1848), pp. 3-6; Tihrānī, *Ṭabaqāt*, II, pp. 420-23. The latter source recognizes him as a successor to Anṣārī who achieved "authority in teaching" (*al-marja'īyat-i fī al-tadrīs*).

53. Tihrānī, *Ṭabaqāt*, II, p. 421.

54. Ibid., I, p. 438. In this biography of Shīrāzī, Āqā Buzurg summarized his own work *Hadayyat al-Rāzī ila Mujadid al-Shīrāzī* (Najaf, 1388/1968) and that of Muḥammad 'Alī Urdūbādī, *Ḥayāt al-Imām al-Mujadid al-Shīrāzī.* See also his *al-Dharī'a*, VII, p. 116 and XXV, pp. 207-8.

55. *Ṭabaqāt*, I, p. 484.

56. Muḥammad Mahdī al-Mūsavī al-Kāẓimī, *Aḥsan al-Wadī'a*, 2 vols. (Baghdad, n.d.), I, p. 160.

57. *Ṭabaqāt*, I, p. 439.

58. *Hadayyat al-Rāzī* lists the biographies of close to 360 of Shīrāzī's students. See also Vā'iẓ Khayābānī, *'Ulamā'*, p. 48; Ḥabībābādī, *Makārim*, III, p. 888.

59. *'Ulamā'*, pp. 80-82; *Ṭabaqāt*, I, pp. 409-11.

60. Kāẓimī, *Aḥsan*, I, pp. 162-63; *'Ulamā'*, pp. 50-52.

61. Anṣārī, *Zindagānī*, p. 85.

62. Shīrāzī's works mostly consist of commentaries on the works of his teacher, Anṣārī. He also wrote a general work of jurisprudence on earnings (*makāsib*) and contracts (*mu'āmalāt*) (*Ṭabaqāt*, I, p. 441; *makārim*, III, p. 887).

63. For his family background, see Ḥasan Fasā'ī, *Fārsnāma-yi Nāṣirī* (Tehran, 1313/1896-97), II, p. 54; Amanat, *Resurrection and the Renewal*, Chapter II and the cited sources.

64. *Ṭabaqāt*, I, p. 274; Yahyā Kirmānī, *Farmāndihān-i Kirmān*, Bāstānī Pārīzī, ed. (Tehran, 1344/1965), pp. 26, 50.

65. *Ṭabaqāt*, I, p. 440; *Makārim*, p. 886.

66. *Takmalat al-Amal al-Āmil*, MS cited in *Tabaqat*, I, p. 440.

67. For the correspondence between the *'ulamā'* during the Regie episode, see Shaykh Ḥasan Karbalā'ī, *Tārīkh-i Dukhānīya ya Tārīkh Inḥiṣār-i Dukhānīyat*, I. Dihgān, ed. (Arak, 1333/1954); also cited in I. Taymūrī, *Taḥrīm-i Tanbākū* (Tehran, 1328/1949). N. R. Kiddie, *Religion and Rebellion, the Iranian Tobacco Protest of 1891-1892* (London, 1966), and F. Ādamīyat, *Shurish bar Imtiyāznāma-yi Regie* (Tehran, 1360/1981), discuss the role of the merchants in persuading the *'ulamā'* to support their cause. See also F. Kazimzadeh *Russia and Britain in Persia, 1864-1914* (New Haven and London, 1968) pp. 241-301 for the Russian anti-Regie provocations.

68. P. 173.

69. Karbalā'ī, *Tārīkh-i Dukhānīya;* also cited in Taymūrī, *Taḥrīm*, p. 120. It asserts that "all the *mujtahids* of the time were unanimous that this [i.e., Shīrāzī's declaration] was a ruling and not an opinion. The distinction between the two is that compliance with a ruling of a fully qualified *mujtahid* is an obligation for all, whereas the opinion is only obligatory for the deliverer of the opinion (*muftī*) and his emulators.

70. On the merchants' initiative in Shiraz, which was taken in spite of the *'ulamā''s* early reluctance, see M. H. I'timād al-Salṭana, *Khalṣa yā Khwābnāma*, M. Katirā'ī, ed. (Tehran, 1348/1969), pp. 122-25; 'Abbās Mīrzā Mulkārā, *Sharḥ-i*

Ḥāl, 'A. Iqbāl, ed. 2d ed. (Tehran, 1355/1976), pp. 183-84. For Falāsīrī, see *Fārsnāma*, II, p. 23.

71. Rajab 4, 1309/February 4, 1892. Cited in Muḥammad Nāẓim al-Islām Kirmānī, *Tārīkh-i Bīdārī-yi Īrāniān*, 2d ed., A. A. Sa'īdī Sīrjānī, ed., 3 vols. (Tehran, 1346/1967), I, pp. 34-35.

72. The original Arabic text of this letter appears in Kirmānī, *Bīdārī*, I, pp. 88-92. The Persian translation then in circulation is cited in Taymūrī, *Taḥrīm*. For the English translation, see E. G. Browne, *The Persian Revolution of 1905-1909* (Cambridge, 1910), pp. 15-21.

73. Browne, *Revolution*, 16. The Arabic original reads: *"hibr al-umma, bāriqat al-anwār al-a'āmma, da'āmat al-'arsh al-dīn wa lisān al-nāṭiq 'an al-shar' al-mubīn"* (*Bīdārī*, I, 88).

74. Ibid.

75. Ibid., p. 17.

76. See *Bīdārī*, I, p. 12; cf. Browne, *Revolution*, p. 22; Keddie, *Rebellion*, p. 96, n. 1. For Āshtīyānī, see Tihrānī, *Ṭabaqāt*, I, pp. 389-90.

77. Keddie, *Religion and Rebellion*, pp. 114-19; V. A. Kosogovski, *Khaṭirāt*, 'A. Jalī, trans., 2d ed. (Tehran, 1355/1976), p. 177.

78. M. Maḥmūd, *Tārīkh-i Rawābiṭ-i Siyāsī-yi Īrān va Inglīs dar Qarn-i Nūzdahum-i Mīlādī*, 8 vols. (Tehran, 1333-40/1954-61), VI, pp. 1343-44; the memoirs of Muḥammad Bāqir Ulfat written in 1343/1964 (copy in possession of S. A. Arjomand).

79. Ulfat, memoirs; A. Kasravī, *Tārīkh-i Mashrūṭa-yi Īrān*, 13th ed. (Tehran, 1356/1977), pp. 294, 381-85, 496-98; A. H. Hairi, *Shi'ism and Constitutionalism in Iran* (Lieden, 1977).

80. See, for instance, the joint *fatwā* (perhaps an *ijmā'*) on "the prohibition of travelling via the mountain route to Mecca" (*risāla bar ḥurmat-i istiṭrāq az ṭarīq-i jabal bi Macca-yi Mu'aẓẓama* (Sha'bān, 1320/1902). Initiated by Shaykh Faḍlallāh Nūrī, this fatwā is endorsed by twenty leading *mujtahids* of the time. Appearing presumably in the order of seniority, the first in the list, Muḥammad Fāḍil Sharābiyānī, is addressed as "the head of *faqīhs* and *mujtahids*" (*ra'īs al-fuqahā'wa al-mujtahidīn*); the second, Faḍlallāh Nūrī, and the third, Mīrzā Ḥusayn Tihrānī, are addressed as "the head of the nation and the faith" (*ra'īs al-millat wa al-dīn*); the fourth and fifth, Muḥammad Kāẓim Khurāsānī and Muḥammad Ḥasan Māmaqānī, were addressed as "the pride (*iftikhār*) of *faqīhs* and *mujtahids*"; while the rest were referred to as the refuge (*malādh*), the supporter (*ẓhīr*), and the pillar (*'imād*) of Islam and Muslims. This *risāla*, though on a relatively minor issue, demonstrates the tendency to preserve a united clerical front on the eve of the Constitutional movement. It may also be taken, however, as an indication of the ongoing struggle for clerical supremacy in

the decade following the death of Shīrāzī. See also Vā'iẓ Khayābānī, *'Ulamā-yi Mu'aṣirīn*, pp. 77-78.

81. Ulfat's memoirs (extract pp. 6-9). See also Āqā Najafī Qūchānī, *Siyāḥat-i Sharq*, 2d ed. (Tehran, 1362/1983), pp. 455-82, who gives an amusing account of the student's dependence on Khurāsānī and Yazdī for their subsistence.

82. Muḥammad Bāqir Ulfat marks the death of Mullā Muḥammad Kāẓim Khurāsānī as the end of an era of intervention by the *'ulamā'* in the political affairs of Iran; an era which he believes had started some twenty years earlier with the tobacco protest of 1891-92 (memoirs, extract p. 12).

CHAPTER 6

Constitutionalism and Clerical Authority

ABDOL KARIM LAHIDJI

This misconception of the role of the *'ulamā'* in the Constitutional Revolution of 1906-11, and the presumption that they were the leaders of the Constitutionalist movement have distorted historical reality considerably. This chapter analyzes the political action of the *'ulamā'* in this period as a *reaction* to the Constitutionalist movement which had been initiated by others. That the position taken by the *'ulamā'* was usually a reaction to prevailing political developments is nowhere better illustrated than in the attitude toward the judiciary reforms of the Constitutionalists. Therefore, this chapter focuses on the impact of the Constitutional Revolution in general, and of the judiciary reforms in particular, on the authority of the Shi'ite *'ulamā'* and its consequences for the latter's political activities during the first and the second Majlis.

While there is no doubt that a number of clerics, *'ulamā'*, and *marāji'-i taqlīd* (sources of emulation) were influential in bringing constitutional government to Iran, their role in the Constitutional movement of 1905-11 needs to be qualified by the following four points:

1. The *'ulamā'* did not initiate the movement.

2. Their intent was not to institute popular rule, a government that emanated from the will of the people, for they were either ignorant of such a political system or their goal was to make constitutionalism conform to Islamic doctrine.

3. What motivated them to act was the basic desire to limit the privileges and authority of the Qājār king. Some clerics, such as the *mujtahid* of Tehran, Sayyid 'Abd Allāh Bihbahānī, were more concerned with their prestige and position and with augmenting their own power, and they viewed the growth of their own rights and privileges as dependent

upon restricting those of the king.

4. Only when the objectives of the reformers and Constitutionalists dawned on them did the clerics cry "Sacrilege!" and "Woe to Islam!" and, but for a few exceptions, they fought and agitated against the order based on national sovereignty and the government of law.

1. The Role of the *'ulamā'* in the Constitutional Revolution

The rise of the clerical agitation against the state began with the Naus affair in 1905. The Belgian M. Naus, who was Minister of Posts and Director of Customs in Iran, appeared at a masquerade dressed in clerical robes and a turban. A picture of him in costume circulated in Tehran. Merchants dissatisfied with Naus's stewardship of customs complained to the *'ulamā'*, and notices were distributed throughout the city which stated: "It is incumbent on every believing Muslim to kill the infidel Naus." In his description of the grievances brought against Naus, the prominent *mujtahid* of Tehran, Sayyid 'Abd Allāh Bihbahānī, wrote to the Prime Minister 'Ayn al-Dawla and requested "that the injustices committed by Monsieur Naus be rectified." Not receiving a reply, Bihbahānī pursued the matter for several reasons, the principal one being his personal dislike of the Prince Prime Minister; "the matter thickened."[1] Bihbahānī was the enemy of 'Ayn al-Dawla and a supporter of a rival former Prime Minister, Amīn al-Sulṭān, the Atābak. On the eve of the ninth day of Muḥarram (March 16, 1905), the month of Shi'ite mourning for the sect's archmartyrs, Bihbahānī took the pulpit and, cleverly playing on the heightened emotional state of his audience, paraded his own cause.

> All clerics and theology students (*ṭullāb*) [no mention is made of the public at all] assembled here share a religious grievance. They insist that I issue a writ for the killing of this damned unprincipled bastard. I see no need to issue such a writ, for the offense he has committed with his impudence against our Prophet and the *'ulamā'* has by itself earned him death at the hands of any believer. There is no reason to condemn him formally. It is never difficult to kill a common cur. Let the matter rest for the time being and go on with your mourning until the answer to a petition to the king demanding the man's dismissal and expulsion arrives.[2]

Bihbahānī adroitly declares Naus a "damned bastard" the shedding of whose blood requires no injunction, but at the same time does not want to assume responsibility for this deed by issuing an injunction. He has another idea and intends to bargain. He writes both to the king and to the *marāji'* in Najaf. The latter strengthens his position by sending him the following telegram:

> The complaint of the inhabitants from the injustices of the Christian Monsieur Naus has reached a level that it cannot be overlooked. Today, your noble being is the supporter of Islam and the well-wishes of the Muslims. In order to protect the honor and property and lives of the Muslims, it is necessary to remove the hand of that oppressor with all his subordinates from the land of the Muslims. The duty of the public is the same. Whoever supports him, in any garb, is corrupt and of the same status [as Naus].
>
> Muḥammad Kāẓim al-Khurāsānī,
> 'Abd Allāh Māzandarānī, the scion of the late Ḥājj Mīrzā Khalīl

A letter to Bihbahānī follows:

> Without the king, may God help him and make him victorious, it is not at all wise to enter into this matter, but you must, out of impartiality, make a representation to the crown prince, may God perpetuate his sovereignty, that the enemy and the in-house thief is intent on the destruction of your capital and your realm. Your Highness is not as heedless as His Majesty, and can fend off these obstacles before the affairs are gradually disrupted and it is too late. Saying this is the duty of the soldiers of prayer (*'asākir-i du'ā*).[3]

The *marāji'* of Najaf are not thinking about a revolution; nor do they have any demands aiming at the establishment of constitutional government, the rule of law, or the revival of the rights of the people. They pray for the continuity of the rule of the king and the crown prince because the clerics are "the soldiers of prayer."

Months go by, the king returns from Europe and the *'ulamā'* are busy with "I wish and perhaps." It is the people who begin to agitate. Leaflets and proclamations such as the following are distributed in the streets and the bazaars:

> The tyranny of the governors in the cities is a calamity. Nothing can be done by numbed and disunited subjects. The only remedy is a sustained initiative by the respected *'ulamā'* who should lead in accordance with Muslim honor so that the people can follow.

At first the *'ulamā'* are encouraged to rise; then they are threatened and warned:

> . . . . then some people will treat the *'ulamā'* in the same way as they treat the ministers.

Finally, they consider the Minister of Court, Amīr Bahādur, the main obstacle to the progress of the movement and request that "the *'ulamā'* publicize a writ for killing him. Shedding the blood of this son of a dog is permissible according to the Sacred Law."

In a petition to Bihbahānī, the revolutionaries, having underscored the responsibility of the *'ulamā'* in the transmission of divine commandments to the people and the protection and explication of the Sacred Law, complain of the corruption, oppression, and immorality, and encourage the *'ulamā'* to join the movement.

> We Muslims have so far been cautious to avoid bloodshed because of our liking for the king. But we are not weaker than any other people. Thanks to Islam, we are capable of confronting the government. As you respected *'ulamā'* are the leaders of our religion and our creed, we make you mediators and intermediaries for our demands. . . .

With the onset of popular agitation, both religious and political authorities are constantly reminded of their responsibility towards the nation. Here are some examples from the proclamations signed by the Islamic Association (*hiy'at-i islāmiyya*), the National Islamic Association (*hiy'at-i milliya-yi islāmiyya*), and the Human Angel (*firishta-yi basharī*):

> The law of the Muslims today consists of the Commandments of the Qur'ān and the Sacred Law of Islam, and the progress and propagation of the commandments of the Sacred Law is the responsibility of the respected *'ulamā'*.
>
> [You (government officials) have] weakened the rightful Islamic state and surrendered the nation and the country of the Muslims . . . to the infidels.
>
> For the past one hundred and fifty years, the self-seeking and Godless spiritual and temporal leaders of the kingdom of Iran have left these sacred rules of Islam unimplemented and disturbed.[4]

While the popular agitators were seeking to induce the participation of the *'ulamā'*, the king made a favorable gesture towards Bihbahānī and the Prime Minister, 'Ayn al-Dawla, sent him some money "for distribution among the theology students." Naus, however, "firmly resisted all the efforts of Sayyid 'Abd Allāh's entourage to blackmail him."[5]

Popular protest gathered momentum, and the religious leaders joined it out of necessity, especially as the rights of one of their members had been violated and their particularistic interests had been ignored. The administration of the Marvī *madrasa* had been taken from the sons of Mīrzā Ḥasan Āshtiyānī and given to the *imām jum'a;* and a stamp duty had been imposed on the stipends of the *'ulamā'*. When the *'ulamā'* took sanctuary in the shrine of 'Abd al-'Aẓīm, in addition to the demand for the removal of Naus, they demanded the restoration of the administration of the Marvī school to the Āshtiyānīs and the removal of the stamp from the *'ulamā'*'s salary vouchers. This indicated that the *'ulamā'* wanted to secure their particularistic rights and were unwilling to pay state tax.

During the *bast*, which finally led to the Shah's rescript, the reformist elements persuaded the *'ulamā'* also to press the government for the establishment of a "governmental house of justice" (*'adālat-khāna-yi dawlatī*). The text of this rescript indicates that the object is to appease the *'ulamā*.

> Your Excellency Atābak A'ẓam:
>
> As we have repeatedly declared, the establishment of the governmental house of justice—in order to carry out the commandments of the Sacred Law and to provide comfort for the citizenry—is above all other objectives. Therefore, we hereby and unequivocably decree that toward execution of this holy intention, the Islamic code of justice, consisting in the determination of the punishments and execution of the commandments of the Sacred Law, be immediately established. . . . And of course, requests such as these from the honorable *'ulamā'* will always be considered so as to increase their prayers (*du'a-gūī*).

The *'ulamā'* return to the capital in victory and are received by His Majesty who bestows his kindness and grace upon them. But discontent is widespread among the people and the distribution of leaflets continues: "You were content with a royal rescript, which today, after two months, still has not taken effect." Or, "Oh *'ulamā'*, do not be silent until your requests are carried out. If you are not concerned about us, pity the oppressed people of Shiraz, Kerman, Isfahan, Tabriz, Kermanshahan, Qumm and Kashan; pity the clerical class so that your name is not sullied with dishonor and it is not announced that you received money and gave up the rights of a nation."[6]

Finally, Sayyid Muḥammad Ṭabāṭabā'ī is forced to act. He writes to the Atābak that the redress of grievances is "only possible with the establishment of a *majlis* (parliament), the unity between the nation and the government, and the cooperation of the *'ulamā'* with government officials." He then warns: "We do not wish to see the historians write that the Qājār rule ended with the reign of Muẓaffar al-Dīn Shāh, Iran perished in that period, and the Shī'a have since become abject, lowly and dominated by foreigners."[7]

The idea of the establishment of a *majlis* did not come from the clerics any more than did that of "the house of justice." According to Dawlatābādī, it was first brought up during the emergency session at the Court by Iḥtishām al-Salṭana, and later gained popularity.[8] Public opinion was influenced by intellectual elements. The clerics as usual were either attracted or intimidated by their followers, without having any knowledge of such progressive demands as the "national parliament," "democracy," "equality," "constitution," and the like. Consequently, in the migration to Qumm, a Shaykh Faḍl Allāh Nūrī is found side by side with Ṭabāṭabā'ī and Bihbahānī. The *'ulamā'* demand the removal of 'Ayn al-Dawla, the theology students taking sanctuary in the British Embassy demand a "parliament of justice (*majlis-i ma'dalat*) for the execution of the commandments of Muḥammad's law," while the leaders of those at the British Embassy and of other students proclaim as their objective the establishment of a national consultative assembly.[9] The popular element is far ahead of the clerical leaders, so much as to write "If the *'ulamā'* give in, they will persist."

The Shah sends a telegram inviting the *'ulamā'* to return. They respond:

> Aggression and injustices of those in charge and their disregard for the execution of the commandments of the Sacred Law, the proliferation of prostitution and immorality, and the commitment of what religion forbids is implanted and kept in your memorious royal mind, and thus the establishment of an assembly and parliament of justice is in order .... This important Islamic objective results in the declaration of the word of truth and therein the increased power of the Islamic kingdom .... It is the *bona fide* request for those who pray [for the king], the honorable *'ulamā'* and the subjects of the king of Islam .... [that such be established] under the supervision, direction and command of the very person of the king of Islam, and the reform of the affairs of the Muslims in accordance with the holy law and the certain commandments of the binding *sharī'a*, which is the official and royal law of the country—be made known and executed.[10]

Ḥusayn Pīrniya, the son of the new Prime Minister, Mushīr al-Dawla, visits those who have taken sanctuary with the suggestion that the parliament should "obey the will of the king and the Shah should not be bound to execute the order of Majlis." Merchants and tradesmen respond that "the Majlis must be the absolute ruler .... and if it passed a law, His Majesty must sign and execute that legislation." Then, in conciliation toward the *'ulamā'*, they say "Majlis should be declared established with the approval and desire of the *'ulamā'*." But the people do not accept, and the Shah is constrained to issue an order for the establishment of a Majlis composed of those selected by the Princes, the *'ulamā'*, the Qājārs, the notables and the nobility, landlords, merchants, and guildsmen in order to "begin to execute the laws of the holy *sharī'a.*" The people, however, tear up copies of the order. Two days later, on the sixteenth of Jumada II, 1325/7 August 1906, another decree is issued stating:

> We hereby order that the aforementioned Majlis in accordance with the description given in the last rescript be properly set up, and, after the election of the members, sections and provisions of the constitution of Islamic consultative assembly be drawn up in accordance with the approval and signature of the elected representatives, so as to bring about the reform of the people of the kingdom and the execution of the laws of the holy *sharī'a.*

The protestors are still not satisfied, and their representatives go to see the Prime Minister. Discussions center around the establishment of the Majlis.

> The Prime Minister said that it must be called an Islamic consultative assembly. One of the representatives, Āqā Sayyid Ḥusayn Burūjirdī, said that it must be a national consultative assembly. The Prime Minister said I won't give the 'national consultative.' Āqā Sayyid Ḥusayn said, with the strength of the nation, we will take the national consultative assembly. After lengthy discussions, it was decided that the representatives should have another conference with Mushīr al-Mamālik and Muḥtasham-al Salṭana. After these discussions, the result of the conference was that it would be the National Consultative Assembly.[11]

The *'ulamā'*, facing a *fait accompli*, return to Tehran. Dawlatābādī comments: "They are not happy with the events and know that the situation will not end to their advantage because the legislation and the establishment of the national consultative assembly would not only limit the authority of the government and the monarchy, but it would also put an end to their own unlimited influence which they have acquired through their relation to the Sacred Law."[12]

The first steps towards the etablishment of the national parliament get underway, and the first confrontation between the progressive front and the religious front begins because, as stated earlier, the latter had no clear conception of Constitutionalism and a national parliament.

Disagreements that surfaced between the two factions during the drafting and approval of the electoral law will not be discussed here. The Majlis was convened and the Fundamental Law approved (December 30, 1906), a law that aimed only at the supervision of the process of the establishment of the Majlis and the definition of its functions and jurisdiction. According to its Article 16:

> All laws necessary to strengthen the foundations of the State and Throne and to set in order the affairs of the Realm and the establishment of the Ministries, must be submitted for approval to the National Consultative Assembly.

There is no mention of the rights of the people, nor of the principle of national sovereignty, as there is no mention of the principles of separation of powers, responsibility of government to the parliament, the Judiciary Power, and many other fundamental rights. Thus, the Majlis decided to proceed with the Supplement to the Fundamental Law in 1907. Its draft was prepared and was brought to the Majlis and caused much debate. It was said that "the Qur'ān is our Fundamental Law. Another person corrected this by saying that that book is the foundation of religion, whereas the Fundamental Law determines the principles of the state and the limits of government and the rights of the nation."[13] Bihbahānī showed the way and set the precedence for the use of the "legal ruse" (*ḥīla-yi shar'ī*) in Majlis.

> You should never state that they did so in this or that state, and we should do the same. The common people do not understand, and it is insulting to us. We have laws and we have the Qur'ān. I do not want to say do not name the country. Name it and mention it, but explore the matter so that it becomes clear that what they have done has been based on wisdom and derived from our Sacred Laws."[14]

Finally, the solution was found in the supervision of the clerics, which was not included in the Fundamental Law. From the beginning of the establishment of Majlis, it was decided that three *mujtahids* who were not among the representatives—i.e., Ṭabātabā'ī, Bihbahānī, and Shaykh Faḍl Allāh Nūrī—would appear in Majlis and "without the advanced approval of two of the most prominent *mujtahids*, Sayyid Muḥammad Ṭabāṭabā'ī and Sayyid 'Abd Allāh Bihbahānī, none of the important issues would be resolved."[15]

The idea of supervision was that of Shaykh Faḍl Allāh. Another cleric stated in its justification: "There will not be any rule of the customary law that would oppose and be contradictory to any rule of the Sacred Law," and customary laws "would not change the rules of the incumbent and for the forbidden" and if "some subjects and the execution of the primary rules of the Sacred Law become impractical, it would be possible, with the approval of the *'ulamā'*, to replace the primary rules by secondary ones according to the principle 'necessity allows what is forbidden.'[16]

The excellencies persuade the majority of Majlis to accept their juristic authority, and Shaykh Faḍl Allāh's draft is approved.

> Art. 2. At no time must any legal enactment of the Sacred National Consultative Assembly, established by the favour and assistance of His Holiness the Imam of the Age (may God hasten his glad Advent!), the favour of His Majesty the Shahinshah of Islam (may God immortalize his reign!), the care of the Proofs of Islam (may God multiply the like of them!), and the whole people of the Persian nation, be at variance with the sacred principles of Islam or the laws established by His Holiness the Best of Mankind (on whom and on whose household be the Blessings of God and His Peace!).[17]

In terms of ordering of priorities, the will of the people is placed after the "assistance" of the Hidden Imam, "the favor" of the Shah, and the "care" of the *'ulama';* and its significance and effect is determined by this ordering.

Another confrontation involved the freedom of religion. In Article 1 of the Supplement to the Fundamental Law, it was stated:

> The official religion of Iran is Islam, according to the orthodox Ja'farī doctrine of the Ithnā 'Ashariyya (Twelver Shi'ism), which faith the Shah of Iran must profess and promote.

This was another point that was conceded to the clerical front, and that created a negative reaction outside the Majlis. The editor of *Ḥbl al-Matīn* who had written "laws that were instituted thirteen hundred years ago were for Arabs of the Arabian peninsula and not for the people of Iran and for this time," was tried and convicted for committing "evident forbidden acts."[18]

Article 8 on equality of rights also created a scandal. It was said that the rights of the Muslims and non-Muslims are not equal in the Sacred Law. Ṭabāṭabā'ī was in favor of equality of political rights. Eventually they resorted to a legal ruse, and approved the following:

"The inhabitants of the kingdom of Iran have equal rights before the law of the state," which implied the persistence and continuity of the duality of laws, religious and secular, and, therefore, the duality of sovereignty.

The clerics even opposed compulsory education as contrary to the *sharī'a;* and under Article 18 on freedom of education, a proviso for the absence of prohibition by the Sacred Law was entered. They similarly opposed the freedom of the press and associations. The pertinent Articles were eventually approved as follows:

> Art. 18. The acquisition and study of all sciences, arts and crafts is free, save in the case of such as may be forbidden by the Sacred Law.
> Art. 20. All publications, except heretical books and matters hurtful to the perspicuous religion [of Islam] are free, and are exempt from the censorship. If, however, anything should be discovered in them contrary to the Press law, the publisher or writer is liable to punishment according to that law . . . .
> Art. 2. Societies (*anjumans*) and associations (*ijtimā't*) which are not productive of mischief to religion or the State, and are not injurious to good order, are free throughout the whole Empire . . . .

The Articles on the Powers were more sensitive. As regards the Legislative Power, in addition to Article 2, which assured the supervision of the jurists (*fuqahā'*), under Article 27 they stated:

> The legislative power, which is specially concerned with the making or amelioration of laws. This power is derived from His Imperial Majesty, the National Consultative Assembly, and the Senate, of which three sources each has the right to introduce laws, provided that the continuance thereof be dependent on their not being at variance with the standards of the Sacred Law, and on their approval by the Members of the two Assemblies, and the Royal ratification. . . .

Thus, the king was given the right to introduce laws, and the validity of the laws passed by the Majlis was made conditional upon not being at variance with standards of the Sacred Law—the authorities for determining the conformity to the standards of the Sacred Law being the jurists who were to be present in the Majlis in accordance with Article 2.

The contentions over the definition of the Judiciary Power will be considered in Section (3) of this chapter.

Generally speaking, the victory of the progressives in the first stage of the Constitutional Revolution rang an alarm bell for the *'ulamā'.* In

Ādamiyyat's words, they discovered that "once the Constitutionalists gained the upper hand vis-à-vis the Court of Muḥammad 'Alī Shāh, it would not be long before their turn would come, meaning they should know their superiors . . . . the *mujtahids'* assistance toward the people's objective was neither serious nor sincere. They pretended to lead the people towards that objective because they were afraid they might be forced by the people to follow them."[19]

2. Two Clerical Responses to Constitutionalism

The *'ulamā'* did not generally have a clear idea of constitutional government and national sovereignty because their understanding of the foundations of new political philosophy was limited. The clashes between the progressive reformist and the clerical fronts over the Supplement to the Fundamental Law also produced differences in the clerical front and eventually resulted in divisions and factionalism. These were compounded by the rivalry for leadership, especially between Shaykh Faḍl Allāh and Sayyid 'Abd Allāh. In any event, the *'ulamā'* became divided into two groups: those who tried to reconcile constitutional government and a legislative assembly with the principles and commandments of the Sacred Law, and those who put forth the idea of "religiously legitimate constitutionalism" (*mashrūṭa-yi mashrū'a*), and became allies of the absolutists. We will briefly mention the views of Mīrzā Muḥammad Ḥasan Nā'īnī and Shaykh Faḍl Allāh Nūrī as representatives of these two groups, respectively.

Nā'īnī is an Uṣūlī jurist and the author of *Tanbīh al-Umma va Tanzīh al-Milla* (Warning to the Community of Believers and Purification of the Nation). In this book, he endeavors to legitimize the constitutional order with the methods of religious jurisprudence. He divides government into "arbitrary" or "subjugating" (*isti'bādiyya*) and "constitutional" or "limited." In the first kind of government, the monarch is the absolute ruler and owner of the people; whereas in the second, the basis of government is "general interests." Government is thus like "guardianship (*vilāyat*) and trust," and, as with other kinds of guardianship and trust, it is conditional upon the "absence of transgression and excess" as regards the subject of guardianship. He then turns to the structure of constitutional government and states that with the institution of the Fundamental Law, "the extent of domination of the ruler and the freedom of the nation, and the recognition of the rights of all classes of inhabitants of the country" are determined according to the requirements of religion. The elected body of the representatives of the nation will constitute the

National Consultative Assembly, and, as the Shī'a consider the political affairs of the community of believers among the functions of the Deputies of the Imam, it suffices that a few of the *mujtahids*, or others authorized by them, be included in the elected body. The foundation of Nā'īnī's view is therefore guardianship and trust. The ruler is the guardian (*valī*) or trustee (*amīn*) of the people, and "departing from the function of guarding and trust keeping. . . causes permanent dismissal" of the trustee.[20]

Even though he opposed "subjugating" governments and considers "submission to the arbitrary commands of the leaders of sects and nations presented as religion" a kind of subjugation, Nā'īnī's view is problematical. This is so because, on the one hand, he respects the freedom and rights of the nation only within the limitations of the "requirements of religion," and on the other, because he sanctions the guardianship of the jurists—as authorities for determining the compatibility or incompatibility of parliamentary legislation with the Sacred Law—over the National Assembly, which is the organ of the sovereignty of the people. Yet this is another form of subjugation: subjugation to immutable rules whose understanding and interpretation is within the competence of a small group and not the people in general. Therefore, he runs into a contradiction on the issue of equality and argues as follows: "The principle of equality of the people of the country applies only to the laws enacted for the regulation of the deeds of the functionaries, not for the general removal of distinctions among them!" Elsewhere, in response to those who consider the writing of the Constitution "opening shop in competition with the Lord of the Sacred Law," he states that the objective of the Constitution is the limitation and responsibility of the power of government. "Reprehensible innovation (*bid'at*) and [usurpation of] divine law-making occurs only if the intention of legislation is to create a Sacred Law—i.e., if the laws are given the title of *shar'ī* commandments."[21]

The story of Shaykh Faḍl Allāh, who possessed neither the knowledge of Nā'īnī nor his uprightness and virtue, should be explained in more detail. The *'ulamā'* of Tehran were still in migration in Qumm when the eternal differences between them became more public. Yaḥyā Dawlatābādī writes as follws: "On the return of the gentlemen from Qumm, I went to welcome them in Kahrīzak, three parasangs from Tehran. I met the Shaykh by chance, and we had a pleasant conversation . . . . He said: I know now that if we do not have a constitutional regime, we will not be safe from the foreigners. But the situation is such that our friend (meaning Sayyid 'Abd Allāh Bihbahānī) has made of this issue a source of income and practices lack of restraint in taking people's property. And there is no way to stop him . . . . He asks me to speak with my truly liberal friends to support him in joining the Constitutionalists, leaving Bihbahānī to support the Shah, since he has always supported the government."[22] On the one hand, the Shaykh attends the Majlis and raises the issue of "religiously legitimate Consitutionalism," and, on the other hand, he engages in conspiracies outside the Majlis, takes sanctuary in the shrine of 'Abd al-'Azīm, and publishes his "bills." He writes that the philosophy of Constitutionalism is for "the people to assemble and ask their king to change the arbitrary monarchy, thereby establishing rules regarding government responsibilities, services and court duties, which, from that point on, in their behavior and actions, the king and his servants and retinue would never violate. Finally, thank Almighty God, the late king succeeded, the efforts of the honorable *'ulamā'* were rewarded, and the great Islamic Consultative Assembly was opened. Later, as soon as the discussions in the Majlis began and topics concerning the principle of constitutionalism and its boundaries were raised in the course of the speeches, bills and newspaper articles, certain unexpected issues appeared which became the source of extreme fear and astonishment for the chief clerics, *imam jum'as* and all the religious and the faithful. For instance, in the royal charter, wherein it was stated that we have a National Islamic Consultative Assembly, the term 'Islamic' was omitted . . . . The irresponsible, immoral and irreligious group formerly known as Bābīs and those who deny religious law and believe in nature . . . (state in the newspapers) that the religious law must be modified, certain secondary rules must be changed into better and more appropriate ones, and the laws that were established to meet the needs of one thousand three hundred years ago must all be made to conform with the situations, conditions and needs of today. These include the lifting of prohibitions against intoxicants, the spread of prostitution, the opening of schools for women and elementary schools for girls, and the spending of funds set aside for religious mournings and pilgrimages to the holy sites on building factories and roads and streets . . . and that all the nations on earth must have equal rights, the infidels and Muslims must be equal in value of their blood . . . . " Then, addressing the people, he states: "Had you ever heard of a Jew [being allowed] to sodomize a Muslim child?" [Assuming that there would have been no problem had the person been a Muslim] or of "a Jew having pulled off the head cover of a Muslim girl?" or . . . of dragging your spiritual leaders by force in the Majlis in line with European women" and of "those foreign customs, such cheering and all those inscriptions of 'long live, long live (long live equality) and (equality and brotherhood).' You could write on one 'long live the Sacred Law,' 'long live the Qur'ān.' " And once again he dramatically relates his discussion to the Majlis: "We see that in the Majlis, they have brought in the legislative books of the European parliaments and based on their need for law, they have expanded them, not realizing that the European nations had not devised sacred laws . . . . But we, the followers of Islam, have a heavenly and eternal Sacred Law, which is so dignified, proper, perfect and firm that it cannot be abrogated . . . . Therefore, our need, the need of the Iranian people, to devise a law is merely in terms of the affairs of the monarchy, which, in the course of world events, have been separated from the course of religious law and, as the religious jurists explain, the government has become a government of injustice and, as politicians are wont to say, it has become a dictatorial government." Then, he proceeds with his proposals: "In the regulations (not the Constitution) of the Majlis, after the term 'Constitution,' the word *mashrū'a* (legitimate/in accordance with the Sacred Law) must be inserted. Secondly, in the chapter concerning the conformity of the laws of the Majlis to the sacred religious laws and the article concerning the supervision of a committee comprised of the just (*'udūl*) religious jurists in every era over the Consultative Assembly must be included . . . . Also, the Consultative Assembly by no means has the right to appoint that committee of the just religious jurists . . . . And a chapter concerning the implementation of all religious injunctions in regards to the Bābī sect and other atheists and heathens must be included in the regulations." Concerning the freedom of the press, he states: "This law does not coincide with our religious laws . . . . The printing of the books of the Frenchman Voltaire, which are all comprised of insults against the prophets, . . . are all prohibited in the Koranic law." In connection with this issue, he resorts to the injunction of Akhūnd Khurāsānī, which states: "Adversities are continuously on the increase, and are due mainly to the excessive impudence of heretics and non-believers and the spreading of heathenism and atheism, which are the result of the supposition of freedom of the pen and expression, which has become the source of all destruction." In another bill he writes: "The Majlis is the grand house of Islamic consultation and is established with the grateful help of the Islamic leaders and the general deputies of the Imam and is founded to serve and assist the court of the Twelver Shi'ite government and protect the rights of the followers of the Ja'farī sect. It is impossible for the parliaments of Paris and England to influence the Majlis into copying from them the law of freedom of ideas and the pen and change religious laws and injunctions." Upon the escalation of the protest of people, when he finds his position threatened, he states: "I do not by any means deny the National Islamic Consultative Assembly. Rather, I consider myself to have been more involved in its establishment than anyone else, because none of our great religious scholars who are residing in the vicinity of the holy shrines of Iraq and other countries supported it, and through reasoning and offering evidence, I have gained their cooperation." In support of his views, he resorts to another decree from the sources of emulation in Najaf (Khurāsānī and Māzandarānī): "In the regulations [i.e., Constitution], they have agreed to the inclusion and legality of political articles and procedures to conform to the pure religious laws. This is one of the necessary articles, which preserves the Islamic nature of this principle .... It is necessary to include another permanent article to reject these atheists, implement divine injunctions in regards to them, and prevent the spread of prohibited acts."[23] Elsewhere, he writes: "It is not obligatory to obey the Majlis. Obedience is obligatory to God, the messenger of God, the Imams and those who are deputies of the Imam—i.e., the *'ulamā'*. Obviously, this Majlis is none of the above; but it is a government by consultation, which is not obligatory for the Ja'farī sect to obey if it is headed by other than God or one of the other three groups." And: "In which school in Vienna or Paris was this inauspicious term, freedom, taught and in which store was this colorful merchandise found, that has been sold, like a beautifully designed but biting and deadly snake, to the poor Iranian people?" And: "Freedom and equality belong to their forged laws and imagined suppositions. Other religions and religious laws are not worth considering and are unworthy of Islam and the followers of Islam .... It is astonishing that by confusing the issue they spread the notion that the seekers of Islam are dictatorial; of course they must be dictatorial. Islam and every religion is autocratic."[24]

The conflicts become heated and the provocations of the Shaykh come to fruition. The bazaar merchants begin to think about closing down the bazaars. The association of guilds extends an invitation to the religious scholars and the ministers. The speaker of the session is Mīrzā Yaḥyā Dawlatābādī, who states: "Shaykh Faḍlallāh opposes neither the Majlis nor the Constitution; he is neither an opponent of the Constitution nor is he concerned about religion. Rather, he has an argument with his honorable colleagues who pay no attention to him and have supposed that he is dead. The Shaykh says: 'I claimed to be superior to you; it did not work out. I consented to be your ally; it did not happen. Now, I am satisfied to be your inferior, and still you will not take me into your game. After all, I am one of you, your colleague. You are sitting on that seat of power; sit a little closer and allow me to sit at the side.' "[25] Bihbahānī leaves the session in protest and the differences become deeper. The Shaykh dauntlessly engages in fighting *"mashrū'a"* (religious legitimacy) and joins Muḥammad 'Alī Shāh. The absolutist faction determines to put an end to the matter. They fire cannons at the Majlis, kill the liberals or torture and jail them.

Ṭabāṭabā'ī is arrested and then released to "go and reside in Daraka in Shemiran." And Bihbahānī is exiled to Kermanshah.

The reaction of the sources of emulation in Najaf to this national tragedy is astonishing and shows their views concerning the people's rights, national rule, and the government of the king protected by Islam. In a telegram, the three sources of emulation (Akhund Khurāsānī, Shaykh 'Abd Allāh Māzandarānī and Ḥājjī Mīrzā Khalīl) consider "cooperation with the opponents of the Constitution, no matter who they are, whether in high or low positions, to be aggression against the Muslims and the commoners [and against] this righteous principle, [and thus] belligerency against the Imam of the Age." This included the king, the courtiers, and the whole of the absolutist faction; and the rule regarding such belligerency is clear in the Qur'ān. However, in another telegram addressed to the Regent, Kāmrān Mīrzā, expressing disappointment regarding "the destruction and annihilation of the sacred National Assembly, the exile of Muslims, the bloodshed of, insults against and exiling of the grand religious leaders," they point out that they "are afraid for His Imperial Majesty." In another telegram to Mushīr al-Salṭana, the Prime Minister, they state: "We have no purpose but to protect the realm of Islam, the independence of the country, the survival of the Shi'ite monarchy, the elimination of injustice and the improvement of the conditions of the worshippers." Muḥammad 'Alī Shāh responds:

> When in amending the Constitution, the agents of corruption saw that the religion of the inhabitants of Iran is the Ja'farī rite and the law of Aḥmad, salutations to him, and that religious freedom would no longer be possible for them, through deception, conspiracies and contrivances . . . in the name of traditionalism and superstition, they disguised their intentions in the garb of Constitutionalism in order to temporarily prevent the public from religious mourning and certain charitable acts, which are the foundations of the sacred religion, and established the Bābī association and began to speak about the freedom of this group. When I realized that they might weaken the administration of the foundation of the Prophet's sacred religion, I found it necessary . . ., firstly for religion and secondly to preserve the monarchy, to prevent them.

The sources of emulation respond to "His Majesty, may God perpetuate his kingdom," express their sorrow at the traitors having left a poisonous effect on him, and consider "the protection of Islam and the independence of the Twelver Shi'ite government, may God strengthen it, in not deviating from the laws of the Constitution," hoping that "the mischief makers continue to allow His Majesty to nurture the religion and administer the country." The country is in the fever of revolution, and Tabriz is the vanguard of the movement. The sources of emulation continue to send telegrams, this time through the Prime Minister to the "sacred presence of His Majesty, whose kind treatment of his subjects is the favor God grants onto those subjects" and express their anxiety because the people "have begun to speak boldly in regards to the position of the monarchy" that "the position of the Islamic monarchy" has become a means "to destroy the foundations of religion," and about Azarbaijan, which is lost.[26]

Another group of religious scholars in Najaf explain and clarify Constitutionalism in a decree: "Within Islam and the firm injunctions of the Koran . . . there is no opposition to restricting government administration. What is meant by the National Consultative Assembly is a building prepared in which the prominent people of the nation can consult in regards to what is beneficial or harmful to the country. The existence of these two issues in the governing Islamic monarchy is in accordance with Islamic laws and in conformity with the injunctions of the Koran, not contrary to them, because the result is to restrict the absolute acceptance of a government of injustice and regulate the chaotic bureaucracy of the government so as to benefit rather than harm the Islamic country." In explaining freedom, it states: "What is meant by liberty is the freedom of the entire populace from any sort of uncontrolled domination and force . . . and this matter has no relationship to allowing debauchery and removing control from actions forbidden by religious law." In the Constitution, "all Islamic standards" have been observed and "that law is summed up in two areas: first, the control of government property and administration, with restrictions and regulations determined by the trustees of the nation; and secondly, consideration made in regards to the penalties, compensations and other punishments of the kind, which must be in accordance with determinations made in the sacred religious laws." In regards to the definition of Constitutionalism, the three sources of emulation in Najaf issued a decree as follows:

> Constitutionality and the freedom of Iran mean the government and the nation not deviating from the laws but conforming to special and general injunctions taken from the religion and based on the implementation of divine laws . . . and preservation of religious and national principles, prevention of what Islam prohibits, and the proliferation of justice . . . . In the second chapter of the Supplement to the Fundamental Law, which we signed earlier, the necessity of the opposition of the laws therein to religious injunctions has been clearly stated . . . and no person with corrupt intentions or a corrupter shall have the power, God forbid,

> to meddle in this affair and, by eliminating the laws and injunctions of the Ja'farī sect or by forging a law, to create atheism and heresy, in violation of the Constitution and the principle of Iranian Constitutionalism, thereby establishing autocracy in another cursed form by the most abominable of vile men.[27]

The words of the *'ulamā'*, which indicate their views about Constitutionalism, require no interpretation. In any case, Tehran is conquered, and the case of Shaykh Faḍl Allāh's life is concluded with his execution (July 1909). This statement is ascribed to him: "I was neither a supporter of autocracy nor was Sayyid 'Abd Allāh, a Constitutionalist, nor a Sayyid Muhammad. They opposed me and I opposed them."[28]

3. Constitutionalism and the Juristic Authority of the *'ulamā'*

Sayyid 'Abd Allāh enters Tehran victoriously. Dawlatābādī pays a visit to him and warns him against interfering in politics. He says: "You have no rival in the position of religious authority. It would be appropriate for you to regulate the administration of religious law without any sort of involvement in political affairs and to keep religious and civil laws separate."[29] But the Sayyid does not agree to give up his position of power and he, too, loses his life over leadership.

Dawlatābādī's warning about the separation of religious and secular judiciary must have touched a nerve. The issue was intimately bound with the professional interest of the *'ulamā'*, who considered judiciary office their legitimate monopoly as heirs to the Prophet and the Imams. This they had insisted upon during the deliberations on the Supplement to the Fundamental Law in 1907. From the very beginning, Akhūnd Khurāsānī had warned: "It is certain that their excellencies have so arranged and corrected the chapters of the Fundamental Law as to assure their agreement with the standards of the Sacred Law as regards the trials and punishments." In the draft of the fundamental law, the Judiciary was envisioned as an independent power. Two factions openly struggled over the issue. The pro- and anti-Constitutionalist *'ulamā'* were united in their view. Ṭabāṭabā'ī stated: "With the establishment of (secular) courts of the Judiciary, what will be left for the *'ulamā'* to do?" In Bihbahānī's view: "All the judiciary organization concerns the execution of the commands of the Sacred Law. The Judiciary has no business other than the execution of the laws and commands of the *sharī'a.*" Even Naṣr Allāh Taqavī, a member of the commission in charge of drafting the Supplement to the Fundamental Law, was the defender of the Sacred Law: "Making laws which are contrary to Islam and whatever abrogates the Sacred Law are clear infidelity (*kufr*). Bihbahānī filibustered the discussion. The Majlis Speaker, Iḥtishām al-Salṭana believed that "there should be no courts other than the courts of the Ministry of Justice, and the fully qualified *mujtahids* should serve in them and receive salaries." He sent a message to Ṭabāṭabā'ī: "Do you not remember we agreed that you should become a judge in the Judiciary and receive a monthly salary?"[30] Finally, according to Dawlatābādī, "the matter turned to wrangling and the Majlis broke up. The news reached the representatives of the *anjumans* who were roused against Āqā Sayyid 'Abd Allāh, and bad-mouthed him at great length. They were set to insult him, and pulled a gun to kill him.[31]

In the end, the *'ulamā'* resolved the issue through ambiguity and cursoriness—in other words, the legal ruse which was the means of reconciling the religious and secular government. This is reflected in the following articles of the Supplement to the Fundamental Law:

> Art. 27. The powers of the Realm are divided into three categories . . . .
> Second, the judicial power, by which is meant the determining of rights. This power belongs exclusively to the ecclesiastical tribunals in matters connected with the Sacred Law, and to the civil tribunals in matters connected with ordinary law . . . .
> Art. 71. The Supreme Ministry of Justice and the judicial tribunals are the places officially destined for the redress of public grievances, while judgements in all matters falling within the scope of the Sacred Law is vested in just *mujtahids* possessing the necessary qualifications.
> Art. 73. The establishment of civil tribunals depends on the authority of the Law, and no one, on any title or pretext, may establish any tribunal contrary to its provisions.
> Art. 75. In the whole Kingdom there shall be only one Court of Cassation for civil cases, and that in the capital; and this Court shall not deal with any case of first instance, except in cases in which Ministers are concerned.
> Art. 83. The appointment of the Public Prosecutor is within the competence of the King, supported by the approval of the religious judge.

Nevertheless, the *'ulamā'* remained unhappy about the concessions they had made in 1907, and even though they did not raise the issue again, it had made them cooler towards the reformers.

Returning now to the events of 1909, the Majlis elections are held and the Najaf sources of emulation write to the *'ulamā'* in Tehran to select the *mujtahids* to represent them.

> Since in accordance with Chapter Two of the Supplement to the Fundamental Law, in order to oversee that the laws discussed and votes cast are not contrary to religious laws, it has been officially determined that twenty just and knowledgeable *mujtahids* will be introduced, within the time required, to the honorable National Assembly, five of whom will be elected by a majority vote or lottery and recognized as members of the Majlis, and accepted or rejected in conformity with the contents of this chapter.

The Majlis is formed and the representatives take oaths before a committee of more than ten *mujtahids* invited to the Majlis. The position of Sayyid 'Abd Allāh increasingly solidifies. He imagines himself to be above the Majlis, the government, and the new-found constitutional system. He "writes a letter of reprimand to the Ministry of Justice" and threatens "the members of the court with chastisement and punishment," for they had summoned the Friday prayer leader because of the complaint of "a member of the weaker sex."[33]

The conflict between the revolutionaries and the moderates or Sayyid 'Abd Allāh and Taqīzāda escalates, and the sources of emulation in Najaf hasten to support Bihbahānī and send the following telegram to the Majlis:

> Because the opposition of the ideology of Sayyid Ḥasan Taqīzāda, which he has pursued separately, against the Islamic ideology of the country and laws of the holy *sharī'a*, is proven to him and the prominent people and his corrupt secrets have been revealed, hence, he is fully dismissed from membership in the sacred National Assembly and of being worthy of the trust of the public that is necessary for that lofty position and is legally and religiously removed from office .... And his exile from Iran is immediately necessary and the slightest forbearance and negligence is prohibited and is considered enmity with the Lord of the Sacred Law.... In his place, choose a religious, patriotic, nationalist trustworthy person of the proper ideology, identify him as a corrupter and being corrupt in the country. Also, notify the brave people of Azarbaijan and other provincial and state assemblies of this divine decree.... Anyone who would cooperate with him will also be subject to the same decree.[34]

This statement clearly shows the views of the gentlemen about the constitutionality of the system of national sovereignty, on the one hand, and the solidification and verification of their own rank and position, on the other. They consider themselves above the Constitution, the National Assembly, and even the people. The dismissal of the Majlis representative by a religious authority did not have any legal basis, and was in fact contrary to Article 12 of the Constitution. This Article of the Constitution endorses the principle of parliamentary immunity; but the "guardian jurist" who does not consider himself to be bound to obey the Constitution and the Majlis, not only issues a decree of excommunication, heresy, and, consequently, the dismissal of the Majlis representative, but also prevents him from "interfering in the affairs of the country and nation," issues a decree for his exile from Iran, instructs the authorities to select another person in "his place," identifies him as a "corrupter of and corrupt in the country," and states that "anyone who cooperates with him is subject to the same decree" and that the decree is a "divine decree."[35]

The murder of Bihbahānī and the dismissal of Taqīzāda from the Majlis creates relative calm, but the events and changes that occur in the country worry the *marāji'*, who write to the Regent, complaining of the reporting of the public appearance of women without the veil in a Tabriz newspaper and requesting the observance of Article 2 of the Supplement to the Fundamental Law: the purge from the press of all that is in opposition to the Sacred Law and the purging of the schools and their syllabi of all un-Islamic elements. As regards the law of the Judiciary,

> absolute care is necessary so that. . . [it is] established on the basis of the facts and truth of the manifestation of justice and safeguarding against injustice, in accordance with the Sacred Law. The position of religious magistrate, which is a divine appointment. . . must fully conform to the principles of the sacred Ja'farī religion . . . and rulings issued must be influenced by and subject to the injunctions of the illuminated Sacred Law . . . and must preserve the unity of all the noble and illustrious *'ulamā'* and the whole nation as it should be.[36]

What the gentlemen have stated as the elimination of "prohibited acts" is what appears on the surface. The fact is that they have just realized the dangers of "freedom" and "civil legal government." The "democratic ideology" is declared corrupt because its doctrine specifies the "equality of all members of the nation before the government and the law, regardless of race, religion, or nationality," the "complete separation of political power from religious power," and the administration and supervision of the government over "all religious endowments."[37]

Certain directives are given in regards to the Ministry of Justice, because the "law of the principles of trials" is being discussed in the Majlis and the high-ranking religious scholars have risen in strong opposition to it. Sayyid Ḥasan Mudarris, who is "the active and notable member of the *'ulamā'* committee," opposes the legislative bill presented by the Minister of Justice, Mushīr al-Dawla Pīrniya, to the Majlis. Mudarris is more lucid than the rest of the committee. He is a political element, intelligent and prudent. His presence in the Majlis is constructive, and in grave situations, he is a mediator and arbitrator between the two factions. He insists on adding his proposal, which includes eight articles, to the law. In this proposal, disputes are divided into three kinds: first, "religious matters, such as conflicts concerning marriage, divorce, kinship, endowments, ownership, appointment of guardians, bankruptcy ruling and legal disputes about which the injunctions of the *'ulamā'* differ in regards to the principle of the ruling. In such disputes, the religious magistrate alone should investigate the matter. Secondly, civil matters, such as disputes concerning government taxes and concessions, to be investigated by the Ministry of Justice courts. Thirdly, common matters, that is, matters other than religious and civil issues, provided there is no doubt whether it is a religious or civil matter, must be referred to the religious courts. In such cases, too, if both parties to the dispute first consent to investigation by a Ministry of Justice court, the court will do so, otherwise, it must be referred to religious courts." In another article, the proposal is made that "in other than religious matters, the consent of both parties in the trial is required for investigation by the Ministry of Justice and without their consent, the Ministry of Justice court has no right to investigate and must refer the case to the religious court."[38]

When discussing the statute of limitations, the religious group rose up in opposition. They said that the statute of limitations would not repeal the commitment and it is not religiously legal to repeal someone's right with a statute of limitations. The supporters would respond that the statute of limitations would not repeal someone's right, rather, it would only prevent the hearing of a claim, and, therefore, the claim is repealed. Mudarris mediated and, addressing the *'ulamā'*, reasoned fallaciously: "Gentlemen, the civil courts consider themselves competent only for a limited period of time. After the passage of this period, the religious courts are competent to investigate the dispute" (quoted in paraphrase). Mushīr al-Dawla and other progressives wanted the new legislation to be established in any form. For this reason, on the one hand, with the help of Mudarris with religious justifications and trickery, they legitimized the legislative proposals; but, on the other hand, they had to yield to Mudarris. Hence, both the law of the principles of trials was ratified together with the eight articles proposed by Mudarris. The religious court was established alongside the civil courts, and one of the *mujtahids* (Sayyid Muḥammad Yazdī) was selected to head the court, with the approval of the *'ulamā'*.

The issue of the finality of religious rules (*aḥkām*) created certain problems. The rulings of the civil courts could be appealed and overturned; therefore, religious rulings had an advantage over civil ones. This caused some discontent. The sources of emulation waited in expectation, and Akhūnd Khurāsānī sent a bill to the Majlis as follows: "Religious disputes must be referred to the honorable *mujtahids* for ruling. In regards to the rulings of the *mujtahids*, no one has the right to appeal or to have a ruling overturned. Appeals and overturning concern trials in the Ministry of Justice and arbitration trials." The Majlis wrote the following response:

> It has been stated that, according to Article 27 of the Constitution, the settling of religious disputes is conferred on the religious courts of the special just *mujtahids* and that other political disputes in the country are conferred on the civil courts. Now it is argued in your illuminated presence that the former arrangement and that article of the Constitution are viewed practically, and that unqualified individuals have taken charge of disputes and the courts of appeal arrogate to themselves the right to overule the verdicts issued by the *mujtahids* whose ruling is binding. In response, the National Consultative Assembly informs your honor: Thus far, no deviation has occurred from the purport of Article 27 and others of the Constitution and as it has been stated in the aforementioned article, religious disputes shall be referred to the courts of the just *mujtahids*, and the verdicts issued by the religious courts are considered decisive and final and shall not be referred to courts of appeal or overturned.[39]

The presence of religious jurists in subsequent sessions of the Majlis as representatives and not "religious overseers," and in religious courts, was solidified and verified. In regard to the failure to implement Article 2 of the Supplement to the Fundamental Law, the *mujtahids* were not concerned, because supervision continued to take place. Sayyid Ḥasan Mudarris was present in the majority of the committees that devised the laws and played a valuable role in new Iranian legislation. In the transitional laws of the penal courts, ratified in Ramaḍān 1330 (August-September 1912), the structure of religious courts was preserved; and concerning the adjudication procedures of these courts, they said: "The clear religious requirements, which are the standards for religious judgement, are the same requirements that have been established in the Sacred Law." (Legislative note following Article 247)

4. Conclusion

The recognition of the juristic authority of the *'ulamā'* and the unquestionable validity of the *sharī'a* in the legislation of the early constitutional period had lasting consequences that extend into the period of modernization of the state under Riḍā Shāh Pahlavī. In Day 1304/December 1925-January 1926, at the dawn of Pahlavi rule, the Fifth Majlis passed the Law of General Punishments. Its first Article states: "The punishment specified in this Law was established with a view to the maintenance national order and are to be implemented in courts of the Ministry of Justice. Offenses discovered and prosecuted in accordance with the Islamic rules are subject to the punishments (*ḥudūd va ta'zizāt*) decreed by the Sacred Law." This law, giving legal legitimacy to the jurisdiction of the Sacred Law and of the clerical authorities was in effect for nearly fifty years, until 1352/1973-4, and a portion of it is still on the books. In order to evade the Islamic punishment decreed for theft, Article 222 of the same law states: "When theft does not meet all the conditions specified in the Sacred Law, but meets the following five conditions, the punishment for the offender is life imprisonment . . . . " What is implied in this article is that if theft does meet the conditions specified by the Sacred Law, the punishment is accordingly the amputation of the fingers. In the area of penal statutes of limitations, acts for which there is no specific Islamic punishment (*ḥadd*) are exempted (Article 279).

Clerical authorities gradually lost their influence in the legal sphere. In 1310/1931, the jurisdiction of the religious courts was restricted to "litigations concerning to the principle of marriage and divorce." But the legal authority of the Sacred Law and the *'ulamā'* was never terminated in principle. Even in the Law of Civil Investigation of 1318/1939, interest was referred to as "damages in delay of payment," a legal ruse to silence the *mujtahids*. In practice, however, the religious courts eventually ceased to exist in the Pahlavi era. But this is another chapter in the history of clerical authority in Shi'ite Iran.

Notes

1. Muḥammad Mahdī Sharīf Kāshānī, *Vāqi'āt-i Ittifāqiyya dar Rūzigār* (Tehran, 1362/1983-4), vol. 1, p. 19.

2. F. Ādamiyyat, *Ideology-yi Nahḍat-i Mashrūṭiyyat-i Īrān* (Tehran, 1355/1976), p. 153.

3. Sharīf Kāshānī, op. cit., vol. 1, pp. 22-24.

4. Ibid., pp. 27, 34-35.

5. Ādamiyyat, op. cit., p. 153.

6. Sharīf Kāshānī, op. cit., vol. 1, pp. 50-51.

7. Ibid., p. 61.

8. Yaḥyā Dawlatābādī, *Ḥayāt-i Yaḥyā*, 3d ed. (Tehran, n.d. [1361/1982-3]), vol. 2, pp. 52ff.

9. Ādamiyyat, op. cit., pp. 167, 169-70.

10. M. Nāẓim al-Islām Kirmānī, *Tārīkh-i Bīdārī-yi Īrāniān*, 3d ed., (Tehran, 1346/1967), pt. 1, pp. 306-7.

11. Ibid., p. 321.

12. Dawlatābādī, op. cit., vol. 2, p. 82.

13. Ādamiyyat, op. cit., p. 413.

14. Ibid., p. 412.

15. M. S. Ivanov, *Inqilāb-i Mashrūṭiyyat-i Īrān*, Persian trans. by Kāẓim Anṣārī, 3d ed. (Tehran, 1357/1978-9), p. 31.

16. Cited in Ādamiyyat, op. cit., p. 416.

17. The translations of the articles of the Supplement to the Fundamental Law are taken from E. G. Browne, *The Persian Revolution* (London: Cass 1966 [1910]), pp. 372-84, with slight modification.

18. Ādamiyyat, op. cit., p. 416.

19. Ādamiyyat, op. cit., p. 422.

20. Nā'īnī, *Tanbīh al-Milla*, cited in Ādamiyyat, op. cit., pp. 233-34.

21. Ibid., p. 242.

22. Dawlatābādī, op. cit., vol. 2, pp. 106-7.

23. Shaykh Faḍl Allāh Nūrī, *Lavāyiḥ*, Ismā'īl Riḍvānī, ed. (Tehran, 1362/1983-84), pp. 27-47.

24. Ibid., pp. 51, 61-62, 65.

25. Dawlatābādī, op. cit., vol. 2, p. 131.

26. Sharīf Kāshānī, op. cit., vol. 1, pp. 204, 209, 222-23, 245.

27. Ibid., pp. 249-52.

28. M.-Q. Hidāyat, Mukhbir al-Salṭana, *Guzārish-i Īrān*, vol. 4, p. 107.

29. Dawlatābādī, op. cit., vol. 3, p. 128.

30. Ādamiyyat, op. cit., p. 418.

31. Dawlatābādī, op. cit., vol. 2, p. 150.

32. Sharīf Kāshānī, op. cit., vol. 2, pp. 444-45.

33. Ibid., 522.

34. Ibid., p. 535.

35. The rank and position of the sources of emulation during the Constitutional period is above all branches of the government and even the wishes and votes of the people. Is the *vilāyat-i faqīh* anything else?

36. Sharīf Kāshānī, op. cit., vol. 3, pp. 599-600.

37. Ibid., pp. 414-16.

38. Ṣadr al-Ashrāf, *Khaṭirātī az Dādgustarī*, cited in M. I. Bāstānī Pārīzī, *Talāsh-i Āzādī* (1347/1968), pp. 515-16.

39. Sharīf Kāshānī, op. cit., vol. 3, p. 645.

CHAPTER 7

Sharī'at Sangalajī: A Reformist Theologian of the Riḍā Shāh Period

YANN RICHARD
Translated by Kathryn Arjomand

A number of recent studies on the religious history of modern Iran present the reign of Riḍā Shāh as a period of unmitigated, stifling repression for the Shi'ite men of religion.[1] However, a more careful reading of the polemical literature published in abundance after the fall of the "tyrant" in 1941 shows that, during this period, the traditional *'ulamā'* knew how to bend their heads to let the storm pass, while at the same time some audacious thinkers attempted to reconcile the intellectual modernism with a renewal of religion. These few reformers were perhaps isolated inside the clerical establishment, but their influence on the new elites of the country was nevertheless not negligible.

My attempt here is not to deny the repressive methods used by the Pahlavī regime to weaken the social power of the *'ulamā'*, but to show through a case study that the situation was not as clear as in Kemalist Turkey. Thus it will be easier to understand why Pahlavī secularism failed to reduce resistance to change among religious circles in Iran. A reformist tendency similar to the Egyptian *Salafīya* can be discerned in Iran, a tendency which identified no more with the traditional *'ulamā'* than with the secular political power.

A close study of Iran after 1941 shows the advent of religious groups on the political scene, both as a regular political force, such as the Islamic wing of the National Front around Āyatallāh Kāshāni, and as extremist activists, such as the Fidā'iyān-i Islām (Devotees of Islam). These groups could not have appeared without some support among the religious circles and the capacity for ideological dispute which only a strong institution can provide.

In the religious literature of the war period, Khumeini's famous book, *Kashf al-asrār* (The Unveiling of the Secrets), in which he refutes a critique of the clerical establishment by 'Alī-Akbar Ḥakamīzāda, reflects some of the controversial issues of that time. Hakamīzāda had discarded his clerical garb and was known in Qumm in the mid-1930s as the editor of the modernist journal *Humāyūn*. In *Asrār-i hizār sāla* (Secrets of a Thousand Years), a pamphlet published in 1943, he took up the subject of modernism in a condensed form, and attacked the *'ulamā'* one last time. He asked them for an accounting of the superstitious beliefs which they had fostered among the believers in order to perpetuate their own power: belief in the intercession of the Prophet and his descendants (*imām, imāmzāda, sayyid*); affirmation of the charisma of the *'ulamā'*; non-recognition of the full legitimacy of temporal power and existing institutions, and of progress and science, and so forth.[2]

This pamphlet was published by the press of Aḥmad Kasravī, the historian and anticlerical proponent of rationalistic purification of religion. At the end of the pamphlet, Ḥakamīzāda directly challenged his former colleagues of Qumm to respond to some precise questions on (1) the value of prayers for intercession made at the tombs of the Imams and the Prophet; (2) the value of bibliomancy and other oracles (*istikhāra*); (3) the actual place of Imamat among the beliefs, as God had not judged it necessary to speak of it in the Qur'ān; (4) the Traditions (*ḥadīth*) which maintain that pilgrimage and mourning ceremonies are more worthy than martyrdom; (5) the limits of the power of the doctor of jurisprudence (*mujtahid*) as representative of the Hidden Imam; (6) the effort of the *'ulamā'* to be independent and free in their preachings; (7) the legitimacy of secular power; (8) the legitimacy of taxes imposed by the secular state; (9) the legitimacy of laws written by men; (10) the justification for the imposition, universally and without change, of the Sacred Law, which was itself in part abrogated during the years of its revelation; (11) the explanation as to why God, after having created the best of His creatures, forbade him the use of his intelligence to understand His commandments; (12) the Traditions which are incompatible with human reason; and (13) the reason for the current lack of interest in religion.

The aggressive tone of Ḥakamīzāda, in a period when there was no censorship to stand in the way of response, gave rise to a vigorous polemical literature from the *'ulamā'*.[3] Khumeinī, who then taught philosophy in Qumm, was solicited during one of his trips to Tehran by a group of bazaar merchants to give a definitive and complete response to Ḥakamīzāda. The result was *The Unveiling of the Secrets.* In this large volume, which refutes point by point the objections of *Secrets of a Thousand Years*, Khumeinī broadens the debate and dismantles the tinselly myth of modernism copied from the West and imposed by the dictatorship of Riḍā Shāh. He names specifically only a few of those he combats: Wahhābism, the extremist Sunni doctrine and traditional enemy of Shi'ism, and its "idolatrous" devotions; a Bahā'ī writer, Mirzā Abu'l-Faḍl Gulpāyigānī[4]; Kasravism, which inspired Ḥakamīzāda (though neither Kasravī nor Ḥakamīzāda is mentioned even once, both are easily recognizable). Finally, at least four times[5] Khumeinī explicitly attacks Sharī'at Sangalajī.

As I propose to demonstrate, Sangalajī was the most dangerous of the opponents for Khumeinī. First, he was not vulnerable through any allegiance to the politics of Riḍā Shāh or ideological compromise (like Ḥakamīzāda). He never was an apostate (like Kasravī). Above all, though he was influenced by Wahhābism, Sangalajī reaffirmed his adherence to the Shi'ite community and put his competence as an extremely cultivated doctor of the faith to the defense of Islam against Westernization and materialism, ceaselessly returning to the Qur'ān.

The Life of Sangalajī[6]

Mīrzā Riḍā Qulī was born in 1890 (according to some accounts, 1892) in Sangalaj (Tehran), into a noble family that had served the Qājārs. His grandfather, of the same name,[7] had studied theology because, being blind, he could not remain in the service of the state. The father of our Riḍā Qulī, Shaykh Ḥasan Sangalajī (d. 1931), continued in the same religious profession and made a name for himself in Tehran. He seems to have supported the fundamentalist resistance of Shaykh Faḍlallāh Nūrī, who was his cousin,[8] against the Constitutionalists in 1908-9 without having played an important role. The two men of religion were neighbors in the Sangalaj quarter, a natural hollow in the center of Tehran. After the victory of the revolutionaries, Shaykh Ḥasan sent his children to propose to Shaykh Faḍlallāh that he take refuge at their house. Upon the execution of Shaykh Faḍlallāh, Shaykh Ḥasan preferred to remove himself from the scene by departing on *Ḥajj*.

Sharī'at Sangalajī received a solid, traditional training in theology in Tehran. He followed the teaching of Shaykh Muhammad-Riḍā Tunkābunī (d. 1965, the father of Muhammad-Taqī Falsafī), and was the student of Shaykh 'Abd al-Nabī Mujtahid Nūrī in Islamic jurisprudence (*fiqh*), of Mīrzā Ḥasan Kirmānshāhī in philosophy (*ḥikmat*), of

Shaykh 'Alī Mutakallim Nūrī in scholastic theology (*kalām*), and of Mīrzā Hāshim Ishkivarī in mysticism (*'irfān*). Little is known about the four years he spent in Najaf (1917 to 1921) with his brother Āqā Muhammad-Mahdī. Iraq was then the arena of violent events, connected to the English attempt to establish a protectorate and the 1920 revolt led by the Shi'a. There is no evidence that Sharī'at took an active part in this revolt.

In Najaf, Riḍā-Qulī Sangalajī is said to have written his first book, whose title is not known. The book was welcomed by the Āyatallāh Āqā Sayyid Muhammad-Kāẓim Yazdī, a great Shi'ite theologian of that time, who gave its author the surname of Sharī'at, "sacred law."[9]

When he returned to Tehran, Sharī'at took his place at the family mosque of Sangalaj, where he had begun to preach before his trip to Iraq. He was very quickly solicited by the authorities, especially after Riḍā Khān became Riḍā Shāh and the number of *'ulamā'* with whom the latter could have "normal" relations shrank.

It was at Sangalaj before their stay in Iraq that Ḥasan Sangalajī and his eldest son met the proud Riḍā Khān, then an officer of the Cossack Brigade. In 1917, Sharī'at and his father reportedly performed together the marriage ceremony of Riḍā Khān and Tāj al-Mulūk, the daughter of a fellow Cossack officer who was to become the mother of Muhammad-Riḍā and the other Pahlavī princes. Despite his distance from any political movement and his obvious lack of worldly ambition, it seems that Sharī'at all his life kept confident relations with the new regime established by Riḍā Pahlavī.

This indicates the distance between Sangalajī and most of his fellow clerics. It is well known that the authoritarian measures taken by Riḍā Shāh to accelerate secularization—notably, in the areas of education, justice, compulsory military service and dress codes—angered the men of religion. When he needed the support of the *'ulamā'*, especially after the attempt to establish a republic, Riḍā Shāh had cultivated the image of himself as a pious man. But he quickly belied this image. Thus, for example, he lost the sympathy of Abu'l-Qāsim Kāshānī. The only high-ranking theologian who kept courteous and mutually deferential relations with the founder of the new dynasty was Mīrzā Muhammad Husayn Nā'īnī (d. 1936), who lived in Najaf—where he could pretend not to notice certain conflicts.[10] Riḍā Shāh even occasionally considered Nā'īnī as his *marja'-i taqlīd*. In some instances, the tension resulting from the politics of "modernization" could be temporarily defused. Accomodating themselves to an uncomfortable situation, the *'ulamā'* preserved their most vital interests. Shaykh 'Abd al-Karīm Hā'irī Yazdī (d. 1937) kept silent even when certain issues erupted into open confrontation in order to set forth his task of reorganizing the religious center of Qumm.[11]

Several members of the new regime regularly met Sangalajī, such as the Minister of Justice 'Alī Akbar Dāvar, his disciple and student. It is worth noting that Dāvar was charged with drafting the Iranian civil code. Sharī'at told him to systematize the classic works on Shi'ite law, such as *al-Lum'at al-Dimashqīya* of Shamsuddin 'Āmili, the First Martyr (executed in 1380), in order to extract the "Islamic civil law." This was, by and large, accomplished. Dāvar tried to draw Sangalajī closer into official functions; he planned to create for him the post of President of the High Court of Justice. But Sangalajī, quoting to him the verse of Hāfiẓ,

> Go lay your nets for a different bird
> For the nest of the phoenix hangs far too high[12]

declined this offer which did not correspond to his real preoccupations. It is said that Sangalajī never in all his life accepted gifts offered him by authorities or believers, not even in the form of revenues from religious endowments. Certainly he lived austerely and drew his income only from his private teaching. His reputation for integrity attracted to Sangalajī many intellectuals who mistrusted the traditional *'ulamā'*.

I have been able to collect the testimony of several of Sharī'at Sangalajī's "disciples" who were also drawn, in the same period, to the group of Dr. Taqī Irāni (the famous "53" marxists imprisoned in 1937) or to Aḥmad Kasravī. Although discretion is necessary in naming the surviving disciples among Sangalajī's regular audience, we can cite men such as the following:

Asadallāh Rū'īn Mubashshirī, lawyer and philosopher, militant for human rights, who became Minister of Justice in Bāzargān's cabinet (1979). Mubashshirī edited and published a number of Sangalajī's lectures. He once organized a meeting between Sangalajī and Aḥmad Kasravī. (The conversation finished abruptly on account of the radicalism of Kasravī, who stalked out of the house as his interlocutor refused to ignore the differences between Sunnis and Shi'ites).

'Abd al-Vahhāb Tunkābunī. This intrepid cleric (d. 1360/1981) published a large volume that publicized Sharī'at's ideas on the End of Time, and he continued until his death to defend the same ideas.[13]

Muhammad-Javād Mashkūr, scholar with a broad range of scientific achievement, particularly in linguistics and heresiology. Nephew of Sharī'at, he is the only one of his circle to have continued scholarly work on Islam, and he teaches at Tehran University.

Muhammad-Taqī Falsafī, famous religious preacher who took his first lessons in rhetoric with Sangalajī. Falsafī became a quasi-official personality in the Islamic Republic, despite his collaboration with the Shāh's regime in the 1950s.

Husayn-Qulī Musta'ān, famous journalist and editorialist of the newspaper *Ettelā'āt*, who delivered a eulogy for Sharī'at on Radio Tehran several days after his death.

'Ali-Pashā Ṣāliḥ, secretary to the Ambassador of the United States (his brother Allāhyār Ṣāliḥ was later named Ambassador to Washington by Musaddiq). During the war, when Sangalajī was denounced as pro-Nazi and the Soviets wanted to arrest him, Ṣāliḥ persuaded the American Ambassador, George Allen, to intervene on Sangalajī's behalf. 'Alī-Pashā Ṣāliḥ is also a translator into Persian of Browne's *Literary History of Persia.*

Aḥmad Fardīd, a philosopher who was later to become the guiding spirit behind Āl-i Aḥmad and his critique of the West (in his well-known *Qarbzadegi*, "Westoxication").

A number of important intellectuals followed the teachings of Sharī'at, some of whom went on to take widely divergent ideological positions. But despite the ideological flexibility of his influence, we must keep in mind that Sharī'at presented for most of his listeners a dynamic view of Islam which was, at least on some points, in conflict with the official Islam of the clerical establishment.

Sangalajī's audience was sufficiently large and eager that the Thursday night meeting in his Sangalaj mosque became regular and quasi-ritualistic. The mosque was enlarged in 1931, and Sharī'at gave it the name of *Dāruttablīgh-i Islāmī* (Center for Islamic Propaganda, a name later copied in Qumm by Āyatallāh Sharī'at-Madārī). In 1938, when Riḍā Shāh razed the insalubrious quarter of Sangalaj and rebuilt it as a large public garden (*Pārk-i Shahr*), Sharī'at obtained a plot of land on Farhang Avenue where he constructed a mosque in modern style, imitating the Wahhābī mosque without minaret. In the main hall, a gallery of mid-height allowed women to attend the meetings without mixing with the men. Two or three hundred people in all could meet there. It is in the crypt of this mosque that Sharī'at was later buried, his grave commemorated merely with an engraved marble wall plaque. Sharī'at's younger brother, Muḥammad (d. 1981; he was a professor of *fiqh* at the Faculty of Law of Tehran University), added to the south part of the yard a new, styleless building flanked by two minarets, which he named the Arch of the Qur'ān (*Ravvāq-i Qur'ān*). Today, in 1986, a local revolutionary committee occupies the mosque. They have established headquarters in Sharī'at's funeral chamber, where posters now cover the inscriptions. Only the faience tiles, visible from the street, indicate *"Dāruttabligh-i Islāmī."*

A figure respected by the intelligentsia, Sangalajī was invited in 1932 to meet with the Indian poet and philosopher Rabindranath Tagore when the latter, returning from Europe, came to Iran to raise funds for his Bengali university.[14] The meeting was organized as a formal occasion in the presence of a number of establishment intellectuals. However, the debate ended rather abruptly, and the two men parted without understanding each other's position.

Sangalajī's popularity and impartiality overshadowed his colleagues, who were already irritated by the bold doctrinal positions of this freelance theologian. Contrary to Ḥakamīzāda and Kasravī, Sangalajī invoked strictly religious arguments, using numerous Qur'ānic citations, against the Shi'ite *'ulamā'*. During his lifetime, he suffered anathematization (*takfīr*). Dr. Mubashshirī relates that he once invited Sangalajī to his home, but his mother refused to prepare a meal when she learned who her guest would be; she left the house, and upon her return purified or threw out everything that could have been soiled by this "enemy of Islam." Sharī'at himself affirms in the introduction to one of his books that his enemies tried to kill him.

> Having suffered a great deal, I understood the meaning of the phrase, "happiness comes through the pain one endures." Indeed, I was envied by my colleagues for that which God bestowed on me: an inclination for scholarship and the practice of virtues. This is why they sought by every means to torture me; they slandered me, insulted me, more than Yazīd and Shāmir [Shimr] had been slandered and insulted. And on two occasions they sought to kill me, but the Lord protected me.[15]

(After the fall of Riḍā Shāh in 1941, a certain Shaykh Qulī, employee in the military arsenal, was sent by a cleric hostile to Sharī'at to kill the latter in his mosque. The would-be assassin reportedly repented when he heard Sharī'at speaking on Islam.)[16]

In January and February 1938, Sangalajī performed the rites of pilgrimage to Mecca. At Najaf, on his way, he was repelled by the filthiness of the town. He wrote his impressions of the journey in a copy of a book by Muhammad-Husayn Āl-i Kāshif al-Ghiṭā' which he received from the author at that time, and beseeched Muslims to respect the rules of cleanliness and hygiene which are in the spirit of the Qur'ān (ritual purity), instead of spending their lives in sterile discourse.

In those last years of his life, Sharī'at saw the political liberation created in Iran by the invasion of the British and Soviet armies and the collapse of Riḍā Shāh's dictatorship. The new, twenty-one-year-old Shāh, Muḥammad-Riḍā Pahlavī, summoned Sangalajī and his two brothers to the palace in order to consult with them. Sharī'at reportedly told the sovereign to take a lesson from the example of his father, who would not have been obliged to abdicate had he been loved by his people.

Sharī'at had a difficult life. In his fifties, much weakened, he was carried away by typhus (on 15 Day 1322/9 Muḥarram 1363 [*tāsū'ā*]/6 January 1944). Two years later, his younger brother Āqā Muḥammad-Mahdī, professor of Kalām in the Faculty of Theology at Tehran University, fell victim to the same epidemic. However, the real death of Sharī'at without doubt consists in the silence with which he has come to be treated: aside from a few articles in newspapers and a commemorative volume edited in 1945, his name is little by little being erased from history. The *'ulamā'* have never accepted that this reformist theologian be remembered as one who played a role in the religious consciousness of modern Iranians.

Sangalajī's Thought

Three principal themes run through Sharī'at's thought:

(i) the necessity of a more rigorous return to monotheism, eliminating the belief in sacred intermediaries such as the Imams and their descendents;

(ii) accordingly, the suppression of later beliefs which encumber Shi'ite dogma, such as the belief in the Return of the Hidden Imam before the Last Judgment (*raj'at*); and

(iii) the condemnation of superstitious practices which derive from man's natural tendency to return to polytheism, and which prevent Muslims from confronting in a positive way the Western World.

Monotheism

This is the central message of Islam, and it is not surprising that modern Muslim reformists have insisted on the necessity of stripping away the nonessentials of their religion in order to recapture the original inspiration of the faith. The problem is less simple in Shi'ism than in Sunnism, given the quasi-supernatural status conferred on the Imams, particularly the Twelfth Imam, whose Occultation is considered miraculous and quasi-divine.

Sangalajī devoted an entire book to the problem of monotheism. In this treatise, entitled *Tawḥīd-i 'ibādāt—Yaktāparastī* (The Unity of Worship—Monotheism), he attacks different forms of associationism (*shirk*): the cult of saints (*imāmzāda*); superstitions concerning rings and precious stones (he writes that he had only recently disengaged himself from these during his journey to Mecca); the "sacred power" attributed to trees, rocks, and so forth; sacrifice offered to other than God (in the same way that, for Christians, Jesus offered himself for the sins of men, so bad Shi'ites believe that Ḥusayn died to wipe clean their faults); vows other than for God, and prayers and supplications addressed to other than God; astrology; portents, and so on.[17]

The bulk of the book is devoted to the subject of the extremist cult of prophets and saints, who often are deified as Christ is by Christians. According to Sangalajī, to set up such intermediaries between the Creator and the created—asking them to defend us, nourish us, heal us, etc.—is to take other than God as *valī* (protector); this is an impiety. The saints must not be considered as ministers who transmit to the sovereign the requests of the humble, who have access only to them. God is closer to the believers than their jugular vein (Qur'ān 50: 15-16), and He knows all the recesses of their hearts. He does not need informers or intermediaries. He must not be compared to bad kings! Prophets and saints are sent to us as instructors, not as intercessors. For some, recourse to these intercessors has gone to the point of their attributing to the latter a particle of divinity (*rubūbīyat*), before which they prostrate themselves. This belief in intercession (*shifā'at*) originates in pre-Islamic paganism and in religions of priests. It is contradictory to the mission of the Prophet. It is as if one said to a child, "You must learn your lessons at school but do not be afraid of the master; if you do not learn well, I will intercede for you."[18] This ignores the fact that intercession is ineffectual without realization of the merits of which we are capable, and without the accord of God.

A second major theme in Sangalajī's thought is the importance of the Qur'ān, which is the subject of his second book, *Kilīd-i fahm-i Qur'ān* (Key to the Understanding of the Qur'ān).[19] The work is not a "commentary" on the Holy Book, but an analytic introduction to it written, says Sangalajī, to rectify certain errors. As he puts it in the introduction, it was through constant immersion in the Qur'ān that he eventually had the sense that God granted him the power to comprehend it.

First, without much difficulty, Sangalajī refutes the widely held opinion that the Qur'ān had been tampered with by the Sunnis; in fact, the canonical version edited by 'Uthmān was accepted by 'Alī and the Shi'ite doctors. Those who dispute the authority of the Qur'ān are sowers of dissension in the community.[20] Moreover, it is necessary to proceed from the principle that the Qur'ān, revealed for the guidance of man, is comprehensible. The simplistic explanations of those who hold that the Qur'ān would not be respected if fully understood must be rejected. In order to understand the Qur'ān, we must know how it was revealed—the history and civilization of the Arabs at the time of the Prophet. What we need to know is clearly expressed in the text itself. This certainly consists not in positive knowledge, as do microbiology or astronomy, but in the ethical foundations of belief. He writes

> The Koran makes man righteous. Its purpose is to set people on the right path: when they attain this, everything they do will be just and all knowledge they develop will be good.[21]

Sangalajī then develops his conception of the "inner" and the "apparent" meaning (*bāṭin/ẓāhir*) in the Qur'ān. The "inner" meaning is not "what the esoterists have said, which is contrary to reason and logic and therefore blasphemous," says Sangalajī.[22] Rather, it is the "intended" meaning and the very object of the Qur'ān itself, to which we come after eliminating the meanings induced by our passions. Finally, each man must practice the effort of interpretation (*ijtihād*), for he must understand the divine commandments and apply them in the concrete context of his own life. Imitation is a vice to be rejected.

Above all, Sangalajī writes, the fundamental principles concerning the Creator can be found in the Qur'ān: divine unity, the path that leads to God, and knowledge of man's spiritual destination (*ma'ād*). We also find there information concerning the Saints and evil men (Pharaoh, Korah [*Qārun*], the people of Loth, etc.), rules governing eating, marriage, the organization of society, and so on which are necessary for the well-being of believers; information about everything that is instrumental to preserving our bond with God, our reason (*'aql*), and life for ourselves and for future generations.

The Qur'ān, according to Sharī'at, addresses the masses and invites them to improve themselves morally. When the masses are morally sound, they produce doctors, philosophers, and kings who are just and good. The philosophers, says Sangalajī, think it the opposite: they want to create a perfect elite believing that the masses would improve as a result.

The Qur'ān is truly a guide to the understanding of the reality of things, a guide for learning to think, says Sangalajī. It opposes man's congenital laziness, the failure to utilize the intelligence, and therefore opposes "imitation" (*taqlīd*), that is, the simple repetition of the thoughts and actions of the ancients. The entire Qur'ān, says Sangalajī, is a paean to the intelligence and to knowledge. Consider, then, the priests who have always turned men from science, claiming that it conceals God. Even Rūmī once praised ignorance and simplicity of mind;[23] great men can make great mistakes, this is why we need the Infallibles! As for the sclerosed doctors of law (*mutafaqqiha-ye jāmid*), they have diverted Muslims from speculative and philosophical studies and natural history; it is they who have led us into our present state of decadence.[24]

Broadly speaking, imitation (*taqlīd*) impedes the functioning of reason.[25] Man inclines naturally towards imitation: a son imitates his father, who likes the son to repeat what he himself has done. We confer upon imitation a sacred virtue which it does not have. And imitation is a difficult habit to give up; as the mind loses youthful agility and becomes dull with age, it is attracted all the more to imitation. The elderly man has invented justifications for his behavior all his life, and he is not prepared to reorient himself. Sedentary people who have little contact with those around them are even less touched by change than others. All this impedes freedom of thought, just as the passions (*havā*) do. Now Islam liberates us from obedience to all that is not God, and makes all men equal; no one is perfect and, therefore, no one is a model to be imitated.

The Qur'ān praises science and the *'ulamā'*. In order to prevent sluggishness of mind, it commands Muslims to meet each year for the pilgrimage to Mecca, and forbids obedience to the ancients and to priests. In terms of the latter, the Sufis, for example, so developed the principle of authority that for them the faithful (*murīd*) are to the *shaykh* "as cadavers are to the washer of the dead": utterly without will. There is no absolute model in humanity; the sole model is the Qur'ān, which gives freedom to man's spirit and to reason. Only those interested in keeping men prisoners of superstition prevent them from developing their intelligence.

Rejection of the Belief in the Return of the Dead

We repeatedly encounter in Sangalajī's writings very trenchant positions on eschatology. It was for his denial of the traditional Shi'ite beliefs concerning Return (*raj'at*) that the theologian became known and was rejected by most of his colleagues. However, he avoided publicizing his refutation of the traditional tenets directly or with too much insistence. This was the work of one of his close disciples, 'Abd al Vahhāb Farīd Tunkābunī, in two books, *Eslām va raj'at* (Islam and Return), 1939, and *Islām chunān ki būd* (Islam As It Was), 1978.[26]

According to the traditional Shi'ite eschatology, belief in Resurrection is affirmed many times in the Qur'ān and is a part of the creed.[27] Resurrection is designated by several terms: *ba'th* (awakening), *qiyāma* (the action of rising up, resurrection), *ma'ād* (final return, future life), *i'āda-yi ma'dum* (return from physical annihilation—the stumbling block of all the rationalist approaches to corporeal resurrection), *ḥashr* (assembling for the Day of Judgment), and *rujū‘* (return to life). Many philosophical and theological discussions have sought to elucidate how a body annihilated after its separation from the soul could return to physical existence. Some spiritual thinkers in Islam have responded to these dilemmas of literal interpretation by invoking an analogue of the physical body, more perfect, incorruptible, which would be the receptacle of future life.

The Shi‘a have insisted much more than the Sunnis on the importance of future life (*ma‘ād*). It is, with Imamate, one of the Principles of the Faith (*uṣūl al-dīn*). This insistence may be connected to the fact that the Imam, being hidden, already belongs to the other world in a sense. Sunnism, on the other hand, pays more attention to the community of believers already legitimately governed. The parousia of the Mahdi occupies an important position in Shi‘ite eschatology, as it makes possible the victory of those who were previously oppressed. Though texts are not all explicit, the Shi‘a generally believe that the Hidden Imam will return before the Resurrection. Many share, too, the belief in a Return (*raj‘at*) of the righteous and the sinners before the Last Judgment, as one reads in a classical text of Shaykh al-Mufīd (d. 413/1022).

> (§ 8) The Imamis agree that a large number of the dead must come back to earth before the day of Resurrection, though they diverge over the meaning of "return". . . .
> (§ 53) I profess that God will return [or give back] to this sublunar world a number of the dead in the form they had, so as to glorify some and blame others, to distinguish those who believe in the truth from those who do not, the oppressed from the oppressors—and this at the moment when the Mahdī of the Family of Muhammad appears.[28]

However, the Shi‘ite philosophers and mystics showed little or no interest in the topic. There is no mention of it, for instance, in ‘Abdurrazzāq Lāhījī's (d. 1072/1661-62) *Gawhar-i Murād* (the Pearl of the Quest).[29]

Though in his commentary on the Qur'ān Sangalajī is careful not to tackle directly the question of the Return (*raj‘at*) of the saints and the damned before the Resurrection, there is an intimation of his real belief concerning Resurrection. Nothing was created by chance, he argues, and as man is the most perfect being of creation, it is to be expected that the moral and intellectual perfection which his soul achieves on earth be perpetuated in another form after death and the destruction of the body. The Qur'ān gives several proofs of Resurrection (*ba‘th*). Moreover, the Resurrection and Final Return (*qiyāmat va ma‘ād*) of which the Qur'ān speaks do not consist in the annihilation of the body and its re-creation; they involve only a change in form. Death is merely the passage from one nature into another. If Muslims read the Qur'ān, they would cease arguing on this matter. There are several "degrees" of resurrection. It can be the transformation of the universe at the end of time; for each man, it is the day of his death.

When, in his public lectures of 1934, Sharī'at Sangalajī dared denounce as anti-Islamic—because offensive to reason—the belief in the avenging return of the Twelfth Imam, he did not touch on essential dogma concerning Resurrection; he merely conceded to common sense a right of surveillance over doctrinal formulation, an attitude adopted with more discretion by a number of his predecessors.[30] The theological confirmation of his orthodoxy was settled in 1934 by the chief Shi'ite dignitary of the time in Iran, Shaykh 'Abd al-Karīm Hā'irī Yazdī. In response to a question, the Shaykh pronounced the following decision (*fatvā*), which was published in the journal *Humāyūn:*

> I myself believe in Return (*raj'at*) generally speaking, owing to the numerous traditions which attest to it. However, this belief does not belong to the binding principles (*ḍarūrīyāt*) either of faith or of religion. If one does not believe in it, he is not excluded from faith or religion. The evocation of such problems produces harmful dissension among believers.[31]

Despite this indirect backing, many theologians reacted strongly against Sangalajī whom they anathematized, upholding the traditional Shi'ite position on *raj'at* in Shi'ism. The polemic did not cease until the 1940s.[32]

Although he was neither a revolutionary theologian nor a complete innovator in attacking superstition, particularly the cult of saints and the belief in Return and in the revenge of the good on the evil, Sangalajī threw into disequilibrium the entire edifice of Shi'ite clerical power. In the manner of Kasravī, whom he strongly resembles on a number of points, he often repeated that these superstitions played a deplorable social role, locking believers into doctrinal categories closed to reason; that they were the principal cause of dissension among Muslims, and that they were perpetuated by parasites who profited from them. He was concerned that such Shi'ite beliefs hindered dialogue with the Sunnis. In religions of priests (*kāhinān*), he maintained, the latter claim supernatural powers so as to appear indispensible.[33] The influence of these religions, notably Judaism, had diverted Islam from its rigorous monotheism.[34]

The Condemnation of Superstitious Practices

If Sangalajī seems to adopt the funerary rules or architecture of the Wahhābīs, it is because he wants to strip away all noncanonic religious practices which needlessly encumber the life of the believer and prevent civil society from reconciling the demands of modern life with tradition. An example of this is reflected in the following anecdote. One day in a mosque, seeing a soldier remain standing during the prayer, Sharī'at wondered why he did not join the others. The soldier, indicating his high leather boots, explained to Sharī'at the difficulty of removing them for the rituals of ablution. "Don't let that hold you back!" responded the theologian, "In certain cases it is permissible to do the ablutions on the leather of the shoes or boots." This liberty taken with the letter of ritual obligation (which prescribes that ablution be made on the skin) shocked the *'ulamā'*. "You are surprised that I would have a soldier pray in his boots," Sharī'at answered them, "because you would rather let yourself be crushed by those boots."

Sharī'at was particularly hostile to superstition. We must avoid two dangers, he says: the belief that the causes of the sensible world are self-sufficient, and there is no place for the divine will; and the belief that anything in the world can act magically on anything else, like a horseshoe or an agate ring acting on men's destiny.

He applies this logic to the cult of the dead: one must abandon superstitious practices by refraining from praying on tombs, from building monumental tombs, and from repairing tombs. However, it is good to meditate beside the tombs of the Prophet and the Imams.[35]

In summary, all unreasonable and superstitious practice must be avoided.

> Islam was the religion of the intellect, of logic and of nature (*fiṭrat*); the religion of monotheism and the destruction of idols; the religion of virtue and of morals; the religion of patience and of courage, of science and of rectitude. Islam was the law of humanism; it gave man freedom of spirit, of knowledge and intelligence. Islam delivered man from the slavery of priests. It recognized no intermediary between the Creator and the created. Islam annulled the cult of stones [idols] and the cults of anything other than God. When a man became Muslim and took refuge in the Koran, he no longer needed an intermediary between himself and God. Islam has forbidden blind imitation (*taqlīd-i kūrkūrāna*). It opposed action based on personal opinion (*ẓann*).[36]

This last statement shows Sharī'at's opposition to the principle of imitation which is accepted by the majority of the Twelver Shi'a. Sangalajī exhorts believers to recover the original inspiration of Islam and to abandon superstitious practices, many of which were developed in Shi'ism during the Safavid period.[37]

Though himself a member of the *'ulamā'*, Sharī'at did not identify with his peers; he undertook a reform which threatened their moral authority. Even though his formation was in the clerical tradition, he had positive contact with the modern world, which he knew little but whose force he presumed. Having sought before all to preserve the essential religious values of the Qur'ān, he discovered that these values retain their full actuality once disencumbered of the iron collar of later clerical traditions. From his point of view, Islam should not abdicate before the modern world, taking refuge behind a doctrine of asceticism or withdrawal. Nor should it lose its identity. The following lines of Farīd Tunkābunī summarize well this attitude of Sangalajī:

> Those who take the sublunar world as a prison for the believer are ignorant men who wrongly consider themselves Muslims. Even some doctors of religion—those who consider the understanding of religious truths their prerogative—present Islam as contrary to progress, to civilization and endeavor; hostile to all the exigencies of man's social life. They formally present Islam as a monastic creed and an ascetic philosophy, in the name of which they push the masses towards laziness, lassitude, dirtiness, misery, mental rigidity, abjection, and above all to distraction and ignorance—in a word, to misfortune in all its forms. They have so interpreted this pure creed that only a few extremists can be considered its adherents. In addition, another group whose number is on the increase has recently appeared. This group shows the greatest concern regarding the estrangement of Islam: they consider Islam in accord with all the features of the false civilization of the West and are constantly set on reconciling its timeless precepts with the opinions of any ignoramus issuing from that land [the West].[38]

Conclusion

Sangalajī's response to modernism and to the sclerosis of the traditional *'ulamā'* should not be seen as a fortuitous phenomenon. First, Sangalajī himself lived in Iraq and travelled in Hijāz, where he read the works of contemporary Arab theologians. There is some indication in Sangalajī's work of a profound influence of the Wahhābī movement, which was then in full effervescence (Ibn Sa'ūd occupied Mecca in 1924). Despite the strongly anti-Shi'ite character of Wahhābī doctrine (the prohibition of the cult of saints, sack of Karbalā in 1802, and destruction of the Shi'ite cemetery of Baqī' in 1924), this rigoristic Ḥanbalite doctrine appealed to Sangalajī in its fundamentalism and its opposition to *taqlīd.* Sangalajī had no doubt read attentively the books of Ibn Taymiyya (d. 728/1328) and Ibn Qayyim (d. 751/1350).

In Sunnism during the same period, this current of ideas also influenced a thinker whose ideas are not without similarity to Sangalajī's: Rashīd Riḍā (1865-1935). Having been affiliated with the Sufi Naqshbandī order, which he later rejected, Riḍā continued in Cairo the work of the modernist Shaykh 'Abduh (1849-1905),[39] but with a much more fundamentalist slant. According to him, only a return to the Islam of one's ancestors (*salaf*) could put a halt to the decadent state of Muslim society. It may be noted that Rashīd Riḍā aspired to a reconciliation between Sunnis and the Shi'a, after ridding the two doctrines—especially Shi'ism—of what he characterized as the fantastic and mythological contributions of converted Jews.

Sangalajī's audience during his lifetime was limited. He proposed a high-level ideological debate to an elite steeped in the Islamic tradition but not enslaved to antiquated clerical forms. It is significant that 'Alī Sharī'atī's father, Ustād Muhammad-Taqī Sharī'atī, himself an agent of Islamic renewal in Mashhad, never read a line of Sangalajī in that period, though he had heard of him.[40] Farīd Tunkābunī, who carried on his master's ideas up to the Islamic Revolution, does not represent a large movement; he is an original theologian, independent but isolated.

One can attempt to draw a parallel between Sangalajī and 'Alī Sharī'atī, whose criticism of "Safavid" Shi'ism often recalls that of his predecessor. However, to my knowledge, Sharī'atī never referred to Sangalajī and it is possible that he had never heard of him. They seem to develop similar or parallel arguments for the reform of Islam, but Sharī'atī, who received a Western education in France in the 1960s, devoted himself to social issues which Sangalajī carefully avoided.

Curiously, it is in a recent polemical work that Sharī'at Sangalajī's name has resurfaced. In a book violently opposed to 'Alī Sharī'atī, published in the spring of 1362/1983, an ideologue/historian of the Islamic Republic attempts to trace the development of the "Muslim Protestantism" which, according to him, infects the Iranian Islamic revolutionaries. In the course of his indictment, he accuses Sangalajī—placed side by side with Kasravī—of executing a colonialist plan to corrupt Islam.[41] This late attack on Sangalajī demonstrates that the present clerical establishment remains sensitive to the criticism of a reformist who died forty years ago, and that the Islamic revival has followed numerous paths which are sometimes contradictory. At any rate, Sangalajī's books are not entirely forgotten. His *Key to the*

Understanding the Koran, printed for the third time in 1966, was printed again in the Islamic Republic, and I found copies of it in a bookshop of the Guardians of the Revolution in Tehran in 1983.

Notes

1. See, for example, Shahrough Akhavi, *Religion and Politics in Contemporary Iran: Clergy-State Relations in the Pahlavi Period.* (Albany: State University of New York Press, 1980); 'Alī Davānī, *Nahḍat-i rūhāniyūn-i Īrān*, II (Tehran: Bunyād-i farhangī-yi Imām Riḍā, [1360/1981]), pp. 107-70.

2. ['Alī-Akbar] Ḥakamīzāda, *Asrār-i hizār sāla* ([Tehran]: Peymān, 1322/1943).

3. See, for example, Muḥammad-'Alī Himmat-Ābādī, *Risāla-yi pāsukh-nāma-yi islāmī—Radd bar Asrār-i hizār-sāla* ([Tehran]: 'Ilmī, 1364/1945).

4. Rūhallāh Khumeinī, *Kashf al-Asrār* (n.p.: n.d.), p. 132. On Abu'l-Faḍl Gulpāyigānī, see D. MacEoin, "From Babism to Baha'ism . . . " *Religion* 13 (1983): 229 ff.

5. Ibid., pp. 57, 64, 77, 333.

6. Sources: Abu'l-Ḥasan Baygdilī, ed., *Bi-munāsibat-i yakumīn sāl-i raḥlat-i Sharī'at, majmū'a-īst ḥāvī-i ash'ār va maqālāt-ī ki dānishmandān-i Īrān dar rithā-yi ān marḥūm surūda va-yā nivishta-and* . . . ([Tehrān], 1323/1945) (Hence quoted *Yakumīn sāl* . . .); anonymous, "Sharḥ-i ḥāl va āthār-e marhum hājj Sharī'at Sangalajī," *Majmū'a-yi Shāhīn*, 2, (Tehrān 1326/1947), pp. 120-24. I wish to thank some of those who kindly agreed to talk to me about Sharī'at, notably his two sons and Dr. Javād Mashkūr. To my knowledge, the only Western study in which Sangalajī is discussed is Amir Abbas Haydari, "Some Aspects of Islam in Modern Iran with Special Reference to the Work of Sangalajī and Rāshid," unpublished M.A. thesis, Department of Graduate Studies, McGill University, Montréal, August 1954.

7. According to another source, he was named "Riḍā-Qulī" after a mystic Shaykh of whom his father was a *murīd.*

8. See Muḥammad-Ḥasan Sharīfuddīn Mashkūr, "Nām va nasab-i marhūm-i Sharī'at Sangalajī," *Ayanda*, XII, 1-3, (1365/1986), p. 73.

9. Ibid.

10. See A. Hairi, *Shi'ism and Constitutionalism in Iran. A Study of the Role Played by the Persian Residents of Iraq in Iranian Politics* (Leiden: Brill, 1977), p. 149.

11. See A. Hairi, "Hā'irī, Shaykh 'Abd al-Karīm Yazdī," *E.I.2, Suppl.;* Akhavi, op. cit., pp. 41-42. Muḥammad Sharīf-Rāzī, *Ganjīna-yi dānishmandān*, I

(Tehran: Islāmīya, 1352/1973), p. 294, describes Hā'irī at the end of his life as a man exhausted by strife.

12. "Borow īn dām bar morq-ī digar nih / Ki 'Anqā-rā buland-ast āshiyāna," *Divān-i Hāfiẓ*, Qazvini-Ghani, ed., n° 428.

13. See 'A. Farīd, *Islām va raj'at* ([Tehran] 1318/1939), idem., *Islām chunān ki būd* (n.p., 1357/1978).

14. See Ḥusayn-Qulī Musta'ān, "Ṣuḥbat bā doktor Tagore," *Īrān*, n° 3798, 16th year, 18 urdibihisht 1311 (also in *Yakumīn sāl* . . . , pp. *kāf-alif* to *kāf-zā*).

15. Sharī'at Sangalajī, *Kilīd-i fahm-i Qur'ān* (Tehran: Dānesh, 3rd printing, 1345/1966), p. 5.

16. The Lankarānī brothers were well known for their hostility to Sharī'at; Muḥammad Lankarānī strove against the influence of Wahhābism in Iran (see Muḥammad-Sharīf-Rāzī, op. cit., IV (Tehrān, 1353/1974), p. 546. On Ḥusayn Lankarānī, see ibid., VII, p. 29, n° 7.) Another known enemy of Sharī'at was Hājj Mīrzā 'Abdallāh Vā'iẓ Subbuhī.

17. *Tawhīd-i 'ibādāt — Yaktāparastī*, 2d ed. (Tehran, 1362/1943).

18. Ibid., p. 138.

19. *Kilīd-i fahm-i Qur'ān* (*Key to the Understanding of the Qur'ān*) (Tehran, 1st ed., 1361/1942). A third edition is enlarged by a treatise on the *Barāhīn al-Qur'ān* (Proofs of the Qur'ān) (Tehran, 1345/1966-7). I quote from the latter.

20. On this issue, see H. Löschner, *Die dogmatischen Grundlagen des ši'itischen Rechts* (Erlangen-Nürnberg, 1971), pp. 70 ff.; J. Eliash, "The ši'ite Qur'ān, a Reconsideration of Goldziher's Interpretation," *Arabica* XVI (1969): 15-24.

21. *Kilīd-i fahm-i Qur'ān*, p. 38.

22. Ibid., p. 44.

23. Ibid., p. 165.

24. Ibid.

25. Ibid., pp. 162 ff.

26. See n. 13 above.

27. On the issue of the resurrection of the body in Islam, see, for example, L. Gardet, *Dieu et la destinée de l'homme* (Paris, 1967), pp. 259 ff.

28. al-Mufīd, *K. avvā'il al-maqālāt*, translated from the French by D. Sourdel, "L'imamisme vu par le Cheikh al-Mufīd," *R.E.I.*, XL, 2 (1972), pp. 217-96. See also Shaykh al-Mufīd, *Kitāb al-Irshād, The Book of Guidance*, translated by I. K. Howard (London, 1981), pp. 552 ff. A recent Shi'ite synthetic

study which takes the standard traditional position and includes many references has been published by Muḥammad-Riḍā al-Ṭabasī al-Najafī, *al-Shī'a va'l-raj'a*, vol. 1, 3d ed. (Najaf, 1385/1966); vol. II, 2d ed. (Najaf, 1395/1975). (With my thanks to M. Ishkivarī from the Mar'ashī Library in Qumm.) One can see the origin of this eschatological belief in the Bahrām Varjāvand, justice-maker of the Zoroastrians.

29. See 'Abdurrazzāq Lāhījī, *Gawhar-i murād*, lithograph ed., 1271 (reprinted Tehran: Islāmīya, 1377/1958), especially pp. 430 ff., on eschatology.

30. See a later report on the 1935 lectures where he comes back to this issue in *"Nashrīya" 5.*

31. *Humāyūn*, Qum, Bahman 1313/shavvāl 1353/1935, p. 1. On this journal, see above.

32. See, for example, 'Alī-Naqī Faiḍ al-Islām Iṣfahānī, *Pāsukh-nāma-yi Izgolī* (Tehrān: Kitābkhāna-yi Īrān, 1353/1935); idem, *Rahbar-i gumshudagān* ([Tehran]: Islāmīya, 1359/1940). He does not name Sangalajī, but certainly is alluding to him. On pages 26 and 176, he deridingly refers to Sangalajī's "Center for Islamic Propaganda" as "Center for Foodstuffs," *Dār al-irtizāq*. Elsewhere he responds word for word to Farīd Tunkābunī's book, *Islām va raj'at.*

33. *Tawḥīd-i 'ibādāt*, p. 138.

34. *Kilīd-i fahm*, p. 91; 'A. Farīd, *Islām va raj'at*, pp. 79ff.; idem; *Islām chunān ki būd*, p. 4ff. This opposition between pure pristine Islam and Islam that has been corrupted by Jewish converts is a common polemical theme in the *Salafīya.* See A. Hourani, *Arabic Thought in the Liberal Age*, 1798-1939 (London-Oxford-New York: Oxford University Press, 1970), p. 231; J. Jomier, *Le commentaire coranique du Manār. Tendances modernes de l'exégèse coranique en Egypte* (Paris: Maisonneuve, 1954); G. Vajda, "Isrāiliyyāt," *E.I.2, s.v.*

35. *Tawhīd-i 'ibādāt*, pp. 155-156.

36. Ibid., p. 169.

37. Ibid., p. 171.

38. *Islām va raj'at*, p. 20.

39. An explicit comparison of Sangalajī to 'Abduh is made by 'Alī Javāhirulkalām, *Yakumīn sāl. . .*, p. 91. Farīd often quotes 'Abduh and Riḍā.

40. Interview in Mashhad, May 1982.

41. 'Alī Abu'l-Ḥasanī (Mundher), *Shahīd Moṭahharī ifshāgar-i tawṭa'a-yi ta'vīl-i "ẓāhir"-i diyānat bi "bāṭin"-i ilḥād va māddīyat, bi ḍamīma-yi Naqd-ī az ustād-i shahīd bar "Islām-shināsī"-yi Doktor Sharī'atī* ([Qumm], daftar-i intishārāt-i islāmī (1362/1983), pp. 36, 42, 302, 305, and particularly 170ff.

CHAPTER 8

Ideological Revolution in Shi'ism

SAID AMIR ARJOMAND

The Constitutional Revolution and its Impact

Around 1800, an *'ālim* who had emigrated to India during the first years of Qājār rule could write about the spread of Deism and secularism in Western Europe in amazement and with the detachment of an observer at safe distance.

> Nowadays all the Europeans are followers of the philosophers, and are impertinent[1] in matters of religion. The church bells toll once a week on Sunday and the lowly and the masses go to temples. The priests are also present. The sages and the leaders profess to the unity of God but consider the other principles of religion such as Prophecy and Resurrection myths, likewise with praying and churchgoing. . . . The forsaken nation (*ṭā'ifa*) of France, may God slay them, have even gone further. They deny the incumbent obligations, consider their property and wives lawful to one another, and are excessive in their insistence on the eternity of the world. They are thus persistently advancing along the path of error and misfortune, and have indeed outdone the ancient and modern heretics.[2]

A century later, the *'ulamā'* found themselves deeply embroiled in Asia's first modern revolution, and henceforth had to face Deism and the "insistence on the eternity of the world"—i.e., materialism—at home. The old view of the *'ulamā'* as the proponents of Constitutionalism is clearly misleading.[3] Constitutionalism in Iran was a movement against the absolutist monarchy whose initiators called upon the *'ulamā'* to exercise their independent religious authority and to assume the leadership of the nation (*millat*). The monarch had patently failed to defend the nation against foreign encroachments, and as the nation was conceived as no other than the Shi'ite community of believers, it was time for the religious authorities to live up to their position of leadership (*riyāsat*) of the Shi'ite nation on behalf of the Hidden Imam, and to defend her against the imperialism of the infidels. Constitutional reform of government was the surest means of reversing the present decadence and stemming the increasing dominance of the European infidels over the Shi'ite nation of Iran.

The above perception of the objective situation and the corresponding normative obligation of the Shi'ite religious leaders gained general acceptance and, coupled with the endemic power struggle between the hierocracy and the state and the *'ulamā'*'s material interest in opposing the state,[4] was sufficient to put the Shi'ite religious authorities in the forefront of the protest movement which resulted in the creation of the Majlis and the establishment of the Constitution of 1906. However, the goal the Constitutionalist movement succeeded in achieving—i.e., the creation of a parliamentary system of government—brought the *'ulamā'* face to face with a complete novelty. Constitutional democracy, established as the new means for achieving the old end of defending the Islamic nation of Iran, was as novel in theory as it was unfamiliar in practice. Novelty causes bewilderment which can only be overcome by making sense of it. This can usually be done in more than one way. The Shi'ite *'ulamā'* fall into four groups according to the way they made sense of the novelty of parliamentary democracy. The way each group made sense of parliamentary democracy, as defined in 1906 and put into practice in 1907, determined its position toward Constitutionalism.

There is some correlation between the social, positional, and, especially, generational variation within the clerical body and the four orientations toward Constitutionalism. More important than this correlation are the temporal shifts from one category to another, with the progressive definition of the goals of the Constitutionalist movement.[5] But the most important fact about the four typical clerical reactions to Constitutionalism is that they cover the whole range from enthusiastic support to violent opposition. This very fact attests to the novelty of the experience, and is alone sufficient to demolish a number of views which are still held, though not equally widely. It makes it impossible to assert that the *'ulamā'* were and remained unified in their action, that they had a clear idea of the goals of the Constitutional movement from the outset, and that there is or can be only one Islamic position on parliamentary democracy.

Here are the four positions with their respective logic:

1. The staunch traditionalists opposed all novelty categorically and refused to grant that the goal of protection of Islam could either be reached or would justify the new means of constitutional reform of government. This group consisted mostly of the old *mujtahids*, typically without much popular following, who refused to join the protest movement against monarchy in 1905 but did join the traditionalist anti-Constitutionalist movement launched by Shaykh Faḍl Allāh Nūrī (d. July 1909) in 1907.[6]

The dominant ideal interest of the *'ulamā'* was the protection of the realm of Islam. Their dominant material interest could before long be seen as the preservation of their juristic authority and judiciary prerogatives. Those who initially accepted constitutional reform of government as the means to the end of the protection of the realm of Islam (*ḥifẓ-i bayḍa-yi islām*), became divided into three groups during 1907 and the first half of 1908 when the purpose of the parliament and the principles of parliamentary democracy became commonly known and discussed. The logic of this division can best be understood by singling out the dominant material and ideal interests of the *'ulamā'* and considering their interplay.

2. The anti-Constitutionalists became aware that the reform of the judiciary system entailed its secularization and thus posed a serious threat to their material interests; they were even more alarmed by the spread of foreign ideas and manners, and came to believe that Constitutionalism meant the spread of anarchy and immorality, and would thus weaken Islam. Thanks to the effective leadership of Shaykh Faḍl Allāh Nūrī, this group grew in strength during the first two years of constitutional government and came to comprise the majority of the *'ulamā'* by the time of the short-lived restoration of autocracy in June 1908.

3. The Constitutionalist *'ulamā'* continued to believe that the Constitutional reform of government was necessary to protect the realm of Islam, but they were also bent on preserving their juristic authority as fully as possible, and in fact made their support for the Constitution conditional upon the recognition of their judiciary prerogatives. This is an important group and has been the focus of popular and scholarly attention during the past decades. However, the conditionality of their support for Constitutionalism has not been adequately understood. Nor has their success in securing the recognition of their juristic authority in the parliamentary legislation of the first decade.[7]

4. The unconditional Constitutionalists realized that reform threatened the judiciary prerogatives of the *'ulamā'* but considered this a worthwhile price to pay for the strengthening of the Shi'ite nation of Iran. This group consisted almost entirely of the young clerics,

including a group of students surrounding Ākhūnd Khurāsānī.[8] Although this group did not sway the religious establishment, it is nevertheless important in that many of its elements discarded their clerical garb and played an important role in the modernization of the Iranian state in the subsequent decades.

The ideological impact of the Constitutional Revolution on the second and the third group are represented in Chapter 16 of this volume. It consisted of two fundamentally opposed political theories. The theory advocated by Nūrī, the leader of the Islamic traditionalist group, considered Constitutionalism a ploy for imperialistic cultural domination and condemned all parliamentary legislation as transgression on God's prerogative and the *'ulamā'*'s exclusive right to interpret the Sacred Law. The theory put forward by Khalkhālī, a representative of the clerical supporters of the Constitution, on the other hand, legitimated parliamentary democracy in Islamic terms but restricted its jurisdiction to matters not covered by the Sacred Law. Khalkhālī argues that Constitutionalism, like all forms of government, is not part of any religion, and pertains to the temporal sphere of life. The rule of law and constitutional government is in no way incompatible with Islam. He even goes further and maintains that the Europeans have taken their laws and constitutions from the Qur'ān and the words of the Imams.[9] The impact of the nationalism of the Constitutionalist ideology[10] on Khalkhālī's views should also be noted. He emphasizes the necessity of union between the king and the nation to preserve Iran's independence and to prevent foreign domination, and his economic nationalism is pronounced. He advocates the building of railroads and the exploitation of the country's natural resources to further economic development, and suggests that even part of the revenue from the religious endowments should be used to this end.

Although many of the *'ulamā'* initially sympathetic to Khalkhālī's position were won over to the traditionalist camp in 1907-1908 as a result of the gradual clarification of issues—both by the practice of constitutional government and by Nūrī's cogent exposition of the fallacies of the argument for the compatibility of parliamentary democracy and the Shi'ite Sacred Law—some *'ulamā'* remained in the Constitutionalist camp, and a greater number returned to it when the Shah's attempt to restore autocracy with Nūrī's enthusiastic support collapsed in July 1909. Many of Khalkhālī's ideas are reiterated in a tract published by another *'ālim*, Mīrzā Yūsuf Shams al-Afāḍil Kāshmarī Tūrshīzī, in 1911. Like Khalkhālī before him, Kāshmarī makes a basic distinction between secular and religious matters, matters concerning man's livelihood (*umūr-i ma'āshiyya*) and those concerning the Hereafter (*umūr ma'ādiyya*). He argues that constitutional government rests on the principle of consultation (*shūrā*) which is sanctioned in the Qur'ān. The principle of consultation is restricted to the ordering of the matters of livelihood and does not extend to other-worldly matters. "Therefore, the Constitution does not bear on other-worldly matters and its legitimacy derives from the ordering of the matters of livelihood." This should be done by an assembly elected by popular majority vote. Its members are called "the representatives and deputies of the nation," and their place of gathering "the National Consultative Assembly or Parliament."[11] As the understanding of the principles of the unity of God is left to the individual reason and derivative practical norms, and problems of worship are settled through the emulation (*taqlīd*) of the more learned, "so is the ordering of man's livelihood entrusted to politics and the consultation of the wise." Both the ordering of the matters of livelihood and consultation as its means are desired and sanctioned by the divine Law-giver.[12] Concern for the reform and modernization of the state is also present in Kāshmarī's tract, as is economic nationalism.[13] Finally, like Khalkhālī before him, Kāshmarī minimizes the secularizing potential of parliamentary legislation.[14]

Whereas the importance of the anti-Constitutionalist *'ulamā'* was until recently either not recognized or was minimized, much has been made of the role of the Constitutionalist *'ulamā'* in the literature. Still, the exact nature of the synthesis of Constitutionalism and Islam has not received enough attention—hence the above remarks and Chapter 16, Section 2. Nor has their success in safeguarding their juristic authority—hence Chapter 6 by Lahidji. To do so, they limited the secularization of the judiciary by actively participating in the effort to reform the legal system. Ḥājj Shaykh Muhammad *mujtahid*, son of a famous *marja'-i taqlīd*, Shaykh Zayn al-'Ābidīn Māzandarānī (d. 1309/1891-92), for instance, became the Chief Justice of the Supreme Court of Appeal, and drafted a plan for its reform and reorganization in conformity with Shi'ite jurisprudence which was completed in December 1910 and proposed to the Majlis.[15]

Equally deserving of attention are the views of the young clerics and seminarians who constitute the fourth group, the enthusiastic and unconditional supporters of the Constitutionalist movement. Like the previous group, the unconditional Constitutionalists considered the rescuing of Iran from its present decadence and the protection of the realm of Islam the foremost urgent goal of all reform. Their nationalism was more pronounced than that of the first group. But what clearly distinguished this group from the previous is their lack of concern for safeguarding clerical authority and preserving its judiciary jurisdiction. In fact, they are the only group to extend the idea of reform to the religious establishment itself. It was not only the absolutism of the monarchy and its subservience to foreign powers but also the negligence, conservatism, and ritualism of the religious authorities that were responsible for the present decadence of Islam and Iran. Reform should therefore be extended from governmental agencies to religious institutions. In a tract published in 1910, Shaykh Asad Allāh Māmaqānī, a student of Ākhūnd Khurāsānī who had represented him at the Constitutionalist *anjuman-i sa'ādat* in Istanbul in 1908-09, proposed that the Shi'ite centers of learning be moved from the Ottoman Iraq to one of Iran's holy cities—Mashad or Qumm—and the Shi'ite educational system be thoroughly reformed on the model of 'Abduh's reform of al-Azhar in Egypt.[16] He even dared to touch upon the religious taxes, which were exclusively controlled by the Shi'ite religious authorities, and suggested that they be spent on the reorganization of the army and the national educational system.

> We want to know whether the Imam, peace be upon him, would be content with the rescuing of the Muslim country through whose survival and independence Islam and Muslims and signs of Islam would be preserved, or not? . . . Would the Imam not be content if the religious taxes are collected to pay off the Russian debt, which has reduced and humiliated Islam and the Muslims, so that infidelity does not conquer Islam?[17]

Some eight years later, Māmaqānī's rhetorical exhortations and modest reform proposals turn into a full-scale scathing attack on the foundations of clerical authority in Shi'ism. In *Religion, Functions and the Method of Government in Shi'ism*,[18] he maintains that government in society has the same place as Imamate in religion.[19] During the Occultation of the Imam, the function of the maintenance of law and order and policing (*umūr ḥisbiyya*) devolves upon "the just believers"—not the *'ulamā'*—and the proper form of government is therefore the one based on consultation (*shūrā*).[20] This government is the only agency with the legitimate right to control the religious endowments,[21] and to appoint judges.[22] By contrast, jurisprudence has never been the exclusive domain of Imamate, and referring to a jurist has always been voluntary.[23] The jurists have no right to interfere with government, and their intervention in politics is destructive.[24] As *ijtihād* is based on knowledge, following a dead *mujtahid* is permissible, as the reliability of his knowledge does not depend on his being alive. A council of jurists, each with specialized knowledge in a specific area, would be more competent to publish a manual of applied religious law than a single *marja'*, as is currently done.[25] Above all, Māmaqānī denies the validity of the *'ulamā'*'s claim to General Deputyship of the Imam and adduces Shaykh Murtaḍa Anṣārī's support in this regard.[26] Finally he turns to a direct attack on Shi'ite clericalism. The Shi'ite *'ulamā'* who claim to have the keys to heaven, have called themselves "clergy" (*rūḥaniyyūn*) in imitation of Christian priests. The book ends with a catalogue of doctrinally unfounded extentions of the juristic authority of the *'ulamā'* in contemporary Shi'ism and a litany of abuses of clerical authority in its practice.[27]

Advocacy of reform and the attack on Shi'ite clericalism was taken up by Sharī'at Sangalajī (d. 1944) in the 1930s and given a completely apolitical direction.[28] For an echo of Māmaqānī's political ideas, we would have to wait until the late 1970s. Writing in exile in 1982, the ousted President of the Islamic Republic of Iran, takes a step further than Māmaqānī's view on the equivalence of government and Imamate. He speaks of the generalization of the Imamate as the participation of each man and woman in government of the monistic (*tawḥīdī*) society, and hence their participation in determining the direction of its movement.[29]

As for the development of Shi'ism in the present century and the ideological revolution of the 1970s and 1980s, neither Māmaqānī nor Sharī'at Sangalajī hád any appreciable impact. Rather, it was Nūrī's Islamic traditionalism that contained the seeds of future developments.

Clerical Publicists in the Pahlavī Era

After the suspension of the Majlis and the occupation of northern Iran by the Russians at the end of 1911, the *'ulamā'* withdrew from the political arena to the mosque and the *madrasa* in disillusionment. The *marāji'-i taqlīd* generally held aloof from Iranian politics, though they did play the role of the "natural leaders" in the Shi'ite rebellion against the British in Iraq in 1921. With Iraq no longer in Muslim (Ottoman) but in British hands, Qumm indeed became a center of Shi'ite learning. The institution of *marja'iyyat* was in fact consolidated by the retrenchment of the *'ulamā'* into the centers of learning. Mīrzā Muḥammad Ḥusayn Nā'īnī (d. 1936) and Shaykh 'Abd al-Karīm Ḥa'irī (d. 1937) dominated the 1930s, Sayyid Abu'l-Ḥasan Iṣfahānī (d. 1946) and Ḥājj Āqā Ḥusayn Ṭabāṭabā'ī Qummī (d. 1947), the 1940s. After the death of the last two, there gradually developed the unprecedented emergence of a unitary *marja'-i taqlīd*, that of Ḥājj Āqā Ḥusayn Ṭabāṭabā'ī Burūjirdī (d. 1961). As Burūjirdī's biographer correctly points out, the leadership (*riyāsat*) of the Shī'a devolved entirely on him, "and such leadership has not materialized for any one of the *marāji'-i taqlīd* from the time of the Lesser Occultation to the present."[30]

The few clerics who turned to publicistic writing in this period were motivated by the menace of secularism, and a sense of imminent destruction akin to Shaykh Faḍl Allāh Nūrī's. Constitutionalism had taken, and these clerics took credit for having been its promoters,[31] but they bemoaned the take-over of constitutional government by forces conspiring to annihilate Islam through the spread of secularism, immorality, libertinism, and foreign ideas and manners. The most important early figure among these clerical publicists was a *mujtahid* of Tehran, Sayyid Asad Allāh Khāraqānī (d. 1936). Reacting against the incipient secularization of the judiciary, he published a treatise in October 1916 on the Islamic legal system. The book was reissued with the endorsment of three other *mujtahids* in 1919, and reprinted with the approval of the Ministry of Education in 1922.[32]

In a long introduction to this technical treatise, Khāraqānī seeks to explain "how it is that Islamic rules (*aḥkām*) are derelict and not paid any attention to whatsoever, and how anti-Islamic rules are current."[33] Of the divine Islamic rules, he says the following:

> Muslim brethren, know that the honor and independence of your nationality are related to these rules which are the distinctive feature of your Islamicity (*islāmiyyat*). With the abrogation of these rules, Islamicity is removed from your society and you will be the abject slaves of the foreigners and condemned by the enemies of religion, as our other Islamic brothers are caught under the domination of foreigners. . . .
>
> Today the enemies of Islam are overthrowing the flags of Islamic sovereignties by political (*polītīkī*) means. They satisfy their enmity to the Noble Koran by abrogating its rules, and are taking their revenge from us for the wars of the first century [the wars of Islamic conquest] by instilling differences through divisive diplomatic (*diplomātī*) statements with the assistance of a few among us.[34]

Under the heading "What kind of law does Iran want?" Kāraqānī divides the country into three groups who want three kinds of law: First, there is

> the honorable, rational, believing, fair and patriotic Iran . . . the law of this Iran is the Islamic political law and equal rights which combines the world and the Hereafter. It is in accordance with the requirements of the temperament of the dominant Iranian element, which has become a second nature, and in accordance with the first principle of the Fundamental Law.

> Second, the rational Iran, with a materialistic leaning (*ṭabīʿī maslak*), without attachment to God, the Hereafter and religion but attached to Iran, the fatherland, and the honor of humanity. The law of this Iran consists in the translations of numerous laws from different nations of the world from which the sages and scholars of Iran choose what is in agreement with the Iranian temperament and customs and make it into a law. This is the second type of legislation which is contrary to religion but not contrary to reason, national honor and patriotism.
> Third, the materialist (*ṭabīʿī*), egoistic (*shakhṣparast*) Iran, irresponsible toward Islam, the fatherland, reason and honor. The law of this Iran consists in the following: that a person who knows foreign languages should translate foreign law . . . correctly or incorrectly, in accordance to the law of Islam or contrary to it, in accordance with the Iranian temperament or contrary to it, and a few others enslaved by passions (*havā-parast*) . . . should ratify it and another group should boast about executing such a law, concealing its enmity toward Islam. The current laws are of this third kind. They do not correspond to any religious, civil, rational and logical law . . . but are imitation of foreigners. By evidence, the execution of the laws of the industrial and materialist states of Europe in Iran has not had and will not have any results other than the corruptions of the morals, theft, anarchy and embezzlements in governmental agencies. It is therefore necessary for the Islamic nation to rise in the holy Islamic movement of *jihād* in order to eliminate the laws that originated in the minds and mouths of the foreigners and issued forth through the mouths of their imitators. . . .[35]

Khāraqānī bitterly complains of "the private sphere of Tehran" which is filled by the materialist enemies of Islam and dishonorable traitors to the Iranian nation. "The dissemination of anti-Islamic laws" is likened to "poisonous shells of the monstrous looking cannons of the foreigners fired from Tehran."[36] Khāraqānī considered two kinds of law legitimate, the Sacred Law which is restricted to God, and worldly material law. As regards the latter, "no one other than the nation has the right to legislate, and the legislative body must be from the people themselves and not dependent on the foreigners."[37] He insists however, that the current laws are of neither of these two kinds.[38]

Khāraqānī's more general book, *The Effacement of the Imaginary and the Brightening of the Certain. The Way to Renew the Islamic Greatness and Power* is, despite its subtitle, deeply pessimistic. It begins with a discussion of the decline and decadence of Muslims of all sects. This he sees in the context of a more universal trend of the spread of secularism. He sees world history as the arena of contention between two opposing ideas: religion and materialist philosophy. The struggle between the theologians and the materialists (*mādiyyīn*) is decisive proof that the scholars of all religions have not tried and endeavored to counter the materialists and are not doing so."[39] The present age is the age of Ignorance (*jāhiliyya*) because of the division among the Shī'a and because it is impossible to "forbid the evil." The silence of the believers and the *'ulamā'* "in this fourteenth century which is the century of the onslaught of the materialists on the believers in God and of the destruction of the foundation of Islam" is not permissible. Foremost among the remedies proposed by Khāraqānī is the execution of the Islamic penal code "with utmost severity and without any consideration for the connections and worth of the individuals."[40]

In 1923, Khāraqānī was joined by a younger cleric, Shaykh Muḥammad Khāliṣī (d. 1963). He was the son of one of the two *marāji'* expelled from Iraq by the British during the summer of that year, and began his publicistic activity in Iran with a series of sermons in Tehran. In 1924, he took a leading part in the demonstrations against Republicanism.[41] Like Khāraqānī, Khāliṣī is alarmed by the menace of secularism which he considers the chief weapon of British imperialism. The European powers, and Britain especially, have a grand design for the Islamic countries—to connect them to Christianity, and failing that, to turn them away from Islam into materialism and naturalism. This they have undertaken through direct missionary activity, but much more effectively, through the spread of materialism and naturalism by the Muslims themselves. This latter insidious means for destroying the foundation of Islam is chosen according to the rule that "iron must be cut with iron."[42] In such dire circumstances, the *'ulamā'* are engrossed in the minutae of the Sacred Law concerning rituals, and the modern intellectuals are unaware of the plot to destroy Islam.

> Islam is under pressure and discomfort between the necktie and the water for ablutions. You moderns, come and understand religion, and you the believers, come to the line of science and information. The foundation of religion is the protection of the realm of Islam, and the realm of Islam cannot be protected without science.[43]

The remedy is Islamic Reform on the intellectual plane, and pan-Islamic unity on the political plane.

As the secularizing intentions of Riḍā Shāh's government became unmistakable in the late 1920s, a few other clerics joined Khāraqānī, especially to write in protest against the secularization of the judiciary and the license granted to women.[44] Riḍā Shāh, however, reacted firmly, and Khāraqānī, Khāliṣī and others were persecuted and banished.[45]

Khālişī survived Khāraqānī by many years and resumed his publicistic activity after the fall of Riḍā Shāh in 1941. He managed to publish eighteen numbers of a newspaper, *Nūr* (The Light) until his request for a franchise was turned down,[46] but he continued to write, preach and hold Friday congregational prayers. Khālişī regarded the revival of the Friday congregational prayer as the cornerstone of his mission, and attacked the majority of the Shiʿite *'ulamā'* who questioned its incumbency during the Occultation of the Imam. Like his contemporary, Sharīʿat Sangalajī,[47] Khālişī was influenced by the Salafī movement in the Sunni world, and became increasingly critical of the Shiʿite *'ulamā'*. He attacked the majority of the Shiʿite *'ulamā'* not only for their political quietism but also on intellectual grounds, going so far as to consider the science of rational jurisprudence as practiced by the school of Shaykh Murtaḍā Anṣārī an aberation from the pristine teachings of Islam which had resulted from following "the superstitions of Greek philosophy."[48]

In his *Truth of Veiling in Islam*, published in 1948, Khālişī discusses the rules of the Sacred Law regarding the veil. He criticizes the obscurantist believers who insist on the complete coverage of women and maintains that the face, the hands and the feet need not be covered. This much lack of coverage is sufficient for the participation of women in society. Beyond this, the result is corruption, as is the case especially in Tehran where "the official governmental agencies, clubs, swimming pools, theatres and cinemas consist mostly of vulgar, uncovered, bare and naked women."[49] The eventual result can only be the destruction of Iranian society.

The situation of women is the result of the dilapidation of Islamic teachings which had become evident to Khālişī during the three previous years of residence in Tehran. He had been appalled both by the gap between "the class claiming modernity" and "the class affecting religiosity" which could only be removed if both sides would submit to the rules of Islam. Khālişī was particularly alarmed by the presence of the Bahāʾīs, Communists, and materialists among the government functionaries.

This brings us to the typical feature of the 1940s and 1950s. The chief menace to the Shiʿite tradition defended by the clerical publicists was no longer the vague but ubiquitous secularism and materialism, but their concrete embodiment in the Bahāʾī sect and the Tudeh Party.[50] Khālişī devoted much of his energy to combatting these manifestations of apostasy and atheism. His *Bandits of Right and Truth or those who return to Barbarism and Ignorance*, published in 1951, is a detailed refutation of a critique of religion that had been published by the Tudeh Party under the title of the *Guardians of Magic and Myth*. He admits that he is forced to abandon his usual offensive missionary posture and is forced to assume a defensive one to fend off the attack of "the mad and irresponsible Communists."[51]

Khāliṣī did not gain much following among the Shi'ite *'ulamā'* and remained fairly isolated in Kāẓimayn, Iraq, where he had returned after World War II. Nevertheless, he is an interesting figure, combining the non-conformism of Māmaqānī with the activism of Khumeinī. In his activism, Khāliṣī may well have influenced Khumeinī and his followers. Such influence can be documented in one important instance: the unprecedented assumption of the title of Imam. On the front page of the Persian translation of one of Khāliṣī's books by one of his followers, the author is referred to as "the warrior in the path of God, Imam, Āyatullāh al-'Uẓmā Āqā Ḥājj Muḥammad Khāliṣī" (*al-mujāhid fī sabīl Allāh, al-imām*, etc.)[52] The appelation "Imam" is truly striking, even though it is used in an Arabic phrase in a Persian sentence.

While the clerical publicists attended to the evils of Bahā'ism and Communism, 'Alī Akbar Tashayyud, a lay intellectual, wrote to demonstrate the intimate links between Shi'ism and Iranian nationalism. He maintained Iran's tri-color flag was born during the rebellion of Mukhtār in Kūfa from 685 to 687, which he described as the first government of "the Twelver (*sic*) Imāmī Shī'a."[53] In another work, he even went so far as to maintain that the Shi'ite population of Jabal 'Āmil in Lebanon belong to the Iranian race, being the descendants of the Iranians exiled there at the time of Mu'āwiya.[54]

The 1960s was a decade of fateful change in Shi'ism. Sayyid Maḥmūd Ṭāliqānī, who had been active in the 1950s and had published an edition of Nā'īnī's tract with an introduction, brought out Khāraqānī's *The Effacement of the Imaginary* in 1960. In his introduction, Ṭāliqānī sets the tone for the new publicistic style of the *'ulamā'*. Islam is clearly distinguished from and contrasted with nationalism, and the term "Islamic Revolution" makes its appearance.[55] The Communists are not simply to be vituperatively attacked as was done by Khāliṣī. Ideological notions that underlie their political appeal—notably, revolution and social justice—are to be assimilated and appropriated by the clerical publicists in order to create a distinctive Islamic ideology.

The death of the supreme *marja'-i taqlīd*, Āyatallāh Burūjirdī in 1961 ushered in the new wave of publicistic activity. Ṭāliqānī and a group of younger *'ulamā'* that included Murtaḍā Muṭahharī, Sayyid Muḥammad Bihishtī, Sayyid Mūsā Ṣadr, and Sayyid Murtaḍā Jazā'irī, formed a society in Tehran.[56] Meetings began with the recitation of the Qur'ān and were devoted to a series of lectures followed by discussions. The lectures were then published in *The Lecture of the Month in*

Pointing to the Straight Path of Religion in March 1961, an interesting lecture was delivered by a young cleric, Sayyid Muḥammad Bihishtī. The subject of his talk was the believing intellectuals interested in reform whose mission was to reverse the decline of Islam and to awaken the Muslims after ten centuries of slumber. Bihishtī argued that a movement in this direction had begun in Iran some fifty to sixty years earlier, but its advocates had committed an important error. These reformers had adopted a hostile attitude toward the believers. This was now to be put right; and the first step in this direction was the coming of two hundred students from the University of Tehran to Qumm for the service on the fortieth day of Burūjirdī's death. Bihishtī claimed on the basis of personal observation in important Iranian cities that a new stratum of believing intellectuals interested in reform had emerged. This group was no longer a handful of individuals but had become quite numerous. It was therefore necessary to establish links between the Shi'ite center of learning in Qumm and the universities.[57]

In this period, with Burūjirdī's position as the supreme religious leader vacant and with more than half a dozen Grand Āyatallāhs competing to fill it, the idea of the reform of the religious institution, specialization of *ijtihād*, and the possible formation of a council of specialist jurists were discussed by the same group of clerical publicists.[58] Yet another cleric wrote a scathing critique of religious authorities, which was published pseudonymously somewhat later.[59] In the spring and summer of 1963, Āyatallāh Rūḥallāh Khumeinī, one of the contenders for Burūjirdī's position, stole the thunder from the debating societies by challenging the Shah outright. The result was the unsuccessful uprising of June 1963 which was bloodily suppressed. Publicistic activities of Ṭāliqānī and his associates were suspended after the uprising but resumed in the latter part of the 1960s. Mahdī Bāzargān, a lay Islamic publicist, was with the group of clerical publicists from the beginning. In the late 1960s, the clerical publicists were joined by another lay intellectual, 'Alī Sharī'atī (d. 1977) who soon began to outshine them and acquired wide popularity among the younger generation.

The ideal of the reform of religious leadership was dropped once Khumeinī had demonstrated the power and effectiveness of its older form. His person and example spurned the opposite tendency, and set in motion a vigorous movement of traditionalist clericalism. In 1970, Khumeinī himself apart, at least two clerics put forward theories of Islamic government based on the *vilāyat* (mandate) of the jurists on behalf of the Hidden Imam. In *The Fundamental Law of Islam*, a veteran anti-Bahā'ī publicist, Ḥasan Farīd Gulpāygānī, exploited the double meaning of the term *ḥukūmat*—government in ordinary Persian, judgeship in the technical Arabic of Shi'ite jurisprudence—to put forward a comprehensive theory of theocratic government.

> The fully qualified *mujtahid*, in addition to occupying the high position of the jurisconsultancy (*fatwā*)—which means that the king and the beggar must follow him (*taqlīd*) in all personal and social aspects of life—is entitled to the high function of theocratic government (*ḥukūmat shar'iyya*).
>
> Religious sovereignty comprises the two important branches of judgeship and *vilāyat*. . . . During the times of dissimulation (*taqiyya*) and Occultation, when government is in practice in the hands of usurpers and oppressors, both these branches in combination have been entrusted to the just jurist and *mujtahid*. The latter must, if possible, take over the reins of Islamic government and establish order and justice among the Muslims. And the Shi'ite nation must obey them.[60]

Gulpāygānī then mentions some of the specific instances of the *vilāyat* of the jurists in Shi'ite jurisprudence, and exhorts his readers to refrain from resorting to the judiciary machinery of the illegitimate government and to refer their problems to the *mujtajid*s instead. In the same vein, though in a more technical style and with substantiating references to such earlier jurists as Shaykh 'Alī al-Karakī, Sayyid Muḥammad Baḥr al-'Ulūm, and Shaykh Murtaḍā Anṣārī,[61] Shaykh 'Alī Tihrānī puts forward the principle of the *vilāyat-i faqīh* as the foundation of Islamic government.[62] It is important to note, however, that both Gulpāygānī and Tihrānī consider the *vilāyat* as the *collective* authority of the body of jurists and not that of any supreme jurist.

A portentous opening for the decade. Some of the Shi'ite *'ulamā'* were now ready to take the bull of secularism by the horns. They were ready for the effort to subjugate the chief agent of secularization, the modernized state, on the basis of the traditional clerical authority distinctive of Shi'ism.

The Islamic Revolution of 1979

The Islamic revolution in Iran was led by the Shi'ite *'ulamā'* in order to defend and preserve Shi'ism. They acted as the custodian of a religious tradition they considered threatened with corruption if not disappearance. Paradoxically, however, their attempt to restore and revitalize the Shi'ite tradition has constituted a true revolution in

Shi'ism. I characterized the movement led by Āyatallāh Khumeinī as "revolutionary traditionalism."[63] It should be emphasized, however, that the Islamic revolution in Iran has not only been a political revolution but equally a religious revolution. Shi'ite revolutionary traditionalism in Iran has brought about an ideological revolution *in* Shi'ism.

The concern for the restoration of the pure and authentic Islam is evident in the Preamble to the Constitution of the Islamic Republic of Iran. It states that after the earlier political movements of the present century, the movements against autocracy (1905—11) and the nationalization of oil (the late 1940s and early 1950s) became stagnant "because of their deviation from authentic Islamic positions." A great deal of emphasis is put on the authenticity of the ideology of Khumeinī's movement in comparison with the earlier movements.[64]

In their relentless *Kulturkampf* against Westernized intellectuals and the "syncretic" thought (*iltiqāṭī*) of the Islamic modernists, Iran's ruling clerics have claimed legitimacy as the authoritative interpreters of Islam in general and of the Shi'ite tradition by creating an Islamic *ideology* whose cornerstone is a novel theory of theocratic *government*. This major innovation has far-reaching ramifications. It has set in motion a profound transformation of the Shi'ite political culture which constitutes a watershed in the history of Shi'ism and will undoubtedly continue for decades to come.

There has been remarkable consensus among the Shi'ite jurists throughout the centuries regarding the interpretation of the "Authority Verse" of the Qur'ān (4: 59). The major Shi'ite Qur'ān commentaries, al Ṭūsī's (d. 1067) *Tibyān*,[65] al-Ṭabrisī's (d. 1153 or 1158) *Majma' al-Bayān*,[66] and Muqaddas Ardabīlī's (d. 1585) *Zubdat al-Bayān*,[67] assert that "those in authority" (*ulu'l-amr*) are neither the secular rulers (*amīrs*) nor the *'ulamā'*—neither of whom is immune from error and sin—but rather the infallible (*ma'ṣūm*) Imams, 'Alī and his eleven descendants. The Shi'ite consensus on the interpretation of the Authority Verse continued to hold until our time and down to the onset of Khumeinī's formulation of a new Shi'ite political theory. It is worth quoting the most influential contemporary Qur'ān commentary, Ṭabāṭabā'ī's *Tafsīr al-Mīzān* (written in the 1950s and 1960s) on Verse 4: 59.

> Therefore "those in authority" must refer to the individuals from the *umma* who are infallible [*ma'ṣūm*], whose recognition depends on the explicit designation of God or his Messenger, and to whom obedience is incumbent. All this corresponds only to what have been related from the Imams of the House of the Prophet, may peace be upon them, as "those in authority."

> As for the assertion that "those in authority" are the rightly-guided caliphs, the lords of the swords (*amīrs*), or the *'ulamā'* who are followed in their sayings and views, *it can be completely refuted. . . .*[68]

The Shi'ite notion of authority implied in the above interpretations of the Authority Verse was not confined to Qur'ān commentaries but also informed the Shi'ite jurisprudence. Shaykh Murtaḍā Anṣārī (d. 1865), for instance, in his discussion of authority sought, first, "to demonstrate how absurd it is to reason that because the Imams should be obeyed in all temporal and spiritual matters, the *faqīh* are also entitled to such obedience; and second . . . that in principle no individual, except the Prophet and the [infallible] Imam, has the authority to exert *wilāya* over others."[69] As has been pointed out, the *Uṣūlī* movement finally established the religious and juristic authority of the *'ulamā'* on behalf of the Hidden Imam. As a consequence, a number of highly specific functions of the Imam covered in the medieval treatises in jurisprudence, such as the Muḥaqqiq al-Ḥillī's (d. 1277) *al-Mukhtaṣar al-Nāfi'* under the rubric of *Wilā' al-imāma*,[70] were now said to devolve, during the Occultation, upon the Shi'ite jurists by virtue of their collective office of "general vicegerency" (*niyābat 'āmma*).

There is little discussion of *vilāyat* in the context of government and the maintenance of order in the Shi'ite writings of the twentieth century other than in Nā'īnī's treatise.[71] In one instance in the 1920s, it is said that "according to the general opinion, the Shi'ite *'ulamā'* are the representatives of the Imam of the age and the lieutenants of the *valī-yi shar'*, and true sovereignty (*salṭanat vāqi'ī*) is only theirs." The same author proceeds to explain that this true sovereignty puts the *'ulamā'* above politics: "[as] in the opinion of the common people (*anẓār-i 'āmma*) the *'ulamā'* and leaders of the Shi'ite religion are the lieutenants of the Imams and deputies of the Imam of the age, their position is holier than to allow them to interfere and participate in political affairs with tyrannical and usurping rulers and emirs."[72] By contrast, in the early 1930s, an important jurist identifies "the person in authority (*valī-yi amr*), the general shepherd and the person with absolute responsibility" as "The Imam or the ruler of the time (*sulṭān-i vaqt*)."[73] But usually, the discussion of *vilāyat* remained highly technical and specific. Khāliṣī's treatment of *valiy 'āmm* in the early 1950s does not introduce anything significant into the discussion of the topic. Having affirmed that the *valiy* is in fact the Hidden Imam, whose longevity (over 1100 years) should not be subject to doubt, he adds that during the Occultation, "whoever knows the most about the commandments of Islam is the best qualified for government" on the condition that he observes the principle of consultation (*shūrā*), as had done the Queen of Sheba.[74] There follows a short section on *vilāyat ḥisbiyya* consisting of the following statement: if the "fully qualified mujtahid" is unable to undertake government, *vilāyat* becomes one of the *umūr ḥisbiyya* (matters concerning the maintenance of order and policing) and, as such, incumbent upon the just believers. If the just believers are not available, whoever rises to undertake the function of government, no matter how corrupt, should be supported and obeyed so long as he does not contravene the *sharī'a*, and disobeying him is forbidden because the maintenance of order requires the prevalence of *vilāyat 'āmma.*[75] Note that Khāliṣī speaks of the *vilāyat 'āmma* and does not use the term *vilāyat al-faqīh.* A systematic summary of the topic in Shi'ite jurisprudence specifies seventeen instances for the *vilāyat* (mandate) of the religious judge (*ḥākim*), including the implementation of the punishments of the Sacred Law, judging, guardianship of the insane, authority over the estate of the heirless, divorcing of a woman whose husband has disappeared, some authority with regard to general endowments, and the authority to issue a variety of receipts. This mandate is discussed along the *vilāyat* of the legatee, of the father or paternal grandfather, the *vilāyat* of "the just believers," and finally, of policing (*ḥisba*). The last category comes closest to the functions of government. A number of instances are specified as requiring the permission of the religious judge—i.e., the fully qualified jurist—others are said to require no such permission.[76] By the end of the 1960s, the *vilāyat* transferred from the Imam to the jurists had these highly specific and well-defined connotations.[77]

In his bid to overthrow the Shah from exile in early 1970, Khumeinī took a bold step by asserting that the *vilāyat-i faqīh* went beyond these specific types of authority and included a general right to rule. The *vilāyat-i faqīh* thus assumed the meaning of the mandate of the jurist to rule. Khumeinī extended the arguments of the early *Uṣūlī* jurists, which were designed to establish the *legal* authority of the *'ulamā'* on the basis of a number of Traditions from the Prophet and the Imams, to eliminate the duality of religio-legal and temporal authority altogether. Having firmly rejected the idea of the separation of religion and politics as instilled by imperialist plotters, Khumeinī argues that during the Occultation of the Imam, the right to rule devolves upon the qualified *'ulamā'.* This formulation still preserved the Shi'ite juristic pluralism, as *vilāyat* was presented as the collective prerogative of all Shi'ite jurists, or at least all the *marāji'-i taqlīd.* About a year later, Khumeinī attempted to reduce this juristic pluralism to a unitary theocratic leadership to be installed by an Islamic revolution. Having reaffirmed that the *'ulamā'* "possess with respect to government all that the Prophet and the Imams possessed," Khumeinī maintains that

> *wilāya* falls to *al-faqīh al-'ādil.* Undertaking a government and laying the foundation of the Islamic state (*al-dawlat al-islāmiyya*) is a *kifā'ī* duty [i.e., duty of the community and not of any specific individual] incumbent on just *fuqahā'.*
>
> *If one such succeeds in forming a government it is incumbent on the others to follow him. If the task is not possible except by their uniting, they must unite to undertake it.* If that were not possible at all, their status would not lapse, though they would be excused from the founding of a government.[78]

In less than a decade, Khumeinī's theory was embodied in the Constitution of the Islamic Republic of Iran. On the basis of a revolutionary reinterpretation of *vilāyat-i amr* and an equally revolutionary reinterpretation of Imamate as the principle of continuous (*mustamarr*—i.e., uninterrupted by the Occultation of the Twelfth Imam) theocratic leadership, the ruling jurist is identified as the *valī-yi amr*, and his supreme office is interchangeably defined as "Imamate" and "leadership" (*rahbarī*). The Constitution defines the Islamic Republic as an order based on the belief in:

> 1—the one God (there is no god but God) and the restriction of sovereignty and legislation to Him, and the necessity of submission to His command. . . . 5—Imamate and continuous leadership, and its fundamental role in the perpetuation of the Islamic revolution (Article 2).

Article 5 asserts that during the Occultation, "*vilāyat-i amr* and the Imamate of the *umma* is upon the just and pious . . . jurist." A commentator on the Constitution unabashedly declares that the *ulu'l-amr* refers equally to the Imam and the Deputy (*nā'ib*) of the Imam, and the Deputy of the Imam is the jurist who is installed in this position with the necessary conditions.[79]

The clerical ideologues have sought to link the Islamic revolution irrevocably to the establishment of supreme clerical sovereignty. In the words of the late Āyatallāh Muṭahharī, "the analysis of this revolution is not separable from the analysis of the leadership of the revolution." Or, as another Islamic ideologue has remarked more recently, "This revolution is the integrations of religion and politics, or better put, it is the refutation of the colonialist idea of 'separation of religion from politics.' "[80]

Incidentally, it is interesting to note that no mention is made of the principle of consultation (*shūrā*) or democracy as a defining characteristic of the Islamic Republic. The principle of *shūrā* makes its appearance only in Article 7. Madanī's commentary[81] explains the subsidiary role of consultation. The principle of consultation is accepted, but as a subsidiary to the principle of Imamate. "Islamic consultation is only possible when Imamate is dominant. In other words, consultation is at the service of Imamate." The Qur'ānic verse 3: 153 (*wa shāwirhum fi'l-amr* etc.) is said to imply that the actual decision-maker is the Prophet, who was also the Imam. The commentator adds that the advocates of the *shūrā* during the drafting of the Constitution either did not firmly believe in Islam or were contaminated by "syncretic" thinking, and were trying "to link the *shūrā* to the principle of national sovereignty."

As we have seen, Khumeinī's theory of theocratic government extends the *Uṣūlī* norm of juristic authority as elaborated in the nineteenth century into a new sphere previously not covered by it: government. At this juncture, it is interesting to note that the term *Akhbārī* is used only as a pejorative label to designate the apolitical, "stagnant," and "superstitious" orientation of those clerics who do not subscribe to the politicized and ideological Islam of the militant *'ulamā'* and who reject the concept of *vilāyat-i faqīh.* Secular theories of government such as democracy and sovereignty of the nation apart, Khumeinī's theory of the Mandate of the Jurist is open to two forceful objections. The first is that the mandate or authority of the Shi'ite *'ulamā'* during the Occultation of the Twelfth Imam cannot be extended beyond the religio-legal sphere to include government. The second objection is that the mandate in question refers to the *collective* religio-juristic authority of *all* Shi'ite jurists and cannot be restricted to that of a single supreme jurist nor, by extension, to a supreme council of three or five jurists (as envisioned in the Constitution of the Islamic Republic). The above doctrinal objections to *vilāyat-i faqīh* had in fact been voiced by the *marāji'-i taqlīd*, Khu'ī, Sharī'at-madārī, Qummī, and a number of other Āyatallāhs. Therefore, the first obstacle to be removed to pave the way for the universal acceptance of *vilāyat-i faqīh* in its novel form was the Grand Āyatallāh Sharī'at-madārī, its most important critic in Iran. In April 1982, in a move unprecedented in Shi'ite history, some seventeen out of the forty-five professors of the Qumm theological seminaries were prevailed upon to issue a declaration "demoting" Sharī'at-madārī from the rank of Grand Āyatallāh. In May-June 1982, the leading pro-Khumeinī clerics further decided on a purge of the pro-Sharī'at-madārī *'ulamā'* and of other "pseudo-clerics" reluctant to accept *vilāyat-i faqīh.* The Society of Militant Clerics was put in charge of confirming the true clerics.

Hand in hand with the demotion of Sharī'at-madārī and the silencing of clerical opposition went a sustained effort to promote the theory of *vilāyat-i faqīh.* Āyatallāh Khaz'alī, who presided over a series of seminars convened for the discussion of *vilāyat*, would confirm the principle that "the Jurist (*faqīh*) is the lieutenant of the lieutenant of the lieutenant of God, and his command is God's command" (March 1982). Throughout May and June 1982 (and subsequently), the newspapers would regularly publish the martyrs' profession of faith in *vilāyat-i faqīh* and their praise for the Imām and the militant clergy. Statements to the effect that obedience to the *'ulamā'* as "those in authority" is incumbent upon the believer as a religious duty, were often excerpted from the will and made into headlines in bold letters.

The *Imām Jum'a*s have incessantly preached in the doctrine of *vilāyat-i faqīh* and have enjoined their congregations to obey the *'ulamā'* as a matter of religious obligation. A headline on the front page of the daily *Iṭṭilā'āt* in the early days of December 1983 can be taken to represent the culmination of this trend. It was a statement by the Prosecutor General and referred to Khumeinī as *valī-yi faqīh* (the ruling jurist) as synonymous with *valī-yi amr*—an astonishing phrase in view of the fact that, as we have seen, the term *valī* has never been used in the Shi'ite tradition in this general sense except to refer to the twelve Imams. But the most important measure taken to enshrine the novel doctrine of theocratic government has been to teach it at schools. *Vilāyat-i faqīh* is now taught at schools throughout the country as a part of the compulsory course on Islamic ideology from the first grade of high school onward. From August 1983 onward, numerous conventions organized by revolutionary foundations and Islamic associations would pass resolutions endorsing and pledging full support to the concept of *vilāyat-i faqīh*, and declaring obedience to the *faqīh* a religious obligation.

It should be evident that Khumeinī's attempt to subordinate juristic pluralism in the form of the voluntary submission of the Shi'ite believers to the Grand Āyatallāhs as *marāji'-i taqlīd* has been at the expense of the latter.[82] The relationship between the interpretation of the new supreme leadership as *vilāyat-i amr* and the old positions of *marja'-i taqlīd* remains a thorny theoretical issue. Khumeinī himself could not put forward any juristic argument, and he justified his position on the purely pragmatic grounds of the necessity of maintenance of order in society. Recent discussions have not gone beyond Khumeinī's pragmatic justification of the superiority of one *faqīh* over the others. Sayyid Jalāl al-Dīn Madanī, for instance, conceives of the relationship between the supreme leadership and the *marja'iyyat* as one between the general and the particular: the supreme leader has to be a *marja'-i taqlīd*, but not every *marja'-i taqlīd* can undertake the supreme leadership. Furthermore,

> the maintenance of order in society necessitates that when the Leader or the Leadership Council is accepted, all should obey a single authority in social and general problems of the country within the framework of the Islamic Constitutions. Such obedience is implied in the title of *'valī-ye amr'* and 'Imamate of the *umma'* and applies to all members of society without exception, and in this respect the *mujtahid* and the *non-mujtahid*, the *marja'* and the non-*marja'* are in an equal situation.[83]

Despite this accommodation, however, the future of the institution of *marja'iyyat* is in question. Doubts have been raised as to the legitimacy of individual as distinct from collective *ijtihād* now that, for the first time in the history of Shi'ism, an Islamic order has been created. One need only draw out the implications of this typical passage to understand that the institution of *marja'iyyat* has a dark future:

> With the establishment of Islamic government *marja'iyyat*, in practice and officially, took the form of leadership and rule over society; and the *vilāyat-i faqīh*, which in past history had almost never been applied from the position of government, and had always been realized in a defective and incomplete manner, with this revolution reached perfection in practice and occupied its true station.[84]

Some other notable changes in the political ethics of Shi'ism should also be mentioned. Despite the theoretical permanence and immutability of the *sharī'a*, its provisions have been subjected to change, either imperceptibly or as a result of heated juristic controversy. The function of leading the Friday congregational prayer was one of the functions of the Imam which the early Shi'ite jurists declared in abeyance during the Occultation. In a treatise on practical jurisprudence written with a view to its implementation in the local Shi'ite state of Sarbidaran in northeastern Iran, Makkī al-'Āmilī, the First Martyr (d. 1384) ruled that the congregational prayer should be led by the deputy of the Imam even if the latter be a jurist.[85] With the establishment of a Shī'ite empire by the Safavids, the decisive majority of the Shi'ite jurists followed al-Karaki's ruling in favor of holding the congregational prayer during the Occultation of the Twelfth Imam.[86] Safavid monarchs themselves occasionally prayed behind the congregational prayer leaders.[87] During the Qājār period, Friday congregational prayer lost much of its sociopolitical significance because the prayer leaders were among the very few religious functionaries appointed by the Shah, and, therefore, had an ambiguous relationship with the autonomous Shi'ite hierocracy headed by the *mujtahids*. During the Pahlavi era, as we have seen, the activist Khāliṣī made the resuscitation of the congregational prayer the centerpiece of his Islamic revivalist mission. Since the revolution, the Friday congregational prayer has been vigorously revived and fully institutionalized as one of the main pillars of the Islamic theocratic state.[88] The media regularly cover the Friday congregational prayers, which are routinely described as "the unity-creating and enemy-smashing congregational prayer" held in "the meeting-place of the lovers of God." The Friday sermon (*khuṭba*), in Tehran as well as in the remotest towns, has emerged an important political instrument for announcing governmental policies and mobilizing popular support for them.

Ḥajj, another cardinal pratical tenet of Islam, has been given a pronounced political interpretation. In a typical remark, the *imām jum'a* of Rasht has asserted that "the political dimension of *ḥajj* is higher than its devotional dimension."[89] Consistently with this political reemphasis, Khumeinī has in recent years, to the great chagrin and alarm of the Saudi authorities, repeatedly enjoined the Iranian pilgrims to turn *ḥajj* into a forum of protest against imperialism, and to raise the cry of the "disinherited" of the earth against the world-eating *ṭāghūt* and the Great Satan, namely, the United States.

Not surprisingly, there has been an emphatic renewed stress on the incumbency of "enjoining the good" and "forbidding the evil" since the Islamic revolution. *Al-'Urwat al-Wuthqā* of Muḥammad Kāẓim Ṭabāṭabā'ī Yazdī (d. 1919), which has served as the model for all the subsequent treatises on practical jurisprudence (these are required to establish Shi'ite doctors as *marja'-i taqlīd*), contains no specific section on *jihād*, "enjoining the good" and "forbidding the evil." The treatise appeared in 1912/1330 and, in addition to conforming to the Shi'ite tradition, it perhaps also reflects the disillusionment of the leading Shi'ite religious authority of the period with clerical political activism during the Constitutional Revolution of 1906-11. Ṭabāṭabā'ī Yazdī's de-emphasis on political ethics set the tone for the authoritative interpretations of the practical requirements of Shi'ism in the subsequent half century. This de-emphasis was dramatically reversed with the onset of traditionalist clerical activism in the 1960s. Not only did the topic receive considerable attention, but a major qualification in Shi'ite jurisprudence for "enjoining the good" and "forbidding the evil"—i.e., that their performance entail no harm to the person carrying out these duties—came under heavy attack. Hand in hand with this emphatic insistence on the enjoining of the good and forbidding of the evil went a critical reinterpretation of the Shi'ite tenet of *taqiyya* (self-protection by dissimulation of faith) which clearly makes for quietism and non-assertiveness. *Taqiyya* has been generally denounced and declared impermissible whenever it entails "a corruption in religion."[90]

Since the 1960s, *jihād* has also been predictably brought to the foreground in the discussions of political ethics. It is interesting to note, however, that the basic Shi'ite interpretation of the incumbency of *jihād* has so far remained unchanged; it remains restricted to defensive war during the Occultation of the Twelfth Imām.[91]

Another change in the Shi'ite political ethic, a fairly minor one, took place almost imperceptibly in the early decades of the twentieth century. A collection of the practical rulings of Mīrzā-yi Shīrāzī (d. 1895), the *marja'-i taqlīd* during the tobacco protest of 1891-92, edited by Shaykh Faḍlallāh Nūrī (d. 1909), enumerates ten principal ethical duties (*furū'al-dīn*).[92] The last two, *tavallā'* (friendship [towards 'Alī and the House of the Prophet]) and *tabarrā'* (avoidance [of the enemies of the House of Prophet—i.e., the Sunnis]) had been given currency with the establishment of Shi'ism in Iran, and were emphasized through the centuries of Safavid-Ottoman and Qājār-Ottoman warfare and rivalry. Once such rivalry disappeared in the present century, these provisions of the Shi'ite Sacred Law fell into desuetude. They were omitted from the *furū' al-dīn* during the reign of the first Pahlavī, Riḍa Shāh.

The ideologues of the Islamic revolution have not restored the elevated status of *tavallā'* and *tabarrā'* as *furū'*. They have, however, reinterpreted these terms in line with the central idea of a purely Islamic theocratic state.

> *Tavallā'* and *tabarrā'* mean the friendship of the friends of God and the avoidance of the enemies of God . . . . [they are] the foundation of the independence of the Muslims, an independence based on faith and belief which would cause their bondedness to other Muslims and their lack of dependence on the enemies of God."[93]

The devotional love for the House of the Prophet is replaced by the solidarity for the Muslim *umma*, and the avoidance of the enemies of the Imams, by the avoidance of the non-Muslim world-eating and imperialist enemies of God.

Last, but by no means least, we must turn to the topic of martyrdom—prototypically, that of Imam Ḥusayn in Karbalā. The conspicuous use of the imagery of martyrdom and Karbalā in the revolutionary activism of the recent years should not make us ignore the fact that for many centuries the tragedy of Karbalā constituted an apolitical theodicy of suffering.[94] The idea of the martyrdom of Ḥusayn, the Lord of the Martyrs, as vicarious atonement undoubtedly prevailed over its interpretation as the militant assertion of the Shi'ite cause against oppression and tyranny.[95] A religious book from the last decade of the nineteenth century typically illustrates the conception of Imam Ḥusayn as the vicarious sufferer and other-worldly savior: "The Lord of the Martyrs' ark of salvation is greater than other ships of salvation."[96]

A drastic change in the conception of the martydom of Imam Ḥusayn set in with the clerical agitation of the 1960s. In 1968, Ni'matallāh Ṣāliḥī Najafābādī, a student of Khumeinī's, published the *Shahīd-i Jāvīd* (the Eternal Martyr), offering a radically politicized interpretation of the events of Karbalā. Diverging from the doctrinal Shi'ite position on the infallible Imams' divinely inspired knowledge of the past, present, and future affairs, especially the knowledge of calamities (*'ilm al-balāyā*), Najafābādī denied Ḥusayn's foreknowledge of his fate and maintained that "Ḥusayn began his movement neither to fulfill his grandfather's foreboding, nor in a reckless mood of defiance, but as a wholly rational and fairly well-planned attempt at overthrowing Yazīd."[97] Ḥusayn's martyrdom is thus interpreted as a political uprising against an unjust and impious government, and thus the model for Shi'ite political activism.

The book first acquired fame in 1976, when a group said to be disciples of Najafābādī assassinated Āyatallāh Shamsābādī, the representative in Isfahan of the apolitical Grand Āyatallāh Khu'ī. After the revolution, the book was reissued with a foreward by Āyatallāh Muntaẓirī, Khumeinī's designated successor. Khumeinī himself has excelled in the glorification of martyrdom, at times attaining poetic and mystical heights.[98] He has enjoined martyrdom for Islam as a religious duty incumbent on each and every individual.[99] The youthful Guardians of the Islamic Revolution dutifully acknowledge their eagerness for martyrdom when joining the Corps. This is done in a last will and testament which is published in the newspapers if they attain martyrdom.

Conclusion

The militant *'ulamā'* who followed Khumeinī in the 1960s and 1970s sought to defend and revitalize the Shi'ite tradition through a political revolution. To secure the leadership of this political revolution for themselves, they have revolutionized the Shi'ite political ethos whose distinctive mark had been the secularity of temporal rule and the desacralization of political order.[100] To establish and propagate their new conception of authority, the clerical rulers of Iran have incessantly insisted on the sacred character of all authority and thus the ongoing sacralization of the political order. Here are four examples:

In a lecture on the newly established Islamic order, the late Āyatallāh Muṭahharī emphatically maintained that authority is sacred (*muqaddas*) in Islamic government. This is so because the offices of government and judgeship devolve upon the*'ulamā'*.[101]

Āyatallāh Rabbānī Amlashī, temporary *imām jum'a* of Tehran, would accordingly tell his congregation:

> Obedience to the *vilāyat-i faqīh* is an incumbent duty (*vājib*). In the Islamic Republic obedience to the law is incumbent like the daily prayer and fasting, and disobeying it is like disobeying the Islamic Sacred Law.[102]

Āyatallāh Mishkīnī, the *imām jum'a* of Qumm, takes a step in a different direction to sacralize politics.

> Political activity is an incumbent (*shār'ī*) duty. Today, one of the most important acts of devotion (*'ibādāt*) is political activity because without politics our religiosity (*diyānat*) will not last.[103]

Finally, Āyatallāh Mu'min, member of the Council of the Constitution, takes a further step to sacralize *all* authority, legal and political.

> The legitimacy and legality of whatever is done and whatever institutions exist is due to the fact tht they are buttressed by the *vilāyat-i faqīh*. As the *vilāyat faqīh* is at the head of all affairs and the main guarantor of the current laws of the country, it is the *divinely-ordained duty of all the people* to follow every law which is passed and given to the Islamic government for execution. . . . Disobeying such a law is forbidden (*ḥarām*) as drinking wine is forbidden by Islam.[104]

On occasion, the sacralization of politics even necessitates going beyond the requirement of the Constitution of the Islamic Republic. For instance, according to the Constitution, participation in the elections are voluntary. However, as Madanī points out in his commentary, people are usually enjoined by the Imam and the religious authorities to participate in the elections as Muslims fulfilling a religiously incumbent duty. However, "even though this matter becomes incumbent according to the Sacred Law, non-participation is [punishable] not materially but spiritually!"[105]

The paradox of the actual insignificance of the political ethics in the Shi'ite Sacred Law—the paucity of political provisions which reflect the age-old secularity of political authority and the political order in Shi'ism—against the claim of the Islamic militants that Islam is a total way of life and a total ideology, which is above all political and activistic, has struck some observers. For some nine years, the clerical rulers of Iran sought to resolve this paradox by using the legal distinction between the "primary rules" (*aḥkām awwaliyya*) and "secondary rules" (*aḥkām thānawiyya*). The first derive from the sources of the *sharī'a*, the second from expediency as the prerequisites for the implementation of the primary rules. This device has enabled the Āyatallāhs to "Islamicize" and appropriate an enormous amount of European legal material through the revision of the codes of the Constitutional and Pahlavī periods as laws necessary for the maintenance of order which in turn make possible the implementation of the primary rules of the *sharī'a*. More importantly, both categories of primary and secondary rules were said to be binding on the believer as a religious obligation. Thus, for the first time in Shi'ite history, sacrality was claimed for a category of "secondary commandments" as a result *not* of the juristic competence of the Shi'ite *'ulamā' but of their alleged right to rule.* Finally, in January 1988, the charade of the primary/secondary distinction was discarded, and all governmental ordinances (*aḥkām ḥukūmatī*) were said to belong to the category of immediately incumbent primary rules. All pretense was set aside and clerical rule was officially termed the Absolute Mandate of the Jurist (*vilāyat-i muṭlaqa-yi faqīh*).[106]

Notes

1. *Parda dārand* in the printed text is assumed to be a corruption of *darand.*

2. Mīrzā 'Abd al-Laṭīf al-Mūsavī al-Shūshtarī, *Tuḥfat al-'Ālam* (Lucknow: Shawkat al-Islām, 1216/1801), p. 180.

3. See the Introduction, pp. 15-16 above.

4. See Chapter 6, Section 1 above.

5. See my "The *'Ulamā's* Traditionalist Opposition to Parliamentarianism: 1907-1909," *Middle Eastern Studies*, vol. 17, no. 2 (1981), pp. 174-90.

6. Ibid., pp. 178-80. As examples, we may mention Ḥājj Muḥsin, the *mujtahid* of Arāk, and Mullā Qurbān-'Alī, the aged *mujtahid* of Zanjān.

7. These points are stressed by Lahidji in Chapter 6 above.

8. Āqā Najafī Qūchānī, *Siyāḥat-i Sharq ya Zindigānī-nāma*, R. 'A. Shākirī, ed. (Mashhad: Tus, 1351/1972), pp. 460-61, 517-18.

9. See Chapter 16, Section 1 below.

10. See S.A. Arjomand, *The Turban for the Crown. The Islamic Revolution in Iran* (Oxford University Press, 1988), Chapter 2.

11. Mīrzā Yūsuf Shams al-Afāḍil Kāshmarī Tūrshīzī, *Kalima-yi Jāmi'a dar Ma'nā-yi Shūrā va Mashrūṭa va Majlis-i Shūrā-yi Millī* (Tehran 1329/1911), pp. 17-18.

12. Ibid., p. 26.

13. Ibid., p. 6.

14. Ibid., pp. 54-55.

15. Ḥājj Shaykh Muḥammad *mujtahid*, *Risāla-yi Tamīziyya* (Tehran, 1329/1910).

16. Asad Allāh Māmaqānī, *Maslak al-Imām fī Salāmat al-Islām* (Istanbul, 1328/1910), pp. 40-41. On the Istanbul episode, see 'A.-H. Navā'ī, *Dawlat-ha-yi Īrān*, Tehran: Bābak, 1355/1977, p. 131.

17. Ibid., p. 32.

18. Asad Allāh Māmaqānī, *Dīn va Shu'ūn va Ṭarz-i Ḥukūmat dar Madhhab-i Shī'a*, 2d ed. (*Tehran: Chāpkhāna-yi Majlis, 1335/1956*).

19. Ibid., p. 28.

20. Ibid., pp. 54-58.

21. Ibid., pp. 78-79.

22. Ibid., p. 83.

23. Ibid., pp. 62-63.

24. Ibid., p. 73.

25. Ibid., p. 69.

26. Ibid., pp. 42-48.

27. Ibid., pp. 74ff.

28. See Chapter 7 above.

29. Abol-Hassan Bani-Sadr, "Imamat," *Peuples méditerranéens*, no. 21 (Oct.-Dec. 1982), pp. 36, 38. It is interesting to note that Bani-Sadr, too, diverges from the traditional Shi'ite interpretation of the Authority Verse and considers the executive branch of government the *valī-yi amr* (Ibid., p. 39). The Persian original of this work was apparently written earlier. In his book, *L'Éspérance trahie* (Paris: S.P.A.G.-Papyrus Éditions, 1982, p. 12), Banī-Ṣadr refers to a clandestine edition of *Ta'mīm-i Imāmat* (Generalization of the Imamate) published in September 1978. Similar ideas are found in the publications of the

Mujahidīn-i Khalq. A pamphlet published in August 1979, for instance, speaks of "the divine promise concerning the inheritance and Imamate of the weak (*mustaz'afīn*)." (*Rāhnamūdhā-yī dar bāra-yi Tashkīl-i Shūrāhā-yi Vāqi'ī dar Kārkhānijāt va Mu'assisāt*, p. 10.)

30. Sayyid Muṣliḥ al-Dīn Mahdavī, *Tārīkhcha-yi Zindigānī va Āthār-i Marḥūm-i Āyatallāh al-'Uẓmā Ḥājj Āqā Ḥusayn Ṭabāṭabā'ī Burūjirdī*, appended to *Tārīkh-i Sāmarā'* (Isfahan: Firdawsī, 1381/1961-62), p.155.

31. See, for instance, Ḥājj Sayyid 'Abd Allāh Bilādī Bihbahānī, *Mukhtaṣar Javāb-i Iblāghiyya-yi Āqā-yi Mukhbir al-Salṭana, Ra'īs al-Vuzarā', etc.* (Bombay: Muẓaffarī, 1346/1927), p. 8.

32. Sayyid Asad Allāh Khāraqānī, *Risāla-yi Muqaddasa-yi Qaḍā va Shahādat va Muḥakimāt-i Ḥuqūqī-yi Abadī-yi Islām* (Tehran 1341/1922).

33. Ibid., p. 4.

34. Ibid., pp. 1-3

35. Ibid., pp. 5-6.

36. Ibid., p. 6.

37. Ibid., pp. 8-9.

38. Ibid., p. 11.

39. Sayyid Asad Allāh Mūsavī Mīr-Islāmī [Khāraqānī], *Maḥv al-Mawhūm va Ṣaḥv al-Ma'lūm ya Rāh-i Tajdīd-i 'Aẓimat va Qudrat-i Islāmī*, Maḥmūd Ṭāliqānī, ed. ([Tehran:] Gh.-H. Nūr-Muḥammadī Khamsa-pūr, 1339/1960), p. 7. The sense of decline of traditional learning and the deficiency of the *'ulamā'* in reforming their educational system to meet the challenge of modernity is shared by another clerical author of this period: 'Abd al-'Aziz Jawāhir al-Kalām, *Āthār al-Shī'at al-Imāmiyya*, 'A. Jawāhir al-Kalām, tr., Tehran: Maṭba'a-yi Majlis, 1307/1928-9, pp. 108-09.

40. [Khāraqānī], op. cit., p. 144.

41. [M.] Khāliṣī-zāda, *Sa'ādat al-Dārayn va Kiltā al-Ḥasanayn ya Murāsila-yi Āqā-yi Khāliṣī-zāda bi Janāb-i Āqā-yi Qavām al-Salṭana, Nakhust Vazīr*, n.d. [1943], [? Tehran]: Daftar-i Nashriyyāt-i Dīnī, pp. 18-20; [M.] Malik al-Shu'arā' Bahār, *Tārīkh-i Mukhtaṣar-i Aḥzāb-i Sīyāsī-yi Īrān* (Tehran: Amīr Kabīr, 1984-85/1363), vol. 2: p. 44. Inspired by the example of Mustafa Kemal in Turkey, Riḍā Khān's supporters were planning to change the form of government in Iran from monarchy to republic in February-March 1924. Alarmed by the same example, and especially by Mustafa Kemal's abolition of the Caliphate in the same period, Khāliṣī and other clerics opposed Republicanism and organized the bazaar of Tehran against it. Riḍā Khān abandoned the idea after a number of violent clashes. In the following year, the Majlis abolished the Qājār dynasty and Riḍā Khān himself became king.

42. Āyatallāh-zāda [Muḥammad] Khāliṣī, *Mavā'iẓ-i Islāmī* (Mashhad: Matba'a-yi Khurāsān, 1342/1923), pp. 6-7, 77-78.

43. Ibid., p. 18.

44. Bilādī Bihbahānī, op. cit.

45. Khāliṣī-zāda, *Sa'ādat al-Dārayn*, esp. pp. 34-35.

46. Ibid., pp. 72-74.

47. See Chapter 7, p. 174 above.

48. M. Khāliṣī, *Īrān dar Ātash-i Nādānī*, Persian translation of *Sharar Fitnat al-Jahl fī Īrān* by H.-'A. Qalamdārān, n.d., p. 128.

49. Shaykh Muḥammad Khāliṣī, *Ḥaqīqat-i Ḥijāb dar Islām* (Tehran: Daftar-i Nashriyyat-i Dīnī, 1327/1948), p. 50.

50. Khāliṣī-zāda, *Sa'ādat al-Dārayn*, pp. 55-59, 67.

51. Āyatallāh [Muḥammad] Khāliṣī, *Rāhzanān-i Ḥaqq va Ḥaqīqat yā Bāzgashtigān bisū-yi Barbariyyat va Jāhiliyyat* (Baghdad: Ma'ārif, 1371/1951).

52. M. Khāliṣī, *Ā'īn-i Dīn yā Aḥkām-i Islām*, Persian translation of *al-Islām, Sabīl al-Sa'āda wa'l-Salām* (Baghdad, 1372/1953-54) by H.-'A. Qalamdārān, Qumm: Ḥikmat, n.d. [before 1963].

53. 'Alī Akbar Tashayyud, *Tuḥfa-yi Tashayyud dar Tārīkh-i Avvalīn Imārat-i Shī'a* ([Tehran:] Shihāb, 1324/1945), p. 1.

54. 'Alī Akbar Tashayyud, *Hadya-yi Ismā'īl ya Qiyām-i Sādāt-i 'Alavī, etc.* (Tehran: Chāpkhāna-yi Majlis, 1331/1952), p. 90. It is interesting to note also that Tashayyud emphasizes that the Occultation of the Imam should not be equated with his nonexistence. His Majesty (*A'lā-Ḥaḍratash*) miraculously intervened in the events of this world to protect the Shī'a. Furthermore, he has clarified the duties of the believers by referring them to the *mujtahidīn*. (Ibid., pp. 198-200).

55. Khāraqānī, *Maḥv al-Mawhūm*, Ṭāliqānī's Introduction, p. h.

56. For a discussion of the activities of this group, see Shahrough Akhavi, *Religion and Politics in Contemporary Iran. Clergy-State Relations in the Pahlavi Period* (Albany: SUNY Press, 1980), pp. 117-29.

57. *Guftār-i Māh dar Nimāyāndan-i Rāh-i Rāst-i Dīn* (Tehran: Kitābkhāna-yi Ṣadūq, No. 1 [1340/1961]), pp. 260-62.

58. *Baḥthī dar Marja'iyyat va Rūḥāniyyat* (Tehran, 1342/1962).

59. Naṣīr al-Dīn Amīr-Ṣādiqī Tihrani, *Rūḥāniyyat dar Shī'a* (Tehran, 1349/1970), p. 5.

60. Ḥasan Farīd Gulpāygānī, *Qānūn-i Asāsī-yi Islām* (Tehran: Farahānī, n.d. [1349/1970]), p. 296.

61. Anṣarī's position was in reality contrary to Tihrānī's argument. See p. 193 below.

62. 'Alī Tihrānī, *Madīna-yi Fāḍila dar Islām* (Tehran: Ḥikamat, 1354/1976). This work was completed in Mashhad in December 1970 (Ibid., p. 141).

63. S. A. Arjomand, ed., *From Nationalism to Revolutionary Islam* (Albany: SUNY Press, 1984), Chapter 10.

64. See the Preamble, Chapter 17, pp. 371-72 below.

65. Muḥammad b. Ḥasan al-Ṭūsī, *Tafsīr al-Tibyān*, A. B. Tihrānī, ed., (Najaf: Maṭba'at al-'Ilmiyya, 1957), vol. 2, pp. 236-37.

66. Faḍl b. Ḥasan al-Ṭabrisī, *Tafsīr Majma' al-Bayān*, A. Bihishtī, trans. (Qumm, 1349/1970-71), vol. 5, pp. 202-3.

67. Ardabīlī, op. cit., p. 687.

68. Muḥammad Ḥusayn Ṭabāṭabā'ī, *al-Mīzān fī Tafsīr al-Qur'ān* (Beirut: al-'Ilmī, n.d.), vol. 5, pp. 398-99. The same traditional Shi'ite view is upheld by two less important commentaries on the eve of the Islamic revolution: M. Thaqafī Tihrānī, *Ravān-i Jāvīd dar Tafsīr-i Qur'ān-i Majīd*, 2d ed. (Tehran: Burhān, 1398/1978), vol. 2, pp. 70-73; M. T. Najafī, *Tafsīr-i Āsān* (Tehran: Islāmiyya, 1358/1979-80), vol. 3, pp. 277-81.

69. H. Enayat, "Khumaynī's Concept of the 'Guardianship of the Jurisconsult,'" in J.P. Piscatori, ed., *Islam in the Political Process* (Cambridge: Cambridge University Press, 1983), p. 162.

70. Abu'l-Qāsim Najm al-Dīn al-Muḥaqqiq al-Ḥillī, *al-Mukhtaṣar al-Nāfi'* (Najaf, 1383/1964), p. 273.

71. See Chapter 6, p. 143 above.

72. Jawāhir al-Kalām, op. cit., 105-06. It should be noted that the above is reported as the common opinion and not as that of the jurists, nor as a legal norm backed by Qur'ānic Verses and Imāmī Traditions, as Khumeinī was to do.

73. Muḥammad al-Ḥusayn Āl-i Kāshif al-Ghiṭā', *Rīsha-yi Shī'a va Pāyaha-yi Ān*, 'A.-R. Khusravānī, trans. (Tehran, 1317/1938 [Persian translation of *Aṣl al-Shī'a va Uṣūluha*, 1351/1932-33]), p. 92.

74. M. Khāliṣī, *Ā'īn-i Dīn*, pp. 327-28.

75. *Ibid.*, pp. 328-29. The presumably fuller discussion of the topic in Khāliṣī's *Iḥyā' al-Sharī'a* (Baghdad, 1370/1951-52) has not been consulted. The version used is Khāliṣī's own abridgement of that discussion for a broader public.

76. Muḥammad Sangalajī, *Ḍavābiṭ va Qavā'id va Kuliyyāt-i 'Uqūd va Iqā'āt*, 4th ed. (Tehran, 1347/1968), pp. 134-40.

77. A.A. Nāṣirī, *Imāmat va Shafā'at* (Tehran, 1351/1972), pp. 4-5.

78. N. Calder, "Accommodation and Revolution in Imami Shī'ī Jurisprudence: Khumaynī and the Classical Tradition," *Middle Eastern Studies*, vol. 18, no. 1 (1982), p. 14; emphasis added.

79. J. Madanī, "Ḥuqūq-i Asāsī dar Jumhūrī-yi Islāmī," *Surūsh*, no. 176 (17 Day 1361/January 1983).

80. Ḥaddād 'Ādil in *Iṭṭilā'āt*, 7 Shahrivar 1363 (August 1983).

81. *Surūsh*, no. 175 (11Day 1361/January 1983), p. 41.

82. This explains why the chief opposition to the new theory, as we have seen, in fact comes from the *marāji'*.

83. *Surūsh*, no. 177 (25 Day 1361/January 1983), p. 41.

84. Ḥaddād 'Ādil in *Iṭṭilā'āt*, 2 Shahrīvar 1362 (August 1983).

85. Arjomand, *The Shadow of God and the Hidden Imam*, p. 71.

86. See Chapter 4 above.

87. Muḥammad b. Aḥmad al-'Āmilī al-'Alavī, *Qavā'id al-Salāṭīn*, Library of the Majlis, Tehran, manuscript #516, ff. 163-65.

88. Arjomand, *The Turban for the Crown*, Chapter 8, Section 3.

89. *Iṭṭilā'āt*, 7 Shahrīvar 1362 (August 1983).

90. H. Enayat, *Modern Islamic Political Thought* (London: Macmillan, 1982), pp. 178-81.

91. F. Rajaee, *Islamic Values and World View. Khumayni on Man, the State and International Politics* (New York: University Press of America), pp. 88-91.

92. Faḍlallāh Nūrī, ed., *Su'āl va Javāb* (Bombay, 1893), p. 79.

93. Ḥaddad 'Ādil in *Iṭṭilā'āt*, 25 Murdād 1362 (August 1983).

94. Arjomand, *The Shadow of God*, pp. 164-66, 240-41.

95. Enayat, op. cit., p. 183.

96. Abu'l-Ḥasan Iṣṭahbānātī, *Salsabil* (Bombay, 1894/1312), p. 341.

97. Enayat, op. cit., p. 193. As Kohlberg points out in Chapter 2, the rationalist eleventh-century theologian, al-Mufīd, denied Ḥusayn's foreknowledge of his death, but the traditional position remained unaltered.

98. As in the sermon on the martyrdom of Āyatallāh Bihishtī on June 28, 1981.

99. Rajaee, op. cit., p. 70.

100. This position is elaborated in my *Shadow of God*.

101. *Iṭṭilā'āt*, 14 Day 1362 (January 1983).

102. Friday sermon, 24 Sharīvar 1361 (September 1982).

103. *Iṭṭilā'āt*, 28 Ābān 1362 (November 1983).

104. Ibid.

105. *Surūsh*, no. 187 (27 Farvardīn 1362/April 1983), p. 51.

106. *Jumhūrī-yi Islāmī*, 19-29 Day 1366/January 1988.

PART II

Selected Sources

With editorial assistance
from Kathryn Arjomand

CHAPTER 9

An Annotated Bibliography on Government and Statecraft

MOHAMMAD-TAQI DANISHPAZHOUH

Translated and adapted by Andrew Newman

Manuals of Statecraft
(*Dastūr-i Shahryārī*)

The practical philosophy of statecraft (*kishvardārī va shahryārī*) has been called "civic politics" (*al-sīyāsat al-madanīyya*). Ṭabarī Tūranjī in his *The Hippocratic Treatments* (*al-Mu'ālajāt al-Buqrātīyya*) (Chapter Fifty, Section One) called it "public politics" (*al-sīyāsat al-'āmma*), while Ibn Hindū (d.1019/410) in his *The Fascinating* (*al-Mushawwiqa*) described it as "the establishment of laws and regulations which is the function of Prophecy," intending to refer to its religious roots.[1]

Fārābī (d. 950/339), following Plato, Aristotle, and Iranian culture, discussed "the virtuous city and nation," according to Ibn Rushd (d. 1198/595) in his work on the art of rhetoric. Fārābī, in his *The Enumeration of the Sciences* (*Iḥsā' al-'Ulūm*), *The Book of the Nation* (*Kitāb al-Millā*), and the principles of *The Opinions of the Virtuous City* (*Ārā' al-Madīna al-Fāḍila*), as well as his *Civic Chapters* (*Fuṣūl-i Madanī*), for the most part followed the approach of Plato.

The Brethren of Purity (*Ikhwān al-Ṣafā'*), in the seventh essay on crafts (*ṣanā'i'*) spoke of "prophetic politics" (*sīyāsat-i nabavī*), the establishment of royal laws, preservation of the law of God (*sharī'at*), public politics (*sīyāsat-i 'amm*), and the rule of princes and peasants, as opposed to private politics (*sīyāsat-i khāṣṣ*) or household management (*tadbīr-e manzil*), and natural politics (*sīyāsat-i dhāti*) or ethics (*akhlāq*).[2]

What Ibn Sīnā (d. 1037/429) discussed at the end of his "Metaphysics" (*Ilāhī*) in *The Book of Healing* (*Kitāb al-Shifā'*), which is what Mullā Ṣadrā Shīrāzī (d. 1640/1050) also discussed at the end of his work *The Origin and the Return* (*al-Mabda' wa'l-Ma'ād*), can be termed "the just city" (*madīna-yi 'adīla*). Muḥammad Yūsuf Mūsā in his *Memorial Avicenne* called this the social and political dimension of Ibn Sīnā's philosophy.[3] At the 1954 Conference on Ibn Sīnā, Aḥmad Fu'ād Ahwānī, in a lecture entitled "The Political Theory of Ibn Sīnā," and Jamīl Ṣalībā, in a lecture entitled "The Just City," both presented some of the best research on Ibn Sīnā's thought.[4] To date I have not seen critical studies to equal those of these three scholars.

On this subject, aside from the works of Plato and Aristotle, and the Sassanian and Indian texts which have come down to us, there are two sets of works. First, there are those such as *The Rules for Kings* (*Adāb al-Mulūk*) of Ibn al-Ṭayyib al-Sarakhsī (d. 899/286),[5] taken from the work of the same title by Buzurgmihr, in forty chapters; and *The Book of the Crown* (*Kitāb al-Tāj*), attributed to Jāḥiẓ (d. 868/255), but which al-Sarakhsī stated[6] was written by Muḥammad b. Ḥārith Tha'alabī in 861/247 for Fatḥ b. Khāqān, most likely based on Pahlavī works.[7] There is also *The Gift of the Kings* (*Tuḥfat al-Mulūk*) and *The Admonishment to the Kings* (*Naṣīhat al-Mulūk*), both by Ghazālī; *The Political Treatise* (*Sīyāsatnāma*) of Niẓām al-Mulk; *The Gift of the Kings* (*Tuḥfat al-Mulūk*) of Isfahānī; *The Accoutrements and Ornaments of the Resourceful Kings* (*Sāz va Pīrāya-yi Shāhān-i Purmāya*) by Kāshānī; and *The Divine Treatise on Rule* (*Khilāfatnāma-yi Ilahī*). There are also ten other works in Arabic and Persian which I have discussed elsewhere.[8]

Secondly, there are the "Manuals of Statecraft," or "Mirrors for Rulers" for which the phrase "Mirrors for Princes" is used. The genre could also be called "The Treatise of Advice" (*Pandnāma*) or "The Covenant" (*'Ahdnāma*).

In this connection, aside from the Sassanian period, in addition to the works of advice of Anūshīrvān and others, the counsels of Ardashīr and the letter of Tansar may be cited.[9] I have discussed portions of these in my preface to *Jāvīdān Khirad.*[10] From the Greeks, there is the essay of Alexander and Aristotle, and the latter's *Secret of Secrets*,[11] as well as the counsels of Hadrianus which Ibn Dāya (d. 945/334) included in his *The Greek Covenants* (*al-'Uhūd al-Yūnānīyya*).

The letter of advice (*pandnāma*) of Aristotle to Alexander was translated into Persian by the eleventh/fifth-century writer Mukhtār Kamāl al-Mulk Abū Ja'far Muḥammad b. Aḥmad Zūzanī. There is a copy of this in the Munsha'āt-i Majlis and also in the collection of As'ad

Effendī in Istanbul.[12] Professor Minavi used this to publish the work in the 'Āmirīnāma (pp. 41-52). In the Munsha'āt of Ḥusayn Nakhjavānī (#52/9) there is also a copy of the letter of advice of Aristotle to Alexander which he translated into Persian and later published in *Yaghmā.*[13]

Of the Islamic period manuals (*dastūrnāma-hā*) the following may be cited:

1. The advice of the Prophet (May God Bless Him and His Family) to 'Amr b. Hazm, which for the most part dealt with religious aspects of the issue (of statecraft).[14]

2. The Manual (*Dastūrnāma*) of the Imam 'Alī (Upon Him be Peace) (d. 661/40) to Mālik Ashtar (d. 658/38), the same year for which Najāshī (982-1058/372-450) in his *Rijāl* and Shaykh al-Ṭūsī (995-1067/385-460) in his *Fihrist* cited two authorities, from Abu'l-Qāsim Asbagh b. Nabāta (d. after 721/100) and Abū Bakr Aḥmad b. Marwān Mālikī Dīnawarī (d. 932/320) in *The Social Intercourse* (*al-Mujālasa*) and *The Jewels of Knowledge* (*Jawāhir al-'Ilm*),[15] from Muḥammad b. Ghālib from Abu Ḥadhīfa from Sufyān Thūrī from Zabīdyāmī from Muhājir 'Āmirī. Ibn 'Asākir Dimashqī (d. 1175/571) in his *History of Syria* (*Tārīkh al-Shām*),[16] when he discussed the life of Imam 'Alī (Upon Him be Peace), cited a part of this manual on the authority of Abū'l-Qāsim 'Alawī from Rushā' b. Naẓīf from Abū Muḥammad Ḥasan b. Ismā'īl, the coiner, from the same Dīnawarī. The portion cited can be found in *The Path of Eloquence* (*Nahj al-Balāgha*), *The Gifts of Understanding* (*Tuḥuf al-'Uqūl*), and *The Pillars of Islām* (*Da'ā'im al-Islām*). Ibn 'Asākir's *History* does not contain any letter from Ashtar; the author said the Imam (Upon Him be Peace) wrote this for one of His companions in the city in which he was living. Both Qāḍī Quḍā'ī (d. 1062/454) and Miskawayh Rāzī (d. 1030/421) quoted a portion of the work without naming any sources.

This work of the Imam can be found in *The Pillars of Islam* (*Da'ā'im al-Islām*) of Abū Ḥanīfa Nu'mān Maghribī (d. 973/363), written ca. 959/347; *The Gifts of Understanding* (*Tuḥuf al-'Uqūl*) of Ibn Shu'ba Ḥarrānī Ḥalabī (ca. 947-92/336-82); *The Happiness and the Happier* (*al-Sa'āda wa'l-As'ād*) of 'Āmirī Nīshābūrī (d. 991/381); and *The Path of Eloquence* (*Nahj al-Balāgha*) of Raẓī Baghdādī (completed 1009/400). Maghribī did not mention Ashtar but 'Āmirī did, as did Ḥalabī and Baghdādī. From the evidence of the transmitters, the commentaries, and the translations of the letter, there is no doubt among Sunnī and Shi'ite scholars as to its attribution to Imām 'Alī (Upon Him be Peace). Nevertheless several Orientalist and Arab scholars are of a different mind, for example, Jamīl Sulṭan, Iḥsān 'Abbās, Gustave Richter, and Gerard Salinger.[17] More recently, Wadād al-Qāḍī published an article citing

'Abbās, Richter and Salinger, and discussed the issue. She concluded that the Imam's advice may have been from a book of the words of the Imam by Qāḍī Aflāḥ b. Hārūn Malūsī (alive 909/297 and 920/308), a missionary (*dā'ī*) of the Fatimid Mahdī (909-33/297-322), and that Maghribī took it from this source and included it in his own work.[18] As with the other three scholars, al-Qāḍī has a different idea on the issue which cannot be accepted easily, since Najāshī, Ṭūsī, and Aḥmad Malikī Dīnwarī also quoted from this letter of the Imam.

We also know that Maghribī wrote a long work entitled *The Book of the Elucidation* (*Kitāb al-Iḍāḥ*), a portion of which is extant. The work is similar to the *Kāfi* by Kulaynī (d. 941/329) in that it comprises chains of transmission. Maghribī cited other works known to Imāmī and Zaydī scholars. *The Book of the Elucidation* may have been one of the sources used by Ibn Shahrāshūb (d. 1192/588). If a complete copy of the work is found, another chain for the letter of Ashtar may be found there. Wilferd Madelung has also discussed this issue.[19]

3. The advice (*naṣīḥa*) of Marwān b. Muḥammad (744-49/127-32) to his son 'Abdallāh in 745/128. The author was 'Abd al-Ḥamīd Dabīr Qaysārī (d. 749/132).

4. *The Treatise of the Companions* (*Risālat al-Ṣaḥāba*) of Ibn al-Muqaffa' Irragānī (Arrajānī) (727-59/109-42) written for Manṣūr, the 'Abbāsid Caliph (753-74/136-58).

5. *The Ahwāzī Treatise* (*al-Risālat al-Ahwāzīyya*) of the Imām Ja'far al-Ṣādiq (Upon Him be Peace) (699-765/80-148), for 'Abdallāh Najāshī, the governor of Ahwāz.

6. The advice of Ṭāhir Pūshangī to his son 'Abdallāh in 820/205.[20]

Two social groupings are in evidence in these works. The first comprises men of noble birth and the behavior which the ruler must have. In the advice of Aristotle to Alexander, included in *The Commentary on the Path of Eloquence* (*Sharḥ Nahj al-Balāgha*) of Ibn Abī'l-Ḥadīd al-Madā'īnī (d. 1257/655), there is a discussion on princes (*shahzādigān*).[21] In the advice of Imam 'Alī (Upon Him be Peace) to Ashtar, reference is made to "those endowed with chivalry, of noble descent, people of respectable houses and good backgrounds, people of bravery, courage and generosity."[22] Similarly, in the advice of Ṭāhir Pūshangī there is the phrase "people of respectable houses," and 'Abd al-Ḥamīd Kātib used the phrase "people of houses of dignity (*buyūtāt al-sharaf*), well-known for their virtue and worthy of mention." In Ibn Sīnā's *The Book of Healing* (*Kitāb al-Shifā'*) the phrase "people of standing" (*ahl al-sābiqa*) was used.[23]

A second group comprises various sorts of people. In the advice of Ardashīr, these were of four sorts: military knights and guards of the realm; those employed in the religious institution engaged in abstinence (*parhīzkārī*) and adoration of God (*sitāyish*)—these being the religious scholars and doctors of the law; secretaries, astrologers and doctors who are the embellishments of the realm; and, the peasants, farmers, and artisans who make for the prosperity of the realm.[24] In *The Happiness and the Happier* (*al-Sa'āda wa'l-As'ād*), Anūshīrvān was quoted as having specified four sorts: religious judges, disciplinarians (*parhīzakārān*), and those engaged in relgious adoration (*sitāyish-garān*); military knights and infantry; secretaries for court correspondence and taxes (*kharāj*); and peasants, shepherds, artisans, and merchants. In *The Book of Healing* (*Kitāb al-Shifā'*), Ibn Sīnā mentioned three groups: administrators, workers (*al-ṣunnā'*), and guards—exactly those cited by Plato. The *farmān* of Ashtar mentioned the following: public and private secretaries; middle-level, merciful, judicial administators (*dādgarukārkunān*); tax and capitation-tax (*jizya*) collectors; merchants and artisans; and indigents (*niyāzmandān*). Al-Madā'inī in his commentary on the *Nahj al-Balāgha* reiterated the philosophical foundation of these groups.[25] The Brethren of Purity (*Ikhwān al-Ṣafā*) in various places in their essays, as discussed by 'Umar Farrukh, mentioned nine groups.[26]

Islamic politics may be divided into two elements. The first is the behavior and precepts of the Prophet of Islam (May God Bless Him and His Family) himself, where we know what he did and what foundations he laid in his changing the practices of a given area. In determining these, the sole sources are the Qur'ān, the *sunna*, and his actions and words. These in turn can be determined from Qur'ānic commentaries, genuine statements, traditions, *ḥadīth* collections and *fiqh* of the Imāmī, Zaydī, and the four Sunni schools, and the Ibāḍīyya on such matters as *jihād*, punishments (*ḥudūd*), blood monies (*diyāt*), the resurrection, sharecropping (*muzāra'a*), limited partnership (*muḍāraba*), and treasuries. Portions of works such as *The Star Luminaries of the Akhbār* (*Shihāb al-Akhbār*) of Quḍā'ī, and Daylamī's *The Paradise of the Akhbār* (*Firdaws al-Akhbār*) will prove useful in this connection.[27]

The second element is the political thought of the regimes of Caliphate and Imamate which succeeded the Prophet (May God Bless Him and His Family). This thought inevitably became intermingled with Iranian, Indian, Greek, and Hebrew thought, and elements of these are clearly evident. Some Orientalists such as Grignaschi, Manzalawi, and Rosenthal have written articles on this subject which should be consulted. In his book *The Greek Roots of the Islamic Political Theories* (*al-Uṣūl al-Yūnānīyya li'l-Naẓariyyāt al-Sīyāsiyya fi'l-Islām*), Badawi mentioned some of these.[28] *Index Islamicus* should also be consulted.

There are a number of works useful in a discussion of the political thought of the Islamic Caliphate. These were either translated from Arabic into Persian, or written in Persian, and they include:

1. *Imperial Commands* (*al-Aḥkām al-Sulṭāniyya*) by Abu'l-Ḥasan 'Alī B. Muhammad b. Ḥabīb Māwardī Baṣrī Shāfi'ī (974-1058/364-450), which clearly resembles a work of the same title by Farā' Ḥanbalī (d. 1065/458).

Qiwām al-Dīn Yūsuf b. Ḥasan Ḥusaynī Shāfi'ī Rūmī (d. 1516/922), who wrote commentaries on *Nahj al-Balāgha* and Naṣīr al-Dīn Ṭūsī's *Tajrīd*, translated this work of Māwardī into Persian under the title *The Rules of Monarchs* (*Aḥkām al-Salāṭīn*) or *The Commentary on the Imperial Rules* (*Ta'līq Aḥkām-i Sulṭānī*) or the *Translation of the Imperial Rules* (*Tarjama-yi Aḥkām-i Sulṭānī*), in twenty chapters, for Rustam Bahādur Aqqūyūnlū (1492-95/898-901) in the year 1495/901.[29] Among the best works of this genre which I have read, aside from Ibn Khaldūn's *The Introduction* (*al-Muqaddima*), which is both a work of sociology and among the works of the "Mirror for Princes" genre, there is *The Famous Figures of the Profession on the Characteristics of Kingship* (*Nawābigh al-Silk fī Tabāī' al-Mulk*) by Abū 'Abdallāh Muḥammad Gharnāṭī (d. 1490/896), which reconciled Islamic, Greek, and Iranian thought.[30]

2. *The Lamp of the Kings on Justice and Conduct* (*Sirāj al-Mulūk fi'l-'Adl wa'l-Sulūk*) by Ibn Abī Rundaqa Abū Bakr Muḥammad Sarqasṭī Ṭarṭūsī (1059-1126/451-520). Taqī al-Dīn Muḥammad Ṣadr al-Dīn 'Alī Ṭāliqānī Fārsī Hindī Dakanī translated this work into Persian for 'Abd al-Raḥīm Khān Khānā (d. 1624/1034).[31]

3. *The Sea of Benefits* (*Baḥr al-Fawā'id*), dedicated to Atābag Shām and written between 1156/551 and 1161/557 in Syria. There is a great deal of knowledge in many places throughout this work, especially in "The Book of the King" (*Kitāb al-Sulṭān*) where the author discussed Islamic rule. I translated this work and published it.[32] At that time I had access to only two manuscript copies of the work. I later found a third copy at the Shīrānī Library in Lahore (catalogue, p. 273), and a fourth copy at the University of Holland.[33] The work ought to be republished using these two other copies.

4. *The Gardens of Attitudes* (*Ḥadā'iq al-Sīyar*) by Niẓām al-Dīn Yaḥyā, written for 'Alā' al-Dīn Kayqubād Seljūkī (1210-19/607-16) in ten chapters. There is a copy of this work at Sipahsālār and a microfilm copy at the University of Tehran. The work has also been published. C.H. de Fouchecour has also discussed the treatise.[34]

5. *The Benefits of Conduct on the Virtues of the Kings* (*Fawā'id al-Sulūk fī Faḍā'il al-Mulūk*) by Ishāq Sajāsī, written in 1212-13/609-10 for Atabag Uzbig b. Nuṣrat al-Dīn Pahlavān Muḥammad Atābag Azirbayjānī (1210-25/607-22), in ten chapters. There is a copy of this work

in Paris and the Malik collection; a microfilm copy of the Paris manuscript is available at the University of Tehran.[35] A published version might be prepared from these two copies.

6. *Private and Public Politics* (*al-Sīyāsat al-Khāṣṣa wa'l-'Āmma*) by Abū 'Alī Ḥasan Silmāsī, written for Abu'l-Ḥasan 'Alī Iṣfahānī in 1217/614. The author included the advice of many Greek thinkers.[36]

7. *The Subtleties of Wisdom on Knowledge, Administering Justice, and the Behavior of the King* (*Laṭā'if al-Ḥikma dar Ma'rifat va Mu'dalāt va Ādāb-i Pādishāhī*) by Sirāj al-Dīn Abū'l-Thanā Urmawī (1197-1283/594-682), written for 'Izz al-Dīn Kaykāvūs II, the Seljūk (1246-57/644/55) in 1203/600. The work was based on *The Secrets of the Revelation* (*Aṣrār al-Tanzīl*) of Imam Rāzī.[37]

8. *The Pavilion of Justice on the Rules of Sovereignty* (*Fusṭāṭ al-'Adāla fī Qawā'id al-Salṭana*) by Muḥammad b. Maḥmūd Khatīb, written for Muẓaffar al-Dīn Mas'ūd al-Buyūrk and dedicated to Ghīyāth al-Dīn Mas'ūd b. Kayqāvūs b. Kayqubād b. Kaykhusraw b. Kayqubād (1283-96/682-96) in Aqseray (Nakida) in 1284/683, in eight chapters. Blochet discussed the work and there is a microfilm copy at the University of Tehran.[38]

9. *The Junction of the Two Seas* (*Majām' al-Baḥrayn*) by Shams al-Dīn Ibrāhīm, the *muḥtasib* of Abarqūh, written in 1318/718, in which the author discussed politics from a religious and gnostic (*'irfānī*) viewpoint. This is a fine work. I read a copy at the Bibliothèque Nationale in Paris and have discussed it.[39]

10. *The Treasure of the Kings* (*Dhakhīrāt al-Mulūk*) by Amīr Sayyid 'Alī Hamadānī (1314-84/714-86) on Islamic ethics (akhlāq). The work was based on *The Reviving of the Sciences* (*Iḥyā al-'Ulūm*) and *The Chemistry of Happiness* (*Kīmīyā-yi Sa'ādat*). Hamadānī's work was written with an introduction, ten chapters and a conclusion. There are many copies of the work extant, and it has been published several times. I saw an essay in German by J. K. Teufel on this work in Paris in which he described Hamadānī's life and works. Surūrī has translated this work into Turkish.[40]

11. *Admonitions Pertaining to Shāhrūkh* (*Naṣā'iḥ-i Shāhrukh Shāhī*) by Jalāl al-Dīn Zakarīya b. 'Abdallāh Qā'inī Nāṣafī Bukhārā'ī Hiravī, written in 1410/813 for the treasury of Shāhrukh (1307-1458/707-863), in ten sections and four subsections. There is a copy of the work in Vienna.[41]

12. *The Fountain of Secrets* (*Yanbū' al-Aṣrār*) by Kamāl al-Dīn Ḥusayn Khwārazmī (d. 1435/839). His second work was *The Royal Admonishment*, (*Naṣīḥatnāma-yi Shāhī*) which Muṣtafā b. Khayr al-Dīn translated into Turkish. A copy of the translation is in Paris, and it is cited by Munzavī.[42] The *Yanbū' al-Aṣrār* was published in Tehran in

1981/1360, together with an account of the author's life in the preface. H. F. Hofman has discussed the author and his works in his Oriental Turkish Manuscripts Catalogue.

There are two other works of note connected with Khwārazmī. One was by his son Sharaf al-Dīn Ḥusayn Khwārazmī, and entitled *The Path of the Lovers* (*Jāddat al-'Āshiqīn*), written in 1562/970 and 1565/973. The second is *The Key of the Seekers* (*Miftāḥ al-Ṭālibīn*) by Kamāl al-Dīn Maḥmūd, written in 1542/950.[43] *The Life of Khwārazmī* (*Aḥvāl-i Khwārazmī*), manuscript #168 at the Asfiyya (catalogue, III:164), written in 1564/972 must be this same *The Path of the Lovers*.[44]

13. Shaykh al-Islām Burhān al-Dīn Amīr-i Islām Ghazālī, living in Balkh and alive until 1440/844, dedicated a Persian translation to Mughayth al-Dawla Sulṭān Ḥusayn in the fourteenth/eighth century of the letter of Alexander to Aristotle. A copy of this work is in the British Museum, and the University of Tehran has a microfilm of the manuscript. Nafīsī also mentioned the work several times.[45]

14. *The Gift of the Sultāns* (*Tuḥfat al-Salāṭīn*) by 'Alā al-Dīn 'Alī Muṣannifak Shāhrūdī Basṭāmī Herātī (d. 1466/871), in twenty chapters. He wrote the work for Ulugh Beg Gurgānī (1446-49/850-53).

Ḥājjī Khalīfa Chalabi (d. 1656-57/1067) mentioned this treatise in his Kashf al-Zunūn, and there is a copy of it at the Gulistān Library (#1969). It is also described in Ātābāy's catalogue (p. 169, #68).

The beginning of the work exactly resembles *The Gift of the Kings* (*Tuḥfat al-Mulūk*), in forty chapters, and the little-known *The Gift of the Viziers* (*Tuḥfat al-Wuzarā'*) which is available elsewhere.[46] It is clear these little-known works were done from the work of the same Basṭāmī.

15. *The Gift of the Sulṭāns* (*Tuḥfat al-Salāṭīn*), written for Shāhrukh Tīmūrī (1308-1458/708-863). There is a copy of this in the British Museum (OR 11153), and it has also been discussed in the *Bulletin* and the Meredith-Owens's catalogue.[47]

16. *The Jewels of the Treasure of Marvels* (*Jawāhir Kanz al-Gharā'ib*) by Najm al-Dīn Qāsim b. Muḥammad Madhamikaynī. The work was written in four sections and deals with Islamic politics for four groups, and their relationships, based on the Qur'ān and the *sunna*. There is a copy of this work in the Bibliothèque Nationale which I have read and described in my report on my trip to Paris.[48] This copy was completed in 1429/833, thus the work itself must be of the eighth or ninth/fourteenth or fifteenth century.

17. *The Manners of the Sulṭān* or *The Manners of Rule* (*Ādāb-i Sulṭānī*) (*Ādāb-i Sulṭānāt*) by Hibātallāh Shāh Mīr Ḥusaynī, written for Sulṭān 'Alā al-Mulk, 1477/882. In 1492/898, the author again turned to the work and did a corrected version of it.[49]

18. Jalāl al-Dīn Muḥammad Dawānī Kāzirūnī (1426-1502/830-908), a Shāfi'ī theologian, wrote an essay in Persian on the Office of Justice (*dīwān-i muẓālim*) in Lar, for Niẓām al-Dīn Malik 'Alā al-Mulk, the ruler in the area.[50] To clarify his meanings, the author cited examples from the acts of the Caliphs.

Dawānī also wrote *The Path for the Education of Children* (*Ṭarīq Tarbīyat al-Awlād*), which was published in Tehran in the journal *Taḥqīq dar Mabda'-i Āfarīnish.* A copy done by the author upon the order of Mīrmīrān and dated 1498/904 is at the University of Tehran.[51] In this essay, the author discussed the circumstances of school education according to the Sunni style and mentioned several education essays. In the introduction to his *The Sample of the Sciences* (*Unmūdhaj al-'Ulūm*), he mentioned the names of his teachers. He wrote, "I read the 'Forty *Ḥadīth*' (*Arba'īn*) of al-Navāvī, 'The Record of Fiqh' (*Muḥarrar al-Fiqh*) and Bukhārī's *ḥadīth* collection, as well as the commentary on the *Mukhtaṣar* of Ibn al-Ḥājib and the glosses of the Sharifs on them, and I have permission (*ijāza*) to teach from them."

These two works reveal the teaching style of the Iranian Sunnis.[52] Dawānī also wrote the essay "The Inspection of the Army" (*'Arḍ-i Lashkar*), which is very useful and has been published twice.[53] He wrote two treatises on justice in which he may have used the essay "On the Nature of Justice" (*Fī Māhīyat al-'Adl*) which Miskawayh Rāzī wrote for Abū Ḥiyān Tawhīdī. M. S. Khān published this work by Rāzī, with an English translation based on manuscript #137 at Āstān-i Quds-i Raḍavī.[54] He has also written two essays on the treatise.[55]

Both of these works by Dawānī have been discussed by Munzavī, Tihrānī, and Nafīsī.[56] They have also been cited in the catalogues. Munzavī suggested that Dawānī in fact wrote four treatises on justice. After carefully inspecting the manuscript copies and the catalogues, I have concluded that Dawānī wrote one essay on justice dedicated to Sulṭān Ya'qūb Bahādur Khān Bāyandurī (d. 1490/896), with an introduction on the deputyship of man (*khilāfat-i insān*) in two sections, the first in which he stated that man has two strengths, and the second in which he discussed the different types of justice according to Aristotle. The conclusion to the work discussed the embodiment of action and ethics.

There are manuscript copies of this work at the following locations:

a. Faculty of Letters, University of Tehran, Ḥikmat 119/9, copy dated 1562/970, (Catalogue, II:40).

b. Malik Library, 6192/22, copy dated 1648/1058, in fifty-eight folios, twenty-three lines each.

c. Majlis Library, 5180/42, copy dated 1658/1069, folios 407-12 (Catalogue, XV: 34); copy 4023/5, from the thirteenth/nineteenth century, folios 42-51 (Catalogue, XI: 120).

d. Punjab Public Library, Lahore, 170 Jala 279/9, copy dated 1693/1105, folios 51-54.[57]

e. Āstān-i Quds, Manṭiq 113/11 (Catalogue, Manṭiq I:32); Akhlāq, 215, 7225, eleven folios, fifteen lines each; Akhlāq, 216, 5979.[58]

f. Paris, SP 143/3, folios 176-85, copy dated 1500/906. A microfilm copy of this manuscript is available at the University of Tehran.[59]

g. University of Tehran, 1928/10, folios 308-25, copy dated 1539/946 (Catalogue, VIII:544). This is the second essay of Dawānī, and was sent with Amīr Shams al-Dīn Muḥammad to India for the *Pādishāh* of Gujirāt Sulṭān Maḥmūd (1458-1511/863-917). The beginning and the end of copy #1021/5, dated 1532/939 in Tabriz, folios 33-37 (Catalogue III:669) are identical with those of the first work.[60] The work has been published twice.[61]

There is a third version of this essay, with an introduction, five chapters, and a conclusion, and dedicated to Ya'qūb Bahādur. There is a copy of this third version at the Faculty of Letters, University of Tehran, Ḥikmat 253/11, dated 1540/947 (Catalogue, II:56).

Dawānī wrote another essay on justice for an unnamed Indian ruler. This essay has an introduction on the portrait (*naqsh*) of man, a section on justice with a chapter on virtues, and a conclusion on the perfection (*kamāl*) of justice. This essay was sent to India with Shams al-Dīn Muḥammad.

There are manuscript copies of this work at the following locations:

a. Faculty of Letters, University of Tehran, Ḥikmat 253/12, copy dated 1540/947 (Catalogue, II:57).

b. Faculty of Letters, University of Tehran, Ḥikmat 119/1, copy dated 1562/970 (Catalogue, II:40).

c. Majlis Library, 4868/1, copy dated nineteenth/thirteenth century, folios 311-13 (Catalogue, XIII:311). This copy has no introduction and a shorter ending.

d. Āstān-i Quds, Manṭiq 113/10 (Catalogue, Mantiq I:32). The work was published in *Taḥqīq*.[62]

19. *The Behavior of the Kings* (*Sulūk al-Mulūk*) by Khwāja Mullā Faḍlallāh Rūzbihān Khunjī Iṣfahānī Shāfi'ī. This work was written at the command of the ruler of Bukhara Abu'l-Ghāẓī 'Ubaydallāh Bahādur Khān Uzbeg Shaybānī in 1514/920. The work is one of the best religio-political manuals of the Shāfi'ī and Ḥanafī schools. There are copies in Tashkent and Leningrad. The work was published in India in 1966 with a very useful preface in English.[63]

20. *The Constitution of the Sultanate* (*Dastūr al-Sulṭana*) by Abu'l-Faḍl Munshī Shīrāzī, written for Sulaymān Khān (d. 1556/964) on

civic (*madanī*) and canonical (*shar'ī*) politics. The treatise comprised five sections: monarchy (*salṭanat*) and formal government (*ḥukūmat-i ṣūrī*); their conditions; the situation (*ḥāl*) of kings and rulers; the necessity of considering and commiserating with one's subordinates; biographies of prophets and messengers who held formal and intellectual positions of rule justly.

There is a copy of this work in Paris.[64]

21. *The Conduct of the Rulers* (*Siyar al-Salāṭīn*) by Hāshim b. Muḥammad Ḥusaynī, in five sections:

a. on the conditions of justice and the rules of civility and kindness, and the rights of subjects (*ru'āyā*);

b. on the organization of government and the methods of statecraft;

c. on affection for the Family of the Prophet (May God Bless Him and His Family and those of His House), and deference to the advice of the capable learned men (*'ulamā'*), the assemblies of the perfect pious men (*maḥāfil-i ṣulaḥā-yi kāmil*), those endowed with virtue, and the companions of the way;

d. on consideration of the opinions of devoted ministers and faithful and just emirs, and esteeming soldiers and well-meaning functionaries (*khidmatkārī-yi dawlatkhwāh*); and

e. on protecting the realm, the politics of rule (*salṭanat*), and being on guard against powerful and treacherous enemies.

There is a copy of this work at the University of Leyden, and I have discussed it in the *Bulletin*.[65]

22. *The Constitution of the Kings* (*Dastūr al-Mulūk*) by Abu'l-Qāsim Naṣr b. Aḥmad Shādānī Nīshābūrī, in twelve chapters. There is a copy of this work at the Tāshkent Institute, and I have described it in the *Bulletin*.[66]

23. *The Manners of the Rulership and the Vizierate* (*Ādāb-i Salṭanat va Vizārat*) in two chapters.[67]

24. The essay "Politics and Manners of Kings and the Vizierate" (*Sīyāsat va Ādāb-i Mulūk va Vizārat*), in three sections, each with three chapters.[68]

25. *The Rules of the Rulers* (*Qavā'id al-Salāṭīn*) by Muḥammad 'Abd al-Ḥasīb 'Āmilī Iṣfahānī, a Shi'ite scholar (d. 1709/1121). The treatise was dedicated to Shāh Sulaymān Ṣafavī (d. 1694/1105) and was written in 1670/1981. There is a copy in the Ṭabāṭabā'ī collection at the Majlis Library (#516, in 253 pages, with the first folio missing). The University of Tehran has a microfilm copy of this copy (II:145). I mentioned this treatise in the *Jāvīdān-i Khirad*, in my discussion of the works of Shamsā Gīlānī.

'Āmilī greatly praised the Shāh in the work, in the beginning and in the ninth rule (p. 169). Also in this rule he mentions his own ancestor

Shaykh 'Alī Karakī (d. 1533/940) and says that when he came to the court at Isfahan, the Shāh went out to meet him. The Shāh put Karakī's *fatvās* into effect, and ordered that three hundred servants accompany him in his retinue to propagate the law (*tarvīj-i shar' kunand*). The Shāh placed Karakī next to him on his throne and dismissed one of his own *ṣadrs*, a scholarly man, because he quarreled with Karakī. The Shāh gave Karakī a grant (*suyūrghāl*) valued at eight or nine hundred *tūmāns*.

The author also mentioned his ancestor Sayyid Dāmād (Mīr Dāmād, d. 1630-31/1040) (p. 160), Shāh Ṭahmāsb (d. 1576/984), Shāh 'Abbās I (d. 1628/1037) (p. 161), and Sayyid Aḥmad 'Āmilī, his own father, to whom the Shāh was very kind after the death of Sayyid Dāmād. The author said that he himself had been a close associate of the court (*az nazdīkān-i darbār*) (p. 163) and mentioned Shāh 'Abbās II (d. 1667/1077) (p. 164).

In this work, Shi'ite political thought is intermingled with Greek and Sassanian thought in the recounting of stories of Iranian kings and Caliphs of earlier periods. Even if the Persian style of this work is not altogether pleasing, it merits publication since it is an invaluable document for the Safavid period.

26. *Royal Rules* (*Qavā'id-i Sulṭānī*) by Sulṭān Maḥmūd Kashānī, dedicated to Shāh Sulṭān Ḥusayn (d. 1722/1135). The work comprises an introduction and twenty rules. U.C.L.A. has a copy of this work (M408), which I have read and described.[69]

27. *The Manners of the Rulers of the Behavior of the Rulers According to What is Established in the Sayings of the Guiding Imams* (*Adāb al-Wulāt yā Sulūk al-Wulāt 'alā Mā Qurar fī Aḥādīth al-A'imma al-Hudā*) by Muḥammad Bāqir Majlisī (d. 1699/1111). In this work Majlisī included Persian translations of the covenant (*'ahd*) of Ashtar and the already-mentioned Ahwāzīyya essay of the Imām Ja'far al-Ṣādiq (Upon Him Be Peace).[70]

28. Ja'far b. Muḥammad Qadī Mashadī wrote a commentary on the covenant of Ashtar in 1694/1106 and dedicated it to 'Imād al-Dawla Muḥammad Mu'min Khān Ishik Aghasībāshī of the Dīvān-i A'lā.

The covenant is considered important by the Imami and Fatimid Shī'a. Aside from the early fourteenth/eigth-century translation done by Āvī which I have published, in the introduction to that translation I listed thirty-one translations and commentaries which, together with these two of Āvī and Mashadī, make a total of thirty-three Persian translations of and commentaries on this work.

29. *The Gift of the Kings* (*Tuḥfat al-Mulūk*) by a scholar of the period of Muḥammad Shāh Qājār (1834-47/1250-64) and dedicated to the Crown Prince. The work comprises an introduction, five chapters, and

a conclusion, including a quote from the advice of the Sassanian Ardashīr.

There is a copy of this work at the Gulistān Library (#181/1268)[71] and also in the collection of Dr. Asghar Mahdavī (#551), which I have described in the *Bulletin*.[72]

The piece of advice of Ardashīr is: "There is no king without men of distinction (*rijāl*), and there are no men of distinction without wealth (*al-māl*), and there is no wealth without subjects (*ra'īya*), and there are no subjects without justice." This quote appeared in Aristotle's *Secret of Secrets*, and has also been attributed to the Imam 'Alī (Upon Him be Peace).[73]

30. *The Behavior of Kings* (*Sulūk-i Mulūk*) by Mīrzā Muḥammad Ḥusayn Ṣadr-i Dīvānkhāna b. Mīrzā Faḍlallāh Qazvīnī (d. 1867/1284). Qazvīnī was minister plenipotentiary of Iran to Russia between 1850/1267 and 1853/1270, and in 1853/1270 he acquired the title 'Aḍud al-Mulk. He was also Minister of Pensions and Endowments and twice became superintendent of the Āstān-i Quds, once in 1870/1287.[74] This work dealt with the rules (*qavā'id*) of the country and the royal court, and was written ca. 1851/1268.

There is no *hamza* anywhere in the work, and both *The Advice of the Kings* (*Naṣīḥat al-Mulūk*) and a *qaṣīda* appear in the text without dots. I have seen a copy of those works in the Gulistān Library. It is described in the *adabī* and *'irfanī* catalogue of Atabay of Pakistan's Salṭanatī Library (p. 456, 16/187).

31. An essay on politics by 'Alī b. Muḥammad Tabrīzī, dedicated to Nāṣir al-Dīn Shāh (d. 1896/1313). The essay was completed in 1966/1283 and is in a foreign style (*ravish-i farangān*). There is a copy at the Malik Library (Catalogue, p. 485) which I have discussed in the journal *Tārīkh*.[75]

32. *The Spirit of Islam or The Straight Path* (*Rūḥ al-Islām yā Ṣirāt-i Mustaqīm*) by Prince Niẓām al-Mulk Mīrzā Malkum Khān the Armenian (1833-1908/1249-1326), and written in 1876/1293.[76] I described this work and six extant manuscript copies of it in *Tārīkh*.[77]

Malkum praised Islamic politics in this essay and cited evidence to affirm the certainty of the prophethood of Muḥmmad (May God Bless Him and His Family). In the margin of the Paris copy, there is a portion of the French Constitution on the rights of man, translated into Persian by Malkum.[78]

33. *The Nāṣirian Law* (*Qānūn-i Naṣirī*) by Mīrzā Muḥammad Sa'īd Khān Anṣārī Mu'taman al-Mulk Ashlaqī Garmrūdī (1815-83/1231-1301).[79] The author gives a very clear exposition of Iranian politics and political philosophy in a European style.

34. *The Behavior of the Kings* (*Sulūk-i Mulūk*) by 'Abbās Qulī

Khān Sipihr Kāshānī (d. 1921/1340), written for Muẓaffar al-Dīn Shāh (d. 1907/1324) perhaps in 1898/1316. The author included advice and counsel from earlier kings on the basis of which he outlined a path and style of statecraft.

The author's life is discussed in *al-Dharī'a* and Mushar's *Mu'allifīn.*[80] The Millī Catalogue also has a description of this work.[81]

35. *The Garden of the Truth* (*Būstān al-Ḥaqq*) by an unknown liberal (*āzādāndīsh*) scholar, written in 1905/1323 in a new style (*ravish-i jadīd*) on Islamic statecraft. The work comprised several sections (*aṣlāḥ-yi shajara*), each with subsections (*furū'āt*), each of which is in turn subdivided.

36. I have discussed in *Tārīkh*,[82] a political treatise or a work of advice, a copy of which is at the Majlis Library. I saw another copy of this work at the Majlis.[83] The text of this copy, as with other copies, including one at the University,[84] contains no author's name. However, on the title page of the Majlis copy, the work is attributed to Sayyid Jamāl al-Dīn al-Afghānī.

In the work, the foundation of Islamic politics is laid on the basis of the accepted tradition (*maqbūla*) of 'Umar b. Ḥanẓala of the words of the Imam Ja'far al-Ṣādiq (Upon Him be Peace).[85] It is not possible that this work is by 'Abd al-Bahā' 'Abbās Effendī to whom it is attributed; it may not be by al-Afghānī either. In several places in the work the phrase "O Iran!" is used. The ending suggests that there must be a second volume. I have seen a version of this work published together with Aḥmad Faqīhī's *The Guidance of the Contented* (*Hidāyat al-Muktafī*).[86]

In the catalogue of Meridith Owens (p. 351), there is mention of *The Secrets of the Invisible on the Means of the City* (*Aṣrār al-Ghaybīyya lī asbāb al-Madīna*) in the name of 'Abd al-Bahā' 'Abbās.[87] That is this work which is attributed to him. Scholars now need to examine the copies which I have discussed here and in *Tārīkh* to study and judge this work.

37. A political treatise by a scholar dedicated to Aḥmad Shāh Qājār (1909-25/1327-42). The work is in eleven sections and dates from the early Constitutional period. The author mentions Plato, Aristotle, Cicero, and Rousseau.

I have described a copy of this work found at the University.[88] I do not know whether there are other copies extant.

38. *The Foundation of the Kingdom* (*Qiwām al-Mulk*) discussed in the Millī Catalogue. The work is in twenty-seven chapters. I have not seen this work, and do not know what it is.[89]

39. *The Treasure* (*Dhakhīrah*) *of Governor General Mister Warren Hastings* by Muḥammad Waṣīl Jā'īs on Islamic law (*fiqh*) and politics. The work is in two sections, divine decrees and imperial laws. There is a

copy at the India Office in London, details of which were provided by Ethé in his catalogue.[90]

40. Sixty-one rules of statecraft, written in an Indian style. There is a copy of this work at the University of Tehran (#9281).

City Government and Police
(*Shahrdārī va Shahrbānī*)

While at Harvard University, I was fortunate to come upon a number of published treatises on police administration (*ḥisbat*) on which I prepared notes. In Iran, having consulted other sources, I was able to produce the following.

Mawārdī in his *Aḥkām al-Sulṭāniyya* and Ghazzālī in his *Iḥyā' al-'Ulūm* discussed the topic of city government and police. Ibn al-Ḥājj Abū 'Abdallāh Muḥammad 'Abd Rayy Fāsī Mālikī (d. 1336/737), in the beginning of his *The Respected Law* (*al-Shar' al-Sharīf*),[91] and also chapters twenty-one, twenty-four, and thirty-eight of *The Final Degree* (*Nihāyat al-Rutba*)—which I will discuss below—discussed what was relevant to draper (*bazzāz*), and the teacher (*mu'addib*) of children. In *The Behavior of the Kings* (*Sulūk al-Mulūk*), Khunjī discussed both the superintendent of police (*dārūgha*) and municipal officer (*muḥtasib*) (chapters three and four). In the *Khiṭaṭ* of al-Maqrīzī (d. 1441-42/845), there is also mention of the *muḥtasib* (I:463). Al-Shahādī Ibrāhīm Disūqī wrote *Ḥisba in Islam* (*al-Ḥisba-fi'l-Islām*) at the end of which he discussed *muḥtasibs*, including al-Maqrīzī and Badr al-Dīn Maḥmūd 'Aynī Ḥalabī (d. 1451/855), who were themselves *muḥtasibs*.[92]

Nicola Ziadeh has published *Ḥisba and the Muḥtasib in Islam* (*al-Ḥisba wa'l-Muḥtasib fi'l-Islām*), subtitled *Texts Collected and Edited*.[93] This book contains a good historical preface. Walter Bernauer also discussed the issue,[94] using item #2 below. Bernauer also published another work on the subject.[95] In the catalogue of French works, by Ṣabā and also that of Pākdāman and 'Abd al-Ḥamd, there is mention of work on the subject in French.[96]

Perhaps the oldest works on the subject were those of Ibn al-Ṭayyib al-Sarakhsī, *The Large Book on Dishonest Practices and the Profession of Ḥisba* (*Kitāb al-Aghshāsh wa Ṣinā'at al-Ḥisba al-Kabīr*) and *The Small Book on Dishonesty and the Profession of Ḥisba* (*Kitāb al-Ghashsh wa Ṣinā'at al-Ḥisba al-Ṣaghīr*). Al-Sarakhsī is the Iranian philosopher and liberal thinker mentioned by Ibn Nadīm. These two works are no longer extant, and must be considered part of Iranian culture. Franz Rosenthal has published a book on this Iranian philosopher, and two articles,[97] as did Mīnavī in the *Jāvīdān-i Khirad*, which is still not completed.[98]

In the Persian period, 'Alī Muḥammad Bukhārī wrote *The Guide for the Market Police* (*Murshid al-Muḥtasib*). The work is in two chapters, with a conclusion (folios 117-40, #C1478 of the Leningrad Oriental Institute of Manuscripts).[99]

The following is a list of *ḥisbat* works in Arabic:

1. *Police Administration* (*al-Ḥisba*) by Ḥasan Uṭrūsh (844-916/230-304), a Zaydī leader of Ṭabaristān. The work is OR 3804 (folios 285-92) at the British Museum, and it has been published.[100]

2. *The Final Degree on the Quest for the Police Administration* (*Nihāyat al-Rutba fī Ṭalab al-Ḥisba*) by Jalāl al-Dīn, or Taqī al-Dīn Abu'l-Biqā Abu'l Najīb Abū'l-Faḍā'il 'Abd al-Raḥmān b. Naṣr b. 'Abdallāh b. Muḥammad Shīzārī Nabrāwī Shafī'ī (d. 1193/589), an arbitrator (*dāvar*) in the city of Tiberius. The work was written for Ṣalāḥ al-Dūn 'Ayyūbī. He also wrote *The Practical Procedure on the Politics of the Kings* (*al-Minhāj al-Maslūk fī Sīyāsat at-Mulūk*) which has been translated into Turkish.[101]

Nihāyat al-Rutba was written in four chapters. There are fourteen manuscript copies of the work extant,[102] eight of which are in Egypt. The work has been published in Beirut and Cairo.[103]

3. *The Origin of Administration* (*Niṣāb al-Iḥtisāb*) by 'Umar b. Muḥammad 'Iwaḍ Bukhārā'ī, an Ash'arī advisor (alive before 1215/612 to 1239/637). The work contained citations from *The Memorial of the Saints* (*Tadhkirat al-Awlīyā'*). The work is in forty-five chapters, and was published in Calcutta in 1830.[104]

A copy of the work is discussed in the catalogue of the Arabic manuscripts of the India Office.[105] Copy #12 of the Asifiyya Library in Hyderabad is an older copy. The copy at the Iraqi Museum in Baghdad was completed in 1668/1079 by Aḥmad b. Shaykh 'Alī, that in Egypt in 1601/1010 by Shams al-Dīn Ḥājj b. Sa'd al-Dīn from copies at the Treasury and Public Waqf in Baghdad and the Tīmūrī Treasury (#11171). Together with other copies, there are some twenty copies of the work extant. It has also been translated into Turkish.

Because the work contained some discussion of music, Amnon Shiloah mentioned it in his music catalogue and said the author was a Syrian Hanafi and was living in Bukhara in 1526/933.[106]

4. *Administration in Islam, or the Task of the Islamic Government* (*Al-Ḥisbā fī'l-Islām aw Waẓīfat al-Ḥukūma al-Islāmiyya*) by Ibn Taymīyya (d. 1324/728). This work has been published several times.[107]

5. *The Signposts of Proximity on the Judgements of Administration* (*Ma'ālim al-Qurba fī Aḥkām al-Ḥisba*) by Ibn al-Ukhūwwa Ḍiyā' al-Dīn

Muḥammad Qurshī Maṣrī Shāfiʿī (1250-1328/648-729), in twenty chapters. The work has been published twice.[108] In many places the text is identical with Nabrāvī's *The Final Degree.*[109]

6. *The Final Degree on the Quest for Police Administration* (*Nihāyat al-Rutba fī Ṭalab al-Ḥisba*) by Ibn Bassām, a fourteenth/eighth century *muḥtasib*. As he said in the preface and in many places in the text, the work is identical to that of Shītarī Nabrāvī, though material was added in this work to expand it to 118 chapters. The oldest known manuscript copy of this work is dated 1461/866. The treatise was published in the journal *Mashriq.*[110] Muḥammad Kurd ʿAlī has written an essay on the work.[111]

Ḥusām al-Dīn Sāmarāʾī published the treatise in Baghdad in 1968 based on the manuscript copies of Aḥmad-i Salas, #1307, done by ʿAlī Qarrāfī in 1461/866 and the Tīmūrī Treasury, #25, done by Ismāʿīl b. Muḥammad Shashī in 1903/1321. The copy at the British Museum is also mentioned.

7. *The Record of the Judgement on the Organization of the People of Islam* (*Taḥrir al-Aḥkām fī Tadbīr Ahl al-Islām*) by Ibn Jamaʿā Badr al-Dīn Abū ʿAbdallāh Muḥammad Yanbūʿī Ḥamawī Shāfiʿī (d. 1416 or 1429/819 or 833).[112]

8. *The Gift of the Inspector and the Wealth of the Reflector on the Protection of Religious Practices and the Changing of the Disapproving* (*Tuḥfat al-Nāẓir wa Ghanīyyat al-Dhākir fī Hifẓ al-Shaʿāʾir wa Taghyīr al-Munākir*) by Abū ʿAbdallāh Muḥammad ʿAqabānī Tilmisānī Andalusī (d. Tilmisān, 1466/871) in eight chapters and a conclusion. The work has been translated into French and published, based on two manuscript copies at the Zaytūn Mosque in Tunis (#2978) written in Syria in 1783/1198.[113] I read this work and found it very useful.

9. *The Manners of Administration* (*Ādāb al-Ḥisba*) by Abū ʿAbdallāh Muḥammad Saqaṭi Mālaqī in eight chapters. The work has been published by Lévi-Provencal and G. S. Colin.[114]

From this work ʿAbd al-Raḥmān b. ʿAbd al-Qādir Fāsī (1630-58/1040-69) wrote his own *The Substance of the Principles of the Sciences* (*al-Uqnūm fī Mabādī al-ʿUlūm*) which is a poem in the *rajaz* meter, in nine chapters, on the science of *ḥisba.*[115]

10. *The Judgements of Administration* (*Aḥkām al-Iḥtisāb*) perhaps by Yūsuf Ḍīyāʾ al-Dīn. There is a copy in the Tīmūrī collection at the National Library in Cairo, Egypt.

11. *Three Andalusian Treatises on the Manners of Administration and al-Muḥtasib* (*Thalāth Rasāʾil Andalusīyya fī Ādāb al-Ḥisba waʾl-Muḥtasib*) published by Lévi-Provencal, with additional research and editing.[116] The three essays are:

a. "A Treatise on Judgement (*al-qaḍā'*) and Administration" by Ibn 'Abdūn Muḥammad b. Aḥmad Tajībī,

b. "The Manners of Administration and *al-Muḥtasib*" (*Ādāb al-Ḥisba wa'l-Muḥtasib*) by Aḥmad b. 'Abdallāh b. 'Abd al-Ra'ūf, and

c. "Administration" (*al-ḥisba*) by 'Umar b. 'Uthmān b. al-'Abbās Jursīfī.

Lévi-Provencal also translated and published an essay of Ibn 'Abdūn in the *Journal Asiatique.*[117]

12. *What is Preferred on the Study of the Secrets and the Uncovering of the Veils on the Science of the Strategems* (*al-Mukhtār fī Kashf al-Asrār wa Hatak al-Astār fī 'Ilm al-Ḥiyal*) by Zayn al-Dīn 'Abd al-Raḥmān b. Abī Bakr 'Umar Jawbarī Dimashqī in thirty chapters, written for the Atabag of the armies in Syria, Sham Beg, and dedicated to Malik Mas'ūd Artaqī, the ruler of Āmid and the fortress of Kīfā in 1221/618 and 1222/619. In 1223/620 the author was living in Harran, in 1228/626 in Egypt, and in 1262/661 in Iconium.

This essay deals with the deceitfulness of magicians of different groups. Chalabi mentioned this work (V:483) and de Goeje and Fleischer have also dealt with it.[118] Fleugel, in his Vienna catalogue (II:501, #1434) described copy NF154 of the work. The work has been published twice, in Damascus in 1884/1302 and in Egypt in 1898/1316.[119]

13. *The Intimation to the Advantages of Commerce* (*al-Ishāra ilā Maḥāsin al-Tijāra*) by Abū Faḍl Ja'far b. 'Alī Dimashqī. The work was published in Cairo in 1900/1318 based on a copy dated 1174/570.

14. *The Judgements on the Marketplace* (*Aḥkām al-Sūq*) by Abū Zakarīyā Yahyā b. 'Umar b. Yūsuf Kanānī Jiyānī Qurṭubī Sūsī Mālikī (828-901/213-89), the dialectician. I have read this treatise, and it was cited in *The Gift of the Inspector*. It has been published in Egypt.[120]

15. *The Facilitation on the Judgements of Price-Setting* (*al-Taysīr fī Aḥkām al-Tas'īr*) by Qāḍī Abu'l-'Abbās b. Sa'īd Marākishī. The author mentions the work of Saqaṭī.[121]

War

Among the topics related to statecraft are war and battles with enemies; something of these are researched in *fiqh*, but there are also separately written treatises.

During the Qājār period, while European knowledge was coming into Iranian places of learning, treatises on war and its instruments began to be composed, just as before, especially in the Safavid period.

In the midst of Iranian conflicts with the Russians and the British, the demand for this type of work became great. Examples of this genre include:

1. *The Abbasid Gift* (*Tuḥfah-yi 'Abbāsī*) by Mīrzā Abu'l-Qāsim Rashtī Qummī (d. 1815/1231), written *jihād* for 'Abbās Mīrzā.[122]

2. *The Sword of Islam* (*Ḥusām al-Islām*) by Muḥammad b. 'Abdallāh Zanjānī, written for Fath 'Ali Shah (d. 1834/1250). The work was composed in Arabic in 1817/1233 and included a commentary on *jihād*, in eight sections.[123]

3. *The Judgements of Jihād* (*Aḥkām al-Jihād*) by Mīrzā 'Īssā Qā'im Maqām Farahānī (d. 1821/1237).[124]

4. *Treatise on Jihād* (*Jihādīyya*) by Ḥājjī Mullā Muḥammad Riḍā b. Muḥammad Amīn Hamadānī (d. 1831/1247). The work included an introduction, eight sections, and a conclusion.[125]

5. *The 'Abbasid Portions* (*Sihām-i 'Abbāsīyya*) by Ḥājjī Mīrzā Āghāsī, *Ṣadr-ī A'ẓam* of Iran (1751-83/1165/98).[126]

6. *Treatise on Jihād* (*Jihādīyya*) by Ḥājjī Muḥammad Karīm Khān Kirmānī, a Shaykhī scholar. The author composed this work in 1855/1272 at the order of Nāṣir al-Dīn Shāh (d.d 1896/1313) when the British had taken Bushire.[127]

At the library of the Āstān-i Quds, there is a collection of three essays:[128]

1. The Book on Jihād of the "Gardens of the Issues and the Pools of the Proofs" (*Rīyāḍ al-Masā'il wa-Hīyāḍ al-Dalā'il*) by Sayyid 'Alī Ṭabāṭabā'ī, with a preface on the necessity of supporting the Shah of Iran. The work was composed at the request of the Regent, 'Abbās Mīrzā.

2. A reply to a series of questions on the issues of *jihād* and shackles (*ribaṭ*), the essence (*bayḍa*) of Islam, and the emigration (*muhājirat*) by an unknown scholar.

3. "Commandments on the Jizya" (*Aḥkām al-Jizya*) by Mīrzā-yi Qummī, already mentioned and published in his "The Booties of the Days" (*Ghanā'im al-Ayyām*).

Perhaps it was due to the fear of foreign influence that a number of religious scholars, such as Ṭabāṭabā'ī mentioned above, aligned themselves with the Qajar court to arouse the power of the government to drive out the foreigners. The works of this group included:

1. An essay on sovereignty and the necessity of obeying the *sulṭān* by the same Ḥājjī Mullā Muḥammad Rizā Hamadānī.[129]

2. *The Necessity of the Rulership* (*Vujūb-i Sulṭanat*) by Ḥājjī Mīrzā Muḥammad Munshī Nā'īnī, written for Nāṣir al-Dīn Shāh.[130] This man likely was not Mīrzā Muḥammad Munshī Nā'īnī, the author of "History and Tales" (*Tārīkh va Ḥikāyāt*).[131]

3. *The Necessity of Offering Prayer for the Shāh* (*Vujūb-i Du'ā-yi*

Pādishāh) by Mīrzā Qāḍī Muḥammad Saryazdī (d. 1895/1312).[132]

Notes

Translator's note: Wherever possible I have attempted to supplement the bibliographical data given in the original text.

1. *Jāvīdān Khirad* (Journal of the Anjuman-i Falsafa), vol. III, no. 2, p. 31.

2. See also H. Enayat, "An Outline of the Political Philosophy of the Rasā'il of the Ikhwān al-Ṣafā," in Naṣr, S.H., ed., *Ismā'īlī Contributions to Islamic Culture* (Tehran, 1977), pp. 23-49. (Translator.)

3. Muḥammad Yūsuf Mūsā, *Memorial Avicenne,* 6 vols. (Cairo, 1952-63/1372-83). The work contains a preface in Arabic and French, and useful notes at the end.

4. *Jashnnāma-yi Ibn Sīnā* (Tehran: 1952-/1331-), vol. III, 1954.

5. See Franz Rosenthal, *Aḥmad b. al-Ṭayyīb al-Sarakhsī* (New Haven, 1943), p. 81. (Translator.)

6. al-Sarakhsī, *Ādāb al-Mulūk*, pp. 48, 93, 126, 129.

7. Ibn Nadīm, *al-Fihrist*, p. 212 (hereafter Ibn Nadīm); *Hunar va Mardum*, 101:45; Amnon Shiloah, *The Theory of Music in Arabic Writings (900-1900). A Descriptive Catalogue of Manuscripts in Libraries in Europe and the United States* (hereafter, Shiloah), (Munchen, 1979), #47.

8. See my preface to *Customs of the Capital* (*Rusūm Dar al-Khilāfa*), and my two articles on ethics and politics in the *Bulletin de la Bibliothèque Centrale de l'Université de Tehran* (*Nashrīya Kitābkhāna-Markazī-yi Dānishgāh-i Tihran*) (hereafter, *Bulletin*), I:211-18; *Farhang-i Iran Zamīn*, XIX:261-84; Aḥmad Munzavī, *Catalogue of the Manuscripts at the Ganjbakhsh Library*, (Islamabad, 1974-79); and Aḥmad Munzavī, *Catalogue of Persian Manuscripts* (*Fihrist-i Nuskhahā-yi Khaṭṭī-yi Fārsī*) (hereafter, *Catalogue of Persian Manuscripts*), 3 vols. (Tehran, 1969-75/1348-54).

9. See M. Mīnavī, trans., *Nāma-yi-Tansar* (Tehran, 1932/1311). The letter has also been translated into English by M. Boyce, in his *Letter of Tansar*, (Rome, 1968), with a very useful preface.

10. *Jāvīdān Khirad*, Persian translation by Sharaf al-Dīn 'Uthmān Ibn Muḥammad Qazvīnī, edited with an introduction by M. T. Dānishpazhouh, (Tehran: Anjuman-i Falsafa, 1980/1359).

11. See below, n. 71, for the translation by Badawī.

12. Majlis, #2901; see also Dānishpazhouh, Moḥammad-Taqī, *Catalogue of Microfilms at the Central Library of the University of Tehran* (hereafter,

University Microfilms) (Tehran, 1969/1348), II:229; *Journal of the Faculty of Letters, University of Tehran,* (*Majallah-yi Dānishkada-yi Adabiyyāt*), VIII, p. 17, #3.

13. *Bulletin* IV:342, 346-50; *Yaghmā* V:31-34.

14. Dānishpazhouh, preface to *Jāvīdān Khirad* (Tehran, 1980/1359), p. 43.

15. C. Brockelmann, *Geschicte der arabischen Literatur*, 2 vols. and 3 supplements (hereafter, Brockelmann and *Supplement*) (Leiden, 1937-49), I:154; *Supplement* I:249, 497.

16. Pp. 236-37.

17. Jamīl Sulṭān, *Études sur Naḥj al-Balāgha* (Paris, 1940); Iḥsān 'Abbās, *al-Sharīf al-Raḍī* (Beirut, 1959/1379), pp. 52-58; Gustave Richter, *Studien zur Geschicte der alteren arabischen Furtenspiegal* (Leipzig, 1932), p. 86; Gerard Salinger, "The *Kitāb al-Jihād* from al-Qāḍī al-Nu'mān's *Da'ā'im al-Islām,*" Ph.D. thesis, Columbia University, 1935, preface, p. 8.

18. Wadād Al-Qāḍī, "An Early Fatimid Political Document," *Studia Islamica* 48 (1978): 71-108.

19. Wilferd Madelung, "The Sources of Ismā'īlī Law," *Journal of Near Eastern Studies* 35/1 (1976): 29-40.

20. Ṭabarī, *Annales*, year 206, p. 1058. See also my prefaces to the translation by Āvī of the *farmān* of Ashtar, the *Jāvīdān Khirad* of Miskawayh Rāzī, and the second edition of *Akhlāq-i Muḥtashamī* of Naṣīr al-Dīn Ṭusī.

21. Ibn Abi'l-Ḥadīd al-Madā'inī, *Sharḥ Naḥj al-Balāgha*, M. A. Ibrāhīm, ed., 20 vols. (Cairo, 1959-64/1379-84), II:319. See also the essay by Grignaschi in vol. 19 of *Bulletin d'Études Orientales*, Damascus.

22. *Naḥj al-Balāgha*, III:101.

23. Muḥammad Kurd Alī, ed., *Raṣā'il al-Balāgha* (Cairo, 1954/1374), pp. 197, 199; *Al-Shitai*, p. 22.

24. Iḥsān 'Abbās, ed., *'Ahd Ardashīr* (Beirut, 1967), pp. 63, 78, 131.

25. al-Madā'inī, *Sharḥ Naḥj al-Balāgha*, II:418. See also M. T. Dānish-pazhouh, ed., *Akhlāq-i Muḥtashamī* (Tehran: Tehran University Press, 1960/1339), preface, p. 37.

26. 'Umar Farrukh, *Ikhwān al-Ṣafā, Dirāsa Taḥlīlīyya* (Beirut, 1945/1365), p. 132.

27. Brockelmann, I:343, 344. (Translator.)

28. Cairo, 1954-/1374-. (See below, n. 71.)

29. See the preface to the French translation of 1915; *Bulletin* I:235, 259.

30. *Akhlāq-i Muḥtashamī*, the second preface, p. 22.

31. *Jāvīdān Khirad*, preface p. 38; *Bulletin* I:297; Shiloah, 257; *Bengal Catalogue*, II:354, #4981; *Catalogue of Persian Manuscripts*, #1571.

32. Tehran: Bungāh-i Tarjuma va Nashr-i Kitāb, 1966-67/1345.

33. See my discussion in *Bulletin* X:227, 260.

34. Ibn Yūsuf, *Madrasa-yi Sipahsālār Catalogue* (Tehran), IV:295 (hereafter, *Sipahsālār*); *University Microfilms*, I:74; *Farhang-i Īrān Zamīn*, XXV; C. E. de Fouchecour, "Ḥadāyiq al-Siyar, un miroir des princes de la cour de Qonya au VIIe-XIIIe siecle," *Studia Islamica* 1 (1972): 219-28.

35. E. Blochet, *Catalogue des Manuscrits Persans de le Bibliothèque Nationale*, vol. II (Paris, 1912), #758; Iraj Afshār and M. T. Dānishpazhouh, eds., *Catalogue of the Malik Library* (Tehran), p. 572, #4094; *University Microfilms*, I:145; *Catalogue of Persian Manuscripts*, #1452.

36. *University Microfilms*, I:404; *Catalogue of Persian Manuscripts*, #1635.

37. *Rāhnamā-yi Kitāb*, XVI:536.

38. E. Blochet, *Catalogue des manuscrits turcs* (Paris, 1932-33), II:169; *University Microfilms*, #5641.

39. *Bulletin* IX:285; see also Sa'īd Nafīsī, *The History of Poetry and Prose in the Persian Language Until the End of Tenth Century Hijri* (*Tārīkh-i Naẓm va Naṣr dar Zabān-i Fārsī ta Pāyān-i Qarn-i Dahum Hijrī*) (hereafter, *The History of Poetry and Prose*) (Tehran, 1965-66/1344), p. 192.

40. *Catalogue of Persian Manuscripts*, 161; preface to Tehran, 1358 edition.

41. Fluegel, *Vienna Catalogue*, I:289, #1858.

42. *Bulletin* IX:313; *Catalogue of Persian Manuscripts*, 708, 1717.

43. Munzavī, *Catalogue of the Manuscripts at the Ganjbakhsh Library*, 2100, 2142.

44. Astouri, I:973-74; *Tashkent Catalogue*, III:318-19; *Samarqand Catalogue*, p. 44.

45. Charles Rieu, *Catalogue of the Persian Manuscripts at the British Museum*, 3 vols. and supplement (London, 1879-95), 447; *University Microfilms*, I:123; *The History of Poetry and Prose*, 325, 639, 789.

46. Nos. 691, 70-76, 78-80 in the catalogue by Ātābāy.

47. *Bulletin* IV:66; G. M. Meredith-Owens, p. 12.

48. AF 99, Blochet, IV:95, #2141; *Kitābdārī*, no. 9, Central Library of the University of Tehran.

49. *Bulletin* V:416; *Catalogue of Persian Manuscripts*, 1514.

50. University of Tehran, copy 1021/6, dated 1532/939. See my *Catalogue of the Manuscripts of the Central Library of University of Tehran* (hereafter, *Catalogue of the Manuscripts at the Central Library*) (Tehran, 1951-78/1330-57), III:662, #7265/21, copy dated 1598/1005.

51. *Taḥqīq dar Mabdā'-i Āfarīnish* (Tehran, 1342), X:24-26; *Catalogue of the Manuscripts at the Central Library*, III:667, #1010/23.

52. M. T. Dānishpazhouh, ed., *Catalogue of the Manuscripts of the Library of the Faculty of Letters* (Tehran) II:55-57.

53. University copy #4864/51, #7265/5, #119/14 Ḥikmat, at the Faculty of Letters, University of Tehran; *Catalogue of Persian Manuscripts*, #3588.

54. Leiden, 1964.

55. M. S. Khān, "An Unpublished Essay of Miskawayh on Justice," *Zeitschrift der Deutschen Morgenlandischen Gesellschaft* (*ZDMG*) 112/2 (1962): 309-318.

56. *Catalogue of Persian Manuscripts*, #1447; al-Tihrānī, Āghā Buzurg, *The Means to the Writings of the Shi'a* (*al-Dharī'a ilā-Taṣānīf al-Shī'a*) (hereafter, *al-Dharī'a*), 25 vols. (Tehran and Najaf, 1934-39/ 1353-98), XV:236; *The History of Poetry and Prose*, p. 265 and elsewhere.

57. Manṣūr Iḥsān 'Abbās, *Catalogue of Persian Manuscripts at the Punjab Public Library*, 2 vols. (Lahore, 1966), II:11.

58. *Catalogue of the Manuscripts of the Library of Āstān-i Quds-i Raḍavī* (*Fihrist-i Kutub-i Khaṭṭī-yi Kitābkhāna-yi Āstān-i Quds-i Raḍavī*) (hereafter, Āstān-i Quds) (Mashad), VI:445-46.

59. Blochet, I:109, #153; *University Microfilms*, I:535, #754, 1612-20.

60. *Bulletin* I:221.

61. *Paris Yearbook*, 1324 Sh., based on a copy dated 1532/939; *Taḥqīq dar Mabda'-i Āfarīnish*, VIII:13-28, dedicated to Ya'qūb Bahādur Khān, in 6 sections.

62. *Taḥqīq dar Mabda'-i Āfarīnish*, 1343, II:1, pp. 13-23.

63. *Sulūku'l-Mulūk* (*A Manual of Government based on Islamic Principles*), M. Nizamuddin, ed., Hyderabad- DN. A.P., 1386/1966.

64. AF 135, dated sixteenth/tenth century, in Blochet, II:39, #769.

65. P. de Jong, and M. J. de Goeje, *Catalogus Codicum Orientalium Bibliothcae Aacademiae Lugduno Batavae*, vol. IV (Leiden: Brill, 1866), pp. 222-23; *Bulletin* X:260.

66. Catalogue of Tashkent Institute, III:153, #2094; *Bulletin* IX:137.

67. *Catalogue of Persian Manuscripts*, 1514.

68. University, #1943.

69. *Bulletin* XI, XII:69.

70. See above, and my introduction to Āvī's translation of the *farmān* of Ashtar, p. 35.

71. Ātābāy's catalogue 209, #75.

72. *Bulletin* II:66; *Catalogue of Persian Manuscripts,* 1563.

73. A. R. Badawī, *The Greek Roots of the Islamic Political Vision* (*al-'Uṣūl al-Yūnānīyya li'l-Naẓarīyyāt al-Sīyāsīyya fī'l- Islām*), vol. I (Cairo, 1954/1374), pp. 126-28.

74. *Al-Dharī'a,* IX:604; M. Bāmdād, *A History of the Men of Distinction of Iran* (*Tārīkh-i Rijāl-i Īrān*) (hereafter, Bāmbād), 6 vols. (Tehran, 1968-72/1347-51), III:381.

75. See, *Tārīkh, Journal of the Faculty of Letters, University of Tehran,* I:2, p. 221, for my description of this work.

76. *Catalogue of Persian Manuscripts,* 613; 'A. Anvār, *Catalogue of the Manuscripts at the National Library* (*Fihrist-i Nusakh-i Khaṭṭi-yi Kitābkhāna-yi Millī*) (hereafter, Anvār), 10 vols. (Tehran, 1965-79/1344-58), V:391, #2275, copy dated 1880/1297.

77. *Tārīkh,* I:2, pp. 218-21.

78. Blochet, I:51, #79.

79. *Tārīkh,* I:2, 212-23; II: 53-525.

80. *Al-Dharī'a,* IX:429, XII:230; Khānbābā Mushār, *The Authors of Printed Books* (*Muallifīn-i Kutub-i Chāpī*), 6 vols. (Tehran, 1961-66/1340-45), III:697.

81. Anvār, I:335; Catalogue of Persian Manuscripts, 1633.

82. Majlis Catalogue, X:371: *Tārīkh,* I:2, pp. 221-22.

83. Majlis, #1464/9719/17822, copy dated nineteenth/thirteenth and twentieth/fourteenth centuries, in ninety-two pages. The work has Arabic titles and phrases, with a colored border, and a chart of gold and lapis.

84. Catalogue, XVII:133, #8430.

85. See the article by Joseph Eliash, "Misconceptions Regarding the Juridical Status of the Iranian *'Ulamā',*" *International Journal of Middle East Studies* X/1 (February 1979): 9-25, especially pp. 14-15. (Translator.)

86. Muḥammad 'Alī Shīrāzī, ed., Bombay, 129, p. 8; Majlis Catalogue, 616/150, p. 101, #538090.

87. In twenty-two folios, thirty-one lines each, copy dated 1911, OR 8686; *Bulletin* IV:624.

88. Catalogue XVII:190, #8671.

89. Anvār, IV:484, #1990.

90. 88. Hermann Ethé, *Catalogue of the Persian Manuscripts in the Library of the India Office*, vol. I (Oxford, 1903), #2614, #2615.

91. Shiloah, 113.

92. Cairo, 1963/1382.

93. Beirut, 1963.

94. Walter Bernauer, "Memoir sur Les Instituts de la Police chez les Arabes, les Persans, et les Turce," *Journal Asiatique*, 1860-61, vol. V/15, pp. 461-509; vol. V/16, pp. 114-190.

95. "Notice Particulaire sur la Charge de Muḥtasibe," *Journal Asiatique*, V/16 (1860), pp. 347-92, and no. 18 (1861), pp. 56-76.

96. Muḥsin Ṣabā, *Bibliographie francais de l'Iran*, Tehran, 1951/1330, p. 62; Nāṣir Pākdāman and 'Abd al-Ḥamīd 'Abd al-Ḥamd, *Bibliographie francais de civilisation Iranniene* (Tehran, 1972-74/1351-53), II:254.

97. Franz Rosenthal, *Aḥmad al-Ṭayyib al-Sarakhsī*, New Haven, 1943, p. 81; see also Franz Rosenthal, "From Arabic Books and Manuscripts, VI. Istanbul Material for al-Kindī and al-Sarakhsī," *Journal of the American Oriental Society* (*JAOS*) 76 (1956): 27-31; "From Arabic Books and Manuscripts, VIII. As-Sarakhsī on Love," *JAOS* 81 (1961): 222-24.

98. *Jāvīdān Khirad*, I:1, pp. 9-18.

99. *Catalogue of Persian and Tajik Manuscripts at the Asian Peoples' Institute, Soviet Science Academy* (Moscow, 1961), p. 542.

100. B. B. Seargant, *Bulletin of the School of Oriental and African Studies* XXXVIII (1943): 1-34; F. Sezgin, *Geschicte des arabishchen Schrifttums* (hereafter, Sezgin), 7 vols. (to date) (Leiden, 1967), I:567, Arabic translation of Sezgin, II:307.

101. *Bulletin* IX:19; XI, XII:409.

102. Including copy NF 272 in the Vienna catalogue of Fleugel, III:263, #1831.

103. Sayyid Baz 'Araynī, Beirut, 1969/1389; Cairo 1965/1364. The Cairo edition included a register of *ḥisbat* by Qāḍī Fāḍil, taken from *Ṣubḥ al-A'shī* by Abū'l-'Abbās Aḥmad al-Qalaqashandī, 14 vols. (Cairo 1918-22), X:260. There are three short texts on *ḥisbat* in French by the Crusaders, with Arabic translations.

104. The journal *Majma'-i 'Ilmī*, Damascus, XVII:438, the essay by K. 'Awwad. Sāmarā'ī's preface to Ibn Bassam's *Nihāyat al-Rutba*, Baghdad, 1968, p. 6.

105. III, section 3, #1693.

106. Shiloah, #233; Brockelmann, *Supplement* II, 4427.

107. Beirut, 1967/1387, with a preface by Muḥammad al-Mubārak; Damascus, 1967/1387, with a study on the work, and a separate section covering the *ḥadīth* extracted from the work; Cairo, 1900/1318.

108. English translation by R. Levy, London, 1938; and in Egypt in 1976.

109. Shiloah, 1490.

110. 1907, no. 10.

111. *Al-Muqtabis*, 1908, no. 3.

112. Published and edited by H. Kofler, *Islamica* VI (1934): 319-414; VII (1935): 1-34.

113. *Bulletin d'Études Orientales*, Damascus, no. 19 (1965-66).

114. *Un Manuel hispanique de ḥisba. Traite d'Abū 'Abdallāh Muḥammad b. Abī Muḥammad al-Sakati de Malaqa sur la surveillance des corporations et le repressions des fraudes en Espange Musulmāne*, Paris, 1931.

115. E. Lévi-Provencal, *Catalogue of Arabic Manuscripts at Rabat*, II, #284, folio 58, a photo of which is included in the 1931 edition of the work.

116. *Trois traites hispaniques de ḥisba*, Cairo, 1955.

117. "Le Traité d'Ibn 'Abbās," *Journal Asiatique* (April-June 1934): 177-299.

118. M. J. de Goeje, "Gaubari's 'Entdecke Geheimnisse'," *ZDMG* XX (1866): 485-510; Fleischer's comment on this article, *ZDMG* XXI (1867): 274-76.

119. Preface of Colin and Provencal (see n. 112 above), p. 7.

120. M. A. Mekki, *Journal of the Egyptian Institute of Islamic Studies*, 1954/1375, IV/1-2: 59-151.

121. Lévi-Provencal's preface (see n. 115 above), p. 12. See also the discussion of *ḥisba* in M. Keyvani, *Artisans and Guild Life in the Later Safavid Period* (Berlin, 1982), pp. 68-70. (Translator.)

122. Āstān-i Quds, V:381; Ātābāy, Royal Library Catalogue, #45.

123. Ātābāy, p. 569, #266.

124. Majlis Catalogue, III:66; Āstān-i Quds, II:39.

125. Anvār, II:435, #900.

126. Bāmdād, II:203; Āstān-i Quds, II:76; *Al-Dharīʻa*, XII:260.

127. Sipahsālār, I:413, IV:129; Catalogue of Works of Aḥmad Aḥsā'ī and other Shaykhs, II:221.

128. Āstān-i Quds, V:404, #601.

129. Ātābāy, p. 567, #265; al-Tihrānī, Āghā Buzurg, *Ṭabaqāt A'lām al-Shīʻa*, XIII:541.

130. Malik Library Persian Manuscript Catalogue, 475, #5256; Majlis-i Sinā Catalogue, II:53: *al-Dharīʻa*, XXV:23; *Catalogue of Persian Manuscripts*, 1712.

131. Ātābāy, 152, 464.

132. Anvār, II:31, 537/1; *University Microfilms*, 5015; and University, 5036.

CHAPTER 10

'Allāma al-Ḥillī on the Imamate and Ijtihād

Translated and edited by John Cooper

Jamāl al-Dīn Ḥasan b. Yūsuf b. 'Alī b. al-Muṭahhar al-Ḥillī (d. 1325/726) is the best representative of medieval Shi'ism for our collection. His statement on the Imamate, derived from the mercy (luṭf) *of God according to the principles of Shi'ite rational theology, represents the definitive doctrinal position. Furthermore, it is as concise as it is authoritative. His statement on* ijtihād, *on the other hand, marks a break with the traditional rejection of the principle. The traditional Shi'ite yearning for certainty in legal norms is in the background, and the justification of* ijtihād *is cautious, the aim being to establish the* permissibility *of* ijtihād, *in particular the "specialized" kind. This falls far short of advocating* ijtihād *of the "absolute" kind* (muṭlaq) *discussed in Chapter 5 on the nineteenth century. Nevertheless, as the first explicit endorsement of* ijtihād, *the statement is a hallmark in the evolution of clerical authority in Shi'ism. (Ed.)*

On the Imamate[1]

The Imamate is a universal leadership (*riyāsa*) by a single individual in religious and secular matters.

It is a matter which is incumbent upon God, for it is a divine mercy (*luṭf*), and every divine mercy is incumbent upon Him, so the Imamate is incumbent upon Him.

As for the minor premise, it is necessary because we necessarily know that when people have a leader (*ra'īs*) he holds them back from acts of disobedience and spurs them on to acts of obedience, so that the people end up nearer to right behavior and further from corruption.

As for the major premise, it has been proved earlier.

Let it not be said [as say our opponents] that divine mercy is only incumbent upon God when nothing else takes the place of the Imamate, but when something else [i.e., rule by others] takes its place it is not incumbent. . . . Or that, since the Imamate is only a divine mercy when the Imam manifestly has power so that the benefit of the Imamate, which is the restraining of the disobedient, can be had from him, it is not incumbent upon God when the Imam is concealed and his power is withheld, because the benefit is not there.

For we say that the recourse which intelligent people have in all countries and times to appointing leaders for the preservation of order shows that there is no other way than the Imamate. And the aspects of evil are known and delimited, for we are bound by the Law to avoid them, so they must be known, otherwise it would necessarily follow that there was an obligation to do what could not be done; and there is certainly none of these aspects in the matter of the Imamate. And the benefit is there even if the Imam is concealed, because the possibility of his advent at any time is a mercy with regard to the believer who is duty-bound by the Law.

Concerning the Attributes of the Imam

It is necessary that he be infallible (*ma'ṣūm*). If not, there would be an infinite regress [of authority], and since the conclusion is invalid, the premise is too. This is so because what makes the obligation to appoint the leader (Imam) necessary is the possibility that persons bound by the Law may commit an error, and if it were possible for the leader to commit an error he would necessarily require another person to lead him, for it would be a mercy for him and for the community as well, and this continues ad infinitum.

Moreover, he must be infallible because he is the protector of the Sacred Law (*al-shar'*). For the Qur'ān and the *sunna* are insufficient for the elaboration of the divine commandments. And consensus (*ijmā'*) requires a proof for its validity, since its issuance without a proof or a presumptive indicant (*imāra*)[2] necessarily means that a religious opinion is promulgated only on the basis of whim (*al-tashahhī*); moreover, an agreement on presumptive indicants cannot be reached by intelligent people, nor can we completely comprehend all the divine commandments, since there are different opinions concerning most of them. And analogy (*qiyās*) is not a proof; firstly, because it leads to conjecture which often may be mistaken; and secondly, because our Law is founded on bringing together things which are divergent and separating things which resemble one another, and in this case, analogy cannot reach a conclusion. And as for the rule of "absolution from obligation" (*al-barā'a al-aṣliyya*),[3] all legal norms can be referred back to it when there is doubt. Thus, if error was a possibility for the Imam, and he was therefore not infallible, his preservation of the Law would not be reliable.

It is also necessary that he be more excellent than his subjects, since it is wrong that someone who has a superior should have preference over the superior, and since God has said: "And which is worthier to be followed—he who guides to the truth, or he who guides not unless he is guided?" (10:35).

It is also part of this that he should be the most pious (*azhad*), the most God-fearing (*awra'*), the most courageous, the most learned (*a'lam*), and the most honorable.

It is also necessary that he be explicitly designated (*manṣūṣ 'alayh*), since we stipulated that he be infallible and infallibility is one of the hidden matters of which no one but God is informed, so it is necessary that he be appointed by explicit designation (*naṣṣ*) and in no other way.

That the Imam After the Prophet is 'Alī b. Abī Ṭālib

The 'Allāma al-Ḥillī details twelve proofs based on the text of the Qur'ān (5:55) "Your walī *is only God, and His Messenger, and those who perform the prayer and pay* zakāt *while bowing down [in prayer],"*[4] *on Traditions from the Prophet, and on 'Alī's fulfilment of the condition already mentioned. Similar proofs are briefly given for the Imamate of the rest of the twelve Imams. Finally, al-Ḥillī turns to the proofs for the possibility and necessity of the continuing concealment of the Twelfth Imam.*

And now the Occultation of the Imam, peace be upon him. He does not appear in public or privately because of fear for his life from his enemies, and of fear for his friends. As for the expediency of his concealment, only God the Exalted has the knowledge.

The length of his life is not improbable. In past times and centuries, there were persons who lived long lives, longer than his, and it is established that God is able to do whatever is destined possible, and there is no doubt in his persistence, peace be upon him, for a long time, nor any improbability.

The necessity of his existence, peace by upon him, obtains with certainty [as does] his long life through explicit texts proving it from the Prophet, peace be upon him, and the Imams which have been repeatedly related among the Imamiyya. Furthermore it is certain because of the necessity of the appointment of the leader (*ra'īs*) in all times, and the necessity of his infallibility.

Concerning Ijtihād[5]

Section 1—The Mujtahid.

a. In ordinary language *ijtihād* means "exerting oneself to the utmost of one's ability in order to accomplish a difficult action," and in the technical language, "the jurist's exerting himself to the utmost of his ability to attain a probable opinion (*ẓann*) about a ruling in the Sacred Law." The most probably valid kind of *ijtihād* is the specialized kind (*al-tajziya*).[6] It is approved because the incumbency to act in accordance with *ijtihād* in the legal rules (*aḥkām*) necessarily exists when the *ijtihād* is practiced in the case of one rule, and the obligation to perform one's religious duty excludes the possibility that what is known be made to depend on what is not known.

b. The correct opinion is that the Prophet, peace be upon him, was not obliged by God to practice *ijtihād:* because God has said: "[Your companion—i.e., the Prophet] . . . does not speak out of caprice" (53:3); because he is able to attain certain knowledge and thus is not allowed to act on the basis of probable opinion (*ẓann*); because whoever opposes him is an unbeliever while someone who opposes a *mujtahid* is not an unbeliever; because he depended on divine inspiration (*al-waḥy*) in the commandments; and because if he were permitted to practice *ijtihād*, so also would Gabriel, peace be upon him, and the absolute certainty of divine inspiration would be removed. . . .

c. The criterion for being a *mujtahid* is that the legally obligated person should have the ability to establish proofs for matters pertaining to the rules of the Sacred Law. This can only be accomplished when certain things have been achieved:

i. He should have knowledge of the Arabic language and of the meanings of the words used in the religious law, not all of them, but of what is needed for elaborating proofs; and if the *mujtahid* consults a valid source at his disposal for the meanings of words that is allowed.

Comprised in this is knowledge of syntax (*al-naḥw*) and of the inflexions (*al-taṣrīf*), because the religious law is in Arabic, which cannot be understood without a knowledge of these two subjects, and that without which something obligatory cannot be accomplished is itself obligatory.

ii. He should know God's intention when He expresses something; and this can only be accomplished if he understands that God does not speak in such a way that the meanings of what He says cannot be understood, nor by using expressions which He intends to be understood in other than their ostensive meanings without an explanation. This can only be accomplished if the *mujtahid* understands that He is Wise—and that this depends on God's knowledge of evil and His being free from it—and knows that the Prophet of God, peace be upon him, spoke the truth, and knows the principles of theological dogmatics—which is not feasible on the basis of the Ash'arite doctrines.

iii. He should know the Traditions which indicate the rules of the Law either by memory or by reference to true sources; and he should know the circumstantial biographies of the transmitters of Tradition (*aḥwāl al-rijāl*) so that he can know the sound reports from the defective. He should also know those parts of the Book from which the injunctions are deduced—these are the "five hundred" verses; it is not stipulated that he should have them memorized, but he should know their significance and their places so that he can find them when he looks for them.

iv. He should know the consensus (*ijmā'*) and where it occurs so that he does not give legal pronouncements against it.

v. He should know the intellectual proofs such as "absolution from obligation" (*al-barā'a al-aṣliyya*) and "continuance of conditions" (*al-istiṣḥāb*) and so forth.[7]

vi. He should know the conditions for elaborating a demonstrative proof.

vii. He should know what abrogates and what is abrogated [i.e., in the text of the Qur'ān and in *ḥadīth*], the general and the specific (*al-'āmm wa'l-khāṣṣ*), what is contextually unrestricted in meaning and what is contextually restricted (*al-muṭlaq wa'l-muqayyad*), and other ways of arriving at the injunctions.

viii. He should have the ability to deduce the rules of the *sharī'a* from the matters of the principles of law.

Section 2—The Matters in Which the Mujtahid Practices Ijtihād.

These are all the rules of the Sacred Law for which there is no certain proof (*dalīl qaṭ'ī*). They are derived as the rational rules (*al-aḥkām al-aqliyya*) of the Law, excluding those rules whose belonging to it is known through a "certain proof," such as the obligation to perform the ritual prayer and to pay *zakāt*.[8]

Section 3—The Rules of Ijtihād.

a. The scholars are in agreement that there is only one correct opinion in rational matters, except al-Jāḥiẓ[9] and al-'Anbarī,[10] who were of the opinion that every person who practiced *ijtihād* with respect to rational issues produced a correct opinion, not in the sense of a correspondence with the truth but in the sense of a reprehensible error being eliminated. But the true opinion is the first, because God made the search for knowledge a duty and set up a proof for it, and whoever is incorrect therein still has to discharge his duty.

As for problems in the Law, the truth is that there is only one correct opinion for them, which is that which corresponds in reality with God's commandment. A group of theologians, such as al-Ash'arī, Abū Hudhayl,[11] and the two Jubbā'īs[12] were of the opinion that every *mujtahid* was correct because, according to them, God did not have a determined commandment in matters in which *ijtihād* is practiced. However, they all agree, except Bishr al-Marīsī,[13] that one who commits an error is pardoned.

According to us, if one of two presumptive indicants preponderates over the other, it makes the action obligatory, and the one who opposes it is in error; but, if it does not preponderate, the belief of both *mujtahids* as to the preponderance of his presumptive indicant is an error. Likewise, the person duty-bound by the Law is obligated, not by a rule in the religion which is arrived at through whim nor by something he cannot do, but in such a way that is specifically incontrovertible, or else preferable, and if there is no preponderance, the rule is either to refrain from action (*al-tasāquṭ*), or to choose (*al-takhyir*), or to have recourse to something else. In any case, the rule is specific, one who opposes it is in error, and there is only one correct opinion.

b. *Novel Occurrences.* If a case occurs to a *mujtahid* concerning himself, he should act as his *ijtihād* directs him; if the presumptive indicants are equal, he should choose or go back to his *ijtihād.* If it is connected with someone else, and is of a kind in which a settlement is involved, such as property, the two parties should make an agreement or take their case before a judge (*ḥākim*) to decide between them, and no repeal is permitted after judgment. If no settlement is involved, as in a divorce of such a kind that one of the parties believes it to be correct and the other does not, they should take their case before an adjudicator who is neither of the two, regardless of whether the person concerned (*sāḥib al-wāqi'a*) is a *mujtahid*, or a judge, or neither, for a judge cannot judge in his own favor against another, rather he should himself appoint someone to act as a judge between them.

If the novel occurrence happens to someone who is a follower (*muqallid*), he should refer to the jurisconsult (*al-muftī*). If there are many, he should refer to that on which the jurisconsults agree. If they disagree, he should act according to the more learned (*a'lam*) and the more pious (*al-azhad*). If there are two equally learned and pious, he should choose . . . .

c. If the *mujtahid* gives as a proof the proof for his original answer about a legal question, he does not need to repeat the *ijtihād;* otherwise, he should carry out *ijtihād.* If it goes against the first *ijtihād*, he should rule according to the second one, and inform the seeker of the legal opinion that he has revoked the first one. If he does not carry out *ijtihād*, how can he base anything on the first one and issue a legal ruling according to that *ijtihād*? This is the most probably correct opinion.

Section 4—Concerning the Jurisconsult (*al-muftī*) *and the Seeker of Legal Opinion* (*al-mustaftī*).

a. Faith (*al-īmān*) and just conduct (*al-'adāla*) are stipulated as conditions on the *muftī* and the judge (*ḥākim*), because without them there is no place for trust. Also stipulated is knowledge, for giving legal opinions and judging without knowledge is judging in matters of religion only on the basis of desire and speaking against God what is not known.

Does someone who is not a *mujtahid* have a legal opinion according to what he relates from a *mujtahid*? The best opinion is that if he relates it from a dead *mujtahid* he is not permitted to act according to it, because a dead person has no opinions; and, because of this, consensus does not hold if it contradicts a living person. But if he relates it from a living *mujtahid* and he has heard it from his mouth, it is permissible for him, and for others also, to act according to it; similarly, if he has heard it from a reliable informer from the *mujtahid.* If the *mujtahid* has written the legal opinion to him, the best view is that he is permitted to act according to it if he feels the written opinion is safe from error and forgery, otherwise not.

b. The truth is that the ordinary person is permitted to follow (*taqlīd*) a *mujtahid*'s opinion in the practical norms of the Sacred Law (*furū' al-sharī'a*) contrary to the opinion of the Mu'tazilīs of Baghdad. Al-Jubbā'ī permitted it in matters in which *ijtihād* could be practiced but not in other matters.

According to us, God's words: "[It is not for the believers to go forth totally;] but why should not a party of every section of them go forth [, to become learned in religion, . . .]" (9:122) require that some members of the party, or group, should instruct, while it is permitted for the others to follow them. The grounds for this are that when novel occurrences happen to an ordinary person, either he has no legal duty to do anything with them—this is invalid according to consensus—or he is duty-bound by the Law, either through deriving a proof for what he should do, or through implementing the rule of "absolution from obligation"—but this is invalid according to consensus—or through some other means, and this is either incumbent on him when his intellect is perfectly developed—but this is invalid according to consensus—or when the novel occurrence imposes the duty to do what he cannot do [—which is well known to be invalid].

As for questions in the principles of religion (*uṣūl*)[14], the truth is that following (*taqlīd*) another's opinion is forbidden here. A group of the jurists (*fuqahā'*) permitted it. According to us, the Prophet, peace be upon him, was commanded to acquire knowledge, and so it is incumbent upon us. Also *taqlīd* which is not known to be true is wrong, because it contains the possibility of error. And the Prophet, may God bless him and his family, accepted the two testimonies of faith (*shahāda*) from the Bedouin, because he knew that they comprised certainty in the principles of the religion, even though he was not able to express these proofs and to answer objections.

c. It is incumbent on the ordinary person (*al-'āmmī*) to practice *taqlīd* in the practical norms of the Law if he is not capable of practicing *ijtihād*. If he is capable of practicing *ijtihād* by striving to acquire the sciences without which he cannot practice *ijtihād*, he can choose between his *ijtihād* and asking for a legal opinion; similarly if he is a knowledgeable person who has reached the degree of *ijtihād*, and he has carried out *ijtihād*, he is not permitted to have recourse to the opinion of a *muftī*. But if he has not carried out his own *ijtihād*, one opinion is that *taqlīd* is permitted him; another that he should only follow one more learned than himself; another that he may practice *taqlīd* in what concerns himself specifically, but not when he gives legal opinions; another, that he may do so in what concerns himself when there is a limitation in time. The most probable opinion is that it is forbidden, because he is able to attain probable opinion in a stronger way, so it is incumbent upon him. The reason of the greater strength of his own *ijtihād* is the possibility that lying may afflict the *muftī*.

d. The one who asks for a legal opinion is not obliged to know that the *ijtihād* of the *muftī* is correct because of God's word: "Question the people of Remembrance [if it should be that you do not know]" (16:43). It is incumbent on him to follow whomever he deems most likely to be a *mujtahid* and pious, and this probability is only perceived by the person who asks for a legal opinion by observing the *muftī* delivering legal opinions to an assembly of people and by the agreement of Muslims to consult him and to revere him. But if the person asking for a legal opinion deems it likely that the *muftī* is not learned and more pious, he is forbidden to seek a legal opinion from him, according to consensus, because he is in the same position as the *mujtahid* when he investigates a presumptive indicant. And if two or more persons issue legal opinions for him, if they concur there is no problem; but if they do not, he should try to find out which is the more learned and the more pious and follow him; if they are equal, he is free to choose; if one of them has more knowledge and the other more piety, the more learned is to be selected. The most learned will be known through his forbearance and through other manifest evidence, not through his search for knowledge itself, for this is not something for the ordinary person to judge. If a scholar is not able to practice *ijtihād*, he is not allowed to issue legal opinions according to the opinion of another *mujtahid*, living or dead; nor may the ordinary person follow someone when a more excellent person exists, because the supposition about his being correct is weaker. If two *muftī*s are equal and the ordinary person follows one of them, he is not permitted to turn away from him in that ruling on which he consulted him; the preferable opinion is that he is permitted to turn away from him and follow the other in any other ruling.

There follows Section 5 on differences among the mujtahidīn.

Notes

1. Translated from Chapter 11 of al-'Allāma al-Ḥillī's *Nahj al-Mustarshadīn fī Uṣūl al-Dīn*, Sayyid Aḥmad al-Ḥusaynī and Shaykh Hādī al-Yūsufī, eds. (Qumm: Majma' al-Dhakhā'ir al-Islāmiyya, n.d.), pp. 62-67.

2. *Imāra* (lit.: "sign") is used technically to mean an indicant which leads to a probable opinion (*ẓann*) being formed about the existence of that which it indicates. Since the evidence of an *imāra* is probabilistic, there is necessarily always doubt, and, therefore, disagreement among people, about the existence of what it indicates.

3. *Al-barā'a al-aṣliyya:* the principle in Islamic jurisprudence whereby, if the *ḥukm*, or legal value, of an act according to the *sharī'a* cannot be determined, the value is as it was before the knowledge brought by the *sharī'a.* Nearly all Sunni jurists are of the opinion that there are no legal values outside the *sharī'a;*

but for Shi'ite jurists (as for Mu'tazilī theologians), the legal values of certain acts can be determined by the intellect.

4. This translation follows the traditional Shi'ite interpretation of the verse according to which the third *walī*, after God and Muḥammad, is 'Alī, who, on one occasion, gave *zakāt* to a poor man while in the bowing position during the performance of a ritual prayer.

5. Translated from Chapter 12 of al-'Allāma al-Ḥillī, *Tahdhīb al-Wuṣūl ilā 'ilm al-Uṣūl* (Tehran 1308/1890-91), pages unnumbered.

6. *Ijtihād* can be either a competence in the entire field of the law or a competence in only some parts of it. It is this second kind which is meant here.

7. For *al-barā'a al-aṣliyya*, see note 3 above. *Al-istiṣḥāb* is another principle in Islamic jurisprudence whereby a situation is deemed to remain the same as long as it has not been demonstrated to have changed or to have ceased to exist.

8. Such matters are known for certain because they are commanded by the text of the Qur'ān; there is thus no doubt about them, given the certainty of the ostensive meaning of the Qur'ān.

9. (Ca. 160/776-255/868-69); the famous man of letters and Mu'tazilī theologian of the Basran school.

10. 'Ubayd Allāh b. al-Ḥasan b. al-Ḥusayn al-'Anbarī (105/723-168/785); a Basran jurist and Traditionalist.

11. Abu'l-Hudhayl al-'Allāf (d. 226/840-41 or 235/849-50); the first systematic theologian of the Mu'tazilī school.

12. Abū 'Alī (d. 303/915-6) and his son Abū Ḥāshim (d. 321/933) were famous Mu'tazilī theologians.

13. (D. 218/833); a prominent theologian of the Murji'a; he was born in Kufa, but lived most of his life and died in Baghdad.

14. As opposed to the *furū'*, the "branches," which are the practical norms of the divine law.

CHAPTER 11

Two Decrees of Shāh Ṭahmāsp Concerning Statecraft and the Authority of Shaykh 'Alī Al-Karakī

Translated and edited by Said Amir Arjomand

Shāh Ṭahmāsp, the second Safavid monarch, ascended the throne in 1524 at the age of ten and ruled Iran until 1576. He was a pious man, and his long reign was of crucial importance for the definitive penetration of Iran by Twelver Shi'ism, which had been established by his father, Ismā'īl I, at the onset of Safavid rule in 1501. The two *farmāns* translated below give us a fairly complete picture of the political culture of the new Shi'ite empire and the precise accommodation of Twelver Shi'ism and clerical authority within it.

The first decree, frequently and fondly referred to by subsequent Shi'ite scholars as a key endorsement of their clerical authority[1], is in fact a grant of extensive lands, tax immunities, and revenue from the mint of Ḥilla to Shaykh 'Alī 'Abd al-'Ālī al-Karakī (d. 1534/940), and is addressed primarily to the governors and officials of the Arab Iraq. The text was copied from the original by the author of *Mustadrak al-Wasā'il.*[2] The decree was issued by the young monarch in 1533, the year before al-Karakī's death and during the intense struggle between the latter and the *ṣadr*, Mīr Ni'matallāh Ḥillī, mentioned in Chapter 4, Section 1. In it, Ṭahmāsp refers to Shaykh 'Alī as the Seal of the *Mujtahidīn*, Proof of Islam, Guide of the People, and the Deputy of the Imam, and grants him the power of appointment and dismissal of religious and military officials and anywhere in the country. All officials and notables of the realm are ordered to consider him "their guide and model" and to obey him in all affairs. It should also be noted that Shaykh 'Alī is twice referred to as the *shaykh al-Islām*.

The document illustrates the personal nature of delegated authority in Iranian patrimonialism, and the consequent lack of clear differentiation of its scope. The same document grants Shaykh 'Alī broad religious and political authority and specific proprietary and fiscal rights and immunities. It also confirms a previous endowment (*vaqf*). The chief interest of the document from our point of view is in fact its endorsement of the religious authority of the foremost Shi'ite *mujtahid* of the time which Ṭahmāsp was seeking to institutionalize and make supreme in his realm. The authority of the Seal of the *Mujtahidīn* rests on his unparalleled knowledge of the Sacred Law as the heir to the sciences of the Prophet and the Deputy of the Imam, which makes him the model, the exemplar, and the guide of the people. Noteworthy among the terms used to designate the supreme religious authority of the realm is "the Deputy of the Imam," also used in the decree cited in Chapter 4, Section 1. The term had been given currency by al-Karakī in his controversial discussion of the extent of the juristic authority of the *'ulamā'* during the Occultation of the Imam.[3] The chroniclers of Shāh Ṭahmāsp's reign define the term *nā'ib-i imām* as the "jurist who has all the qualifications for giving authoritative opinion" (*faqīh-i jāmi' al-sharāyiṭ-i fatvā*).[4] As the reader of the volume by now knows, these terms were destined for a long history in the evolution of clerical authority in Shi'ism.

In practice, al-Karakī in turn delegated his authority to his "deputies", referred to in this and other documents. The year before this decree was issued, al-Karakī had secured the appointment of one of his students, Amīr Mu'izz al-Dīn Muḥammad Iṣfahānī (d. 1545-46/952), as the *ṣadr*. Amīr Mu'izz al-Dīn was in Isfahan at the time. In an instance of exercise of the authority to appoint religious functionaries granted him by the king, "His Excellency, the *Mujtahid* of the Age, appointed deputies and representatives for [the new *ṣadr*] until his arrival at the sublime threshold."[5] Furthermore, exercising his authority specifically as the Deputy of the Imam, al-Karakī instituted the Friday congregational prayer—hitherto considered in abeyance during the Occultation of the Imam by many jurists—and appointed congregational prayer leaders throughout Iran.[6]

The second decree does not bear a date but can safely be assumed to have been issued later. The Persian text used for this translation was published by Danishpazhouh on the basis of a lithograph edition of 1887-88/1305.[7] Danishpazhouh does not venture to suggest a date for it, but the decree was most likely issued in the middle part of the sixteenth century, when Ṭahmāsp had survived the internecine tribal warfare of the early years of his reign and emerged as the great monarch at whose court such distinguished supplicants as Humāyūn Shāh of India and the Ottoman Prince Bayazīd took refuge. In any event, the date of its issue is not significant from our point of view, as it sets forth general principles of government and statecraft under patrimonial monarchy. It contains a large number of ethical precepts on the proper conduct of the officials, and a number of specific directives including two interesting ones regarding women and homosexuals (Articles 63-64). The norms regulating the political economy of patrimonialism—promotion of agriculture and handicraft (Articles 24-25), protection of the animal resources of the country (Articles 68-69), maintenance of fair prices and prevention of hoarding and speculation in grains (Articles 52, 56-57)—are also set forth. Employment of spies as an important technique in statecraft receives considerable attention (Articles 46-49). Governors and headmen are made responsible for the security of roads and streets, and for the restitution of all stolen property to the owners in the areas under their jurisdiction (Articles 53-54). Of special interest is the responsibility of the officials for the welfare and education of orphans (Articles 65-66). Ṭahmāsp took great interest in the welfare of orphans, and, incidentally, in their upbringing as orthodox Shi'ites under "pious male and female teachers of Shi'ite persuasion."[8]

The articulation of the principles of patrimonial government and Shi'ite religion in the document requires some brief comments. The prohibition of wine and music (Articles 58-60) represent Ṭahmāsp's decision to follow the Shi'ite Sacred Law. Article 55 assigns the administration of the property of those deceased without an heir to the governors. The Shi'ite Sacred Law considers this one of the functions of the Imam. In the nineteenth century, this function was deemed to devolve upon the Imam's General Deputies during his Occultation.[9] Finally, the emphatically informal and discretionary norms of patrimonial justice (Articles 8, 20) offer an interesting contrast to the formalized norms of the Sacred Law and to its rigidly fixed punishments.

The last sentence of the decree is of great retrospective interest. It typically refers to the Safavid Dynasty as the House of *Vilāyat* (Authority), the very term Khumeinī was to appropriate for the *'ulamā'* in his theory of the sovereignty of the jurist four centuries later.[10]

The Decree Concerning Shaykh 'Alī al-Karakī

In the name of God, the Merciful, the Compassionate, O Muḥammad,

O 'Alī, the royal decree has been made effective:

Since the dawn of the rising sun of the eternal rule (*dawlat*) [of the Safavids] and of the appearance of the auspicious banners of honorable glory, without whose concordance the hand of Providence does not mark with felicity the book of lives of the happy ones, we consider the elevation of the banners of the sublime Prophetic Law (*sharī'a*)—from the effect of the appearance of whose sun the marks of oppression and ignorance become removable from the space of the world and its inhabitants—supportive of the pillars of sovereignty and rules of success; and we consider the revival of the customs of the Law of the Lord of the Messengers and the showing of the rightful path of the infallible Imams, God's benedictions be upon them—which have, like the truthful morn, lifted the darkening dust of the innovation of the opponents [i.e., the Sunnis]—as preliminaries to the appearance of the sun of the spread of justice and the nurturing of religion, the Lord of Time (*ṣāḥib al-amr*), peace be upon him. The path for reaching this goal and the origin [*sic*] of attaining this security is undoubtedly the following of and obedience to the *'ulamā'* of religion who, aided by learning and proselytizing, protect and preserve the Law of the Lord of the Messengers, through whose guidance and direction all mankind can reach the realm of instruction from the straits of abjection and astrayness, and from whose bounteous benefits the darkness of ignorance is removed from the pages of the minds of the people of imitation (*ahl-i taqlīd*), especially in this bounteous and privileged age [in] which [such guidance] is reserved for the rank of the [divinely] guided Imams[11], peace and praise be upon them, and the highly positioned seal of the *Mujtahidīn*, Heir to the sciences of the Lord of the Messengers, Protector of the Religion of the Commander of the Faithful [i.e., Shi'ism], the Kibla of the pious faithful, the Exemplar of expert *'ulamā'*, the Proof of Islam (*ḥujjat al-islām*) and of the Muslims who directs the people unto the clear path, Erector of the banners of the indelible Law (*sharī'a*) who is obeyed by the great governors in all times, and Guide (*muqtadā*) of all the people of the time, the Clarifier of the permissible and the forbidden, the Deputy of the Imam (*nā'ib al-imām*)—peace be upon Him—who has clarified the difficulties of the rules of the community of believers and the rightful laws; may he not come to an end, like his elevated victorious namesake, 'Alī. The highly positioned *'ulamā'* of all quarters have bowed their heads in humility at the threshold of his sciences and are honored by what they acquire from the rays of his beneficent lamp through the use of sciences. Furthermore, the lords and nobles of the time obey and follow the orders and prohibitions of that guide and consider submission to his commands the cause of salvation. They all devote their lofty will and honorable intent to the raising of the position and elevation of the rank of that Excellency.

We decree that the great *sayyids* and the lords and the honorable nobles and the commanders and the ministers and other pillars of the sacred state (*dawlat-i qudsī ṣifāt*) consider the above-mentioned their guide and leader, offer him obedience and submission in all affairs, carry out what he orders and refrain from what he forbids. [They should consider] dismissed whomever he dismisses among the office holders of the religious affairs of the [God-] protected realms (*mamālik-i maḥrūsa*) and the victorious military, and appointed whomever he appoints. [Furthermore,] they should not require any other document in such dismissals and appointments, and should not appoint any person dismissed by him so long as he is not [re]appointed by that Excellency.

We have also decreed that the agricultural estate of Kabīsa and Dawalīb. . . .adjacent to the river of holy Najaf . . . and the cultivated lands of Umm al-'Azamāt and the Kāhin al-Wa'd lands of Ramāḥiyya that he has brought into cultivation be made an endowment (*vaqf*) for him, and for his descendants after him, according to the correct procedure of the Sacred Law as specified in the deed of endowment. And the world-incumbent command has been issued that [the above] be removed from the tax registry of the Arab Iraq, excluded from the revenue and expenditure accounts, be considered His Holy Excellency's endowment and entitlement, and be exempted from all future orders affecting requisition, division, replacement and change of the *suyūrghāls* and land grants. Furthermore, the sum of ten Tabrīzī *tūmāns* from the mint of Ḥilla is established as *suyūrghāl* for His Excellency instead of the tar of Ḥārhīt and Ḥilla which has been His Excellency's *suyūrghāl* in the sum of eight hundred *tūmāns* but which he has given up willingly owing to the difficulty of transportation. The officials must give the above sum priority over all other receipts and drafts and not pay a single *dīnār* to anyone until it has reached his deputies (*vukalā'*) from the mint.

As he has humbly requested, we make His Excellency the gift of Barqāniyya and its surroundings whose tax is seventy *tūmāns* instead of [?] Bahilal . . . with seventy-two *tūmāns* which he had as *suyūrghāl*. We order that Barqāniyya and its surroundings be recognized as the *suyūrghāl* of the above-mentioned Seal of the *Mujtahidīn* from the beginning of the year *'īlān 'īl* and be handed over to his deputies. All its produce for that year is to be handed over to his agents without excuse and without any reduction. . . .

The respected tax accountants, agents, and bureaucrats must remove all the above from the tax registry and exempt them from all dues, especially . . . the tithe, . . . the stamp due, the due of *vizāra*, the due of *ṣidāra*, etc. . . . The officials of the tax bureau of the Arab Iraq must remove their pen from these estates and not set foot in them . . . not inspect them, . . . not impose fines and if a fine is issued, leave it to his agents . . . and consider all the receipts fully and freely due to the above-mentioned Shaykh al-Islām and exempt from taxation as his other *suyūrghāls*.

As the world-incumbent order has been issued prohibiting the central *dushlakāt* bureau from imposing the *dushlakāt*, the *dushlakāt* bureau of the Arab Iraq should similarly consider itself prohibited. . . .

As the above-mentioned source of guidance occasionally turns from holy Najaf to some of the protected realms, [the inhabitants of] Ramāḥiyya especially should do everything possible in offering gifts for the journeys, and consider the above-mentioned personage and his retenue present even in their absence, and discharge all obligations.

When the above-mentioned Guide of the People (*muqtadā yi anām*) is at the foot of the celestial throne, all the lords and nobility, commanders, governors and notables of the protected realms attend to him and he does not visit anyone. The governors of the Arab Iraq should observe the same rule and discharge the duty of attendance, and display utmost politeness in every way. They should not greedily expect the above-mentioned Shaykh al-Islām to visit them and to go out to welcome them; and, needless to say, they should not require his attendance at their sessions.

Furthermore, it is decreed that the arrears of the previous year from the mint be cleared without delay; that the coinage of the city of the believers, Ḥilla, be entrusted to the deputies of His Excellency; and that the mint not operate without their presence and all disagreement with them be avoided. And as, according to our order, the produce of Barqāniyya and its surroundings, inclusive of the due of the landlord and of the state, is established for the above-mentioned holy personage, this obligation should be respected and discharged, the [?]monetary equivalent (*'avaḍ*) of the seed [?not] be demanded. No receipt or document of whatever date or wording has any validity in this regard. [The officials] should consider His Excellency permitted to order the punishment of any person who opposes this decree and does not comply, and should assist him in this matter to the utmost . . . they should observe the above-mentioned orders and the decree issued in Muḥarram 936 [October-November 1529] in every detail, not seek to deviate from it, and consider the offender accused and banished and . . . rejected by this dynasty . . . [the grants and dues] should be considered binding and payments be made annually without requiring new documents; and the thanks and complaints of his deputies and agents be given great weight.

Written on 16 Dhi'l-Ḥijja, 939/July 9, 1533.

On the margin: The above order and all the orders regarding the above-mentioned Guide of the People is to be considered signed and effective, the offender accursed and banished. Ṭahmāsp.

The Ordinance of Shāh Ṭahmāsp on the Law of Sovereignty (salṭanat)

The universally incumbent decree for the obedient world [emanating] from the source of benevolence and the mine of royal compassion is hereby promulgated for those in attendance at the threshold of the rulers (which is the place of prostration), the functionaries of the court (which is the people's place of hope) from among the noble brothers and children, the Beglerbegs, the governors and the deputies (*khulafā'*) [of the Ṣafavī order], the great generals, commanders and Khans, and other officials, ministers, secretaries, minor and major tax agents, commanders of the fortresses, elders of the tribes, aldermen (*kalāntarān*), village headmen, road-keepers, and all the attendants at the Caliphal threshold and the officials of the important quarters and regions to obey. In addition to what is known to them of the laws of the sovereignty and Caliphate that govern our justice-based nature and admired royal conduct, they should assume responsibility for the implementation of this directive, which is issued from the seat of glory, and make it the basis for the ordering of the lives of the subjects and the cities without deviating from it by a hair's breadth:

1. Briefly, that they seek divine satisfaction and be needful of God's threshold in all affairs, be they customs, transactions or acts of worship, bend themselves and others towards this goal in so far as possible so that they apply themselves to tasks with sincerity and without ulterior motives.

2. That they avoid isolation—as this is the way of desert-dwelling dervishes—but not develop the habit of appearing in public and frequenting constantly either—as is the way of the trades people (*bāzārīyan*); in short, that they not relinquish moderation and keep to the middle and the mean.

3. That they respect and hold dear those promoted by God among the righteous and valuable thinkers and *'ulamā'*.

4. That they get accustomed to being awake morning, evening, midnight, and day.

5. When they are not preoccupied with the affairs of the people, let them read the books of the masters of Sufism and sincerity, like the books on ethics which are spiritual medicine. Let them not become accustomed to vacationing, relaxation, and comfort-seeking, which

resemble the state of the dead and of women and not the habit of men and the living.

6. That they be firm and patient so as not to be outdone by . . . the enticements of the dishonest and the fraudulent. The best of the acts of worship is the ordering of the affairs of the people: friendship or enmity, kinship or otherness are to be disregarded and everyone's problem be handled with good will and an open heart.

7. That they assist and be charitable to the poor, the abject, the needy, especially the withdrawn and the isolated who are without access and do not voice their request as much as they are capable.

8. That they scrutinize the offenses, errors, and violations of the people one by one according to the standards of justice. By the same standard of justice, they should exactly determine the retribution for each offense, deciding which is to be ignored and which investigated and punished. Many a small offense requires a heavy penalty, and many a grave offense can be overlooked.

9. That, with the appropriate gradation, they admonish the offenders mildly or upbraid them rudely; and if nothing comes of admonishment and warning, proceed with arrest, corporal punishment, and cutting of limbs on the appropriate scale. They should not make brave in killing, and only do so after ample deliberation, as the head of the executed cannot be grafted back on. Whenever possible, they should send the offender deserving execution to the celestial threshold [of the king] with the truth of the case, and be bound by and execute whatever verdict is issued. However, if keeping the offender or sending him would cause disorder, let them execute him in the place of punishment as a lesson to the evil-doers.

10. That they refrain from skinning and burning and the severe punishments . . . The desert of each class of people is in accordance with its status. With a person of high nature, a sharp look is the equivalent of killing, and with the lowly, even mutilation is of no avail. . . .[12]

16. In granting justice and interrogating the plaintiff, they should initiate action themselves in so far as they are capable.

17. That they make a list of the supplicants so that those who come early not be subjected to the discomfort of waiting.

18. That they show no haste in punishing a person reported to have done wrong and in pursuing the matter, as many are the slanderers and fabricators of calumny and few are the well-thinking tellers of truth.

19. They should not lose their reason during fits of anger (*ghaḍab*), but work slowly and with patience. They should allow a few of their attendants and intimates who are known for wisdom and propriety to utter the word of truth[13] at times when anger and distress take the upper

hand and the wise remain silent.

20. They should develop the habit of overlooking offenses in so far as disorder is not likely to result. Most individuals have committed some offense; some could become bolder as a result of punishment while others would impose banishment on themselves with the loss of honor. There are some who must be punished without any offense and others who should be overlooked despite a thousand offenses. Punishment (*sīyāsat*) is the most delicate of the functions of sovereignty, and should be carried out with calm, deliberation, and wisdom.

21. They should constantly be informed about major and minor conditions and situations concerning them and their jurisdiction, as kingship and commandership and government is no other than policing (*pāsbānī*).

22. They should not swear, as swearing implies the attribution of lying to oneself and of suspicion to the person addressed.

23. They should not become accustomed to cursing people, as this is the manner of the rude and the lowly.

24. They should endeavor to promote agriculture, to strengthen and assist the subjects with the provision of seed, and to treat them well so that the number of cities, townships, and villages be increased every year. They [should govern] so lightly that all arable land be brought under cultivation.

25. They should then endeavor to increase the production of perfect and valuable goods and work diligently . . . on the directives of the tax agents. They should treat the humble subjects individually and show concern for them.

26. They should never renege on a promise or an undertaking.

27. They should forbid the soldiers or others ever to descend on people's houses without their consent.

28. They should not [completely] trust their reason in the conduct of affairs, and consult a person wiser than themselves. Even if such [a wise person] is not forthcoming, they should still proceed with consultation, as the correct and true path is often found through ignorance.

29. They should not consult many, as the correct and insightful mind is God-given and cannot be acquired by reading or through the passage of time.

30. They should not refer any task that can be done by their attendants to their children, and should not personally undertake what can be done by their children. This is so because they can compensate for what others fail to do, but it is difficult to make up for their own failure.

31. They should befriend well-wishers from every class.

32. They should not be excessive in sleeping and eating in order to step beyond the station of animals and to reach the rank of humanity.

33. They should not be obstinate, mischievous, wicked, or vindictive. They should not make their chests the prison of rancor . . . They should laugh and joke infrequently.

34. They should not adorn their body or attire;

35. and should choose something less than what they can afford.

36. They should endeavor to spread knowledge and art and education so that talent from [all] classes of people is not wasted.

37. They should make an effort to educate the old families.

38. They should not ignore the discipline and equipment of the army.

39. Their expenditure should be lower than their revenue. Anyone whose expenditure exceeds his income is a fool. Anyone who balances the two is not a fool, but neither is he wise. . . .[14]

44. They should be informed about their confidants and servants to assure the latter do not abuse their closeness to act tyrannically.

45. They should avoid the slick-tongued who dishonestly do the work of enmity in the garb of friendship. . . .

46. They should constantly be informed by spies.

47. They should not trust the word of a single spy, especially in the case of probability, as honesty and impartiality is rare.

48. They should appoint several spies for each matter, without any one of them knowing about the others, and should hear their reports separately. . . .

49. The spies should be unknown.

50. They should constantly exercise the army.

51. They should not be eager about hunting and travel, and [hunt] only occasionally for exercise, soldierliness, and recreation.

52. No one anywhere in the protected realms should take corn from the subjects to hoard it out of greed. If such should appear, it would rouse the wrath of the ruler.

53. They should make every effort for the security of roads and thoroughfares. Every step of the roads of the protected realms is the responsibility of the governors and the headmen. They must pursue thieves and robbers in settled areas or on roads so that no trace is left of the pickpocket, the night thief, and the larcenist.

54. They must either find the thieves or compensate for whatever is stolen or plundered themselves.

55. They should investigate the property of the absent and the deceased from whatever religion and denomination. If there is an heir, the property should be handed over without anyone hovering around it. If there is no heir, the property should be turned over to a trustee with

the notification of the notables of each quarter, a trusteeship be set up, and the truth be reported to the sublime threshold. If a lawful heir appears, the property should be transferred to him or her. Utmost care and benevolence should be exercised in this regard lest contentment (*sīr-chashmī*) disappear and what goes on in the Ottoman realms gradually appear here too.

56. They should try to keep the prices down and should not allow the rich to buy a lot and hoard out of greed and to push up the prices gradually against the interests of the victorious state.

57. They should prevent trade in the essential grains.

58. They should persistently see to it that there is no trace of wine;

59. and so punish its consumers, sellers, and carriers in order to set an example for others.

60. Other than in the royal kettle-drum houses of the protected realms, no musical instrument is to be played. If it transpires that anyone has made an instrument of any kind, that person is guilty.

61. They should spare no effort in celebrating the Feast of Nawrūz (New Year), the two feasts [of Sacrifice and the Breaking of the Fast], the birthday of the Prophet, and other Feasts.

62. In the days of Feasts, kettle-drums should be played in the cities.

63. Women should never ride horses unless it is absolutely necessary, and when they do ride by necessity, they should not sit on the saddle and should not hold the reins in their own hands, in so far as possible.

64. Homosexuals and women, however old, should not attend the shows of the Qalandar dervishes and other players. Even though we have not forbidden these groups to perform, they are forbidden to bring children over twelve into their shows.

65. They should investigate in every town and village of the protected realms. Whenever they find an orphan without relatives, they should raise him or her. If the orphan is very young, he should be entrusted to a trustworthy wet-nurse; and after he reaches the age of discernment, they should appoint a qualified teacher for the male and a chaste widow for the female, and entrust the orphans to them for education. A boy for whom learning a profession and a craft is appropriate and hereditary should work in the day and come to the teacher in the evening. The officials of every district should inform its religious and secular judges of the state of expenditure of state funds on the necessities of the children monthly and without delay. Every year on the Nawrūz, two appropriate suits of clothes should be given to the children and the teachers individually, and on the first of Mīzān (Libra), one suit of winter clothes.

66. For marrying the orphans, all the necessities of life and suitable equipments should be provided from the funds of the exalted state. The

tax officials and headmen should carry out this directive and pay the allowances in every town and district, whether there are one hundred orphans or one, and report to His Majesty year by year and name by name.

67. They should execute the regulations for the Judiciary (*dār al-qaḍā'*) . . . , and the regulations on transactions . . . that have already been issued in two Imperial decrees.

68. Lambs and goats should not be slaughtered in any place . . . before they are six months old. Let no one make disease and possibility of death an excuse for slaughtering.

69. The owners and renters of beasts of burden should not unnecessarily load more than one hundred Tabrīzī *mans* on a camel, no more than eighty *mans* on a mule, and no more than fifty *mans* on donkeys. In all matters they should choose what is closer to the law of moderation and justice.

The honorable secretaries should enter this decree whose acknowledgement is incumbent in the eternal registers, and the noble Beylerbegs, governors and deputies (*khulafā'*) should send copies of it to their tribal, rural, and urban districts, and have its august content proclaimed loudly. This sacred decree should be engraved in stone and erected in a prominent location in three or four important cities of Iraq and Azerbaijan so that the law of sovereignty (*qanūn-i salṭanat*) remain in the world as a memorial to the House of Prophethood and *Vilāyat* (Authority) [i.e., the Safavid Dynasty], and in order to increase the intelligence of the administrators of all times.

Notes

1. Khātūnābādī, op. cit., p. 461; Yūsuf ibn Aḥmad al-Baḥrānī, *Lu'lu'at al-Baḥrayn* (Bombay, n.d.), p. 153; Muḥammad Bāqir al-Khwānsārī, *Rawḍāt al-Jannāt*, A. Ismā'īliyān, ed. (Qumm, 1970/1391), vol. 4, pp. 262-65; Muḥammad Ḥusayn al-Nūrī al-Ṭabrisī, *Mustadrak al-wasā'il* (Tehran 1903/1321), vol. 3, pp. 432-34; Gulpāygānī, *op. cit.*, pp. 299-300.

2. Vol. 3, pp. 432-34. A defectively edited version of the decree has been published in Mīrzā 'Abd Allāh Afandī al-Iṣbahānī, *Riyāḍ al-'Ulamā' wa Ḥiyāḍ al-Fuḍalā'*, S. M. al-Mar'ashī and S. A. al-Ḥusaynī, eds., Qumm: Maṭba'at al-Khayyām, 1980-81/1401, Vol. 3, pp. 455-60. On one point, this version offers a significant variant to our reading which is noted below (n. 11).

3. See Madelung, op. cit. (1981); Modarressi op. cit. (1983), pp. 50-59.

4. Ḥasan Rūmlū, *Aḥsan al-Tavārīkh*, C.N. Seddon, ed. (Baroda: Oriental Institute, 1931), p. 255. The definition in *Khulāṣat al-Tavārīkh* (under the year 940) is virtually the same.

5. Ibid., p. 313.

6. Muḥammad Tunikābunī, *Qiṣaṣ al-'Ulamā'* (Tehran: 'Ilmiyya Islāmiyya, n.d.), pp. 347-48, citing Ni'matallāh Jazayirī's (d. 1701) *Ghawwās al-La'ālī.* Both *Aḥsan al-Tavārīkh* and *Khulāṣat al-Tavārīkh* define the term *nā'ib al-imām* in the context of the institution of congregational prayer during the Occultation. (See n. 4 above for references.)

7. M. T. Dānishpazhūh, *"Ā'īn-i shāh Ṭahmāsp-i ṣafavī dar qanūn-i salṭanat," Barrasī-hā-yi Tārīkhī*, VII, no. 1 (1972/1351), Introduction, pp. 121-29; the text, pp. 130-38.

8. Iskandar Beg Munshī, *Tārīkh-i Ālam-ārā-yi 'Abbāsī*, I. Afshār, ed. (Tehran 1971/1350), vol. 1, p. 123.

9. Such is the opinion of Shaykh Muḥammad Ḥasan Najafī (d. 1850/1266) in *Jawāhir al-Kalām*, cited in Ḥusayn 'Alī Muntaẓirī, *Kitāb al-Khums* (Qumm, n.d. [1981 or 1982]), p. 347.

10. See Chapter 8 above and Chapter 17 below.

11. The *Riyāḍ al-'Ulamā'* version (p. 456) reads as follows: "especially in bounteous age when a personage of elevated status who belongs to the rank of the [divinely] guided Imams, etc."

12. The ensuing articles are on the ethics and etiquette of proper conduct towards the subjects for the officials.

13. The phrase *"khabithiyyat navarzand"* in the text is assumed to be corrupt.

14. The ensuing articles reiterate the necessity of keeping one's word and promises, and commend avoidance of villains.

CHAPTER 12

The Muqaddas al-Ardabīlī on Taqlīd

Translated and edited by John Cooper

The text translated below is by Mullā Aḥmad Ardabīlī, the Muqaddas (d. 1585/993), and is excerpted from the chapter on "Enjoining the Good and Forbidding the Evil" in his commentary on the Qur'ān, Zubdat al-Bayān.[1] *It is significant for its refutation of the arguments against* taqlīd, *and for formally conjoining the ideas of* ijtihād *and* taqlīd. *This conjunction greatly enhanced clerical authority in Shi'ism. If* ijtihād *legitimized the juristic authority of the* 'ulamā', taqlīd *made compliance with their injunctions and opinions an ethical obligation for the laity. Ardabīlī's argument is still cautious, he uses the term* iqtidā' *as an alternative to* taqlīd, *and takes pains to establish that the* taqlīd *of the jurist is different from the reprehensible* taqlīd *forbidden by the Qur'ānic verses.*[2] *Nevertheless, a new trend has set in. The layman is no longer the voluntary seeker of legal advice* (mustaftī) *of the medieval Shi'ite literature,*[3] *and is gradually assigned the fixed legal status of "follower"* (muqallid) *as subject to clerical authority.* (*Ed.*)

"But the unbelievers forge against God falsehood, and most of them have no understanding" (5:103), that is to say the unbelievers fabricate lies about God by making what is permitted unlawful and vice versa, and they say falsely that God made it thus. They do not know what is permitted from what is unlawful . . . nevertheless they follow their forefathers and do not hear what is reasonable, as is understood from God's words: "And when it is said to them: 'Come now to what God has sent down, and the Messenger,' they say: 'Enough for us is what we found our fathers doing.' What, even if their fathers had knowledge of nought and were not guided?" (5:104) . . . , which means that following a model (*al-iqtidā'*) is only correct for someone who knows that the model is rightly guided and knowledgeable, and that is known only through a proof. Thus nothing but proof suffices in following a model (*taqlīd*).

Taqlīd is not permissible as an equivalent for an appeal to God and to the Prophet, indeed it is in no circumstances permissible as long as the model is not rightly guided; thus it is indicated that it is allowed when the follower knows that the model is rightly guided. Contained in this is permission for *taqlīd* in a general sense, and this is not unlikely, but it is not a true kind of *taqlīd*, because the *muqallid* does not know that he is rightly guided nor that the one he follows is, unless by means of a proof which demonstrates that the model and the *muqallid* guide rightly and are rightly guided, respectively, and that there is right guidance and direction in following the model. In that case, it does not count as blameworthy *taqlīd*, nor even as *taqlīd tout court*, since he is really following a proof, for in following a proof there is no difference between whether what is followed is a person or not. For this reason they say that *taqlīd* is the acceptance of someone else's word without a proof of why it should be accepted. However, *taqlīd* of the prophets, or even the *taqlīd* of *mujtahid*s, is not *taqlīd* in this general sense, but rather the demonstration, as in the case of the *mujtahid*, of the truth of a matter through a proof. Indeed, this kind of following is given the name *taqlīd* in another sense, not in the sense in which it is blameworthy and not permissible.

Taqlīd of a *mujtahid* is therefore proper and permissible; indeed, it is obligatory once a proof for it has been established, such as the *mujtahid*'s ability to derive legal judgments (*ijtihād*). This is obvious and explained in the principles of jurisprudence (*uṣūl*); and this is the meaning of *taqlīd* to be understood from verse 5:104 (quoted above) and from similar verses. The kind of *taqlīd* which is not permissible and is blameworthy is the like of that which God's words, "Do not follow that of which you have no knowledge" (17:36), and similar verses indicate, that is, "Only say or do that which you know to be permissible." The meaning of this is *taqlīd* without a known proof. This then is *taqlīd*, and in this explanation is combined the permissibility of *taqlīd* and impermissibility; the permissibility of acting on the basis of probable opinion (*ẓann*) and the impermissibility of acting thereupon. . .; and the permissibility of *taqlīd* in legal matters (*furū'*) and the impermissibility of probable opinion and *taqlīd* in dogmatics. . . .We have claimed that knowledge produced for a *muqallid* by *taqlīd* in legal and other matters, when it is through a proof, is like following the Infallible [Imam], as when it is said of a *mujtahid*: "This is the legal opinion which the *muftī* gave; every legal ruling which the *muftī* gives is true and must be acted upon." The first premise is posited, the second is established by a proof and by divine command, so the conclusion is scientifically established, so consider this.

God's words: "They follow only *ẓann*, and they are only liars" (6:116) demonstrates the impermissibility of acting on probable opinion (*ẓann*) in dogmatics, not in legal matters, which are based on *ẓann*, for the meaning of [the verse] is, according to what is in al-Kashshāf,[4] that they follow only their supposition that they were partners with God, which is a question of dogmatics not law, and they are only liars, surmising falsely that they were partners, for the opening of the verse demonstrates the unfitness of anything apart from God for Lordship (*rubūbiyya*).

The proof of the impermissibility of *taqlīd* and following of the ignorant and those surpassed in knowledge, and that *taqlīd* definitely belongs to the rightly guided, is established by the words of God: "Is he who guides to the truth the more worthy to be followed, or he who does not guide unless he is guided himself" (10:35). . .Furthermore, "What ails you then, how you judge" (10:35), which means: "You do not judge by anything but the truth if you are just", that is, there is no doubt that the one who guides by himself is the more worthy.

The impermissibility of *taqlīd* of an ignorant and inferior person, on the assumption that the superior person exists, can be deduced from this verse, even if the ignorant person is more pious; and because of this some scholars hold this opinion.[5] Similarly with the priority of the superior in learning in leading the ritual prayer, and likewise in the narration of Tradition. . . .It is also possible to deduce the impermissibility of *ijtihād* for the Prophet or Imam, since they are able to attain knowledge from God, and similarly the impermissibility of *ijtihād* for him who is able to get knowledge from them, and indeed the impermissibility of accepting probable opinion at all when one can attain certain knowledge.

Also, proving this are God's words: "And most of them follow only probable opinion (*ẓann*); indeed, surmise is of no avail for attaining the truth."

It might be supposed from the ostensive meaning of the verse that it indicated an absolute prohibition on acting on, and following, *ẓann*, because of the ostensive meaning of "indeed, probable opinion (*al-ẓann*) is of no avail for attaining the truth." At first glance, it seems to have a general meaning, although it is a singular endowed with a definite article not ostensively because of generality.[6] But if the utterance was to do with the unbelievers in relation to beliefs, indeed to the principles of religion (*uṣūl al-dīn*), and the repudiation of *ẓann* in such matters, it would only be permissible to act and rely upon it following a proof indicating its permissibility which was stronger than, or equal to, a proof forbidding it, just as is established by reason in the case of acting in legal matters through *ijtihād* and *taqlīd*, because otherwise there would necessarily result distress and harm (*al-ḥaraj wa'l-ḍarar*), both of which are excluded by reason and by texts (*al-'aql wa'l-naql*), and one would be charged to do what one cannot do. It is also established by several verses of the Qur'ān and Traditions, indeed by consensus, since there is no longer anyone who would at the same time say that *taqlīd* was forbidden and also affirm *ijtihād*. . . .

Notes

1. Mullā Aḥmad Muqaddas Ardabīlī, *Zubdat al-Bayān fī Aḥkām al-Qur'ān* (Tehran, 1966/1386), pp. 343-47.

2. It is interesting to note that even in Ṭahmāsp's decree of 1533/937 (Chapter 11, Section 1, above), the term used for "following" is not *taqlīd* but *iqtidā'*, which has clear connotations of voluntariness.

3. See Chapter 10, Section 2, above.

4. The famous commentary on the Qur'ān by al-Zamakhsharī (d. 1144/538).

5. I.e., the opinion that if there is a choice of whom to follow, the more learned should be followed in preference to the more pious.

6. A singular noun with the definite article (*al-*) can be taken in Arabic to stand collectively for all things it denotes.

CHAPTER 13

Two Seventeenth-Century Persian Tracts on Kingship and Rulers[1]

Translated and edited by William C. Chittick

The two works translated below represent the views of two of the most respected *'ulamā'* of the Safavid period, Mullā Muḥsin Fayḍ Kāshānī (1007-90/1600-79) and Mullā Muḥammad Bāqir Majlisī (1037-1110/1628-99). Fayḍ was the son-in-law of the great philosopher Mullā Ṣadrā (d. 1050/1640), and himself both an outstanding philosopher and an authority in the religious sciences. Majlisī was the foremost scholar of *ḥadīth* of the period and for the most part avoided philosophical approaches to his material. The two works were written with different goals and from sharply divergent points of view, yet they draw two deeply harmonious pictures of the proper role of kings and rulers in society.

Fayḍ Kāshānī. Mullā Muḥsin Fayḍ was born in Kashan. He relates that he studied with a large number of teachers, but did not find the qualifications he was searching for until he met Mullā Ṣadrā in Qumm (1033/1623-24 or 1034/1624-25).[2] Under Mullā Ṣadrā, Fayḍ busied himself with spiritual discipline (*al-riyāḍa wa'l-mujāhada*), "until I gained clear vision (*baṣīra*) in the various esoteric sciences (*funūn 'ilm al-bāṭin*)."[3] After spending eight years with Mullā Ṣadrā in Qumm, Fayḍ married Ṣadrā's daughter. Invited by Shah Ṣafī (1038-52/1629-42) to come to Isfahan, he refused. Then he was invited by Shah 'Abbās II (1052-77/1642-67).

I wavered between accepting that command and rejecting it

> because of the afflictions it entailed through the sons of this world and their affairs. I kept on stepping forward with one foot and stepping back with the other until I finally made up my mind to go to his presence because of the possibility of propagating the religion. So I went to him, and when I met him I found him to be much better than I had heard; he gathered together the kingly virtues and was adorned with inward and outward perfections.[4]

Though Fayḍ was treated well at the king's court for some years, his high position made him many enemies who gradually caught the Shah's ear. He withdrew from courtly circles around 1065/1654-55.

Fayḍ is the author of 116 works in a wide variety of fields, including Qur'ān commentary, *ḥadīth*, jurisprudence, principles of jurisprudence, supplications, ethics, philosophy, and theoretical Sufism (*'irfān*). His enormous *al-Wāfī* is considered, along with Majlisī's *Biḥār al-anwār* as one of the four great books on *ḥadīth* written by the moderns.[5] Fourteen commentaries have been written on his *Mafātīḥ al-sharā'i'* in jurisprudence. Mishkāt, speaking for the tradition of the philosophically oriented Shi'ite *'ulamā'*, considers him one of a handful of major figures in the history of Islam who have brought together the perspectives of philosophy and the *sharī'a*.[6]

Fayḍ's "Kingly Mirror" translated below is a perfect example of the type of contribution Mishkāt has in mind, though this may not be too obvious, since it is written for a popular audience and, therefore, avoids references either to the Qur'ān and the *ḥadīth* or to the intellectual tradition which has shaped the coherent world view which so clearly underlies the text.

Majlisī. Mullā Muḥammad Bāqir Majlisī is probably the most famous of the *'ulamā'* of the Safavid period. His father, Mullā Muḥammad Taqī Majlisī was himself a well-known scholar. Born in Isfahan, Majlisī became the Shaykh al-Islām of the city in 1098/1687 for the last years of the reign of Shāh Sulaymān (1077-1105/1667-94) and the early years of Shāh Sulṭān-Ḥusayn (1105-35/1694-1722) until his death in 1110/1699. During this period he was in charge of the religious affairs of Persia, so his pronouncements on the benefits and dangers of dealing with kings have the ring of first-hand experience, even if they do take the form of quotations from the Imams.

Majlisī's most famous work is *Biḥār al-anwār*, a twenty-six-volume compilation of *ḥadīth*. Majlisī also wrote a dozen other Arabic works, including a twelve-volume commentary on al-Kulaynī's *al-Kāfī*. His fifty-three Persian works are concerned mainly with translating the collected wisdom of the Prophet and the Imams into the language of the people. They cover a large variety of topics, but are drawn mainly from the "transmitted" (*naqlī*) sources, not from the intellectual (*'aqlī*) tradition of which Fayḍ was a representative.[7] The contrast between the two approaches is obvious in the two works translated below.

The Kingly Mirror

by Mullā Muḥsin Fayḍ Kāshānī

Introduction

"The Kingly Mirror" (*Ā'īna-yi shāhī*), was written in 1060/1650 at the request of Shāh 'Abbās II. As Fayḍ reports in his bibliographies of his own works, it is based largely upon an Arabic work he had written three years earlier, *Ḍiyā' al-qalb*, "whose like has never been seen."[8] The basic structure and argument of the two is identical. The Arabic text is not quite twice as long, the added material being mainly in the form of Qur'ānic verses and *ḥadīths* quoted to support the argument. The Arabic text is obviously written for the *'ulamā'* and those conversant with the language of scholarship; not only does Fayḍ quote many supporting texts, he also writes in a precise and almost aphoristic language that shows he assumes the reader is trained in logical discourse and has no need of long clarifications. In contrast, the simplicity and clarity of the Persian text show that it was written with a nonspecialist audience in mind. The arguments are developed generously and fluently, with many more words being employed than is really necessary. The supporting texts are neither quoted nor mentioned.

Fayḍ's approach is typically philosophical and even Sufi in that he considers kingship as one of a number of interrelated phenomena all of which center on the human self. In other words, he investigates kingship in its total context within God's creation, not as something that can be isolated from religion, psychology, or cosmology. Kingship is one form of rulership, he tells us, and its overall significance cannot be assessed until we know what a ruler is, what the object of rule is, and how ruling takes place.

"The Kingly Mirror" investigates the nature of those things which issue commands (*ḥākim*) that human beings may either follow or reject. Fayḍ is dealing in a general fashion with the concept of *ḥukm*, a term which is used technically in a number of disciplines, principles of jurisprudence perhaps being the most relevant. The term *ḥākim* might be rendered as "ruler," "sovereign," "governor," "judge," or "commander";

I chose the last because it seems to do the most justice to English usage and the various senses of the term that come out in the text.

Text

Worthy gratitude and incumbent praise must be strewn before that Lord who made the designations of the revealed law coincide with the requirements of intellect and who subordinated both the nature and habit of the possessor of the perfect intellect to his intellect. Innumerable blessings be upon the soul of the prophets, the leader of the pure, who undertook to perfect the creatures with the most perfect intellect and the most complete revealed law, and upon the household of inerrancy and purity—through love and obedience toward whom God has caressed the delivered persuasion, the Shi'a.

Now to the point: The most noble mind of the most holy, exalted, independent highness, the sun of leadership's sky, the shining orb of religion's firmament, the scion of Muḥammad's family, the descendant of 'Alī's clan, the confirmed by divine confirmation, Shāh 'Abbās the Second—God join his empire to the empire of the Twelfth Imam, upon whom be peace!—turned toward hearing a few words of the subtleties of true knowledge and the elegancies of wisdom, which are appropriate for the illumination of the heart and the nourishment of the soul. This least supplicant, Muḥammad ibn Murtaḍā known as Muḥsin, had earlier written a treatise in Arabic called *Ḍiyā' al-qalb* on knowing the human rational soul and training it through commanders in order to know the Lord and His lordship among men. I thought it appropriate to present its contents to that unique one of the age. Hence I have translated its gist and offered it as a gift to that paradise-like assembly. Since the meaning of kingship displays itself therein, and since it is ascribed to the king who is religion's patron, it came to be named the "Kingly Mirror." Hopefully, it will attain to the exalted station of acceptance.

Introduction

Know that as long as man is held by the bonds of this perishing life, he has no choice but to obey (*farmānbar*) five commanders (*ḥākim*) which the Lord of the world has put in place to train him and charged to strengthen him. The Lord has given him the choice to follow whichever commander he likes, but he cannot leave the command (*ḥukm*) of all of them. Obeying some will lead to his ascending to exalted degrees, and obeying others will lead to his falling into the nethermost pits.

Two of these commanders are inside: intellect (*'aql*) and nature (*ṭab'*). Two are outside: revealed law (*shar'*) and common law (*'urf*). The fifth comes from outside and becomes established on the inside, that is, habit (*'ādat*), which is actualized through repetition and familiarity. Sometimes one of these gives a command contradictory to the command of another; at such times the obeyer may not know which he should obey to achieve his best interest (*maṣlaḥat*), so he remains in bewilderment. Sometimes a command is given and it is not known who has given it. Sometimes obeying one of the commanders will lead to loss, but the obeyer cannot go outside of its command; so he is forced to seek refuge in the Lord, who is the "Best of Commanders" (Qur'ān 95:8), in order to repel its evil.

These introductory remarks show that no one can escape the necessity of [I-V] knowing these five commanders, one by one; [VI] knowing his own self, which is obedient to them; [VII] knowing the levels of the commanders in excellence (*sharaf*) and virtue (*faḍīlat*); [VIII] knowing the wisdom in their being given sovereignty (*salṭanat*) over man; [IX] finding the way to one's own best interest in spite of the differences among the commanders; [X] separating the command of some of them from that of others, given the fact of confusion; [XI] recognizing some of the favors of the Best of Commanders which aid and assist in this affair; and [XII] knowing how to seek refuge in Him—majestic is His majesty! Therefore this treatise has been written to explain these matters and has been arranged in twelve chapter, in the order mentioned.

Chapter I

On Knowing Intellect. Intellect is of two kinds. The first is "innate" (*ṭabī'ī*) and is possessed by man from his original creation. It is a faculty within him through which he can perceive things that he can only reach through thought. Through this faculty man is distinguished from other animals. The second is "acquired" (*muktasab*), since it must be gained. It is a faculty in man through which he can discern between those works which will give him profit in the hereafter and those which will give him loss. Hence he performs the works useful for the hereafter even if they result in a loss for him in this world, and he refrains from works that are harmful for the hereafter even if they result in a profit for him in this world. This faculty comes together around the time of puberty (*bulūgh*). Day by day it is made firmer with the help of correct knowledge and right activity, which have been and are gathered through the aid of the innate intellect, while the angels guide and help the person from within. Both of these intellects are found in different degrees. Some people have been given more perfect intellects, others less perfect intellects; in the measure of the intellect's perfection and imperfection religious duties are prescribed, and to this extent people will be called to account.[9]

Chapter II

On Knowing the Revealed Law. The revealed law is a divine command sent for the servants in order that whoever accepts and obeys may gain everlasting happiness and eternal pleasures. Some of its commands are considered incumbent and necessary. Whoever does not accept and obey them becomes worthy of divine punishment and deprivation from the eternal pleasures. Some were made into supererogatory works. Whoever obeys them will find a reward and reach high degrees, but no punishment is necessary for the person who does not obey. Among the things considered incumbent, some were made the pillar of the religion and the supporting pole of the revealed law; whoever does not obey them leaves the religion.

Some of the commands were clearly explained, so that no one would be left with any excuse to refrain from obeying them. Some were made obscure and ambiguous, so that the servants would be tested and tried through them. Whoever observes caution in them [by obeying them] will be given high degrees in the hereafter as a reward, but whoever does not observe caution will be deprived of those high degrees. Or rather, it sometimes happens that because of the inauspiciousness of not observing them, he will also be deprived of success in obeying the incumbent commands.

In obedience people are diverse because of a diversity of levels in firmness of belief, abundance of certainty, purity of sincerity, and degree of submitting the body to everything that must be done and not done. Some believe and obey with heart, tongue, body, and soul, like the faithful who have true faith. Some deny with the heart and accept with the tongue, like the hypocrites. Some deny with the tongue and believe with the heart, like those ingrates who recognize the truth but deny out of envy or pride. Some deny with both heart and tongue, like the active unbelievers. Some admit with both, but they have a perverted understanding of the commands, like those who have gone astray. Some admit with both and understand correctly, but they do not submit to everything that must be done and not done, like the disobedient and the ungodly. Then each of these groups has many degrees and innumerable levels.

Chapter III

On Knowing Nature, Which is also Called Caprice (*hawā*).[10] Nature is a faculty in man through which he counts one thing as appropriate and agreeable and considers another as incompatible and disagreeable, whether in fact it be agreeable or disagreeable, that is, whether it brings him benefit or loss. That which he considers agreeable he tries to bring to himself; wanting that thing is known as "concupiscence" (*shahwat*). That which he considers incompatible he tries to push far from himself; not wanting it is known as "irascibility" (*ghaḍab*). If doing that thing is opposed to the requirements of intellect and the revealed law, then Satan by means of his whispering seeks help from imagination and fantasy or makes use of deception, guile, arrogance, and enmity to overcome intellect and the revealed law and bring the person out from under their command. Though Satan cannot command people independently, such that he would then have to be considered one of the commanders, through misguidance he displays to caprice the agreeable as disagreeable and the disagreeable as agreeable, and then caprice commands.

Chapter IV

On Knowing Habit. Habit is a faculty that incites man to do something which, through repetition and familiarity, has become agreeable to his intellect or caprice after the thing was not agreeable or after its agreeableness increased over what it had been before. It makes no difference whether this thing is conformable with the requirements of intellect or the revealed law, whether it is acceptable to the wise, and whether it is useful. Following habit strengthens and increases the thing, while holding oneself back weakens and decreases it, to the extent that it may be put to the side and eliminated.

Chapter V

On Knowing Common Law. Common law is a set of commands (*dastūr*) which the generality of people have established among themselves. They have made acting in accordance with it incumbent and necessary, while they consider opposing it ugly (*qabīḥ*). Even if acting in accordance with it is disagreeable to nature and difficult, everyone thinks of another reproach with which to oppose nature.

This set of commands differs according to the diversity of times, countries, and peoples. Sometimes it conforms with intellect, revealed law, and nature, and sometimes not. Sometimes it is acceptable to intelligent people, and sometimes not. Adhering to that which is not conformable to those three things and not acceptable to this group is stupidity, unless for the sake of self-protection (*taqiyya*)[11] or the fear of loss.

If common law comprises conquering force (*ghalaba*) and mastery (*istīlā'*), then it is called sovereignty (*salṭanat*). Every society (*ijtimā'*) must have sovereignty in order for the collectivity to be put into order (*niẓām*) and the means for the people's livelihood to be arranged.

The difference between the revealed law and sovereignty is that sovereignty sets aright the collectivity of individual souls and puts in order the means for their livelihood so that they can exist in this world, and nothing more; it comes into existence from individual souls, who can make mistakes. But the revealed law sets aright the whole collectivity and puts in order both this world and the next world, while leaving the right situation for both this world and the next in its own place. Hence the revealed law necessarily teaches society that there will be a return to another world above this world, an everlasting and eternal world which is true happiness; and that this cannot be actualized without turning one's desire away from the passions and pleasures of this world. So the revealed law distinguishes between works that will be useful in the hereafter and those that will not be useful or will be harmful; it makes people hope for the rewards of works and warns them of their punishments. This law cannot come into existence except through perfect intellects which are protected from mistakes and lapses. Therefore, the acts of sovereignty are incomplete and are only completed through the revealed law, while the acts of the revealed law are complete and have no need for sovereignty.

Moreover, the profit of most of the affairs of sovereignty are outside the person who is commanded, while the profit of the affairs of the revealed law are inside his own person. For example, sovereignty commands the display of pomp and splendor (*tajammul*) for the sake of onlookers who are outside of the person who does the displaying. The revealed law commands the daily prayers and fasting, the profit of which goes to those who pray and fast.

In short, in relation to the revealed law sovereignty is like the body in relation to the spirit, or like the slave in relation to the master. Sometimes the sovereign listens to the revealed law and obeys it, sometimes not. Whenever the sovereign obeys the revealed law and follows its commands, the outward appearance of the cosmos, known as the "Kingdom" (*mulk*), follows the inward reality of the cosmos, known as the "Dominion" (*malakūt*).[12] Sensory things come under the shadow of intelligible things and parts move toward the whole. People desire "the abiding deeds of righteousness,"[13] and renounce the perishing, ephemeral things; they gain relief from harmful things and acquire good deeds as habits. Each day that passes is better for man than the previous day. Day by day God guides the servants, aids them, and gives them success, especially the king who urges his subjects to follow the revealed law, and follows it himself. It sometimes happens that for this reason so many of the lights of the Dominion descend upon the heart of the king that he gains the vision of that plane; yearning to be like spiritual beings takes him to such exalted degrees that, just as he is a king in this plane, so also he becomes a king in that plane. Why? Because he has brought about the guidance of a large number of the subjects, so his spiritual reality must constantly receive effects and replenishments from their spiritual realities.[14]

But whenever the sovereign does not obey the revealed law, intellects are made prisoners of the senses and the Dominion is subjected to the Kingdom; the low cease to show humbleness and obedience before the high. People desire perishing things, renounce the abiding deeds of righteousness, and acquire evil qualities as habits. Each day that passes is worse for man than the previous day. Day by day God leaves the servants more alone and takes guidance and aid away from them. In short, the opposites of the things mentioned above take place. We seek refuge in God from that!

Chapter VI

On the Explanation of Knowing the Self (*khwud*), which is the Subject which obeys (*farmānbar*) the Five Commanders. The self is the human rational soul (*nafs-i nāṭiqa*), which in reality makes up the human being. The self does not remain in a single state, but rather fluctuates (*munqalib*) between intellect and nature, such that whichever dominates over the person becomes identical with him; [hence] the self is called the heart (*qalb*).[15] If the intellect dominates through the help of the angels, the person becomes an angel in attribute, since the intellect and the angel are derived from a single reality.[16] If nature dominates over him in respect of concupiscence, he becomes a beast in attribute and enters into the ranks of livestock, for concupiscence is the stuff of beastliness. If nature dominates in respect of irascibility, he will become a predatory animal in attribute and enter into the ranks of the beasts of prey, since irascibility is the meaning of predatoriness. If he should be dominated in respect of duplicity, guile, falsehood, and deception, he will become one of the human satans, since the reality of satan is united with these meanings.[17]

In respect of being dominated by the five commanders, the soul has four levels: If it incites itself to ugly actions and inappropriate speech, it is called the "soul that incites to evil." If it places one foot forward and blames itself for committing forbidden acts and accomplishing acts of disobedience, it is called the "blaming soul." If it moves one more step and sees its own loss, to the extent that it makes itself perform good deeds and always sketches praiseworthy pictures on the tablet of its own consciousness, it is called the "inspired soul." If it should advance still further so that it passes beyond bewilderment and fluctuation, having gained ease with the intellect and reached the beginning of the waystation of tranquility, then it is called the "tranquil soul."[18]

You should know that these commanders are always at war with each other inside man, and each is tormented by the others. The ranks of the angels constantly stand opposite the ranks of the satans; the soldiers of good and right continue to fight and struggle with the troops of evil and corruption until the coming of the final moment and the end of all hopes. In the final state, the felicitous person is he in whom the soldiers of the angels have dominated and conquered the army of the satans, while the wretched person is he in whom intellect has been overcome by nature and conquered by caprice.

Since the heart, in keeping with the root of its primordial nature (*fiṭrat*), was created pure and subtle, it stands in an equal relationship to accepting the traces of angelic and satanic qualities. If the heart is able to withstand the army of the satans, it will keep the hand of untrue opinions and false suppositions far from itself and follow the path of gaining similarity to the character traits of the pure and assuming the moral attributes of the wise, thus becoming the seat of angels and the place of descent for celestial messengers. But if the heart follows concupiscence and irascibility, which are the concomitants of nature and caprice, and if it lets Iblis come and go within itself, then it will reach the point of being the nest of satans and the playground of Iblis's children.

Chapter VII

On the Explication of the Levels of the Commanders in Nobility and Excellence. There is no doubt that intellect and the revealed law are nobler and more excellent than the other commanders. Of these two, intellect is more excellent, more knowledgeable, and nobler if it has reached perfection, since through intellect one can know the reality of each of the commanders and discern them from one another. If there were no intellect, the revealed law would also not be known. In reality, intellect is a revealed law within man, just as the revealed law is an intellect outside of man. The most honored favor which God has given to His servants is intellect. Why? Because it is the substance of life and the foundation of subsistence. From it come understanding and knowledge, and through it can be preserved and witnessed the way of professing God's Unity (*tawḥīd*). Through its illumination one can see, and through its guidance one can reach high degrees. In short, the source of all goods and the origin of all perfections is intellect.

Below intellect and revealed law in nobility and excellence stand nature and habit. For nature and habit put the body in order, while intellect and the revealed law put the spirit in order. It is clear that the body was created to serve the spirit. So intellect and the revealed law are more excellent than nature and habit. The relationship of nature to habit is like that of revealed law to intellect; indeed, habit is a nature from outside, just as nature is a habit from inside. In the same way that intellect and the revealed law aid each other and gain strength from each other so that each is perfected and completed through the other, nature and habit help each other and gain strength from each other, to the extent that they seem to be a single thing.

Common law is lower than all of these, but in spite of its lowness, it commands all of them, dominating and overpowering them in most people. Both intellect and the revealed law say that it should be followed, so long as it does not conflict with their laws. But when it does conflict, it must be avoided, unless by reason of self-protection or fear of loss.

Chapter VIII

On the Explication of the Wisdom of the Mastery of these Commanders over Human Beings. Know that the fundamental goal in the creation of man is for his rational soul to advance, little by little, until it reaches the perfection that is fitting for it. The body was created to be the soul's instrument in actualizing this perfection. The ultimate end of this perfection is for man to know and recognize existence as it is, to bring together in himself all the existent things, and to gather together all created things in his own world through a gathering that is free of the stain of dispersion and a unity that is rid of the color of multiplicity.[19]

That is why the peerless God placed in man's constitution examples from the three worlds, that is, intellect, imagination, and sense perception; He gave him a share of each of these so that day by day he will put each of his limbs and faculties to work in its own place, and little by little he will subject the lower to the nobler, until finally he will lift his head out from the collar of all existent things, so that to him will belong everything that occurs within each. In reality, he becomes the soul of the heaven and the earth and the spirit of all existent things, high and low. Nor is this a place for surprise, since the human reality possesses along with unity and noncompositeness the perfection of all-comprehensiveness (*jāmi'iyyat*), such that it actualizes all the existent things of the world of generation and corruption, that is, animals, plants, and minerals. It accomplishes the work of all three of these. So why should it not be able to traverse God's path so that, having travelled on the Straight Path, it reaches a place where its all-comprehensiveness and all-inclusiveness increase even more? It is clear that one reaches this high station by following intellect and the revealed law and puts on this beautiful cloak with the help of doctrine and practice.

The wisdom of nature's being given mastery over man is that during this period [of spiritual growth] nature serves the body and protects the physical constitution so that the spirit can control the body with ease. The spirit throws away everything that is contrary and opposed and brings near to itself everything that is agreeable and conformable. But this cannot be accomplished without the help of habit; it becomes easy with the assistance of the praiseworthy moral traits that habit actualizes.

The profit of the mastery of common law over man is that it helps and aids him to follow the other commanders. Were there not the halter of the common law, the mount of the body would bolt and find it easy to follow the various forms of concupiscence. Then immersion in perishing pleasures, which contradict the basic goal, would increase day by day. For example, if people were secure from the backbiting of the backbiters and the spying of the faultfinders and if they did not fear the criticism of their peers and relatives, they would not be so careful about preserving themselves from ugly acts and mortal perils, nor would they persevere as they should in acts of obedience and worship. From here it should be obvious that the wretched have a tremendous part to play in perfecting the felicitous; people receive benefits from their enemies that they could never receive from their friends.

Chapter IX

On the Explication of Which Commander it is in one's Best Interest to Follow when the Commanders Differ. When the intellect is perfect, it has priority over the other commanders. As long as it is present, none of the others can command. Hence, if another should command something opposed to it, one must not listen. Why? Because it is nobler and more excellent than all the others and always conforms to the revealed law, while the other commanders are subordinate to it. Moreover, intellect has no need for weighing and distinguishing alternatives, since it knows no contradiction or obscurity. However, this intellect pertains exclusively to the prophets and the friends of God (*awliyā'*).

A person who does not have this perfect intellect must give priority to the revealed law over all else, since the revealed law stands in the place of the perfect intellect for the person who does not possess it. Hence the owner of an imperfect intellect must follow the revealed law. In other words, if a person finds the law in conflict with his own intellect, he must consider his own intellect mistaken and not criticize the revealed law.

After intellect and the revealed law, a person must follow nature and habit. Since both of these have been placed in the human body in order to preserve it for a time so that the spirit can acquire perfection and attain to the utmost perfection that is appropriate to it, whenever their commands differ, the command of that one which is more pertinent to this aim must be given priority. Thus the person will have shown greater obedience to his Creator and accomplished more toward the best interest for which he was created. If both are equal for this aim or neither is pertinent, he can give priority to whichever one he wishes, since in this situation obeying and disobeying them are the same.

Whenever common law aids intellect and revealed law more than nature and habit, it must be given priority over them. In the same way, whenever it aids the one of the two that is more pertinent to preserving the body, it has priority over the other.

In short, since the aim of placing the commanders within man was for the World of the Kingdom to serve the World of Dominion, the forms of concupiscence to be subjugated to intellect, and man to gain next-worldly perfections in this world so that he will have comfort and enjoyment in the next world and be freed from punishment, every work which brings this about or is useful for it must be accomplished, everything which destroys it or harms it must be avoided, and everything which is neither useful nor harmful must be considered indifferent.

Chapter X

On Separating the Commanders from each other when there is

Confusion among them. In some people there is a reality similar to intellect which makes them seek to acquire their livelihood. The common people name this "intellect" or "sensible conduct" (*rushd*). In the same way, in the midst of the commands of the revealed law there is a command which some people imagine to be the revealed law, whether because of a mistaken judgment or having learned it from someone who is unqualified. Both of these must be attached to caprice and nature. Therefore man must know the intellect well and learn the revealed law properly from its qualified spokesmen so as not to fall into these doubtful areas.

If ever any one of the five commanders should leave its original nature and purity and become mixed with another, such that the mixture brings about confusion, the possible kinds of confusion are ten in number, resulting from the multiplying of each by the others and eliminating the repetitions.

If a person should learn, though it be through intermediaries, the regulations of the revealed law from the Prophet and his executors—upon them be peace—all of whom are protected [by God] from error and lapses and were placed [among us] for the guidance and instruction of the creatures; if he does not let any of the other commanders influence the revealed law—i.e., he does not allow nature, habit, and common law to mix with it; if he refuses to formulate an independent opinion (*ijtihād*) based on his own imperfect intellect; and if he does not consider it permissible to deduce a view by interpreting (*ta'wīl*) ambiguous verses; then he will be delivered from confusing the revealed law with the rest [of the commanders]. If in this affair he also employs the commands of the revealed law in a manner that is appropriate and fitting with sincere intention, and if he remains steadfast in that in a single state, accomplishing the rules of conduct and prescriptions, he will leave aside all confusions.

If he is not able to do this, he should look and gaze upon the commandment of that commander which is commanding him. If the commander's view in this command is firmly fixed upon sheer truth and takes into account his situation in the next world—even if this should be in the form of the work of this world—then he should know that this commander is sheer intellect. Naturally he should follow it and thank God. If the commander's view is fixed upon this world, he should know that it is sheer nature, or nature mixed with satanity, or caprice, or intellect contaminated with one of these, or revealed law adulterated with caprice, or common law unacceptable to the intellect, or the base habit of the foolish. In any case, he certainly has to refrain from that command and not follow it.

If he does not know what the commander has in view, and he is bewildered in trying to discern it, he must refer to the perfect intellect, that is, he must consult with the possessor of the perfect intellect or someone who is near to such a person in intellect, if possible. If not, he must plead and beg at the threshold of the Creator and ask the Divine Side to guide and instruct him or to guide him to a guide. Beware! Without thorough consideration let him not undertake anything before the reality of the situation becomes clear to him. Why? Because it often happens that Satan displays pure evil in the form of plain good to the view of his companion and in this way pulls him to wretchedness. Hence no one has any choice but to investigate every thought that passes through his heart in order to see if it derives from the inspiration of the angel or the whispering of Satan, even if that thought should take the form of an act of worship. The investigation can be done in the manner mentioned.[20]

Chapter XI

On Remembering some of the Favors of the Best of Commanders which aid and assist in this Affair. Every servant has no choice but to know that he has an omniscient Lord and an omnipotent Creator who has bestowed upon him the robe of existence, generously given him the character of judgment, gracefully endowed him with seeing eyes and hearing ears, conferred upon him a speaking tongue and strong limbs, and appointed for him a wakeful heart and an aware intellect, that he might separate good from evil and discern gain from loss. He must know that he has need of God Himself for life and subsistence, of His help in the degrees of the spiritual path, the ascent, and the truth, of His facilitation and grace in obeying His commandments, and of His protection and preservation in refraining from His prohibitions. He must know that nothing whatsoever is hidden from Him, whether large or small, manifest or concealed. Whenever the servant knows this through the "knowledge of certainty" (*'ilm al-yaqīn*) or contemplates it through the "eye of certainty" (*'ayn al-yaqīn*), his business will reach a place where he never neglects his Lord and never forgets Him in any state. On the contrary, in most times and the great majority of states he will busy himself with meditation (*fikr*) and remembrance (*dhikr*) of Him. In all states he will call upon Him, in every hope he will seek access to Him, in each sort of concern he will address Him and speak to Him, and in every kind of retreat he will converse intimately with Him. Little by little he will reach a place in contemplation and careful watchfulness where he is completely cut off from everything other than God and joined with Him; he will have no need for anyone else and will be connected only to Him. Once he wins this high station, God will bring him near to Himself and place him in His own neighborhood. He will raise up his worth and exalt his degree. He will add him to the string of His friends, commingle him with His pure devotees, bring him into the ranks of the angels, and caress him with everlasting joys and eternal felicities.

Chapter XII

On How to Seek Aid from the Divine Side. In the *ḥadīths* of the inerrant Imams (God's blessings be upon them all!) it has been mentioned that the servant will find the best access to the Divine Side, have his prayers answered, and gain victory over enemies—whether in the Lesser Struggle (*jihād-i aṣghar*), which is the war with outside enemies, or the Greater Struggle (*jihād-i akbar*), which is the war with one's inner enemies—by seeking access to the Seal of the Prophets, who is the leader of the pure, and all the Imams of guidance (God's peace be upon them!). In other words, he should mention them by name in intimate prayer to God and seek his need and object of supplication through their rank and high standing. The reason for this is that in past times and previous nations, seeking access revolved around them. Whenever a tremendous affliction happened, an enemy appeared, a person's task became difficult, a sin was committed, grief and heartache arrived, or days of hardship became long, people would seek access to the high standing of these great ones and seek blessing through their famous names. They were the constant salve of their wounded hearts and undid the locks of their closed doors. The past prophets constantly borrowed lights from them and the cavalry of the messengers turned their attention toward the kibla of their spirits. Adam's repentance was accepted through the blessing of their blessed names, Noah's ark was [delivered with their aid, Abraham] reached the station of friendship [through their help],[21] Moses found the degree of speaking with God and election through the blessing of fulfilling their covenant, Jesus son of Mary reached the level of being the spirit of God through the light of knowing them, and the Holy Spirit plucked fresh fruit in paradise from the gardens of their knowledge.[22]

Hence the Shi'a, the community which is the object of mercy and which is their community, the delivered persuasion which is ascribed to them, are much more worthy [than previous religious communities] of seeking access to the side of God through their rank and of making them their intercessors in that Court. Hence, if the situation of one of the Shi'a should become constrained, he must plead and beg at the Creator's court and say:

Oh God, though I am a sinner
    and the shame and disgrace of sin
    have left me not the face to ask, yet [I say]:
By the high standing and rank
    of the great ones of Thy Court
and by the exaltation and proximity
    of those brought near to Thy Threshold
    —those whose love
    Thou hast placed in my heart
    through the bounty of Thy mercy,
those whom
    Thou hast allowed
    my spirit to recognize,
        Muḥammad,
        'Alī,
        Fāṭima,
        Ḥasan,
        Ḥusayn,
        'Alī ibn al-Husayn,
        Muḥammad ibn 'Alī,
        Ja'far ibn Muḥammad,
        Mūsā ibn Ja'far,
        'Alī ibn Mūsā,
        Muḥammad ibn 'Alī,
        'Alī ibn Muḥammad,
        Ḥasan ibn 'Alī,
        and the Standing Proof
        (the blessings of God be upon them all!)—
protect me from disobedience and error,
give my soul refuge from Satan and caprice,
forgive my sins,
make my enemies miserable and disappointed,
increase [?] my understanding,
and through Thy kindness and compassion
    caress this poor needy one.
For their measure with Thee is greater
    than that Thou wouldst reject the supplication
        of him who seeks access through them
    or deal badly with him,
        whatever bad he might have done.

*

Every sin and every fault
that from me has appeared
and will appear
forgive, by those people pure
of every sin
and every fault.
Through Thy bounty place me
in their neighborhood,
since in my heart love for them
has found a place.

The Fountainhead of Life (extracts)[23]
by Mullā Muḥammad Bāqir Majlisī

Introduction

The following passages are taken from one of Majlisī's many Persian works written for a popular audience, *'Ayn al-ḥayāt*. It is a long commentary (606 pages in the printed edition) on a testament given by the Prophet to Abū Dharr al-Ghifārī (d. 31/652), one of the leaders of the "faction of 'Alī" among the Prophet's Companions and an important traditionist in Sunni as well as Shi'ite sources.[24] Majlisī cites the Arabic text of the hadith section by section, writing a detailed commentary on each of the issues that it raises. Most of the text consists of quotations of other *ḥadīths* from the Prophet and the Imams. The book is divided into fourteen major parts dealing with a wide range of topics, such as intention versus works, the objects of faith (including a good deal of theological and cosmological material), the nature of prophecy, the Imamate, eschatology, ethics, virtues and vices, abstinence, piety, fear of God, supplications, the excellence of the Qur'ān, and the rules of Qur'ān recitation. One long section, most of which is translated below, discusses the role of kings and rulers in society. It is inspired by the third part of the following passage from the Prophet's testament:

> Oh Abū Dharr! Part of magnifying God is to honor (*ikrām*) the aged Muslim, to honor those who carry and act in accordance with the Qur'ān, and to honor the just king (*al-sulṭān al-muqsiṭ*).[25]

As stated above, most of Majlisī's text is taken up by translations of *ḥadīths*. These are linguistically rather loose, but on the whole quite accurate in conveying the sense of the *ḥadīth* in fluent Persian. Majlisī is perfectly aware that he is not writing for the *'ulamā'*, who expect every *isnād* to be in place, but rather for the mass of the people who are interested in increasing their religious knowledge. His task is not to produce a scholarly or literary masterpiece, but a work accessible to all. He writes

> I have not attempted to produce beautiful texts and precise translations. Rather I have tried to render the contents of the texts in expressions easily understood, and to solve with brevity the difficulties in those passages in need of commentary and explanation where it is not simply a case of understanding the meaning of the words. Thereby the totality of the believers and the generality of the Shi'a may have a full share and perfect portion from this divine repast and lordly benefit.[26]

One of the methods Majlisī follows in translation is to render a single word by two synonyms, in keeping with the habit of many Persian writers down to the present day and as illustrated in the last sentence just quoted. In translating the texts I have followed the Persian, though I have also compared the texts with the original Arabic where possible; the sources for most of the Arabic texts—which Majlisī often translates in blocks from *Biḥār al-anwār*—are provided in the notes. With one exception (n. 66) the only serious discrepancies between the original and the translation are instances where Majlisī has dropped parts of the text; these are duly noted.

Finally, it should be kept in mind that the original sources for the vast majority of the *ḥadīths* quoted go back to the fourth/tenth century and the works of two of the three major Imamite authorities, Shaykh al-Ṣadūq (d. 381/991-92) and al-Kulaynī (d. 329/950-51). The *ḥadīths* provide a fair cross-section of the types of *ḥadīth* found in the standard works. In other words, the views that Majlisī presents are nothing new to Shi'ism, but represent the earliest sources of the tradition.

Text

The Third Spring[27]

On the Explication of a few of the situations of rulers (*salāṭīn*) and commanders (*umarā'*), on associating (*mu'āsharat*) with them, and on their justice (*'adl*) and injustice (*jawr*). The mention of this will flow in several streams.

The First Stream

On the Explication of their Justice and Injustice

Know that the justice of kings and commanders is one of the greatest benefits of the people. Their justice and righteousness (*ṣalāḥ*) give rise to the righteousness of all God's servants and the flourishing state of the cities, while their ungodliness (*fisq*) and lewdness (*fujūr*) disrupt the order of the affairs of most of the world's inhabitants and incline most people toward their condition.

(1) Thus it is related by a trustworthy chain of authority that the Messenger of God said, "If two groups in my community are righteous and worthy, my community will also be righteous; and if they are corrupt, my community will also be corrupt." The Companions asked him who they are. He replied, "The jurists (*fuqahā'*) and the commanders."[28]

(2) By another chain of authority it is related that the Prophet said, "For two people there will be no intercession: the possessor of sovereignty (*salṭanat*) who does wrong, works injustice, and transgresses, and the person who exceeds proper bounds (*ghuluw*) in religion and leaves the religion."[29]

(3) It is related that [the sixth] Imam Ja'far al-Ṣādiq said, "I have hope for the deliverance of those in this community who recognize my right (*ḥaqq*), except for three groups: the possessor of kingship who works injustice, the person who innovates (*bid'at*) in the religion according to his own desire, and the ungodly person who commits sins openly and does not care."[30]

(4) It is related by a trustworthy chain of authority that the Prophet said, "At the resurrection, the fire of Gehenna will speak to three people: the commander, the Qur'ān reciter, and the man of wealth. To the commander it will say, 'Oh you whom God gave kingship and domination, but you were not just toward those under you!' Then it will steal him away like a chicken who takes a sesame seed. To the Qur'ān reciter it will say, 'Oh you who adorned yourself beautifully in the eyes of the people, but acted with disobedience in the presence of God!' Then it will steal him away. To the man of wealth it will say, 'Oh you whom God gave the spaciousness of the lower world and then sought to borrow a little of that from you, but you did not lend it and were miserly!' Then it will steal him away."[31]

(5) It is related that the Commander of the Faithful ['Alī] said, "Be on guard for your religion against a possessor of kingship who imagines that obeying him is obeying God and disobeying him is disobeying God. He is lying, for he is in the midst of nothing but disobedience toward his

Creator, and it is not necessary to obey someone who disobeys God. Obedience is only mandatory toward God, the Messenger, and those in authority (*ulu'l-amr*),[32] who are the inerrant (*ma'ṣūm*) Imams. God commanded that the Messenger must be obeyed because he is inerrant, purified from sin, and does not command to disobedience. God commanded that those in authority should be obeyed because they are inerrant, purified of evils and sins, and do not command the people to disobedience."[33]

(6) In another *ḥadīth*, it is transmitted that 'Alī said, "There is a mill in Gehenna that is turning." He was asked what it grinds and replied, "Lewd men of knowledge (*'ulamā'*), ungodly Qur'ān reciters, wrongdoing tyrants, traitorous viziers, and lying chiefs and leaders."[34]

(7) In another *ḥadīth*, he said, "Six people will be chastised for six traits: the Arabs for ardent tribalism, landholders and owners of farms for arrogance, commanders and kings for injustice, jurists and men of knowledge for envy, merchants for treachery, and peasants for ignorance."[35]

(8) It is related by trustworthy chains of authority that the Messenger of God said, "There are seven people whom I have cursed and whom every prophet whose prayers have been answered before me has cursed: a person who adds something to the Book of God; a person who denies God's foreordination and destiny; a person who opposes my Sunna and produces innovation; a person who considers it lawful (*ḥalāl*) to wrong my family and to take by force[36] their rights, though God has declared this unlawful (*ḥarām*); a person who through coercion becomes the master of the people in order to exalt a group whom God as abased and to abase a group whom God has exalted; a person who takes possession of the common property of the Muslims for himself and considers this lawful; and a person who considers unlawful something that God has declared lawful."[37]

(9) It is related by a trustworthy chain of authority that the Prophet said, "The first persons who enter Gehenna will be a commander and possessor of mastery who does not do justice, a property owner who does not give God His right, and a poor person who is proud and arrogant."[38]

(10) It is related by a trustworthy chain of authority that [the eighth] Imam Riḍā said, "When rulers lie and issue unrightful decrees, rain is imprisoned in the sky. When kings act with injustice, their dynasty will be thrown down. When people forbid the alms-tax, four-legged animals will perish."[39]

(11) It is related that the Messenger said, "No one becomes a commander over ten people or more without his being brought at the

resurrection with his hands manacled to his neck. If he is a good-doer, his hands will be freed, but if he is a bad-doer and wrongdoer, more manacles will be added."[40]

(12) By another chain of authority it is related that the Messenger said, "If anyone is made the leader of a people and does not act well among them, God will imprison him at the edge of Gehenna one thousand years for every day he was their ruler."[41]

(13) It is related by a trustworthy chain of authority that Ziyād Qandī came to see Imam Ṣādiq. The Imam asked him, "Oh Ziyād! Have you been appointed by the Caliphs of injustice?" He replied, "Yes, Oh son of the Messenger of God! I am a chivalrous man and do not gather possessions. That which I bring together I give to my brothers in faith, spending it on them as a brother." The Imam said, "If you do this, then, when your ego calls you to do wrong (*ẓulm*) to the people while you have power over them, remember the power of God over punishing you on the day when the wrong you did toward the people has passed and its sin remains for you."[42]

(14) It is related by a trustworthy chain of authority that Imam Ṣādiq said, "When God gives kingship to someone, He appoints for him a period of nights, days, months, and years. If the kings should do justice among the people, God commands the angel who is placed in charge of the sphere of their empire to turn the sphere slowly; hence the days, nights, months, and years of their empire become long. But if they should work injustice and wrongdoing, God commands the angel to turn it quickly. So the days, months, and years of their empire pass quickly."[43]

(15) It is related by a trustworthy chain of authority that ʿAlī said to Nawf Bikālī, "Accept my advice: Never become headman, leader, commander, tithe-collector, or officer!"[44]

(16) It is related by a trustworthy chain of authority that Imam Riḍā said, "Justice and good-doing are the sign of long blessings."[45]

(17) It is related by a trustworthy chain of authority that Imam Ṣādiq said, "There are three people who will be the nearest to God on the Day of Resurrection until He finishes settling the accounts of the creatures: A person who in the state of anger is not moved by his power to wrong someone under him, a person who judges or walks between two people and does not incline by a single barley-corn to the one or the other, and a person who speaks the truth, whether it be to his loss or his benefit."[46]

(18) It is related by a trustworthy chain of authority that Imam Ṣādiq said, "Justice is sweeter and more wholesome than water found by a thirsty man! How spacious and conducive to plenty and well-being is justice, even if it be but little!"[47]

(19) In another *ḥadīth*, Imam Ṣādiq said, "Justice is sweeter than honey, softer than butter, and more fragrant than musk."[48]

(20) It is related that [the fifth] Imam Muḥammad Bāqir said, "My father counselled me as follows at the time of his death: 'My son, beware of wrongdoing (*ẓulm*) toward someone who has no help against you but God.'"[49]

(21) It is related that Imam Ṣādiq said, "When a person wakes up and does not have in his mind to do wrong toward anyone, God forgives his sins on that day, unless he should unrightfully spill someone's blood or consume the property of an orphan unlawfully."[50]

(22) It is related by sound chains of authority that the Messenger said, "Avoid tyranny (*ẓulm*), for it is the shadows (*ẓulumāt*) of the Day of Resurrection", that is, it will result in darkness on that day.[51]

(23) It is related by a trustworthy chain of authority that Imam Ṣādiq said, "No one commits a wrong without God afflicting him by reason of that wrongdoing in himself, his property, or his children."[52]

(24) In another *ḥadīth*, he said, "God revealed to one of His prophets, in whose country there was a tyrannical king, 'Go to this tyrant and tell him that I have not appointed him to spill the blood and take the property of the people. On the contrary, I gave him power to keep from Me the sound of the weeping of the wronged. Surely I will not refrain from coming to their aid in the wrongs that have been done to them, even if they are unbelievers."[53]

(25) In another *ḥadīth*, Imam Ṣādiq said, "The wronged person takes more from the religion of the wrongdoer than the wrongdoer takes from the property of the wronged." Then he also said, "A person who does evil toward people knows that evil has also been done toward himself. Surely the child of Adam reaps only what he sows. No one has reaped bitter from sweet or sweet from bitter."[54]

(26) The Commander of the Faithful said, "What bad provisions for the Day of Resurrection—transgression and wrongdoing against the people!"[55]

(27) It is related by a trustworthy chain of authority that a person came to Imam Muḥammad Bāqir and said, "From the time of Ḥajjāj [ibn Yūsuf] to now I have been the governor of the people. Is my repentance acceptable?" The Imam did not answer. The man repeated the question. The Imam replied, "Your repentance is not acceptable until you give to everyone who has a right his right."[56]

(28) It is related that the Messenger said, "If a person wrongs someone and cannot find him to compensate him for it, he should pray for forgiveness for him, since that is the wrongdoer's expiation (*kaffāra*)."[57]

The Second Stream

On the Explication of the Associating of Commanders with Subjects (ra'āyā) *and on the Explication of a few Rights* (ḥaqq) *that the Subjects have against them*

(29) It is related by a trustworthy chain of authority that [the fourth] Imam 'Alī ibn Ḥusayn said, "The king must know the rights of the subjects against him. They have been made subjects since God has made them weak and given him power. Hence it is incumbent upon him to act with justice among them and to be like a compassionate father toward them. If they should do something in ignorance, he should forgive them and not punish them, thanking God for the power He has given him over them."[58]

(30) It is related by a trustworthy chain of authority that Imam Ṣādiq said, "When a person is put in charge of the affairs of the Muslims and acts with justice, leaves the door to his house open, removes the curtains and the veils from between himself and the people, investigates the people's affairs, and takes care of their business, then God will change his fear at the Resurrection to security and take him into paradise."[59]

(31) It is related by a trustworthy chain of authority that Imam Muḥammad Bāqir went before [the Caliph] 'Umar ibn 'Abd al-'Azīz. The latter said, "Counsel me!" The Imam replied, "Oh 'Umar, open the doors to your house and place no doorkeeper between yourself and the people. Help those who have been wronged and correct the misdeeds that have been done against the people."[60]

(32) It is related by a trustworthy chain of authority that the Commander of the Faithful said, "If a governor keeps himself veiled from the people and does not take care of their affairs, at the resurrection God will not take care of his needs. If he takes a gift from the people, he has stolen, and if he takes a bribe, he has associated another god with God."[61]

(33) It related that Imam Ṣādiq said, "If a person is put in charge of one of the affairs of the Muslims and leaves them unattended, God will leave him unattended."[62]

In this connection there are many *ḥadīths*. But since they are of no use for most people, we will content ourselves with this amount. Anyone who wants [to know more about] the proper modes of behavior (*ādāb*) of commanders and rulers should refer to the clear letters which the Commander of the Faithful wrote to the governors and commanders of outlying areas, especially the long letter he wrote to Mālik Ashtar[63] and the letters he wrote to Sahl ibn Ḥunayf and Muḥammad ibn Abū Bakr.[64]

You should know that in this world God has given everyone a sovereignty (*salṭanat*). Thus the Prophet said, "Each of you is a shepherd and each of you" at the resurrection "will be asked about his flock"[65] and how he conducted himself with it. Thus God gave kings power over their subjects, commanders and ministers power over some of the subjects, and owners of farmlands and property power over a group of farmers. God bestowed upon him who has houses, servants, wives, and children authority and abundance over male and female slaves, servants, women, and children, and He made him the means of their daily provision. He appointed the men of knowledge (*'ulamā'*) shepherds of the seekers of knowledge, making the seekers the flock of the men of knowledge. He gave everyone power over certain animals, and made each individual the governor of his own faculties, limbs, and organs, so that he may keep them busy with affairs that will not result in their punishment in the hereafter. God also put works, moral qualities, and acts of worship under the authority of each person and commanded each to observe them. Hence there is no one in this world who does not have a share of governorship and rule and under whose command there is not found a certain group. In associating with each kind of subject there is an injustice and wrongdoing. Everyone has been given certain blessings worthy of that over which he has been given power. In keeping with that blessing each person has been asked to show gratitude. Gratitude for each blessing results in an increase in the amount of that blessing. Gratitude for each lies in this: He associates with each blessing in the manner that God has commanded and observes the rights that God has set down for them. When he does this, God increases the blessing. If he shows ingratitude, God takes it away.

Thus, if kings show gratitude for their power and domination and if they observe the state and rights of the subjects, their kingdoms will last. Otherwise, they will soon disappear. Thus it has been said that a king will remain while he is an unbeliever, but not while he is a wrongdoer. The same can be said about someone who has slaves and servants. If he should treat them wrongly and fail to observe their rights, his control over them will soon be taken away. If a possessor of knowledge should act badly with his flock, his knowledge will soon be taken away from him; otherwise, it will be increased. If a person employs his limbs and organs to disobey God, they will soon be overcome by afflictions and he will cease reaping benefit from them. Reward and punishment in the hereafter depend on observing or not observing these rights. If someone would like details about these rights, let him refer to the long *ḥadīth* about rights that has been recorded from Imam 'Alī ibn Ḥusayn.[66]

The Fifth Stream

On the Rights of Kings,
and on Observing those Rights,
Praying for Kings to be made Righteous,
and Avoiding their Fits of Anger

Know that kings who follow the true religion have many rights upon the subjects, for the kings guard and defend them and repel the enemies of religion from them. Kings preserve and protect their religion, life, property, and honor. Hence people must pray for them and recognize their rights, especially when they act with justice.

Thus the Prophet said in this noble *ḥadīth* [upon which this commentary is being written], "Part of magnifying God is to honor . . . the just king," even though he is apparently referring to the Imam and those connected to him, since another *ḥadīth* has the same content and "just Imam" in place of "just king."[67] Other *ḥadīths* will be mentioned shortly.

If kings oppose the way of righteousness and justice, people must pray that they be set aright, or they must set themselves aright in order that God may set the kings aright, for the hearts of kings and of all creatures are in the hand of God. Tyrannical and wrongdoing kings must also be obeyed unconditionally, while self-protection (*taqiyya*)[68] in respect to them is mandatory: People must protect themselves from them and not make themselves objects of their wrath.

(34) Thus [the fourth Imam] Sayyid al-Sājidīn says in the "*ḥadīth* of rights," "The king's right upon you is that you know that God has made you a trial (*fitna*) for him. God is testing him by giving him power and kingship over you. You must know that you are obligated not to make yourself the object of his wrath and anger and thereby throw yourself to destruction and become his partner in his sin through the harm and punishment which he brings down upon you."[69]

(35) It is related by a trustworthy chain of authority that Imam Ṣādiq said, "After Nimrod threw Abraham into the fire and exiled him from his kingdom, Abraham entered the kingdom of the king of the Egyptians. He had built a trunk and placed Sarah within it so that no one would gaze upon her. In that kingdom he reached a tithe-collector. When the man came to take the tithe from Abraham's property, he told Abraham to open the trunk so that he could see what is inside it. Abraham replied, 'Calculate as you wish and take its tithe.' The man replied, 'I will not be satisfied until you open the trunk.' When Abraham opened the trunk, the tithe-collector asked who this was in the trunk. He replied that this was his wife, the daughter of his mother's sister.

"When the tithe-collector saw her beauty and loveliness, he reported the situation to the king, who ordered that they be brought before him. When Abraham entered the court of the king, the king ordered him to open the trunk. Abraham replied, 'My honor and cousin is in this trunk. Whatever I have I will sacrifice in order not to open it.' The king insisted, so he opened the trunk. When the king saw the beauty and loveliness of Sarah, he extended his hand toward her. Abraham said, 'Oh God, hold back his hand from my honor.' Immediately the king's hand withered; he was not able to stretch it toward Sarah, nor was he able to pull it back. The king said, 'Did your God do this to my hand?' Abraham replied, 'Yes. My God is a jealous God who is the enemy of the forbidden. He came between you and my honor.'

"The king said, 'Pray to God to return my hand. If he answers you, I will not turn toward your wife.' Abraham prayed and the king's hand became healthy again. Again the king looked upon Sarah and stretched out his hand, and again Abraham prayed and his hand became withered. Then the whole story repeated itself a third time. When his hand was mended the third time, the king showed Abraham great honor and respect and said, 'Go wherever you like. But I have one request from you.' Abraham asked what it was. He replied, 'I have a beautiful and intelligent Egyptian slave girl. Allow me to give her to Sarah to serve her.' So he gave Hagar, the mother of Ishmael, to Sarah.

"Abraham went his way, and the king came out to escort him. Abraham went ahead, the king following behind in order to show respect for him. In the midst of the way a revelation reached Abraham: 'Stop, and walk not in front of the tyrannical king!' Abraham stopped and said to the king, 'My Lord has just sent me a revelation that I should honor you, put you in front of myself, and walk behind you.' The king replied, 'I bear witness that your Lord is merciful, clement, and generous.'"[70]

(36) The Prophet counselled the Commander of the Faithful as follows: "There are eight people who, if they are abased and made lowly, have none to blame but themselves: A person who makes himself present at a meal without having been invited, a guest who orders around his host, a person who seeks good from his enemies, a person who seeks bounty and beneficence from the base, a person who places himself between two people in their secret matter which they have not shared with him, a person who shows contempt for a king, a person who sits in a place where he has not the worthiness to sit, and a person who speaks to someone who does not listen to him."[71]

(37) It is related that Imam Ṣādiq said, "If anyone disputes with one of these three people, he will be laid low: father, king, and creditor."[72]

(38) It is related by a trustworthy chain of authority that the Prophet said, "God says, 'I am God other than whom there is no god. I created

kings and their hearts are in My hand. If a people obey Me, I will make the hearts of kings compassionate toward them, and if a people disobey Me, I will make the hearts of kings angry toward them. Busy yourselves not with cursing kings! Repent toward Me of your sins and I will incline their hearts toward you and make them compassionate.'"[73]

(39) It is related by a trustworthy chain of authority that Imam Ṣādiq said, "When God wants good for certain subjects, He appoints for them a compassionate king and ordains for him a just vizier."[74]

(40) It is related by a trustworthy chain of authority that [the seventh] Imam Mūsā Kāẓim said to his partisans (*shīʿīyān*), "Oh partisans, do not make yourselves lowly by failing to obey your king. If he is just, ask God to preserve him, and if he is tyrannical and unjust, ask God to set him aright. Surely your righteousness lies in the righteousness of your king. Surely a just king is like a compassionate father. So desire for him what you desire for yourselves, and dislike for him what you dislike for yourselves."[75]

(41) It is related that the Prophet said, "He who fails to obey the king has failed to obey God, for God says, 'Throw not yourselves by your own hands into destruction' (Qur'ān 2:195)."[76]

(42) It is related by a trustworthy chain of authority that Imam Ṣādiq said, "If a person resists a tyrannical king and is thereby afflicted by an affliction, God will not give him the wages of that affliction, nor will He give him patience in its severity."[77]

The Sixth Stream

On the Explication of the Corruptions
Caused by Proximity to Kings;
on not Depending on their Nearness;
and on the Prohibition of Aiding Tyrannical Rulers,
Being Content with their Tyranny,
Eating their Food,
and Praising them

Know that proximity to kings and commanders results in loss in this world and the next. In this world a few days of authority and reputation are polluted by a hundred thousand lowlinesses and trials. These quickly pass and the person is miserable in this world and the object of God's wrath in the next. In order to know this it is sufficient to witness the diverse states of the lords of empire and the speed of the disappearance of their empires. If a person has any news of their states, he will know that in spite of their authority and reputation they have not a moment of ease, and they envy the situation of the poor and the helpless.

The corruptions which proximity to kings and commanders brings about are many:

1. Helping them in wrongdoing. It is perfectly clear that it is impossible to address them a great deal without helping them in certain acts of wrongdoing.

2. Affection and love toward them. Frequency of association causes love and affection, but God says: "Lean not on," that is, incline not toward, "the wrongdoers, or the Fire will touch you" (Qur'ān 11:113). *Ḥadīths* forbidding amicable relations with them are many.

3. Approving their ugly acts. This also comes about by frequency of association. A person who approves an act of wrongdoing is a partner in it.

4. Through frequently witnessing their blameworthy dealings, a person will no longer see their ugly states but will even consider them beautiful. This will lead to his inclination and desire for those works and acts, and soon he also will be afflicted by them.

5. In their gatherings one must not appear to go against the customs of common usage. Following the customs in such a gathering means that whenever they utter some vanity or desire some ugly thing, one must praise and extol it. But this is nothing but hypocrisy and inventing lies against God and the Prophet.

6. If a wrong is committed in their gathering, according to the common usage a person cannot forbid it. And a person who wants to be a favorite and companion must speak in confirmation of their words. Thereby he abandons "forbidding evil" (*nahy az munkar*), and this is a major sin.

7. The person will want them to continue in their wrongdoing so that he may remain honored by them; or, he will want honor through their friendship, which is also not permissible.

8. The person must enter into their houses, which are of doubtful legitimacy, walk upon their doubtful carpets, and eat their doubtful morsels. All of this will lead to hardness of heart. Or rather, through frequent mixing with them the person will come to know for certain that all these things are forbidden; he will no longer have any doubt concerning their legitimacy, yet he will still have to overlook the things which have been misappropriated.

There are many other causes of corruption which this treatise does not have the scope to mention. Concerning the above meanings there are many *ḥadīths*:

(43) It is related by a trustworthy chain of authority that Imam Ṣādiq said, "A miser has no ease, an envier has no pleasure, kings have no faithfulness (*wafā'*), and a liar has no manliness."[78]

(44) It is related by a trustworthy chain of authority that the Prophet said, "Of all people, kings have the least faithfulness; of all people, kings have the fewest friends."[79]

(45) It is related by a trustworthy chain of authority that Imam Ṣādiq said, "If you should have a friend who is appointed to a governorship and you find him acting toward you one-tenth of the way he used to, he is not a bad friend."[80]

(46) It is related by a trustworthy chain of authority that Imam Mūsā Kāẓim said, "Four things corrupt and harden the heart and cause hypocrisy to grow in it, just as water causes a tree to grow: listening to music and song, speaking ugly words, entering the houses of kings, and hunting (*ṭalab al-ṣayd*)."[81]

(47) It is related that the Prophet said, "Whoever keeps company with a king is being tempted; the closer he is to the king, the farther he is from God."[82]

(48) It is related that Imam Ṣādiq said, "The possessor of abstinence (*wara'*) is he who abstains from the things prohibited by God and avoids doubtful things. If he does not avoid doubtful things, he will fall into forbidden things out of ignorance. A person who sees an evil (*munkar*) without disapproving of it while he is able to do so has loved to see God disobeyed, and anyone who loves to see God disobeyed has openly shown enmity toward God. A person who wants wrongdoers to remain has loved to see God disobeyed, though God has praised Himself for destroying wrongdoers (Qur'ān 6:45)."[83]

(49) It is related by a trustworthy chain of authority that the Commander of the Faithful said, "The wrongdoer, the person who aids him in his wrongdoing, and the person who approves his wrongdoing are all partners in wrongdoing."[84]

(50) It is related that Imam Ṣādiq said, "Jesus said to a group of the Children of Israel, 'Help not the wrongdoer in his wrongdoing, or your excellence will be nullified.'"[85]

(51) It is related that the Prophet said, "If a person praises a tyrannical king and humbles himself before him out of desire for this world, he will be his companion in Gehenna. If a person directs a wrongdoer to wrongdoing, he will be the companion of Haman[86] in Gehenna. If a person should contend on behalf of a wrongdoer or aid him, when the angel of death comes to him he will say, 'Good news to you: God's curse and the fire of Gehenna!'"[87]

(52) It is related by a trustworthy chain of authority that Imam Muḥammad Bāqir said, "Do not be present at a gathering where a tyrannical king beats or kills someone out of wrongdoing and enmity or acts wrongly toward him unless you help him. For it is incumbent upon the

believer to help the believer if he should be present. But if you are not present and know nothing about it, there will not be a complete argument against you."[88]

(53) It is related by a trustworthy chain of authority that Muḥammad ibn Muslim said, "One day Imam Muḥammad Bāqir passed by and saw that I was seated before one of the judges of Medina. The next day I went to see the Imam. He said, 'What was that gathering in which you were seated yesterday?' I replied, 'May I be your sacrifice! That judge honors me and I sometimes sit with him.' The Imam said, 'What makes you sure that no curse will descend upon him from God, encompassing everyone in the gathering?'"

(54) When the Commander of the Faithful was dying, he charged Imam Ḥasan saying, "Love the righteous person for his righteousness, and humor the godless person to preserve your religion from his evil, but have enmity toward him in your heart."[89]

(55) It is related that Imam Ṣādiq said, "If a person excuses a wrongdoer in his wrongdoing, God will turn him over to someone who will wrong him, and if he prays for the removal of that wrongdoing, his prayer will not be answered and he will not be given the wages of the wronged."[90]

(56) It is related by a trustworthy chain of authority that the same Imam said, "At the resurrection the helpers of the tyrannical rulers will be kept in pavilions of fire until God is finished with the accounts of the creatures."

(57) In another *ḥadīth*, Imam Ṣādiq said, "It is part of 'leaning on the wrongdoers' (Qur'ān 11:113) to go before a tyrannical king and pray for his long life so much that he puts his hand into a sack and gives a reward."

(58) It is related by a trustworthy chain of authority that the Prophet said, "On the Day of Resurrection a caller will call from the direction of God, 'Where are the tyrants and their helpers?' Anyone who placed a tuft of cotton in their inkwells, tied shut a sack for them, or put ink into their pens will be gathered with the wrongdoers."[91]

(59) The Prophet said, "No servant is brought near a king without going far from God, nor does he gain more possessions [without his account being more severe, nor do his followers increase] without his satans increasing."[92]

(60) The Prophet also said, "Beware! Avoid the courts and entourage of kings. Whoever is nearer to their courts, entourage, and followers is farther from God; whenever a person chooses the king over God, God will take away his abstinence and leave him bewildered."[93]

(61) It is related by a trustworthy chain of authority that Imam

Ṣādiq said, "Guard your religion through abstinence, strengthen your religion through self-protection, and through God become free of seeking your needs from kings. Know that if a believer displays humility before a king or before someone who is opposed to him in religion out of desire for what that person has of this world, God will throw him into obscurity, consider him His enemy, and leave him to his own devices. If he should acquire something of this world, God will take away the blessing of that thing. If he spends any of that property for the *ḥajj*, the *'umra*, or freeing slaves, it will not have any reward for him."[94]

(62) It is related that Imam Ṣādiq said, "If a person should help a wrongdoer against a wronged person, God will remain angry with him until he desists."[95]

The Seventh Stream

On the Explication of Several Reasons for which a Person may go to the Houses of Rulers and Commanders

Know that sometimes associating with them and entering and leaving their houses becomes mandatory, for several reasons.

1. Self-protection (*taqiyya*), as was mentioned earlier. If a person by not going to see them should fear losing his life, property, or honor, it is necessary to see them in order to repel that loss. The inerrant Imams (God bless them!) used to come and go at the houses of the 'Abbāsid Caliphs (curses be upon them!) and their relatives by reason of self-protection, and when speaking with them they would agree with them and humor them.

2. That his goal in going should be to repel a loss from someone who has been wronged or to benefit a believer. For this reason sometimes it is mandatory and necessary, as was seen in various *ḥadīths* in the chapter on going to the aid of the wronged and taking care of the needs of the believers.[96] Or rather, if a person has the power to remove a wrong from a believer, but he takes into account his own honor and reputation and does nothing, he is a partner in that wrong and will be punished; God will make him lowly.

(63) Thus it is mentioned in a *ḥadīth* that everything has an alms-tax (*zakāt*), and the alms-tax of position and reputation is that a person spend it in taking care of the needs of his brother believers. Just as property increases through giving the alms-tax, so position and honor spent in the way of God will increase; and just as property disappears when the alms-tax is not paid, so also reputation disappears by refusing to spend it, and God will make the person lowly.[97]

(64) In the same way it is related by a trustworthy chain of authority that Imam Mūsā Kāẓim said, "The Prophet said, 'Present to me the need of someone who cannot present his need to me himself. Surely when a person presents to a king the need of another who is not able to present it, on the Day of Resurrection God will steady his feet on the Narrow Bridge.' "[98]

(65) It is related by another trustworthy chain of authority that the Prophet said, "If I should fall down a mountain and be broken into pieces, that would please me more than that I should support one of the works of the wrongdoers or walk upon one of their carpets, unless it be in order to allay the grief of a believer, free a prisoner, or pay the debt of a believer. Surely the least that will be done to the helpers of the wrongdoers is that their heads will be placed in tents of fire until God is finished with the accounts of the creatures."

(66) It is related by a trustworthy chain of authority that Imam Ṣādiq said, "There is no tyrant who does not have with him a believer for the sake of whom God will repel the evil of that tyrant from the Shi'a, but the share of that believer in the hereafter will be less than all other believers because of his companionship with that tyrant."[99]

(67) It is related by a trustworthy chain of authority that Imam Mūsā Kāẓim said, "God has friends with kings, by reason of whom He repels loss from His friends."

3. That he go before kings with the aim of guiding them, if they have the capacity to be guided, or to learn a lesson from their states.

(68) It is related by a trustworthy chain of authority that Imam Ṣādiq said, "Luqmān used to go to the houses of judges, kings, commanders, and rulers and preach to them. He used to have compassion toward them because of the affliction by which they were afflicted and the fact that they had fastened their hearts upon the passing considerations of this world. So he would learn from their states and take benefit from their dealings, and through that he was able to conquer his own lower soul and struggle against its desire and caprice."[100]

Notes

1. My thanks to the editor of this volume, who suggested I translate this material and provided me with the texts.

2. Fayḍ Kāshānī, *al-Maḥajjat al-bayḍā' fī iḥyā' al-Iḥyā'*, S.M. Mishkāt, ed., 4 vols. (Tehran: al-Maktabat al-Islāmiyya, 1339-40/1960-61), vol. IV, pp. 6, 11.

3. *Al-Maḥajjat al-bayḍā'*, IV, p. 7.

4. Ibid., IV, pp. 8-9.

5. Ibid., I, p. 24; the other two are *Wasā'il al-shī'a* by Shaykh Muḥammad ibn al-Ḥasan al-Ḥurr al-'Āmilī (d. 1104/1692-93) and *Jawāmi' al-kalim* by Muḥammad ibn al-Sayyid Sharaf al-Dīn, known as al-Sayyid Mīrzā al-Jazā'irī (a teacher of both Majlisī and Ḥurr 'Āmilī).

6. Ibid., I, p. 23.

7. On Majlisī's works, teachers, and students, see the introductory volume (numbered "0") to the new edition of *Biḥār al-anwār* (Qumm and Tehran, 1376-94/1956-74).

8. *Al-Maḥajjat al-bayḍā'*, vol. II, p. 12, no. 29. *Ā'īna-yi shāhī* was printed along with two other Persian treatises by Fayḍ, *Tarjamat al-ṣalāt* and *Ulfat-nāma* (Shiraz: Chāpkhāna-yi Mūsawī, 1320/1941). *Ḍiyā' al-qalb* was lithographed along with five more of Fayḍ's short Arabic treatises in Tehran, 1311/1893-94.

9. Allusion to a fundamental principle of Islamic law, stated most succinctly in the Qur'ānic formula, "God charges no soul save to its capacity" (2:286).

10. Nature is the philosophical term, "caprice" the Qur'ānic term. For example, "Obey not him whose heart We have made neglectful of Our remembrance, so that he follows his own caprice" (18:28); "Who is further astray than he who follows his own caprice without guidance from God?" (28:50).

11. Or, "dissimulation of one's faith." Cf. note 68.

12. These are standard cosmological terms derived from the Qur'ān, referring to the two fundamental kinds of created things. The Kingdom is the visible, sensory, or corporeal world; the Dominion is the invisible, intelligible, or spiritual world.

13. Reference to Qur'ān 18:46 and 19:76.

14. The last four sentences, beginning with "Day by day," are clearly directed at the Shah, since they have no parallel in the Arabic original.

15. As a verbal noun, the word "heart" (*qalb*) means fluctuation and change. There are allusions to the fluctuation and constant transformation of the heart in the *ḥadīth*, and many Sufis—especially Ibn al-'Arabī and his followers—devote a good deal of attention to the heart's changing nature.

16. Again, this is a standard cosmological teaching, found, for example, in philosophers such as Avicenna and the Sufis.

17. This paragraph is derived, most likely without any intermediaries, from Ghazzālī's *Iḥyā' 'ulūm al-dīn* III.1.5; cf. Fayḍ's own revision of the *Iḥyā, al-Mahajjat al-bayḍā' fī iḥyā' al-Iḥyā'*, III, pp. 14-15. Part of the *Iḥyā'* passage is translated by R.J. McCarthy in *Freedom and Fulfillment* (Boston: Twayne, 1980), pp. 376-78. Mullā Ṣadrā refers to the same threefold division of wretched souls in some of his works; cf. J.W. Morris, *The Wisdom of the Throne* (Princeton: Princeton University Press, 1981), pp. 144ff.

18. These four stages are commonly described in Sufi works, and, as Fayḍ points out carefully in *Ḍiyā' al-qalb*, the terms are derived from four Qur'ānic verses (12:53, 75:2, 91:8, and 89:27, respectively).

19. Parallel passages in the writings of the philosophers are plentiful, for example, Ibn Sīnā, *al-Najāt* (Cairo: Maṭba'at al-Sa'āda, 1938), p. 293; translated in A. J. Arberry: Avicenna, *On Theology* (London: J. Murrray, 1951), p. 67. Cf. Mullā Ṣadrā, *al-Asfār*, 1282/1865-66, p. 853.

20. From this point on, the text of *Ḍiyā' al-qalb* diverges completely from the present work, though the spirit is not much different.

21. The two passages within brackets are not in the printed text but are demanded by the context; something to this effect has probably been dropped by a copyist or the editor.

22. Cf. Majlisī, *Biḥār al-anwār*, vol. 26, pp. 319ff., Chapter 7: "That the prayers of the prophets were answered through their seeking the aid and intercession of the Imams". The first *ḥadīth* cited there, from Imam Ṣādiq, corresponds largely with the present passage.

23. Majlisī, *'Ayn al-ḥayāt*, Tehran: Kitābfurūshī-yi Mūsā 'Ilmī, 1333/1954, pp. 487-92, 499-506; pp. 492-99 deal rather indirectly with the topic and were dropped to save space.

24. The full text of the *ḥadīth* is given by Majlisī in *Biḥār al-anwār*, vol. 74, pp. 73-91; he quotes it from Ḥasan ibn Faḍl al-Ṭabarsī (sixth/twelfth century), *Makārim al-akhlāq* (Iran, 1376/1956-57), pp. 537ff.; and Shaykh al-Ṭā'ifa al-Ṭūsī (d. 460/1067-68), *al-Amālī* (Iran, 1313/1895-96), II, pp. 138ff. On Abū Dharr, cf. A.J. Cameron, *Abū Dharr al-Ghifārī: An Examination of his Image in the Hagiography of Islam* (London: Luzac, 1973).

25. *'Ayn al-ḥayāt*, p. 446; *Biḥār al-anwār*, vol. 74, p. 85.

26. *'Ayn al-ḥayāt*, p. 3.

27. The first and second "springs" concern the first and second topics mentioned in the *ḥadīth* quoted above, that is, the aged and the Qur'ān.

28. *Biḥār al-anwār* (hereafter, BA), vol. 72, p. 336, no. 1. From Shaykh al-Ṣadūq, *al-Khiṣāl*, Iran, 1302/1884-85, vol. I, p. 20. In the notes that follow, all references to BA are from volume 72 (*mujallad* XVI, *abwāb* 31-96), unless otherwise indicated. The original sources of the *ḥadīths* are supplied as given by the editors of BA.

29. BA 336.3; Ṣadūq, *al-Khiṣāl* I:33.

30. BA 337.6; Ṣadūq, *al-Khiṣāl* I:59.

31. BA 337.7; Ṣadūq, *al-Khiṣāl* I:55.

32. Reference to Qur'ān 4:59; "Oh believers, obey God, and obey the Messenger and those in authority among you."

33. BA 337.8; Ṣadūq, *al-Khiṣāl* I:68. Abbreviated.

34. BA 338.14; Ṣadūq, *al-Khiṣāl* I:142. Abbreviated.

35. BA 339.15; Ṣadūq, *al-Khiṣāl* I:158.

36. Reading *ghaṣb* for *ghaḍab*.

37. BA 339.17; Ṣadūq, *al-Khiṣāl* II:6.

38. BA 341.22; Ṣadūq, *'Uyūn akhbār al-Riḍā* (Iran, 1318/1900-01), II:28.

39. BA 341.23; Shaykh al-Ṭūsī, *al-Amālī* (Iran, 1313/1895-96), I:77.

40. BA 341.24; Ṭūsī, *al-Amālī* I:270.

41. BA 343.34; Ṣadūq, *al-Amālī* (Iran, 1300/1882-83), p. 259. Abbreviated.

42. BA 341.26; Ṭūsī, *al-Amālī* I:309.

43. BA 342.29; Ṣadūq, *'Ilal al-sharā'i'* (Iran, 1321/1903-4), II:253.

44. BA 342.30; Ṣadūq, *al-Khiṣāl* I:146. Abbreviated.

45. BA 26.9; Ṣadūq, *'Uyūn akhbār al-Riḍā* II:23.

46. BA 26.7; Ṣadūq, *al-Amālī*, p. 215.

47. BA 36.32; Kulaynī, *al-Kāfī* (Iran, 1375/1955-56), II:146.

48. BA 39.37; Kulaynī, *al-Kāfī* II:147.

49. BA 308.1; Ṣadūq, *al-Amālī*, p. 110.

50. BA 323.55; Kulaynī, *al-Kāfī* II:331.

51. BA 309.7; Ṣadūq, *al-Khiṣāl* I:83. Abbreviated.

52. BA 313.23; Ṣadūq, *Thawāb al-a'māl* (Iran, 1375/1955-56), p. 243.

53. BA 331.65; Kulaynī, *al-Kāfī* II:333.

54. BA 328.58; Kulaynī, *al-Kāfī* II:334. Abbreviated.

55. BA 309.4; Ṣadūq, *al-Amālī*, p. 267.

56. BA 329.59; Kulaynī, *al-Kāfī* II:331.

57. BA 320.44; Shaykh al-Mufīd (d. 413/1022), *al-Ikhtiṣāṣ* (Iran, 1379/1959-60), p. 235; also BA 313.27; Ṣadūq, *Thawāb al-a'māl*, p. 244.

58. BA, vol. 71, p. 5; Ṣadūq, *al-Khiṣāl* II:126ff. This is a portion of a nine-page *risāla* on "rights" (*ḥuqūq*).

59. BA 340.18; Ṣadūq, *al-Amālī*, p. 148.

60. BA 344.36; Ṣadūq, *al-Khiṣāl* I:51.

61. BA 345.42; Ṣadūq, *Thawāb al-a'māl*, p. 233.

62. BA 345.41; Ṣadūq, *Thawāb al-a'māl*, p. 232.

63. Translated in W.C. Chittick, *A Shi'ite Anthology*, Albany: SUNY Press, 1981, pp. 68-82.

64. Majlisī gives the text of the letter to Muḥammad ibn Abū Bakr in BA, vol. 74, pp. 385-91; Mufīd, *al-Majālis*, pp. 152ff, and Ṭūsī, *al-Amālī* I:24ff.

65. This *ḥadīth* is well documented in Sunni sources, for example, Bukhārī, Jum'a 11, Janā'iz 32, Istiqrāḍ 20, and so forth.

66. This is the *ḥadīth* of "rights" mentioned above; BA, vol. 71, pp. 1ff. For a complete translation, see the introduction to W. C. Chittick, *The Psalms of Islam* (London: Muhammadi Trust, 1988).

67. BA 137.5; Faḍlallāh ibn 'Alī al-Rāwandī (d. 580/1184-85), *al-Nawādir* (Najaf, 1376/1956-57), p. 7.

68. *Taqiyya* is to hide one's true faith and specifically one's attachment to the Imams out of fear for life or property. It is often translated as "dissimulation," but I prefer the literal sense of the term since it makes the point more clearly.

69. BA, vol. 71, pp. 4-5; Ṣadūq, *al-Khiṣāl* II:126ff.

70. BA, vol. 12, pp. 45-47; from Kulaynī, *al-Kāfī*, *al-Rawḍa* 370-73. The story is extracted from a much longer narrative and the text is then much condensed.

71. BA 371.12; Ṣadūq, *al-Khiṣāl* II:40.

72. BA 338.10; Ṣadūq, *al-Khiṣāl* I:91.

73. BA 340.21; Ṣadūq, *al-Amālī*, p. 220.

74. BA 340.19; Ṣadūq, *al-Amālī*, p. 148.

75. BA 369.2; Ṣadūq, *al-Amālī*, p. 203.

76. BA 368.1; Ṣadūq, *al-Amālī*, p. 203.

77. BA 372.16; Ṣadūq, *Thawāb al-a'māl*, p. 222.

78. BA 338.13; Ṣadūq, *al-Khiṣāl* I:130.

79. BA 340.17; Ṣadūq, *al-Amālī*, p. 14.

80. BA 341.25; Ṭūsī, *al-Amālī* I:285.

81. BA 370.10; Ṣadūq, *al-Khiṣāl* I:108.

82. BA 371.13; Ṭūsī, *al-Amālī* I:270.

83. BA 369.6; Ṣadūq, *Ma'ānī al-akhbār* (Iran, 1379/1959-60), p. 253.

84. BA 312.16; Ṣadūq, *al-Khiṣāl* I:53.

85. BA 370.6. Majlisī gives a reference to Ṣadūq, *Ma'ānī al-akhbār*, but

the editors note that they were not able to find the text of the *ḥadīth* in that work.

86. The vizier of Pharoah, mentioned in six Qur'ānic verses.

87. BA 369.3; Ṣadūq, *al-Amālī*, p. 256. Abbreviated.

88. BA 17.2; Abū Ja'far Muḥammad ibn 'Abdallāh al-Ḥimyarī, *Qurb al-asnād* (Iran, 1370/1950-51), p. 26.

89. BA 369.4; al-Mufīd, *al-Majālis* (*al-Amālī*) (Najaf, 1351/1922-23) p. 129; Ṭūsī, *al-Amālī* I:6. To "humor" someone (*mudārāt*) is taken as a near synonym of "self-protection" (*taqiyya*); cf. BA, vol. 72, chapter 87, which is called "al-Taqiyya wa'l-Mudārāt" (pp. 393-443).

90. BA 372.21; Ṣadūq, *Thawāb al-a'māl*, p. 244.

91. BA 372.17; Ṣadūq, *Thawāb al-a'māl*, p. 232.

92. BA 372.18; Ṣadūq, *Thawāb al-a'māl*, p. 233. The phrases in brackets, taken from the Arabic, were apparently dropped from the Persian text.

93. BA 372.19; Ṣadūq, *Thawāb al-a'māl*, p. 233.

94. BA 371.15; Ṣadūq, *Thawāb al-a'māl*, p. 220.

95. BA 373.22; Ṣadūq, *Thawāb al-a'māl*, p. 244.

96. *'Ayn al-ḥayāt*, pp. 492ff.

97. This seems to be a free translation and interpretation of BA, vol. 93, p. 9.5, a passage from the *Tafsīr* attributed to the eleventh Imam, Ḥasan al-'Askarī (Iran, 1315/1897-98), p. 166.

98. BA 384.3; Ṭūsī, *al-Amālī* I:206.

99. This seems to be identical with a portion of BA 379.40; Sadīd al-Dīn Abū Alī ibn Ṭāhir al-Sūrī, *Qaḍā' ḥuqūq al-mu'minīn*. However, the Arabic text has in the second part, "Such will have the greatest share of reward on the Day of Resurrection."

100. BA, vol. 13, p. 410; 'Alī ibn Ibrāhīm al-Qummī (d. 329/940-41), *Tafsīr* (Iran 1313/1895-96), pp. 506ff. These sentences are condensed from the midst of a long narrative.

CHAPTER 14

Lives of Prominent Nineteenth-Century 'Ulamā' *from Tunikābunī's* Qiṣaṣ al-'Ulamā'

Translated and edited by Hamid Dabashi

Qiṣaṣ al-'Ulamā' *is a rare and precious document on the lives and culture of the Shi'ite* 'ulamā' *during the first half of the nineteenth century. Its author, Mīrzā Muḥammad b. Sulaymān Tunikābunī (b. 1235/1819-20, d. 1302/1885), completed it in 1290/1873-74.*[1] *Except for Narāqī, he had studied with all the figures whose biographies are presented below, and writes about their times and circumstances with the insight of a scholar in the inner circles, and the naïveté and bluntness of a native of the Caspian coast. The result is a remarkably candid and revealing picture of life in the Shi'ite centers of learning and their surrounding world. (Ed.)*

Ḥājjī Mullā Aḥmad Narāqī

He was one of the most famous religious authorities of Iran, and an eminent Muslim scholar. . . . He also had an excellent poetic predisposition.

When his noble father [Mullā Mahdī Narāqil] passed away, the students of his father appointed Mullā Aḥmad as their teacher. At the time, he was not a particularly knowledgeable person. He taught [Taftāzānī's] *Muṭawwal* and [Shaykh Zayn al-Dīn's] *Ma'ālim [al-Uṣūl].*

Then he migrated to the holy shrines of the Shi'ite Imams in Iraq. He studied with Baḥr al-'Ulūm, Āqā Sayyid 'Alī, and other students of Āqā [Muḥammad] Bāqir [Bihbahāni]. He told Ḥājjī Sayyid Muḥammad Shafī' Burūjirdī that he and his father had attended Āqā Bāqir's lectures together.

He was originally from Narāq, but resided in Kermān. He wrote many books. His *Minhāj al-Uṣūl* is in two volumes. He has a very important book on the principles of jurisprudence. His *Sharḥ Tajrīd al-Uṣūl*, a commentary on his father's [*Tajrīd al-Uṣūl*], is in six volumes. His other books are: *Miftāḥ al-Uṣūl; Mi'rāj al-Sa'āda*, a thorough and comprehensive book on ethics, originally by his father in Arabic, translated by Mullā Aḥmad into Persian on Fatḥ 'Alī Shāh's request; *Sayf al-Umma*, written to negate certain accusations of the English missionary Henry Martyn, the Christian *Padri* (father) who had raised certain doubts about the validity of Islam and propagated them in Iran. This *Padri* had disguised himself and studied with Mullā 'Alī Nūrī. Then he levelled these accusations against Islam. Many religious scholars responded to his accusations.... The third book is Mullā Aḥmad Narāqi's *Sayf al-Umma.* The Ḥajjī consulted with ten Jewish scholars. He also collected many books on the Torah and other such sources from the library of the Jewish Mullā Mūshih. Then he talked to many members of the Jewish community. Finally he wrote his book, in which he deals extensively with ancient prophets [i.e., those before Muḥammad]. These three books are truly remarkable in their refutation of the superseded (*bāṭila*) religions.

Mullā Aḥmad's *'Awāyid al-Ayyām* is on the general doctrines of jurisprudence. I have written extensive glosses on this book. Mullā Aḥmad's *Mathnāvī*, which he composed after Rūmī's model, is known as *Ṭāqdīs*. It is beautifully composed in terms of its stories and anecdotes. In his *Mustanad al-Shī'a*, Mullā Aḥmad has rationally discussed many Shi'ite sources of jurisprudence. This is a very good book, containing many minute and subtle points. He was an *Uṣūlī, par excellence* [i.e., he believed in the rational foundation of juridical doctrines, as opposed to *Akhbārīs* who considered the Prophetic and Imamite Traditions sufficient ground for such doctrines to be legally binding]. However, very often he went to extremes in diverging from what was commonly held by his *Uṣūlī* peers. For example, as with the Hanafites [and contrary to the Shi'ites] he considered grape juice to be pure between its first and third boiling, as opposed to requiring three complete boilings....

It is reported that this Ḥajjī Mullā Aḥmad on a number of occasions expelled the local governors of Kāshān. Fatḥ 'Alī Shāh summoned the Ḥājjī to his court and admonished him for his intrusion in matters of the state by expelling his appointed governor. When the Ḥājjī saw that the king became extremely angry, he rolled his sleeves, raised his hands, and with tears in his eyes he said, "Almighty God! This tyrant king appointed a tyrant governor over the people. I prevented this tyranny. And now this despot is angry with me!" As Mullā Aḥmad was about to curse the king, Fatḥ 'Alī Shāh suddenly raised and grabbed the Ḥājjī's hands and pulled them down. Then the king began to apologize to Mullā Aḥmad, and catered to his wishes. He appointed another governor for Kāshān who was acceptable to Mullā Aḥmad.

It is reported that Ḥājjī Mullā Aḥmad had a son of whom he was particularly fond, and who became so ill that the Ḥājjī was utterly hopeless and ran into the streets in despair. Suddenly he ran into a dervish who asked him why he was so desperate. The Ḥājjī said, "My son is hopelessly sick." The dervish assured him there was nothing to be worried about. Then he struck the ground with his pointed stick and read the opening chapter of the Qur'ān without any attention to proper rules of recitation. He then exhaled heavily and said, "Ḥājjī! Go on now, your son is cured!" The Ḥājjī was startled, but thought perhaps the dervish was right. He returned home and saw his son had recuperated. The Ḥājjī was truly amazed and tried to find the dervish. They looked in vain for the dervish everywhere in Kāshān. Several months later, the Ḥājjī saw the dervish in a street. He said to him, "Dervish! Although you are a man who has traversed the Sufi path, and have a curing breath, you did not recite the opening chapter of the Qur'ān that day properly and correctly. You ought to be more diligent in your religious (*shar'iyya*) duties!" The dervish replied, "Now that you did not like our recitation of the opening chapter, I'll read it back." Then he mounted his stick on the ground and recited the opening chapter again. He exhaled heavily and told him, "Go!" The Ḥājjī went home and found that very son ill. And he died from this illness.

Ḥājjī Mullā Aḥmad had a son by the name of Ḥājjī Mullā Muḥammad who was also a jurisconsult. Once His Majesty Muḥammad Shāh was sick. Ḥājjī Mullā Muḥammad wrote His Majesty a letter from Kāshān and inquired about his health. His Majesty responded that his illness was over and that he had regained his health. The Ḥājjī again wrote, "Now that Your Majesty is healthy, and since health is the highest manifestation of the divine bounty, it is proper if, according to the noble words of the Qur'ān, *Therefore of the bounty of thy Lord be thy discourse* (94:11), the news of your health be brought to Muslim countries." His Majesty responded, "This Qur'ānic verse contradicts the famous Prophetic tradition which says, *Conceal your wealth, your travels, and your faith!* How would you resolve this contradiction?"

Ḥājjī Mullā Muḥammad responded, "Since the word 'bounty' (*ni'ma*) is singular and in the genitive case (*Muḍāf*), it indicates a general implication; whereas the authentic Tradition of *Conceal your wealth [etc.]* is particular. And logically, whenever a general and a particular contradict each other, the general must be interpreted on the basis of the particular. And since 'bounty' does not include 'travel' or 'faith' [then the Qur'ānic passage, which is general, overrides the Prophetic Tradition, which is particular, and you must acknowledge this bounty by making your health publicly known]." Muḥammad Shāh was extremely pleased with this answer and rewarded Mullā Muḥammad appropriately.

I heard that once a governor was sent to Kāshān by the king. Now, this governor had not met Ḥājjī Mullā Aḥmad before. After the arrival of the governor, and before he had actually met the Ḥājjī, something happened that caused animosity between them. The Ḥājjī was thus officially suspected. After a while, the Ḥājjī went to the governor's mansion, nobody accompanying him, with his cloak over his head and his stick in his hand. When the Ḥājjī arrived, the governor was gambling with someone—playing backgammon and chess. Nobody from Kāshān was present in that wretched place. The Ḥājjī entered and greeted them. The governor was quite disgusted to see a person of the religious rank in such a gathering. The Ḥājjī sat at the doorstep. The governor greeted him high-handedly, and proceeded to gamble. Then the governor and his partner got into a fight over the game they were playing. Ḥājjī arbitrated between them according to the rules governing the game of chess. The governor was pleased and said sarcastically, "Ākhūnd! Obviously you are not that dogmatic, and you know something about this game." Then he proceeded to talk to the Ḥājjī. Suddenly, somebody who was a native of Kāshān came in and saw that the Ḥājjī was sitting in a lowly place at the doorstep. He realized that the governor had not recognized the Ḥājjī. He then somehow conveyed to the governor that this was Ḥājjī Mullā Aḥmad. Extremely embarrassed by the way he had acted, the governor stood up, kissed the Ḥājjī's hand, led him to the highest place in the room, and begged his forgiveness. At any rate, that very encounter resolved their hostility.

It should be mentioned that Mullā Aḥmad was known for not having studied under many masters, and for having arrived at so many fine juridical findings by virtue of his own intelligence and wit. *But God knows best!* His jurisprudential orientation was quite different from that of the majority of the well-known authorities. The reason is that he very frequently resorted to ill-documented sources in order to substantiate his argument, and this is not prudent. It is much better to rely on well-known sources, and follow the opinions of the authoritative jurisconsults in documenting juridical injunctions. Even in referring to the Traditions of the noble Imams, peace be upon them, reliance on well-known sources has been recommended.

Ḥājjī Sayyid Muḥammad Bāqir Shaftī

Ḥājjī Sayyid Muḥammad Bāqir ibn Sayyid Muḥammad Taqī Mūsavī-i Shaftī-i Dashtī [Rashtī; henceforth referred to as Sayyid or Ḥujjat al-Islam] lived in Isfahan. He was known as Ḥujjat al-Islām (Proof of Islam), and was unique in his days as a leader of the community. His command of Arabic was excellent, as was his knowledge of astronomy, jurisprudence, and biography. . . . He was unrivaled in austerity, piety, and abstinance. He was extremely knowledgeable . . . , and had a proverbial memory. He composed many books. His *Maṭāli'al-Anwār* is a commentary on the book of *ṣalāt* (ritual prayer) in Muḥaqqiq-i Ḥillī's seven-volume *al-Sharāyi'*, and it still does not cover *ṣalāt* in its entirety. Each volume consists of almost twenty thousand lines of poetry. [There follows a discussion of Shaftī's treatises].

His lectures were impeccable in precision and profundity. He would elaborate on the legal verdicts of the jurisconsults and make use of many logical possibilities in interpreting their positions. Many people attended his lectures. However, he used to give very few lectures—two or three times a week, or perhaps even fewer. Some days he did not lecture at all. Ocassionally, as he was teaching, the parties involved in a legal suit would storm into our classroom and disrupt his lectures. Ākhūnd Mullā Ja'far Nazarābādī of Qazvīn used to say, "I transcribed the sections of ritual purity and ritual prayer of *Sharḥ-i Kabīr* (The Great Commentary) when I was a student of the Ḥujjat al-Islām's and his lectures were being interrupted by parties involved in a dispute and we did not have anything to do. I had the sections of ritual purity and ritual prayer from *Sharḥ-i Kabīr* with me, and I would simply transcribe them." I too attended the lectures of Ḥujjat al-Islām Shaftī for almost a year. He used to talk to me quite often. He was a close friend of my father's. He decided to give me my *ijāza* (certificate). He took my copy of the chapter on *ṭahārāt* (ritual ablutions) from the book of *Badāyi'* and kept it for a week. On a Thursday that he had intended to give me my *ijāza* he passed away. Consequently, I sought to obtain my *ijāza* from his students, so that I could authenticate my credentials through him.

It is impossible to relate the degree of Ḥājjī Sayyid Muḥammad Bāqir's piety . . . . He knew the Fifteen Supplications [attributed to 'Alī, the first Imam] by heart, repeating them constantly in tears . . . . I was in the service of His Excellency for a year and never heard him recite any other prayer. . . . At any rate, the supplications of this noble soul were so intense that he would cry and mourn all night long until dawn. He would wander around his library until morning in despair, as if he were insane: praying and supplicating, beating on his head and chest. This master of religious piety would cry and moan so loudly that the neighbors would have heard him if they were awake. Towards the end of his life, he cried and supplicated so much that he got a hernia. He had to wear a truss, and no physician could cure him. Finally, he was told that crying was religiously forbidden to him, as it would worsen the hernia. Then whenever he would go to the mosque, the preachers would not go to the pulpit as long as he was sitting there, but would wait until he left. If a preacher went to the pulpit while he was still in the mosque, Sayyid Muḥammad Bāqir would not leave, but stay and cry. . . . *May God grant us success in [matching] his supplications.* [There follows another anecdote about Shaftī's intense prayers and supplications].

At any rate, he was always alone in his library. A servant would sleep at his doorstep. His oil lamp had two wicks: one thick, the other thin. He would turn on the thick wick when he was awake, and when he went to sleep he would turn on the thin wick. When he woke up he would again turn on the thick wick. He would turn on the lamp before the complete sunset—as soon as the sun disappeared. He would turn off the lamp at sunrise. It is said that this kind of practice brings good luck and prosperity, and the Prophetic Tradition of *No extravagance in [using] the lamp light* supports this claim. Ḥujjat al-Islām Shaftī would always go to public baths on Wednesdays. There is a Prophetic Tradition regarding this, too. It is also commonly held that going to the barber on Wednesday increases one's prosperity. It is said that during all the time that he attended the Friday prayers, Ḥujjat al-Islām Shaftī never missed a prayer, except the day his son, Sayyid Hāshim, passed away. That day he missed his noon prayers. . . .

As for his legal verdicts, they were of the highest degree of certitude. He was extremely cautious in issuing legal verdicts. It would also take him quite some time. Sometimes, cases would take more or less a year to settle. He possessed an incredible judicial perspicacity. . . . Among the amazing cases that Ḥajjat al-Islām Shaftī handled is one that concerns a woman who approached his Excellency and said, "The mayor of such and such a village has illegally taken possession of my property." The mayor was sent for. He denied any wrongdoing, and produced fourteen legal judgments from fourteen judges in Isfahan, all of whom had rejected the woman's claim. The Sayyid examined the verdicts. Then he piled them together and put them in front of himself. He turned to the woman and said, "The mayor is an honest man and he is right." The woman started to cry and moan. Then the Sayyid attended to other cases. As he was conducting other cases, he asked the mayor, "Have you purchased this property?" "No," he replied. "But is ownership possible only through purchasing?" The Sayyid said, "No. Not necessarily." The Sayyid again attended to other cases. After a while he asked the mayor, "Have you inherited this property?" The mayor responded, "No. But is ownership possible only through inheritance?" The Sayyid said, "No. I have properties that I have not received through inheritance." He again resumed his other cases. After a while he asked the mayor, "Have you received this property as a settlement in a dispute, or did somebody leave it to you in his will?" "No," he answered. "But is ownership possible only through such arrangements?" The Sayyid replied "No." In the same manner, and as he was attending to other cases, he mentioned all the possible legal formulae according to which the mayor could have owned the property. But he denied all of them, and said none was actually applicable. Then the Sayyid asked him, "Then what makes your claim over this property valid?" The mayor answered, "There is no need for anything to substantiate my claim. The sky just opened up and the property fell into my lap." The Sayyid said, "How come the sky does not send anything down for me? Go away and return the property of this woman's children! You have appropriated it illegally." Then the Sayyid tore the fourteen verdicts into pieces and, on the woman's request, wrote a verdict of his own to the mayor ordering him to return the property to the woman. [There follows the description of another case.]

The third case is also quite interesting. Somebody brought a man to his court and said, "This is Āqā Ḥasan, and he owes me four hundred *tūmāns*." The Sayyid asked the defendant to respond. The latter said, "Āqā Ḥasan owes the plaintiff money, but I am not Āqā Ḥasan!" The Sayyid did not pursue it any further, and attended to other cases. As the litigants and the witnesses were arguing back and forth, he suddenly turned to the former defendant in the midst of all the confusion and said, "Āqā Ḥasan!" The defendant answered, "Yes!" The Sayyid continued, "Get up and pay this man his four hundred *tūmāns*!" Then they both left his court. The point is that the Sayyid caught the defendant off-guard; if he were innocent, he would not have responded. At any rate, there are too many such incidents in His Judicious Excellency's court to be recorded here.

Nobody can believe how poor His Excellency was at the beginning. When a student of Baḥr al-'Ulūm in the holy city of Najaf, the Sayyid was a close friend and confidant of Ḥājjī Muḥammad Ibrāhim-i Kalbāsī.

One day Ḥājjī Kalbāsī came to pay him a visit and found him lying down on the ground. It became evident that he had passed out from hunger. The Ḥājjī then rushed to the bazzar, bought him some food, and made him eat until he recovered. . . .

And as for his wealth after this period of poverty, apparently His Excellency was extremely rich. God Almighty demonstrated His will to His Excellency so that it would be a lesson to everybody, as well as a token of credence to figures of authority. A wealthy man from the village of Shaft sent His Excellency a considerable sum of money to spend as he wished. A portion of the money was to belong to His Excellency, and the rest was to be invested during His Excellency's lifetime. The proceeds would belong to him personally. After the death of His Excellency, the principal would be spent for specified causes. The Sayyid invested this money, and in a short period of time it generated considerable interest. If, for example, he lent some money with a house as its collateral, on the due date he would appropriate that property immediately.[2] Then he would either keep the property or sell it. He also had stables of camels and mules. His residence was the house of the late Āqā Muḥammad Bīd-ābādī, a Ṣūfī master who was also known as an alchemist. His house extended from one block to another, and it contained many living quarters. The Sayyid had seven sons and every one of them had interior and exterior living quarters of his own. Their expenses were provided separately. There were seventeen excellent horses in the stable of his eldest son, Āqā Mīr Zayn al-'Ābidīn. The number of persons in the household of the Ḥujjat al-Islām, not including the retinue of his sons, was close to one hundred. He had many male and female servants and wives, and a considerable number of villages and properties, and much real estate. In the city of Isfahan he is reported to have owned four hundred caravansaries. He is also said to have owned two thousand shops. . . . In brief, he had to pay an annual tax of seventeen thousand *tūmāns* just for his villages in Isfahan. Fatḥ 'Alī Shāh, may he rest in peace, once told the Sayyid, "We will waive the taxes from your villages." His Excellency said, "Would you deduct that figure from the total sum of the annual tax of Isfahan? Or will the total figure stay the same?" The King replied, "The total tax of Isfahan will not be lowered; it will have to be divided among other villages." The Sayyid said, "I will not accept that my taxes be divided among other villages and paid by other people. This is an injustice, and I will have none of it. I will pay the taxes on my villages myself."

From every city and every village inside and outside Iran religious taxes were dispatched to Isfahan for the Sayyid, and he would distribute them among the poor. Once Fatḥ 'Alī Shāh was residing in the palace of Haft Dast, which is in the suburbs of Isfahan. He was looking at the countryside through his binoculars when he saw an elephant loaded with goods. He told his retinue, "An elephant is being sent to us." But he saw the elephant being led towards the city and away from his encampment. The king asked about the owner of the elephant and the goods it carried. He was told that the elephant was from the Muslim merchants and public officials of India, dispatched for the Ḥujjat al-Islām, and that its load was the various religious taxes that the merchants had sent for the Ḥujjat al-Islām to spend as he willed. The king did not say anything, but he did not like that. When the elephant was taken to the Sayyid, and he was told of the incident with the king, he received the goods . . . and sent the elephant for the king. At any rate, none of the early or contemporary Shi'ite authorities were as wealthy as the Sayyid. . . .

There were several reasons for the Sayyid's reputation. One was the high praises of Āqā Sayyid Muḥammad, who had responded to the question of whether Āqā Sayyid Muḥammad Bāqir was a source of authority in jurisprudence: "Do not ask me about his authority, ask him about mine." The other reason is the high opinion of Mīrzā-yi Qummī in response to Fatḥ 'Alī Shāh's request: "Recommend to us an impeccable religious authority to bring to the royal mosque in Tehran to perform the Friday prayers, and under whose leadership we can perform our prayers." Mīrzā-yi Qummī had responded, "I do not know anyone better or more meritorious than Āqā Sayyid Muḥammad Bāqir-i Shaftī-i Rashtī who resides in Isfahan." Then the king wrote to the governor of Isfahan to prepare the Sayyid and sent him to Tehran. The governor asked around about who this Sayyid Muḥammad Bāqir was. When he found out, he sent a messenger to tell him, "The king has asked for you. Get ready, and I shall arrange for your travel." The Sayyid refused to comply. The governor was surprised by his asceticism, and went to see him personally and ask him to go. The Sayyid still refused. The governor said, "We have to obey His Majesty's wishes. We are not in a position to oppose his will." The Sayyid responded, "I shall not go by choice!" The governor was disappointed, and wrote to the king. This incident engendered confidence in him on the part of the king, until His Majesty came to Isfahan. The Sayyid was taken to see him. The king said to the Sayyid, "Ask me for a favor!" The Sayyid did not ask for anything. The king insisted. Finally, the Sayyid said, "Now that you insist, my request is that you command the royal kettle-drum house be closed down." The king did not say anything. When the Sayyid left, the king told Amīn al-Dawla, "What a strange Sayyid he is! He asks me to close down the imperial kettle-drum house which is the symbol of royalty." Amīn al-Dawla begged His Majesty's pardon. When the king came to Isfahan the following year, the Sayyid went to see him. After he left, the king told Amīn al-Dawla, "This Sayyid is not the Sayyid I saw the last time. He has become very shrewd" . . . .

Although he was very small in physical stature—thin, short, and frail—it frequently happened that even when he was not in a state of ritual fasting, he did not eat anything for lunch. He would perform his morning prayers in the mosque. Then he would attend to legal disputes which were brought to him until noon. Then he would engage in his noon prayers with the same ritual ablution that he had performed in the morning. Occasionally, he would even perform the evening prayers with the same ritual ablution. And he would not eat anything, other than an occasional mint sherbet in the middle of the day. But he would, every once in a while, eat lunch. And this indeed was the cause of much astonishment!

When Muḥammad Shāh came to Isfahan, the Sayyid, riding on a camel, went to see him. As was his custom, Sayyid 'Alī-Naqī 'Arab was leading him while reciting from the Qur'ān with a powerful and beautiful voice. In the Haft Dast palace, Muḥammad Shāh was watching this from afar. When the Sayyid approached the encampment, Sayyid 'Alī-Naqī recited this verse: *Say: O Allāh! Owner of Sovereignty! Thou givest sovereignty [unto whom Thou wilt, and Thou withdrawest sovereignty from whom Thou wilt. Thou exaltest whom Thou wilt, and Thou abasest whom Thou wilt. In Thy hand is the good. Lo! Thou art Able to do all things]* (Qur'ān 3:26). When he reached the section, *Thou exaltest whom Thou wilt*, Muḥammad Shāh said, "Undoubtedly, it is the Majesty of God's Will that has ennobled this man so much and given him so much glory!" . . . When the Sayyid reached the vicinity of the royal encampment, Sayyid 'Alī-Naqī was reciting this verse: *[Till, when they reached the Valley of the Ants, an ant exclaimed:] O ants: Enter your dwellings lest Solomon and his armies crush you [unperceiving]* (Qur'ān 27:18). All of a sudden, the people in the encampment—the soldiers, gentries, and all—stormed forward. The overwhelming majority of them could not reach the Sayyid to kiss his hands. They mostly could only kiss his mule, or the hoof of his mule. Muḥammad Shāh was astounded. When the Sayyid reached the royal entrance, the following Verses were being recited: *Lo! [We have sent unto you a messenger as witness against you, even as] We sent [unto] Pharaoh a messenger. But Pharaoh rebelled against the messenger, [whereupon We seized him with no gentle grip]* (Qur'ān 73:16).

As for his enjoining the lawful, he personally executed seventy people for legal transgressions. But he administered legal punishments not involving execution even more frequently. When he issued a death sentence for the first time—it was a case of pederasty—nobody would execute the order. Finally, he stood up and struck a blow himself. It was not fatal. Then somebody else came forward and cut off the head. The Sayyid himself performed the ritual prayers for the executed. As he was praying, he fainted.

Once he went to Mecca during the reign of the Egyptian Muḥammad 'Alī Pāshā. He used to frequent with the Pāshā. He took the Fadak garden [i.e., the estate of 'Alī and Fāṭima which was confiscated by Abū Bakr] and returned it to the *sayyids* in Medina.

His Excellency excommunicated (*tafsīq*) three contemporary religious authorities. One was Ḥājjī Mullā Asadullāh Burūjirdī, a student of the late Āqā Sayyid Muḥammad. He had already attained his *ijāza*, and the daughter of Mīrzā-yi Qummī was his wife. A number of religious authorities from Burūjird, such as Ākhūnd Mullā 'Alī, persuaded the Sayyid to excommunicate him, and he did. The second person was Mīrzā Muḥammad Taqī Nūrī, a brilliant student of Ḥājjī Kalbāsī who had also briefly studied with Āqā Sayyid 'Alī. He was very ignorant in the principles of jurisprudence. He resorted to ill-documented sources [i.e., Traditions]. For example, on the question of the dilution of the ritual water, he maintained that impurity ascends from a lower to a higher level. This is contrary to the customary position; nay, in fact there are two received legal consensuses against it. . . . He also smoked the nargila at the pulpit during the fasting month of Ramaḍan. He did not consider smoking as nullifying the state of fasting. Shaykh Ḥasan ibn Shaykh Ja'far, and the author of *Madārik*, among others, have also issued legal injunctions proclaiming that smoking does not nullify the fast. Rationally, this seems to be the case, while it would be very difficult to argue otherwise. However, issuing injunctions to this effect and smoking in public during the month of Ramaḍan is not proper for a jurisconsult. At any rate, this Mīrzā Muḥammad Taqī Nūrī issued many controversial injunctions that are contrary to jurisprudential principles. However, in enjoining the lawful he was second to none and quite remarkable. Yet a group of people from Nūr came to the Ḥajjat al-Islām and challenged his credibility, and the latter excommunicated them. . . . The third person whom the Sayyid disqualified from issuing legal verdicts was Ḥājjī Mullā Ṣādiq-i Rashtī. This Ḥājjī was a learned man in all respects. He was an eloquent preacher. He was superior to all the religious authorities in Rasht in every way. He was a student of the late Āqā Sayyid 'Alī. He lived for one hundred and eighteen years, and was in full control of his senses. [There follows a description of Ḥājjī Mullā Ṣādiq-i Rashtī.] At any rate, some people from Rasht got together, came to the Ḥujjat al-Islām and challenged his qualification to issue legal verdicts. Consequently, His Excellency the Sayyid officially excommunicated him. When the Ḥājjī heard about this, he went to the pulpit and reproached the Ḥujjat al-Islām. It is also quite possible that the Sayyid had made a mistake. In fact both of them were upright and righteous. But God knows best. . . .

Ākhūnd Mullā ʻAlī Akbar Khwānsārī reported, "One day I went to see the Ḥujjat al-Islām in his library. There was so much gold piled in front of him that he could hardly be seen behind it. That wealth—which he could spend as he wished—was an obstruction between us. He asked for a nargila to be brought for me. As I started smoking the nargila, he sent for the needy and the *sayyids.* Immediately a crowd formed. The Sayyid gave a fistful of the money to each person. I had not yet finished the nargila when he had distributed all the money. Enchanted and astounded, I said, 'You have such an abundant flow of the Imam's property!' His Excellency replied, 'That is correct. Usually sons do take such liberties with their father's property.' "[3]

On the day of Ghadīr-i Khumm [i.e., the anniversary of ʻAlī's nomination as Prophet Muḥammad's successor] the merchants of Isfahan would send, each according to his ability, one or two hundred *tūmāns* to His Excellency to be distributed among the poor. Once during the Qadīr celebration, he went to the mosque and climbed up to the pulpit. Around him were put bags full of money—gold, silver, and coins of all kind. He commanded that the poor be gathered at one entrance of the mosque, come to him one by one, take their share of the money, and leave from the other door. Then a crowd of needy people gathered. He gave each a fistful of money, until the money was entirely spent. It took him almost an hour to distribute the money to the poor. They figured it was about eighteen thousand *tūmāns* that he had given to the poor in an hour. He had designated two of his shops—a bakery and a butcher shop—for the poor. . . . It is said that from one thousand people to two thousand families received their bread and meat from His Magnanimous Excellency. . . .

The year that Rasht was struck by a plague, a considerable amount of property was collected which did not have any owner or inheritor. Fatḥ ʻAlī Shāh went to see the Sayyid and told him, "I have too many mouths to feed and I am very poor. Give me some of the money that was collected in Rasht!" The Sayyid had twenty thousand *tūmāns* of this money delivered to His Majesty in Rasht. Every year he would send money for the poor living in Medina. He assisted the seminary students considerably. He even catered to high public officials, the nobility, merchants, and princes by giving them loans. He had a mosque constructed in the Bīd-ābād neighborhood. . . . During the time of the late Fatḥ 'Alī Shāh, who was particularly helpful, kind, and considerate to the religious authorities, the king went with the Sayyid to the site of the mosque and requested to be included in construction of this mosque. The Sayyid did not accept. His Majesty said, "You cannot afford to finish this construction!" The Sayyid replied, "I have my hands in the treasury of God Almighty!"

The year he died, I was in Isfahān. That year Amīn al-Dawla claimed that His Excellency owed him twenty thousand *tūmāns*. He responded, "You had given me this money to distribute among the poor in compensation for the tyrannies you have committed;[4] and I have done as you asked." Amīn al-Dawla said, "I had simply entrusted that money with you." The Sayyid replied, "I am under no moral obligation to return your money. But now that you do not concede, I accept the expenses myself. Let what I have paid to the poor be from my own money!" And he put it in his will that twenty thousand *tūmāns* from his properties be given to Amīn al-Dawla, to reimburse his loan. . . .

When His Majesty [Muḥammad Shāh] came to see that most learned of all religious authorities at his house, fanfare and kettle-drums announced his arrival. As the Sayyid was coming to his door to welcome His Majesty, he heard the sound of fanfare and kettle-drums. He raised his hands towards the sky and said, "O God! Do not permit the humiliation of the descendants of [Fāṭima] Zahrā more than this!" And he returned inside.

Among the signs of his miraculous powers (*karāmāt*) is that as he passed away from this world and rushed to meet the judgment of God Almighty, His Majesty Muḥammad Shāh came to Isfahān and caused him more than thirty thousand *tūmāns* in damage. He treated his family with utmost disrespect. He commanded Ākhūnd Mullā Muḥammad Taqī Ardakānī, who had sought a haven in the Sayyid's house, to be taken to Tehran. But it was not before long that His Majesty passed away, and that his prime minister, Mīrzā Āqāsī, was dragged in the soil of humiliation. Another time, some followers of Satan and enemies of the path of Muḥammad, the Seal of the Prophets, poisoned the food that he regularly ate. The cook gave some of that food to a cat and it died. From then on, his kitchenwares were locked. Once, too, the governor of that region promised four villains one hundred *tūmāns* each to go to the Sayyid's residence during the night and murder him. The villains climbed the walls of his residence and approached his library. They hid under a tree in front of the library and saw that the Sayyid was sitting there, with barely a shirt on. A lamp was lit, and a prayer book was open in front of His Excellency. He was praying and crying lamentably, like a cloud in spring. One of them charged his gun, and aimed at the chest of His Excellency. Suddenly, he was petrified and began to tremble in fear. His hands began to shake and the gun was about to fall down. He motioned to his accomplice, who took over the gun. But the same condition struck the second one. They both began to cry, and departed. His Magnanimous Excellency never noticed them.

Towards the end of his life he became quite ill, and the physicians could not do anything. On a Thursday, he developed strangury. At his death bed, Ḥājjī Kalbāsī came to pay him a visit. The Sayyid sat for a while. Ḥājjī Kalbāsī said farewell to His Excellency at his death bed and left. The Sayyid performed his ritual ablutions, and stood up for his noon prayers—both mandatory and supererogatory. Then he passed out. He had on the top of his prayer rug a piece of clay from Imam Husayn's shrine. He ate it, and instantly the bird of his soul flew to the sacred nest. Ḥājjī Kalbāsī had not yet reached his house when he was told of the Sayyid's rushing to the presence of his most noble and pure ancestors. The Ḥājjī passed out from this horrible news. When he regained consciousness, he came to the Sayyid's house and lamented for him. Ākhūnd Mullā 'Alī Akbar Khwānsārī performed the ritual ablution on his corpse. Then they kissed his most sanctified hands, and shrouded him. He was buried, according to his will, in a place he had prepared next to the mosque. *May God be content with him, for the sake of his right through his most noble and infallible ancestors!*

Āqā Sayyid Ibrāhīm ibn Sayyid Muḥammad Bāqir al-Mūsavī [al-Qazvīnī]

He was my teacher. He was very famous, and unique among his peers. In principles of jurisprudence, applied law, and biography he was truly unrivalled. Nobody among the great teachers even came close to him. Students at all levels attended his lectures and benefited from his scholarly acumen and jurisprudential perspicacity. He resided near the shrine of Imam Ḥusayn, and taught at Madrasa-yi Sardār, which was adjacent to this shrine. At times, up to one thousand students attended his lectures. . . .

His writings include *Ḍawābiṭ al-Uṣūl* in two volumes. It is said that he wrote this book in two months in Mecca. This book is considered among his miracles. He wrote it in the year of plague. He composed this book in such a way that on most of the pages, the lines begin and end with the same letter. For example, on one page every line begins with "a" and ends with "n" or "l." In this manner, he wrote the entire course of the principles of the jurisprudence in two months. Composing the original manuscript in that manner . . . cannot be but the sign of Divine providence and grace. . . .

After Sharīf al-'Ulamā' died, Sayyid Muḥammad Bāqir married one of his wives. She could not bring him any children, however. He had a number of daughters from another wife, one of whom, with Āqā Sayyid's approval, was married to the late Mullā 'Alī Muḥammad, a brilliant student of his. This Mullā 'Alī Muḥammad sat in judgment, led the public prayers, preached, and taught while Sayyid Ibrāhīm was still alive. When Sayyid Ibrāhīm passed away, Mullā 'Alī Muḥammad married his wife, the one who had also been Sharīf al-'Ulamā''s wife. *What you do to others, others will do to you!* At any rate, it was not before long that some people from Mullā 'Alī Muḥammad's hometown invited him over and poisoned him. He was survived by two sons from one of his wives. . . .

Sayyid Ibrāhīm used to say that there are three kinds of *ijtihād.* The first is to explore the issue thoroughly, relate it to all the stated opinions and the significance of consensus on the topic, then to proceed to express the logic behind these positions, and finally to choose one of them and thus conclude the issue. The second is to provide exhaustive logical explanations, and to elaborate on the rationale behind the legal injunctions more than in the previous case, and to cite a few secondary proofs as well. The third is to elucidate thoroughly all the universal principles upon which the legal issue under discussion rests, and, in providing proofs, to be so exhaustive as to render the legal injunctions totally, or at least partially, indubitable. The jurist should provide secondary proofs *ad infinitum,* and then be so thorough in weakening the opposite position as to render it almost inevitably annulled. . . .

It should also be known that one of the reasons we have argued against the necessity of imitating the most learned *mujtahid* (*taqlīd-i a'lam*), and have actually written a treatise on "imitation" (*taqlīd*), is that the educational background of the jurisconsults—in terms of the preliminaries of *ijtihād,* principles of jurisprudence, and other such prerequisites—differs. Each one of the jurisconsults is an expert in one or the other of these fields: one is good in Arabic, the other in biography; one in principles of jurisprudence and in persuasive arguments, and yet another in rational sciences; one in "preliminaries," the other in "ritual obligations," and yet another in "legal transactions." Thus, in all fairness there is no single person who is the most learned in all areas of jurisprudence and its preparatory disciplines, and in all these at one and the same time.

His Excellency Sayyid Aḥmad Āqā Sayyid Ibrāhīm is the one who approved my *ijtihād*. However, he did not give me an *ijāza* (certificate) to transmit Prophetic and Imamite Traditions; and I did not ask for it either. Although my *ijāza* to issue legal opinion inevitably qualifies me to transmit Traditions too. . . .

When we were in the *'atabāt* (holy cities in Iraq) the Master [Āqā Sayyid Ibrāhīm] was superior to all other religious authorities, and was the *marja'* (source of imitation) for all the believers. During that time, close to seventy students attended the lectures of the late Shaykh Muḥammad Ḥasan, may he rest in peace, the author of *Jawāhir al-Kalām;* and close to twenty attended those of Shaykh Murtaḍā, may God elevate his status. The Master, however, was more famous than others. Now, it just happened that somebody died in Shiraz, and according to his will some four thousand *tūmāns*, a third of his inheritance, were brought to the Master. The late Shaykh Muḥammad Ḥasan came all the way from Najaf to the Master's house and said, "I shall not leave this house until you give me my share of the money." So the Master gave him four hundred *tūmāns*.

After the death of the late Hujjat al-Islām, the treatise of the late Master was published in Qazvīn. The first run was not enough for that city. The treatise was published a second time. As the second printing was being prepared, our Master died.

After His Excellency Āqā Sayyid Ibrāhīm passed away, the late Shaykh Muḥammad Ḥasan Najafī, may God elevate his status, became very famous. Initially, the late Shaykh Muḥammad Ḥasan refused to endorse the injunctions of the late Master, until he became more acquainted with the students of his Excellency, and endorsed their *ijtihād*. The students then verified the *ijtihād* of the Master, and in turn the Shaykh verified the *ijtihād* of Āqā Sayyid Ibrāhīm. And this process of verifying the *ijtihād* of a master by those of his students is truly strange! Particularly in view of the fact that the Master was much superior to the Shaykh in the principles of jurisprudence, in biography, and in Arabic; nay, in fact, in jurisprudence and piety His Excellency was superior to the Shaykh. Perhaps initially the Shaykh did not know the Master that well. But God knows best!

The Master's degree of asceticism was such that despite a substantial sum—more than twenty thousand *tūmāns*—that he received as religious taxes from India, as well as from Iran and Arabia, he lived in poverty. Other than his daily sustenance, which he kept to a minimum, he did not possess anything, nor did he accumulate any wealth.

Now, one of His Majesty Fatḥ 'Alī Shāh's daughters, Ḍiā' al-salṭana, was very famous, beautiful, and wealthy. Fatḥ 'Alī Shah had asked the late Ākhūnd Mullā Ḥasan Yazdī, the author of *Muhayyij al-Aḥzān*, to give Ḍiā' al-salṭana in marriage to his son. The Ākhūnd refused, arguing, "We subjects are not worthy of His Majesty's daughter living in our house." As everybody knew, Fāḍil-i Qummī, the author of *Qawānīn al-Uṣūl*, had a son. The late Fatḥ 'Alī Shāh asked that one of his daughters be married to this son. After the House of Parliament was abrogated, the Mīrzā asked God, "If the princess is to marry my son, then I wish he were dead!" Having thus prayed, the Mīrzā's son was found drowned and dead in the small pool of their house. At any rate, after Fatḥ 'Alī Shāh passed away, Ḍiā' al-salṭana went to the holy shrines. First, she sent a message to the late Āqā Sayyid Muḥammad Mahdī, the son of Āqā Sayyid 'Alī Ṭabāṭabā'ī, asking him to marry her. The Sayyid refused. This Āqā Sayyid Mahdī was a very ascetic person. Then Princess Ḍiā' al-salṭana went and asked Shaykh Muḥammad Ḥusayn, the author of *al-Fuṣūl fī 'Ilm al-'Uṣūl*, to marry her. The Shaykh, too, refused. Finally, she sent somebody to the Master, asking him to marry her. The Master replied, "Your expenses, Princess, are quite high. I am very poor and cannot afford you!" The Princess responded, "I shall not ask you for any expenses; I shall in fact pay for your expenses as well as those of your wife!" His Excellency responded, "I have a family who has lived with me through thin and thick. I would have to abandon them if I were to marry you; and that would be abominable!" The Princess sent another message: "You can live with your wife; my only objective is to bear your name." The Master still refused, and disappointed her completely. . . .

In the "Book of Fasting" in *Dalā'il al-Aḥkām*, the Master argued that under two conditions smoking nullifies the fast. On its margin, however, he wrote that smoking apparently does not nullify the fast! Now, when I was preparing a manuscript of the Master's "Book of Fasting" and reached this point, I went to see him, may God elevate his status. I asked him, "Do you not consider the smoking of the nargila as nullifying the fast!?" He said, "I have never issued any injunction to that effect!" I said, "Well, in your book you have argued that smoking nullifies the fast; yet, on the margin, you have indicated that apparently smoking does not nullify the fast!" He replied, "I have simply provided the argument; I have not issued any legal injunction to that effect. Nobody should attribute such an injunction to me."

As for his extraordinary deeds (*karāmāt*), there are quite a number of them. Among them is his having seen Fāṭimah [the Prophet's daughter and 'Alī's wife] in a dream, and her giving him pen and ink to write on jurisprudence, as was mentioned earlier. The other sign was when he consulted the Qur'ān to write a treatise for his legal constituency in Persian, and, as we have pointed out, the following verse came up:

[Say: Lo! As for me, my lord hath guided me unto a straight path,] a right religion, the community of Abraham, who was no idolater (Qur'ān: 6: 161). Another sign of his miraculous powers is a very famous incident. Some people from India wrote to him and asked for a treatise for the guidance of their conduct. His Excellency dispatched a treatise to them. Those who were sent to carry this treatise were caught in a storm at sea on the way back to India. The ship and all its passengers and cargo were about to be drowned in the sea. In order to save the ship and her passengers, much of the cargo was thrown into the sea. The package in which the treatise was kept was also thrown into the sea. The ship and her passengers reached India safely, and they reported the incident to those who had requested the treatise. Once again the Indians wrote to His Excellency, "The treatise was thrown into the sea, please send us another one!" His Excellency thought of having another treatise transcribed to be sent to India again. But after a while, a letter was received from India stating, "We have received your package, including the treatise." It went on to say, "The exact detail of this is that one day we were walking along the shore. All of a sudden we saw a strange sea animal lying there dead and with his belly swollen. We cut his belly and found a package inside. We opened the package and found your treatise and all that you had sent us intact. Water had not penetrated it, nor had your treatise been damaged. . . ."

Among his magnanimities, other than what has been mentioned, I was also witness to the following: When the Master was in the holy city of Najaf attending the lectures of Shaykh 'Alī, he saw Amīr al-Mu'minīn 'Alī, peace be upon him, in a dream commanding him to go to Karbalā. Because the dream was not a proper proof, His Excellency did not abide by it. He had the same dream a second time; this time Ḥaḍrat-i Amīr [i.e., 'Alī] told him that his first dream was authentic. He was also somewhat angry with him. The Master did not heed this time, either. Then he saw Ḥaḍrat-i Amīr in a dream for the third time, commanding him to go and reside in Karbalā. This time His Excellency complied and went to reside in Karbalā.

One of the strange incidents that happened between the Master and Shaykh Muḥammad Ḥasan Najafī, the author of *Jawāhir*, is as follows: In response to a request from the people of Shiraz, the Master sent Hājjī Shaykh Mahdī Kujūrī, who was one of his most distinguished and brilliant students, to that city with a full recommendation. After he reached Shiraz, Shaykh Mahdī started to teach *Ishārāt al-'Uṣūl*, a book by the late Hājjī Muḥammad Ibrāhīm Kalbāsī. Now, Ḥājjī Kalbāsī was of the opinion that issuing legal injunctions is a very difficult enterprise, and that many people who claim competence in issuing such injunctions are not really qualified to do so. The Ḥājjī would thus admonish whoever claimed to be a *mujtahid* and a judge. Now, since Shiraz is the twin city of Isfahan, and since Shaykh Mahdī was teaching the Ḥājjī's *Ishārāt al-'Uṣūl*, the latter by and large ignored Shaykh Mahdi. At any rate, once, when I myself was present in Isfahan, Ḥājjī Kalbāsī began to boast about his publications in a sermon and said, "Yes, there is this Mullā in Shiraz who has recently started teaching my *Ishārāt*, and many people attend his lectures." To make a long story short, in Shiraz there used to be a Mullā who was not all that learned, yet he was very famous and the late Shaykh Muḥammad Ḥasan Najafī used to support and write recommendations for him. Now, Ḥājjī Shaykh Mahdī was far superior to that Mullā. At any rate, Ḥājjī Shaykh Mahdī wrote in detail to the Master, told him all about the situation and asked him, "to intervene on my behalf with Shaykh Muḥammad Ḥasan and ask him to write me letters and recommend me to the people of Shiraz so that I may do better!" The Master intervened on his behalf with Shaykh Muḥammad and wrote to him: "Shaykh Mahdī is learned and judicious. You ought to support him!" Shaykh Muḥammad Ḥasan responded, "You are only one witness; I shall need another to verify that he is actually a *mujtahid.*" The Master did not respond. Now, this Shaykh Muḥammad Ḥasan had a small house in Karbalā that he occupied whenever he came there for special pilgrimage. Next to that house lived somebody from Shiraz. This neighbor passed away, and as his religious tax he transferred his house to Ḥājjī Shaykh Mahdī. Ḥājjī Shaykh Mahdī wrote to the Master and asked him to take care of the house for him, and attend to it in whatever way necessary. In the meantime, Shaykh Muḥammad Ḥasan wrote to the Master requesting, "My house is small. Please give me that Shīrāzī's house which is next to it." The Master responded, "Ḥājjī Shaykh Mahdī has authority over that house. You kindly write to him, and he shall transfer the house to you." Consequently, Shaytkh Muḥammad Ḥasan wrote a kind letter to Shaykh Mahdī confirming his *ijtihād!* The Master wrote the detail of the incident to Shaykh Mahdī, too, asking him to "transfer the house to Shaykh Muḥammad Ḥasan now." Consequently, Shaykh Mahdī transferred the house to Shaykh Muḥammad Ḥasan. One should not think that Shaykh Muḥammad Ḥasan refused to acknowledge the *ijtihād* of Shaykh Mahdī for any personal reasons, or because the latter was a student of the Master, or that he finally acknowledged him in order to get that house. The actions of Muslims are to be presumed righteous. Perhaps, as in the case of the distinguished author of the *Jawāhir al-Kalām*, Shaykh Muḥammad Ḥasan did not initially appreciate the significance of Shaykh Mahdī. And then he was assured.

Another incident that occured between Shaykh Muḥammad Ḥusayn, the author of *[al-] Fuṣūl [fī 'Ilm al-'Uṣūl]*, and the Master is briefly as follows: One of the *'ulamā'* presided over a marriage ceremony. The two parties involved in the marriage got into a quarrel. Then the Master, may he rest in peace, issued a judgment nullifying the marriage contract on the basis that the bride was under age. But Shaykh Muḥammad Ḥusayn took issue with the opinion of the Master and issued his injunction pronouncing the marriage valid. The dispute went on for quite some time. Finally, the case was taken to the jurisconsults in Najaf. There, Shaykh 'Alī Muḥaqqiq-i Thālith, the son of Shaykh Ja'far Najafī, supported the Master's position and issued his opinion in favor of nullifying the marriage contract. Other jurisconsults in Najaf followed suit, and the issue was thus concluded.

The Master died in 1264/1847 from cholera. The people of Karbalā sanctified his body by carrying it around the shrines of Imam Ḥusayn, the Prince of the Martyrs, and that of His brother 'Abbās. A huge crowd gathered, and the body was taken through the streets. While people were in tears and anguish, he was buried in a special tomb, next to his house, and adjacent to the court of Imam Ḥusayn's shrine. . . .

Shaykh Murtaḍā Shūshtarī al-Anṣārī the Most Learned of the Scholars (*a'lam al-'ulamā'*)

After the late Shaykh Muḥammad Ḥasan, the leadership (*riyāsat*) of the Shi'ite community was entrusted to him. He never sat in judgment, nor did he give anybody *ijāza* of *ijtihād*. . . .

He was truly a founding figure in the principles of jurisprudence: in the categories of "the validity of conjecture," "the principle of exemption," and in "association." He lived close to eighty years, like Shaykh Muḥammad Ḥasan, may he rest in peace, and may God illuminate his tomb.

Ākhūnd Mullā Āqā Darbandī

A brilliant jurisconsult, Ākhūnd Mullā Āqā Darbandī was a student of Sharīf al-'Ulamā'. He was extremely ill-tempered and obnoxious. Every once in a while he would start talking about numerous criticisms that he had of a particular juridical point. Then the late Sharīf al-'Ulamā' would say, "You just give us one solid argument and forget about the rest". . . . Then he would get into a debate with his teacher and make him quite angry. The Ākhūnd himself would get angry, too. Sharīf al-'Ulamā' would then expel him from his class. Students would grab him and throw him out of the class. He would stop at the door and say, "Well, I may be thrown out, but I don't believe a word of what he says. He is utterly wrong." Then Sharīf al-'Ulamā' would ask his students to beat him.

At any rate, the Ākhūnd would not come to the class for a few days. Then his fellow students would go to Sharīf al-'Ulamā' and say, "Ākhūnd Mullā Āqā is really a knowledgeable man. Would you please consider letting him back?" Sharīf al-'Ulamā' would agree, with the condition that he not utter a word. Then he would come and would not say anything for a few days. But he would again get into a discussion, and the same cycle would be repeated.

Once there was a disagreement among the students as to what juridical issue they should discuss. They finally decided on a topic. But Mullā Āqā disagreed and said, "You must discuss the question of 'the legal validity of conjecture,' otherwise I am going to let you all have it!" Sharīf al-'Ulamā' admonished him.

Sharīf al-'Ulamā' and his students once went to Sāmarra on a pilgrimage. One night they were resting in a place. Here again Mullā Āqā got into a fight with another student and became very upset. He had some kind of weapon, with which he started to chase the man. The petrified student escaped into Sharīf al-'Ulamā''s tent, with Mullā Āqā after him. Sharīf al-'Ulamā' admonished Mullā Āqā and ordered him to leave.

At any rate, Mullā Āqā was well-versed in the rational sciences (*ma'qūl*), but quite an expert in traditional sciences (*manqūl*). Āqā Sayyid Ibrāhīm used to say on many occasions, "Ākhūnd Mullā Āqā is among the masters of the principles of jurisprudence. Consult with him." In theology and philosophy, his intellectual contributions were in conformity with the religious doctrines. He was also quite extraordinary in biography. As to rhetoric, I have not seen anyone even come close to him—Arab or Persian. The same is true of his knowledge of the Arabic language.

His publications include *Kitāb-i Khazā'in* (The Book of Treasures) in three volumes . . . on jurisprudence. Once Shaykh Muḥammad Ḥasan came to Karbalā on a special pilgrimage. Ākhūnd Mullā Āqā went to see him. The Shaykh said to him, "My *Jawāhir al-Kalām* (Jewels of Words) is a very good book; have you read it?" The Ākhūnd responded, "There are many such jewels in our Treasures."

The Ākhūnd spent quite some time in Karbalā, teaching every

once in a while. I used to attend his lectures, but he was so ill-tempered that they used to be interrupted.

His other book is *Iksīr al-'Ibādāt fī Asrār al-Shahādāt*, which is an extremely good book . . . on Karbalā tragedy and its interpretation. . . . He also wrote *Sa'ādāt al-Nāṣiriyya* on [Nāṣir al-Dīn] Shāh's request. This is a short book in Persian which is of some merit. He was quite good in reciting the tragedy of the Lord of the Martyrs Ḥusayn ibn 'Alī. He would cry so much on the pulpit that he would faint. In 'Āshūrā, he would take off all his clothes and wear only a towel around himself. Then he would smear his head with dust, and his body with mud, and go to the pulpit in that very condition. He was indeed quite sincere in his devotion to the sacred Imams, beyond anything we have seen in our time.

He knew the science of Elexier and had actually written a treatise on the subject. . . .

One day a nobleman asked his opinion about Rūmī, and whether he was a Muslim or an infidel. He replied, "I really do not know, but there is a line of his which is quite true:

> The people of this world, high and low
> May God's damnation be upon them all!"

When His Majesty Nāṣir al-Dīn Shāh came to visit him, he told the king, "You are a Muslim ruler; why don't you trim your mustache as is religiously prescribed?" His Majesty complied with the Ākhūnd's wishes and instantly asked a barber to trim his mustache accordingly.

The Ākhūnd handled the texts of religious sciences with utmost respect. So much so that whenever he picked up Shaykh-i Ṭūsi's, may God be satisfied with him, *Tahdhīb [al-Aḥkām]* or anything of that sort, he would kiss them and handle them reverentially, just as the Holy Book. He used to say that books of the Traditions are as sacred as the Qur'ān.

He lived for eighty or ninety years, and died in Tehran. He had many debates with his adversaries; there is no reason why we should not relate some of them . . . .

Mullā Āqā . . . reports, in his *Iksīr al-'Ibādāt:*

> Once I was invited to the house of the most learned Sunnī scholar in Baghdad, Shihāb al-Dīn Sayyid Maḥmūd 'Arūsī—or 'Alūsī according to some texts. He welcomed me very warmly. He was the highest religious authority (*Muftī*) in Baghdad. There was also a certain 'Abd al-Raḥmān Kurdī who was known for his asceticism and piety. But the Muftī was known as a worldly man.
>
> One day Muftī 'Alūsī was not home, and I went to see Mullā 'Abd

al-Raḥmān. I told him to ask me any question he had about anything. The Muftī [*sic*, i.e., Mullā 'Abd al-Raḥmān] said, "Who are you to answer my questions!? You can ask me if *you* have any question!" He waited for a while and then asked, "Why do you Shi'ites curse Yazīd?" I became very upset and said, "A Muslim should not ask a Muslim such questions. May Yazīd and his father Mu'āwiya go to hell!" When the Muftī [*sic*, i.e., Mullā 'Abd al-Raḥmān] heard this, he became very angry. Now, his house opened onto a crowded street in Baghdad. He started yelling and screaming, and people gathered around us. He said, "How dare you curse the Uncle of the Faithful [Mu'āwiyya, Muḥammad's brother-in-law] in Baghdad, the capital of the Islamic world, the center of the Sunnīs!? You better defend yourself as to why you curse him, or else I will have you executed immediately!" I said, "You are not in any position to have me executed. It is incumbent upon you to curse Yazīd and Mu'āwiyya, too; and whatever is incumbent needs no proof. Have you forgotten what 'Allāma Taftāzānī has said in his *Sharḥ al-Maqāsid*, in sections where he deals with Imamate and hostility to 'Alī and his family?" The Muftī [*sic*] asked: "What has Taftāzānī said?" I said, "He has argued that there is no doubt that some of the Prophet's companions harassed his family. Thus, not every companion of the Prophet is infalliable; and not everybody who met the Prophet was a good person. But it is not really seemly to curse them; that would be detrimental to Islam. But those tyrants who have come after them, everything testifies to their guilt. Thus God's curse, and that of everybody else, be upon them all!"

Then I asked, "Is this the gist of what Taftāzānī has said or not?" He replied, "Yes it is, but who is he, and who cares what he has said; I am infinitely more knowledgable than he was. You will have to support your argument with Qur'ānic verses and Prophetic Traditions." I said, "If I produce clear Qur'ānic verses in this regard, as well as a number of Prophetic Traditions, do you commit yourself to curse Yazīd and Mu'āwiyya?" He answered, "Yes!"

I made him promise, and then I said, "God Almighty has said in Sūrah al-Aḥzāb: *Lo! those who malign Allāh and His Messenger, Allāh hath cursed them in the world and the Hereafter, and hath prepared for them the doom of the disdained* (Qur'ān; 33:57). He asked, "And how would that support your argument?" I said, "Has it not been reported in your own sources that Muhammad, peace and God's blessings be upon him, said, *'Alī! Your fight is my fight; your peace my peace; your flesh my flesh; your breath my breath; and whoever fights you fights me, and he who fights me fights God*? He said, "Yes, we have this Tradition." Then I said, "Has it not been recorded in your own sources that the Prophet said: *'Ḥusayn is from me and I from Ḥusayn; His flesh is my flesh and his breath my breath*? He answered, "Yes, it is thus recorded." I said, "Has it also not been repeatedly recorded in your own sources that the Prophet said: *Fāṭima is a piece of me; whoever hates her hates me, and whoever bothers her bothers me*? He answered, "Yes, it is thus reported." Then I said, "Can I rest my case?" He dropped his head and did not utter a word. I wanted to leave. He asked me if I would please stay for half an hour. I sat. He ordered me fresh coffee and the nargila. I asked him, "What subject of the principles of jurisprudence are you lecturing on these days?" "The section on 'judgment and the judge,' from 'Aḍudī's *Sharḥ*," he replied. I took him on that and argued forcefully against "the unity of reason and the reasoned." He was grounded as an ass in mud.

Then I came back to the Muftī's house, who had just come and was waiting for my arrival. He put his arms around my shoulder and said, "May dogs shit on Yazīd's beard and that of Mu'āwiyya too! Who dares oppose their being cursed!?" I asked him, "How did you find out?" He answered, "A number of my servants were present. But why did you not practice 'prudent self-protection' (*taqiyya*)? That cursed 'Abd al-Raḥmān almost had me killed because I publicly cursed that impertinent Yazīd." I said, "Efendi, nobody practices 'prudent self-protection' more than I do, but the protection of the Commander of the Faithful ['Alī], peace be upon him, is my protecting citadel."

Ākhūnd Mullā Āqā began teaching Ibn Abī al-Ḥadīd's commentary on the *Nahj al-Balāgha* when he was only twenty years of age. As he has stated in his *Asrār al-Shahāda,* he used to have persuasive discussions with Abū Bakr and 'Umar, and with Ibn Abī al-Ḥadīd—in his dreams.

Notes

1. Vā'iẓ Khiyābānī, *'Ulamā'-i Mu'āṣirīn* (Tehran: Islāmiyya, 1366/1947), pp. 12-13.

2. Since the value of the collateral, in this case a house, is usually more than the borrowed money, its lawful appropriation on the maturity date is a legal mechanism through which the prohibition of usury is circumvented.

3. Half of the *Khums* is given to the leading Shi'ite authorities as "the share of the Imam" (*sahm-i Imām*) to be spent at their discretion. Since Ḥujjat al-Islām Shaftī is a *sayyid,* he refers to this share as his father's property.

4. *Radd-i maẓālim:* payment to a *mujtahid* to secure forgiveness for the committed acts of tyranny.

CHAPTER 15

An Exchange Between a Mujtahid *and a Qājār Official*

Translated by Hamid Dabashi

Extant letters constitute an important and still largely untapped source for Iranian history in the nineteenth century. A number of letters throw considerable light on the articulation of religious and political authority in the last quarter of the nineteenth century.[1] *Of these, the following correspondence between Ḥājj Mullā 'Alī Kanī and Mīrzā 'Abd al-Vahhāb Khān Āṣif al-Dawla has been chosen.*[2] *The letters are not dated, but they must have been written between 1301/1883-4 when Mīrzā 'Abd al-Vahhāb Khān Shīrāzī acquired the title of Āṣif al-Dawla upon being appointed the governor of Khurāsān, and his death in 1304/1886-7. The exchange is remarkable for the light it throws on the conceptions of* ijtihād *and* taqlīd *in practice. Mullā 'Alī Kanī (d. 1306/1888), the powerful* mujtahid *of Tehran who was mourned by the populace as the "deputy of the Prophet,"*[3] *had pushed the exercise of clerical authority to its limits by issuing, in 1873, an injunction* (fatvā) *making the dismissal of Prime Minister Mīrzā Ḥusayn Khān Mushīr al-Dawla incumbent* (vājib) *on account of the extensive concession for railway construction and exploration of mines granted to Baron Reuter.*[4] *'Abd al-Vahhāb Khān Āṣif al-Dawla, a man of considerable learning and a tough-minded and ambitious Qājār official, was fully the* mujtahid*'s match for pointing out the limits of clerical authority. Though an abstemious man who prayed and fasted regularly,*[5] *he had no hesitation in insisting that, as a layman, he had the right to choose any* mujtahid *he wanted to follow in religious matters, and that the sole and sufficient source of his own authority in office was the mandate from the monarch. (Ed.)*

Kanī to Āṣif al-Dawla

May it be brought to the attention of Your Excellency: There are two questions which I wish to pose in order to solicit your opinion (*istiftā'*). Please write your answers in the margins. The first question: In minor matters (*far'iyya*) of Divine commandments, do you act upon your own judgment (*ijtihād*) or do you imitate (*taqlīd*) a source of authority? If you imitate an authority, who is that authority? As you have a very low opinion of all religious scholars (*'ulamā'*), consider them ignorant and slander them, then certainly they cannot be imitated and you must exercise *ijtihād* yourself. If so, it is not really necessary to degrade the other *mujtahidīn.* Moreover, it is incumbent upon the *mujtahid* to be well-versed in the opinions of the previous generations of *'ulamā'* so that he would not contradict the Consensus (*ijmā'*). You have been repeatedly heard to voice your opinion against the Consensus, to say the least.[6]

The second question is this: It is necessary to delimit the jurisdiction and specify the authority (*riyāsat*) that has been delegated to you. Now, I have been told your authority is limited to commercial matters. Infringement is infringement. If by "merchant" we refer to its common meaning, that is, that individual who trades goods from one place to another and who is engaged in wholesale and not retail, then your authority is rather limited to such cases when, for example, two merchants have a dispute or a discrepancy in their accounts. But this is not what you are usually engaged in. Why should the cloth-seller, the greengrocer, the herbalist, and so forth be subject to your authority? And if your authority is not so delimited, so far as one party of a litigation is a merchant it warrants the judgment of Your Excellency. But if by "merchant" the reference is made to just any party involved in the transactions of buying and selling, covered by the Sacred Law, then the authority is totally with Islam. . . . What is His Excellency 'Aḍad al-Dawla doing, what is His Excellency the Regent all about? What is the Minister of Interior doing? And so forth and so on.

It is obvious that all commercial guilds, nay indeed just about everybody, deals with merchants. The cobbler and the stoker of a bath-furnace buy tobacco and loin-cloth from the merchant; so does the masseur in a public-bath buy pumice stone and blade. Is everybody then under your authority, and are you entitled to collect the merchants' claim from them? And do you have this authority based on your own personal orders, without any reference to the Sacred Law?

In view of what has been said in the first question—even though the main part of the latter question and answer should be addressed to the person who has given you this general leadership (*riyāsat-i 'āmma*)[7]—my intention is to seek your opinion, and to see whether or not such indeed is the case. Please write the answer in the margins. I shall not inconvenience you any further.

Āṣif al-Dawla to Kanī

May it be brought to the attention of Your Excellency: Your servant delivered your written message to me. You have asked me two questions. As to the first, whether I am a *mujtahid* or a follower [*muqallid*]: Neither are you entitled to ask nor am I required to answer, but obviously I am a follower. As to your question "whom I imitate": Again, neither are you entitled to ask nor am I obligated to respond, but I imitate Ḥājjī Shaykh Murtaḍā, may God elevate his status, with the permission of the living *mujtahid*.[8] As to your assertion that I dislike the *mujtahids* and that I slander them, I could not determine exactly whom you have in mind. Certainly, I have never told you in person of such things, so you could not be quoting me directly. But if somebody else has attributed these assertions to me, you should have modified your question accordingly, so the liar would have been identified. If by these religious authorities you mean those who are outside the capital, as for example those in Iraq or in other parts of Iran, they think very highly of me, and have their utmost confidence in me. I have the documents of their favorable opinion about me at my disposal; they are ready for your inspection, if this is what you wish. If you refer to those in the capital, the phrase "all the *mujtahids*" is useless; one will have to be more specific. His Excellency Ḥājjī Mullā Muḥammad Ja'far, may God Almighty keep him safe; His Excellency Ḥājjī Mīrzā Mahmūd, may God Almighty keep him safe; His Excellency Mirzā Ḥasan, may God Almighty keep him safe; His Excellency Ḥājjī Āqā Muḥammad, may God Almighty keep him safe, and others have been quite generous with their favors towards me, and I with my sincerity towards them. This is what I believe to be the case, and you can seek their opinion too.

Yes, I dislike those who are not *mujtahid* scholars, but falsely claim to be, and indeed are among *Those who hoard up gold and silver and spend it not in the way of Allāh [unto them give tidings (O Muḥammad) of a painful doom,] On the day when [it will (all) be heated in the fire of hell, and] their forehead and their flanks and their backs will be branded therewith (and it will be said unto them): Here is that which ye hoarded for yourselves. Now taste of what ye used to hoard* (Qur'ān 9:34-35). God dislikes them, too, and so does the Messenger of God (Muḥammad). If they lie, and not be a *mujtahid*, then they invoke *the curse of Allāh upon those who lie* (Qur'ān 3:61).

As to your second question, asking about my position and office: That, sir, has nothing to do with you; that is the prerogative of His Majesty's Exalted Essence, may our spirits be sacrificed for him. The appointment, dismissal, and delimitation of my authority and that of those like me is entirely vested in his sanctified opinion.

But if I too were to indulge in asking questions which I am not entitled to ask, I would have inquired whether, if I have an excessive desire for worldly matters, it is not out of the ordinary. But what about you, sir, why do you design all kinds of schemes for the capital and the provinces? Wherever there is water, land, a shop, or a mill, it is somehow religiously endowed; one way or another you appropriate it. On one specific occasion, there is the record in your handwriting in which you have indicated that a certain will is not valid. And then in your own handwriting you have prepared another will—not quite unlike the one that Ḥājjī Mullā Hādī, may he rest in peace and may God elevate his status, had drawn for the inheritors of Ḥājjī Muḥammad Javād the silk-merchant and now belongs to the inheritor—and as recorded on the back of the document, you personally hold one-third of the whole as collateral. And then by appealing to Mīrzā Khalīl's reputation, you secure a guardianship in your own name, which is again like Ḥājjī Mullā Hādī, may he rest in peace, who, in his own handwriting and with his own seal, dismissed him from guardianship. I am in possession of that document. If one-third of a living and present inheritor's property can be thus appropriated, then every living person should be asked for one-third of his property.

And if every hearsay can be repeated, I have also heard from Tehrani merchants that some twenty years ago Ḥājjī Murtaḍā, may God elevate his status, was asked if a person who studies and becomes a *mujtahid*, and then abandons his studies for a few years, and his preoccupation be primarily in water, land, aqueduct, garden, mill, and shop, whether the mental capacity to pass judgment will remain with him or not. He said "I do not know, but whenever I leave Najaf to go to Karbalā for pilgrimage, in my return I detect some lapses in my mind."

You had requested that I should respond on the margin of your letter, but because it became evident that before I even had a chance to respond, some had already seen your letter or a copy of it, and then had reported its content with some discrepancy, I kept the original which is in the handwriting of Your Excellency. I wrote the response with my own handwriting on the margin of a copy of your letter, so that both my letter and yours shall be safeguarded against distortion. I shall not infringe upon your time any further.

Notes

1. For an interesting example, see the letter written by the *mujtahid* Ḥājj Mullā Muḥammad Ṣādiq Qummī to Nāṣir al-Dīn Shāh in 1292/1875: [H.] Modarresī Ṭabāṭabā'ī, "Ḥājj Mullā Muḥammad Ṣādiq Qummī Faqīh-i 'Ālīqadr-i Dawra-yi Qājār va Nāma-yi Aū bi-Nāṣir al-Dīn Shāh dar Shikva az Maẓālim-i 'Ummāl-i Dawlat," *Vahīd*, vol. 12, no. 3 (1352/1973), pp. 211-19.

2. Published in C. Ghani, ed., *Yaddāshthā-yi Duktur Qāsim Ghanī*, vol. 9 (London, 1982), pp. 422-25.

3. Muḥammad Ḥasan Khān I'timād al-Salṭana, *Rūznāma-yi Khāṭirat*, I. Afshār, ed., Tehran: Amīr Kabīr, 1350/1970, p. 596.

4. H. Algar, "'ALI KANĪ," *Encyclopaedia Iranica*, vol. 1 (London: Routledge & Kegan Paul, 1985), p. 866.

5. He could not resist gambling, however. M. Bamdād, *Tārīkh-i Rijāl-i Īrān*, vol. 2 (Tehran: Zavvar, 1347/1968), pp. 301-17, esp. 307-08.

6. In other words, you cannot be a *mujtahid*.

7. Kanī's question is of course sarcastic. He wishes to imply that general rulership—i.e., general deputyship—is the prerogative of the *mujtahid* and, therefore, no person could legitimately have granted it to Āṣif al-Dawla.

8. According to the Shi'ite law, Āṣif al-Dawla needs the permission of a living *mujtahid* in order to continue his imitation of a *mujtahid* whom he used to follow but who has passed away.

CHAPTER 16

Two Clerical Tracts on Constitutionalism

Translated and edited by Hamid Dabashi

The two tracts on constitutional government presented in this chapter, offer two diametrically opposed Islamic view points. The first, written by a Constitutionalist 'ālim *shortly after the ratification of the Supplement to the Fundamental Law in October 1907, legitimizes constitutional government both as a means for the protection of the realm of Islam, and as an end in itself, embodying the Islamic political principles. This legitimation, however, follows the spirit of the Supplement in safeguarding the religious and juristic authority of the* 'ulamā', *and restricts the scope of parliamentary legislation to matters not covered by the Sacred Law. It is also interesting to note that majority vote or consensus are not considered valid per se.*

The second tract was written about a year later after the restoration of autocracy by its most important clerical supporter. Its author, Shaykh Faḍl Allāh Nūrī was the leader of the anti-Constitutionalist 'ulamā' *and reacts sharply to the ideas expressed in the first tract. He sees Constitutionalism not as the means for protecting Islam, but on the contrary, as the ploy for the destruction of Islam and the spread of irreligion, Bābī heresy, materialism and foreign ideas. Whereas the Constitutionalist Khalkhālī presents popular representation and parliamentary legislation as embodiments of the true spirit of Islam, Nūrī strikingly highlights their imported and alien quality, and whereas Khalkhālī considers equality the divine principle of creation of the world, Nūrī fulminates against equality and freedom as pernicious principles that destroy the solid pillar of the Sacred Law. Parliamentary legislation, Nūrī argues forcefully, implies the denial of the perfection of Muḥammad's Revelation and Sacred Law and their full adequacy for all times and all places, and is therefore contrary to Islam. Incidentally, Nūrī also argues that the* marāji'-i taqlīd *had no authority to endorse constitutional government. This endorsement was not binding on their followers because such matters were beyond the scope of the juristic authority of the* marāji', *and, in fact, constituted undue interference with the ruler's right to govern the kingdom. (Ed.)*

A Treatise on the Meaning of Constitutional Government

by

Sayyid 'Abd al-'Aẓīm 'Imād al-'Ulamā' Khalkhālī

On the Meaning of Constitutional Monarchy and its Benefits

In The Name of God, The Merciful, The Compassionate

Boundless and immeasurable praise and gratitude is due to the Worshipped One and the Sovereign of the sovereigns who has established the law of justice, fairness, and the principles of equality under His Sovereignty. And benedictions and greetings are worthy of that Messenger who is the propagator of divine rules and the executer of divine laws. And salutations beyond limit are appropriate for his family, who are the disseminators and exponents of the rules of the Eloquent Qur'ān.

When I, the humblest of all descendants of the Prophet, 'Imād al-'Ulamā', originally from Khalkhāl and residing in Najaf, returned to my country of origin some time ago in order to perform a pilgrimage to the shrine of the Eighth Imam and attend to some other necessary matters, I found the inhabitants of Iran disturbed, confused and bewildered by the baseless tyranny of absolutism, so much so that . . . they have now become Constitutionalists. With the great effort of the sacred National Consultative Assembly, they have established councils (*anjumanhā*) in the capital as well as in other cities, and have devoted all their efforts to the establishment of the Constitution and the uprooting of tyranny and absolutism. But because the objective and ideology (*marām*) of the Constitutionalists have not yet become quite clear to some absolutists, and because the Constitutionalists' rightful demands—hidden and concealed—have not been recognized as they truly are, I found some intelligent and knowledgeable individuals, as well as some perspicacious observers, bewildered. So much so that they considered this problem of Constitutionalism as pertaining to issues of faith and belief, referring to it as the Constitutionalist "school" (*madhhab*) and "religion." The advocates of this apposite opinion are accordingly accused of lacking in conviction, being of lowly nature, and wanting in intelligence. Furthermore, a considerable number among the masses who have not understood its meaning and description properly, refer to it as "the interrogation room!"

Consequently, I felt obliged to explain, explicate, interpret, and comment upon the truth of this question to the degree that I understand it, and in a lucid, clear, and concise manner, equally understandable by both the elite and the masses, . . . so that confusion and doubt is dispelled from them and they come to recognize that the issue of Constitutionalism is in no way related to faith or religious beliefs, and that considering it a religion is due to lack of deliberation and insight into the essence of this matter, and also to a lack of comprehensive knowledge about the main subject of this problem. . . .

You should know that according to the word of God, exalted and sanctified, *Surely We created man of the best stature* (Qur'ān 95:4). God Almighty adorned man in the best manner, so that He thus praised His own Essence: *Blessed be Allāh, the Best of Creators!* (Qur'ān 23:14). Then He honored man with the gifts of knowledge and speech: *He hath created man. He hath taught him utterance* (Qur'ān 55:3-4). And in another verse: *[He] Teacheth man that which he knew not* (Qur'ān 96:5). Because of this goodness of creation in his essence, and with knowledge and speech as his attributes, and according to the verses: *Verily We have honored the Children of Adam. We carry them on the land and the sea, and have made provision of good things for them, and have preferred them above many of those We created with a marked preferment* (Qur'ān 17:70), God distinguished man from His other creations. And in pre-eternity (*azal*) He made the angels closest to His presence prostrate to him: *And We created you, then fashioned you, then told the angels: Fall ye prostrate before Adam* (Qur'ān 7:11).

Therefore, God established laws and limitations in matters pertaining to livelihood (*ma'āsh*) and the other-worldly destination (*ma'ād*) according to man's capacity and competence, so as to sustain the rank of humanity, and to perfect man's knowledge, speech, and understanding. These in turn enable man to attain the highest stages of nobility, achieve the farthest positions of sanctity, secure eternity in the Paradise, become worthy of approximity to the Beneficence of His Highest Unity, and avoid inclusion among *Those [who] are as the cattle—nay, but they are worse!* (Qur'ān 7:179), and *Thinketh man that he is to be left aimless?* (Qur'ān 75:36). Upon reaching the stage of intelligence and maturity,

God made it incumbent upon man to comply with the rules. He established and stipulated His commands upon historical exigencies, and upon man's capability and endurance so that he could comply. . . .

In these incumbent commands, God has not made any distinction among his obedient servants. Prophets and messengers, serfs and kings, the old and the young, men and women, servants and masters, religious authorities and the masses, descendants of the Prophet and non-Arab Muslims, the rich and the poor, are all equal and partners in their obligations, according to the laws of justice, fairness, and equality. As God has not distinguished among the individuals in creating them, so has He not discriminated in stipulating rules with which they must comply, with the exception of those activities that have been demonstrated by the attributes peculiar to the Prophets. As for men, they have competed with each other in their position of obedience and compliance to the commands of His Unity to the limits of their understanding, and to that degree they have increased their state of bliss, as He has said: *Lo! the noblest of you, in the sight of Allāh, is the best in conduct* (Qur'ān 49:13). And just as in this world, where He has rendered His incumbent commands on the basis of justice, fairness, and equality, so will He treat His obedient servants with justice when they are attended to in the Day of Judgment in His court, wherein he has stipulated the modes of conducting interrogation, requiring witnesses, making a claim, rebuking it, and appealing; thus preventing the possibilities of absolutism and tyranny. . . .

In short, the Creator of the universe has directed His obedient servants towards the laws of justice and equality in this world; and in the world to come, too, He shall treat them by the standards of righteousness in the court of justice. He repeatedly points out in the Noble Qur'ān that *Allāh is no oppressor of His bondmen* (3:182; also, 8:51; 12:10; 41:46; 50:29). He has also prohibited tyranny to His obedient servants, and has directed them towards justice and equality, as He has said: *Lo! Allāh enjoineth justice and kindness* (Qur'ān 16:90). . . . And it is important to note that God's commandments to His obedient servants are all due to His kindness, because on such commandments are based the continuity of the universal order, the comfort of mankind, . . . and the perfection of humanity.

God did not establish His inhibitions and commandments upon man once and for all from the time of Adam to that of the Seal of the Prophets. Instead, God has set man's obligations according to the exigencies of each age, and based on man's capability, endurance, inner disposition, and his state of civility. . . . He then has sent a messenger in every age in order to propagate and execute those laws. . . . [There follows the Islamic account of the completion of the prophetic period with Muḥammad and the perfection of Revelation in the Qur'ān.]

The Glorious Qur'ān is comprehensive of all religious laws, and it contains all political and social regulations; so much so that no one needs any other heavenly book or political regulations in doctrinal, political, or social matters. Considered carefully, the principles of the European laws are obviously derived from the Glorious Qur'ān, the Traditions of the Imams, and the books of Shi'ite jurists. This Glorious Qur'ān of ours is the highest miracle of all prophets and messengers. The miracles of other prophets were peculiar to themselves and died with them, whereas the Glorious Qur'ān is an everlasting miracle. Until *the day when the trumpet is blown* (Qur'ān 6:73), it shall remain in force. So far as this Glorious Qur'ān is upheld, the Islamic religion is upheld, and the Messenger of this community shall be no other than he who brought this Glorious Qur'ān: *There shall be no prophet after me* (Prophetic Tradition).

Thus it became evident that this saved community of Muslims is the best and completest of all communities: *You are the best community that hath been raised for mankind* (Qur'ān 3:110). And the Prophet of this community, who is Muḥammad ibn 'Abd-Allāh, God's salutations and benedictions be upon him, is the best and most perfect of Prophets and the Seal of all Messengers and Prophets: *Muhammad is not the father of any man among you, but he is the messenger of Allāh and the Seal of the Prophets; and Allāh is ever Aware of all things* (Qur'ān 33:40). And the Book of their commanding laws which is the Qur'ān is the best and most completed of all revealed Books. . . .

This Noble Qur'ān is divided into thirty sections. Five hundred of its verses are on punishments and commandments; some parts of it are on the recognition of Divinity and the description of His Highest and Sacred attributes; approximately one third of it is warnings of Hell and tidings of Paradise. . . . The rest is on political matters, admonitions, and stories. But the purpose of God Almighty in such stories as those of Joseph and Potipher's wife or Moses and the daughters of Reu'el . . . is not storytelling. Instead, as He says, *In their stories verily there is a lesson for men of understanding* (Qur'ān 12:111). . . . His objective is to awaken man from the sleep of ignorance, so that he ponders on the matters of this world and thinks about the other. . . .

God Almighty sent these five hundred verses of political commandments to the pagans gradually through His messenger and over the course of twenty-three years. If He had propagated these commandments among them instantaneously, the uncivilized pagans would not have forsaken the religion of their forefathers and imposed so many demands upon themselves. He approached them so cautiously that those wild people became civilized and obedient, to the point of reaching the *day [that] I have perfected your religion for you* (Qur'ān 5:3).

God Almighty has described Muhammad as the Seal of the Prophets, who is the noblest of all creatures and the Universal Intellect: *Nor doth he speak of (his own) desire. It is naught save a revelation that is revealed* (Qur'ān 53:3-4). God Almighty has also directed Muhammad towards consultation: *And consult with them upon the conduct of affairs* (Qur'ān 3:159), so that He, sacred as He is, not be suspected of absolutism.

After this introduction, we would like to say that the modern rulers of the nations will have to conform in their sovereignty and kingship, and in attending to their subjects, to the True King and the Eternal Power, and make the Creator of this universe the model of their conduct. As God is not a tyrant Himself, He is not tolerant of any of His creations perpetrating it on another: *If ye judge between mankind, judge justly* (Qur'ān 4:58). Therefore, rulers in every age must necessarily establish the order of their government and the laws of their leadership in accordance with the exigencies of that very age and attend their subjects with justice and fairness. They should not impose extended and unbearable punishment or immeasurable tyranny upon their subject; nor should they punish without reason or indict before ascertainment; nor should they consider people their slaves to be bought and sold; nor should they behave according to their whim. Since God Almighty has prevented His messengers from such actions, then the rulers are, *a fortiori*, so obligated. Moreover, God Himself has not treated His creations whimsically or arbitrarily. He has established His authority on the law of justice and the principle of equality; nor has He demanded from anyone more than he is capable. He punishes the transgressor only after He has measured his actions, provided witnesses and arguments, and proved his sin.

There was a time when sovereignty in this world was based on tyranny, cruelty, transgression, violence, the massacre of relatives, plundering of the enemy's wealth, destruction of civilization, the plucking of eyes, and cutting of hands. In those times these were necessary. But those ages are gone now. In this age, especially in our time, sovereignty is founded on justice, fairness, and the principle of equality, as is obvious from the Europeans. As a result of contacts with foreign countries and of association with civilized nations, and of studying political books and articles, reading foreign and domestic journals, acquiring knowledge of the relationship between the civilized rulers and their respective subjects, and being informed of the desirability and benefits of Constitutional government, the eyes of the Iranians have been opened, their ears alerted, and their tongues unleashed. They do not tolerate tyrannical actions or unruly behavior. They now have their opinions about internal and external affairs, have become a "people of loosening and binding,"[1] supervising their mutual affairs, and capable of acceptance or rejection. They will certainly not tolerate tyranny and transgression anymore. Even if one thousand of them are killed every day, and all their property is plundered, they shall not abandon the issue of the constitutionality of monarchy.

Today all European states have established constitutions and treat their nations in accordance with them. Perhaps it can be said that, today, the Europeans are better and more intelligent than we Iranians. If this Constitutionalism is nonsense and useless, why is it that they have adopted it? And if it be beneficial, why should the Iranians abandon it? The establishment and execution of law in Iran has been very necessary and appropriate, and may lead to the progress of their state and nation in the best of all possible ways, without breaking the continuity of their sovereignty or causing the dispersing of the society of their nation, so that the whole nation remains willingly obedient to the ruler. The protection of the citizens and their rights is the duty of the ruler, and obedience to and protection of the principles of monarchy, and consideration of the rights of the person of the ruler are incumbent upon the people. This is so because the existence of the person of the king is precious for each and every nation, and if a nation were not to have its own sovereignty, it would constantly be lowly and humiliated like the sick and the incapacitated, even if its individual members were millionaires, as are the Jews and the Indians. By contrast, when a nation has its own sovereignty, it is always respected and honored even if all its individual members are poor and wretched, as are the Muslims and the Christians. It is, therefore, incumbent upon the nation to maintain the honor and majesty of its ruler to the best of its ability. If the continuity of sovereignty in a nation be broken, its honor is lost, and the star of its fortune will begin its decline. Gradually the name and reputation of that nation will be forgotten in this world; foreigners will dominate them and show them no mercy, be they of low or high status. This happened to the Sasanids: they lost their name, reputation, religion, and customs, left their beloved homeland and sought haven in India and other countries. The state and the nation should therefore not transgress on each other's rights, as such antagonism will eliminate both the power of the state and the force of the nation, leaving them both in a state of abject humility, and their country in danger of foreign domination. It is necessary for the state and the nation to share the unity of thought and action so that they can progress.

Undoubtedly, His Sacred Majesty the King of Iran, more than any other wise, intelligent, knowledgeable, and trustworthy man, and more than any minister or public official, knows the poverty, indigence, despair, and humility of the subjects in his kingdom. But alas, he is alone and without any assistant! The ignorance of some of the citizens, lack of knowledge and experience on the part of some of the ministers and governmental officials, designs of some absolutists, . . . corrupt individuals, and the two neighboring governments seeking to advance their own infested schemes in order to penetrate Iran with their commercial goods, through some traitors, these factors all combine to prevent His Majesty the king of Iran from executing the law willingly and wholeheartedly so that we would not be considered among the uncivilized and absolutist nations. We beseech His Majesty Our Father to support his subjects wholeheartedly and enthusiastically, to abort the schemes of our neighbors, and to let history remember him for his good name forever.

In the course of what we have said so far, it has become evident that rules and regulations pertaining to human beings fall into two categories: one relates to God Almighty, and is a spiritual matter having to do with faith and religion; the other relates to the person of the ruler, and is a material issue having to do with temporal concerns. And since the parameters of those laws pertaining to God are circumscribed in such regulations as "mutual and unilateral obligations,"[2] that is, religious duties, contracts, rules of inheritance, judgments, debts, wills, marriage and divorce, testimonies, and so forth, then such criteria must also be established for the duties and responsibilities of the ruler. This is necessary so that the subjects are aware of the exact nature of their obligations, and able to strive to abide by them.

As for divine laws and punishments, they are of concern to God and His obedient servants. As we pointed out, it is the great honor of the prophets and the divine emissaries to propagate God's commandments, which they have received through revelation or inspiration, and to disseminate them among their respective communities. God's chief sacred purpose is the perfection of souls, the advancement of character, and the attainment of that state in which *My servant heed me so that I make you like me!* (Sacred Tradition, *Ḥadīth Qudsī*). The obedient creature is therefore to strive in this world in order to achieve salvation in the world to come: *This world is the field [to cultivate, and harvest] in the next* (Prophetic Tradition).

Now, so far nobody has encroached upon such religious duties in any national assembly or any article of the laws of constitutional rule. Nor has any nation been prohibited from practicing its religiously mandated duties. Quite to the contrary, every state supports, financially and otherwise, its subjects, and propagates their religion by constructing temples, mosques, and churches.

As for social transactions, Muslim people, and particularly the Shi'ites, are not in need of any law, because thank God all the rules of transactions, whether primary or secondary, universal or particular, are derived from the sacred *sharī'a*, and it is not necessary to establish anything new. What is crucial is that the *sharī'a* be executed without being hampered by personal ends or concerns, and without its due process being aborted by external pressures, such as personal gains, whimsical satisfactions, or contradictory judgments, as these would lead to intensified hostility, destruction of personal property, trampling of individual rights, harassment of the orphans and the needy, decline of the religious endowments, and would cause social unrest. Thus the execution of law should be generally so that no judge is able to work his way around it with trickery and strategem, and the elite and the masses alike benefit from its application.

So far, no national assembly has ever decreed the terms of commercial transactions to be applied to marriage, or those of alimony to leasing regulation, divorce to property registration, . . . nor that the thief or the criminal or the murderer or the rebel not be punished. . . .

As for the duties and responsibilities of the subjects towards their ruler, it is quite evident that every human being, according to, *Man was created weak* (Qur'ān 4:28), is not independently capable of defending himself against violations of his rights. The existence of a superior authority is inevitable in every human community, so that under the majestic presence of that leader the subjects may live in peace. The leader protects them with justice and fairness against plunder, antagonism, theft, and discrimination, thus establishing and securing the foundations of peace and prosperity, the continuity of their livelihood, and the protection of their lives, honor, property, and children. This leader, having consulted intelligent people in his realm, should constitute some sort of law—according to the contemporary exigencies, reputation of the country, and organization of the society—under one political and social rubric or another, and rule accordingly. He should protect the rights and responsibilities of both himself and his subjects, and rule in peace and with authority. Today sovereignty is of two kinds: (i) absolutist and tyrannical, and (ii) constitutional, that is to say, government with deliberation and consultation. . . .

Our country is rich in natural resources, such as iron, copper, lead, silver, gold, oil, coal, and so forth. But because of the lack of expertise and confidence they are all left useless under the ground, and we Iranians live in abject poverty and despair. If Iranians knew the exact meaning of wealth, they would inevitably strive to attain it. But since they are in want of law, expertise, industry, schools, and teachers, and because they lack guidance, support, means and mobilizers, they have no wealth. They are engaged in nothing but superstition, pomposity, and futile activity. They do nothing but smoke opium in teahouses and listen to the stories of Rustam[3] and Ḥusayn the Kurd.[4] They have no profession but begging, or being dervishes and wasting their time with Sufism. From the paper on which they write their Qur'ān to the shroud in which they bury their dead, they need the infidel and the foreign nations. They import everything, from clothes to household appliances. Iranians would not be in need of foreign imports, were they to manufacture and be content with their own goods such as: the fabrics of Isfahān, the velvet of Kāshān, the silk of Khurāsān, the wool of Yazd and Kirmān, the knitwear of Rasht and Gīlān, the carpets of Sulṭānābād and Kurdistān, the lamb skin of Shīrāz and Arabistān [Khuzistān], the chintz of Burūjird, the leather of Hamadān, the silver-looking copper pots of Tehran, the cotten clothes of Māzandarān, and the woolen shawls of Khalkhāl and Āzarbāijān. They would not forfeit seventy five million [*tūmāns*?] a year to foreigners for counterfeit and defecting goods; nor long for commercial shipments and English goods, to arrive in Bandar-i Anzalī, Bushihr, and Ahvāz, and for caravans from Caucasia and Baghdad. . . .

Rulers are of two types: either he is naturally intelligent and prudent, or stupid and tyrannical. If he is of the first type, he can manage his country and prevent it from downfall. If he is of the second type, he will lose control of his kingdom, gradually degrading himself. The administration of the country will slip from his hands, his kingdom will be lost and foreigners will scheme for his land.

You should study and learn from the books of history. Read about Shāh Ṭahmāsp and Sulṭān Ḥusayn of the Safavids, and compare them with Nādir Shāh of Afshār, and see how those two rulers, despite the nobility of their family and their political and financial power, led Iran to its decline with their lack of political and administrative acumen. And how that Kurdish peasant [meaning, Nādir Shāh!] emtpy-handedly, and only with his innate intelligence and political perspicacity, brought Iran, after so many defeats and humiliations, back to its lost glory. . . .

The Meaning of Constitutional Monarchy

In this type of government, the king himself appoints a number of nobles; and people, too, elect a number of representatives. These two assemblies deliberate and act on matters of national significance. They recognize the authority of the king. The responsibilities of the king are: appointing the members of the senate, the officers of the army, the honorific titles, the ministers, and the joint chief of staff; the proclamation of war; the acceptance of peace; and the verification of all bills that the two assemblies under particular circumstances pass.

Whenever ministers or governors disobey their mandates, commit illegal acts or treason, or deviate from their responsibilities, they will be impeached in the assemblies. And if their treason is proved, they will be accordingly punished. Countries that share this kind of government include: The United Kingdom, Germany, Italy, Japan, and other European [*sic*] states. In these countries all matters of national significance are referred to impartial men of wisdom and intelligence and public-spirited representatives. The person of the king is not independent in his administration of the matters of national importance. The enforcement of His Majesty's opinion will have to be verified by the national assembly. His Majesty's opinion will have to be considered among those of the members of the national assembly. Because it has been the considered opinion of the political and social scientists that the intelligence and wisdom of one person cannot sufficiently manage the affairs of the country; and that it is impossible for him to be informed of the major and minor problems of the state; and that without consultation he cannot pass proper judgment. Nor has His Majesty delegated the affairs of the state to a few autocratic ministers who in turn will plunder the people with utmost tyranny and deposit their money in foreign banks. This will lead to nothing but the furthering of the interest of those ministers, the poverty and despair of the subjects, and a bad name for the king. Thus a number of political thinkers have made the nation the king's equal and supporter so that they can assist him in matters of national concern. But this is achieved under certain conditions, chief among which is the establishment of equality and the institutionalization of justice . . . so that a right opinion is abiding even if it comes from a peasant or a sailor, and a wrong opinion is dismissed even if it is issued from the king or the prime minister. . . .

No king or governor can exact a penny from a subject other than the established taxes. Yet since government and state cannot operate without an army or a bureaucracy, and because these need money, then there must inevitably be an annual revenue, whether it is called tax or otherwise, to be collected by state officials in order to pay for such governmental expenses. These must be paid collectively because they are for the general welfare of the people and the protection of the national borders. But the exact figure of this tax must be calculated by experts with particular attention to the necessary expenditure of the state. . . .

In short, the innumerable violations perpetrated in an absolutist state are restricted, nay completely eliminated, in a Constitutional government. Having collected a certain amount of money, in proportion to its needs and with equity and justice, the state shall also be very cautious in expending it. It will not pay undeserved salaries to anybody. Nor will it give improper governorship, status, position, or titles to anybody. . . . Nor will anybody be dismissed from his position unless and until his crime or treason has been proven. . . .

Such just and equitable laws and regulations will attract people to their government, bring the state and the people closer together, induce unity, create security in the country, and lead to the establishment of beneficial schools and industries. Every year, thousands of our children will be educated and lead an intelligent and prosperous life, and they will not be forced to buy their food, beverages, clothes, and carpets from the infidels and import them from the outside. With the advancement of ideas and sciences, railroads will be constructed in the country. Underground resources will be discovered; factories will be opened; commerce and agriculture will prosper; and in a short time, wealth will be generated among the people. And with an increase in national wealth, commercial transactions will be created in the country, and the financial power of the state will increasingly grow, and that will lead to a more powerful army and navy; border posts will be strengthened, and the citizens of this country will be respected in foreign lands. . . .

It follows from what we have said that rules pertaining to government have nothing to do with the rules and obligations of the Sacred Law; and that they are not in opposition to the Sacred Law in any major or minor way, but are instead entirely like the "specification of subjects."[5] Now, as to the truth and inevitability of the major premise—i.e., the preservation of Islam, the permanence of the Shi'ite faith, and the continuity of the Shi'ite government—this is evident to every intelligent or ignorant person. As to the minor premise—i.e., what kind of ideas and theories, mechanisms and procedures today are more conducive to the permanence of the Shi'ite faith and the continuity and prosperity of the Shi'ite government—that is a real question whose assessment is up to the spiritual leaders and the experts in political and social issues. Thus the propagation of such ideas and theories, mechanisms and procedures, and the establishment and execution of such laws is not contradictory to the sacred *sharī'a*. To accept or reject the validity of such laws has nothing to do with religious beliefs. Thus Constitutionalism is not in any way a religion among other religions. For example, if someone were to say that today a railroad is necessary for the prosperity of the country, or that a textile factory is needed in Iran so that Muslims will not have to buy shrouds for their dead from the infidels, . . . it is ludicrous to say that this person is of the railroad persuasion or that his religion is textile factory. . . ! Similarly, if the majority of people were to say that the intervention of His Majesty in matters of national significance will have to be in accordance with the rules of justice, and in such a way that judicious people will approve, that he should not be a tyrant, and that he should not delegate the administration of the country to a few misguided and unjust governors—whose injustices induce their wretched subjects to leave their country and emigrate to foreign lands—it would not be fair to distort their rightful opinion and suggest that they are corrupted infidels.

At any rate, absolutist government, tyrannical violation, and arbitrary actions in this day and age will lead nowhere except to the decline, humiliation, poverty, and desperation of the state and the people. . . . Consider the present situation of the Iranian, Ottoman, Chinese, and Turkish states, and compare them with their past! You will see how they have lost their past glory. . . .

The benefits of Constitutional monarchy are world-conquest, nurturing of the subjects, increase in political power, security of the country, growth of the population, consolidation of kingship, and wealth and dignity. Compare the past and present of the Europeans! You will see how the most ill-behaved people of the world have become well-mannered; how the barbarians have become civilized; how the inferiors have become dignified; how the naked animals of America have put on the dress of respectability, honor, wealth, and industry; how the bandits and thiefs of the British Isles have attained dignity, power, majesty, and honor . . . and how the wild beasts of Japan roam with the air of power and strength. . . .

Absolutist monarchy has declined, great progress has appeared in Constitutional monarchy; and the latter has not reached this state other than through the establishment and execution of law. On this law is founded the achievement of justice, equality, propagation of knowledge, establishment of schools, industry, . . . arms, . . . and electricity, ... Today, victory in battlefields cannot be achieved through the techniques of Kāva,[6] and those of Rakhsh[7] and Rustam, with such instruments as spear, arrow, mace, armor, sling, millstone, and sword, ... Instead, it depends on science. If the muzzle of the cannon is targeted towards the enemy camp according to the science of geometry, then the cannon balls will destroy the enemy even if the gunner is a paralyzed cripple.

Are so many rational, traditional, logical, and perceptual proofs not sufficient for the validity of Constitutional monarchy in Iran? Of course, those who deny this viability are among those *who purchase error at the price of guidance, so their commerce doth not prosper, neither are they guided* (Qur'ān 2:16). And as for the absolutist tyrant, may God grant him salvation: *O God! Guide my people; because they do not know!* (Prophetic Tradition).[8]

On Certain Issues That Are in Need of Elaboration

First, today Constitutional monarchy in Iran is like a tree which has just been planted, or a baby just born of her mother. It will have to be taken care of carefully and protected for quite some time, before it can come to fruition for the Iranians. Thus the Iranians should not be disappointed because of certain disturbances, confusions, or debates. Such events are part of any change from . . . one situation to another. The departure of absolutism and arrival of Constitutionalism is like the spring succeeding the autumn: green leaves will not grow unless the yellow leaves have fallen down; rains of mercy will not pour down unless there are clouds and thunder . . . .

It is incumbent upon us to strive for our own rights, as well as for the comfort of our children, and not be intimidated by these disruptions. We should not be disappointed, but do our best to establish this Constitution. Whenever Constitutionalism has been established in any government, such events, or even worse, have appeared perforce. Blood has been shed and properties plundered before Constitutionalism was established and disseminated. Study European history so that you can see how much those brave and courageous patriots suffered before they achieved their goals. But the Iranians have gained this treasure without any pain . . . for which they have to be grateful, and ask God's benedictions for His late Majesty Muẓaffar al-Dīn Shāh. We must also pray day and night in the month of Ramaḍān for the continuity in the rule and kingdom of His Sacred Majesty Muḥammad 'Alī Shāh Qājār, may God lengthen his life and perpetuate his kingdom and sovereignty, who has recorded this reputation in history. *O God! Protect him with your ever-vigilant eyes, and annihilate his enemies completely!*

Second, the laws of the Iranians must be in conformity with rules of the sacred law; and whatever is in opposition to rules of the Sacred Law should not be recognized as law, nor executed. It is politically necessary that a concise law be drafted and executed for a specified period of time in customary (*'urf*)[9] matters with particular reference to the existing conditions of the Iranians. After the Iranians are accustomed to the rule of law, and have savored the sweet taste of justice, security, . . . and equality . . . then it would be appropriate for them to constitute a detailed law, or add to what they already have, with specific reference to their contemporary conditions. If they then wish to translate and act according to the European law in its entirety, the following two problems will arise. First, many European laws are against the sacred *sharī'a*, and certainly the Iranians will not abide by them. Second, the Europeans have established and lived according to the law for some seven hundred years. They have ammended and perfected their laws according to their specific national vicissitudes. It is also for quite some time that they have grown accustomed to and recognized the advantages of the rule of law, so that they now live happily and enthusiastically under its restrictions and demands. But how can the Iranians, who for six thousand years have lived barbarously like unbridled camels, be told to abandon their former habits and act in such a way that will immediately, not gradually, lead them from tyranny and barbarism to the highest degree of civilization? The execution of the European laws in Iran would therefore have no rationale, religious or otherwise. Should it be argued that in Iran we presently lack the necessary expertise to draft our own law, and that we cannot but translate the laws of the Europeans, then I shall humbly suggest that, first of all, the Qur'ān, the Traditions of our Imams, peace be upon them, and the books of Shi'ite jurists, may the blessings of God Almighty be upon them, contain all religious, customary, political, and civil laws. It is very easy to collect and classify them. Second, if for the lack of time or for any other reason, this task cannot be undertaken, a selected number of European laws that are not in opposition to religious principles should be translated and legislated. Attention should also be paid to the details, not to overdo them, however, in such a way that people are so unduly overburdened that they give up the whole idea.

Third, given the essence of the sacred National Assembly, which requires every law to be constituted through consultation, voting, and the consensus of all, or that of the majority, the following three conditions must be observed. First, the prerequisite of consultation is that intelligent people consult with each other, and not the ignorant with the ignorant or the intelligent with the ignorant, because nothing will come of the latter two cases. Thus, all the representatives without any exception must be knowledgeable of what is good and what is bad for the general public, of the principles according to which the borders of the country must be protected, of how to protect the general interest of the kingship, and of the overall responsibilities of the state. They should also be knowledgeable in political matters, thorough on customary (*'urfī*) issues, and acquainted with religious (*sharʿī*) questions, as the objective is to bring the laws into conformity with the rules of the *sharīʿa.* Second, taking the vote of all, or that of the majority, is contingent upon all the representatives, without any exception, being men of firm opinion and independent judgment, capable of both approval and rejection, insightful, quick-witted, and open-minded. If the majority lack independent judgment and opinion, or if this faculty is restricted to just five or ten or a selected group, then Consensus or majority vote is invalid and meaningless. Third, Consensus or majority vote necessitates both the completion of the total number of representatives stipulated by the law, and their actual presence in the sacred National Assembly when it convenes. Otherwise, there will be no quorum. . . . If any of these requirements are not met, the responsibility of the sacred Assembly has not been fulfilled, and its legislations cannot be . . . binding. Thus all the representatives must be civilized, mature, wise, intelligent, knowledgeable, quick-witted, fair, open-minded, pious, just, eloquent, and courageous. They should not pursue their own interests and passions but devote their energies to the public interest, and to the security and prosperity of the country, so that through their exalted efforts the general welfare of the public is served in the best way possible.

Since the responsibility of the sacred National Assembly is legislation, and since law is to be universally applicable . . . , the representatives of every city are to be present in the sacred National Assembly, and no National Assembly should convene in any city other than Tehran. However, as I shall explain presently, in every city there must be a council (*anjuman*) of professional groups.

Fourth, in every city there should not be more than one council, for which every professional group (*ṣinf*) of people elects a representative. The members of this council in turn select one of their own as president. They will also select a member whom they dispatch to Tehran as their representative to the National Assembly. Whenever necessary, every constituency should refer to its own local council (*anjuman-i baladī*). The members of the council, in turn, refer to their representative in Tehran, who should keep them informed of the activities of the National Assembly. The members of the local council report these activities to their constituency. No constituency should bypass the local council and directly contact their national representative. Should they do so, the directives issued by the representative will be contrary to the priorities of the local constituency, and as such will not be implemented but instead cause confusion and rebellion. However, if a constituency has a complaint against its own local council, then their direct contact with their representative is justified. No more than one representative should be dispatched from a city to Tehran, because, the larger the number of their representatives, the more disagreement will arise among them. . . . The sparks from this flame could even gradually reach the capital and disrupt the activities of the sacred National Assembly. . . .

Fifth, the formation of a council in every city is absolutely necessary. In this council, no more than one representative should participate from each professional group. The benefits of such councils are indeed innumerable: many people from different walks of life come to know each other, their differences are dissolved, their ideas unified, inspirations shared; affinity, kindness, and comradeship appear among them and cause them to be more public-spirited. . . . This shall make them more experienced for the second round of elections, so that they elect representatives who are knowledgeable and have been actually tested.

Sixth, the patriotic and pro-Constitution representatives must have a good reputation and be independently wealthy. They should be truly devoted to their country and the sacred Assembly. . . .

Seventh, His Sacred Majesty, the King of Iran, is today the crowned ruler, magnanimous father, protector, and sympathizer of this uncivilized nation. It is incumbent upon every single individual to observe the high level of his dignity and status. Whether openly or secretly, publicly or privately, in gatherings or from the pulpits, he should not in any way be insulted or talked about impolitely. Certain accusations cannot in any way be levelled against him. So far, whatever people have requested from his court, His Majesty has generously granted. But we beseech His Sacred Majesty to support his subjects not only verbally but genuinely and in deed, and to provide them with executive power. This unification of the two will grant monarchy its proper dignity, protect the rights of the nation, and expediate the prosperity of the country and the progress of the state.

Eighth, the responsibility of every minister is to execute the rules pertaining to their respective ministries. They should not give special consideration to anybody or anything, nor should they heed any special request, nor should they fear anyone. . . .

Ninth, in every town a fully qualified and just *mujtahid* should be appointed to supervise and attend to matters covered by the *sharī'a*. If there is no fully qualified *mujtahid* in a city, a just *'ālim* must be designated. But if his justice cannot be ascertained, either through election or by ballot, one of the *'ulamā'* must be chosen as the authority in the Sacred Law. As for customary matters (*umūr-i 'urfiyya*), they fall under the jurisdiction of the Ministry of Justice, which shall attend to them according to the [secular] law.

Tenth, the honor of every group of people and the dignity of every individual are to be respected by everybody, because these are among the chief benefits of Constitutional government. The respected members of the National Assembly, the honorable ministers, the exalted officers of the military, the venerable religious authorities, the noble and honorable princes, the reputable tradesmen, and other dignified merchants, they all must be respected according to their rank and position. Their honor and dignity must be observed. They should not in any way be slandered. . . .

Eleventh, there is absolutely no doubt about the fundamental beliefs of the Muslim nation. . . . It is absolutely a blasphamous sin to debase the religious doctrines, or ridicule the way of the Twelver Shi'ism . . . , or to insult the religious authorities, deride the pious, or slander the Muslims. As we pointed out earlier, the only right religion today is Islam, as God Almighty has said: *Lo! the religion with Allāh (is) Islam* (Qur'ān 3:19). And in another verse: *This day have I perfected your religion for you [and completed My favour unto you,] and have chosen for you as religion AL-ISLAM* (Qur'ān 5:3). Further: *And whoso seeketh as religion other than Islam it will not be accepted from him* (Qur'ān 3:85). The import of this sacred verse is the designation of Islam as the universal religion. . . . Consequently, no Muslim, and no Twelver Shi'ite, should ever speak of freedom of religion, because matters pertaining to religion are quite restricted. The religious obligations of the believers are equally clear, and the law in this particular regard is the Qur'ān. Constitutionalism, as we have pointed out, has to do with customary matters (*'urfiyyāt*) and those pertaining to the obligations of monarchy. Indeed, such matters as enjoining justice and fairness, forbidding tyranny and prejudice, prohibiting gambling, admonishing drinking, curbing the propaganda of the absolutists, and eliminating corruption are all necessary, and with specific stipulations fall under the domain of "enjoining the good and prohibiting the evil."

Twelfth, nowadays the best kind of commerce and trade is to obtain such concessions as railroads, mining, and setting up factories. These are of utmost benefit and advantage because by having a job, the poor will become independent and the rich more wealthy. The beggers will be employed and rescued from destitution. Long distances will be shortened. . . . People will become rich, the state dignified, the country prosperous, and the wretched happy. . . .

Thirteenth, it is necessary and beneficial to establish educational and professional schools in every city. Today the Iranians should do their utmost in this regard, so that innocent children, and poor orphans, will not waste their precious lives on street corners—gambling, horsing around, playing marbles, and flying pigeons;[10] and so that when they grow up and get married, their profession will not be that of a begger, porter, or a thief. . . .

Fourteenth, there are many private religious endowments in Iran instituted by the state or the public. but, alas, their administrators treat these endowments as their property, and when they pass away they are considered as inheritance and as such transferred to their inheritors. The unfortunate donor's will is not acted upon even though his heirs have been deprived. . . . The deeds of endowment are often torn up, the status of the endowment is obliterated and it is sold as lawful property. . . . Thus, in order to preserve the principle of the religious endowments, as well as their proceeds after the deduction of the expenditures, a pious and just person should be appointed to supervise them in every city. All religious endowments—whether they are instituted by the state or the public—should be recorded in official registers. The superviser, with the permission of a *mujtahid*, should see to it that the specific purpose of the donors are in fact carried out. If there is an extra income from these endowments for which no expenditure has been specified, he should spend some of it on educational and professional schools for poor and orphaned children so that they can become educated and learn a profession. The rest should be sent to Tehran to be put in the national treasury of the religious endowments. With this money, an army of fifty thousand armed soldiers should be organized and be stationed on the borders in order to protect the country. Thus, not only the wishes and privileges of the donors and the beneficiaries of religious endowments have been attended to, but the proceeds, which used to be plundered, are spent on social and beneficial matters of general use to all Muslims and thus Islam itself. Since the action and participation of the supervisors are with the permission of the *mujtahids* in accordance with the *sharī'a*, there will be no dilemma. Moreover, because the conduct of the administrator is supervised under the principle of "the administration of the endowment being contingent upon just conduct,"[11] should a breach of trust occur, the administrator will be removed and a substitute appointed so that nobody can complain of any foul play.

Fifteenth, no wealth will be generated for this nation unless the development of this country is advanced by the construction of railroads, the establishment of factories, the excavation of underground resources, and the acquisition of knowledge of commerce and agriculture. These cannot be achieved without confidence in and security from the state; and this security cannot be attained other than through the use of three separated powers: the legislative, the judicial, and the executive. As for the legislative power, which is to establish and amend laws, it is the prerogative of the National Assembly in matters pertaining to the national budget; and in other matters it is divided among His Majesty the King, the House of Representatives, and the Senate. That is to say, each one of these three powers can draft a law, but its establishment is contingent upon its conformity to the rules of the Sacred Law, the ratification of both houses, and the signature of His Imperial Majesty. As for the judicial power, whose function is the recognition of rights, it is the prerogative of the religious courts in religious matters (*shar'iyyāt*), and that of the courts of the Ministry of Justice in customary matters (*'urfiyyāt*). As for the executive power, which is to execute the laws and regulations, it is the prerogative of the king, in whose name and under whose command the ministers and governmental officials should perform their tasks. . . .

These three powers should always be separated to bring about wealth, prosperity, and the security of the community; and whatever anarchy, poverty, impotence, and depression of commerce and agriculture exist in a country is due to the mixing of these three powers.

Some friends who were kind enough to visit my humble residence occasionally asked me about the completion of this book. In all humility I responded that it is finished. It was their esteemed wish that I should not let this book be buried in oblivion like my other writings, and that it should be published for the benefit of the young and old. . . . I accepted their heartily spoken words as fatherly admonitions and proceeded to have this book published and distributed. The benefits of this book cannot be overstated. Suffice it to say that no book has been published on Constitutionalism which is more useful to inform the learned and the ignorant, the young and the old, of the benefits of Constitutional government.

There is nothing more left to be said, and here I shall drop my pen. *O God Almighty! Save our king, assist our religious scholars, protect our representatives and ministers, purify our aspirations, render our objectives attainable, and facilitate our duties! By the infalliable Prophet and his family!*

Written in the blessed month of Shawwal 1325 [November-December 1907], in the capital city of Tehran. Published in the Royal Printing House.

Book of Admonition to the Heedless and Guidance for the Ignorant

(Kitāb Tadhkirat al-Ghāfil va Irshād al-Jāhil)
by
Shaykh Faḍl Allāh Nūrī

When an innovation appears in this world, it is imcumbent upon the man of knowledge to demonstrate his wisdom; otherwise the curse of God shall be upon him.

The Book of Admonition to the Heedless and Guidance for the Ignorant

In the Name of God, the Merciful, the Compassionate

All praise belongs to Him. And then, this humble servant of the binding Muḥammadan Law (*shar'*) wishes to bring to the attention of brothers in religion and friends in spirit that, although the preservation of the worldly order is in need of law (*gānūn*),[12] and the affairs of every nation (*mullat*) that has entered the realm of law and acted accordingly are regulated on the basis of the governance of their law, it is clear to all believers that the best of all laws is the Divine Law. This needs no proof for the Muslims. Fortunately, we the Shi'ite sect have the best and most comprehensive Sacred Law, because it is the Law revealed by God to His noblest Messenger and the Seal of His Prophets: *This day have I perfected your religion for you and completed My favor unto you* (Qur'ān 5:3).

Alas, our people have never been interested in getting to know this Law, despite the fact that it contains whatever a people needs. It is as if we have become particularly fond of ignorance. Furthermore, it is obvious that our Divine Law is not limited to acts of worship but, on the contrary, embraces every major and minor political issue, down to the indemnity for a minor abrasion. Consequently, we will never be in need of man-made law, especially in view of the fact that we are Muslims and must organize our worldly affairs in such a way as not to disturb our situation in the Day of Judgment. Thus the requisite law can only be the Divine Law, because of its dual orientation, that is, because it regulates both this and the other world. Anyone who thinks it is possible and feasible for a group of wise and judicious men and a number of politicians to come together and, through consultation, make a law that meets these two objectives and is also acceptable to God, is obviously not a Muslim. There cannot be Islam without the acceptance of Prophethood and the acceptance of Prophethood is not conceivable without rational proof. The rational proof of Prophethood is no other than our need for such a Divine Law, and our ignorance and incapacity to determine it ourselves. If we consider ourselves capable of creating this Law, we would then have no rational proof of Prophethood. A person who thinks that historical exigencies alter or complement some elements of that Divine Law is outside of the Islamic creed. Our Messenger is the Seal of the Messengers, and his Law is the completion of all sacred laws. And the "seal" is the person to whom has been revealed whatever is right for the believer until Doomsday; and he has thus perfected the religion. Believing in the possibility of perfecting the Divine Law is therefore obviously in opposition to the fundamental belief in the perfection and completeness (*khātimiyyat*) of the Prophet's religion. And challenging this completeness is a sin, according to the Divine Law. . . .

Thus imposing man-made law, whether in general or in particular, is contrary to Islam, and legislation is the prerogative of a Messenger. It is for this reason that every time a Messenger was appointed it was to bring a Law. Consequently, every time a new Prophet appeared he reaffirmed some of the previous Laws and superseded others, until the Seal of the Prophets, may God's benedictions be upon him and his family, was appointed and expressed God's religion completely. Consequently, he is the Seal of the Prophets, and the Divine Law that he has brought will never be deficient, even in relation to all times and all peoples. This is according to the Revelation and not because of any personal opinion: *Nor doth he speak of (his own) desire. It is naught save an inspiration that is inspired* (Qur'ān 53:3-4). . . .

The inference is that the Muslim has no right to legislate (*ja'l-i qānūn*). By God! I could never believe that somebody could actually sign a man-made law, and accept anything but the Divine Law for the Islamic country, or that anyone could consider the exigencies of our time in opposition to some elements of the Divine Law, and yet profess to the completeness and perfection of the religion of Muḥammad, may God's benediction be upon him and his family.

Yes, if an individual wanted to establish a rule in his personal affairs, its acceptance or rejection is not up to anybody else, as its domains do not extend to include the general public, except when it involves a prohibition to which the principle of "forbidding the evil" in the Divine Law becomes applicable. Consequently, should the ruler of Islam (*sulṭān-i Islām*) graciously decide to issue a directive for the conduct of his officials in order to prevent the oppression of his subjects—and this only in matters of minor importance—it would be very good for everybody and every locality. But its ratification and execution is not related to the function of the General Deputies (*nuvvāb-i 'āmm*) [i.e., of the Hidden Imam], or of the Proofs of Islam (*ḥujjaj-i Islām*) [i.e., the religious authorities]. The latter's function is restricted to the derivation of the general commandments (*aḥkām*)—that are the substance of the Divine Law—from its four sources, and their communication to the masses. The four sources are: the Qur'ān, the Traditions, Consensus (*ijmā'*), and Reason (*'aql*). Furthermore, this function has to be performed according to the prescribed procedure, the chief procedural rule being the avoidance of analogy (*qiyās*)[13] and discretionary approval (*istiḥsān*)[14] in their derivations, as the determination of divine commandments through analogy and discretionary approval is forbidden in Shi'ite Sacred Law.

Consequently, regarding the parliament, people wanted to establish, in order to follow their natural disposition and make laws according to majority vote, if their objective were to make (*ja'l*) new laws—and indeed this body was being called "legislative"—even disregarding the problem of validating its propriety, it was in opposition to the profession of the Prophethood [of Muḥammad] and the completeness and perfection of our religion. And if the objective were to institute law (*qānūn*) in accordance with the *sharī'a*, first of all, this was not at all within the jurisdiction of that group and fell completely outside the limits of their responsibility; secondly, it was a case of rational discretionary approval (*istiḥsān-i 'aqlī*), and as such prohibited (*ḥarām*). If their objective were to make laws for minor matters regarding the functioning of the government officials, it would in no way include matters of general concern (*umūr-i 'āmma*),[15] that falls under the authority of the religious lawmaker (*shāri'*). In which case, why did they invoke the names of the Qur'ān and the *sharī'a*; and why did they seek the stamp of approval from the Proofs of Islam? And why did they call anybody who opposed this legislation the adversary and enemy of the Hidden Imam? Finally, if their objective were to determine, execute, and resuscitate the Divine Law, what do the masses (*'avāmm*) and different groups have to do with this matter, and why were they being consulted on "matters of general concern"? Why did they [i.e., the legislators] never mention anything about the justifying proofs from the Sacred Law? In cases of opposition, why did they attack whoever dared to raise the question of compatibility of laws with the *sharī'a*?

My dear brother! If their intention were the implementation of Divine Law, and if the purpose of Constitutionalism were to preserve the Islamic commandments, why did they want to base it on equality and freedom, as each of these pernicious principles is the destroyer of the fundamental foundation of the Divine Law? The foundation of Islam is obedience, not freedom; and the basis of its commandments it the differentiation of collectivities and the assemblage of the different elements, and not on equality.

Consequently, in obedience to Islam, we should consider equal whoever is considered equal in the Divine Law; and treat differently every group that is differentiated from every other. This must be done in order to avoid religious and worldly corruptions. Do you not know that equality necessitates, among other things, that the misguided and misleading groups be treated with similar respect as the Shi'ite sect, whereas the Divine Law makes the execution of the apostates incumbent, their wives irrevocably divorced from them, and their property transferable from their inheritors to Muslims! Their corpse commands no respect, requires no ritual washing, no shroud, no prayers, no burial, and their body is impure. All commercial transactions with them are prohibited and annulled; and their work requires no compensation. As for the Jews, the Christians, and the Zoroastrians, they have no right to retribution [in response to injury by a Muslim]; and their blood money is eight hundred dirhams.

If the purpose had been the execution of the Divine Law, they would not have demanded equality between Muslims and infidels, would not have intended to eliminate so many distinctions that separate different groups in the Divine Law, and would not have designated "equality" as the law of their land. In view of the fact that any change in the Islamic commandment is the prerogative of the Messenger through revelation, and that only so long as the Seal of the Messengers had not been appointed, then you who wish to be considered equal to the Muslim in the Islamic land become a Muslim. . . . Otherwise, by the command of Almighty Creator you will be debased and oppressed in the Islamic land. Since no retribution is exacted with force and tyranny from a Muslim for the blood of an infidel, what is it that allows changing the Divine Law, and making a law against it, even for one instance? Opposing the Divine Law with one's act is a sin; but changing it is infidelity, as it implies that the Divine Law is inappropriate for this age. So you who have sought equality and wanted to make it the law, if you are claiming to be a prophet, or if you are denying Prophethood altogether, or are finding the commandments of the Messenger mistaken—upon him and his family be the benedictions of the Almighty—then say it outright so that I can rest my case.

My dear brother! Do you not know that for many reasons freedom of the press and freedom of speech are opposed to the Divine Law?

Do you not know that its result is that the infidels and heretics can propagate their blasphemies in their speeches and papers, insult the believers and denounce them, and implant doubts in the pure hearts of the wretched masses? My dear, if the ultimate concern of this inauspicious and mischievous principle were not to grant absolute freedom, then why were the sheets of blasphemy not censured? Every journal was filled with accusations against Islam and the Muslims; no governmental organ was void of infidelity. Had it not been for "freedom," that damned, cursed, heretic Jamāl,[16] and that deceitful Fakhr al-Kufr and their likes[17] would not have spread so many blasphemies from their pulpits, in their gatherings, and in their papers. And people would not have listened to that heretic [Sayyid Jamāl Vā'iẓ] as if they were dead wood. . . . Alas, the stupidity of people!

My dear! Had "freedom" not been granted, that villain would not have denied so many truths in public. He would have not, for example, said, "People! Demand your rights! Nobody mints any coin in the Day of Judgment. The Mullahs have just made this up. . . ." That heretic would not have dared to write that the pillars of Islam are two: Unity (*tawḥīd*), which means unification and concord, and Justice (*'adl*), which means equality. That other would not have said that religious tax (*zakāt*) is only required on the four grains, and nothing more . . . ; and that accursed Ṣūr[18] would not have written that appeal to any kind of honorific title is tantamount to polytheism. Nor would they have said that that house of sin, nay blasphemy, [i.e., the Majlis] is as sacred as the exalted Mecca . . . ; nor would that infidel have said that the law is as sacred as the Qur'ān; nor would that unbeliever have written in the paper that we have to act according to the Qur'ān and today this law is our Qur'ān, and the Majlis our Ka'ba, or that one should be faced in its direction in the moment of death.[19] Oh may God shut up your mouth!

Had it not been for "freedom," that usurer, who is said to have murdered others and committed suicide, would not have been referred to as a martyr in Muslim gatherings. Blasphemies would not have been uttered in his eulogy, nor the religious authorities of the past insulted, nor the most sacred principles of Islam openly desecrated. Woe unto us Muslims! They would have respected our lord and master Abu'l-Faḍl[20] and that very epiphany of piety, the Commander of the Faithful ['Alī] . . . , would have considered Shi'ism their honor . . . . , and would not have paid the highest price for ['Abd al-Raḥīm] Ṭālibof's *Masālik* [*al-Muḥsinīn*],[21] which puts forward the method for the annihilation of Shi'ism.

Had it not been for "freedom," that villain would not have written that the Qur'ānic Law is no longer adequate and that we must make thirty thousand regulations to satisfy the requirements of today's administration. Had it not been for "freedom," so much immorality would not have spread in public places. Had it not been for "equality," they would not have visited the house of the infidels in friendship and consolation; and they would not have uttered those blasphemies from the pulpits. Had it not been for "equality," those heretics would not have killed a few Muslims for the murder of a Zoroastrian. They would not have shouted "Long Live Islam!" while doing this, as in our Divine Law there is absolutely no place for such punishments.[22] Woe unto the misguided action of us Muslims when we take it upon ourselves to defend Islam; that we should hear such patent lies attributed to the infalliable Law-giver and still support that Constitution. Have we not yet understood that this small group of people wanted to change the Law and religion of Islam by fraud and misrepresentation, as that Samaritan [Aaron] destroyed the religion of Moses by first attracting people to the God of Moses, peace be upon him, then saying this calf is that god.[23] The stupid people accepted this. . . .

If this group had no aim but to implement the Divine Law, why was their penal code contrary to the latter? Do not say that it was a state law! As if the state could defy the Divine Law with impunity, considering itself beyond its jurisdiction, make a law and implement it in the country and thus render the Divine Law outmoded. If the purpose were to protect Islam and the Muslims, why then have they turned the Ministry of Justice into the hotbed of such infamous individuals, and why did they appoint that godless, faithless, scurrilous person a judge? . . .

My dear! If the purpose [of Constitutionalists] were to enforce Islam, England would not have supported it. And if they wanted to act according to the Qur'ān, they would not have deceived the masses, taking refuge in unbelief and considered the English their friends, supporters, and confidants; while there are a number of verses in the Qur'ān that command us not to consider infidels our supporters, friends, or confidants.[24] Who would be so stupid, may I ask, to believe that infidelity would support Islam, that this Christian Malkam[25] would be such a supporter of Islam and call for Islamic justice, whose very foundation, incidentally, is the differentiation of rights of individuals? Yes, he would support justice as "equality" and "freedom": the two principles upon which tyranny (*ẓulm*) is established. . . .

My dear! If the purpose were to preserve the *sharī'a*, they would not have said that they wanted a Constitution (*mashrūṭa*), but would not permit the word *mashrū'a* [i.e., according to the *sharī'a*] be put next to it. If the enforcement of Islam were in this endeavor, why were individuals known for their piety, asceticism, and faith, as well as the

Islamic principles themselves, being ridiculed and debased, while the benighted sects and the atheists of all kinds became bold and powerful, and the signs of unbelief became manifest? And why would they glorify Zoroastrianism and the ancient Persian kings in their journals—considering them, who were the scum of all nations, a noble race? Why would they not ban so many blasphemy-ridden journals that weakened the faith of the Muslims? . . . .

My dear wretched brother! You should know that the truth of Constitutionalism is that the representatives of the provinces, as elected by the subjects themselves, gather in the Capital. They constitute the legislative body of the state, look into the contemporary exigencies and draft a law, independently and by the vote of the majority, to legislate whatever appeals to and pleases their majority according to their insufficient intelligence and regardless of compatibility or incongruency with the Sacred Law. The only stipulation is that all articles of the law should be founded on the two inauspicious principles of the "equality" and "freedom" of all the citizens. Other than this, whatever you have heard is sheer lie.

Out of hypocrisy and necessity, they have written in the Constitution that its articles must comply with the Sacred Law. But they have also stipulated that all articles of the Constitution are changeable. Among these articles is the article on the compatibility with the Sacred Law. They have not exempted this article . . . and it is merely to silence us that now they talk about the Sacred Law. . . .

My dear! Have you sworn by the Qur'ān to support such corruptions? Then know that your oath by the Qur'ān to support the Constitution is indeed like your swearing by the Qur'ān to oppose the Qur'ān. The foundation of the Qur'ānic commandments is differences among the groups of individuals, and yet you have sworn by the Qur'ān to support "equality." The basis of the Qur'ān is the circumscription of the pen and the tongue, and yet you have sworn to support giving them "freedom." The Qur'ān has mandated that a Muslim cannot be punished for injuries inflicted against an infidel, yet you have sworn to support the establishment of the rights to such punishment (*qiṣāṣ*) for the infidels. . . .

Should it become evident that you have made a mistake, and what you have sworn to is not religiously sanctioned . . . then you are not bound by that oath. It is forbidden by the Sacred Law to act upon that oath once you realize that you are better avoiding it. The recognition of this mistake does not fall within the domain of "imitation" (*taqlīd*). Thus if a thousand *mujtahids* were to write that the foundations of this Majlis are the "enjoining the good and prohibiting the evil" (*al-amr bi'l-ma'rūf wa'l-nahy 'an al-mankar*), the implementation of the Divine Law, assistance to the oppressed . . . and the protection of Islam, but you see this is not the case, . . . the statement of the *mujtahids* is in no way binding. . . .

Do you not see how Islamic beliefs have been weakened among the people? Do you not know that according to the Divine Law if performing an obligatory act requires forbidden means and a preparatory step (*muqaddima*), then that obligation must not be performed, because what is forbidden cannot be the preparatory step for an obligatory duty. Now, let us suppose what they intended to achieve were an obligatory duty. However, because its consolidation depended upon the dissemination of unbelief and propagation of prohibited immorality, and upon creation of much confusion and anarchy, it was forbidden (*ḥarām*) for us to support it. But alas! Woe unto us who heard them when they said this tree should be watered with blood, and did not admonish them and even supported them on account of the mistakes of some dignitaries.[26]

Why do you people act as if you were ignorant!? It is not up to the religious judge (*hākim-i shar'*) to decide "the specification of the subject" for you.[27] This is your responsibility. If a thousand religious judges were to call this animal a sheep and you knew it was a dog, then you will have to say it is a dog and consider it impure.

My dear! Repent from those oaths that were contrary to the Sacred Law if you are a Muslim. Such oaths and acting according to them is religiously prohibited; and none of the Shi'ite *'ulamā'* has ever sanctioned swearing to do something which is prohibited by the Sacred Law and is the source of religious or temporal corruption. They all say that our Divine Law mandates that such oaths are religiously forbidden. I do not know why you people are so reluctant to learn about the Divine Law which has been given to you Shi'ites!

My dear! Suppose this Constitution were not based on making new laws, which is infidelity (*kufr*). Yet there were those Representatives who would express their opinions about matters of general concern (*umūr-i 'āmma*), that is, matters pertaining to all citizens of the state, and would in fact consider anything other than matters of general concern outside their domain of responsibility. Then why are the members of the Majlis called "representative" (*vakīl*)? Do you not know that in matters of general concern representation (*vikālat*) is impermissible, and that such matters pertain to guardianship according to the Sacred Law (*vilāyat-i shar'īyya*)? That is to say, intervening in matters of general concern and public welfare is the prerogative of the [Hidden] Imam, peace be upon him, or his General Deputies. It is no concern of others. Any other person's intervention in these matters is forbidden (*ḥarām*) and is the usurpation of the seat of the Prophet, upon him be God's salutations and benedictions, and of the [Hidden] Imam, peace be upon him. Have you not heard that our Imams have said that during the period of Occultation corruption will reach a point where those who have no authority to speak on matters of general concern will do so?

My dear! Do you not know that if an unqualified person sits in this seat of authority, it is obligatory to oppose him and forbidden to support him? Do you not know that [the occupation of the seat of authority] by anyone other than the General Deputies is the usurpation of the right of Muḥammad and his House?[28]

My dear! What qualification does the Zoroastrian have for sitting in the seat of authority in matters of general concern!? To make matters worse, what are the infidels—residing in the Islamic realm—and heretical and apostate groups doing in the sacred precinct of such seats of authority!? But what can I do when the first to appear in that Assembly were those very heretical sects [i.e., the Bābīs]? Their enthusiasm was the greatest and they were the strongest members of this movement. Indeed, that Assembly they called the Majlis was good for nothing; its members could not vote against the position of other congregations of unbelief and atheism. In fact, it was quite clear to those who possess insight that the members of the Majlis were being manipulated by these sects.

My dear! When so many rotten fruits are grown on this tree, how can it please the Imam of the Age? Do you think that there is a Muslim left who still doubts the forbiddenness of this Constitution after so many clear indications? . . . . Or that there is an intelligent person who does not know and understand that they will extend this Constitution through its laws to a point where nothing will remain of Islam? Particularly if these new schools and those infidel preachers continue as they have done during the past two years; and some of the present teachers continue to teach in them!? I really do not know what the Islam of those children would be like. . . . All this being the case, I do not think that there is a Muslim left who would doubt the incumbency of annihilating this foundation.

My dear! If you got involved in this matter for worldly ends and thus forgot all about your religious responsibilities, believe me, you made a mistake. Finally, when the Constitutional regime exacts taxes from the subjects and citizens of the state, these are going to be ninety per cent . . . but the tax will be imposed piecemeal and with all kinds of excuses. For example, the city government is going to demand money from you annually under all kinds of rubrics. And every governor, according to the Constitution, is entitled to demand contributions twice a year. The Ministry of Justice, too, is going to collect money in one way or another. And so forth and so on. Consequently, the subject has to suffer and the National Bank has to make a bundle so that their[29] commerce is put in order. All philanthropic activities will be abandoned by law. . . .

My dear! Suppose they wanted to support the Islamic government. Then why did they do so much to weaken the ruler who is the refuge of Islam, even though they had no military power? They have particularly annihilated the army during these two years. Why did they slander the ruler of the Muslims with all kinds of stupid accusations? By God, His Majesty has demonstrated much tolerance, patience, and attention to his subjects! He witnessed so much and remained patient. They did what they did to the honor of the country, and he remained patient. They slandered the religious authorities of today, and he remained patient; they offended the religious authorities of yesterday, and he remained patient. But it is evident that patience is not appropriate in such matters as insulting the religious and doctrinal principles, or conspiring to bring about the annihilation of the Islamic government, especially when it is witnessed that a number of Muslims are indecently executed for having been defiled by killing a Zoroastrian—and this deed is called the Divine Law! But since *evil cannot but return*, and our rights have a powerful protector and a strong guardian, thank God, the king of us Muslims abandoned patience by the command of Islam, and, with utmost dignity demanded the incarceration of a small number of infamous and corrupt individuals. But those corrupted infidels refused.... They killed His Majesty's emissaries with a hand-grenade; they shot innocent people, and erected strong barricades.... His Majesty the king... hesitated long beyond prudence in the hope that these infidels and corrupt groups would abandon this Constitution without antagonism and bloodshed, but they did not. Consequently, with utmost care for the preservation of Muslim lives and, God be praised, with the approval of the guardian of the Muslims [i.e., the Hidden Imam], he destroyed that house of corruption [i.e., the Majlis]..., dispersed its members, and incarcerated the corrupt individuals, or put them under house arrest.[30]

Where is he who ascended the pulpit of the Prophet, may God's salutations be upon him and his family, to say: "O! You people of Iran! The Constitution has arrived according to the law of nature, and nothing can prevent it, as all canons of the world cannot stop nature." Wherever you are, look how four cotton canons with the will of the Creator, the Sustainer, and the Evolver of nature dispersed the elements of that nature to so many pieces that there is no trace of it. . . . Where are those infidels who wanted to implement the laws of the materialists in Iran according to contemporary exigencies, and even those as understood by their half-witted intelligence, and who wanted to educate children "naturally"? Where are those who used to say and write that Iranian children must go through a compulsory education in modern schools, with a new script and in the ancient Pahlavi language so that they would not be able to read those books that religious authorities had written during the Safavid period which caused this inauspicious difference between the Shi'ites and the Sunnites? They argue that it was for political purposes that the Safavids disseminated this division between the Muslims, and the *'ulamā'* fabricated these books for their own interest. It is necessary to destroy these books, because they are the origin of this false division; and there is only one way to achieve this goal, and that is what we have asserted [i.e., changing the script and language and establishing modern schools].

Thank God, before it was possible for you to render these books obsolete, the Master and Lord of us Shi'ites [i.e., the Hidden Imam], with the powerful hand of His Islamic Majesty, annihilated your very foundation and dispersed you all. You infidel liars, I might ask, did any of those religious authorities who wrote during the Safavid period say anything without documenting it!? Then look at [Muḥammad Bāqir] Majlisī's *Baḥār* [*al-Anwār*] and other such books: whatever they have reported is fully documented by their sources; and most of these sources, which are equally acceptable to both Shi'ites and Sunnites had been written nine hundred or a thousand years earlier. These are the impertinences for which God destroyed your House of Parliament. But, thank God, the number of casulties was not as high as it could have been, and the Muslim lives were spared despite the fact that they were protecting the infidels. . . . At present, it is incumbent upon us Muslims to express our gratitude every day and night for this great blessing. We should ask our Creator to perpetuate this victory so that such nonsense and blasphemies are not uttered on the pulpits, in gatherings, and in streets, or published in journals; the sacred precincts of Muslims are not turned into a center for infidels, unbelievers, and hoodlums; people are not induced towards worldly ends from the pulpit; the unbelievers and Muslims are not treated equally as regards rights and punishments in the Islamic country; these vile tongues and pens are not unleashed again; and the Muslims are exalted and the infidels are debased. It is incumbent upon you from now on to study the science of the Divine Law, so that you would know that the Divine Law is sufficient for us, and that it is the best and most complete of all laws.

You poor souls! Get to know the Islamic Law, and act according to it. Be content with the wishes of your Creator, so that you would benefit both in this and in the other world. You Shi'ite *'ulamā'*! Act according to the duties of your servitude to your faith! Your Majesty! You King! You Sovereign! Redouble your protection of the Divine Law and the dissemination of the Islamic justice! And you preachers of the Muslims! No longer accept that lies be attributed to God and the Messenger, God's salutations and benedictions be upon him, from the Messenger's pulpit. It is incumbent upon you to rectify the corruptions of those infidels! You people! Know that ignorant world-seeking individuals have put the eyes and ears of your heart into the sleep of ignorance with craft and diabolical mischief. Nay, they have even robbed you of your physical senses. Open your eyes and listen with your hearts' ears! Distinguish between one who changes things for the better and one who changes things for the worse! Do not be fooled by a few hoodlums and thugs who have gathered together in Tabriz![31] Look into their acts, and do not be so greedy as to expect to harvest wheat from barley seeds.

My Shi'ite brothers! Know and be informed; listen and contemplate: you should set aside the desires of your worldly and carnal soul, which result in nothing but evil, and know that for the disposition of our country Constitutionalism is a fatal disease, a terminal injury. Not only is it contrary to the principles of our Islam, but also our Iran which has three characteristics as a result of which the establishment of Parliament cannot but create unbearable confusion and anarchy. One of these characteristics is the existence of many religions, the other the smallness of the army, and the third the multiplicity of tribes. Foreign countries do not share these three characteristics. Their armies are large and there are no religious divisions, as the multiplicity of their religious sects is unified under the rubric of infidelity. *Because infidels are of one nation.* As a result there is no genuine animosity among their religious sects. As for their tribes, everybody knows that they have all become sedentary. But in our Iran, it is the confrontation between light and darkness—Islam on the one hand, and apostasy and infidelity, on the other—each of these two is constantly at odds with the other. All the different sects in Iran harbor utmost hostility towards a small Twelver minority [*sic*] on whose annihilation and extinction they are bent. Furthermore, it is quite evident that some of these sects are similarly hostile to each other. . . . Therefore, the establishment of this inauspicious Constitution will inevitably lead to such confusion and anarchy in our country that nobody will be able to have control over his life, wealth, dignity, or honor. . . . It is also clear what a small minority the believing Twelver would become. *Verily there are very few people who are with God.* The eventual result will be that no trace of this group will remain. From the true Islam there will remain nothing but a name. Or perhaps there will remain nothing but the name of new heretical sects in Islam [i.e., the Bābīs].

This would be the situation in cities and other inhabited parts of Iran. As for the highways and villages, they will all be closed down and abandoned, because of the insurgence of the tribes and the highway robbers who will surface from every corner. . . .

Yes, if we begin to support the exalted sovereign of our country and, with His Majesty's steadfast determination, prepare an equipped standing army of half million, and have a sufficient number of them stationed in every city, every highway, and every tribe, and have a good number of them assigned as His Majesty's personal guard, then confusion and anarchy may be prevented [despite] the establishment of this Constitution which is in opposition to the Islamic religion.

But you, my brothers, make me wonder why you are not heedful of your future and your salvation in the other world, uprooting yourselves as you do with your own hands! I am even more amazed by the confusion and support of the great residents of Kufah [i.e., Shi'ite religious authorities]. Even more surprising is their calling this circus a holy war and those who have been killed in it martyrs! Their excuse is nothing but what they call tyranny. My dear brothers! Does the removal of tyranny constitute a case for holy war? Who punishes a crime which has not been committed? I do not understand what tyranny can occur which is more important than the annihilation of Islam, massacre of the Muslims, and destruction of these respected properties! Perhaps new revelations have descended upon them! *Because I do not find anything of that sort in what has been revealed to the Messenger.* And most surprising of all, they call opposition to this inauspicious Constitution—this evil tree that must be raised with the shedding of Muslim blood—"waging war against the Imam of the Age!"

By God, I am ashamed by the understanding of a certain European. Although they have advanced nothing but their physical senses and faculties of disputation, and their minds are darkened with thick and multiple covers . . . , that European was still intelligent enough to say this:

> Parliament and the National Consultative Assembly, which to us Europeans is such a precious gem, has been established in this world for almost four hundred years. We have liked this gem, have voluntarily chosen and established it as our creed, and are very proud of it. Now, you Muslims have a creed and a path whose master you call the Imam of the Age; and complying with it is complying with the Imam of the Age and opposing it opposing His Lordship. Your creed is in complete

> opposition to ours. You do not consider us Muslims because we have selected Constitutionalism and do not in any way believe in the creed and path of you Muslims. Recently, you Muslims have decided to implement our creed in your country. Now we are baffled as to why you consider opposition to our creed opposition to your Imam of the Age. It is opposition to your own previous creed [i.e., Shi'ism] that is opposition to your Imam of the Age, and not opposition to Constitutionalism which is our creed.

My dear brothers! Please consider this argument! Perhaps the matter would be clarified for you. You Twelver Shi'ites! Have you not heard and seen enough abominations? Can your Islamic disposition still tolerate these hoodlums running the show? Is it justice that the notables of your nation be trampled on by scoundrels!? Did you see how during the past two years we lost the gift of complete security that we had enjoyed in our cities and highways? Is it appropriate for us to inflict ourselves once more with that calamity and become instruments for the advancement of the ends of these heretical sects? Will you again accept that those blasphemies and distortions of the Qur'ānic verses be spread among the people!?

You believers! You used to exonerate yourselves by arguing: "We were trapped unknowingly." Well, do not let it happen again now! You people of reason! And you protectors of the right path! Do not consent that, on the Prophet's pulpit, so many blasphemies and lies be attributed to God and His Messenger, God's salutations and benedictions be upon him and his family. It is incumbent upon you to rectify the corruptions of those infidels!

You merchants! Do not pursue worldly matters so much! . . . Do not practice usury! . . . You retailers! Do not sell short! Do not mix good and bad merchandise, so you can sell it to your clients undetected! Do not lust after this world so much!

You people! Do not hesitate to attend the public prayers and listen to preaching! Give up the perishable goods, and acquire the everlasting goods! Do not tolerate indecency from your wives and daughters! Do not let them out of the house except with chaste attire; not with these improper veils! Men have strong sexual desires, they are not ascetics. There are many unmarried men on street corners. Where is your manly honor? Women with improper veils are engaged in transactions in the streets and bazaars, and nobody admonishes them. Be fearful of God! Be fearful of calamity! Be fearful of tormenting punishment! You will die! And you will all be accountable! Be mindful of that Day of Judgment, too! You who have believed in God, follow the right path! *We seek protection with God from the evils of ourselves, and from the evils of Satan, and from the evils of all those who have evils.*

Zayn al-'Ābidīn, known as Malik al-Khaṭṭatin (the Master of caligraphers), wrote this treatise, in the year 1326/1908-9.[32]

Notes

1. *Ahl-i ḥall va 'aqd:* "People of loosening and binding," a juridical term meaning those who are familiar with the Qur'ān and the *ḥadīth*, and are of a sound mind.

2. *'uqūd va īqā'āt:* "mutual and unilateral obligations," a juridical term. *'aqd* is a contractual obligation for the implementation of which two parties must consent, e.g., marriage, or a commercial transaction. *īqā'* is a contractual obligation for the implementation of which only one party needs to consent, e.g., divorce and wills.

3. "Rustam," the national hero in the Iranian mythology, immortalized in Firdawsī's (d. 1020) *Shāhnāma;* popularized by public recitation (*naqqālī*) of his heroic deeds.

4. "Ḥusayn the Kurd of Shabastar," popular hero from the Iranian folkloric romances. Stories of his adventures are recited in public gatherings, e.g., in teahouses.

5. *Ta'yyn-i mawḍu'āt* (in contrast to the determination of rules [*aḥkām*]): an activity that can be undertaken by ordinary persons and does not require juristic competence or authority.

6. "Kāva the Blacksmith," a hero in Iranian mythology, immortalized in the *Shāhnāma.* He mobilized a resurgence against Ḍaḥḥāk, the usurper king, and installed Faraydūn, the rightful king, to power.

7. "Rakhsh," Rustam's horse.

8. Prophetic Tradition; very similar to Christ's statement: *Father, forgive them: for they know not what they do* (Luke, 23:34).

9. Khalkhālī persistently distinguishes between "the custom" (*'urf*) and "the Sacred Law" (*shar'*). For him, the Constitutional law falls within the former category.

10. *kabūtar-parānī:* "flying pigeons," a game played in Iran. It involves a very skilled individual who collects a number of pigeons on his roof and trains them to respond to his various commands.

11. *mashrūṭiyyat-i tawliyyat bi-'idālat.* The administrator of the endowment must be a just person, otherwise he is legally prevented from administering the endowment.

12. The word "law" poses a particular problem in this treatise. Shaykh Faḍl Allah uses *shar'* always for "religious law," but *qānūn* sometimes for "civil" or "constitutional" law, and sometimes, as in *qānūn-i ilāhī*, for the Sacred Law. In this translation the uppercase "Law" has been preserved for *sharī'a* or *qānūn-i ilāhī*, and the lowercase "law" for *qānūn*, in the sense of the civil or constitutional law.

13. *Qiyās:* "analogy," is a source of law in Sunni jurisprudence. It is not recognized as valid in Shi'ite jurisprudence. In opposition to *qiyās*, Imam Ja'far al-Ṣādiq (83/702-148/765) is believed to have said: *kana awwalu ma qāsa Iblīs* (The first who analogized was Satan).

14. *Istiḥsān:* "discretionary approval," it has been forbidden in Shi'ite law as a source of juridical injunctions. It postulates the possibility of instituting a new law on the basis of its benefits for the Islamic community, regardless of any specific Qur'ānic or Traditional commandments to that effect.

15. *Umūr-i 'āmma:* "matters of general concern," presumably, those matters pertaining to the General Deputyship (*niyābat-i 'āmma*) of the Hidden Imam.

16. Sayyid Jamāl al-Dīn Vā'iẓ (1279/1862-1326/1908), a famous Constitutionalist preacher who was a Bābī.

17. Shaykh Faḍl Allāh is here referring to a number of the leading Constitutionalist *'ulamā'*, including Mīrzā Fakhr al-Dīn Shaykh al-Islām, Ḥājjī Mīrzā Ibrāhīm, Ḥājjī Mīrzā Ya'qūb, Ḥājjī Muḥammad Ḥusayn, and Mīrzā Ibrāhīm Arbāb, who were the leaders of the movement in Azarbāijan.

18. Jahāngir Khān Ṣur-i Isrāfīl (1292/1875-1326/1908), the founder of *Ṣūr-i Isrāfīl*, a leading Constitutionalist journal. After the bombardment of the Majlis in 1326/1908, Ṣūr-i Isrāfīl was captured and murdered by Muḥammad 'Alī Shāh's police.

19. When a Muslim is in his/her deathbed, he/she should face Mecca.

20. 'Abbās ibn 'Alī, Abu'l-Faḍl (d. 61/680), the fourth son of 'Alī (d. 40/660). He was killed in Karbalā fighting in Ḥusayn's army.

21. *Masālik al-Muḥsinīn*, a book by Hājj Mullā 'Abd al-Raḥīm Ṭālibof (1250/1834-1328/1910), one of the leading reformists during the Constitutional period.

22. Allusion to the execution of the murderers of the Zoroastrian Constitutionalist Arbāb Firaydūn in December 1907. According to the *sharī'a*, as Nūrī points out, they should only have paid eight hundred *dirhams* in blood money for killing a Zoroastrian.

23. Reference to the Qur'ānic passage (20:85f) in which the Jewish Sāmirī had instigated a calf-worshiping sect among the Jews when Moses was on Mount Sinai. The Qur'ānic passage has slight variations with the Biblical

narrative (Exodus 32:1-35) in which Aaron leads the rebellion. In the Qur'ān, Aaron is only admonished by Moses for not being able to prevent the schism.

24. Shaykh Faḍl Allāh has in mind Qur'ān 3:28, 5:51 (similar passages are also found in 4:139, and 4:144, etc.).

25. Mīrzā Malkam Khān Nāẓim al-Dawla (1249/1833-1326/1908).

26. Allusion to the support for Constitutionalism by such high ranking religious dignitaries as Ḥājj Mīrzā Ḥusayn Tihrānī, Ākhūnd Mullā Muḥammad Kāẓim Khurāsānī, and Shaykh 'Abdullāh Māzandarānī in Najaf, and Sayyid Muḥammad Ṭabāṭabā'i and Sayyid 'Abdullāh Bihbahānī in Tehran. See Chapter VI above.

27. See note 5 above.

28. Shaykh Faḍl Allāh's rhetorical logic leads him to interrupt and resume a single train of thought intermittently. In order to preserve this logic, I have refrained from editing his discourse so that a set of related ideas concur.

29. Shaykh Faḍl Allāh frequently uses the conspiratorial "they," "them," and "their." These presumably refer to the Bābīs and the materialists who, according to Nūrī, were the chief manipulators of Constitutionalism.

30. Muḥammad 'Alī Shāh ordered the bombardment of the Majlis on Tuesday, 23 Jumādī al-Awwal, 1326/23 June 1908.

31. Allusion to the rebellion of the Constitutionalists against Muḥammad 'Alī Shāh in Tabriz, under the leadership of Sattār Khān (d. 1332/1913). The rebellion was prompted by the bombardment of the Majlis.

32. The tract was written after the bombardment of the Majlis on June 23, 1908, and before the end of the year 1326 (January 22, 1909)—in all probability, during the second half of 1908.

CHAPTER 17

*Clerical Authority in the Constitution of the Islamic Republic of Iran**

In the Name of Allah, The Compassionate, the Merciful.

We sent aforetime our apostles with clear signs, and sent down with them the Book and the Balance that men may uphold justice . . . (*Qur'ān 57:25*).

Preamble

The Constitution of the Islamic Republic of Iran sets forth the cultural, social, political, and economic institutions of Iranian society on the basis of Islamic principles and norms, which represent the earnest aspiration of the Islamic *Umma.* This basic aspiration was made explicit by the very nature of the great Islamic Revolution of Iran, as well as the course of the Muslim people's struggle from its beginning until victory, as reflected in the decisive and forceful slogans raised by all segments of the populations. Now, at the threshold of this great victory, our nation, with all its being, seek its fulfillment.

The basic characteristic of this revolution, which distinguishes it from other movements that have taken place in Iran during the past hundred years, is its ideological and Islamic nature. After experiencing the antidespotic constitutional movement and the anticolonialist move-

* Excerpts from the translation published in *Al-Tawhid*, vol. 3, no. 1 (1406/1985), pp. 130-92. Based on the translation by H. Algar (Mizan Press: Berkeley, 1980).

ment centred on the nationalization of the oil industry, the Muslim people of Iran learned from this costly experience that the obvious and fundamental reason for the failure of those movements was their lack of an ideological basis. Although the Islamic line of thought and the direction provided by militant religious leaders played an essential role in the recent movements, nonetheless, the struggles waged in the course of those movements quickly fell into stagnation due to departure from genuine Islamic positions. Thus it was that the awakened conscience of the nation, under the leadership of the eminent *marja'-i taqlīd*, Āyatallāh al-'Uẓmā Imam Khumeinī, came to perceive the necessity of pursuing an authentically Islamic and ideological line in its struggles. And this time, the militant *'ulamā'* of the country, who had always been in the forefront of popular movements, together with the committed writers and intellectuals, found new impetus by following his leadership. (The beginning of the most recent movement of the Iranian people is to be put at 1382 of the lunar Islamic calendar, corresponding to 1341 of the solar Islamic calendar [1962 of the Christian calendar]).

The Dawn of the Movement

The devastating protest of Imam Khumeinī against the American conspiracy known as the "White Revolution," which was a step intended to stabilize the foundations of despotic rule and to reinforce the political, cultural, and economic dependence of Iran on world imperialism, brought into being a united movement of the people and, immediately afterwards, a momentous revolution of the Muslim nation in the month of Khurdād 1342 [June 1963]. Although this revolution was drowned in blood, in reality it heralded the beginning of the blossoming of a glorious and massive uprising, which confirmed the central role of Imam Khumeinī as an Islamic leader. Despite his exile from Iran after his protest against the humiliating law of capitulation (which provided legal immunity for American advisors), the firm bond between the Imam and the people endured, and the Muslim nation, particularly committed intellectuals and militant *'ulamā'*, continued their struggle in the face of banishment and imprisonment, torture and execution.

Throughout this time, the conscious and responsible segment of society was bringing enlightenment to the people from the strongholds of the mosques, centers of religious teaching, and universities. Drawing inspiration from the revolutionary and fertile teachings of Islam, they began the unrelenting yet fruitful struggle of raising the level of ideological awareness and revolutionary consciousness of the Muslim people. The despotic regime which had begun the suppression of the Islamic movement with barbaric attacks on the Fayḍiyya Madrasa, [Tehran] University, and all other active centers of revolution, in an effort to evade the revolutionary anger of the people, resorted to the most savage and brutal measures. And in these circumstances, execution by firing squads, endurance of medieval tortures, and long terms of imprisonment were the price our Muslim nation had to pay to prove its firm resolve to continue the struggle. The Islamic Revolution of Iran was nurtured by the blood of hundreds of young men and women, infused with faith, who raised their cries of *"Allāhu akbar"* at daybreak in execution yards, or were gunned down by the enemy in streets and marketplaces. Meanwhile, the continuing declarations and messages of the Imam that were issued on various occasions, extended and deepened the consciousness and determination of the Muslim nation to the utmost.

Islamic Government

The plan of the Islamic government based upon *vilāyat al-faqīh*, as proposed by Imam Khumeinī at the height of the period of repression and strangulation practiced by the despotic regime, produced a new specific, and streamlined motive for the Muslim people, opening up before them the true path of Islamic ideological struggle, and giving greater intensity to the struggle of militant and committed Muslims both within the country and abroad.

The movement continued on this course until finally popular dissatisfaction and intense rage of the public caused by the constantly increasing repression at home, and the projection of the struggle at the international level after exposure of the regime by the *'ulamā'* and militant students, shook the foundations of the regime violently. The regime and its sponsors were compelled to decrease the intensity of repression and to "liberalize" the political atmosphere of the country. This, they imagined, would serve as a safety valve, which would prevent their eventual downfall. But the people, aroused, conscious, and resolute under the decisive and unfaltering leadership of the Imam, embarked on a triumphant, unified, comprehensive, and countrywide uprising. . . .

The Vilāyat *of the Just* Faqīh:

In keeping with the principles of governance [*vilāyat al-amr*] and the perpetual necessity of leadership [*imāma*], the Constitution provides for the establishment of leadership by a *faqīh* possessing the necessary qualifications [*jāmi' al-sharā'iṭ*] and recognized as leader by the people (this is in accordance with the *ḥadīth* "The direction of [public] affairs is in the hands of those who are learned concerning God (*'ulamā' bi'llāh*) and are trustworthy in matters pertaining to what He permits and forbids" [*Tuḥaf al-'uqūl*, p. 176]). Such leadership will prevent any deviation by the various organs of State from their essential Islamic duties. . . .

The Judiciary in the Constitution

The judiciary is of vital importance in the context of safeguarding the rights of the people in accordance with the line followed by the Islamic movement, and the prevention of deviations within the Islamic nation. Provision has therefore been made for the creation of a judicial system based on Islamic justice and operated by just judges with meticulous knowledge of the Islamic laws. This system, because of its essentially sensitive nature and the need for full ideological conformity, must be free from every kind of unhealthy relation and connection (this is in accordance with the Qur'ānic verse: "When you judge among the people, judge with justice" [4:58]).

Executive Power

Considering the particular importance of the executive power in implementing the laws and ordinances of Islam for the sake of establishing the rule of just relations over society, and considering, too, its vital role in paving the way for the attainment of the ultimate goal of life, the executive power must work toward the creation of an Islamic society. Consequently, the confinement of the executive power within any kind of complex and inhibiting system that delays or impedes the attainment of this goal is rejected by Islam. Therefore, the system of bureaucracy, the result and product of *ṭāghūtī* forms of government, will be firmly cast away, so that an executive system that functions efficiently and swiftly in the fulfillment of its administrative commitments comes into existence. . . .

Chapter 1: General Principles

Article 1

The form of government of Iran is that of an Islamic Republic, endorsed by the people of Iran on the basis of their longstanding belief in the sovereignty of truth and Qur'ānic justice, in the referendum of Farvardīn 9 and 10 in the year 1358 of the solar Islamic calendar, corresponding to Jamādī al-Awwal 1 and 2 in the year 1399 of the lunar

Islamic calendar [March 29 and 30, 1979], through the affirmative vote of a majority of 98.2% of eligible voters, held after the victorious Islamic Revolution led by the eminent *marja'-i taqlīd*, Āyatallāh al-'Uzmā Imam Khumeinī.

Article 2

The Islamic Republic is a system based on belief in:

1. the One God (as stated in the phrase "There is no god except Allah"), His exclusive sovereignty and the right to legislate, and the necessity of submission to His commands;
2. Divine revelation and its fundamental role in setting forth the laws;
3. the return to God in the Hereafter, and the constructive role of this belief in the course of man's ascent towards God;
4. the justice of God in creation and legislation;
5. continuous leadership (*imāma*) and perpetual guidance, and its fundamental role in ensuring the uninterrupted process of the revolution of Islam;
6. the exalted dignity and value of man, and his freedom coupled with responsibility before God; in which equity, justice, political, economic, social, and cultural independence, and national solidarity are secured by recourse to:

a. continuous *ijtihād* of the *fuqahā'* possessing necessary qualifications, exercised on the basis of the Qur'ān and the *Sunna* of the Infallibles (*Ma'ṣūmūn*), upon all of whom be peace;
b. sciences and arts and the most advanced results of human experience, together with the effort to advance them further;
c. negation of all forms of oppression, both the infliction of and the submission to it, and of dominance, both its imposition and its acceptance.

Article 4

All civil, penal, financial, economic, administrative, cultural, military, political, and other laws and regulations must be based on Islamic criteria. This principle applies absolutely and generally to all articles of the Constitution as well as to all other laws and regulations, and the *fuqahā'* of the Guardian Council are judges in this matter.

Article 5

During the Occultation of the Lord of Time (*Valī al-'Aṣr*) (may God hasten his reappearance), the *vilāyat* and leadership of the *Umma* devolve upon the just [*'ādil*] and pious [*muttaqī*] *faqīh* who is fully aware of the circumstances of his age; courageous, resourceful, and possessed of administrative ability; and recognized and accepted as Leader by the majority of the people. In the event that no *faqīh* should be so recognized by the majority, the Leader, or the Leadership Council, composed of *fuqahā'* possessing the aforementioned qualifications, will assume the responsibilities of this office in accordance with Article 107.

Article 6

In the Islamic Republic of Iran, the affairs of the country must be administered on the basis of public opinion expressed by the means of elections, including the election of the President, the representatives of the National Consultative Assembly[1], and the members of councils, or by means of referenda in matters specified in other articles of this Constitution.

Article 7

In accordance with the command of the Qur'ān contained in the verses: "Their affairs are by consultations among them" (42:38) and "Consult them in affairs" (3:159), consultative bodies—such as the National Consultative Assembly, the Provincial Councils, and the City, Region, District, and Village Councils and likes of them—are the decision-making and administrative organs of the country.

The nature of each of these councils, together with the manner of their formation, their jurisdiction, and scope of their duties and functions, is determined by the Constitution and laws derived from it.

Article 8

In the Islamic Republic of Iran, *al-amr bi'l-ma'rūf wa al-nahy 'an al-munkar* is a universal and reciprocal duty that must be fulfilled by the people with respect to one another, by the government with respect to the people, and by the people with respect to the government. The conditions, limits, and nature of this duty will be specified by law. (This is in accordance with the Qur'ānic verse: "The believers, men and women, are guardians of one another; they enjoin the good and forbid the evil" [9:71]). . . .

Article 91

With a view to safeguard the Islamic ordinances and the Constitution, in order to examine the compatibility of the legislations passed by the National Consultative Assembly with Islam, a council to be known as the Guardian Council is to be constituted with the following composition:

1. six *'ādil fuqahā'*, conscious of the present needs and the issues of the day, to be selected by the Leader or the Leadership Council; and
2. six jurists, specializing in different areas of law, to be elected by the National Consultative Assembly from among the Muslim jurists nominated by the Supreme Judicial Council.

Article 92

Members of the Guardian Council are elected to serve for a period of six years, but during the first term, after three years have passed, half of the members of each group will be changed by lot and new members will be elected in their place.

Article 93

The National Consultative Assembly does not hold any legal status if there is no Guardian Council in existence, except for the purpose of approving the credentials of its members and the election of the six jurists on the Guardian Council.

Article 94

All legislation passed by the National Consultative Assembly must be sent to the Guardian Council. The Guardian Council must review it within a maximum of ten days from its receipt with a view to ensuring its compatibility with the criteria of Islam and the Constitution. If it finds the legislation incompatible, it will return it to the Assembly for review. Otherwise the legislation will be deemed enforceable.

Article 95

In cases where the Guardian Council deems ten days inadequate for completing the process of review and delivering a definite opinion, it can request the National Consultative Assembly to grant an extension of the time limit not exceeding ten days.

Article 96

The determination of compatibility of the legislation passed by the National Consultative Assembly with the laws of Islam rests with the majority vote of the *fuqahā'* on the Guardian Council; and the determination of its compatibility with the Constitution rests with the majority of all the members of the Guardian Council.

Article 97

In order to expedite the work, the members of the Guardian Council may attend the Assembly and listen to its debates when a government bill or a members' bill is under discussion. When an urgent government or members' bill is placed on the agenda of the Assembly, the members of the Guardian Council must attend the Assembly and make their views known.

Article 98

The authority of the interpretation of the Constitution is vested with the Guardian Council, which is to be done with the consent of three-fourths of its members.

Article 99

The Guardian Council has the responsibility of supervising the election of the President of the Republic, the elections for the National Consultative Assembly, and the direct recourse to popular opinion and referenda.

Chapter VIII: The Leader or Leadership Council

Article 107

Whenever one of the *fuqahā'* possessing the qualifications specified in Article 5 of the Constitution is recognized and accepted as *marja'* and Leader by a decisive majority of the people—as has been the case with the eminent *marja' taqlīd* and leader of the revolution, Āyatallāh al-'Uẓmā Imam Khumeinī—he is to assume [the office of] the *vilāyat al-amr* and all the functions arising therefrom. Otherwise, experts elected by the people will review and consult among themselves concerning all persons qualified to act as *marja'* and Leader. If they discern outstanding capacity for leadership in a certain *marja'*, they will present him to the people as their Leader; if it is not possible, they will appoint either three or five *marāji'* possessing the necessary qualifications for Leadership and present them to the people as members of the Leadership Council.

Article 108

The law setting out the number and qualifications of the experts [mentioned in the preceding article], the mode of their election, and the code of procedure regulating the sessions during the first term must be drawn up by the *fuqahā'* on the first Guardian Council, passed by a majority of votes and then finally approved by the Leader of the Revolution. The power to make any subsequent change or a review of this law is vested with the Assembly of Experts.

Article 109

Following are the essential qualifications and conditions for the office of the Leader or members of the Leadership Council:

1. scholarship and piety, as required for performing the functions of *muftī* and *marja';*
2. political and social perspicacity, courage, strength, and the necessary administrative abilities for leadership.

Article 110

Following are the duties and powers of the Leadership:

1. appointment of the *fuqahā'* on the Guardian Council;
2. appointment of the supreme judicial authority of the country;
3. supreme command of the armed forces, exercised in the following manner:
   a. appointment and dismissal of the chief of the joint staff:
   b. appointment and dismissal of the chief commander of the Islamic Revolution Guards Corps;
   c. formation of the Supreme National Defence Council, composed of the following seven members:
      — the President,
      — the Prime Minister,
      — the minister of defence,
      — the chief of the joint staff,
      — the chief commander of the Islamic Revolution Guard Corps, and
      — two advisers appointed by the Leader;

d. appointment of the supreme commanders of the three wings of the armed forces, on the recommendation of the Supreme National Defence Council; and

e. the declaration of war and peace, and the mobilization of the armed forces, on the recommendation of the Supreme National Defence Council;

4. signing the decree formalizing the election of the President of the Republic by the people. The suitability of candidates for the presidency of the Republic, with respect to the qualifications specified in the Constitution, must be confirmed before elections take place by the Guardian Council, and, in the case of the first term [of the Presidency], by the Leadership;

5. dismissal of the President of the Republic, with due regard for the interests of the country, after the Supreme Court holds him guilty of the violation of his constitutional duties, or after a vote of the National Consultative Assembly testifying to his political incompetence;

6. pardoning or reducing the sentences of convicts, within the framework of Islamic criteria, on a recommendation [to that effect] from the Supreme Court.

Article 111

Whenever the Leader or a member of the Leadership Council becomes incapable of fulfilling the constitutional duties of leadership, or loses one of the qualifications mentioned in Article 109, he will be dismissed. The authority of determination in this matter is vested with the experts specified in Article 108.

Regulations for convening a meeting of the experts in order to implement this provision are to be laid down at the first session of the Assembly of Experts.

Article 112

The Leader or the members of the Leadership Council are equal to all other citizens in the eyes of law.

Chapter XI: The Judiciary

Article 157

In order to fulfil the responsibilities of the judiciary, a council to be known as the Supreme Judicial Council will be constituted, which will be the highest judicial body entrusted with the following responsibilities:

1. creation of the necessary organizations for the administration of justice to fulfil the responsibilities specified in Article 156:

2. preparation of bills on judicial matters appropriate to [the form of government of] the Islamic Republic;

3. employment of just and worthy judges, their dismissal, appointment, transfer, their assignment to particular duties, promotions, and carrying out similar administrative duties, in accordance with the law.

Article 158

The Supreme Judicial Council is to consist of five members:

1. the chief of the Supreme Court,

2. the Prosecutor-General,

3. three judges of proven justice and possessing the capacity of *ijtihād*, to be elected by all the judges of the country.

The members of this council shall be elected in the manner to be prescribed by law, for a period of five years, and nothing defers them from being re-elected. The qualifications for the candidates and the electors will be specified by law.

Article 161

The Supreme Court is to be formed for the purpose of supervising the correct implementation of the laws by the courts, ensuring uniformity of judicial procedure, and fulfilling any other responsibilities assigned to it by law, on the basis of regulations to be established by the Supreme Judicial Council.

Article 162

The chief of the Supreme Court and the Prosecutor-General must both be just *mujtahids* well versed in judicial matters. They will be nominated by the Leadership for a period of five years, in consultation with the judges of the Supreme Judicial Council.

Article 163

The conditions and qualifications to be fulfilled by a judge will be determined by law, in accordance with the criteria of *fiqh*.

Article 164

A judge cannot be removed, whether temporarily or permanently, from the post he occupies except by trial and proof of his guilt, or in consequence of a violation entailing his dismissal. A judge cannot be transferred or redesignated without his consent, except in cases when the interest of society necessitates it, that too, with a unanimous vote of the members of the Supreme Judicial Council. The periodic transfer and rotation of judges will be in accordance with general regulations to be laid down by law.

Article 167

The judge is bound to endeavor to judge each case on the basis of the codified law. In case of the absence of any such law, he has to deliver his judgement on the basis of authoritative Islamic sources and authentic *fatāvā*. He, on the pretext of the silence of or deficiency of law in the matter, or its brevity or contradictory nature, cannot refrain from admitting and examining cases and delivering his judgement.

Article 170

Judges of courts are obliged to refrain from executing statutes and regulations of the government that are in conflict with the laws or the norms of Islam, or lie outside the competence of the executive power. Everyone has the right to demand the annulment of any such regulation from the Court of Administrative Justice.

Article 171

Whenever an individual suffers moral or material loss as the result of a default or error of the judge with respect to the subject matter of a case or the verdict delivered, or the application of a rule in a particular case, the defaulting judge must stand surety for the reparation of that loss in accordance with the Islamic criteria, if it be a case of default. Otherwise losses will be compensated for by the State. In all such cases, the repute and good standing of the accused will be restored.

Note

1. By the first act it passed (31 Tīr 1359/ July 1980), the Majlis changed its official name from National Consultative Assembly (*majlis-i shūrā-yi millī*) to Islamic Consultative Assembly (*majlis-i shūrā-yi islāmī*). (*Ed.*)

*Index**

*To avoid redundancy, the titles and authors catalogued in chapter 9 (An Annotated Bibliography) have not been indexed.